CALIFORNIA
WORKERS' COMPENSATION HANDBOOK

A Practical Guide to the Workers' Compensation Law of California

Eleventh Edition

By STANFORD D. HERLICK

Member of the California Bar
Former Instructor, Workers' Compensation Law,
University of California Extension, Riverside

Parker & Son Publications, Inc.
Carlsbad, California

First Edition 1964. Eleventh Edition 1991
Printed in the United States of America

Library of Congress Catalog Card Number 91-67850
ISBN 1-55943-147-4

TABLE OF CONTENTS

PREFACE

The success of a book of this type is in a great measure dependent upon the qualifications of its author. We think the reader will find the Handbook's author uniquely qualified as an expert on the subject of the California Workers' Compensation Law. As an attorney for the State Compensation Insurance Fund, he appeared before the Industrial Accident Commission as an advocate. Later, as a Deputy Attorney General, he represented the Subsequent Injuries Fund. After his appointment as Referee-in-Charge of a commission branch, his duties included hearing and deciding cases and the administration of the branch office. He also served as a Deputy Commissioner, acting as commissioner pro tem in reviewing those decisions of trial referees of Panel II which were before the commission on appeal. His position as a County Counsel involved problems of underwriting, ancillary benefits, and legislation.

Having taken the author's course on this subject, we find that the Handbook parallels his method of instruction—the practical point of view, while covering the meaning and interpretation of the law in a clear and concise way. His classes are composed of the same cross-section of people who will find this volume to be of assistance: doctors, lawyers, hospital and industrial nurses, medical assistants, insurance agents, adjusters, management personnel, union representatives, personnel technicians, safety coordinators, employer insurance department personnel. The course required a text—so in 1962, the author developed the "Comp Primer" which is the predecessor to the Handbook. The Eleventh Edition reflects the most recent developments in the law which affect the workers' compensation program and includes a discussion regarding the report of the National Commission of State Workmen's Compensation Laws which will influence legislation in this field on both state and national levels.

Those who have used the Handbook are in agreement that it is written in a style which is easy to read and understand. In our work with compensation matters, we have found it to be a rapid resource for resolving specific problems and finding the pertinent code sections.

Victor A. Gables, Esq.
Wilford N. Sklar, Esq.

INTRODUCTION

The Handbook

The California workers' compensation law has far-reaching effects. When employees suffer industrial injuries, not only is their welfare and that of their families involved, but so also are the interests of other individuals or groups. These include employers, employees, unions, insurers, brokers, agents, underwriters, physicians, lawyers, industrial relations staffs and various benefits, hospital, or medical plans.

Problems related by students and others in these fields of activity influenced this attempt to provide a text that could serve as a practical guide to the interested layperson and professional as well. Our approach here is to present the scope and operation of this law in a single volume of the handbook type, to include some of the policies of the Division of Workers' Compensation, the Workers' Compensation Appeals Board, and the Office of Administrative Director which may not be readily available from other sources. Statutory references are placed in the margin for easier reading of the text material, and case references are provided on a selective basis.

The marginal references are to sections of the California Labor Code, Rules of the Workers' Compensation Appeals Board, and the Administrative Director, as well as sections of other California Codes covering special situations. These abbreviations will identify the codes and the rules:

LC	—	Labor Code
R	—	Rules of the Workers' Compensation Appeals Board, Administrative Director and Director of Industrial Relations (sections of the California Code of Regulations)
IC	—	Insurance Code
UIC	—	Unemployment Insurance Code
CC	—	Civil Code
CCP	—	Code of Civil Procedure
EC	—	Education Code
EvC	—	Evidence Code
GC	—	Government Code
H&S	—	Health and Safety Code
PC	—	Penal Code
PUC	—	Public Utilities Code
W&I	—	Welfare and Institutions Code
M&V	—	Military and Veterans Code

Historical Background

While the belief that an employer should provide employees with some measure of protection from the effects of work injuries is not new, it has not been extensively held until modern times. During certain periods of recorded history, civilizations have established such a duty by law or custom.

For example, the laws of ancient Babylon controlled wages and hours. Both employers and slave-masters were required to provide for workers during periods of illness and unemployment and to pay their "doctors' fees."

The modern concept of workers' compensation and safety laws originated in Europe as a product of industrialization during the latter part of the 19th century. The idea spanned the Atlantic after a generation, and now every state and territory has such a law. Congress has also legislated programs in various areas of activity in interstate and maritime commerce.

Before the enactment of these special laws, the worker's redress for a work injury was limited to a suit for damages against the employer. He or she had the burden of proving that the employer's negligence caused his or her injury, but if the employer could prove that the employee's own negligence played a part in causing the injury, the employee was denied recovery. This special defense is known as the "doctrine of contributory negligence," and it is a defense in any type of negligence case in most states.

A second defense permitted by the courts was labeled "the fellow-servant rule." Under this rule, if the injury was caused by another employee, the employer was not liable.

The courts also created a third defense known as the "assumption of risk doctrine," which prevented recovery in most cases. The employee was considered as having assumed the risks attendant upon his or her job, and if in the course of regular employment duties the worker was injured, the employer escaped liability. The many uncompensated work injuries caused a serious social and economic situation.

California first dealt with the problem in 1911 by adopting the Roseberry Act, which provided for a voluntary plan of compensation benefits. It was superseded in 1913 by the Boynton Act, which made these benefits compulsory. This enactment, as amended and codified, is the one in force today. Since 1913 then, California workers have been entitled to medical treatment and compensation payments for industrial injuries.

The basic philosophy behind workers' compensation is that industry should provide protection as a cost of doing business and that benefits should be afforded, within defined limits, regardless of the fault of any person. For this reason, in a compensation case the defenses of contributory negligence, assumption of risk, and fellow-servant rule are not available to the employer. The law, in turn, provides the employer with protection against negligence suits based upon industrial injuries if the employer has provided for compensation benefits. California has also enacted safety laws in an effort to reduce the number of injuries, and many employers and insurance companies maintain staffs of safety experts. These laws are contained in the California Labor Code.

The Labor Code permits both the Administrative Director and the Workers' Compensation Appeals Board which comprise the Division of Workers' Compensation to promulgate rules in furtherance of the purposes of the workers' compensation law (Title 8 of the California Code of Regulations).

California has also sought to improve its workers' compensation program through ongoing legislative studies which result in amendments to this law. Study commissions have issued reports in every decade since 1950, and amendatory legislation has resulted. The most far-reaching of such legislation is the Workers' Compensation Reform Act of 1989 (Statutes 1989, chapters 892, 893). This Act applies only to injuries occurring on or after its effective date, January 1, 1990 with certain provisions becoming operative in 1991 and 1992. This Act changes the name of the Division of Industrial Accidents to Division of Workers' Compensation with sub-offices, a new administrative-medical procedure, operative in 1991, for initial resolution of permanent disability and medical questions, a formalized claims procedure, mandatory arbitration and settlement conferences in certain cases, new timeframes for payment of compensation, automatic penalties for late payment, increased monetary benefits, a presumption of spousal dependency in certain death cases, and continuation of death benefit payments to dependent minor children. These and other provisions, including special operative dates are discussed topically in appropriate Handbook chapters.

For recommendations of national and state study commissions, see: Chapter 1, THE CALIFORNIA PLAN, *State and Federal Legislation.*

Chapter 1
THE CALIFORNIA PLAN

§ 1.1   Introduction

Although basically similar, there are some differences among the types of plans existing in the many jurisdictions of the United States. One type of program requires the employer to insure with a monopolistic state agency which also determines entitlement to benefits. (An example of this approach in California is the unemployment insurance law which requires employers to insure with the Department of Employment by paying a payroll tax.) Under such a scheme, any person dissatisfied with the administrative determination may appeal first to the agency, then to the courts. Other states provide for private insurance or a choice between private insurance and insurance issued by a competing state agency. The California plan is of the last type.

Benefits also vary from state to state. Some are low; some are relatively liberal. Some place a limit on the amount of medical treatment; others, like California, provide all necessary treatment without limit. A comparison of benefits has been compiled by the U.S. Chamber of Commerce. Copies may be obtained from the Chamber's Washington, D.C. office.

Depending on the jurisdiction, disputed cases may be decided by arbitration, a court, a commission or a board. One state has established a Workmen's Compensation Court.

§ 1.2   Division of Workers' Compensation; Administrative Director; Workers' Compensation Appeals Board; Workers' Compensation Judges; Arbitrators; Referees

Cal. Const. Art. XIV, Sec. 4

LC 110-137

The California program is based upon a grant of power in the state Constitution to create a liability on the part of the employer to furnish benefits to industrially injured employees without regard to the fault of any person. It also provides that disputed cases may be determined by the courts, a commission, or both. The plan established by the Legislature by statute provided for benefits in case of injury or death resulting from employment and the administration of these benefits by employers or their workers' compensation insurers. Litigation of disputed cases or issues was placed within the jurisdiction of the Industrial Accident Commission, with appeals being taken to the California Courts of Appeal and Supreme Court. The plan was based upon a philosophy of minimum governmental involvement with the claims-handling process, official action being limited to the resolution of disputes by the commission. During the years since the original enactments of 1911 and 1913, there has been a gradual increase in official oversight and regulation, and the Workers' Compensation Reform Act of 1989 brings government into the claims picture at the administrative level with respect to injuries occurring on or after January 1, 1990.

In early decisions, the California Supreme Court defined the Industrial Accident Commission as a court of limited jurisdiction with the unique feature of having special bureaus, such as the Medical Bureau and Permanent Disability Rating Bureau, to assist and facilitate proceedings before it. The fact of an industrial injury was declared essential to the exercise of the commission's judicial authority. The commission had other duties of an administative nature which were legislatively transferred to other agencies in 1945, leaving the commission with the judicial function of resolving disputed cases or issues.

In 1945, legislation was adopted which divided the State of California into two panels for the purposes of enforcement of the workers' compensation law. This legislation provided for an industrial accident commission of seven members appointed by the governor who designated one member to act as chairman. By virtue of statute, the chairman was deemed the chief administrative officer of the Division of Industrial Accidents with the same authority as the director of a state executive department. Three commissioners were assigned to Panel I with headquarters in San Francisco, and three commissioners to Panel II with headquarters in Los Angeles. Geographically, each panel served approximately one-half of the state and functioned as an independent unit.

Because of the large number of cases filed for hearing, the commission early on began appointing attorneys to act as referees to conduct hearings, to take evidence, and make recommended decisions. In 1951, statutory authority was given the commission to delegate to the referees final decision-making authority. In 1955, the referees were also given authority to make final determinations of adequacy of compromise and release agreements. These items of legislation were implemented by commission rule, and, thus, the referee was the trial judge of the commission with the commissioners comprising an appellate tribunal of the first instance.

At each panel headquarters, administrative matters at the trial level were placed under the immediate supervision of a presiding referee. His responsibility included procedures for calendaring and assignment of cases for hearing.

In 1965, the Workmen's Compensation Study Commission filed a report based on extensive investigation and hearings concerning the operation of the California Workmen's Compensation Law. From the recommendations made by this commission, legislation was adopted which changed the name of the Industrial Accident Commission to Workmen's Compensation Appeals Board. This legislation also did away with the two-panel system, providing that the seven members of the new Appeals Board should be headquartered in one location in a centrally located city. San Francisco was selected as that city, and the Appeals Board is now based at and operates from the State Building in San Francisco. Branch offices are located in Los Angeles and other key cities, as discussed below.

The legislation of 1965 also created the Office of Administrative *LC 110-* Director to handle the administrative matters of the Division of Industrial *139.6* Accidents, formerly under the aegis of the chairman of the Industrial Accident Commission. For purposes of administration of the caseload of the Appeals Board, the law provides for a chairman of that body. Five of the seven commissioners must be attorneys. In 1967, further legislation designated the members of the Workmen's Compensation Appeals Board as "commissioners."

In 1974, the term "workmen" was changed to "worker" in Article XIV, Section 4, of the state Constitution and in various sections of the Labor Code. Thus, it is now the "workers' compensation law" and "Workers' Compensation Appeals Board" (also called W.C.A.B.). In 1975, by W.C.A.B. rule, the trial referees were designated "Workers' Compensation Judges" (in 1986 this designation was established by statute in addition to the W.C.A.B. Rules) and Presiding Referees as "Presiding Workers' Compensation Judges." (A workers' compensation judge must be an attorney with five years experience and is selected by competitive examination.) W.C. judges are subject to the California Code of Judicial Conduct. Pro tem judges *LC 123.6* may be appointed to hear particular cases if the parties agree. A pro tem *123.7* judge must be a certified specialist in workers' compensation or be eligible for certification.

LC 5309   LC 5309(c), enacted in 1988, empowers the W.C.A.B. to direct and order workers' compensation judges "[t]o issue writs or summons, warrants of attachment, warrants of commitment, and all necessary process in proceedings for direct and hybrid contempt in a like manner and to the same extent as courts of record." "Hybrid contempt" is defined as "a charge of contempt which arises from events occurring in the immediate presence of the workers' compensation judge for reasons which occur outside the presence of the workers' compensation judge."

LC 121   To assist the W.C.A.B. in its work as an appellate tribunal, the law provides for the appointment of three deputy commissioners who are usually W.C.A.B. judges. The law provides that the seven commissioners and the three deputy commissioners shall operate as panels of three unless it is determined that a case is of such unusual or important status that it should be considered by all seven commissioners *en banc*. The panels must be so constituted that appeals from decisions of the trial judges will not be assigned consecutively to the same panel. In other words, the makeup of the panels

LC 115   must rotate. The Appeals Board has followed this provision, and appealed cases are assigned to panels of three with different personnel than the previous panel. Included in this procedure are the three deputy commissioners. However, a deputy commissioner may not act unless his or her decision is concurred in by at least one commissioner. With this exception, a deputy commissioner may act as a commissioner and may be assigned to a panel.

        The Reform Act of 1989 changed the name of the Division of Industrial Accidents to Division of Workers' Compensation headed by the Administrative Director and created the Office of Benefit Determination (O.B.D.) and the Office of Benefit Assistance and Enforcement (O.B.A.E.), each headed by a Deputy Administrative Director. As a part of the Division

LC 139,
139.2   the Act also establishes the Industrial Medical Council. Increased staffing is
LC 62.5   authorized for the D.W.C. and the W.C.A.B. A revolving fund is set up for financing these agencies with additional assessments of employers being mandated for amounts required over $56,057,000 annually. The Act further provides for the appointment by the W.C.A.B of referees and arbitrators to determine certain issues. (See Chapter 14, PROCEDURE.)

§ 1.3   Appeals Board Branch Offices

        Branch facilities located throughout the state were established by the Industrial Accident Commission. These have been continued and augmented as offices of the Workers' Compensation Appeals Board. Thus, there are W.C.A.B. units located in Redding, Eureka, Santa Rosa, Sacramento, Stockton, Oakland, Walnut Creek, San Francisco, San Jose, Salinas, Fresno, Grover City, Bakersfield, Santa Barbara, Ventura, Agoura, Long Beach, Santa Monica, Norwalk, Los Angeles, Mid-Wilshire (L.A.), Van Nuys, Pasadena, Pomona, Santa Ana, Anaheim, San Diego and San Bernardino. Here, the W.C.A.B.'s judicial powers are exercised by W.C.A.B. judges (one of whom is designated Presiding Workers' Compensation Judge) assisted by staffs of court reporters, stenographers, and clerks.

§ 1.4 Authority of the Workers' Compensation Appeals Board; Liberal Application of Law

The Workers' Compensation Appeals Board has the same authority of *LC 130* enforcement as courts of general jurisdiction. Thus, the Board has the power to adopt rules of practice and procedure, issue subpoenas, make orders necessary to enforce its awards, punish for contempt, appoint guardians ad litem or trustees and conduct investigative hearings.

The Board has concurrent jurisdiction with the general courts to act as *LC 5308* arbitrator of disputes between any self-employing person and an insurer insuring him or her for workers' compensation benefits. The State Compensation Insurance Fund must submit such arbitration matters to the Appeals Board.

By agreement with the United States government, the Board may en- *LC 128* force the Longshoremen's and Harbor Workers' Compensation Act. However, this federal workers' compensation law is administered by the United States Department of Finance.

As the California appellate courts frequently point out, the workers' *LC 3202* compensation law contains a proviso that the law is to be liberally construed to effectuate its remedial purpose. While this is a rule governing the interpretation of the law, the appellate courts have applied it to various legal and factual issues. One of its most significant applications is seen in the *Reynolds* case in which the California Supreme Court decreed that the statute of limitations does not start running against an employee's claim until an employer having knowledge of an injury informs the employee of his or her rights under the workers' compensation law. (See Chapter 14, PROCEDURE.)

§ 1.5 Service Bureaus; Office of Benefit Determination; Office of Benefit Assistance and Enforcement

At the San Francisco, Los Angeles and other of the larger offices, staffs of experts carry out the work of the Division of Workers' Compensation and assist the Appeals Board and its trial judges. The Legal Bureau is located in San Francisco and is composed of attorneys who represent the Appeals Board in the appellate courts and provide other legal services for the division. Doctors assigned to the Medical Bureau examine applicants referred by the Administrative Director, the Workers' Compensation Appeals Board, or its judges in certain cases, and who report their medical findings to the referring official. Likewise, the Disability Evaluation Bureau (formerly, Permanent Disability Rating Bureau) is staffed with specialists trained in the computation of benefits under the workers' compensation law. Their chief duty is to prepare reports of permanent disability ratings based upon disability factors determined by the W.C.A.B. or its judges. Additionally, the specialists pre-pare advisory ratings in nonlitigated cases, help in screening cases for pre-trial conferences, provide assistance to the Medical Bureau, and prepare reports on set-tlement evaluations. Rating specialists are also assigned to the larger branch units.

LC 124
LC 4061-
4067.5

The Reform Act of 1989 places the responsibilities of the Disability Evaluation Bureau and the Rehabilitation Bureau within the Office of Benefit Determination (O.B.D.). The O.B.D. also has authority to make initial determinations under procedure effective in 1991 regarding the findings of qualified or agreed medical evaluators on the issues of permanent disability and medical treatment. The Office of Benefit Assistance and Enforcement (O.B.A.E.) has absorbed the duties of the Claims Bureau and the Information and Assistance Bureau. The O.B.A.E. has authority to audit the performance of employers, insurance carriers, and third-party administrators under the workers' compensation law and assess civil penalties for any failure to comply. The Medical Bureau is an adjunct of the Industrial Medical Council.

LC 129,
129.5

§ 1.6   Rules and Regulations of Administrative Director and Workers' Compensation Appeals Board

LC 5307,
5307.3
R 9700-
10137
R 10300-
10999

The Administrative Director has authority to adopt rules and regulations reasonably necessary to enforce the workers' compensation law. The W.C.A.B. may adopt rules of practice and procedure. The rules of both agencies are set forth in Title 8, California Code of Regulations. Certain of these rules are reproduced in the Handbook as deemed necessary to the dis-cussion.

Administrative Director rules include regulations regarding notices to be given injured workers, including information concerning rights, benefits, and procedures; also procedures relating to employee selection of physician, change of physicians, and medical fees; vocational rehabilitation; definitions of disability and authorization for the permanent disability rating schedule. Supplemental rules have been required to implement the Reform Act of 1989, including claim forms for employees or dependents and attorney dis-closure statements, as well as requirements for claims files of administrators for self-insured employers.

W.C.A.B. Rules of Practice and Procedure govern proceedings before workers' compensation judges, arbitrators and referees. The rules also cover appeals by way of petition for reconsideration and appeals from determina-tions of the Administrative Director and the Rehabilitation Unit.

§ 1.7   Vocational Rehabilitation Unit

LC 139.5

Legislation effective in 1965 provided for voluntary vocational rehabilitation plans. In 1975, vocational rehabilitation was made a mandatory benefit for qualified injured workers, and the Rehabilitation Bureau was designated to administer the program. By regulation, the unit was called the Rehabilitation Bureau; however, the Reform Act of 1989 and supplemental rules have redesignated it the Vocational Rehabilitation Unit. (See Chapter 16, VOCATIONAL REHABILITATION.)

§ 1.8 Industrial Medical Council; Medical Director; Qualified Medical Evaluators

Before 1990, the Medical and Chiropractic Advisory Committee, whose members were appointed by the Administrative Director, served as a liaison between the Division, its Medical Bureau, and the medical, osteopathic, and chiropractic professions. The committee also was an advisory body with regard to medical fees, medical-legal guidelines, standards of care, rehabilitation, as well as selection of independent medical examiners and independent chiropractic examiners. The Reform Act of 1989 has replaced the advisory committee with the Industrial Medical Council.

The Council is an agency within the Division of Workers' Compensation. Members are appointed by the Governor, Senate Committee on Rules, and Speaker of the Assembly. The Council includes physicians and surgeons, both M.D.'s and D.O.'s, two chiropractors, and one doctor of psychology. Of the physicians and surgeons, one must be a specialist in occupational medicine and one a psychiatrist. The Administrative Director is an ex officio member, and the Medical Director (a physician and surgeon appointed by the Council to head the Division's Medical Bureau) serves as executive secretary. Actions of the Council are taken by concurrence of at least eight of the members. The Council recommends physicians for appointment as qualified medical evaluators. The Council has authority to adopt rules and regulations regarding medical evaluations, including standards for evaluating disability and psychiatric injury. Authorized staffing to assist the Council includes an executive director, medical and attorney positions, as well as consultants and office assistants. *LC 139-139.3*

The Council is to maintain liaison with the healing professions, counsel and assist the Administrative Director, assist in recruiting physicians for the Medical Bureau, develop guidelines for determination of disputed clinical fact, suggest standards for improved care of injured workers, study and disseminate information regarding developments in rehabilitation, recommend levels of fees for physicians, monitor and measure costs and frequency of medical services, and appoint advisory committees regarding specialties and psychiatric injuries.

The Medical Director may appoint assistant medical directors to assist in the work of the Medical Bureau, and is to assign qualified medical evaluators for examination and evaluation of injured workers. Reports issued by qualified medical examiners are to be monitored by the Bureau. *LC 122, 139.2*

Qualified medical evaluators (Q.M.E.'s) are appointed to the Bureau's roster by the Council for four-year terms. Appointees must be physicians as defined by LC 3209.3, which includes M.D.'s, D.O.'s, chiropractors and *LC 139.2, 139.3* clinical psychologists. Physicians and surgeons must be board-certified in their specialties, and those in other categories must be certified by an appropriate professional organization. LC 139.2 sets forth conditions for appointment and reappointment, and LC 139.3 prohibits the acceptance of any form of compensation for a referral. Industrial Medical Council rules must include time-frames for appointment of Q.M.E.'s and for their reports after making examinations and evaluations.

§ 1.9   Case Load; Litigation Reduction Program; Information and Assistance Officer

The number of litigated cases filed with the W.C.A.B. is steadily increasing. The present rate is about 100,000 new filings per year. Each case may result in one or more hearings, supplementary proceedings, or decisions.

There are about ten million workers in California and each year about one million industrial injuries. Of these, about 200,000 are lost-time injuries. The ratio of litigated cases to lost-time injuries is approximately 1 to 2. For this reason, the Division of Workers' Compensation is working to reduce the number of litigated cases filed. One means of accomplishing an informal disposition of a claim is the advisory rating procedure whereby both the employer, or employer's carrier, and the employee submit information to the rating bureau. If the employee is represented by an attorney, a judge of the W.C.A.B. will set the attorney's fee. A similar procedure, which will utilize more pre-hearing conferences, is being sought for other issues. However, these informal procedures are not binding, and the employee may file an application or a petition to reopen for new and further disability within five years from date of injury, and carriers and employers may be expected to waive the statute of limitations.

LC 5410, 5803-4

LC 139.6, 5450-5455

As a means of furthering this program, the Legislature in 1977 authorized the appointment of an Information and Assistance Officer. This Officer is to provide information to the public and to assist employers and employees to resolve issues without a formal hearing. He or she may make recommendations on any matter submitted, refer matters to the various bureaus within the Division and, if necessary, recommend that the Administrative Director refer an employee to an independent medical or chiropractic examiner. Submission of a matter to this officer serves to toll or delay the running of any applicable statute of limitations until 60 days after the issuance of his or her recommendation. This procedure does not affect any party's right to commence more formal proceedings before the Workers' Compensation Appeals Board.

LC 5703.5

§ 1.10   State and Federal Legislation

In 1970, Congress enacted the law known as the Occupational Safety and Health Act (OSHA) which sets forth safety standards and enforcement procedures for places of employment. A section of that law created the

National Commission on State Workmen's Compensation Laws. Members were appointed by the President. In 1972, the Commission filed its report with Congress in which it recommended standards for state workers' compensation programs. The report recommended that if the states do not meet those standards, Congress should enact a federal law which would be binding on all the states. The deadline for Congressional action was 1975. Congress immediately upgraded its own Longshoreman's and Harbor Workers' Act, but all attempts to pre-empt the states have met with failure because of opposition to a federal takeover in this field.

Meanwhile, many states have set up study commissions of their own to study the report of the National Commission and to make recommendations to their legislatures. California has responded to the national report legislatively by adopting some of the recommendations and by setting up the State Workers' Compensation Advisory Committee. Legislative changes include:

- Weekly compensation rate of 66²/3% of earnings (previously, 61³/4% of earnings).

- Compensation payable for life in case of total permanent disability.

- Temporary total compensation payable for duration of temporary total disability.

- After two years from date of injury, temporary total compensation is payable per rates in effect when payment is made.

- The waiting period for temporary compensation is three days after leaving work because of injury except where disability exceeds 21 days or there is hospitalization (14 days for injuries occurring on or after January 1, 1990).

- Medical and vocational rehabilitation for qualified permanently disabled workers.

- Employee-selection of physician after 30 days from date of injury.

- Increased allowances for dependents in industrial death cases.

- Uninsured employers' fund for protection of their employees.

- Requirement that employers give notice of workers' compensation rights to their industrially injured workers.

- Compensation coverage for domestic workers, babysitters, gardeners, and other casual labor.

- Informal procedures for resolving disputed cases.

With these changes, California complies with most of the recommendations.

The following recommendations of the National Commission have not been adopted by California:

- Weekly compensation to be 80% of spendable income with a maximum compensation rate of 200% of the statewide average wage. (State Committee does not agree but recommends that maximum compensation rate be 100% of statewide average wage computed each July 1.)

- Adjust current payments of compensation to changes in statewide average wage, regardless of date of injury. (State Committee agrees but does not agree that such changes should be made on any retroactive basis.)

- Waiting period for payment of temporary compensation should be three days from date off work because of injury, but no waiting period if disability exceeds 14 days. (State Committee agrees. California would need to change only the exemption period from the present 21 days to 14 days.)

- Liberalize use of subsequent injuries fund. (State Committee recommends only that the fund be given more publicity; otherwise, California complies.)

- Death allowance to a widow or widower or to minor children to be no less than 50% of the statewide average wage, with the maximum to escalate to 200% of the statewide average wage by 1981; the death allowance to be paid for the life of a widow or widower or until remarriage, a lump sum of two years of payments to be paid on remarriage, and to children until age 18 or to age 25 for any child who is a full-time student; the death allowance to be reduced by any social security benefits received on account of the death of the employee. (State Committee agrees but recommends that the maximum not exceed 100% of the statewide average wage; that a widow or widower be presumed to be dependent only for two years following the employee's death, after which actual dependency would be required; that the social security credit be only for benefits to the extent that the employee did not make contributions.)

- Statute of limitations to be three years after employee knows or should know that the injury or condition is work-related. (State Committee does not agree. The present system is felt to be adequate (i.e., one year with five years to reopen for new and further disability). Committee does recommend eliminating the requirement that a death claim be filed with the W.C.A.B. within 240 weeks from the date of injury.)

- No statute of limitations for necessary medical treatment. (State Committee agrees.)

- Regulation of attorneys' fees; worker to pay for own attorney; states to consider assessing fees to an employer if the "employer or his insurer has acted in an unjustified manner." (State Committee makes no recommendation, indicating that California complies with the basic recommendation of the National Commission regarding control of fees awarded employees' attorneys. California does not regulate fees of attorneys of employers or carriers.)

The Reform Act of 1989 has changed the retroactive period of disability which will justify payment of compensation from the first day of injury from 21 to 14 days, has increased benefits for injuries on or after January 1, 1990, and has provided additional administrative procedures for resolution of disability and medical issues. However, the Legislature has not adopted other recommendations of the National Commission as described above. Thus, we may anticipate further efforts for legislation in this area.

Chapter 2
COMPENSATION COVERAGE—EMPLOYMENT

§ 2.1   Compulsory and Voluntary Provisions

In a general way, we may say that every employer and employee within the State of California is subject to the provisions of its workers' compensation law. The law applies with equal force to citizen and resident alien. Certain employments are excluded because they are within federal jurisdiction, such as longshoremen and harbor workers, ship's crew members, interstate railroad workers, and employees of the federal government.

The law requires that the California employer provide benefits and secure payment. Every type of legal entity may be an employer. Included are individuals, partnerships, corporations, the state, counties, cities, and their agencies. Certain employments are exempt from the compulsory provisions of this law. Employers in such instances may elect to cover their employees, usually by purchasing a workers' compensation insurance policy. It is well to observe here that if voluntary protection is afforded to excluded employees, the employer benefits, for the employee is then limited to his or her remedy under this law and may not bring suit in the general court on the ground of negligence. Further, even though an employer may be able to establish the employment as excluded, the employee may still file an action for benefits with the Workers' Compensation Appeals Board. Insurance, therefore, will save the employer the expense of such litigation, since it may be costly to prove that the employment was excluded. *LC 3300-3301* *LC 3352-3371* *LC 3600-3700* *LC 3600* *LC 4150-4157*

Again, all employments are subject to the workers' compensation law except those expressly exempted by the Labor Code. It should be stressed that covered employment under the code must involve work for pay or other consideration as a prerequisite. If a person does work with the understanding that he is to receive no pay, he is deemed to be a volunteer rather than an employee. Such a volunteer, unless specifically covered by some provision of the Labor Code, is not an employee subject to coverage of the workers' compensation law. In the leading decision of the California Supreme Court on this point, the alleged employer had a policy of workers' compensation insurance, but it was deemed not to cover a volunteer who was at the time of her injury acting as a hostess at the Hollywood Canteen. Other decisions have established that the "work for pay" requirement may be met by the furnishing of any benefit, remuneration, or consideration in exchange for services. Thus, wages may take the form of goods, other services, training, or education. Also, in 1973, the California Supreme Court established the principle that one may be deemed to be an employee under the workers' compensation law so long as the service rendered was furnished on a "non-gratuitous" basis, even though there is no formal employment contract or payment of any type of wages. The court's holding was in the *Laeing* case wherein the claimant was injured while performing a physical agility test or tryout as an applicant for a job. The court differentiated Laeing's activity from the activity in the *Hollywood Canteen* case wherein the injured was a volunteer for patriotic reasons. Laeing, on the other hand, expected to get a job, and the employer, through use of the test, expected to get a qualified employee. It has also been held that this rule does not apply to one merely seeking to file a job application.

While the general rule, subject to the foregoing principles, is that a volunteer is not an employee, and, therefore, excluded from compensation coverage, the Legislature has included certain volunteers within the definition of "employee." (See § 2.5, *Special Included Categories*.)

§ 2.2   Employers

LC 3300, 3301

The term "employer" includes any person or entity which engages the services of a "natural person." It includes an individual employer, a partnership, the legal representative of a deceased employer, a corporation, and any association or organization. It also includes the state and every state agency, every county, every city, and all public and quasi-public corporations and agencies. Specific exclusions from employer-status are afforded to sponsors of bowling teams and private, non-profit, organizations sponsoring persons who perform service as a condition of sentencing by a superior or municipal court, where the persons sponsored are not otherwise employed by their sponsors. Whether a particular "employment" is a covered employment is also governed by the definition of "employee" under the workers' compensation law.

§ 2.3   Employees

LC 3351

The term "employee" includes every person who performs a service for another under any appointment or contract of hire or apprenticeship, express or implied, oral or written, whether lawfully or unlawfully employed. "Employee" includes aliens and minors. Coverage also extends to elected and appointed paid public officers, as well as officers and members of boards of directors of quasi-public or private corporations while rendering actual service for pay. [NOTE: Where corporate officers and directors of a corporate general partnership are the sole shareholders of the corporation, they may be brought under compensation provisions only by a corporate election to do so accomplished pursuant to LC 4151(a)]. As a general rule, it is presumed that *LC 3357* one performing a service for another is an employee, but the law provides that the alleged employer may prove otherwise if there was, in fact, no employment relationship, or if there was employment but in an excluded category. The workers' compensation law contains numerous provisions, some of which exclude and some of which include specific categories of workers or work situations.

§2.4   Exclusions

1. CASUAL EMPLOYMENT. [NOTE: This discussion of casual em- *LC 3351,* ployment is subject to legislation which became effective January 1, 1977, *3352,* and which was amended again effective March 25, 1977, relating to coverage *3354-3356* of employees of homeowners or occupants. This program is treated more fully in item 18, § 2.5, *Special Included Categories*. The discussion which follows describes the circumstances under which casual labor was excluded before January 1, 1977. These provisions continue to be of significance as to injuries occurring before 1977, and also because of the amendments of March 25, 1977, purporting to reinstate this exception where a homeowner or occupant has neither workers' compensation nor liability insurance.]

Before 1977, casual employment, not in the regular course of trade or business of the employer, was exempt and not covered by the workers' compensation law. However, the definition of excluded casual labor contained three provisos or conditions which had to be met, or the employment was not "casual" and was covered by the compensation law. To be excluded, casual employment had to meet *all* of these conditions:

(a) The job *must not* have been in furtherance of the employer's regular trade or business; and

(b) The work must have been completed in *not more* than 10 working days, without regard to the number of employees doing the work; and

(c) The total charge for personal services *had to be less than* $100.00 regardless of the number of employees doing the work.

If any one of the foregoing conditions was not met, the employment was not casual, and the employer was subject to the compulsory provisions of the workers' compensation law.

EXAMPLE: Green operated a fruit and vegetable stand and hired Jones to work there for four hours, at $5.00 per hour, to help unload a truckload of vegetables. Jones was injured while doing this work. This situation would meet conditions (b) and (c), above—i.e., not more than 10 working days and under the $100.00; however, Green would be liable for workers' compensation benefits, because the work was in the course of his regular business.

REMEMBER: Employment was never casual (i.e., never exempt from this law) if connected with a regular business venture of the employer.

[NOTE: If Green had hired Jones to move trash at the Green residence, the employment would have been casual. But, if the trash-moving took 11 days, it would not have been. Or, if Jones had been paid $100.00 or more, it would not have been casual.]

LC 3352(f)
2258.5
2. HOUSEHOLD DOMESTIC LABOR. [NOTE: Before 1977, household domestic service, including babysitting, was an excluded employment. Effective January 1, 1977, this type of employment has been included under the homeowners' and occupants' coverage, as amended March 25, 1977. See item 18 under Section 2.5, *Special Included Categories*.]

Before 1977, household domestic service was excluded, but if the employment exceeded fifty-two hours per week, the employer became subject to the law's requirement to furnish workers' compensation benefits in case of a work injury in the course of such employment. If the actual working time was less than fifty-two hours, the fact that living quarters were furnished did not bring the employment within coverage.

If the domestic work is other than the "household" variety, such as for a hotel or sanitarium, this type of work is protected by the law regardless of the number of hours worked. Where part of the domestic's duties relates to a "household" and part to a business venture on the same premises, entitlement to benefits depends on the particular type of function in which the injury occurred.

The California Supreme Court has held that where a homeowner's liability policy excluded activities which were "incident to a business pursuit," the activity of the homeowner in taking care of the children of another family for pay along with her own children, was not a commercial pursuit, as such, and the injury to one of the children was covered by the homeowner's policy.

LC 3352(h)
3. PART-TIME GARDENERS for private dwellings with several customers were excluded before 1977 if their work for any one customer did not exceed forty-four hours per month. On or after January 1, 1977, such gardeners have coverage under and subject to the limitations of the homeowners and occupants program, as amended March 25, 1977. (See item 18 under Section 2.5, *Special Included Categories*.)

LC 3351,
3352(a)
4. HOMEOWNERS' OR OCCUPANTS' RELATIVES. Any person who is employed by his or her parent, spouse or child to perform work which is incidental to the maintenance, use or ownership of a private dwelling owned or occupied by the employer is excluded from compensation coverage.

5. VOLUNTEERS, as defined in the earlier discussion of the *Hollywood* *LC 3352(i)*
Canteen and *Laeing* cases, are not, as a general rule, employees and therefore
are excluded from compensation coverage. The Labor Code specifically excludes any person performing voluntary service for a public agency or private, non-profit organization who receives no remuneration other than meals,
transportation, lodging or incidental expenses. [NOTE: Certain volunteers are
included by legislation, and certain entities may opt to cover volunteers. See
Section 2.5, *Special Included Categories*.]

In 1953, the appellate court decided a church-volunteer case. Some of
the congregation agreed to donate services to the church on particular days.
For certain other days of service, they were to be paid. The court concluded
that even though one of the men was injured on one of the volunteer days, the
payment of wages for some of the work characterized the arrangement as an
employment.

6. VOLUNTARY SERVICES to a non-profit recreational camp, hut, or *LC 3352(d)*
lodge for meals and lodging only are excluded.

7. SERVICES TO CHARITABLE INSTITUTIONS in return for aid or *LC 3352(b)*
sustenance only are exempt. The purpose is to allow organizations like the
Salvation Army to obtain service from the aided needy, without the risk of
being held as an employer under the law.

However, where the aid is given as regular wages in a work-therapy
program for the mentally retarded, the Court of Appeal has held that the
aided person is an employee, even though his family paid a fee to the
charitable organization equivalent to the amount paid him as earnings.

8. VOLUNTARY SKI PATROLMEN whose only recompense is use of *LC 3352*
ski lift or ski tow or meals or lodging are excluded. Also excluded are em- *(e), (f)*
ployees of ski lift operators when engaged in purely personal recreational activities.

9. DISASTER SERVICE WORKERS registered with an accredited *LC*
disaster council, or impressed into service during a state of war emergency, a *3352.94*
state of emergency, or a local emergency by a person having authority to
command the aid of citizens, are excluded from the compulsory workers'
compensation program but are afforded special coverage under LC 3211.9-
3211.93a and LC 4351-4386 which is dependent upon there being funds
specifically appropriated for this purpose by the Legislature. This coverage *LC 4353-*
sets earnings at maximum, and permanent disability is rated per occupation *4354*
of laborer. The State Compensation Insurance Fund is the adjusting agency. *LC 4381*

10. HONORARY DEPUTIES. One appointed as a deputy clerk, deputy *LC 3352(c),*
sheriff, or deputy constable for his own convenience to serve without pay for *3364*
a county or municipality is not covered. But a sheriff's reserve deputy is covered while on active duty.

PC 4017,
4125.1
LC 3351(e)
LC 3370-
3371

11. CONVICT LABOR (PRISON LABOR). County prisoners are excluded if the county has adopted an ordinance requiring prisoners to perform service for the county. Such labor is covered while doing fire-fighting or fire-suppression work, or if performing work for pay while "on loan" to another public agency. State prisoners have coverage while working as assigned, including work on state roads and highways. (See Section 2.5, *Special Included Categories,* item 8.)

LC 3301

LC 3352(g)

12. SPONSORED SPORTS ACTIVITY is excluded, even though subsistence and equipment are furnished, where participants are not otherwise employed by the sponsor. [NOTE: Sports activity may be covered where sponsored by an employer for the employer's regular employees, or where the degree of control and the manner of making cash payments denote an employment relationship. See Chapter 8, THE INJURY, Section 8.7, *Recreational Activities.*]

LC 3352(k)

13. STUDENT-ATHLETES participating in amateur sporting events sponsored by any public or non-profit school are excluded. This exclusion applies where the student receives no remuneration for participating other than "use of athletic equipment, uniforms, transportation, travel, meals, lodgings, scholarships, grants-in-aid, or other expenses incidental thereto." It is applicable to sporting events sponsored by "any public agency, public or private nonprofit college, university or school." This statutory provision is in response to an appellate court decision holding that college athletes were employees where the coach made special payments to players according to how they performed, the funds being supplied by "boosters" of the college. The resolution of similar cases in the future may depend upon the definition of the statutory term "grants-in-aid."

LC 3352(j)

14. AMATEUR SPORTS OFFICIALS, other than regular employees, are excluded if officiating at amateur sporting events sponsored by a public agency or non-profit organization. A condition of this exclusion is that such an official receive no remuneration other than a stipend for each day no greater than the amount established by the State Board of Control as a per diem for employees of the state. This stipend is presumed to cover the usual expenses involved in an officiating assignment.

LC 3358

15. WATCHMEN paid by subscription by several establishments are excluded.

LC 3351(f)

16. PARTNERS are excluded from the law with one exception. A working partner receiving a salary in addition to his or her share of the profits is entitled to workers' compensation benefits. But if the working partner is a general partner, he or she is excluded unless the partnership has elected coverage under LC 4151(a).

A 1954 appellate decision holds that three brothers engaged in a trucking enterprise (involving the use of a truck owned by one of them) were partners or engaged in a joint enterprise and were not employees. This illustrates the point that working partners are not employees of the partnership unless wages are paid for the work.

A special type of partnership involves workers associating in a partner- *LC 3360* ship to do a specific job for a person. All such worker-partners are employees of the person for whom the work is done. Such an employer is not liable if the worker-partners have provided their own workers' compensation insurance coverage.

An employee of a partnership is considered an employee of each partner; thus an injured employee's sole remedy is under the compensation law, and individual partners may not be held for damages in a negligence action in court. (This holds true, assuming the partnership has complied with the law regarding the "securing" of compensation benefits as discussed in the next chapter.)

17. INDEPENDENT CONTRACTORS are not employees and are excluded. (See subsequent discussion.)

18. OFFICERS OF A CLOSELY HELD CORPORATION are not *LC 3351(c)* deemed to be employees if they are the only shareholders of the corporation. *4151* The corporation may, however, elect to cover such officers.

19. A LAW ENFORCEMENT OFFICER regularly employed in an ad- *LC 3352* joining state who is temporarily deputized to work under the supervision of a *(l), (m),* California peace officer is excluded from coverage under the California *3366, 3367* workers' compensation law. Also excluded are law enforcement officers of the Oregon State Police, Nevada Department of Motor Vehicles and Public Safety, or Arizona Department of Public Safety acting as peace officers in California pursuant to PC 830.32.

§ 2.5 Special Included Categories

These activities are deemed to be employments subject to the workers' compensation law:

1. VOLUNTEER POLICE while on active duty. *LC 3362*

2. SHERIFF'S RESERVE DEPUTIES while on active duty. *LC 3364*

3. Any PERSON ASSISTING A PEACE OFFICER, at the request of *LC 3366* such an officer, in active law enforcement, or as part of the posse comitatus of the county.

[NOTE: A law enforcement officer of an adjoining state temporarily deputized to work under the supervision of a California peace officer is excluded. See item 19, above.]

4. STATE FISH AND GAME RESERVE OFFICERS while on active *LC 3363* duty.

5. VOLUNTEER FIREFIGHTERS while on active duty. *LC 3361*

LC 3365   6. Any PERSON IN ACTIVE FIRE SUPPRESSION WORK OR TRAINING at the request of an officer charged with fire fighting or fire suppression duties. (This does not apply to independent contractors or their employees but does apply to one who contracts to furnish an airplane to a public entity for fire prevention or suppression and to pilot the plane personally.)

LC 3367   7. HAZARDOUS WORK. Any person voluntarily rendering technical assistance to a public entity to prevent a fire, explosion, or other hazardous occurrences at the request of a duly authorized fire or law enforcement officer of that entity is deemed to be an employee of that entity. Rendering technical assistance includes the time of travel of the person to the location of the potentially hazardous condition.

PC 4017,
4125.1   8. CONVICT LABOR (PRISONERS). A county prisoner working voluntarily for a small sum per hour at the direction of the county will be deemed to be an employee of the county, unless the county has adopted an ordinance pursuant to Penal Code Section 4017, requiring prisoners to perform forced labor.

Persons confined in a city jail, as well as those in a county jail, may be required to perform work for a public entity. As to fire prevention or suppression work, prisoners may be required to perform work in a city, a county, or adjoining counties. While engaged in fire-control activities, prisoners are deemed to be employees for the purpose of workers' compensation coverage.

The appellate court has held that in a personal injury action brought by a prisoner against a county, the trial court must determine the issue of employment. If the prisoner is an employee, the W.C.A.B. has jurisdiction. Prisoners "loaned" by one public entity to another public entity are employees of the "borrowing" agency if any type of remuneration is involved, according to an appellate court decision.

LC 3370-
3371
PC 5069   Inmates of state penal institutions are covered for workers' compensation while performing assigned work including work on state roads and highways. Compensation is not paid while the inmate is incarcerated. However, by virtue of a 1988 amendment, benefits may be paid to a dependent spouse (or former spouse) or children of the inmate. If there are no dependents, payment of any temporary compensation will be made to the Uninsured Employers Fund, and any permanent disability payments will be held in trust for the prisoner. If a proceeding is held during incarceration, the workers' compensation judge may appoint an attorney for the inmate at state expense. These special provisions do not apply to county or city prisoners. As a condition of coverage for state prisoners, the law provides that an injury during such work will not be compensable if it results from an assault in which the injured was the initial aggressor.

W&I 883   9. Any YOUTH IN A COUNTY DETENTION CAMP doing fire suppression work.

10. BLIND AND PHYSICALLY HANDICAPPED persons working in state rehabilitation programs.

11. NATIONAL GUARD OFFICERS AND ENLISTED MEN. *M&V 340*

12. APPOINTED SCHOOL VOLUNTEERS, with approval of school district. *LC 3364.5*

13. PUBLIC AGENCY VOLUNTEERS; NON-PROFIT ORGANIZA- *LC 3363.5* TIONS. Unpaid volunteers may now be covered under workers' compensa- *3361.5* tion by public agencies and certain tax-exempt, non-profit organizations upon the adoption of a resolution of the governing body of such an entity. "Service without pay" in LC 3363.6 is defined as without pay except for meals, *LC 3363.6* lodging, and incidental expenses. This also applies to volunteers of a park and recreation district and to volunteers of services to the state under the oil- *GC 8574.1* spill contingency plan.

14. STUDENTS. The Court of Appeal has ruled that a student nurse working under a contract whereby tuition is to be paid by the federal government, and the student is to receive practical training, is an employee of the hospital. The payment of a consideration is not controlling so long as the service to the hospital is not gratuitous.

The Education Code provides workers' compensation coverage for work *EC 51769,* performed by students in school work-experience or community occupational *78249* training programs. The Labor Code requires that the supervising school *LC 3368* district shall provide coverage unless a student receives a cash wage or salary for work from an employer, in which case the employer must provide coverage.

The same conditions of coverage apply to students in work-experience programs conducted by a school district, or in similar programs administered *EC 51769* by the state Department of Education under EC 51769.

15. CONTRACT-AUTHOR where a written contract designates a "for *LC 3351.5* hire" situation, and the employer has ownership of copyright.

16. JUVENILE COURT WARDS engaged in rehabilitative work by *LC* court order for any government entity, including the federal government. *3364.55*

Similar provisions apply to juvenile traffic offenders and probationers *LC 3364.6* doing rehabilitative work on public property, with no temporary compensation and with the minimum compensation rate for permanent disability benefits.

17. WELFARE WORK-TRAINING. Welfare recipients receiving training under the Work Incentive Program handled by the state's Department of Employment Development are covered under a policy obtained by that department.

LC 4206-
4229

Enrollees under an economic opportunity work or work-training program (E.O.P.) are also covered, but have no minimum compensation rate.

LC 3351,
3352

18. HOMEOWNERS' OR OCCUPANTS' EMPLOYEES. Effective January 1, 1977, the Legislature enacted a special law to provide workers' compensation coverage for employees engaged in work-connected activities with respect to private dwellings. Insurance coverage was provided through compulsory homeowners' comprehensive liability insurance. One purpose of the law was to eliminate the problems created by the previous provisions dealing with casual labor, domestic workers, babysitters, part-time gardeners, and others. Because of many unforeseen problems which arose under the new law, once it became effective, it was quickly amended effective March 25, 1977.

Under the law effective from January 1, 1977, through March 24, 1977, every homeowner's liability policy contained workers' compensation coverage unless the homeowner rejected it in writing. Questions arose, such as, whether the law covered employees of renters; whether homeowners without insurance would be liable.

LC 3351,
3352

The statute enacted effective March 25, 1977, now governs these situations, but it presents certain problems of its own, principally with regard to employees of homeowners or occupants who have no insurance. Under this newer version the term "employee" includes any person employed by the owner or occupant of a residential dwelling whose duties are involved with the ownership, maintenance, or use of such dwelling, including the care and supervision of children, or whose duties are personal and not in the course of the trade, business, profession, or occupation of such owner or occupant of a

LC 3355,
3356

private dwelling. The definition of "course of trade, business, profession, or occupation" includes all services tending toward the preservation maintenance, or operation of a business, a business premises, or the business property of the employer engaged in with some degree of regularity, without regard to the trade name, articles of incorporation, or principal place or business of the employer.

Those employees in home-related or personal services categories are not covered under the homeowners or occupants program, if:

LC 3352(a)

a. The employer is the parent, spouse or child of the employee, or

LC 3352(h)

b. The employee is employed for less than fifty-two hours during the ninety calendar days which immediately precede the date of injury, as injury is defined LC 5411 or the date of last exposure resulting in an occupational disease, as occupational disease is defined in LC 5412, or

LC 3352(h)

c. The earnings of the employee are less than $100.00 from the homeowner or occupant-employer during the ninety calendar days immediately before the date of injury, as injury is defined in LC 5411 or the date of last exposure resulting in an occupational disease, as occupational disease is defined in LC 5412.

Notwithstanding the above, an employer may elect to cover the categories of employees who may be excluded under the above provisions pursuant to LC 4151 and 4156.

Also, if the work in question was performed in the course of the trade, business, profession or occupation of the employer, liability for workers' compensation would be assessed against the employer under the general provisions of the workers' compensation law. *LC 3351, 3600*

For home-related and personal employees who are included under this special program, there must be coverage of the employer by a comprehensive personal liability insurance policy. In other words, if the employer of such employees has not obtained a comprehensive personal liability insurance policy, the home-related employee is not entitled to workers' compensation benefits, and may not maintain a proceeding before the Workers' Compensation Appeals Board, nor obtain a recovery from the uninsured employers fund. In this type of situation the employee's only recourse would be to bring a personal injury action in the general courts. In the personal injury action against the homeowner or occupant, the employee would not be entitled to the presumption of negligence on the part of the employer, and the employer would not be deprived of the defenses of contributory negligence, assumption of risk, and the fellow-servant rule. *LC 3351(d)* *LC 3715, 3716*

Further complicating the picture in this home-related type of situation, the Legislature has provided for recognition of three categories of workers who would be entitled to workers' compensation, even though the homeowner or occupant had no type of insurance. The reason for including these categories is stated by the Legislature to be to provide protection for those who, before January 1, 1977, had protection under the casual employee, the part-time gardener, and the household domestic provisions which we have previously discussed. (See Section 2.4, *Exclusions*, items 1, 2 and 3.) Therefore, employees doing home-related or "personal" work who are covered whether or not there is insurance and who have access to the uninsured employers' fund are these:

a. An employee who is engaged in household domestic service while employed by one employer for over fifty-two hours per week. *LC 3715, 3716*

b. One who is engaged as a part-time gardener in connection with a private dwelling where the number of hours for any individual customer regularly exceeds forty-four hours per month.

c. An employee who is considered a casual employee, where the work contemplated is to be completed in not less than ten working days (without regard to the number of persons employed), and where the total labor cost (for personal services only) of such work is not less than $100.00.

LC 3708
In the alternative, an employee in one of these three categories just mentioned may maintain a personal injury action against the employer and have the benefit of the disputable presumption that the employer was negligent, and the employer would not be able to rely upon the defenses of contributory negligence, assumption of risk, and the fellow-servant rule.

IC 11590,
11591
As previously stated, insurance coverage for home-related or personal services is provided by a policy or policies of comprehensive personal liability insurance. Any policy of this type issued or in effect on or after January 1, 1977, must contain a provision covering home-related and personal employments. Any such policy which does not contain a workers' compensation clause will be construed as if such a clause were embodied therein. (The coverage under the liability policy does not apply to any situation where the services are in connection with the employer's trade, business, profession or occupation requiring a regular policy of compensation insurance or permissible self-insurance.)

LC 3550
The homeowner or occupant-employer need not post the notice required by Section 3550 regarding the name of the employer's insurance carrier, or, if the employer is permissibly self-insured, the fact of such self-insurance. In addition, certain penalties provided by law are not applicable where there is involved a failure to secure payment of compensation. There is, however, such a requirement as to the employments listed which show a special type of right for those doing household domestic work for more than fifty-two hours per week; or the part-time gardener working more than forty-four hours per month for an individual employer; or those in casual employment of ten days or more and who have wages of $100.00 or more.

Special provisions for computing minimum earnings for temporary compensation are applicable to injuries arising from home-related work before 1990. The minimum for temporary compensation in these cases is the statutory minimum or 1.2 times the actual earnings from all employers, whichever amount is less. Maximum earnings are determined in the same manner as for other employments. For injuries occurring on or after January 1, 1990, in home-related employment, by virtue of the repeal of LC 4453.1, there is no special minimum limit.

LC 5500.6
As to occupational disease, liability is limited to those employers who employed the worker during the last day of exposure. If no such employer was insured on the last day of exposure, liability will be assessed against the last employer having insurance wherein the worker suffered an exposure. There is no right of apportionment among previous employers. On the other hand, there is a right to apportionment of disability due to a specific injury, non-work related causes, or preexisting disability.

19. FARM WORKERS have been covered under the compulsory provisions of the compensation law since 1959.

20. PARTNERS. For conditions under which working partners may be covered, see *Exclusions*, item 16.

21. PARENT-VOLUNTEERS in a non-profit nursery school program *LC 3363.6* may be covered for workers' compensation.

22. IN-HOME SUPPORTIVE SERVICE for welfare recipients who are *LC 3351.5* entitled to such service at the expense of the state or county is covered for workers' compensation.

23. TRIAL JURORS are deemed employees of the county under appellate court decisions.

24. NEWSPAPER CARRIERS AND VENDORS are included. If inde- *LC 4157* pendent contractors, they may be included by election under LC 4157. Minimum earnings for temporary compensation are deemed to be *the lesser of* the statutory minimum or 1.2 times actual earnings. However, this special minimum is not applicable to injuries occurring on or after January 1, 1990, by virtue of the repeal of LC 4453.1.

§2.6   Jurisdictional Requirement of Employment

The operation of the workers' compensation law and the exercise of authority by the Administrative Director and the Workers' Compensation Appeals Board in a given case depend upon the existence of an injury arising out of and occurring in the course of employment. Therefore, if employment *LC 3600* in a covered category, as previously discussed, is not established, this law does not apply and the Administrative Director and the W.C.A.B. have no jurisdiction. The W.C.A.B. has jurisdiction to determine the issue of employment, and if it finds that there was no employment or that any employment was excluded, its jurisdiction over the matter ends upon making such a finding. (See Chapter 13, JURISDICTION.)

§2.7   Presumption of Employment

When a person claims to have been injured in the course of employment, the alleged employer may deny employment. This denial may be on one or more grounds, such as the following: the alleged employer never hired the claimant; the alleged employee was not on the payroll at the stated time; the employment was excluded by law; they were partners; or the alleged employee was an independent contractor. In such a situation, the *LC 3353,* alleged employee is presumed to be an employee having workers' compen- *3357* sation coverage if he or she shows that he or she performed a service for the alleged employer. This presumption is disputable. That is, in a W.C.A.B. *LC 5705(a)* hearing, the defendant (alleged employer) has the right to counter with evidence tending to show no employment. The applicant (alleged employee) then has the opportunity to present rebuttal evidence to bolster the presumption of employment. Usually, the applicant knows when he or she must meet a non-employment defense, and will put on all the evidence he or she possesses to prove employment, rather than rely solely upon the presumption. This presumption, however, remains as a potent matter of evidence and indicates a legislative policy to resolve any doubts in favor of finding employment where a service was performed.

§ 2.8   Employee or Independent Contractor?

Cases arise in which the paramount issue is whether the applicant for benefits was an employee or an independent contractor. This defense brings into focus several rules of law defining the differences between an employee and an independent contractor.

LC 3353

An employee is one who performs services for another and who is subject to the direction and control of his employer in the manner in which the work is done. The contractor is also retained to perform a service, but he or she is chargeable only with the result and is not subject to the control of the customer in the manner in which the details are carried out. Thus, for example, we retain a "contractor" to build a house according to plans and specifications for a certain price. He performs a service, but we do not have the right to tell him whom to hire or how to carry out the work. We do have the right to a finished product within the contract price. The contractor must provide compensation coverage for his own employees. He, in turn, may retain sub-contractors who are not his employees. The subcontractors, likewise, must protect their employees.

LC 2750.5
3357

Legislation was enacted, effective January 1, 1978, in an endeavor to clarify certain situations and make clear that the burden of proof is on the person who asserts an independent contractor defense. LC 2750.5 provides that any person engaged in work requiring a license under Business and Professions Code Section 7000, and following, are presumed to be employees unless they have the required license. This presumption is in addition to the presumption discussed above under LC 3357. However, the W.C.A.B. has held that the presumption of employment does not apply if the work does not require a license.

The W.C.A.B. and the appellate courts have ruled that if a purported building contractor has no license he or she must be deemed to be an employee. Under these decisions, one who retains an unlicensed uninsured building contractor is considered to be the employer (the "ultimate hirer") of the contractor and any employees of the contractor. If the "ultimate hirer," whether a property owner or a licensed general contractor, has "secured" payment of workers' compensation benefits through insurance or permissible self-insurance, the uninsured employers fund is not liable, and neither the licensed contractor nor his or her employees may maintain a damage suit against the "ultimate hirer." These decisions emphasize the need to ascertain both the license status and the insurance status of any person or firm holding forth as either a general or specialty building contractor. Where both a general contractor and an unlicensed sub-contractor have workers' compensation insurance, an employee of the sub-contractor is an employee of both, and the employee is barred from maintaining a personal injury suit against the general contractor. LC 2750.5 does not require a lack of insurance as a ground for the operation of the presumption of employment in such cases.

A physician who enters into a contract for the performance of health *LC 2750.6* services on behalf of a licensed primary care clinic is presumed to be an independent contractor. This presumption is rebuttable.

The problem of independent contractor news vendors is addressed in LC *LC 4157* 4157, which provides that voluntary coverage for workers' compensation does not affect their status as independent contractors "for all other purposes."

Between the obvious situations we encounter in our personal experiences, there is a myriad of overlapping or confusing relationships which have come before the Appeals Board and the courts. As a result, certain tests or guideposts have been established. In addition to evidence of the parties' intentions, there are many factors tending to substantiate *employment*. For example, the one receiving the service:

1. Controls the details or manner of doing work.

2. Has the right to terminate relationship.

3. Pays salary or wages.

4. Makes deductions made for unemployment disability insurance and Social Security.

5. Furnishes materials or tools.

6. Requires performance during specific days or hours.

Factors tending to prove an *independent contractor* relationship are that the one receiving the service:

1. Lacks control over details.

2. Has no right to terminate relationship before completion of work.

3. Makes payment by contract price, lump sum, specific fee or percentage commission.

4. Makes no deductions for unemployment disability insurance and Social Security.

5. Does not furnish tools or materials, the one doing the work furnishing these items.

6. Except for contractual deadlines, has no control over working hours.

Also, the person doing the work:

7. Is an expert, the customer knowing little or nothing about how to do such work.

8. Has regular business or special license and performs service for many customers.

9. Holds forth as professional person such as doctor, lawyer, accountant, registered nurse, architect.

No single factor is decisive of the question, for the affairs of men and women are seldom clear-cut. Many ambiguous situations develop. One field of endeavor has created quite a bit of litigation on this issue; namely, the "sales business." A real estate or insurance broker or agent holds a state license. He or she may associate with a firm, go into business, or hire out as a salesperson. He or she may be paid by commission, and if he or she does not sell anything, no income is received. Such cases usually are decided on the extent of control held or exercised by the claimed employer. Some brokers retain no control, and, aside from giving another broker or agent access to listings or leads and the telephone, furnish nothing and require nothing. If the associate sells, they both get a portion of the brokerage fee. This type of relationship has been found to be that of independent contractor.

On the other hand, brokers with sizeable businesses require continuity of operation, and while the salesperson may be left relatively free in his or her choice of territory, method of contract, or advertising, he or she is required to be in the office one or two days per week and, in the case of realtors, to put up signs and flags and to show a particular property at designated times. These requirements may be contained in oral instructions, a contract, or an office manual. Here we find aspects of both relationships, but the factor of control plus the Labor Code presumption would point to a finding of employment.

Any type of work or profession may, of course, present such conflicting situations. *The most important factor is control and the extent of it.*

Another interesting example is set forth in an opinion of the Court of Appeal. The owner of a chain of small eateries decided to abandon his role as employer with all its problems of regulation and taxation. By suitable documents, he and his employees changed their relationship to that of lessor-lessees. Under the lease agreement, the lessor was merely to collect rent, and the lessees were now operators of the business. The documents, however, required certain hours of work, business policy, specific income of the lessees, with the rest going to the lessor as rent. The court looked through the documents, calling them a subterfuge, and found that the so-called lessees were still employees. The California Supreme Court has likewise ruled that share-farmers harvesting crops as ostensible independent contractors under a written agreement are employees of the farmer for whom the work is done. The Court of Appeal has ruled that an employer may not change the status of an employee to that of an independent contractor by illegally requiring him to provide for his own withholding taxes and workers' compensation insurance. In these cases, the determining factor was control.

The California Supreme Court has ruled that granting artistic freedom to staff writers does not constitute lack of control. Thus, salaried writers of teleplays and stories for the "Lassie" TV series were determined to be employees. A 1989 decision of the Court of Appeal applies this principle to salaried actors, determining that they also are employees.

§ 2.9 Election to Cover Exempt Employments

An employer whose operation or workers are exempt from the workers' compensation law may nevertheless elect to provide workers' compensation coverage. This can be accomplished by giving the workers and the state notice of such election or by purchasing a policy of workers' compensation insurance.

LC 4150-4156

An election to provide coverage applies only to "employees." Thus, an election will not provide coverage for an independent contractor or a volunteer not expressly covered by the law, for these relationships are not "employments." This is the reason there are so many code sections permitting coverage of various types of volunteers. If an employer, potential employer, broker, or agent is in doubt on a question of employment, that is, whether to insure or not to insure, this writer's advice is to insure by purchasing both a workers' compensation and a comprehensive personal liability policy. The insured is then protected as to both suits at law and actions before the Appeals Board. This conclusion is based upon the many cases seen in which the element of control rules out an independent contractor relationship, or lack of a monetary interest in a venture on the part of the applicant makes it unlikely that he or she is a partner. Where excluded employment is the defense, there is very often some fact or arrangement which brings the injury within the operation of the workers' compensation law.

§ 2.10 Identity of Employer—Joint Employment

Problems arise where a party alleges that two or more persons or firms are joint employers of an injured worker. For example, it has been held that a municipal court judge is an employee of the state rather than the county in which the court is located, even though the county pays the judge's salary. Again, control is the most important consideration. The determination of the issue of joint employment affects questions of liability for compensation or liability for damages for claimed negligence. These matters are discussed in more detail in Chapter 3, INSURANCE, and Chapter 12, DAMAGE SUITS—SUBROGATION.

Chapter 3
INSURANCE

§ 3.1   Introduction

All employers subject to the compulsory provisions of the law, as discussed in the previous chapter, must "secure" payment of benefits. This is done by insuring with an insurance carrier which may be either an insurance company or the State Compensation Insurance Fund. Certain employers may qualify to self-insure, that is, guarantee payments without purchasing insurance.

Employers in the exempt category may elect to come within the law by "securing" payment as outlined above or by giving notice of election.

On or after January 1, 1977, no policy providing comprehensive personal liability insurance is to be issued or renewed without containing a proviso or clause for coverage against liability for payment of workers' compensation regarding home-related or personal services which are not in the course of the employer's regular business. Under these policies are covered those employers who are owners or occupants of residential dwellings. Regulations which govern rates classifications and a rating system for workers' compensation insurance are not applicable to this special type of coverage. A regular policy of workers' compensation insurance which is issued to cover a business or professional enterprise does not cover the home-related workers included in the special homeowner's or occupant's program. For a more complete discussion of this program, the legislation, and extent of coverage, see the discussion in Chapter 2, Section 2.5, *Special Included Categories*, item 18.

Regarding the effect of legislation dealing with fraudulent claims, see Chapter 9, PENALTIES, § 9.18, *Fraudulent Claims*.

§ 3.2   Insurance Premiums

Most employers secure payment of benefits through insurance premiums which are subject to a degree of regulation through the Insurance Commissioner's power to set minimum premiums. Such minimums are set for each type of occupation covered and are set forth in a manual which is used by all carriers selling workers' compensation insurance. The premium is expressed for each $100 of payroll.

Examples (from 1984 manual):

1. Automobile or Automobile Truck Dealers:
   - All but sales personnel . . . . $ 4.16
   - Salesmen 1.32
   - Dismantling 11.75
2. Chimney Construction Workers 15.69
3. Hotel Employees 5.91
4. Raising or Moving Buildings or Structures . . . 22.58
5. Clerical Office Employees 0.53

One can gauge the relative degree of occupational hazard, according to the opinions of underwriters, by comparing rates for various occupations. The spread in rates emphasizes the need for careful analysis of the employer's operations to place them in the correct premium category. Many agents and brokers provide a service to clients by double-checking the carrier's determination of premium.

IC 11732.5, 11734   The Insurance Commissioner may, after a public hearing, change a classification or system if credible actuarial and economic evidence indicates a need for change to assure that the code requirements are met. The expense provision for all classifications of risks and premium rates must be uniform as to all insured employers. For the years 1990, 1991, and 1992, the expense provision must be 34%, 33%, and 32.8%, respectively.

IC 11745   The Workers' Compensation (Insurance) Rate Study Commission is to study issues set forth in IC 11746 and render a report of its findings by March 1, 1992. The issues referred to include criteria for providing adequate coverage for workers and expeditious handling of claims, a reasonable rate of return for insurers, lowest net cost to employers, competition among insurers and availability of coverage to employers. The study is to include a review of experience in other states including those having exclusive state funds.

The employer must keep adequate records so that the insurance carrier may determine the correct classification of employees and amount of payroll. If records are not sufficient, the carrier may charge the rate for the highest category of the employees involved in the employer's activities. An employer's payroll and job-classifications may be audited or inspected by the insurer. The California Workers' Compensation Insurance Rating Bureau *IC 11750.3* may also conduct inspections and test audits. Further, if the Department of *IC 11736.5* Industrial Relations, the Employment Development Department, or any other *LC 90.7* state department or agency makes a final determination that an employer has *UI 1141.5* not properly reported payroll to such department or agency, the Insurance Commissioner may order the insurer or the insurance rating bureau to conduct an audit and require payment of the correct premium.

However, if an insurer's determination of classification would increase *IC 11743* an employer's premium, the employer is entitled to notice of such determination and also of his right to appeal the determination. This notice requirement does not apply to increases resulting from rate-changes made by the Insurance Commissioner.

Also, an insurer may not increase premiums by changing policy classi- *IC 11743.1* fication unless one of the following conditions is met: (a) Notice is given the insured or the insured's agent or broker during the affected policy period. (b) The insured, agent or broker agrees to the changes. (c) The insured, agent or broker should have known that the previous classifications were improper. (d) The change is due to an audit or inspection initiated within one year after the policy period. (e) The change is due to officially published classification assignments. (f) The previous classifications were the result of fraud or material misrepresentation of the insured. (g) The insured fails to cooperate in a payroll audit or inspection. If a workers' compensation insurer changes classifications so that additional premium is due exceeding 25% of annual premium, the insurer must permit the insured employer to pay the additional premium in monthly installments over a one-year period. This alternative is not required if the reclassification is the result of official action.

[NOTE: Insurance Code Section 756, permitting civil penalties to be assessed against an employer for unlawful misrepresentation of payroll, was repealed by the 1988 Proposition 103, effective November 9, 1988. Other remedies of an insurer in such a case were not affected. Effective January 1, 1992, any per- *IC 11670* son who misrepresents any fact in order to obtain workers' compensation *11880* insurance at less than the proper rate is guilty of a misdemeanor or felony depending upon the circumstances and a possible fine not to exceed $50,000.]

IC 11736   No premium may be lower than the rates determined by the Insurance Commissioner. Further, premiums may not be reduced by refunds except in the following instances:

IC 11738   1. If the insurer has a surplus after allowing for overhead and reserves, it may issue a refund only out of such surplus, on a participating plan. The appellate court holds that refunds are legal only when participating, and this means a share of the earnings without reference to the price paid for the insurance. Where a dividend agreement is not sharing, it is not participating. The participation clause must be set forth in the insurance policy.

IC 11738.5   An insurer's plan for issuing refunds or dividends under participating policies may not be discriminatory. Insurers must file annual confidential reports with the California Workers' Compensation Insurance Rating Bureau showing premiums, losses, and dividends paid, including data on premium size and loss-ratio categories.

IC 11776   2. The State Compensation Insurance Fund does issue refunds, for, as a state agency, it is prohibited from making a profit. Its income is used for overhead, payment of claims, maintenance of a surplus account, and the rest is refunded.

3. California operates on the merit system, and savings to employers are allowed by applying credit to premium rates for good experience records. If an employer's accident rate is low, he can realize savings through efficiency. Thus, there is a definite monetary incentive for an employer to be safety-conscious. An employer does not qualify for the merit plan until his payroll reaches $500 annually.

[NOTE: The Court of Appeal has ruled that recovery of a judgment for damages by reason of the fraud of an insurance agent for a workers' compensation insurance company does not constitute an illegal refund by that insurance company to the plaintiff employer. The fraud involved the promise of the agent that by switching to his company the plaintiff would save $6,000 through use of a cost-plus contract.]

In 1956 the Insurance Commissioner issued his "Ruling 67" which permitted insurance carriers to offer employers further savings in compensation insurance premiums through "package deals" of various types, termed retrospective rating plans, and a premium discount plan. This ruling was upheld by the California Supreme Court, but was nullified in 1957 by amendments to the Insurance Code. Ruling 67 would have permitted employers savings reflected by total loss experience either in multi-state operations or in multi-line (different types of insurance) policies. This plan was fought in court by the State Compensation Insurance Fund and other carriers who operated only in California. The court's decision points out that 68% of California workers' compensation coverage is written by California companies, including the 24.78% written by the Fund which can only write intrastate.

The restrictions placed in the Insurance Code are these:

Sec. 11732.2: No classification of risks, premium rates, or merit rating may reflect premiums or experience under any other type of insurance held by an employer (casualty or liability).

Sec. 11732.3: Nor may they reflect any experience or premium under any compensation insurance policy written under the laws of any other state.

Sec. 11732.4: There can be no discount by reason of any reduction of the expense provision in classes of risk.

Secs. 11732 and 11732.5: The expense provision in premium rates or classification risks shall be uniform as determined by the Insurance Commissioner.

The legislation nullifying Ruling 67 leaves the premium picture rather rigid. Employers with sizeable premiums thus search for ways of effecting savings through self-insurance. While insurers can issue refunds under a participating plan, they are limited by the requirement that the cost of operation reflected in minimum premiums must be uniform for all industries.

In one case, a utility and its carrier worked up this scheme: records would be kept on an 18-month basis, and the carrier would return all premiums, less total losses and reserves, and a 25.5% charge for administrative costs (cost-plus contract). The Supreme Court held this to be an illegal transaction because under the law, following the 1957 restrictive legislation, the only possible refund must be based on a participating plan, so stated in the policy, and the refund can be made only out of "surplus earnings" at the end of the policy period.

The code specifically prohibits the payment of any part of the insurance premium by the employee. Self-employing persons may obtain insurance *LC 3751* which provides the same protection as workers' compensation. Also, working *IC 11657* partners or working individual employers (sole proprietors) and working members of their families may be covered under a policy, along with other employees. If such an employer is covered for compensation benefits under *IC 11843-* his or her own policy, the premium is based upon all income he or she re- *11846* ceives from the business, subject to minimum and maximum limits set forth in the official insurance manual. The premium rate is to be based upon the highest rated classification for any duty undertaken by the self-employed person and in no event is to be less than that for executive supervisors of contractors. (See California Workers' Compensation Manual.) Either a court or the W.C.A.B. may act as arbiter between a self-employing person and the *LC 5308* insurance carrier. The State Compensation Insurance Fund may also issue *IC 11846* such policies and coverages and must submit to arbitration of any dispute by the W.C.A.B.

§ 3.3   Partial Coverage

LC 3750

IC 11657

An employer may insure any part of his risk. An example is the so-called "medical-ex policy" by which an employer insures the liability for monetary benefits but remains self-insured for the medical benefits. Permission for this arrangement must be obtained from the Director of the State Industrial Relations Department, otherwise the employer may be considered uninsured for benefits excluded from the policy.

§ 3.4   Insurance Coverage for Employer Groups

IC 11656.6

Certain employers with a common trade or business may purchase workers' compensation coverage under a group policy. Statutory permission for this type of coverage applies to agricultural enterprises, building and construction industry, transportation and warehouse industry, timber and lumber industry, public agencies providing water service, sheltered workshops and rehabilitation facilities licensed under LC 1191.5, all other enterprises for which the principal payroll (i.e., 51% or more of the payroll) develops under a single manual rate.

§ 3.5   Re-insurance

Many insurance carriers, self-insured employers, and legally uninsured public agencies, themselves, obtain other insurance to guard against the larger losses. This is known as "re-insurance" (or "excess coverage") and covers all losses over a certain amount. Approval by the Department of Insurance is required. Such coverage of a self-insured employer must be in excess of $96,500 per event or any one occupational disease claim. Re-insurance premiums depend, of course, on the amount of risk to be covered and are an added item of overhead.

§ 3.6   Employer's Duty

LC 3760
LC 6409
LC 6412

The employer is not relieved of duty entirely by insurance. An employer must post notice at each place of employment giving the name of the insurance carrier, the date of expiration of the policy, the telephone of the nearest office of the Labor Commissioner, along with an invitation to employees to call the Labor Commissioner's office if the coverage under the insurance policy has expired. Most notices contain the name of the doctor to whom the employees are referred in case of emergency. An employer must also report injuries to the insurer and to the Department of Industrial Relations on forms provided for this purpose. The first treating physician also renders a first report of injury. The report made out by the employer is confidential and is inadmissible in any proceeding before the Workers' Compensation Appeals Board. The doctor's report is admissible and is a very important piece of evidence.

LC 3752-3759

The employer must see that benefits are furnished. An employer is relieved of this duty if the insurance carrier assumes control of the case. Anything an employer does in an industrial accident case is binding on the insurer unless the insurer has given written notice that it has assumed liability and will not be bound by the acts of the employer. Such written notice is rarely given so that in most cases the employer may continue to bind the insurer. The effect of this principle will become apparent in later chapters.

§ 3.7 Subrogation

Since an insurer "stands in the shoes" of its insureds, it not only assumes the employer's liabilities, it also has all the rights the employer may have. Thus, if the employer has a right of action against a third party who may have caused an employee's injury, his insurer becomes possessed of, that is, subrogated to, this right. (See Chapter 12, DAMAGE SUITS—SUBROGATION.) *LC 3850-3864*

IC 11662

§ 3.8 Uninsurable Risks

In two instances the employer is not protected by insurance. These are:

1. Penalty for causing the employee's injury through serious and wilful misconduct. However, an employer may insure against the expense of defending a charge of serious and wilful misconduct. Thus, an insurance carrier may defend its insured in such a case, but the employer will be required to pay any award of a penalty issued by the W.C.A.B. *IC 11661*
LC 4553

2. Penalty for illegal hiring of a minor. (See Chapter 9, PENALTIES.) *IC 11661.5*
LC 4557

§ 3.9 Joint (General—Special) Employment

In some cases there is a problem in identifying the actual employer. In other cases the employee may be working for more than one employer at the time of the injury. For instance, Ajax Trucking Co. leases a truck to Smith for a few days and allows one of its drivers to operate the truck on condition that Smith pay the driver his regular daily wage. This situation is called a "general-special" employment. The special employer is Smith. If the driver suffers an industrial injury, both employers are liable. As between the workers' compensation insurance carriers of the two employers, that of the general employer is liable unless the special employer had the employee on its payroll. (If one of the employers is self-insured, that employer is deemed to be an insurance carrier for the purposes covered by IC 11663.) In our example, then, Smith's carrier would be liable. Such joint employment can occur in any industry; cases have arisen in the trucking, entertainment, and construction industries. *IC 11663*

§ 3.10 California Workers' Compensation Insurance Rating Bureau

The California Workers' Compensation Insurance Rating Bureau (CWCIRB) is an advisory bureau composed of members from the insurance industry. Insured employers and labor are also represented on the Bureau's *IC 11750-11759* governing committee. The Bureau maintains a record of all employers covered by workers' compensation insurance, including names of insurers, policy numbers and periods of coverage. In cases involving many employers, such as industrial disease cases, the employers' carriers can be ascertained. The Bureau also compiles data for determination of minimum premiums and makes recommendations to the Insurance Commissioner. The Bureau then issues a manual of the minimum premiums established by the commissioner. This manual, called the "California Workers' Compensation Insurance Manual," also includes interpretations concerning coverage, premiums, endorsements, and regulations of the Insurance Commissioner. It also includes samples of approved endorsements to workers' compensation insurance policies. It can be obtained from the Bureau's San Francisco office.

IC 11752.6   Many records and statistics are kept. One of the most important is a record of the number of injuries for each employer. An insurance carrier may thus ascertain with more certainty the type of risk involved and charge accordingly or refuse the risk. Insured employers have the right to obtain all policyholder information in the Bureau's files concerning their own coverage, including loss experience, claims, classification assignments, rates, policy contracts, rating plans and systems, and manual rules. Notice of a request for such information is to be given the carrier. Denial of a request is appealable to the Insurance Commissioner. The address of the Bureau is Spear Street Tower Suite 500, One Market Plaza, San Francisco, California 94105.

§ 3.11   Disputed Coverage

LC 5300   When an insurance company denies insurance coverage of an injury, a three-way dispute results involving the employee, the employer, and the alleged carrier. The Workers' Compensation Appeals Board determines the issue and, if necessary, may order reformation of an insurance policy to accord with the true situation. Since policy terms are those of the insurer, policy language is interpreted against the insurer, especially if ambiguous. However, if the terms are clear and not ambiguous, the terms and conditions will be given effect.

§ 3.12   Insurer's Bond and Reserves

IC 11690-11720   Insurance carriers are regulated by the Insurance Commissioner in accordance with the provisions of the California Insurance Code and commissioner's rules. In order to qualify as an admitted workers' compensation insurer in California, a carrier (except the State Compensation Insurance Fund) must deposit a bond or securities with the commissioner in an amount which will cover claims reserves. That is, an amount determined on the present value of estimated future payments and loss expenses computed at 6 percent interest. It must also be sufficient to reflect 65% of net earned compensation premium for the three years previous to December 31. If the amount computed on necessary reserves exceeds $50,000, the amount of the bond or securities shall not be more than double the amount so computed, and in any

IC 11699

event shall not be less than $100,000. Every insurance carrier must remain in a solvent condition with regard to its reserves and other liabilities.

The securities which a carrier may deposit in lieu of a bond are "cash *IC 11715* instruments," approved letters of credit, approved interest-bearing securities, approved stocks readily convertible to cash, investment certificates, share accounts in a savings and loan association with deposit insurance, certificates of deposit or savings deposits in a bank licensed to do business in California. Bonds and deposits are reviewed annually, and the commissioner may order any necessary increase of a bond or deposit of securities. Carriers may have security deposits in other states if those states have reciprocal laws.

Reserves are funds set aside to cover claims and are determined by the insurer's claims department. Each claim is considered separately and a reserve computed based upon probable liability. For instance, suppose Fred Smith makes a claim for an industrially caused hernia condition. The claims examiner can anticipate that if the claim is valid, the insurer will furnish six weeks' compensation and medical care. As the benefits are discussed in later chapters, keep in mind how the correct computation of benefits would affect setting up reserves.

Reserves must be adjusted from time to time, for the condition of the injured employee may prove to be different than first anticipated. The necessity for a fairly accurate appraisal by the insurer's claims department is paralleled, if litigation results, by the same requirement on the part of the attorney representing the employer or carrier and the attorney representing the employee before the Workers' Compensation Appeals Board.

§ 3.13 Reports; Audits; Solvency; Liquidation; Guarantee Association

Insurance carriers must file reports with the Insurance Commissioner's office which has authority to audit their financial condition as well as all other aspects of their business including claims-handling and reserves. The commissioner may enforce corrective measures when necessary. If it appears that a carrier is insolvent or precariously close to insolvency, the commissioner may take over its operation or liquidate its assets as a receiver. This action may be taken administratively or through court action. This authority includes resolving claims, enforcing a bond against its sureties, or liquidating any securities deposited in lieu of a bond.

An insurer may be audited by the Office of Benefit Assistance and *LC 129,* Enforcement (O.B.A.E.) of the Division of Workers' Compensation with re- *129.5* spect to the adequacy of furnishing benefits to injured workers or dependents. Payment may be ordered by O.B.A.E., penalties assessed, or action taken against the insurer's certificate.

IC 1063-
1063.145

The Legislature has created the California Insurance Guarantee Association (CIGA) to provide additional protection to insureds and claimants under policies written by admitted insurers in the fields of workers' compensation, liability, vehicle, fire, and certain other coverages. (See IC 1063 and 1063.1(c)(1)-(9).) The association is financed by assessments levied against the premiums received by members for included coverages. These assessments are to be recouped through a separately stated premium-surcharge. Any insurer, including the State Compensation Insurance Fund, writing policies in the protected categories must be a member of the association. Payment will not be made on the first $100 of a claim, nor that portion of any claim over $500,000, except in the case of workers' compensation claims. There appear to be no limits on the amount of a valid workers' compensation claim.

IC 1063.1

CIGA is not liable for the obligations of an insolvent insurance carrier under federal ocean marine laws or the Longshore and Harbor Workers' Compensation Act. These exclusions are effective as to occurrences on or after January 1, 1988. Also excluded from CIGA coverage are premium adjustments made pursuant to a retrospective rating plan, and any amount awarded as punitive damages.

IC 1063.1

While claims under insurance retroactively covering known losses are not paid by CIGA, claims under a special excess insurance policy covering the continuing obligations of a formerly self-insured employer are an exception to that exclusion.

In *Isaacson v. C.I.G.A.*, the California Supreme Court held that the Insurance Guarantee Association has no liability for a separate settlement by an insured where CIGA has settled the claim filed against it for a reasonable amount. The Court of Appeal held in *Reed v. C.I.G.A.* that CIGA is not liable where an insured of the defunct insurance carrier allows a default judgment to be entered against him. However, the court in *Carver v. W.C.A.B.* has held that CIGA is liable in a workers' compensation case for a 10% penalty under LC 5814 for the failure of an insolvent insurance carrier to pay compensation.

§ 3.14   Endorsements and Policy Exclusions

Regulations filed by the Insurance Commissioner have dealt with a previously troublesome area of the compensation practice. Before the changes, the standard approved workers' compensation policy form permitted exclusion of relatives of an employer and corporate officers and directors. To cover such excluded personnel, it was the duty of the employer to see that those individuals were named in the policy with changes effected only by written notice to the insurance carrier. There were other permitted exclusions. Under the regulations, however, the basic policy covers all employees except those excluded by endorsement. This changes the emphasis so that the carrier must bring the situation to the attention of the employer to ascertain whether some type of employee or worker should be excluded. The difficulty with the previous practice was that if a standard policy were delivered to an employer with the exclusion of relatives and corporate officers contained in it without notice to the employer, the employer might go for some time without realizing that a certain class of employees was not covered. As to excluded employees, an employer is considered uninsured unless he or she covers them with some other policy of workers' compensation insurance. There was also the possibility that an injured employee might file with the Workers' Compensation Appeals Board claiming a penalty for wilful non-insurance. The new rules make it more difficult to be uninsured in this manner; however, it still behooves an employer to carefully check any policy of workers' compensation insurance when it is delivered.

When a limiting endorsement is placed upon a policy of workers' compensation insurance, one of the following statements must be contained in boldface type or typewritten in capital letters:

"ENDORSEMENT AGREEMENT
LIMITING AND RESTRICTING THIS INSURANCE"

or

"DOES NOT INSURE"

or

"DOES NOT EXTEND TO OR COVER"

or

"DOES NOT APPLY"

The character of any limitation must be printed in boldface or typewritten caps in the margin. Also, every limiting endorsement must contain the following footnote in bold-face or typewritten caps:

"FAILURE TO SECURE THE PAYMENT OF FULL COMPENSATION BENEFITS FOR ALL EMPLOYEES AS REQUIRED BY LABOR CODE SECTION 3700 IS A VIOLATION OF LAW AND MAY SUBJECT THE EMPLOYER TO THE IMPOSITION OF A WORK STOP ORDER, LARGE FINES, AND OTHER SUBSTANTIAL PENALTIES (Labor Code Section 3710.1, et seq.)."

Limiting endorsements may be utilized only on forms approved by the Insurance Commissioner. These forms may be found in Title 10 of the California Administrative Code, Sections 2269.1 through 2269.14. Each *IC 11659* workers' compensation insurer must submit its limiting endorsement forms to the California Workers' Compensation Insurance Rating Bureau for approval. The form will be deemed approved by the Insurance Commissioner unless within 30 days of the date of submission the Insurance Commissioner notifies the insurer that the form is disapproved. Such forms will be deemed approved until 10 days after the date of a written notification of disapproval.

One approved endorsement form provides for exclusion of coverage for serious and wilful misconduct and penalty for illegal employment of a minor, insurance for which is prohibited by the Insurance Code. Other permitted endorsements may provide for:

1. Under a workers' compensation and employers' liability policy, exclusion under coverage B—employers' liability—"with respect to any employee employed in domestic employment not described in the declarations unless the policy applies under coverage A with respect to such employee."

2. Exclusion of employee who may also be a member of the partnership named as the insured employer in the policy, even though such person is a silent member of the partnership or a working member of the partnership receiving wages irrespective of profits from the partnership, unless such person is specifically named in the policy or in an endorsement.

3. Exclusion of relatives in the following degree: relatives of the employer or spouse, namely, spouse, child by birth or adoption, stepchild, grandchild, son-in-law, daughter-in-law, parent, stepparent, parent-in-law, grandparent, brother, sister, stepbrother, stepsister, half-brother, half-sister, brother-in-law, sister-in-law, uncle, aunt, nephew or niece; if at the time of injury such relative resides in the household of the employer or spouse, or is a child under the age of 12, unless such relative is included specifically by name in the schedule in the policy or by endorsement to the policy.

4. Exclusion of medical benefits under LC 4600. (This is the so-called medical-ex policy.)

5. Exclusion of named employees or categories of employees or particular operations or locations of the employer—if the employees are otherwise covered.

6. Exclusion of any liability of the named employer other than as a partnership "jointly and not severally."

These exclusions do not contain any approved form of endorsement to exclude officers and directors of corporate employers. These and other employees may be excluded from a particular policy only if the employer affirms to the insurer in writing that any such employee (or liability) is otherwise insured or is lawfully uninsured. In 1969, Labor Code Section 3351 was amended to provide that the term "employee" does not include the officers and directors of a corporation if they are the sole shareholders. Compensation coverage for such officers or directors is elective.

It should be stressed that any lack of clarity in policies or ambiguities resulting from tacking on exclusionary endorsements will be construed against the insurer. In the absence of any provision or endorsement to the contrary, a policy is presumed to cover all employees in all businesses operated by the insured employer. A general provision, such as covering "all employees, including construction or extension of lines," will control over a specific exclusion if the employee is injured doing the type of work described in the general provision of the policy.

If a limiting endorsement is attached to an insurance policy in such a way that it cannot be read and understood by the average person, it will not be given effect by the W.C.A.B. or the courts. In one case, the limiting endorsement was attached by staples so that the reader had to form a cylinder by pressing the paper and read it upside down. In another case, the language was so confusing that an official of the insurance company could not explain the meaning to the court. In both cases, limiting language was held ineffective and full coverage was ordered.

§ 3.15 Basic Rights and Obligations of Insurers

Under the provisions of the Boynton Act, as now codified in the Labor and Insurance Codes, the insurer assumes a direct and primary liability under its policy. Where a policy of insurance contains exclusions from coverage but also a clause covering defense of all claims arising out of the operations of the insured, the insurer has the duty to defend, which is broader than the duty to indemnify. Any doubts concerning this liability will be resolved in favor of the insured. An insurer may have the duty to defend, even though it may not have the duty to pay any judgment or award rendered. Where, however, under a liability policy the liability of the insured under the workers' compensation law is excluded, the duty to defend does not include the duty to furnish a defense to an action filed before the Workers' Compensation Appeals Board. But where a workers' compensation insurance policy includes coverage for employers' liability, a defense must be provided the employer in a lawsuit filed by an employee even though liability may ultimately be found to be excluded under the terms of the policy.

If an agent of an insurer makes representations that excluded employees may be covered with the same type of insurance under another policy, these representations will be deemed to be included as terms and conditions of a so-called major medical policy which, as issued, contains an exclusion of industrial injuries.

Where an insured in applying for insurance misstates a material fact regarding the type of risk to be covered, the carrier will not be held liable for a loss sustained by reason of such unknown risk. The misstated or undisclosed risk defense has been applied in the compensation field, but since premium is determined by payroll audit, a defense based upon a policy exclusion is more difficult to maintain if the carrier has accepted a premium on such an audit. Acceptance of the premium after an opportunity to review the books and records of the employer may *estop* the carrier from denying coverage and also indicate that the activity involved in the exclusion was not material to the actual risk being insured.

The effect of an agent's acceptance of a premium with an application for insurance is to bind the carrier as of the date indicated by papers or other evidence of agreement, rather than some later date after the insurance carrier has passed judgment upon the applicant's insurability. Any requirement that issuance is dependent upon the carrier's approval must be clearly stated to the applicant for insurance. Insurance transactions are construed in the light of a layman's reasonable understanding of the time and extent of the coverage.

It has been seen that the employer has a basic liability as does the insurer under the workers' compensation law, and thus the employer may, in effect, bind the carrier in certain instances where agreements or benefits have been furnished. Similarly, under general insurance law, if an employer under group policies conducts certain of the administration for the carrier, the employer may bind the carrier. A master policy issued with certificates of coverage to the employees will be construed consistent with any enlargement of coverage indicated by the certificate. However, where an employer is ordered into receivership, and the receiver takes over the employer's property and the operation of his or her business without notification or payment of premiums to the insurance carrier, a receiver, as the new employer, must secure workers' compensation benefits. The insolvent employer and his or her former workers' compensation insurance carrier have no further interest or liability. (However, the result might be different if the carrier accepted a premium with knowledge of the change of employer.)

§ 3.16   Agents and Brokers

An insurance agent acts on behalf of the insurer and may bind the company by written or oral representation that the customer is insured. A broker acts for the customer, and his or her representations do not bind any particular insurance carrier. He or she may place insurance with any carrier who will accept the coverage. However, a course of dealings may show that an insurer has considered the acceptance by a particular broker as binding. As between employer-customer and agent or broker, both types of insurance salespersons or firms may incur a liability if a policy is not issued in accordance with the agreement or if policy limits are changed by an agent or broker without a request by or the approval of the client. However, absent an agreement or representation, an agent or broker is not a "blanket insurer" for every possible risk which a customer might encounter.

§ 3.17   Homeowners or Occupants; Personal Liability Insurance Coverage

The Insurance Code provides that every personal liability insurance policy issued or renewed on or after January 1, 1977, must contain a provision covering the policyholder's workers' compensation liability arising from his or her status as an employer of persons performing home-related work. This coverage applies specifically to duties incidental to the ownership, maintenance, or use of a residential dwelling, including the care and supervision of children, where such duties are personal to the policyholder and are not in the course of the trade, business, profession, or occupation of the policyholder. The premium charge for this special coverage is not to be separately stated in the charge for the personal liability policy.

The present provision does not permit the policyholder to reject workers' compensation coverage, but it does not make it mandatory to have such insurance. Where homeowners or occupants do not have such insurance and hire persons to do home-related or personal work, the provisions of LC 3715(b) come into play and permit certain of such employees the option of civil suit against the employer in case of a work injury, or to workers' compensation rights enforceable against both the employer and the state's uninsured employers' fund. The employees who qualify for these rights are those who would have so-qualified under the provisions in effect before 1977 regarding casual employment, household domestic service, and part-time gardeners. As indicated in the previous chapter, it behooves the homeowner or occupant (renter) to have a personal liability policy as a part of his or her insurance package before hiring anyone to work in home-related or personal activities. (For a more detailed discussion of the coverage and rights of those engaged in home-related work, see Chapter 2, COMPENSATION COVERAGE-EMPLOYMENT, § 2.5, *Special Included Categories*, item 18.) *IC 11590-11593*

§ 3.18   Employee Contribution Prohibited

The law provides that no employer "shall exact or receive from any employee any contribution, or make or take any deduction from the earnings of any employee, either directly or indirectly, to cover the whole or any part of the cost of [workers'] compensation. . . ." Violation of this provision is a misdemeanor. Also, per the Court of Appeal, deduction of a pro rata amount of the cost of workers' compensation insurance from an employee's wages or salary results in a loss of the employer's immunity from personal injury actions brought by employees injured in the course of employment. *LC 3751*

Compensation may not be reduced by other benefits, unless specifically permitted by law in special situations. But, if an employer provides supplemental benefits, credit for worker's compensation may be a part of the supplemental program. The important point is that basic workers' compensation benefits not be reduced. *LC 3752*

§ 3.19   Failure to Insure; Uninsured Employers' Fund

If an employer fails to "secure" payment of benefits by insurance or self-insurance, the employer is deemed to be wilfully uninsured. Certain penalties may be assessed by the Appeals Board if an employee is found to be entitled to workers' compensation benefits. The penalties are a 10% increase in the award and payment of the employee's attorney's fees. If the employer shows that the failure to insure was not wilful, the 10% penalty is *LC 3710 et seq.*

LC 3700.5

not assessed, but the employer must pay the attorney's fee. Any uninsured employer is also guilty of a misdemeanor if the employer knew or should have known of the requirement to "secure" these obligations.

LC 3706-3732

An injured employee of an illegally uninsured employer has several remedies. He or she may bring a personal injury action in the general courts, and may pursue workers' compensation benefits by claim and by filing an application with the W.C.A.B., including the right to join as a party to a W.C.A.B. proceeding the Uninsured Employers' Fund (U.E.F.). This Fund was created to provide workers' compensation benefits to injured employees of illegally uninsured employers who do not or cannot meet their obligations when their employees are injured in the course of employment. The fund pays basic benefits. It is not liable for any penalties or interest assessed

LC 3716, 3716.2

against the employer or for any medical treatment furnished by the state under the California Medical Assistance Program. It is not liable for benefits or contribution in occupational disease or cumulative trauma cases unless no employer during the period of actionable exposure or injury was insured, self-insured, or legally uninsured. Also, the Fund is not liable in any case involving an unlicensed uninsured building contractor, or his or her employees, where the "ultimate hirer" (whether property owner or general contractor) has "secured" payment of compensation through insurance or permissible self-insurance.

In *Rymer v. Hagler*, the Court of Appeal ruled that a final finding of insurance coverage determined by a workers' compensation judge precludes a personal injury action against the employer under LC 3706 on the basis of res judicata and collateral estoppel. In that case, a workers' compensation action and a personal injury action were instituted by the employee against the employer. In the W.C.A.B. proceeding, the applicant moved for dismissal of the insurance carrier as a party. The judge ruled that the carrier had coverage by admission and by estoppel. No petition for reconsideration was filed by the applicant, and the judge's finding became a final decision, even though the case in chief was never tried and was dismissed by the applicant.

The Uninsured Employers' Fund is administered by the Director of Industrial Relations and is financed with public funds and any recoveries or civil penalties the Director is able to obtain from uninsured employers. The law provides the Director a number of avenues to pursue in obtaining such recoveries. The Director of Industrial Relations may make a *prima facie* determination of failure to secure workers' compensation benefits, subject to due process procedures and appeal.

The W.C.A.B. has ruled in *U.E.F. v. W.C.A.B.* (1989) that the filing of a petition in bankruptcy under Chapter 7 by an uninsured employer does not automatically stay W.C.A.B. proceedings as against the Uninsured Employers Fund. In many cases involving an uninsured employer who has filed a petition in bankruptcy, it has been necessary to obtain an order from the bankruptcy court lifting the automatic stay of other proceedings against the bankrupt in order to move forward with a W.C.A.B. proceeding even where the principal purpose of the proceeding is to obtain benefits from U.E.F. The decision in *U.E.F. v. W.C.A.B.* should obviate the necessity to apply to the bankruptcy court for such orders where U.E.F. liability is in view.

The Appeals Board has the authority to assess a 10 percent penalty *LC 5814.1* against an uninsured employer to be applied to any discretionary payments made by the Director from the Uninsured Employers Fund. This penalty is payable to the Director and is in addition to any penalty assessed against the employer under Section 5814.

The employer upon being served with the application may be required to *LC 3715* furnish the W.C.A.B. with a bond to cover any award for benefits as determined by the Appeals Board. If the employer fails to pay the award or furnish a bond within 10 days after being notified, the employee, or his dependents, may apply to the Director of Industrial Relations for payment of the award from the Uninsured Employer's Fund. Upon payment, the Director has a liquidated claim for damages against the employer in the amount fixed by the Appeals Board. The Director may file an action against the employer to collect the amount so paid. A certified copy of the record of the W.C.A.B. proceedings must be attached to the complaint. The record constitutes *prima facie* evidence of the truth of the facts therein contained. The defendant is given 10 days to file his or her appearance. The case receives preference on the trial calendar. The Director of Industrial Relations has the discretion to compromise any suit against the employer which he believes will best serve the interests of the fund under his control. The Director may also seek to recover for the employee penalties and interest for which the Fund is not liable. In seeking recoupment from an uninsured employer, the Fund may enforce liability against any "parent" of a corporation under Corporations Code Section 175, and any substantial stockholder of the corporation.

In handling a claim for compensation benefits, the Director, with notice, *LC 3715,* may bind the uninsured employer in an approved compromise and release *5106* agreement with the injured worker or by way of a stipulated award. If the employer objects, the Director's action will not bind the employer unless the W.C.A.B. determines that the employer is liable. On request of the Director, the W.C.A.B. may order the employer to pay the Fund the commuted value of an award of installment payments. Per a Court of Appeal decision, the Director may obtain reimbursement from the "ultimate hirer" if a purported building contractor-employer is unlicensed and uninsured. See discussion of "ultimate hirer," Chapter 2, EMPLOYMENT, Section 2.8, *Employee or Independent Contractor.*

The Fund also has subrogation rights against third-party wrongdoers under LC 3850, et seq., for which the statute of limitations is one year from *LC 3732* the date on which the Fund pays or becomes obligated to pay compensation.

Damage recoveries from third parties obtained by the Fund are not to be reduced because of any negligence of the employer, and the W.C.A.B. is not to consider any employer negligence in regard to approval of settlements or credit issues involving third-party recoveries.

In third-party personal injury actions, the Fund's subrogation or lien rights are not reducible by the comparative negligence of either the employer or the employee. The Director may settle or waive a claim as the Director deems necessary for the best interest of the Uninsured Employers' Fund.

LC 3706, 3708.5

When an employee maintains a personal injury action against an uninsured employer, a copy of the complaint must be served upon the Uninsured Employers' Fund. If the employee recovers a judgment, the employer will be credited with any compensation paid. The judgment must include a reasonable attorney's fee fixed by the court. The Fund has a lien against the judgment to the extent of compensation paid. No satisfaction of judgment is valid unless the Director is given the opportunity to perfect the Fund's lien.

If the Appeals Board determines that a claim has been filed against an uninsured employer, the Administrative Director is to file, with the office of the county recorder in any county in which the employer has property, a certificate prepared and furnished by the Appeals Board showing the date of the application, the name and address of the employer and the fact that the employer has not secured payment of workers' compensation benefits as required by law. Upon recordation, the certificate constitutes a valid lien in favor of the Director of Industrial Relations and has the same force, effect, and priority as a judgment lien. A copy of the certificate so filed must be served upon the employer by the W.C.A.B. If payment has been made or bond posted by the employer, the Administrative Director is to cancel the lien of record. The Administrative Director may also obtain a superior court judgment by filing a certificate with the county clerk.

[NOTE: The Uninsured Employers' Fund has no liability as to injuries to employees of uninsured homeowners or occupants arising from home-related or personal services except in these instances: qualified domestic service, part-time gardeners, and casual employment. For details, see Chapter 2, EMPLOYMENT, Section 2.5, *Special Included Categories*, item 18.]

LC 4401-4418

Asbestos Workers' Account. This account within the Uninsured Employers' Fund was established to assure payment of workers' compensation in cases arising from industrial exposure to asbestos. Claimants must demonstrate that they were exposed to asbestos and suffer from asbestosis. Claimants must also file an application with the W.C.A.B. against any known employer or to determine employment where employer-identity must be determined. Benefits covered are temporary total compensation, medical treatment, permanent total disability compensation, and death benefits. (Benefits not payable from the Account may be sought as against an employer.) Dependents are limited to a dependent spouse and minor children. The statute of limitations in an asbestos case is one year from date of death. Compensation is to be paid in installments and may not be commuted to a lump sum. The Account has lien rights, collection rights against employers, and lien rights and subrogation rights in actions against third-party wrongdoers. This program terminates as of December 31, 1989, unless extended by the Legislature. However, the authority of the Account to recover payments and costs made prior to that date is continuing.

§ 3.20 Self-Insurance; Security Fund

An employer in the private sector (i.e., a nonpublic agency employer) may elect to be self-insured for workers' compensation if able to meet various criteria. Permission must be obtained from the Director of Industrial *LC 3701,* Relations who, if the employer qualifies, will issue a certificate of consent to *et seq.* self-insure. In order to qualify, an employer must be solvent, pay fees based upon the number of employees, and post a bond or securities in an amount sufficient to secure 125% of estimated workers' compensation liability plus an additional 10% of the estimated liability to cover administrative and legal expense, the minimum deposit being $220,000. If an applicant for a certifi- *LC 3701.7* cate of self-insurance has had a period of unlawful uninsurance, additional security and penalties may be required. Securities which may be deposited in lieu of a bond include cash, securities, cash and securities, cash and a bond, or an approved irrevocable letter of credit. The Director may use funds from deposited security to pay claims for compensation if the employer has failed to make timely payment. Disputes regarding the use of these funds are resolved by the Director with there being the right of review in a superior court mandate proceeding. A private employer who has ceased to be self-insured has continuing liability for compensation for obligations accruing dur- *LC 3702.8* ing the period of self-insurance. Security must be maintained to cover this liability. Such an employer may obtain insurance to cover claims relating to previously unreported injuries. A self-insured employer who ceases to be self-insured may purchase special excess insurance to cover continuing obligations, in which case the deposit is held for three years. Upon the posting of the policy, the Security Fund obligation is discharged, and the California Insurance Guarantee Association (CIGA) must be notified.

A self-insured employer must file an annual report with the Director, *LC 3702.1,* and a third-party administrator is required to estimate the total accrued lia- *3702.2* bility of each client for use in the annual report. The Director may conduct audits of self-insured employers. The cycle for audits by the Office of Self- *LC 3702.6* insurance Plans is three years. A self-insurer may be audited by the Office of *LC 129,* Benefit Assistance and Enforcement (O.B.A.E.) of the Division of Workers' *129.5* Compensation with respect to the adequacy of furnishing benefits to injured workers or dependents. Payment may be ordered by O.B.A.E., and in flagrant cases penalties may be assessed and action taken against an employer's certificate of self-insurance.

The certificate of consent may be revoked for good cause after a hearing. "Good cause" includes insolvency, impaired solvency, failure to *LC 3702*

LC 6401.7

LC 3702 (b)

maintain the security deposit, failure to pay assessments for the Self-Insurers' Security Fund, frequent or flagrant violations of safety laws (including wilful failure to maintain an injury prevention program), failure to properly administer workers' compensation obligations. Improper administration includes habitually forcing workers to take less than is due or causing unnecessary resort to the W.C.A.B., dishonesty, or administration in a manner which could cause injury to the public or those dealing with the employer. If a revocation is based upon the private employer's lack of financial strength, failure to fulfill obligations, or dishonesty, the employer may not challenge or appeal the Director's decision unless the employer has "in effect insurance against liability to pay compensation."

LC 3740-3747

Every private permissibly self-insured employer must be a member of the Self-Insurers' Security Fund, a non-profit mutual benefit corporation governed by a seven-member board of trustees. Six trustees are representatives of private self-insurers. The seventh trustee is the Director of Industrial Relations. The fund is financed by assessments against members on a pro rata basis, and liability for assessments continues for three years beyond cessation of self-insured status. Upon order of the Director, this fund will assume the workers' compensation liability of an insolvent self-insurer, except that the fund will not be liable for any penalties. The fund may seek reimbursement from the insolvent employer and may look to the self-insurer's bond or security deposit. In addition, the fund has the same subrogation rights as the employer in actions against third parties under LC 3850.

In *Self-Insured Employers' Security Fund v. ESIS, et al.*, the Court of Appeal held that an officer of a self-insured corporation is not personally liable to the Fund for deficiencies in the corporation's workers' compensation liability reports.

Regulations implementing statutory requirements for self-insurance are set forth in Title 8, California Code of Regulations, sections 15200 and following.

§ 3.21   Government Agencies; Insurance and Self-Insurance

LC 3700

IC 11870-11872

The government of the State of California, all state agencies, and all local governmental agencies (i.e., counties, cities, special purpose, or taxing districts) must "secure" payment of workers' compensation benefits. They may either insure or self-insure. Their form of self-insurance is also called "legal uninsurance," for they thus far are not required to post bond or deposit securities as are private self-insurers. When a state or local public agency obtains insurance, the carrier is usually the State Compensation Insurance Fund. The Fund may also act as an adjusting agency for the state and state agencies as self-insured entities, represent them in workers' compensation proceedings and seek recovery from third parties, including the maintaining of court actions.

A self-insured local agency (but not the state or state agency) must obtain a certificate of consent from the Director of Industrial Relations. The fees are paid by the state. Such agencies are subject to revocation of their certificates for the same reasons as are private self-insureds. As an added incentive for making timely payment under compensation awards, if a self-insured local public agency unduly delays or refuses payment of amounts awarded, the W.C.A.B. is to assess a penalty in the form of an attorney's fee incurred in enforcing the award, in addition to any 10% penalty under LC 5314.

LC 3700(c), 3702

LC 5814.5

§ 3.22   Self-Insurance Administrators

A private or public self-insured employer may retain the services of an independent firm to act as administrator of the employer's workers' compensation program. Such administrators must be certified by the Department of Industrial Relations, and certification is subject to revocation for cause. Admitted insurance carriers are exempt from this requirement. In order to qualify for a certificate of consent, a self-insurance administration business or firm must demonstrate competency to provide such service. Administrators and claims personnel may be required to take a written examination approved by the Director of Industrial Relations. A separate certificate is required for each business location. A certificate may be revoked for good cause on the same grounds set forth in LC 3702 for self-insurers, as previously discussed. The Director is authorized to levy a fine of $50-$500 for each violation in lieu of revocation.

LC 3702.1

LC 3702.7

Third-party administrators are also subject to audit by the Office of Benefit Assistance and Enforcement (O.B.A.E) of the Division of Workers' Compensation with respect to the adequacy of furnishing benefits to injured workers or their dependents. Payment may be ordered, and in flagrant cases penalties assessed and action taken against an administrator's certificate.

LC 129, 129.5

§ 3.23   Workers' Compensation Requirement for Building Permit

A contractor or owner is required to show evidence of insurance for workers' compensation or a certificate of permissible self-insurance in order to obtain a building permit from a city or county. A permit is not to be issued if proof is not so presented, although an applicant for a permit may certify to having no employees. A county has been held liable for a worker's loss through an uncompensated work-injury where such proof was not required of the contractor or owner before the issuance of a building permit.

LC 3800 H&S 19825-19827

§ 3.24   Workers' Compensation Requirement for Highway Carrier Permit

Highway common carriers, including cement carriers and highway permit carriers, must file proof of insurance or permissible self-insurance for workers' compensation with the Public Utilities Commission as a condition of issuance, transfer, or retention of a permit to do business. Highway carriers

PUC 460.5, 1063.5, 3553, 3554

having gross annual earnings of $350,000 or more must file an annual statement with the Commission identifying the workers or owner-operators hired or engaged during the reporting period. If a highway carrier had no employees subject to the Workers' Compensation Law, a sworn statement to that effect must be filed.

Chapter 4
MEDICAL TREATMENT

§ 4.1   Introduction

An industrially injured worker has the right to select his or her own physician after 30 days from the date on which the injury is reported to the employer. In the words of the statute, "After 30 days from the date the injury is reported, the employee may be treated by a physician of his or her own choice or at a facility of his or her own choice within a reasonable geographic area." The law also requires employers to notify all employees of their rights with respect to medical treatment. In addition, if an employee has notified his or her employer in writing before the date of injury that he or she has a personal physician, the employee has the right to be treated by that physician from the date of injury. The right to be treated by one's personal physician at the outset also accrues if the employer has failed to post notice of workers'

LC 4600

LC 4603.5

R 9780(h)
*LC 3550-
3552*

compensation rights as required by LC 3550. "Personal physician" is defined as a doctor of medicine or osteopathy who, before the injury, directed the medical treatment of the employee and maintains the employee's medical records and medical history.

The amendment to LC 4600 granting the right of employee-selection of physician was effective January 1, 1976, and has been held to apply to all cases after that date regardless of the date of injury. Before 1976, the law assigned full medical control to employers or their insurance carriers. An employer or carrier could lose medical control if the treatment was not adequate. LC 4600 now gives the employer or carrier medical control only for a period of 30 days after receiving notice (or equivalent knowledge) of an industrial injury. However, the employee has the option of leaving medical control with the employer. (The Worker's Compensation Institute has pointed out that in 70% of the cases treatment does not go beyond 30 days and that many employers have had a policy of permitting employees to choose their own physicians.)

LC 4603.2   If an injured worker selects his or her own physician or medical facility, the employee or the treating physician must immediately notify the employer of the physician's name and address, and, within five working days of the initial examination, the physician must submit a medical report to the employer. Thereafter, the physician must submit periodic reports. The employer or compensation carrier is obligated to pay bills rendered for the physician's services after receipt of the required reports.

LC 4601   The employee has a right to one change of physicians on request, the new physician to be selected and furnished by the employer. Upon receiving such a request, the employer must within five working days provide the employee an alternative physician or, if requested by the employee, a chiropractor. "The employee is also entitled, in any serious case, upon request, to the services of a consulting physician or chiropractor of his or her choice at the expense of the employer."

If before injury a worker has notified the employer of his or her personal chiropractor, i.e., one who has regularly treated the employee and maintained appropriate records, on the employee's request for change of physician, the alternative physician is to be the personal chiropractor.

LC 4603

R 9780-
9787

If, after 30 days from the date the employer receives notice of injury, the employee decides to select his or her own physician or medical facility, the employer or carrier, upon reviewing the medical reports from the employee's physician or from the employer's or carrier's examining physician, may wish to retain medical control. If so, the employer or carrier must petition the Administrative Director, who, upon a showing of good cause, may order a change of physicians. When the Administrative Director finds that there is good cause, the Director issues an order to that effect and may direct the employer or carrier to furnish the employee a panel of five physicians or, if requested by the employee, a panel of four physicians and one chiropractor competent to treat the particular case. The employee must select one from this panel to treat his or her industrial injury. Under R 9786(d)(3), the Administrative Director may merely "issue an order requiring employee to select employer designated physician." This rule puts the burden upon the employee to request the panel. The granting of such a request appears to be discretionary on the part of the Director. Regarding possible sanctions for involvement in a fraudulent workers' compensation claim, see Chapter 9, PENALTIES, § 9.18, *Fraudulent Claims*.

§ 4.2 Administrative Director Rules

The Administrative Director has authority to adopt rules regarding medical treatment. Rules have been adopted regarding employee-selection of physician, "reasonable geographic area," and transfer of medical treatment. These rules as amended are set forth below, verbatim:

§ 4.2(a) Article 5: Transfer of Medical Treatment

Definitions. As used in this Article: *R 9780*

(a) "Employer" includes insurers as defined in Division 4 of the Labor Code, and any person performing the duties of an employer under Division 4, Part 2, Chapter 2, Article 2 of the Labor Code, or this Article;

(b) "Employee" includes an attorney or other representative authorized by the employee to exercise any right under Division 4, Part 2, Chapter 2, Article 2 of the Labor Code, or this Article;

(c) "Physician" has the meaning defined in Labor Code Section 3209.3;

(d) "Facility" means a hospital, clinic or other institution capable of providing the medical, surgical, chiropractic or hospital treatment which is reasonably required to cure or relieve the employee from the effects of the injury.

(e) "Reasonable geographic area" within the context of Labor Code Section 4600 shall be determined by giving consideration to:

(1) The employee's domicile, place of employment and place where the injury occurred;
(2) The availability of physicians in the fields of practice, and facilities offering treatment reasonably required to cure or relieve the employee from the effects of the injury;
(3) The employee's medical history;
(4) The employee's primary language.

(f) "First aid" is any one-time treatment, and any follow-up visit for the purpose of observation of minor scratches, cuts, burns, splinters, etc., which do not ordinarily require medical care. Such one-time treatment, and follow-up visit for the purpose of observation, is considered first aid, even though provided by a physician or registered professional personnel.

(g) "Emergency treatment" is that medical treatment reasonably required by an injured employee immediately following an industrial injury or illness, which, if delayed, could decrease the likelihood of maximum recovery.

(h) "Personal physician" means a doctor of medicine, or a doctor of osteopathy, who prior to the injury has directed the medical treatment of the employee and who retains the employee's medical records and medical history. "Personal physician" includes a corporation, partnership or association of such doctors of medicine or osteopathy.

(i) "Employee-selected physician" includes personal physician and physician of facility selected by the employee more than 30 days from the date the injury is reported.

R 9780.1   **Employee Selection of Personal Physician.** If an employee wishes to be treated by a "personal physician" selected pursuant to Labor Code Section 4600, the employee shall notify his employer in writing. The notice need not be in any particular form, and may be in a form reasonably required by the employer and shall advise the employer of the name and address of such personal physician. Nothing in this Article shall prohibit an employer from permitting an injured employee to be treated by a physician of the employee's choice.

R 9780.2   **Employer's Duty to Provide First Aid and Emergency Treatment.** Where an employee has notified his or her employer in writing prior to the date of injury that he or she wishes to be treated by a personal physician pursuant to Labor Code Section 4600, and Section 9780.1 of this Article, the employer shall continue to have the duty to provide first aid treatment, and appropriate emergency treatment reasonably required by the nature of the injury or illness. Thereafter, if further medical treatment is reasonably necessary, the employee may be treated by his or her personal physician at the expense of the employer.

R 9781   **Employee's Request for Change of Physician.** An employee's request for change of physician pursuant to Section 4601 of the Labor Code need not be in writing. The employer shall respond thereto promptly, and in the manner best calculated to reach the employee, and in no event later than 5 working days from receipt of said request. Except where the employee is permitted to select his or her own physician or facility to provide medical treatment, the employer shall advise the employee of the name and address of the alternative physician, or chiropractor if requested, the date and time of an initial scheduled appointment, and any other pertinent information. The employer may confirm its response in writing.

R 9782   **Notice to Employee of Right to Choose Physician.** Every employer shall advise his employees in writing of their right to request a change of treating physician if the original treating physician is selected initially by the employer; to be treated by a physician of his or her own choice 30 days after reporting an injury; and to direct initial medical treatment, other than appropriate emergency or first aid treatment, by designating a personal physician and notifying the employer in writing of his or her choice prior to the injury. This duty may be satisfied by incorporating such advice in a notice, if posted in a conspicuous manner at all places of employment, or by any other regularly used means of communicating information to employees.

Duties of the Employee. Upon selecting a treating physician or facility *R 9783* pursuant to Labor Code Section 4600 30 days after reporting the injury, the employee shall immediately notify the employer of the name and address of the physician or facility selected. The employee shall not be penalized for failure to so notify the employer if the selected physician or facility promptly gives notice to the employer of the commencement of treatment or if the employer receives this information promptly from any source.

If so requested by the selected physician or facility, the employee shall sign a release permitting the selected physician or facility to report to the employer as required by these rules.

Duties of the Employer. In addition to the duty of the employer to give *R 9784* notice pursuant to Sections 9782 or 9880, upon being notified of the name and address of the employee-selected physician or facility, the employer, after treatment has commenced, shall promptly authorize such physician or facility to provide all medical treatment reasonably required to cure or relieve the employee from the effects of the industrial injury, furnish the name and address of the person to whom billing for treatment should be sent, and provide such other information as is required by this Article.

The employer shall also arrange for the delivery to the selected physician or facility of all medical information relating to the claim, all X-rays and the results of all laboratory studies done in relation to the injured employee's treatment.

If the employee-selected physician or facility fails to provide adequate medical reports pursuant to Section 9785, the employer shall promptly notify said physician or facility of the requirements of Section 9785.

Duties of the Employee-Selected Physician. The physician or facility *R 9785* chosen by the employee who undertakes to provide treatment pursuant to Labor Code Section 4600 shall:

(a) Within 3 working days after undertaking to provide such treatment notify the employer of the name and address of such treating physician or facility, and

(b) Within 5 working days following initial examination submit a written report to the employer to include:

(1) The name and address of injured employee;

(2) The employee's medical history as obtained by the physician;

(3) Findings on examination;

(4) The subjective complaints reported by the employee;

(5) The planned course, scope and duration of treatment;

(6) If appropriate, the estimated return-to-work date for regular or modified work;

(7) An opinion as to whether residual permanent disability is to be anticipated and, if possible, an estimate of its extent;

(8) An opinion as to whether the employee will eventually be able to engage in the occupation being performed at the time of injury.

(c) At reasonable intervals (which shall not be less frequent than every 45 days) during the active treatment submit progress reports to the employer which shall include an explanation of the need for continuing treatment and a reasonable estimate of the course, scope and duration of such treatment.

(d) Report promptly to the employer when:

(1) The employee's condition permits return to modified or regular work;

(2) The employee's condition requires him or her to leave work;

(3) Hospitalization or surgery is indicated or recommended;

(4) The employee's condition becomes permanent and stationary;

(5) The employee's condition undergoes a previously unexpected significant change (this report shall contain a statement of the proposed course of treatment required, if any, by the change);

(6) The employee is referred to another physician for consultation.

(7) The employer reasonably requests additional appropriate information.

(e) Any controversies concerning this section shall be resolved pursuant to Labor Code Section 4603 or 4604, whichever is appropriate.

R 9786   **Employer's Petition for Order Requiring Employee to Select Employer-Designated Physician.**

(a) An employer desiring a change of employee-selected physician pursuant to Labor Code Section 4603 shall file with the Administrative Director a Petition for Order Requiring Employee to Select Employer-Designated Physician. Said petition shall be filed on a form and in a manner prescribed by the Administrative Director.

Said petition shall be accompanied by proof of service thereof and of any supportive documentary evidence filed therewith on the employee or, if represented, the employee's authorized attorney or representative, and upon the employee-selected and currently treating physician or chiropractor.

(b) Good cause shall be shown by a statement of facts deemed to constitute same with supportive documentary evidence (medical reports, affidavits and declarations, etc.).

Good cause includes, but is not limited to:

(1) A clear showing that the treating physician has regularly failed to comply with Section 9785 of this Article;

(2) A clear showing evidenced by medical reports that current treatment is inappropriate and that the employer is prepared to offer more effective treatment to cure or relieve from the effects of the injury or illness;

(3) A clear showing that the employee-selected physician or facility is not within a reasonable geographic area.

Good cause shall not include a showing that there is no present need for medical treatment to cure or relieve from the effects of the injury. The employer's contention that the employee is no longer in need of medical treatment to cure or relieve from the effects of injury or illness should be directed to the Workers' Compensation Appeals Board, not the Administrative Director, in support of a Petition for Order Requiring Employee to Select Employer-Designated Physician.

(c) As soon after service of such petition is possible, and in no event more than 20 days thereafter, the employee, his or her representative, or the treating physician may file with the Administrative Director and serve upon the employer and all other parties, a response to said petition. If the responding party wishes the contents of said response, and any supportive evidentiary documents to be considered by the Administrative Director as evidence relating to the issue of good cause, said response should be verified in the manner set forth in Section (a), Subsection (9) of this Section.

(d) The Administrative Director shall, within 25 days of the receipt of the petition if no response is filed, or within 20 days of the receipt of the response, either:

(1) Dismiss said petition, without prejudice, for failure to show good cause or to meet the requirements of this Section;

(2) Deny said petition pursuant to a finding that there is no good cause to require the employee to select an employer-designated physician.

(3) Grant said petition and issue an order requiring employee to select employer-designated physician pursuant to a finding that good cause exists therefor; or

(4) Set the matter for hearing before the Administrative Director or a member of the Administrative Director's staff for hearing and determination or refer the matter to the Workers' Compensation Appeals Board for hearing

and determination by a Workers' Compensation Judge of such factual determinations as may be requested by the Administrative Director.

(e) The employer's liability to pay for medical treatment by the employee-selected physician shall continue until an order of the Administrative Director issues granting the petition.

(f) The foregoing provisions of this Section notwithstanding the Administrative Director may elect to attempt informal adjustment of the employer-employee dispute as to treating physician. The Administrative Director may extend the time specified in Subsection (d) within which to act upon the employer's petition for a period not to exceed 30 days.

R 9787   **Appeal from Administrative Director's Order Granting or Denying Petition for Order Requiring Employee to Select Employer-Designated Physician.**

Any order denying or granting the employer's petition whether issued with or without hearing, shall be final and binding upon the parties unless within 30 days from service thereof the aggrieved party petitions the Workers' Compensation Appeals Board for relief in the manner prescribed by the Board's Rules of Practice and Procedure. [See Chapter 15, APPEALS.]

§ 4.2(b)   Article 6: Consulting Physician, Certification of

R 9796   **Certification of Consulting Physician, How Initiated.**

When an injured employee requests an employer to secure certification of a consulting physician under Labor Code Section 4602, the employer shall direct a letter in triplicate to the Division of Industrial Accidents, attention Medical Director, 455 Golden Gate Avenue, San Francisco, California 94102, containing the following information:

(a) The name and address of the injured employee;

(b) The name and address of the consulting physician chosen;

(c) The field of practice of the consulting physician.

R 9799   **Criterion for Certifying Competence.**

The criterion to be followed by the Administrative Director in certifying the competence of the consulting physician chosen by the injured employee is that the field of practice is related to the injury or the problem for which consultation was requested.

R 9802   **Notification by Administrative Director.**

The Administrative Director will notify the employer and employee as to competence of a consulting physician within twelve (12) days of the date of the receipt of the request for such certification.

§ 4.3   Authority of the W.C.A.B.

The Labor Code provides that the Appeals Board has jurisdiction over any controversy relating to the furnishing of medical treatment under LC 4600-4605. Presumably, this authority will extend to any case in which the Board's jurisdiction has attached by virtue of the filing of an application. Since the jurisdiction of the Board involves a judicial power conferred by the State Constitution, it may be concluded that its jurisdiction over the medical aspects of a case will be exclusive. According to a decision of the Court of Appeal, the Board's jurisdiction is recognized in the rules through its appellate authority. Thus, even though a proceeding is pending before the W.C.A.B., an employer or carrier must petition the Administrative Director if medical control is sought.

LC 5304, 4604
R 10950

§ 4.4   Employers' Basic Duty; Adequate Treatment

The provision for employee-selection of physician was added to LC 4600 without changing the basic requirement that an employer furnish all necessary medical treatment to the employer's industrially injured workers. LC 4600 further provides that in "the case of his or her neglect or refusal seasonably to do so, the employer is liable for the reasonable expense incurred by or on behalf of the employee in providing treatment." It therefore behooves the employer to provide treatment immediately and, if the employee elects to select his or her own physician after the 30-day period, to monitor closely the treatment prescribed by the self-procured doctor. The employer or carrier can utilize the medical reports required of the self-procured doctors and also the reports of examining physicians selected by the employer or carrier. There has been no change in LC 4050-4054 which gives an employer or carrier the right to periodic examinations of an injured employee.

LC 4600

LC 4050-4056

The primary obligation of the employer, on receiving notice of a work injury, is to arrange for initial medical treatment. If the employer is permissibly self-insured, the employer will continue to administer the case; if insured, administration will be turned over to the insurance carrier, usually by filing the employer's report of injury and providing the carrier with a copy. Most doctors realize that they should also report any injury to the carrier. The carrier may retain the first doctor or refer the injured employee to other physicians.

LC 4600

The employer's duty to provide treatment includes all medical, surgical, nursing and hospital care reasonably required to cure or relieve from the effects of the injury. Treatment also includes any necessary medicines, medical or surgical supplies, crutches, apparatus, or prosthesis.

LC 4600, 3209.5

The appellate courts have said that treatment under this law must be adequate. It is adequate if seasonably offered and is comprised of diligent effort within extant medical knowledge. To state it differently, treatment is not adequate if there are unreasonable delays or if it does not include a correct diagnosis and all measures indicated to cure or relieve.

The employee is not required to ask for medical treatment. He or she is required to give the employer notice of the injury. It is then the duty of the employer to see that treatment is provided or offered.

There is no monetary limit to the amount of medical treatment to be furnished, if the treatment is necessary. If needed, therefore, an employee may be given such care for life. He may receive lifetime hospital, institutional, or private nursing care, or he may be provided with glasses, hearing aids, braces, or artificial limbs, along with repair and replacement, as the case may warrant.

§ 4.5   Notice of Injury—Exception

LC 5400

An employee must give the employer notice of an industrial injury before the employer's obligation arises to furnish medical care. This notice is not required if the employer has knowledge of the injury from any source. Also, it has been held that employer-knowledge of facts which indicate exposure, stress, or bodily difficulty suffered by an employee in his or her work is

LC 5402

equivalent to notice. And knowledge of supervisory personnel, or of a claims or insurance office of the employer would be equivalent to employer-knowledge. Other situations are foreseeable wherein application of equitable

LC 5403

considerations and the liberal-construction rule would excuse a failure to give the required notice. For example, suppose that an employee is injured to the extent that he cannot communicate the facts to anyone. If treatment is rendered for a considerable period, may the employee recover its cost? The code does not give the answer. The Court of Appeal in the *Simien* case clarified this type of situation. In this case, the employee had been struck on the head. His condition was not at once apparent, though people in daily contact with him noticed that he had become very irritable. Further medical investigation, including an operation, revealed a hematoma causing pressure on the brain. Removal of this blood deposit relieved his symptoms. It was the opinion of the court that the employee should recover the cost of treatment, the basis being that as between employer and employee, both of whom were ignorant of the actual condition, the employee should not bear this financial burden.

§ 4.6   Self-Procured Treatment—Loss of Medical Control

LC 4600

Prior to 1976, a considerable body of law developed interpreting the provision of LC 4600 that an employer is liable for the reasonable cost of self-procured treatment if the employer fails to provide adequate care. The principles established by appellate court decisions will be applicable to many situations under LC 4600 as amended, especially where the employer has medical control, such as during the first 30 days after receiving notice of injury; where the employee has opted for treatment selected and furnished by the employer; and where the employer has retained medical control.

These principles will also be pertinent to cases in which an employer endeavors to terminate medical treatment (whether selected by the employer or the employee) by the employer's administrative action, by way of a petition to the Administrative Director or by way of a petition to terminate filed with the W.C.A.B. A discussion of these principles follows.

It has been said that an employer terminates treatment at his peril. This statement refers to the right of the employee to recover the cost of treatment *LC 4600* which he has obtained on his own if the employer fails to furnish adequate treatment. Section 4600 provides that the employer must provide treatment which is necessary to cure or relieve the effects of an industrial injury— seasonably. If he does not, he is liable for the reasonable medical expense incurred by or on behalf of the employee. Decisions of the appellate courts and the Board define "seasonably" as immediately after receiving notice of injury. Where treatment is furnished, it must be adequate. If the employer cuts off treatment too soon, or if the employee is released without a proper diagnosis, the employer has then relinquished medical control over the case to the employee. The employer may be liable for treatment at private rates which could have been furnished at fee-scheduled rates. These rules do not mean that by terminating treatment an employer is necessarily acting wrongfully, for the reports of the examining or treating physicians may justify such action. But if the employee proves through other physicians, to the satisfaction of the Appeals Board, that further treatment is or was necessary, the employee is entitled to recover the cost of such treatment. If the Appeals Board awards reimbursement for self-procured medical treatment and orders the employer to furnish further treatment, the employer resumes medical control. Should the employer or carrier again fail to give adequate treatment seasonably, the same issue may arise.

There are instances in which an employer, upon receiving knowledge of an injury does nothing, thinking the employee not to be badly hurt. This employer has relinquished medical control at the outset.

Another type of case is the one in which the employer tells the employee to go to "a doctor." Here the employer has expressly given the employee control over the treatment. This may not be strictly in the category of self-procured treatment since such arrangement has been ruled to constitute the furnishing of treatment. In effect, the employer has made the employee an agent, and the employee, in procuring the treatment, creates an obligation which is binding on the employer.

When an employer loses medical control, it may be regained if suitable treatment is offered which the employee accepts. In most instances, medical control is regained when the Appeals Board orders the furnishing of additional treatment. But if the employee makes an issue of medical control, the Appeals Board must make a determination whether termination of self-procured treatment would be detrimental to the employee. Relevant to this issue are the factors of physician-patient confidence, nature of the injury and treatment, qualifications of the physician, and the nature of the treatment offered by the employer. Upon appropriate findings, the Board has authority to order the continuation of self-procured treatment at the employer's expense.

§ 4.7   Notice of Self-Procured Treatment

LC 4600

LC 4603.2

LC 3202

Under the law applicable to self-procured medical treatment prior to 1976, where an employer failed to provide adequate care, or expressly refused to provide treatment, the injured worker was not required to give the employer (or insurance carrier) notice that she had obtained or was about to obtain her own medical care. If the employer's failure or refusal was erroneous, the employee would be entitled to recover the reasonable cost of such medical treatment. Under LC 4600 as amended, a question arises whether an employee must now give notice of all self-procured treatment because of the provisions of LC 4603.2. This section requires that upon selecting a physician, the employee or the doctor must notify the employer and give the employer the name and address of the doctor who must issue periodic reports to the employer. By its terms, Section 4603.2 applies to the provisions of Section 4600 allowing the employee to choose a personal physician after the 30-day period.

A basic principle applied by the W.C.A.B. and the appellate courts is that the law will be liberally construed so as to extend compensation benefits "for the protection of persons injured in the course of their employment." For this reason, it may be concluded that existing principles will be applied where the employer refuses to provide any medical care, as where the employer denies liability or denies the occurrence of an injury in the course of employment. They would also apply where the employer has medical control during the first 30 days after receiving notice or knowledge of an injury and where the employer has regained medical control on order of the Administrative Director or the W.C.A.B. It appears that the requirement that the employee give notice of his or her selection will apply where the employer or carrier has accepted the claim and is willing to provide treatment. Where disputes arise over the need for treatment or the adequacy of employer-furnished treatment, one may expect the prior rules to be applied.

As a practical matter, where the employer has medical control, the employee would do well to notify the employer or insurance carrier and give a reasonable time for treatment to be furnished before embarking upon a program of self-procured treatment. In the usual case, notice of the injury is sufficient. The most difficult problems arise after some treatment has been furnished. An employee may go to his or her own physician before having been released by the employer's doctor, and if so, he or she probably would not be reimbursed. The employer may be offering treatment, but the employee, through a misunderstanding, may not realize it. Employees often move without notifying the employer or carrier of a new address. On receiving the information, the employer may authorize the treatment. In any event, the employee can clarify the situation by writing or phoning the claims department of the employer or carrier.

The largest percentage of cases is handled by claims examiners for insurance carriers. A self-insured may have a claims department or it may utilize the services of an adjusting firm. Most of the employee's contact will therefore be with claims personnel. Notices and questions can be referred to the claims examiner who should then take appropriate action.

§ 4.8   Emergency Treatment; First Aid

Under the safety provisions of the Labor Code, the employer must provide adequate first aid supplies where five or more persons are employed   *LC 2440*
or where power machinery is used. The duty to provide both first aid and emergency medical care is implicit in the rules. An employer must provide   *R 9780.2*
these services even where an employee has qualified to be treated by his or her own personal physician. "First aid" is defined as temporary treatment for   *R 9780(f)*
"minor scratches, cuts, burns, splinters, etc., which do not ordinarily require medical care." "Emergency treatment" is defined as medical treatment   *R 9780(g)*
required "immediately following an industrial injury or illness, which, if delayed, could decrease the likelihood of maximum recovery."

Emergency treatment is reimbursable whether or not the employer has knowledge of the injury. The decisions on this point are based upon the rationale that it is assumed the employer would have furnished such care, and it would be unfair not to reimburse the employee. When the emergency is over, the employee may not continue self-procured treatment and must give the employer notice of the injury.

Emergencies may also arise during the course of treatment provided by the employer. In such cases the employee is required to contact the physician appointed to the case, if reasonably available. The nature of the emergency and reasonableness of the conduct of the employee would be determinative factors. It has been held by the California Supreme Court that an employee may not use an emergency as an excuse for changing physicians when an employer entitled to medical control was providing the necessary treatment.

Emergency medical personnel are entitled to prophylactic medical   *H&S*
treatment to prevent the onset of disease when exposed to contagious   *1797.186*
diseases while performing first aid.

§ 4.9   Agreements for Medical Treatment

Treatment of injuries includes all medical, surgical, and hospital services specified in Labor Code Section 3209.5 and any other form of   *LC 3209.7*
therapy, treatment, or healing practice agreed upon voluntarily in writing between the employee and his or her employer. The agreement may be entered into at any time after employment by completing a form approved by

the Department of Industrial Relations. The agreement must contain a description of the healing practice and designation of individuals and facilities qualified to administer it. By entering into such an agreement, the employee does not waive any rights conferred by law, nor does the employee forfeit any benefits to which he or she might otherwise be entitled. The employer and employee each reserve the right to terminate the agreement upon seven days' written notice. No liability is incurred by the employer except as required under the workers' compensation law upon proof of an industrial injury.

§ 4.10   Award for Continuing or Lifetime Medical Treatment

LC 5803

If an employee has been awarded continuing or further medical treatment in a finding which is general, that is, without reference to a specific kind of treatment, the W.C.A.B. retains jurisdiction to determine the type of medical treatment to which the employee is entitled. The order may include chiropractic treatment if the record indicates that it is the only type of treatment which will benefit the employee.

LC 4600

In a proper case, the employee may be awarded lifetime medical treatment. An award may be in general form, or it may limit the entitlement to a specific mode of treatment. Any award for dentures, glasses, braces, or artificial members arising from a bodily injury also provides for repairs and replacements. In a severe case, the medical award might provide for lifetime hospital or institutional care or a private nurse.

LC 4607

LC 4607 provides that if an employer or carrier unsuccessfully petitions the W.C.A.B. to terminate an award for continuing medical treatment, the applicant will be awarded reasonable attorney's fees for legal services required in resisting the petition.

§ 4.11   Other Conditions

Additional treatment must be rendered if necessitated by any negligence on the part of the physician or other practitioner furnished by the employer. There may be complications not related to injury which must nevertheless be dealt with in order to adequately treat for the injury. The employee is also entitled to treatment for such conditions. Examples would be pneumonia secondary to bed confinement, a pre-existing focus of infection which may be prolonging the symptoms from the industrial injury, or an injury resulting from activity prescribed by the treating physician.

§ 4.12   Travel Expense

LC 4600, 4621

Medical examination or treatment includes reasonable expenses of transportation, meals and lodging. Transportation expense is based upon 21 cents per mile or 24 cents per mile for state employees by the state personnel department per GC 19820, whichever is higher, from the employee's home to the place of examination or treatment and return, plus any bridge tolls.

Should the employee lose any wages in submitting to an examination at the request of the employer or Appeals Board, he or she is entitled to a day's temporary compensation for each day's wages lost. When an employer or carrier schedules a medical examination of an employee, the mileage and bridge tolls are to be paid in advance along with the notice of the time and place of the examination. Allowable travel expense includes reasonable cost of travel involved in obtaining necessary medications. If travel for medications necessarily involves a great distance, mileage for such travel must be paid, according to an appellate court decision.

§ 4.13 Damage to Medical Appliances

The term "injury" includes damages to any artificial members, dentures, eyeglasses, and medical braces of all types. Thus, if the employee suffers no injury to his or her person, but does sustain damage to the described artificial appliances, he or she is entitled to repair or replacement. *LC 3208*

Exception: eyeglasses and hearing aids will not be repaired or replaced unless injury to them occurs as an incident of an otherwise disabling injury. By W.C.A.B. interpretation, the disablement need not be extensive, for this provision is liberally construed to allow the benefit if the damage is accompanied by any bodily injury.

§ 4.14 Furnishing Medical Appliances

It should be kept in mind that an employee's entitlement to medical appliances by reason of bodily injury is broader than that involved in injuries to such an appliance. In cases of bodily injury, the employee is to be furnished everything necessary in treatment of the industrial injury. It may include glasses or artificial eyes in eye injury cases, dentures necessitated by injuries to the mouth or, as the case may be, braces, crutches, and wheelchairs. *LC 3209.5, 4600*

§ 4.15 Medications

Medications may be awarded if necessary, but the Board rarely awards mere palliatives, a term applying to medicine without any proven curative power and which afford only temporary relief. However, it may be noted that the language in LC 4600 is "cure or relieve," so that the basic question is whether the medication is reasonably necessary under the circumstances revealed by the medical reports. Common palliatives are aspirin, narcotics, tranquillizers, novocaine and, in some situations, cortisone derivatives. If an employee becomes addicted to drugs administered during treatment, the employer may be held liable for the cost of curing the addiction. (Regarding travel expense in obtaining medications, see previous discussion, § 4.12, *Travel Expense*.) *LC 4600*

§ 4.16   Nursing or Household Help; Spouse or Relative as Nurse

If medical opinion supports the conclusion that an employee's condition requires special nursing or household help in connection with treatment, the employer or carrier is required to furnish it.

A question which is not uncommon concerns the entitlement of an employee's spouse or relative to payment for private or practical nursing care. The rule is that the claim will not be allowed unless the employer has agreed to utilize such services. As a practical matter, most of these situations are ironed out before any dispute arises. Where a dispute results, some arrangement for future services may result, even though the claim for past services may not be valid.

An agreement to employ the injured's spouse as a practical nurse may be inferred from the actions of the parties if there is a need, and the employer or insurance carrier has knowledge of the situation. In a 1972 decision of the Court of Appeal, the court affirmed an award in favor of the employee's wife on these facts: the insurance carrier's doctor told her that her husband would be better off at home than in a care-facility. She followed the doctor's instructions in how to care for the employee. The court specifically stated that it was not necessary under these circumstances that the wife forego other paid work in order to be paid for her work as a practical nurse, as had been suggested in a 1948 case.

§ 4.17   Refusal of Medical Treatment by Employee

LC 4056   An employee cannot collect compensation for any disability caused by an unreasonable refusal of medical treatment. Further, if death is caused from refusing treatment without good reason, the surviving dependents will not be allowed any death benefits. If such unreasonable refusal aggravates the disability, the employee is not entitled to compensation to the extent of such aggravation. In that situation, the question is how much disability would have resulted had the employee accepted treatment. This question is one for the Appeals Board to resolve and is often a difficult one.

The question of whether the refusal of treatment is reasonable or unreasonable is a decision for the Board. Ordinarily, the defense is raised when surgery is declined. The employee may have already undergone major surgery because of the injury and is apprehensive about a second session. The doctor may have stated the chances for improvement from the procedure are only 50-50. The employee may have a psychological problem. In such instances, it would be difficult to find the refusal to be unreasonable. If the reason is based upon personal dislike of the doctor or a desire to choose his or her own physician where the employer has medical control, the refusal would be unreasonable. This issue is the basis for many settlements.

There are several court decisions regarding refusal of medical treatment on religious grounds. The most recent case involved a disability retirement under a public retirement system. The record indicated that the condition causing the disability could be readily eliminated by medical treatment. The Court of Appeal decided that the employee had a constitutional right to exercise her religious beliefs and could not be required to undergo treatment contrary to such beliefs; as such she was entitled to the disability pension. In an earlier case under the workers' compensation law, the Court of Appeal issued a decision holding that refusal of treatment on religious grounds was unreasonable and that compensation benefits were properly denied. In that case, a man received serious injuries on the job, and he was rushed to the hospital. There, he refused blood transfusions on religious grounds. It was established that the transfusions would have saved his life, and the widow was denied benefits. The appellate court held that this ruling does not constitute an interference with religious freedom, that workers' compensation benefits are not a part of that concept. This previous decision was brought to the court's attention in the retirement case, but the court stated it would not follow a decision it felt to be wrong. To the extent that these two decisions are in conflict, the final decision rests with the California Supreme Court which has not yet spoken on the issue. However, it may be pointed out that in the retirement case, there was no law requiring the employee to undergo treatment; whereas, under the workers' compensation law, there is a statutory, affirmative, duty that an injured worker submit to medical and, if necessary, surgical treatment. Further, the penalty for an unreasonable refusal is also made clear in LC 4056.

In a 1973 decision, the Court of Appeal held that since the employer involved did not offer the injured employee medical treatment, the employer could not base a defense of the employee's refusal to accept surgical treatment offered by a county welfare department.

§ 4.18   Definition of Physician

Under the provisions of the Labor Code, the term "physician" includes medical doctors (physicians and surgeons holding an M.D. or D.O. degree), psychologists, optometrists, dentists, podiatrists, physical therapists, and chiropractic practitioners licensed by California law. This recognition is limited to the scope of practice permitted to each licensee under the law, and does not permit any licensee to represent or advertise any broader scope of practice than permitted by his or her particular license. To be considered as a "physician" under the Labor Code, a psychologist must meet these requirements: (1) a doctor's degree in psychology and two years' clinical experience or meet the standards of the National Register of the Health Service Providers in Psychology, and (2) allow for "appropriate medical collaboration when requested by the employer or the insurer."

LC 4600, 3209.3- 3209.8

If referred by a licensed physician or surgeon with the approval of the employer, the employee may receive the services of a licensed marriage counselor, family counselor, child counselor, or clinical social worker for treatment of a condition arising out of an industrial injury. However, these social service practitioners may not determine disability. Unless an employer has failed to provide any medical treatment, the employer is not liable for such a consultation and report procured by the employee without the employer's consent.

Acupuncturists are included in the term "physician" and approved to treat industrial injuries. An acupuncturist must hold a certificate issued per Business and Professions Code Section 4925 et seq. (This authorization is effective until January 1, 1993.) However, they are not authorized to determine the extent of disability.

An appellate court has ruled that medical treatment and medical reports from physicians located outside this state are authorized by the California workers' compensation law.

§ 4.19   Medical Fee Schedule; Payment for Medical Treatment

LC 5307.1

The Medical Fee Schedule adopted by the Administrative Director is *prima facie* evidence of the value of medical services provided under the workers' compensation law. Fees for medical services which exceed fee schedule rates must be substantiated and may not be higher than the physician's usual and customary fees. The Director is to review this schedule biennially. If there is a dispute over fees, and if the physician testifies pursuant to the employer's or carrier's subpoena, and if the judge determines that the fee charged was reasonable, then the physician is entitled to a reasonable fee for testimony. Except for laboratory, X-ray, and other diagnostic tests, the Medical Fee Schedule does not apply to medical-legal

LC 4608

services (medical reports; see subsequent topics). [NOTE: In billing an employer or carrier, a pharmacy may utilize an exact copy of the claim form required by the employer or carrier.]

R 9791-9792

The medical fee schedule adopted by the Administrative Director fixes values for certain categories of medical services. In order to determine the correct fee, these values are applied to the relative value units set forth in the 1974 revision of the 1969 California Relative Value Studies, Fifth Edition, Revised, as reprinted by the California Workers' Compensation Institute in 1982 and successive supplements or modifications. (The Institute's address is 120 Montgomery Street, San Francisco, CA 94104.)

The values (unit conversion factors) set by the Administrative Director effective July 1, 1987 are:

Medicine Section	$6.15
Surgery Section	$153.00
Radiology Section:	
Total Service	$12.50
Professional Component	$1.95

Pathology Section $1.50
Anesthesia Section $34.50

[NOTE: Failure to submit all required medical reports including interim or R 9784,
progress reports may result in a delay in receiving payment for medical 9785
services. Regarding possible penalties under the fraudulent claims legislation,
see Chapter 9, PENALTIES, § 9.18, *Fraudulent Claims*.]

For injuries occurring on or after January 1, 1991, payment to an LC 4603.2
employee-selected physician must be made within 60 days after receipt of the
physician's billing and any required medical reports. If not so paid, the
amount paid must be increased by 10% plus interest at the rate for judgments
in civil actions. An employer or carrier may challenge a billing by filing a
contest thereof with the W.C.A.B. As part of the contest, the employer or
carrier may request an audit of items included from a hospital outpatient or
independent diagnostic facility. The penalty provision does not affect any
employee claim for a penalty under LC 5814. Any penalty or interest paid by
an insurance carrier will be considered in any classification of risks and any
system of merit rating for determining premium in the same manner as an
increase in compensation under LC 4650(d).

Disputes regarding medical, medical-legal or hospital fees may be re- LC 4903.4
solved in a separate proceeding which may include binding arbitration by
agreement of the parties including the employee if remaining a party to the
dispute.

If an employee files a claim per LC 5401, a provider of medical services LC 3751(b)
having knowledge of a claim may not collect money directly from an
employee for medical services unless the claim is rejected and the provider
has received written notice of the rejection and has provided the employee
with a copy of the notice. A medical provider who violates LC 3751(b) is
liable for three times the amount unlawfully collected, plus reasonable
attorney's fees and costs.

§ 4.20 Medical Examinations

The employer has the right to require periodic examinations of the
employee. Though rarely exercised, the employee has the right to have his or LC 4050,
her own physician present during the examinations. The employee must also 4052
report for an examination ordered by the Appeals Board. There are certain
penalties for failure to report for these examinations. They are:

1. If the examination is at the employer's request, the employee's right
to begin or maintain a proceeding before the Appeals Board is suspended. LC 4053

2. If the examination is at Appeals Board direction, the employee's right
to compensation is barred for the period of the refusal. LC 4054

The examination must be scheduled with due consideration for the
employee's convenience, condition and ability to attend. (Regarding travel

expense and compensation for medical examinations, see prior discussion, Section 4.12, *Travel Expense.*)

LC 4050 provides that if an injured employee does not cooperate by submitting to medical examinations, his proceeding may be suspended. However, the W.C.A.B. may not dismiss the case on that ground. Such a dismissal is beyond the Board's authority. Further, it is error to dismiss a proceeding without giving the applicant notice and an opportunity to be heard on the issue.

LC 4600

The law permitting employee-selection of physician after 30 days from date of injury underscores the importance of the right of an employer or insurance carrier to request periodic examinations by their own physicians. In this way they may monitor the treatment being rendered as well as obtain diagnoses, prognoses, and suggestions regarding treatment of choice. Such examinations and the reports thus obtained can be useful to the treating physician and could also be used as a basis for any petition for change of physician filed by an employer or carrier.

LC 9040

Employers must provide for medical examinations for workers having possible exposure to carcinogens. Examinations must be in accordance with the requirements of 8 Cal. Code of Regulations Secs. 5208-5210.

An appellate court has determined that it is an abuse of discretion for an employer to require an employee to travel 185 miles for a medical examination when there are many physicians specializing in the worker's condition within the region near the worker's home.

The method of measuring psychiatric elements of disability is determined by criteria set forth in psychiatric protocols adopted by the Division of Workers' Compensation. Copies may be obtained from the office of the Division's Medical Director.

LC 28,
139.2,
4061-
4067.5

Medical or chiropractic examinations may be ordered by an Information and Assistance Officer or the Medical Bureau in matters submitted for administrative recommendations. The W.C.A.B. and its judges have authority to order examinations by independent medical examiners (I.M.E.'s) or agreed medical examiners (A.M.E.'s) in cases before them for determination. The Code has been amended so that the term "independent medical examiner" now means "qualified medical evaluator," (Q.M.E.), and "agreed medical examiner" becomes "agreed medical evaluator" (A.M.E.). Official authority is subject to the provisions of LC 139.2 and 4061-4067 regarding submission of permanent disability and medical issues to such evaluators for initial determination. (See Chapter 14, PROCEDURE, for details.)

R 10606

LC 4628

R 10606 (W.C.A.B.) requires that the name and function of any person assisting a physician in examining a worker or in preparation of a medical report be included in the report. (See Chapter 14, PROCEDURE, § 14.23, *Contents of Medical Reports.*) Similar requirements have been included in the statutory law per LC 4628. This section provides that no person other than the physician who signs a medical report, except a nurse performing routine nursing functions, may examine an injured worker or participate in the nonclerical preparation of the report. However, another person may make an initial outline of a patient's medical history or excerpt prior medical records, in which case the physician must review the outline or excerpts and make any necessary inquiries and examinations in order to identify and determine medical issues. The physician must take a complete history, review and summarize prior medical records, compose and draft the conclusions of the report. No amount may be charged in excess of direct charges for professional services, reasonable costs of laboratory examinations, diagnostic studies, other medical tests, reasonable clerical and other overhead expenses. Failure to comply with these requirements may subject a physician to a civil penalty of up to $1,000 for each violation to be assessed by a workers' compensation judge or the W.C.A.B.

[NOTE: An appellate court has ruled that under R 10606 a physician who fails to identify the name and role of another person participating in the preparation of a medical report may be held in contempt by the W.C.A.B. Regarding possible penalties under the fraudulent claims legislation, see Chapter 9, PENALTIES, § 9.18, *Fraudulent Claims*.]

§ 4.21 Payment or Reimbursement for Cost of Medical Reports

When a disputed case comes before a W.C.A.B. judge, he or she must decide medical questions on medical evidence, that is, medical reports filed *LC 5703(a), 6412* and offered into evidence by the parties to the action. Here, the employee is designated the "Applicant" and the employer and insurance carrier as "Defendants." If the applicant does not wish to submit the case on the defendants' medical reports, the applicant should be ready with his or her own medical reports. For some years, it was difficult for an applicant to *LC 4600* obtain adequate or comprehensive reports because of lack of funds. The Legislature finally amended Section 4600 of the Labor Code to provide that an applicant could recover the reasonable expense of medical testimony, medical reports, examination, X-rays, and laboratory tests required to prove a claim. The California Supreme Court has construed this portion of Section 4600 in a 1963 decision, holding that it is not always necessary for the employee to win the case in order to be reimbursed for such costs. The test, says the court, is whether the medical evidence was reasonably and actually necessary when it was obtained.

"Medical-legal expense" includes any costs incurred by or on behalf of *LC 4620- 4627* any party, the Administrative Director, the W.C.A.B., or workers' compensation judge for X-rays, laboratory fees, diagnostic tests, medical reports, medical records, medical testimony, and, as needed, interpreter's fees for the purpose of proving or disproving a contested claim. An employee or the dependents of a deceased employee have a right to reimbursement for medical-legal expense "reasonably, actually and necessarily incurred." The reasonableness and necessity for such expense are to be determined as of the time when the expenses are actually incurred.

LC 4621   If an employee submits to examination by a physician at the request of the employer, the insurance carrier, the Administrative Director, the W.C.A.B., or judge, he or she is entitled to payment for transportation, meals, and lodging incident to reporting for examination, as provided in LC 4600. It should be noted that this benefit, as set out in LC 4600, is broader than as described in LC 4621, and also includes a day of temporary compensation for each day's wages lost in submitting to examination. See prior discussion, Section 4.12, *Travel Expense.*

LC 4622   When an employer or carrier is liable for medical-legal expense, payment is to be made within 60 days after receipt of billing. If a bill remains unreasonably unpaid beyond that time, it is to be increased 10%, plus interest at 7% per annum. The duty to pay within 60 days arises only if the medical provider or other person submitting a bill for medical-legal expense has included or previously provided any or all reports or other necessary information incident to the services for which the billing is submitted. Also, *LC 4623* the billing must be in a form which complies with LC 4623. It must itemize the charges for review of medical records, compiling the patient's medical history, performing a medical examination, preparing the report, and any necessary research. Also, the bill must show the total charge.

LC 4628   Billing for a medical examination and report must comply with LC 4628 (discussed in the previous topic). This section limits charges to direct charges for professional services, reasonable costs of laboratory examinations, diagnostic studies, other medical tests, reasonable clerical, and other overhead expenses.

If an employer or carrier disputes a charge, an appeal may be filed with the Appeals Board challenging the reasonableness and necessity for incurring the fees, services, or expenses. This appeal must be filed within the 60-day period after receipt of the billing. Written notice of appeal and its basis must be sent to the medical provider, the employee or dependents, or attorney. If the employer or carrier pays the bill within the 60-day period, or an amount consistent with a schedule developed by the Administrative Director, and if the W.C.A.B. upholds the appellant's position, the penalty and interest are not added, and the Board may order "the physician" to reimburse the employer or carrier the amount found to be excessive. The employer or carrier must pay the amount found by the Board to be payable within 20 days after the filing of the Board's order. When payment under the order is requested by the employee or dependent within this 20-day period, and if payment is not made within that time, the payment is to be increased 10%, plus interest at 7% per annum. The penalty provision of LC 5814 (delay or failure to pay compensation due) and the interest provision of LC 5800 do not apply to LC 4620-4627 obligations.

For the period January 1, 1991, until June 30, 1992, fees for initial *LC 4624* comprehensive medical-legal reports charged by independent medical examiners, agreed medical evaluators, treating physicians and qualified medical evaluators are rebuttably presumed reasonable if the charges do not exceed the following:

Orthopedics	$984
Internal medicine and cardiology	$995
Neurology	$881
Psychiatry	$1279
All others	$866

Annually, beginning April 1, 1991, the Administrative Director will publish the range of fees for such reports for the 12 months ending the previous December 31, along with the percentile deemed reasonable after applying one-half the percentage change in the California Consumer Price Index for the 12 months ending the previous June 30. Beginning July 1, 1992, charges of all physicians providing initial comprehensive medical-legal reports are rebuttably presumed reasonable if not in excess of the 73rd percentile of fees as published by the Administrative Director.

Charges may exceed the foregoing amounts if the billing is accompanied by information establishing their reasonableness.

Charges for X-rays, laboratory services, and other diagnostic tests are to *LC 4626* be itemized and billed in accordance with the medical fee schedule previously discussed under the topic of § 4.19, *Medical Fee Schedule*. (The W.C.A.B. has ruled that the cost of copying medical records is a reimbursable medical-legal expense.)

The Administrative Director and the W.C.A.B. are authorized to adopt *LC 4627* any rules deemed necessary to effectuate the provisions of LC 4620-4627 regarding medical-legal expense.

A completed Form 76, "Report of Medical-Legal Charges," is required *R 9793-* to be filed with each medical report. The Administrative Director will utilize *9795* the information so gathered to compile the data required by LC 4623 for determination of reasonable medical-legal expenses.

Disputes regarding medical, medical-legal or hospital fees may be re- *LC 4903.4* solved in a separate proceeding which may include binding arbitration by agreement of the parties including the employee if remaining a party to the dispute.

If an employee files a claim per LC 5401, a provider of medical services *LC 3751(b)* having knowledge of a claim may not collect money directly from an employee for medical services unless the claim is rejected and the provider has received written notice of the rejection and has provided the employee with a copy of the notice. A medical provider who violates LC 3751(b) is liable for three times the amount unlawfully collected, plus reasonable attorney's fees and costs.

For additional discussion of medical reports and cross-examination of physicians, see Chapter 14, PROCEDURE, § 14.21, *Filing Medical Reports: Hospital Records;* § 14.22 *Medical Examiners Appointed by the W.C.A.B.;* § 14.23, *Contents of Medical Reports;* § 14.24, *Late Filing of Medical Reports;* § 14.25, *Medical Reports of Lien Claimants;* § 14.26, *Cross-Examining Physicians.*

§ 4.22   Medical and Hospital Liens

LC 4903
(b)

Medical providers may file for a lien in workers' compensation proceedings for the value of services rendered to an industrially injured worker. The lienclaim procedure is also available regarding charges for medical examinations and reports (medical-legal services). See Chapter 10, LIENS, § 10.3, *Medical and Hospital Liens.*

§ 4.23   Interpreter

LC 4620

An employee is entitled to the services of, or reimbursement for the cost of, an interpreter if necessary for obtaining medical-legal services.

Chapter 5
COMPENSATION PAYMENTS

§ 5.1   Preliminary Considerations

In addition to medical treatment, an employee is entitled to compensation payments while unable to work because of the injury. Thus, an employer or carrier will initiate medical treatment and begin paying compensation after receipt of notice of injury. If the employee loses no time from work, then medical treatment only is furnished. But whether or not there is loss of time from the job, the employee is entitled to a payment for any permanent disability which results and, in certain cases, a life pension.

Compensation benefits are not "damages" for injury. In a given case, an employee might feel benefits should be greater, or an employer might consider them too large since the injury was not caused by any wrongdoing on her part. These reactions to workers' compensation most often occur when the parties attempt to evaluate a case according to the concept for recovery in a negligence action. The compensation law, rather, provides a partial recompense to the employee for loss of earnings or loss of ability to compete in the labor market. The program is intended to minimize the effects of such injuries upon both worker and employer.

The discussion in this chapter covers computation of weekly compensation rates for temporary and permanent disability, determination of earnings at time of injury, and principles governing the payment of temporary compensation, as well as certain collateral benefits or programs. The rules governing rating permanent disability, the number of payments, life pensions, and the subsequent injuries fund are discussed in Chapter 6, PERMANENT DISABILITY.

An injured employee may be a qualified injured worker entitled to vocational rehabilitation and the payment of rehabilitation temporary compensation. Discussion of these benefits is set out in Chapter 16, VOCATIONAL REHABILITATION.

§ 5.2   Date of Injury Controls Benefits

LC 4453.5

LC 4661.5

A general rule in every workers' compensation case is that the date of injury controls benefits. In other words, the law and benefits in effect on the date of injury are applicable to that injury and will not change. This principle was established by the California Supreme Court in the *Charlesworth* case. The *Charlesworth* principle was incorporated into the statutory law in 1972, but the language of LC 4453.5 relates to "time" of injury. Thus, benefits are to be provided as authorized "by the law in effect at the time the injury giving rise to the right to such benefits occurred." In most cases, the "time" of injury is the "date" of injury as defined in LC 5411 and 5412. Any difference in terminology would be pertinent only in unusual cases dealing with occupational disease or cumulative trauma, or successive injuries to the same part of the body under the *Wilkinson* principle discussed in Chapter 6, PERMANENT DISABILITY. A specific exception to the general rule stated above is found in LC 4661.5 which provides that:

> When any temporary total disability indemnity payment is made two years or more from the date of injury, the amount of this payment shall be computed in accordance with the temporary disability indemnity average weekly earnings amount specified in Section 4453 in effect on the date each temporary total disability payment is made unless computing the payment on this basis produces a lower payment becaues of a reduction in the minimum average weekly earnings applicable under Section 4453.

Pursuant to a 1990 Court of Appeal decision, in a case involving continuous exposure to asbestos where two separate conditions are caused by the exposure, there can be two dates of injury, one for determining disability benefits relating to one condition and one for determining death benefits by virtue of industrial death resulting from the other condition.

With these noted exceptions, the general rule, stated practically, is that the benefits applicable to a particular case are those in effect on the date of injury. This approach is utilized in the compensation tables provided in the Appendix.

EXAMPLE: Carolyn suffered a specific injury on December 10, 1983, at which time her earnings of $400 per week entitled her to temporary compensation at the maximum rate of $196 per week. Her disability continued until her return to work on April 15, 1984. On January 1, 1984, the maximum increased to $224 per week, but Carolyn's temporary compensation rate would remain at the lower rate of $196 per week.

The compensation tables in the Appendix cover compensation rates for various periods since 1951. These tables permit the ascertainment of weekly rates according to the formula, and the maximum and minimum limits of weekly rates for earnings, temporary compensation, and permanent disability payments in effect on the date of injury.

> Table A—minimum and maximum limits for injuries on or after April 1, 1974
>
> Table B—values for computing compensation for injuries on or after April 1, 1974
>
> Table C—minimum and maximum limits for injuries prior to April 1, 1974
>
> Table D—values for computing compensation for injuries prior to April 1, 1974
>
> Table E—permanent disability compensation rates for minors

The basic formula for computing compensation for injuries occurring on *LC 4453* or after April 1, 1974, is two-thirds of average earnings, subject to minimum and maximum limits as set forth in Table A. Labor Code provisions govern the determination of earnings and control the minimum and maximum compensation rates by setting limits on the weekly earnings which will be considered. Thus, our starting point in computing compensation is a determination of the employee's earnings at time of injury.

The Court of Appeal holds that where an injured worker sustains another injury while engaged in training under a vocational rehabilitation plan, compensation rates in effect at the time of the training injury are applicable.

§ 5.3 Earnings

"Average earnings" are defined as 100% of the employee's average ac- *LC 4453* tual earnings at time of injury. Earnings have also been equated with "earning capacity" at time of injury.

Problems in earnings arise in the case of transient, temporary, part-time, seasonal, or intermittent workers. Also, when the Legislature changes the compensation rates, more cases involve an issue on earnings. The code reflects the Legislature's attempts to cover the many types of work records which may be encountered and reveals a policy that the employee is not to receive more in compensation than he could have earned if not injured.

The factors to be considered and methods used in determining actual earnings are listed below.

LC 4453(a)   1. If the worker has steady employment of 30 hours or more per week, his or her earnings are based upon the weekly earnings in that job at the time of the injury. A job may be considered as steady if the employer has not placed any restrictions on the period of employment.

EXAMPLE: Frank is hired as a machinist by Acme Aircraft on a 40-hour week at $10 per hour. Nothing was said about how long he would be employed, and it appears to be a permanent position. A few weeks later he is injured on the job. His actual earnings are $400 per week.

LC 4453(b)   2. If the employee has more than one job, total earnings are taken, but they can be no greater than the total time worked in these jobs, multiplied by the rate of pay in the job in which he or she was injured.

EXAMPLE: Black has two jobs. For Ajax Company he works 30 hours per week at $12.00 per hour. For White Company he works 20 hours at $6.00 per hour. He is injured while working for Ajax Company. Black's earnings would be considered as total earnings in both jobs—

30 hours × $12.00 = $360

20 hours × $8.00 = $160

Total $520   per week

This amount does not exceed total hours in both jobs times the Ajax Company rate.

If Black were injured while working for the White Company, the above figure ($520 per week) would exceed total hours in both jobs times the White Company rate of $8.00 per hour; therefore, in this situation his earnings would be taken as—

50 hours × $8.00 = $400   per week

LC 4453(c)   3. If the employee is paid at an irregular rate, by piecework, by commission, or by the week, month, or other period, his or her earnings are averaged over a convenient period, not exceeding one year.

In this category have been placed those employees who are not in steady employment when injured. Included are those sent out from union hiring halls for temporary or short-term employment; seasonal workers, such as found in agriculture and the canning and logging industries; those who limit their availability on the labor market because of illness, other activities, or choice. An issue on earnings occurs in the instances of those whose regular status is that of housewife, student, or pensioner.

It will be noted that the period of time over which this average is to be taken may not exceed one year before the date of injury. Some insurance carriers, as a practical matter, use a 6-month earnings record in determining actual weekly earnings.

EXAMPLE: In one case, compensation was based on earnings over a 9-month period because of the absence of other information. The employee could not supply information, because he had been rendered non compos mentis by the injury. A factor considered here was the report of the last employer that while the work was seasonal, the man was a good worker and was being kept over for a short period past the end of the season.

4. If for any reason, one of the above methods does not seem to apply to a case under consideration, the code permits a determination based upon a *LC 4453(d)* sum which reasonably represents the employee's earning capacity at the time of injury. For this purpose, due consideration is to be given to actual earnings from all sources and employments.

In this way, the law provides the use of some discretion in avoiding results which might seem harsh or illogical if the above methods were adhered to strictly.

In cases involving this point, the appellate courts have said that in determining earnings, we seek the worker's capacity to earn. Factors involved include not only the wages earned and the necessary arithmetic, but also the employee's ability, willingness, and opportunity to work. In effect, in unusual situations, one must size up the individual and his or her good faith in seeking and obtaining employment. (See subsequent topic, The *Montana* Case.)

The appellate court decisions also stress that a change in circumstances or employment pattern is an important consideration. One appellate decision involves a case in which the worker had not worked for some time because of illness. Upon recovering, he returned to work at maximum wages. On the second day of employment he sustained a fatal injury. The court upheld a finding of maximum earnings.

[NOTE: In *Henning v. Industrial Welf. Com.*, the California Supreme Court held that the minimum wage set by the Industrial Welfare Commission must be applied to all employees, and distinctions in minimum wage levels cannot be based on the fact that some workers receive tips.]

5. In computing earnings in any of the above ways, overtime and the value of any incidental benefits enjoyed by the employee by reason of the *LC 4454* employment is counted as a part of the earnings. Reimbursement for expenses is not. Advantages which are recognized include room and board, fuel, tips, uniforms, and bonuses. Fringe benefits which can be taken into consideration in determining earnings are not to include the cost or market value of any savings, wage continuation, wage replacement, or stock acquisition

program, or any employee benefit program for which the employer pays or contributes to persons other than the employee or his or her family (LC 4454).

LC 4456

6. Disability payments of employees on any unemployment relief program of the state or local agencies are determined only upon the earnings in the particular program.

LC 4457

7. Statutory average earnings of workers associated under a partnership agreement for performance of labor on a particular piece of work are deemed to be $40 per week, if earnings are not otherwise ascertainable.

LC 4458,
4458.5

8. Earnings are presumed to be maximum for volunteer firemen, policemen, or persons impressed into fire control service, if injured in the line of such duty.

M&V 340,
340.1,
341
520
562

9. When any officer or enlisted personnel of the national guard, militia, naval militia, national guard reserve, or officer of cadet instruction is injured while on active duty, he or she is entitled to state compensation benefits subject to a credit for any sums paid on account of the injury by the federal government. Earnings are measured by the member's income from all sources during the preceding year, but in no event are they deemed to be less than $2,500 per year. Under certain conditions of duty, a National Guard or militia member may qualify for 26 weeks' military pay and allowances in lieu of workers' compensation.

LC 3364.55
LC 3364.6

10. Earnings of juvenile traffic offenders and wards of the juvenile court who do rehabilitative work on public property are deemed to be minimum for permanent disability compensation, and no temporary compensation is payable. These restrictions do not apply, however, if the juveniles in these categories volunteer for firefighting work or other work which is other than rehabilitative work on public property without pay. (A previous restriction to minimum earnings for inmates of state penal institutions was repealed as of January 1, 1977.)

LC 4453.1

11. For injuries sustained during the period January 1, 1977 through December 31, 1989, by news vendors who purchase the periodicals they sell, the minimum earnings limit for determining temporary compensation is the minimum in effect on date of injury or 1.2 times actual earnings whichever is less. For injuries on or after January 1, 1990, this special minimum no longer applies due to the repeal of LC 4453.1.

12. For injuries sustained during the period January 1, 1977 through December 31, 1989, by those in home-related or personal services categories per LC 3351(d), the minimum earnings limit for determining temporary compensation is the minimum in effect on date of injury or 1.2 times actual earnings whichever is less. For injuries on or after January 1, 1990, this special minimum is no longer applicable due to the repeal of LC 4453.1.

LC 3212-
3212.7

13. Earnings for those in police, firefighting, or other "safety" positions who are entitled to a presumption of industrial injury after termination of

employment (for a period not to exceed 60 months) are deemed to be *LC 3213* "maximum."

§5.4 The *Montana* Case

In 1962 the California Supreme Court decided the *"Montana"* case and injected a new concept into the determination of earnings in employments which are seasonal, intermittent, or temporary. (Montana was the injured employee.) The court concluded that in cases of this type, short-term earnings are to be given great weight in setting earnings for computing temporary compensation; whereas, a longer period of average earnings should be used in the case of permanent disability benefits.

The Labor Code sections just discussed make no such distinction; they define earning capacity at time of injury without relation to the type of benefit. Other sections determine benefits based on that earning capacity. The court in its decision makes such a distinction by attributing the wage-loss theory to both benefits. Permanent disability specialists, in working out the permanent disability rating schedule, as authorized by the code, have never considered the permanent disability benefit a wage-loss payment. It has been looked upon as a payment made to assist in rehabilitation and bears a direct relationship to the extent of permanent disability. It is payable even if the injured suffers no actual wage loss following the termination of his or her temporary disability; i.e., he or she has resumed work in spite of any handicap. But because the court is the final authority on what code sections mean, we must now take it as established that a worker may have one earning capacity for "temporary" and another for "permanent" disability benefits.

The court states that in cases involving intermittent or temporary jobs, the extent of the disability controls wage loss. Thus, if Smith has a job which would last six months and his injury causes him to lose four months of that opportunity while temporarily disabled, the earnings in that temporary job are the measure of his loss and should be taken as his earning capacity. The court then states that permanent disability benefits are usually paid over a longer period, and thus an employee in this category would show a smaller wage-loss over a long period because of his or her proven intermittent showing in the past.

Other decisions have applied the principles of the *Montana* case. In one case the applicant was injured in April of 1967 while employed as a part-time park and recreation instructor for Culver City. She was a U.C.L.A. student on a full-time basis. She worked 10 to 12 hours per week at $2.39 per hour for the city. The work was to continue from April to June, 1967. Because of the injury, the student was prevented from continuing her studies which would qualify her for a teaching credential, and she subsequently obtained her credential and a teaching position in 1968. The W.C.A.B. found earnings to be minimum. On review, the appellate court reversed and remanded the case to the Board to redetermine earnings, giving weight to the factor of the employee's employment opportunities for the future. Such evidence is relevant to earning capacity at the time of the injury for purposes of determining the temporary compensation rate and wage loss for the period involved.

In another case the California Supreme Court held that earnings of the injured employee, following his injury, may be considered in determining earning capacity at time of injury. The basic guideline is the employee's "general overall capability and productivity." A change in circumstances to full-time employment after an injury is an important consideration. The Supreme Court does not say that earnings after injury are determinative, but that they must be considered as relevant to the status of the employee's capability and productivity at the time of injury.

A 1962 appellate court decision goes further and holds that failure to compute earnings according to the *Montana* case can result in the assessment of a 10% penalty against the insurance carrier.

In a case decided at the same time as *Montana*, the Supreme Court rejected the assertion that union scale should determine earning capacity, where a worker has a sketchy work history.

A corollary to the *Montana* principle was established by the Court of appeal in 1967. Even though an employer does not specifically limit the length of job tenure, if the evidence shows that the employer had only occasional need for the employee's services in the past, the employee must prove the likelihood of continuation of employment except for the injury.

§ 5.5   Minimum and Maximum Earnings

LC 4453
4460

As previously indicated, the minimum and maximum weekly rates for the payment of compensation are controlled by setting minimum and maximum limits of earnings which may be considered or utilized in the basic formula: compensation = 2/3 actual weekly earnings. Thus, the Labor Code does not set out the minimum or maximum limits for compensation rates, but, rather, these limits are controlled or changed by controlling or changing minimum and maximum earnings. For this reason, compensation tables show both the limits on earnings and the resulting limits on compensation. The earnings limits also are controlling in utilizing the formulas for wage-loss compensation for temporary partial disability and the life-pension in cases of permanent disability rating 70% or more. Also, it will be noted that earnings limits differ depending on the type of benefit involved.

LC 4453
4460

By way of illustration, the Labor Code sets forth the maximum earnings limit for temporary total and permanent total disability for injuries occurring during the period January 1, 1984 through December 31, 1989, as $336 per week. This earnings limit results in a maximum compensation rate of $224 per week (2/3 × $336 = $224) for these benefits. Maximum earnings for permanent partial disability benefits applicable for injuries occurring during the stated period are fixed at $210 per week, resulting in a maximum compensation rate of $140 per week for this benefit ($2/3 \times \$210 = \$140$). Regardless of how much an employee's earnings may exceed the statutory maximums, earnings may not be considered above the maximum set for each type of benefit. As can be seen, a person may have less than maximum earnings for temporary compensation but maximum for permanent disability benefits.

Minimum earnings for the above period are set at $168 per week for temporary total and permanent total disability resulting in a minimum compensation rate of $112 per week ($2/3 \times \$168 = \$112$) for these benefits. For permanent partial disability benefits for injuries during the stated period, minimum earnings are taken at $105 per week, the compensation rate being $70 per week ($2/3 \times \$105 = \$70$). No matter how much less than these minimum levels an employee's actual earnings might be, earnings will be deemed to be at least the minimum amount set by the code. The establishment of minimum earnings and compensation rates by law represents a legislative policy that there is a point below which compensation should not go in assisting an injured worker during the period of recovery or rehabilitation.

EXAMPLES:

(1) Jones was injured in 1984 when his earnings were $500 per week. For computing temporary compensation (and permanent total disability benefits), his earnings are considered to be maximum, i.e., $336 per week. The compensation rate is maximum, or $224 per week for these benefits, For permanent partial disability, Jones has maximum earnings of $210 per week and a maximum compensation rate of $140 per week.

(2) In 1984, Fletcher had a part-time job in which he earned $75 per week. If he were injured in the course of this employment, his earnings would be minimum, i.e., considered to be $168 per week for computing temporary or permanent total disability compensation with a compensation rate of $112 per week. For permanent partial disability payments, earnings will be taken at the minimum rate, $105 per week, with a minimum compensation rate of $70 per week.

§ 5.6 Computing Compensation Payments for Injuries On or After April 1, 1974

Effective for injuries occurring on or after April 1, 1974, the basic formula for weekly compensation is: Compensation = two-thirds actual weekly earnings, subject to minimum and maximum limits. Table A in the Appendix shows these limits for various benefits for legislative periods since April 1, 1974. Table B provides a method of determining compensation for amounts between these limits. Or, one may multiply earnings by 2 and divide the results by 3. The latter method works well with electronic or pocket calculators.

For purposes of discussion, we set forth the minimum and maximum limits applicable to injuries occurring during the period January 1, 1984, through December 31, 1989. [For these and limits for other periods, particularly those effective during 1990 and those effective as of January 1, 1991, see Tables A and C in the Appendix. In these tables, the limits are grouped according to effective dates for access with any given date of injury.]

1. Temporary total disability compensation: Maximum earnings—$336 per week; maximum compensation rate—$224 per week. Minimum earnings—$168 per week; minimum compensation rate —$112 per week.

2. Temporary partial disability compensation: Maximum earnings for wage-loss compensation formula—$336 per week. Minimum earnings for wage-loss formula—$168 per week. (See subsequent discussion of wage-loss formula.)

3. Permanent total disability compensation: Maximum earnings—$336 per week; maximum compensation rate—$224 per week. Minimum earnings—$168 per week; minimum compensation rate —$112 per week.

4. Permanent partial disability compensation: Maximum earnings—$210 per week; maximum compensation rate—$140 per week. Minimum earnings—$105 per week; minimum compensation rate —$70 per week. [NOTE: If an employee would receive more for a PD rating on the basis of four weeks of compensation for each 1% of the PD rating, with a maximum compensation rate of $52.50 per week based upon maximum earnings of $78.75 per week, employee is entitled to the greater amount. See Chapter 6, PERMANENT DISABILITY.]

5. Life pension: For permanent total disability, i.e., PD rating of 100%, compensation is payable for life, subject to limits set forth in item 3, above. For life pension payable in cases of permanent partial disability, i.e., PD ratings of $70%-99\frac{3}{4}\%$, maximum earnings for the life pension formula—$107.69 per week; minimum is the minimum for permanent partial disability. (See Chapter 6, PERMANENT DISABILITY.) [For compensation rates and limits before April 1, 1974, see subsequent topic in § 5.8, *Computing Compensation Payments for Injuries Prior to April 1, 1974.*]

EXAMPLES:

(1) Frank, who has a steady job with Acme Aircraft at $350 per week, was injured on November 5, 1984. Checking limits shown above or in Table A, we find that maximum earnings are $336 per week and that the maximum compensation rate for temporary disability is $224 per week. No further computation is necessary, for he cannot obtain more than the maximum.

(2) Assume that Frank's earnings were $150 per week. This is less than the maximum earnings for temporary compensation, so we must compute:

$$\begin{aligned}
\text{Compensation rate} \quad &= \quad \text{2/3 of \$150} \\
&= \quad \text{\$100 per week for} \\
&\quad \text{temporary compensation}
\end{aligned}$$

But, this is less than the minimum compensation rate of $112 per week; thus, Frank's rate is $112. We could have obtained the same result merely by noting that Frank's earnings were less the minimum of $168 per week and concluding that he would receive minimum compensation of $112 per week.

(3) When the period of temporary disability has terminated, Frank may have some residual permanent disability for which he may receive payments based upon a permanent disability rating. If his disability is permanent and total (i.e., rates 100%), he will receive weekly compensation payments for life at the rate of $224 per week in example (1). In example (2), he would receive $112 per week for life. However, if the permanent disability is partial (i.e., rates between 0-99¾%, inclusive), in example (1) Frank's earnings would exceed maximum, and his compensation rate would be $140 per week based upon maximum earnings of $210 per week. However, assume example (2). Here Frank's earnings of $150 per week are less than the maximum $210 per week; so his PD rate is computed as 2/3 × $150 = $100 per week. Note that this exceeds the minimum for the permanent partial rate. Thus, his compensation rate for permanent partial disability is $100 per week.

(4) Phil was injured in 1984 while working as a store clerk. His earnings were $174 per week. This amount is less than the maximums and more than the minimums so that his compensation rate must be computed.

$$\begin{aligned}
\text{Compensation rate} \quad &= \quad \text{2/3 of \$174} \\
&= \quad \text{\$116 per week for} \\
&\quad \text{temporary and permanent} \\
&\quad \text{disability benefits.}
\end{aligned}$$

(5) On September 2, 1984, Bill was injured while working in a packing house at a wage of $3.50 per hour. This was seasonal work which Bill had been doing for several years for the same employer. His earnings during any one of these years never averaged more than $100 per week, except that during the 1-year period prior to his injury his annual average was $115 per week. When injured, Bill had been working 50 hours per week for several weeks which, with overtime pay, would amount to $200 per week. His job had about one week to go after which he would be unemployed until the next harvest. Under these facts, Bill's earnings would be taken as $115 per week *LC 4453(d)* under LC 4453(d). These earnings are less than the maximum earnings of $336 per week for temporary and permanent total disability and less than the minimum of $168 per week. Thus, Bill's compensation rate for these benefits is taken at $112 per week. His rate for permanent partial disability benefits is $76.67 per week (2/3 × $115 = $76.67). Earnings for computing any permanent partial disability life pension, assuming his PD rating is in the 70%-

LC 4659

99³/4% range, would be taken as $107.69 per week, the maximum earnings recognized for this benefit per LC 4659(a).

The foregoing approach to determining Bill's earning capacity at time of injury is consonant with a recent appellate court decision. The court points out that the *Montana* principle was inapplicable to a situation which showed a set pattern of employment without future likelihood of change and no loss of immediate opportunity. In the example, the data would be weighted more favorably if Bill could have shown definite prospects of employment in the immediate future or prospects of a positive change in his employment pattern.

§ 5.7   Minors—Permanent Disability Rate

LC 4455

Temporary compensation rates for minors are computed in the same manner as for adults. But, permanent disability compensation rates and earnings are subject to a special provision of the Labor Code. Since 1972, minors are persons under 18 years of age. Before 1972, minors were persons under 21 years of age.

A minor's earnings for permanent disability benefits are deemed to be probable earnings at age of majority in the job in which the minor is injured or in any occupation to which he or she might be promoted if not injured, subject to the limitations previously discussed. If such probable earnings cannot be ascertained, a minor's earnings are deemed to be $105 per week. This figure is applicable to injuries occurring on or after May 7, 1974. This assumed rate is but $20 more than the 1983 minimum rate and the same as the minimum rate effective in 1984. Under the two-thirds formula, this results in an assumed compensation rate of $70 per week for permanent disability benefits. Because of a legislative oversight, for a short period under the new formula, such assumed earnings were $107.69. Thus, for the period 4-1-74 through 5-6-74 the result is an assumed compensation rate of $71.79 for permanent disability benefits ($2/3 \times 107.69 = 71.79$).

Before April 1, 1974, the compensation formula for permanent disability compensation for minors was 65% of actual earnings (rather than the basic formula, 65% of 95% of actual earnings) because of an appellate court interpretation of LC 4455. Therefore, under the old formula, permanent disability rates for minors are slightly higher than those for adults, although temporary compensation is computed the same way for both minors and adults. For injuries occurring 4-1-72 through 3-31-74, the assumed earnings for permanent disability benefits for minors are $107.69 per week for a compensation rate of $70 per week. For injuries occurring 9-18-59 through 3-31-72, these amounts are: assumed earnings, $80.77; compensation rate, $52.50 per week. (See Table E in the Appendix for values for computing minors' PD compensation rates as to injuries occurring prior to April 1, 1974.)

It should be kept in mind that if the facts show that a minor's probable earnings at age 18 (or at age 21 prior to 1972) are less than the assumed earnings figures, the employer or carrier may utilize the probable earnings and in any litigated case present evidence to the W.C.A.B. Also, a minor employee's actual or probable earnings will control if they are larger than the assumed amounts in case of permanent total disability resulting from an injury occurring on or after April 1, 1974.

§ 5.8   Computing Compensation Payments for Injuries Prior to April 1, 1974

Because of the rule that the law and benefits in effect on the date of injury are controlling, it is still necessary to have an understanding of the "old" formula for computing compensation payments. This formula is applicable to injuries occurring before April 1, 1974. Cases under the prior provisions may still be pending for determination or may arise because of the provisions relating to the statute of limitations and the continuing jurisdiction of the W.C.A.B.

LC 4453.5

LC 5405-5410

5803,

5804

As to injuries occurring before April 1, 1974, the compensation rate is 65% of "average earnings," which, in turn, are defined as 95% of actual earnings. Actual earnings are determined under the same rules as previously discussed, but "average earnings" are taken as 95% of the actual earnings so determined. Thus, the weekly compensation rate is 65% of 95% of actual weekly earnings, or 61³/₄% of actual earnings. This simpler method, that is, 61³/₄% of actual earnings, may be used successfully when we are only dealing with compensation rates for temporary total disability or permanent disability. There are two instances, however, wherein "average earnings" must be used; that is the 95% of actual earnings. One instance is in determining wage-loss compensation for temporary partial disability. (See subsequent discussion.) The other is in determining life pensions in cases of permanent disability rating 70% or more. (See next chapter.) For purposes of discussion, we will refer to "statutory average earnings" as being the 95% of actual earnings defined by the code.

LC 4653

4658

Minimum and maximum compensation rates for injuries before April 1, 1974, are set and controlled by minimum and maximum values for "statutory average earnings" contained in the code. To obtain the amount of actual earnings necessary to result in these values for statutory average earnings, one must work backwards using the basic formula: statutory average earnings = 95% of actual earnings. These limits have been changed for various periods of time, and thus it is necessary to ascertain the limits in effect on date of injury. The limits differ for temporary and permanent disability benefits. Table C is provided in the Appendix for this purpose, showing the values for periods since 1951. Table D in the Appendix may be used for computing compensation rates for earnings between the limits in Table C. The following are the most recent limits under the old formula and apply to injuries occurring 4-1-72 through 3-31-74;

LC 4453

4460

1.   Temporary Total Disability Compensation: Maximum actual earnings - $170.04 per week; maximum statutory average earnings

$161.54 per week; maximum compensation rate - $105 per week. Minimum actual earnings - $56.67 per week; minimum statutory average earnings - $53.84 per week; minimum compensation rate - $35 per week.

2. Temporary Partial Disability Compensation: Maximum actual earnings - $170.04 per week; maximum statutory earnings for wage-loss formula - $161.54 per week. Minimum actual earnings - $56.67 per week; minimum statutory average earnings for wage-loss formula - $53.84 per week.

3. Permanent Disability Compensation: Maximum actual earnings $113.36 per week; maximum statutory average earnings - $107.69 per week; maximum compensation rate - $70 per week. Minimum actual earnings - $32.39 per week; minimum statutory average earnings - $30.77 per week; minimum compensation rate - $20 per week. [NOTE: If an employee would receive more for a PD rating on the basis of 4 weeks of compensation for each 1% of the PD rating, with a maximum compensation rate of $52.50 per week based upon maximum actual earnings of $85.02 per week and maximum statutory average earnings of $80.77 per week, employee is entitled to greater amount. (See Chapter 6, PERMANENT DISABILITY.)]

4. Life Pension: Minimum and maximum values for actual and statutory average earnings applicable to the life pension formula for PD ratings of 70% - 100%, inclusive, are the same as set forth in item 3, above. (See Chapter 6, PERMANENT DISABILITY.)

EXAMPLES:

(1) On July 14, 1973, Mary was injured in the course of her employment as an administrative analyst. Her salary was $250 per week. Her actual earnings exceed maximum actual earnings ($170.04 per week); thus, her compensation rate is $105 per week for temporary disability. Her earnings also exceed the maximum actual earnings for permanent disability benefits ($113.36 per week), so that her compensation rate for these benefits is $70 per week, subject to the proviso in item 3, above.

(2) Assume that Mary's earnings were $150 per week. This is less than maximum earnings for temporary compensation; so we must compute.

Compensation rate	=	65% of statutory average earnings
	=	65% of 95% of $150
	=	$61^3/4$% of $150
	=	$92.63 per week for temporary compensation

(3) When the period of temporary disability has terminated, Mary may have some residual permanent disability for which she may receive payments

based upon a permanent disability rating. Under both examples (1) and (2) her earnings exceed the PD maximum resulting in a PD compensation rate of $70 per week, subject to the proviso in item 3, above.

(4) Catherine worked part-time as a clerk in a dry goods store and was injured while getting some stock. The date of injury was January 15, 1974, and actual earnings were $70 per week. This amount is less than the maximums and more than the minimums for both types of benefits; so, the compensation rate must be computed.

$$
\begin{aligned}
\text{Compensation rate} \ &= \ 65\% \text{ of statutory average} \\
&\quad \text{earnings} \\
&= \ 65\% \text{ of } 95\% \text{ of } \$70 \\
&= \ 61\,3/4\% \text{ of } \$70 \\
&= \ \$43.23 \text{ per week for both} \\
&\quad \text{temporary and permanent} \\
&\quad \text{disability compensation}
\end{aligned}
$$

§ 5.9 Temporary Disability—Waiting Period

Temporary disability indemnity (compensation, also referred to as TC or TD) is payable during the period the injured employee is temporarily incapacitated by reason of the industrial injury. Payment continues until he or she has recovered sufficiently to return to work or until his or her condition reaches a stationary point beyond which there is expected to be no improvement. *LC 4650, 4652*

Effective for injuries occurring on or after January 1, 1990, there may be an automatic 10% penalty if payment of temporary compensation is not made within 14 days after the employer receives knowledge of an industrial injury and disability or if any other payment of compensation is not made in a timely manner. See Chapter 9, PENALTIES, § 9.5, *Delay or Failure to Provide Benefits.*

The workers' compensation law provides for a waiting period before payment of temporary compensation must be made. This provision is intended to provide some motivation for an employee to return to work as soon as possible if the injury is not too significant. The law also recognizes that it would be unfair to apply a waiting period in more serious cases and sets forth a so-called "retroactive period" of disability which renders the waiting period inapplicable. Inpatient hospitalization is another factor eliminating any waiting period. *LC 4650, 4652*

The waiting period for injuries occurring during the period April 1, 1974 through December 31, 1989, is three days after an employee leaves work because of an industrial injury. Thus, compensation is payable on the fourth day after the employee leaves work for this reason. The retroactive disability period is 21 days for injuries during this period, that is if temporary disability extends beyond 21 days, compensation is payable beginning on the first day after the employee leaves work. Also, if the employee is hospitalized because of the injury, compensation accrual begins on the first day after the employee leaves work. Note that this provision excludes the day of injury. Thus, for injuries occurring before 1990 no compensation is paid for the day of injury. "Hospitalization" is construed to mean being a bed patient in a hospital. It does not include clinical or emergency treatment which could be performed in a physician's office. No time limit has been placed on the duration; one day would be enough. It is also immaterial when the hospitalization occurs. The Appeals Board has ruled that being scheduled for an overnight hospital stay is sufficient even though the doctor releases the patient early. Further, the days of disability which would eliminate the waiting period need not be consecutive. By way of example, assume that a worker leaves work on the day after his injury. He will not receive compensation for the first three days of disability. If his disability extends beyond 21 days, the employer or carrier would be obliged to pay compensation for the first three days in addition to any other compensation due at that time. The same obligation would arise if the worker were hospitalized at any time after the injury.

LC 4652   Effective for injuries occurring on or after January 1, 1990, the three-day waiting period is retained; however, the retroactive period of disability has been reduced to 14 days. Further, the three-day waiting period includes the day of injury unless the employer pays full wages for that day. The "inpatient" requirement for hospitalization has been retained; thus, the interpretations regarding hospitalization discussed above are still applicable.

Because of legislative changes regarding the waiting period, and because of the rule that date of injury controls benefits, one must ascertain the waiting period provisions in effect for each injury. The present 3-day waiting period applies only to injuries occurring on or after April 1, 1974. Before that date, the waiting period was 7 days with payment of temporary compensation commencing on the 8th day after the employee left work as the result of an industrial injury. For injuries occurring 4-1-72 through 3-31-74, the period of temporary disability which would render the 7-day waiting period inapplicable is 28 days; for injuries 1949 through 3-31-72, 49 days. The hospitalization exception has been in the law since 1959. To assist in determining applicable waiting period provisions, the following table is provided for dates of injury after 9-18-59.

Date of Injury	Waiting Period*	Retroactive Disability Period
On or after 1-1-90	3 days**	14 days
4-1-74 through 12-31-89	3 days	21 days
4-1-72 through 3-31-74	7 days	28 days
9-18-59 through 3-31-72	7 days	49 days

*If employee hospitalized, there is no waiting period.
** Waiting period for injuries on or after 1-1-90 includes day of injury unless full wages paid for that day.

Compensation is payable beginning the first day after leaving work because of injury to state civil service, University of California, and state university and college employees where injury is the result of an act of criminal violence directed at such an employee.   *LC 4650.5*

§ 5.10   Temporary Compensation—Number of Payments

For injuries which occur on or after January 1, 1979, the only limit to   *LC 4656* the number of compensation payments for temporary total disability is the duration of such disability. There is no longer any arbitrary limit to the number of such payments. There is, however, a limit to the number of temporary partial disability compensation payments of 240 compensable weeks within a period of 5 years from the date of injury.

As to injuries occurring before January 1, 1979, the limit is 240 compensable weeks within a period of 5 years from the date of injury, and this limit applies to both temporary total and temporary partial disability.

Since date of injury controls which benefits apply, the previous limitations will continue to be viable regarding payments of temporary total compensation where the injury occurred before January 1, 1979.

In those cases in which the 240-week limit applies, if an injured worker has intermittent periods of disability, they cannot exceed a total of 240 weeks and, further, if the 5-year period elapses, no more temporary compensation is payable even if the worker has less than 240 "compensable weeks" within that period.

If an injury occurred before January 1, 1979, and the injury caused both temporary total and temporary partial disability, the total number of both types of compensation payments may not exceed 240 weeks within the 5-year period. Also, with regard to pre-1979 cases, no temporary compensation is payable after 5 years from date of injury.

The removal of the limit for temporary total compensation for injuries on or after January 1, 1979, will probably not affect the majority of cases, for most injuries do not cause such lengthy periods of temporary disability. It will serve to make possible the payment of temporary total compensation in the previously troublesome type of case in which surgery is performed after 5 years from date of injury. It is important to keep in mind that in many cases entitlement to temporary compensation depends on the opinions of treating or examining physicians.

The Supreme Court in *Nickelsberg v. W.C.A.B.* (1991) has ruled that the removal of the time constraints in LC 4656 regarding payment of temporary total compensation for injuries on or after January 1, 1979, does not permit an employee to petition to reopen an award after five years from the date of injury in order to obtain a further award of such compensation. The court applied the five-year limitation period set forth in LC 5410 and 5804 on petitions to reopen an award and so ruled even though the temporary disability resulted from surgery performed pursuant to an award of further medical treatment. An award for further medical treatment does not amount to an implied award for further compensation for disability resulting from such treatment. The removal of the time limit in LC 4656 was intended only to permit timely awards of temporary total compensation where the disability is continuous.

For injuries occurring prior to January 1, 1990, the first day of disability is the day after the employee leaves work because of a work-injury. In determining the payments to be made, the applicable waiting period must be taken into account. [NOTE: For injuries occurring on or after January 1, 1990, the first day of disability is the day the employee leaves work because of injury, unless full wages are paid for that day.]

It has been the practice to base payment upon a seven-day week; that is, for each calendar day of disability, $1/7$th of the weekly rate is paid. Recent compensation limits have been fixed so as to be evenly divisible by 7 to get a daily rate. (For instance, $224 ÷ 7 = $32; $112 ÷ 7 = $16; $140 ÷ 7 = $20; $70 ÷ 7 = $10.)

EXAMPLES: [NOTE: The following examples have been provided to illustrate situations which might confront the reader, keeping in mind the 5-year jurisdiction of the W.C.A.B. and the fact that there are many "older cases" in which there can be pending, undecided issues.]

(1) Eloise injured her right, major wrist on May 14, 1984, while working as a parts inspector. She left work the same day and shortly thereafter underwent surgery. She was off work until her return on November 9, 1984. Her earnings at time of injury were $350 per week.

Step 1: Check Table A for earnings and compensation limits for this date of injury. Her earnings exceed maximum earnings for temporary total compensation. Thus, her compensation rate for temporary total disability is $224 per week or $32 per day.

Step 2: Check applicable waiting period. The waiting period would be three days, but since temporary disability exceeded 21 days (and also because she was hospitalized for surgery), there is no waiting period, and she is entitled to compensation beginning with the day after she left work because of the injury. Payment would begin with May 15, but the first check would have the waiting period deducted, unless she were hospitalized immediately; then it would not be deducted. Under these facts, she would be entitled to be paid for the first three days as soon as hospitalization is reported and in any event after 21 days of disability.

Step 3: In line with the medical opinion in this case, payments continue until Eloise's return to work. A review of temporary compensation payments will indicate the total paid. This review is useful as a double-check of such payments and is a pertinent procedure in evaluating claims and disability issues. Also, it provides ready information for the W.C.A.B. in the event the matter becomes litigated.

May	—	17 days
June	—	30 days
July	—	31 days
Aug.	—	31 days
Sept.	—	30 days
Oct.	—	31 days
Nov.	—	8 days
Total	—	178 days $+ 7 = 25^3/_7$ weeks

Step 4: Compute total amount of temporary compensation entitlement using either daily or weekly rate.

$178 \times \$32$ per day ($25^3/_7 \times \$224$ per week)

$= \$5,696$

(2) In this example, we assume that a worker, whom we shall refer to as Brown, was seriously injured at work on September 1, 1978, and that the injury caused temporary total disability, Brown leaving work because of injury that same day. At time of injury, Brown's earnings were $300.00 per week. The treating physician released him from treatment, and he returned to work on Monday, March 5, 1979.

Step 1: Check Table A for earnings and compensation limits, since this injury occurred after 4-1-74. The table shows that earnings exceed the maximum of $231.00 per week; therefore, the compensation rate is limited to $154.00 per week.

Step 2: Check applicable waiting period. For this day of injury, the waiting period is three days. Payment will commence on the fourth day of disability, i.e., September 5, 1978. (The first day of disability is the day after an employee leaves work because of injury.) On the 22nd day of disability (or sooner if he were hospitalized before the 22nd day), Brown is entitled to payment for the first 3 days of disability in addition to the current payment.

Step 3: In line with the medical opinion in this case, payments continue until Brown's return to work. Review total period of disability.

Sept.	—	29 days
Oct.	—	31 days
Nov.	—	30 days
Dec.	—	31 days
Jan.	—	31 days
Feb.	—	28 days
March	—	4 days*
Total	—	184 days ÷ 7 = $26^2/_7$ weeks

*Because of use of 7-day week in computations, Saturday & Sunday are included.

Step 4: Compute total amount of temporary compensation entitlement, using either a daily or weekly rate.

184 × $22 per day (or $26^2/_7$ × $154.00 per week) = $4,048

(3) Assume that Jones is injured on January 5, 1976. At time of injury, his earnings were $200 per week. He left work the day of the injury, returning on March 4, 1976.

Step 1: Check Table A for earnings and compensation limits, this injury occurring after 4-1-74. The table shows that the earnings exceed the maximum of $178.50 per week; therefore, the compensation rate for temporary disability is $119 per week.

Step 2: Check applicable waiting period. For this date of injury the waiting period is 3 days. Payment would commence on the 4th day of disability, i.e., January 9, 1976. On the 22nd day of disability, Jones would be entitled to payment for the first 3 days of disability in addition to the current payment.

Step 3: On Jones' return to work, review total period of temporary disability and entitlement.

Jan. — 26 days
Feb. — 29 days (1976 is a leap year.)
Mar. — 3 days
_____
Total — 58 days ÷ 7 = 8²/₇ weeks

Step 4: Compute total amount of temporary compensation entitlement. This can be done by using the daily rate or the weekly rate.

58 days × $17 per day (or 8²/₇ × $119) = $986

(No deduction for the waiting period because disability exceeded 21 days.)

(4) Smith was injured on May 2, 1974, while working as a messenger. His earnings were $3.50 per hour, 40 hours per week, or $140 per week. He was immediately taken to the hospital where he remained for 3 days, after which he continued to be disabled until his return to work on September 14, 1974.

Step 1: Check Table A for minimum and maximum rates for temporary compensation. Smith's wages are less than maximum and more than minimum so that his compensation rate must be computed.

Compensation rate = ²/₃ × $140
= $93.33 per week for temporary compensation

Step 2: Check applicable waiting period. The 3-day waiting period is not applicable here because of the hospitalization. Payment would commence as of May 3, 1974, the first day of disability.

Step 3: Review total period of disability on Smith's return to work.

May — 29 days
June — 30 days
July — 31 days
Aug. — 31 days
Sept. — 13 days
_____
Total — 134 days ÷ 7 = 19¹/₇ weeks

Step 4: Compute total amount of temporary compensation entitlement.

19¹/₇ weeks × $93.33 per week = $1,786.60

(No deduction for the waiting period because of hospitalization and disability exceeding 21 days.)

(5) On February 2, 1974, Bonnie injured her back in the course of her work as a secretary. Her earnings were $175 per week. She continued working for another 3 days when her condition worsened requiring her to leave

work on February 5, 1974. She responded to conservative care and returned to work on March 2, 1974.

Step 1: Check Table C for minimum and maximum rates for temporary compensation (since this injury occurred before April 1, 1974). Bonnie's actual earnings exceed maximum ($170.04); thus, her temporary compensation is $105 per week.

Step 2: Check applicable waiting period. A 7-day waiting period applies. She would not be paid for the first 7 days of disability until disability exceeds 28 days (which it does not in this example).

Step 3: Review total period of disability on Bonnie's return to work.

Feb.	—	23 days
Mar.	—	1 day
Total	—	24 days ÷ 7 = $3^3/_7$ weeks

Step 4: Compute total amount of temporary compensation entitlement.

24 days – 7-day waiting period = 17 days or $2^3/_7$ weeks

17 days × $15 per day (or $2^3/_7$ × $105) = $255

(Waiting period deducted because disability did not exceed 28 days.)

(6) Betty, while employed as a waitress, sustained a severe burn injury in the course of her work on December 4, 1971. At that time, her actual earning capacity was $138 per week. She left work that day and remained off work while receiving extensive medical care. On January 4, 1972, she was hospitalized for 3 days, then continued under her physician's care until her return to work on February 19, 1972.

Step 1: Check Table C for minimum and maximum rates for temporary compensation. Betty's actual earning capacity is less than maximum actual earnings for this date of injury ($141.70) and more than the minimum ($40.48); thus, her rate must be computed.

Compensation rate	=	65% of statutory average earnings
	=	65% of 95% of $138
	=	$61^3/_4$% of $138
	=	$85.22 per week for temporary compensation

Step 2: Check applicable waiting period. A 7-day waiting period applies. Under these facts, Betty would not be paid for the first 7 days of disability initially. Her payments would start on December 12, 1971 (the 8th day after leaving work). However, when hospitalized on January 4, 1972, she would become entitled to payment for the first 7 days. (She would become eligible for this payment without hospitalization on the 50th day of disability, i.e., January 23, 1972.)

Step 3: Review total period of disability on Betty's return to work.

Dec.	—	27 days
Jan.	—	31 days
Feb.	—	18 days
Total	—	76 days ÷ 7 = $10^6/7$ weeks

Step 4: Compute total amount of temporary compensation entitlement.

$10^6/7$ weeks × $85.22 per week = $925.25

(No deduction for waiting period because of hospitalization and disability exceeding 49 days.)

§ 5.11 Change in Rate After Two Years From Date of Injury

LC 4661.5, as effective January 1, 1979, provides: "[W]hen any temporary total disability indemnity payment is made two years or more from the date of injury, the amount of such payment shall be computed in accordance with the temporary disability indemnity average weekly earnings amount specified . . . on the date each such temporary total disability payment is made." A proviso has been added to LC 4661.5, effective as to injuries occurring on or after January 1, 1990, that the section does not apply if payment after two years from date of injury would result in a lower rate because of the reduction of minimum average earnings per amendments to LC 4453. *LC 4661.5*

The Court of Appeal has ruled that this provision applies to any payment of temporary total disability compensation made two years or more from date of injury regardless of the reason the payment was made at such later time. It applies when payment has been improperly delayed or withheld for two or more years, even though the compensation has accrued during a time when rates were lower.

Before 1979, and effective January 1, 1975, this section provided for such payment only where temporary total disability extended for two years beyond the date of injury.

§ 5.12 Disability: Temporary Total—Temporary Partial

So far, our discussion has pertained to computations for temporary total disability. The code also provides for compensation based upon temporary partial disability. Total disability refers to incapacity to do any kind of work; temporary partial disability indicates a condition which permits the employee to perform some occupational function. If the employee is able to obtain some type of work despite his or her partial incapacity, he or she is entitled to compensation on a wage-loss basis. Currently, wage-loss compensation is 2/3 of the difference between earnings on the new job and the actual earnings at time of injury (subject to the maximum and minimum limits for earnings in *LC 4654, 4657*

Table A). The two-thirds formula is applicable to injuries occurring on or after April 1, 1974.

For injuries occurring before April 1, 1974, wage-loss compensation for temporary partial disability is 65% of the difference between the employee's actual weekly income on the new job and the "statutory average earnings" at the time of injury (subject to the maximum and minimum limits for statutory average earnings in Table C).

EXAMPLES:

(1) Mark was injured on the job in 1984 having earnings of $400 per week. He received temporary compensation of $224 per week until his return to a lighter job. He was still undergoing physiotherapy two days per week, the doctor not having given him a full release. Mark worked three days per week (24 hours total) at $6 per hour. He would be entitled to temporary partial compensation. Because his original wages exceeded maximum earnings, the computation of the wage-loss compensation would be determined on the basis of the maximum of $336 per week.

Wage-loss	=	Actual (Max.) earnings minus actual earnings on new job
	=	$336 – $144
	=	$192
Wage-loss Compensation	=	²/₃ wage-loss
	=	²/₃ × $192
	=	$128 per week

This plus his new wage equals a total income of $272 per week. If Mark's prior earnings had been less than maximum, say $300 per week, then the actual wage received would be used.

Wage-loss	=	$300 – $144
	=	$156
Wage-loss Compensation	=	$104 per week
Total Income	=	$248 per week

(2) Assume that Marilyn was injured in 1984 while working as a part-time typist earning $100 per week. While under treatment, she is able to work half-time earning $50 per week. Her previous $100 per week is less than the minimum earnings limit in effect on date of injury which is $168 per week. This latter figure must be used in the wage-loss formula.

Wage-loss	=	Actual (Min.) earnings minus actual earnings on new job
	=	$168 – $50
	=	$118 per week

Wage-loss
Compensation $= \frac{2}{3} \times$ wage-loss
$= \frac{2}{3} \times \$118$
$= \$78.67$ per week

Total income is $\$50 + 78.67$ or \$128.67 per week. This is more than she was earning when injured, but this is the way the concept of minimum earnings and minimum compensation works. When she was temporarily totally disabled, her TTD rate was \$112 (minimum) which was also more than she had been earning. Again, this concept has been held to be consistent with the remedial nature of the workers' compensation program and deemed necessary to sustain an employee while recovering from a work-injury.

(3) Assume that Fred was injured on October 1, 1978, when his actual earnings were \$250 per week; that after a period of temporary total disability his doctor certified him for light work; that Fred obtained work paying him \$90 per week. Reference to Table A shows maximum actual earnings of \$231 for temporary compensation; so this is the figure to be used in computing the wage-loss.

Wage-loss $=$ Actual (Max.) earnings minus actual earnings on new job
$= \$231 - \$90$
$= \$141$ per week

Wage-loss
Compensation $= \frac{2}{3}$ wage-loss
$= \frac{2}{3} \times \$141$
$= \$94$ per week

Note that while Fred's wage-loss compensation seems small, when it is added to the earnings on the new job of \$90 per week, his total income is \$184 per week.

(4) Nancy was injured on August 15, 1972, at which time her wage was \$150 per week. For this date of injury, wage-loss is the difference between actual earnings on the new job and statutory average earnings at time of injury. Checking Table C, we find that the maximum statutory average earnings are \$161.54 per week for temporary compensation. Thus, Nancy's statutory average earnings for wage-loss determination are 95% of \$150 per week, or \$142.50 per week. Some time later, while temporarily partially disabled, Nancy obtains work from her employer paying her \$100 per week.

Wage-loss $=$ Statutory average earnings minus actual earnings on new job
$= \$142.50 - \$100$
$= \$42.50$ per week

Wage-loss
Compensation $=$ 65% of wage-loss
$=$ 65% of \$42.50
$= \$27.63$ per week

This amount in addition to the earnings on the new job results in a total income for Nancy of $127.63 per week.

If a partially disabled employee can perform some type of work, and it appears to the Appeals Board that lack of work is due to his or her own desire, the Board may determine probable earning ability for the purpose of computing wage-loss compensation for partial disability.

On the other hand, partial disability may be such that it effectively prevents the employee from performing any duty for which he or she is skilled. An example would be one whose only calling, experience, training, schooling, and ability is heavy laborer, who suffers an impingement of a nerve by scar tissue in his right palm. True, the only portion of his anatomy which is affected is the palm of his hand, but it prevents him from effective use of the tools of his trade. He cannot accept labor assignments from his union hiring hall. This man might be considered temporarily totally disabled. Under a 1959 decision of the California Supreme Court, he would more accurately be considered partially disabled, but his wage loss would be considered total, entitling him to the maximum compensation rate while off work. In the Supreme Court case, the partially disabled carpenter could do nothing except finish work, which is light carpentry. There was no showing that such light work was available or offered, and thus his wage loss was total.

This decision sweeps away a knotty problem in the case of partial disability, for before this 1959 decision, the Court of Appeal had laid down a rigid requirement in cases in this category. The employee, to obtain total compensation, had to show that no work was available she could do, that she had made a diligent effort to find work, that as a result she was an "odd lot" in the labor market. If she did not present such proof, the commission was required to determine the probable wage she could earn in the type of employment she was physically capable of, whether or not such work was offered. The Supreme Court expressly disapproved the appellate court's views, and the "odd lot" issue has been laid to rest (*Stroer* case).

CAUTION: The Appeals Board has not construed the Supreme Court decision as a directive to pay every partially disabled employee total temporary compensation simply because no work is offered by the employer. The employee should make an effort to obtain employment within his capabilities.

It is at this juncture that many disputes arise. The employer may not be in a position to offer light work or invent some light job. There have been occasions in which the injured has tried to return to regular duty too soon and, as a result, suffers a relapse of the injury. A different case results when the treating physician releases the injured person to return to regular duty. Generally, the employee agrees and returns to the job. When the employee fails to return, it is often difficult to determine whether that failure is due to the physician's premature release or mistake on the part of the employee as to entitlement to further compensation.

If the employer offers light work which the employee can do, and the employee refuses, or is fired for good cause unconnected with injury, temporary partial compensation may be determined pursuant to the wage-loss formula based on the wage earned in light work or a wage the worker could reasonably be expected to earn as partially disabled.

If the employee files an application before the Appeals Board, she may file a report from her own physician, and in most instances the employer will obtain an up-to-date medical report. As a result, there will be a certain number of cases in which the employer will voluntarily resume benefits. Most applications, however, lead to a proceeding before a trial judge whose decision will be based upon the evidence presented at that time. If the employee is not entitled to further temporary benefits, but has residual permanent impairment which affects her working ability, the employee may be awarded a permanent disability payment. In the next chapter we discuss the conditions upon which such payments are made.

§ 5.13 Successive Injuries—Temporary Disability

In 1964, the California Supreme Court held that payment of temporary compensation is not to be apportioned among several employers in whose employ the applicant suffered back injuries. The commission found on conflicting evidence that the last of four injuries caused the applicant's temporary disability and need for treatment. The Supreme Court agreed, pointing out that the payment of temporary compensation is on a wage-loss basis. It was the last injury which resulted in the wage-loss in question. (The employers in a case of this kind may be entitled to an apportionment of liability for a permanent disability benefit. See Chapter 6, PERMANENT DISABILITY, § 6.16, *Apportionment of Permanent Disability*.) However, compensation is not payable for temporary disability due to an intervening pregnancy.

§ 5.14 Temporary Compensation and Rehabilitation

An injured worker who is receiving compensation because of temporary disability may be a candidate for vocational rehabilitation. If an employer or *LC 139.5* carrier knows that an injured worker will not be able to return to his or her occupation, or if temporary disability extends beyond 180 days from the date of injury, the employer or carrier must report this fact to the Vocational Rehabilitation Unit of the Division of Workers' Compensation by completing and filing form RB-1. While any rehabilitation program may be future, this *R 10004* procedure permits early identification of potential rehabilitants. This requirement is in addition to the requirement that an employer or carrier notify the injured worker of his or her right to vocational rehabilitation if found to be a "qualified injured worker" under Administrative Director Rule 10004(b). A qualified injured worker is entitled to temporary compensation while partic- *R 10003(i)* ipating in a rehabilitation program. (See Chapter 16, VOCATIONAL REHABILITATION.)

§ 5.15   Time and Method of Payment; Penalty

LC 4650   Before 1990, the law provided for payment of compensation two times per month. With respect to injuries occurring on or after January 1, 1990, the first payment of temporary compensation must be made not later than 14 days after knowledge of the injury and disability, unless liability has been denied. Subsequent payments are to be made every two weeks on the day designated with the first payment unless the employer continues the employee's wages under a salary continuation plan. [NOTE: Effective January 1, 1991, "salary continuation plan" means a plan paid for by an employer under a collective bargaining agreement, memorandum of understanding or established employer policy whereby an employee is paid on the regular payday not less than the salary provided by the plan and not less than the workers' compensation payments the employee would otherwise receive.] If compensation due is not paid in a timely manner, the amount of the late payment must be increased 10%, without application, and paid to the employee. This penalty is not applicable to any payment due prior to or within 14 days after the date a claim form is submitted. Also, the penalty is not applicable when within the initial 14-day period the employer is unable to determine whether temporary compensation payments are owed and so advises the employee on a form prescribed by LC 138.4. Such a notice must include what information is needed and when the employer expects to have the information required to make a decision. This self-actuating penalty does not apply to injuries prior to 1990. [NOTE: LC 5814 provides for a 10% penalty to be assessed by the W.C.A.B if benefits have been unreasonably refused or delayed. LC 5814 is applicable to both pre-1990 injuries and those occurring on or after January 1, 1990.]

IC 11661.6   Beginning January 1, 1991, if an employer is insured, the employer must reimburse the insurance carrier for any penalty paid under LC 4650 if
LC 4650   the late payment of compensation is due less than seven days after the carrier
(e), (f)   receives the completed claim form from the employer. The carrier is to notify the employer of the obligation to reimburse within 30 days of payment and bill and collect the amount no later than at final audit. There is no obligation to pay or collect such amounts unless their aggregate exceeds $100 during the policy year. The notice to the employer must include a notice of the employer's right to appeal the carrier's decision to the Department of Insurance within 60 days. An employer's obligation to reimburse a carrier for this penalty is not insurable.

LC 4902   A compensation payment must be cash or a negotiable demand instrument. Payment must be made directly to the employee and cannot be made to any other person unless the W.C.A.B. orders such payment to a guardian, trustee or lien claimant. The code reference to negotiable instrument has been amended to provide that the payment of compensation must be made either in cash or by *immediately* negotiable demand instrument, payable in cash without discount.

COMMENT: Apparently some drafts issued by insurance companies have been deemed to be negotiable, although not immediately negotiable because of confirming conditions placed on drafts. By requiring that the instrument be immediately negotiable, the Legislature seems to have ruled out the conditional draft type of instrument.

The method used by one company is not recommended. The document involved was the size of a business letter and was captioned, "VOUCHER." Beneath this, there was an accounting of everything paid to date for compensation and medical treatment. Then, in small print was the statement that when properly signed, the voucher would change into a sight draft for $70. Next came six signatures of company officials. There was a space for the employee's signature which had to be witnessed. At a glance, the document and its eight signatures gave the impression of being a conditional sales contract. Such payment was not cash or a negotiable demand instrument.

A further admonition regarding payment: If a particular method of payment causes undue delay or undue difficulty in negotiating an instrument into cash, a 10% penalty may be assessed by the W.C.A.B. under LC 5814.

§ 5.16 Payment and Acceptance of Compensation Not Due

In paying compensation and furnishing medical treatment after receiving notice of injury, the employer does not thereby admit that he is *LC 4909* under any legal obligations to pay or continue to pay. This provision is designed to protect the employer who mistakenly makes payments for a non-industrial condition suffered by the employee and to encourage prompt payment of benefits. The employer is entitled to credit for any benefits furnished, including credit for any overpayments. Likewise, the employee's acceptance of compensation does not constitute a waiver of any claim he or she may have.

§ 5.17 Payment of Wages

a. Voluntary Payment of Wages

If an employer voluntarily pays wages to the injured employee while he is off work, the insurance carrier is not relieved of its duty to pay compensation. It is not uncommon for an employer to pay the employee the difference between compensation and his or her regular earnings. The parties may agree that employer-payments shall be repaid if any compensation is paid. One self-insured company gives its employees the option of straight compensation or full salary if the employee will agree to credit for the overpayment against any permanent disability award. Another pays the difference between compensation and 90% of wages during the first 90 days of temporary disability. A utility pays into an employees' welfare fund, managed by an employees' committee. From this fund, various benefits are paid including the difference between wages and temporary compensation.

The issue of whether credit is to be given an employer or insurance carrier for wages paid during a period of industrial disability has been determined by the California Supreme Court in a decision which sets up the following principles:

LC 3754

1. Where the employee is paid wages during a period of temporary disability, the employee is not entitled to workers' compensation payments in addition, if the W.C.A.B. finds that the employer paid such wages as a disability benefit and did not intend the wage payment to be a gift.

2. If the employer has a carrier, the employer is entitled to a reimbursement from the carrier to the extent of the compensation which would otherwise have been due the employee, and the lien procedure can be used in this connection. The W.C.A.B. may allow this lien on its motion under LC 4905.

3. A contrary rule would make possible a double recovery by the employee. The W.C.A.B. has authority to determine the type of payment which was made, the purpose for which it was made, and the credit which might accrue to the employer (LC 4909). This decision is consistent with prior appellate decisions holding that a payment of a wage during disability is a benefit paid because of an industrial disability and therefore extends the running of the statute of limitations.

b. Law Officers

LC 4800-4855

Certain law officers are entitled to full salary, not to exceed one year's salary, instead of workers' compensation payments or the rehabilitation maintenance allowance provided for under LC 139.5.

LC 4800-4810

Those qualifying for this special benefit include any "member" whose position falls within the "state safety" class of—

California Highway Patrol
California Department of Justice
also: Harbor Police, San Francisco Port Commission
Firefighter, University of California
Police, University of California

LC 4850-4855

Employees of local government entitled to one-year's salary in lieu of compensation are—

Sheriff and deputy sheriff
Police officer of a city
Investigator in a district attorney's office
Firefighter of a county, city or fire district
Lifeguard of Los Angeles County (full-time only)
Harbor Police, Harbor District (until 1-1-90)

As a condition of entitlement, the local government law officers must be members of either the (State) Public Employees' Retirement System or a County Retirement System under the County Retirement Act of 1937, GC

31450 and following. Officers whose county, city, or district employer has not provided retirement coverage under one of these two systems would not be eligible for this benefit unless the governing body has otherwise provided for it. However, the County of San Luis Obispo may provide this benefit to sheriff and firefighting personnel even though they may not be members of either of the above retirement systems. Also, the governing board of a fire district may waive this requirement as to firefighters employed by the district. *LC 4850.5, 4850.7*

The intent of the one-year salary benefit is as a protection for those in active law enforcement or active firefighting. Thus, those whose positions are clerical, mechanical, or otherwise clearly not within the scope of active police or firefighting work do not qualify for this benefit.

An officer entitled to this benefit is not limited by a "calendar" one-year period if he has intermittent periods of disability. The aggregate of such periods may not exceed one year. However, if an officer retires or otherwise terminates his employment, his right to further salary in lieu of compensation terminates. These special leave provisions apply whether the disability is temporary or permanent, and the officer is also entitled to a rating for any residual permanent disability.

If an officer receiving salary in lieu of temporary compensation is retired, thus terminating the right to such salary, he or she is nevertheless entitled to receive temporary compensation until the condition becomes permanent and stationary.

Effective January 1, 1986, LC 4850 was amended to provide that the payment of salary in lieu of worker's compensation is payable during disability not to exceed one year or such earlier date as the employee is retired on a permanent disability pension and is actually receiving disability pension benefits or advanced permanent disability pension payments. The local *LC 4850.3* government employer may make advance disability pension payments to such employees on the basis of 50% of average annual compensation (salary) during the 3 consecutive years preceding retirement. This amount may be less than 50% if the employee has elected otherwise. If the employee is eligible to receive sick leave, advance pension payments may be commenced only after the employee has exhausted all sick leave payments.

Under LC 4800 and following, a California Highway Patrol officer is entitled to receive salary in lieu of compensation in addition to any permanent disability payments to which he or she is entitled. The statutes are construed to mean that the officer is precluded from receiving both compensation and salary only as to temporary compensation payments. When rated for any permanent disability, he or she may continue to receive the salary for one year along with permanent disability payments.

A city may not terminate a disabled police officer because of physical unfitness for work and thus foreclose a right to salary under LC 4850.

LC 4855   Reserve police officers and firefighters do not qualify for the special salary in lieu of compensation benefits.

The Court of Appeal has ruled that the W.C.A.B. does not have jurisdiction under LC 4801 to determine whether a particular state position is in the safety member category. Such a determination is to be made by the state through the employing department.

c. Vacation and Sick Leave

An employee may take accrued vacation time or sick leave without affecting his or her right to temporary compensation. These fringe benefits are earned by the employee, and the employee may not be penalized for availing himself or herself of them. Many public employees are permitted to go on sick leave if they wish, and their sick leave accounts are credited with the pro-rate value of compensation payments. Accrual and use of vacation and sick leave are matters which can be controlled by company policy or regulation, and many employers have rules governing use of these benefits in industrial accident cases so that a worker does not receive more than wages when added to compensation. These rules also help the employee to retain certain amounts of sick leave or vacation for non-work injury situations. It is recognized that the adoption of such rules by an employer may involve negotiation or meet and confer sessions with employee organizations. Changes in vacation and sick leave plans may be made only on a prospective basis in view of the vested nature of rights already accrued.

EC 44984,   In 1963, the Education Code was amended to grant school employees 60
87787   days' industrial accident sick leave per year on a noncumulative basis.
EC 45192,   However, only so much leave may be taken as will equal full salary when
88192   added to regular workers' compensation benefits.

State employees who are members of the Public Employees' Retirement System or the State Teachers' Retirement System are granted the option of
GC 19869-   workers' compensation or a special industrial disability leave. If the injured
19877.1   state worker uses the special leave, his or her rights under the workers' compensation law thereafter are still intact. (This particular benefit does not apply to employees in the police or firefighting categories who are eligible for salary in lieu of compensation under LC 4800.) The special leave under GC 18120 is up to 22 working days at full salary and thereafter additional leave at two-thirds of salary (without any maximum compensation rate limitation), total leave not to exceed 52 weeks within two years after the employee leaves work because of an industrial injury.

§ 5.18   Retirement Plans

Various retirement provisions are also concerned with industrial injuries and require consideration. Most of the reported cases deal with rights under a statutory plan for public employees. Private plans may be coordinated with workers' compensation by rule or contract. For instance, one company provides that its disability retirement and death benefit shall be payable only to the extent that the recipient does not receive benefits under the workers' compensation law for the disability in question. Similar provisions in California public employee plans were repealed by the Legislature some years ago. Public plans differ from most private plans in that public employees must contribute a portion of their wages (usually 6% to 10%) to help finance benefits.

Considerable litigation has resulted from provisions in some city charters setting up retirement plans with special benefits for service-connected disability retirement. Such a provision which defines these benefits as workers' compensation payments has been held to be effective so that the city may take credit for such benefits as payments of workers' compensation. The rationale here is based upon the fact that a city charter is also a special statute enacted by the Legislature which controls over the general laws. The credit is limited to those pension payments allocable to tax-financing and not to the portion allocable to employee-contributions.

Public plans include:

Public Employees' Retirement System	*GC 20000 et seq.*
Teachers' Retirement System	*EC 22000 et seq.*
County Employees' Retirement Law (Counties may elect to contract with Public Employees' Retirement System.)	*GC 31450, et seq.*
City Plans: May contract with state system or govern own system per a city charter or by ordinance.	*GC 45345, 45300 et seq.*

As a general rule, pension provisions are liberally construed to provide for employees or their families. The following case-examples show various facets of the operation of public plans:

Under a compulsory public retirement program, contributions of the employee are community property except where a statute directs the mode of survivorship. The spouse's community interest is no greater than that created by the employment contract. Thus, where the beneficiary is the "widow," a former wife cannot qualify for benefits, even though she had the status of "wife" during the period when most of the contributions were made.

Payment of full salary for temporary disability under a charter provision constitutes payment of compensation rather than salary. Therefore, the city's deduction of a 6% retirement fund contribution was erroneous.

The 29-year marriage of a couple had been interrupted by a divorce and a 3-year separation. He had retired after the divorce and before their remarriage, and, as a consequence, the widow could not qualify under a provision making a widow's continuation pension dependent upon their marital status for one year prior to the employee's retirement. The court held that the remarriage after retirement reinstated the widow's contingent community property interest in rights under the pension provisions and ordered payment of the widow's allowance.

A widow of a city employee sought retirement benefits but was erroneously told she had no rights under the plan then in effect. The error, based on a legal interpretation, was not intentionally made by the city representatives. Both the municipal claims period and the statute of limitations barred the claim when she finally brought suit. The Supreme Court held that the city was not estopped to rely upon these technical defenses as to past benefits, but that since the obligation to pay the pension was continuous she could reapply for future payments. A Court of Appeal decision which held to the contrary as to the city's right was disapproved. As to future benefits, the city's conduct will be held to closer scrutiny, because this right is of greater magnitude than the claim to past payments. The court must determine whether the public agency employer acted reasonably regarding the advice given. An important holding in this case is that there is a confidential relationship between an employer and a pension-claimant.

A city granted a service-connected disability pension. However, the city also revoked an industrial injury leave granted under an ordinance (full salary) and placed the employee on sick leave status. The employee sued and recovered salary benefits to the date of retirement.

Where a pension plan provides for deduction of workers' compensation payments from a service-connected disability retirement allowance, the plan will be construed so as not to permit deductions for compensation received before retirement. Also, if a plan provides for deduction of compensation from a widow's pension, no such deduction is authorized where the workers' compensation death benefit was awarded to the decedent's son rather than to the widow.

One on disability retirement is not entitled to a service retirement when he later reaches the service retirement age.

If a police and firefighter retirement plan contains no provision for a return of contributions to the employee upon termination of employment before retirement, a member has no vested right in the contributions which he made to the plan. The employee pointed out in this case that the city operated two other retirement systems which did have refund provisions. The court states that the other plans did not affect the police and fire plan which provided for benefits much larger in size than the benefits under the other plans.

A city had authority to contract with the State Employees' Retirement System and to change from its own city-administered plan on a prospective basis. Contributions for extra pay for "hazardous duty" of police and firefighters must be computed and made to the state system by both the employees and the city.

The Court of Appeal holds that where a retirement association is an entity separate from the employing entity, the association is not bound by a Workers' Compensation Appeals Board determination regarding industrial causation of disability. Therefore, if the retirement board decides on conflicting medical evidence that an employee's disability was not service connected, its decision will be upheld. Because of procedural due process of the law requirements, the employee must be afforded a hearing on the question of whether he has suffered a service-connected disability. The Supreme Court has ruled that the Superior Court, in reviewing a decision of a county retirement board regarding a service-connected disability claim, may reweigh the evidence considered by the board. On appeal from the judgment of the court, the judgment will be upheld if supported by substantial evidence.

A retirement system may recover the actuarial value of the retirement benefits due because of disability caused by an injury resulting from the negligence of a third party. The subrogation right is not limited to the payments made to the date of the judgment against the third party. (It should be noted that specific laws or programs setting up retirement plans may limit subrogation rights in certain cases.)

Where a disability retirement right is dependent upon the employee's being "incapacitated for the performance of duty as the result of an industrial disability," the public employee must show that he was incapacitated to the extent of being unable to do *substantially* all the material acts required by his job. If the record shows that an employee can do *substantially* all of the duties of his position he is not so incapacitated and, thus, is not entitled to a service-connected disability retirement, even though his industrial injury resulted in some partial disability.

The heart disability presumption in LC 3212.5 is not applicable to disability retirement cases unless a statute makes it clearly applicable.

§ 5.19 ERISA

The federal Employees' Retirement Income Security Act (ERISA) of 1975 applies to retirement plans and employee welfare plans in the private sector (29 U.S.C. Sec. 1001, et seq.). The purpose of this law is to protect the rights of employees under such plans. It does not require that an employer furnish these benefits; it provides criteria and enforcement procedures where plans are in place. In addition to pension and retirement plans, it covers health, accident and disability benefits, as well as vacation and severance pay arrangements.

ERISA contains broad federal pre-emption provisions. State laws and state court jurisdiction are superseded except that a state's regulation of the insurance business within its borders is not pre-empted. Court decisions have emphasized federal jurisdiction over suits to enforce rights under ERISA, and the U.S. Supreme Court has ruled that federal pre-emption applies to a lawsuit brought in a state court alleging common-law causes of action where the suit is based upon a failure to provide benefits under an employee welfare plan. As a result, many such suits are removed from state courts to federal courts.

An action may be maintained against the administrator of a plan governed by ERISA for return of an unconscionable personal windfall in dealing with plan assets, even though the beneficiaries received all the benefits contemplated by the plan. However, the courts have declared that common-law damage suits are out, and ERISA does not create causes of action for damages. Permissible actions are those enforcing rights in plans under that law.

Chapter 6
PERMANENT DISABILITY

§ 6.1   Introduction

     The framers of California's workers' compensation law recognized that *LC 4658-* it is not always quite enough to provide treatment and temporary compensa- *4663* tion. Quite often an injured employee will need additional assistance in adjusting to working requirements if any permanent physical impairment has resulted from the injury. A measure of assistance is provided by the permanent disability (PD) benefit. Some states limit payment to a statutory schedule; some provide no payment until the employee suffers a loss in earnings after his return to work; others require a considerable waiting period before payments begin. One jurisdiction couples an occupational rehabilitation program with a life pension, payable upon a showing of loss of earnings.

Under the California system, permanent disability is expressed in terms of a rating which is a percentage of total disability, the latter being considered as 100%. In rating permanent disability, consideration is given to the nature of the injury, occupation, and age at time of injury, and diminished ability to compete in an open labor market. The percentages are determined (rated) in accordance with a schedule adopted by the Administrative Director. A permanent disability rating is converted into a number of weeks of compensation utilizing a table of values set forth in LC 4658. The law also provides for a life pension in more severe cases, i.e., if a rating is 70% or more. Permanent disability benefits are payable in addition to any temporary compensation paid.

LC 139.5   In 1965, the legislature recognized the importance of more positive rehabilitative efforts and provided for voluntary rehabilitation programs for injured workers. Effective January 1, 1975, the right to necessary rehabilitation, both medical and vocational, was added as a workers' compensation benefit. Regulations have been promulgated defining "qualified injured worker" for rehabilitation benefits as one who has a permanent or potentially permanent handicap as a result of an industrial injury. (See Chapter 16, VOCATIONAL REHABILITATION.)

§ 6.2   Permanent Disability Benefits

LC 4662   If an industrial injury results in permanent disability which causes a significant handicap in performing work, the injured worker is entitled to a permanent disability rating. This rating will be expressed as a percentage of total disability depending on the severity of the handicap. Total disability rates 100%. Permanent partial disability is a permanent disability which rates less than 100%, and because 1/4 of 1% is the smallest increment used, the range of permanent partial disabilities is 0 – 99 3/4%. Certain conditions, such as bilateral blindness or loss of both hands, are conclusively presumed to be total, i.e., to rate 100%.

[NOTE: Appellate court decisions have established the principle that if a worker has a pre-existing permanent disability which would rate 100%, but he or she is nevertheless working in a job in which he or she sustains an injury, the 100% rating limitation is deemed a fiction and any further permanent disability resulting from the injury must be rated.]

LC 4658   The percentage rating is then converted to a number of weeks of com-
4659   pensation in accordance with the formula in effect on the date of injury. For injuries occurring before April 1, 1972, the conversion formula is 4 weeks of compensation for each 1% of the PD rating. As to injuries occurring on or after April 1, 1972, a more complicated formula applies. Under the "old" method, it is a relatively simple procedure to multiply a rating by 4 to get the

number of weeks of compensation. The "new" method involves a cumulative table intended to provide a smaller recovery for the smaller ratings and increasingly larger recovery for the larger ratings. The table in the code has been used as the basis for a cumulative table prepared by the Disability Evaluation Bureau which may be used to obtain the weeks of compensation for any rating. A later amendment to the code provides that a worker who is permanently totally disabled (i.e., PD rates 100%) will receive weekly compensation payments for life if injury occurs on or after April 1, 1974.

The weekly compensation payment for permanent disability is determined in the same way as the temporary disability payment, although the minimum and maximum limits may be less. Again, these limits are set and controlled by fixing the minimum and maximum earnings which can be considered or utilized in the formula for weekly compensation rates. (See Tables A and C.)

In developing the new conversion procedure, the legislature was mindful that even though the weekly compensation rate was increased to a maximum of $70 per week on April 1, 1972, the reduction in the number of weeks of compensation for smaller ratings could result in a smaller total recovery by an employee than would have been the case under the old formula with the previous maximum compensation rate of $52.50 per week. Therefore, perhaps as a compromise, there is a proviso applicable to injuries occurring on or after April 1, 1972, which retains the old method as an alternative if the employee would get more total dollars with the previous maximum limit of $52.50 per week.

Permanent disability ratings will be converted to the number of weeks shown in chart below for injuries occurring on or after April 1, 1972. [NOTE: *LC 4658* Under the Reform Act of 1989, an amended table is effective as of January 1, 1992; thus, the following values apply to injuries occurring on or after April 1, 1972, to and including December 31, 1991. For the amended table, see subsequent topic in § 6.3, *Conversion Values — Injuries on and after January 1, 1992.*]

PD Rating   Weeks per 1%

0	-	9$\frac{3}{4}$%	× 3 weeks
10%	-	19$\frac{3}{4}$%	× 4 weeks
20%	-	29$\frac{3}{4}$%	× 5 weeks
30%	-	49$\frac{3}{4}$%	× 6 weeks
50%	-	69$\frac{3}{4}$%	× 7 weeks
70%	-	99$\frac{3}{4}$%	× 8 weeks*

(These values are cumulative. Thus, a rating must be separated into this statutory table. Use of components to fit following PD conversion table is recommended.)

*For injuries on or after 4-1-74, if permanent disability rates 100%, compensation is paid for life at the rate for temporary total compensation.

If a rating would result in more value under the prior system of multiplying a rating by 4 weeks, but with a limit of $52.50 per week, the larger of the two computations will be awarded.

The following table provides the cumulative number of weeks for each rating. The figures in "Rating" columns represent percentages of permanent disability.

PERMANENT DISABILITY CONVERSION TABLE

[For injuries 4-1-72 through 12-31-91.]

Rating%	Weeks	Rating%	Weeks	Rating%	Weeks	Rating%	Weeks
1	3.00	9.50	28.50	18	62.25	26.50	103.00
1.25	3.75	9.75	29.25	18.25	63.25	26.75	104.25
1.50	4.50	10	30.25	18.50	64.25	27	105.50
1.75	5.25	10.25	31.25	18.75	65.25	27.25	106.75
2	6.00	10.50	32.25	19	66.25	27.50	108.00
2.25	6.75	10.75	33.25	19.25	67.25	27.75	109.25
2.50	7.50	11	34.25	19.50	68.25	28	110.50
2.75	8.25	11.25	35.25	19.75	69.25	28.25	111.75
3	9.00	11.50	36.25	20	70.50	28.50	113.00
3.25	9.75	11.75	37.25	20.25	71.75	28.75	114.25
3.50	10.50	12	38.25	20.50	73.00	29	115.50
3.75	11.25	12.25	39.25	20.75	74.25	29.25	116.75
4	12.00	12.50	40.25	21	75.50	29.50	118.00
4.25	12.75	12.75	41.25	21.25	76.75	29.75	119.25
4.50	13.50	13	42.25	21.50	78.00	30	120.75
4.75	14.25	13.25	43.25	21.75	79.25	30.25	122.25
5	15.00	13.50	44.25	22	80.50	30.50	123.75
5.25	15.75	13.75	45.25	22.25	81.75	30.75	125.25
5.50	16.50	14	46.25	22.50	83.00	31	126.75
5.75	17.25	14.25	47.25	22.75	84.25	31.25	128.25
6	18.00	14.50	48.25	23	85.50	31.50	129.75
6.25	18.75	14.75	49.25	23.25	86.75	31.75	131.25
6.50	19.50	15	50.25	23.50	88.00	32	132.75
6.75	20.25	15.25	51.25	23.75	89.25	32.25	134.25
7	21.00	15.50	52.25	24	90.50	32.50	135.75
7.25	21.75	15.75	53.25	24.25	91.75	32.75	137.25
7.50	22.50	16	54.25	24.50	93.00	33	138.75
7.75	23.25	16.25	55.25	24.75	94.25	33.25	140.25
8	24.00	16.50	56.25	25	95.50	33.50	141.75
8.25	24.75	16.75	57.25	25.25	96.75	33.75	143.25
8.50	25.50	17	58.25	25.50	98.00	34	144.75
8.75	26.25	17.25	59.25	25.75	99.25	34.25	146.25
9	27.00	17.50	60.25	26	100.50	34.50	147.75
9.25	27.75	17.75	61.25	26.25	101.75	34.75	149.25

PERMANENT DISABILITY CONVERSION TABLE (Cont.)

Rating%	Weeks	Rating%	Weeks	Rating%	Weeks	Rating%	Weeks
35	150.75	45.75	215.25	56.50	286.50	67.25	361.75
35.25	152.25	46	216.75	56.75	288.25	67.50	363.50
35.50	153.75	46.25	218.25	57	290.00	67.75	365.25
35.75	155.25	46.50	219.75	57.25	291.75	68	367.00
36	156.75	46.75	221.25	57.50	293.50	68.25	368.75
36.25	158.25	47	222.75	57.75	295.25	68.50	370.50
36.50	159.75	47.25	224.25	58	297.00	68.75	372.25
36.75	161.25	47.50	225.75	58.25	298.75	69	374.00
37	162.75	47.75	227.25	58.50	300.50	69.25	375.75
37.25	164.25	48	228.75	58.75	302.25	69.50	377.50
37.50	165.75	48.25	230.25	59	304.00	69.75	379.25
37.75	167.25	48.50	231.75	59.25	305.75	70	381.25
38	168.75	48.75	233.25	59.50	307.50	70.25	383.25
38.25	170.25	49	234.75	59.75	309.25	70.50	385.25
38.50	171.75	49.25	236.25	60	311.00	70.75	387.25
38.75	173.25	49.50	237.75	60.25	312.75	71	389.25
39	174.75	49.75	239.25	60.50	314.50	71.25	391.25
39.25	176.25	50	241.00	60.75	316.25	71.50	393.25
39.50	177.75	50.25	242.75	61	318.00	71.75	395.25
39.75	179.25	50.50	244.50	61.25	319.75	72	397.25
40	180.75	50.75	246.25	61.50	321.50	72.25	399.25
40.25	182.25	51	248.00	61.75	323.25	72.50	401.25
40.50	183.75	51.25	249.75	62	325.00	72.75	403.25
40.75	185.25	51.50	251.50	62.25	326.75	73	405.25
41	186.75	51.75	253.25	62.50	328.50	73.25	407.25
41.25	188.25	52	255.00	62.75	330.25	73.50	409.25
41.50	189.75	52.25	256.75	63	332.00	73.75	411.25
41.75	191.25	52.50	258.50	63.25	333.75	74	413.25
42	192.75	52.75	260.25	63.50	335.50	74.25	415.25
42.25	194.25	53	262.00	63.75	337.25	74.50	417.25
42.50	195.75	53.25	263.75	64	339.00	74.75	419.25
42.75	197.25	53.50	265.50	64.25	340.75	75	421.25
43	198.75	53.75	267.25	64.50	342.50	75.25	423.25
43.25	200.25	54	269.00	64.75	344.25	75.50	425.25
43.50	201.75	54.25	270.75	65	346.00	75.75	427.25
43.75	203.25	54.50	272.50	65.25	347.75	76	429.25
44	204.75	54.75	274.25	65.50	349.50	76.25	431.25
44.25	206.25	55	276.00	65.75	351.25	76.50	433.25
44.50	207.75	55.25	277.75	66	353.00	76.75	435.25
44.75	209.25	55.50	279.50	66.25	354.75	77	437.25
45	210.75	55.75	281.25	66.50	356.50	77.25	439.25
45.25	212.25	56	283.00	66.75	358.25	77.50	441.25
45.50	213.75	56.25	284.75	67	360.00	77.75	443.25

PERMANENT DISABILITY CONVERSION TABLE (Cont.)

Rating%	Weeks	Rating%	Weeks	Rating%	Weeks	Rating%	Weeks
78	445.25	83.50	489.25	89	533.25	94.50	577.25
78.25	447.25	83.75	491.25	89.25	535.25	94.75	579.25
78.50	449.25	84	493.25	89.50	537.25	95	581.25
78.75	451.25	84.25	495.25	89.75	539.25	95.25	583.25
79	453.25	84.50	497.25	90	541.25	95.50	585.25
79.25	455.25	84.75	499.25	90.25	543.25	95.75	587.25
79.50	457.25	85	501.25	90.50	545.25	96	589.25
79.75	459.25	85.25	503.25	90.75	547.25	96.25	591.25
80	461.25	85.50	505.25	91	549.25	96.50	593.25
80.25	463.25	85.75	507.25	91.25	551.25	96.75	595.25
80.50	465.25	86	509.25	91.50	553.25	97	597.25
80.75	467.25	86.25	511.25	91.75	555.25	97.25	599.25
81	469.25	86.50	513.25	92	557.25	97.50	601.25
81.25	471.25	86.75	515.25	92.25	559.25	97.75	603.25
81.50	473.25	87	517.25	92.50	561.25	98	605.25
81.75	475.25	87.25	519.25	92.75	563.25	98.25	607.25
82	477.25	87.50	521.25	93	565.25	98.50	609.25
82.25	479.25	87.75	523.25	93.25	567.25	98.75	611.25
82.50	481.25	88	525.25	93.50	569.25	99	613.25
82.75	483.25	88.25	527.25	93.75	571.25	99.25	615.25
83	485.25	88.50	529.25	94	573.25	99.50	617.25
83.25	487.25	88.75	531.25	94.25	575.25	99.75	619.25
						100*	For Life

*For PD ratings of 100% resulting from injuries on or after 4-1-74, compensation will be paid for life at the rate for temporary total compensation.

Note that under the new schedule a rating is to be evaluated in two ways: (1) under the cumulative table (see new conversion table) and (2) under the previous method of 4 × rating, with a maximum compensation rate of $52.50 per week. If the latter computation results in a larger value than that computed under the cumulative table, the greater of the two computations will be awarded to the employee. The following table developed along with the conversion table by the Disability Evaluation Bureau is designed to assist in this type of case. To use this table, one needs the PD rating and the applicable weekly compensation rate for permanent partial disability, keeping in mind the minimum and maximum limits for such weekly compensation rates as of the date of injury. Find the PD rating in the first column and the "reference compensation rate" in the second column. If the employee's actual weekly compensation rate is more than the "reference compensation rate," the employee will benefit by using the conversion table and the actual compensation rate. However, if the actual compensation rate is less than the "reference compensation rate," the employee will benefit by receiving 4 weeks of compensation for each 1% of the PD rating with the weekly compensation rate being subject to a maximum of $52.50 per week. (The table also indicates that PD ratings of 29½% and over should be converted under the "new" method; that is, by using the conversion table.)

REFERENCE COMPENSATION RATE TABLE

- Where actual compensation rate is equal to or greater than reference compensation rate, "new" benefit applies.

- Where actual compensation rate is less than reference compensation rate, "old" benefit applies.

Permanent Disability Rating	Reference Compensation Rate	Permanent Disability Rating	Reference Compensation Rate
.00-9.75	70.00	17.75	60.86
10.00	69.43	18.00	60.73
10.25	68.88	18.25	60.60
10.50	68.38	18.50	60.47
10.75	67.90	18.75	60.35
11.00	67.45	19.00	60.23
11.25	67.03	19.25	60.12
11.50	66.63	19.50	60.00
11.75	66.25	19.75	59.90
12.00	65.89	20.00	59.58
12.25	65.55	20.25	59.27
12.50	65.22	20.50	58.98
12.75	64.91	20.75	58.69
13.00	64.62	21.00	58.42
13.25	64.34	21.25	58.15
13.50	64.07	21.50	57.89
13.75	63.82	21.75	57.64
14.00	63.57	22.00	57.40
14.25	63.34	22.25	57.16
14.50	63.11	22.50	56.93
14.75	62.90	22.75	56.71
15.00	62.69	23.00	56.50
15.25	62.49	23.25	56.29
15.50	62.30	23.50	56.08
15.75	62.12	23.75	55.89
16.00	61.94	24.00	55.70
16.25	61.77	24.25	55.51
16.50	61.60	24.50	55.33
16.75	61.45	24.75	55.15
17.00	61.29	25.00	54.98
17.25	61.14	25.25	54.81
17.50	61.00	25.50	54.65

REFERENCE COMPENSATION RATE TABLE (Cont.)

Permanent Disability Rating	Reference Compensation Rate	Permanent Disability Rating	Reference Compensation Rate
25.75	54.49	27.75	53.35
26.00	54.33	28.00	53.22
26.25	54.18	28.25	53.09
26.50	54.03	28.50	52.97
26.75	53.89	28.75	52.85
27.00	53.75	29.00	52.73
27.25	53.61	29.25	52.62
27.50	53.48	29.50 & Over	—

EXAMPLES:

(1) Assume that Martin is injured on March 4, 1971, with earnings of $150 per week. His injury causes permanent partial disability which rates 40%. Checking Table C we find maximum actual earnings for PD of $85.02 per week and a maximum compensation rate of $52.50 per week. Since earnings exceed maximum, the compensation rate for PD is $52.50 per week. Also, since the injury occurred before April 1, 1972, the PD rating will be converted to weeks of compensation by multiplying the rating by 4.

$$4 \times 40\% = 160 \text{ weeks of payments at } \$52.50 \text{ per week}$$
$$160 \times \$52.50 = \$8,400 \text{ - total to be paid}$$

(2) If Martin's injury occurred on March 4, 1973, the PD conversion table would be used. Here the 40% rating converts to 180.75 weeks. The maximum compensation rate for PD is $70 per week based on maximum actual earnings of $113.36 per week.

$$40\% = 180.75 \text{ weeks of payments at } \$70 \text{ per week}$$
$$180.75 \times \$70 = \$12,652.50 \text{ - total to be paid}$$

(3) Assume that Martin's injury occurred in 1975. The result would be the same as in example (2) above, for Table A indicates a maximum PD compensation rate of $70 per week based on maximum actual earnings for PD of $105 per week, and the conversion table still shows 180.75 weeks of compensation for the 40% rating.

(4) On January 15, 1972, Sylvia suffered a work injury which results in a PD rating of 25%. Her earnings at time of injury were $80 per week. Table C shows maximum earnings for PD of $85.02 per week; thus her compensation rate must be computed.

$$
\begin{aligned}
\text{Compensation rate} &= 65\% \text{ of statutory average earnings} \\
&= 65\% \text{ of } 95\% \text{ of } \$80 \\
&= 61\tfrac{3}{4}\% \text{ of } \$80 \\
&= \$49.40 \text{ per week for PD}
\end{aligned}
$$

Since injury was before 4-1-72, the rating is converted to weeks of compensation by multiplying by 4.

$$4 \times 25 = 100 \text{ weeks of payments at \$49.40 per week}$$
$$100 \times \$49.40 = \$4,940 \text{ - total to be paid}$$

(5) Assume that Sylvia's injury occurred on January 15, 1973. Table C indicates a maximum weekly compensation rate of $70 per week based on actual earnings of $113.36 per week. The compensation rate remains at $49.40 per week based on Sylvia's earnings of $80 per week. Because her PD rating of 25% is less than $29\frac{1}{2}\%$, her potential under the "old" formula of 4 × PD rating must be checked. The PD conversion table indicates that a 25% PD rating is equivalent to 95.5 weeks of compensation. Since the weekly compensation rate is the same as in example (4), we see that Sylvia would have a greater recovery under the "old" method with a maximum limit on the compensation rate of $52.50 per week. Thus, she would receive 100 weekly payments at $49.40 per week. The reference compensation table is designed to short-cut this type of comparison. For a rating of 25%, that table shows a "reference compensation rate" of $54.98 per week. Since $49.40 per week is less than $54.98 per week, the table tells us that the employee will receive more under the "old" formula.

(6) Assume the same factual situation in examples (4) and (5) but with date of injury January 15, 1975. For this date of injury, Sylvia's compensation rate is $\frac{2}{3} \times \$80 = \$53.33$ per week. (This is less than the applicable maximum of $70 per week based on maximum actual earnings of $105 per week.) The "reference compensation rate" for her PD rating of 25% is $54.98 per week. Her computed compensation rate of $53.33 per week is less than $54.98; so she will benefit by use of the "old" method. However, the maximum compensation rate under the "old" method is $52.50 per week. As a result, Sylvia would receive 100 weeks of compensation × $52.50 = $5,250 in total payments.

(7) Jim suffers a hand injury resulting in permanent partial disability rating 10%. His earnings at time of injury, July 5, 1971, were $104.50 per week. His earnings for this date of injury exceed the maximum PD earnings limit of $85.02 per week; thus, his PD compensation rate is $52.50 per week.

$$4 \times 10 = 40 \text{ weeks of compensation}$$
$$40 \times \$52.50 = \$2,100 \text{ - total to be paid}$$

(8) Assume that in example (7) Jim's hand injury occurred on July 5, 1972. For this date of injury, maximum actual earnings for PD are $113.36 per week, and the maximum PD compensation rate is $70 per week. Since Jim's actual earnings are less than maximum, his compensation rate must be computed.

Compensation rate = 65% of statutory average earnings
= 65% of 95% of $104.50
= 61¾% of $104.50
= $64.53 per week for PD

The date of injury being after April 1, 1972, and the 10% rating for PD being less than 29½%, the reference table is checked. For a PD rating of 10%, the "reference compensation rate" is $69.43 per week. Jim's rate of $64.53 per week is less than the reference rate; therefore, the "old" formula applies with a maximum compensation rate of $52.50 per week and total payments of $2,100, as in example (7).

(9) For this example, assume the same facts as in example (7) but a date of injury on July 5, 1975. Now the weekly PD compensation rate is ⅔ of actual earnings. Maximum actual earnings for permanent partial disability are $105 per week, and the maximum PD compensation rate is $70 per week. Since Jim's earnings are slightly less than maximum, his rate must be computed.

⅔ × $104.50 = $69.67 per week for PD

The "reference compensation rate" is $69.43. Jim's rate is more than the reference rate so that Jim will benefit more under the "new" formula. The conversion table shows that a 10% rating is worth 30.25 weeks of compensation.

30.25 × $69.67 = $2,107.52 - total to be paid

(10) On November 16, 1971, Frank sustained a work injury which caused permanent and total incapacity to work, the PD rating being 100%. Earnings were $160 per week. Earnings exceed the maximum earnings for PD of $85.02 so that his compensation rate for PD is $52.50 per week.

4 × 100 = 400 weeks of PD compensation
400 × $52.50 = $21,000 - total to be paid

(Frank is also entitled to a life pension; see subsequent discussion.)

(11) If in example (10) the injury occurred on November 16, 1972, Frank's 100% rating would be converted by reference to the PD conversion table. Also, for this date of injury, Frank's earnings of $160 per week exceed maximum actual earnings for PD of $113.36; thus the PD compensation rate is $70 per week.

621.25 × $70 = $43,487.50 - total to be paid plus life pension

(12) Assume that Frank's injury occurred on November 16, 1975. For this date of injury, compensation payments are made for life if disability is permanent and total, subject to a maximum compensation rate of $119 per week based on maximum earnings of $178.50 per week. Frank's earnings of $160 per week are less than maximum; therefore, his rate must be computed.

$2/3 \times \$160 = \$106.67$ per week for life

(13) Assume that Ernest was injured at work during 1983. Compensation limits for permanent partial disability are $50 per week, minimum, and $130 per week, maximum. Ernest was working at a part-time job paying him only enough to result in a PPD compensation rate of $60 per week. His permanent disability rates 35%. The reference table shows that the conversion table will be used because the PPD rating exceeds $29^1/4\%$.

(14) If in the above example Ernest's PPD rating were 15%, the reference table shows that his weekly compensation rate of $60 is less than the reference rate of 62.69, and thus he will benefit under the "old" method of $4 \times$ the rating $\times$ the maximum of $52.50 per week; $4 \times 15 \times \$52.50 = \$3,150$.

(15) Now assume that Ernest's injury occurred during 1984, and his PPD rates 15%. The compensation limits for PPD are $70 per week, minimum, and $140 per week, maximum. His computed compensation rate of $60 per week is less than the minimum of $70 per week; so, the minimum is applicable. Here, the minimum of $70 is greater than the reference rate of 62.69. So, the conversion table will be used; 50.25 weeks at $70 per week = $3,517.50.

§ 6.3 Conversion Values—Injuries On and After January 1, 1992

The following values for converting a permanent disability rating apply *LC 4658* to injuries occurring on and after January 1, 1992:

PD Rating	Weeks per 1%
0 – 9.75%	3
10 – 19.75%	4
20 – 24.75%	5
25 – 29.75%	6
30 – 49.75%	7
50 – 69.75%	8
70 – 99.75%	9

This change in conversion factors assigns higher values for ratings of 25% or more. The values are cumulative. Thus, a rating must be separated into components to fit the table.

§ 6.4 Life Pension—Injuries On or After April 1, 1974

For injuries occurring on or after April 1, 1974, there are two possible *LC 4658,* categories of life-pension cases: those involving permanent total disability *4659(b)* and those involving permanent partial disability. Permanent total disability takes a permanent disability rating of 100%, and compensation is payable for life at the same rate as for temporary compensation. See Table A, Appendix, for the applicable minimum and maximum limits.

As to injuries resulting in permanent partial disability (PD ratings of 0-99³/4%), if a PD rating is 70% or more, the employee is entitled to a life pension based on a formula utilizing variables determined by the rating and weekly earnings at time of injury. The maximum earnings which may be used in this formula are $107.69 per week; the minimum earnings are as set out in Table A for permanent partial disability. The employee is entitled to a life pension of 1.5% of actual weekly earnings for each 1% the PD rating exceeds 60%. (But, the employee does not qualify for a life pension unless the PD rating is 70% or more.) The following table is based upon this formula:

Rating	Pension (For injuries on or after April 1, 1974)
0 thru 69³/4%*	No Pension
70%	15% of weekly earnings for PPD
80%	30% of weekly earnings for PPD
90%	45% of weekly earnings for PPD
99³/4%*	59.625% of weekly earnings for PPD

*PD ratings are computed to the nearest ¹/4 of 1%.

EXAMPLES:

(1) On January 5, 1984, while on the job, Scott suffered electric burns to his hands rendering them permanently functionless for any type of work. Permanent loss of use of hands rates 100%. His wage at the time was $350 per week. Thus, Scott is entitled to a life pension at the maximum rate of $224 per week for permanent total disability.

(2) If Scott's earnings had been less than the maximum of $336 per week, say $285 per week, then his life pension would be $2/3 \times \$285$ or $190 per week.

(3) James is a part-time courier earning $98 per week. On May 14, 1984, he is involved in an accident while making a delivery for his employer. Multiple injuries result in permanent disability rated at 72%. His life pension would be computed on minimum earnings for PPD of $105 per week.

$$
\begin{aligned}
LP &= (72\text{-}60) \times 1.5\% \times \$105 \\
&= 12 \times 1.5\% \times \$105 \\
&= 18\% \times \$105 \\
&= \$18.90 \text{ per week for life}
\end{aligned}
$$

(4) Peter suffered loss of vision in both eyes on April 15, 1975. At that time, his earnings were $200 per week. Total loss of sight rates 100%. Since Peter is permanently totally disabled, and since his earnings exceed $178.50 per week, he will receive $119 per week for life.

(5) If, in example (4), Peter's earnings were $150 per week, he would receive compensation of $100 per week for life ($2/3 \times \$150 = \$100$).

(6) Alice sustained multiple injuries in a car accident on July 12, 1974, while in the course of her employment. The combined rating for her various permanent disabilities was 99¾%. As shown in the above table, her life pension would be 59.625% of earnings subject to maximum earnings of $107.69 for this formula. Her earnings at time of injury were in excess of this maximum figure.

$$LP = 59.625\% \text{ of } \$107.69$$
$$= \$64.21 \text{ per week for life}$$

Note the difference between this life pension and those in examples (4) and (5) involving a rating just ¼ of 1% larger than Alice's.

(7) George injured his back and hip at work on February 2, 1976. His permanent partial disability rates 78%. Actual weekly earnings were $102.50. His earnings were less than maximum for the LP formula (i.e., $107.69).

$$LP = (78\text{-}60) \times 1.5\% \times \$102.50$$
$$= 18 \times 1.5\% \times \$102.50$$
$$= 27\% \times \$102.50$$
$$= \$27.68 \text{ per week for life}$$

(8) Frances fell in the company parking lot resulting in severe damage to her wrists and knees. Her permanent disability rated 80%. Date of injury was March 15, 1975, and earnings were $250 per week. For the life pension, earnings will be maximum or $107.69 per week. From the above table, the life pension is 30% of earnings [(80-60) × 1.5% = 30%].

$$LP = 30\% \text{ of } \$107.69$$
$$= \$32.31 \text{ per week for life}$$

§ 6.5 Life Pension—Injuries 1959 Through March 31, 1974

For injuries occurring on or after September 18, 1959, to and including *LC 4658* March 31, 1974, the life pension is a percentage of "statutory average earnings" (i.e., 95% of actual earnings at time of injury), subject to the minimum and maximum limits for statutory average earnings as set forth in Table C. The maximum for the period 4-1-72 through 3-31-74 is $107.69 per week based on actual earnings of $113.36; the maximum for the period 9-18-59 through 3-31-72 is $80.77 based on actual earnings of $85.02. An employee whose permanent disability rates 70% or more is entitled to a life pension of 1.5% of "statutory average earnings" for each 1% the rating exceeds 60%. This formula applies to ratings of 70% to 100%, inclusive.

Rating	Pension (for injuries 9-18-59 through 3-31-74)
0 to $69^3/4\%$	*No Pension
70%	15% of statutory average earnings for PD
80%	30% of statutory average earnings for PD
90%	45% of statutory average earnings for PD
100%	60% of statutory average earnings for PD

*PD ratings are computed to the nearest $1/4$ of 1%.

EXAMPLES:

(1) Jones was rendered permanently and totally disabled by a work injury on August 14, 1971. His earnings were $120 per week. Since his earnings exceed the maximum average earnings for PD for this date of injury ($85.02), his statutory average earnings for PD are taken at $80.77 per week. His condition rates 100%; thus, from the table we see that his life pension will be 60% of $80.77.

$$
\begin{aligned}
LP &= \text{60\% of statutory average earnings for PD} \\
&= \text{60\% of \$80.77} \\
&= \text{\$48.46 per week for life}
\end{aligned}
$$

(2) In example (1), if Jones' injury occurred on August 14, 1972, his earnings would exceed minimum for PD, and thus his statutory earnings for PD would be $107.69.

$$
\begin{aligned}
LP &= \text{60\% of statutory average earnings for PD} \\
&= \text{60\% of \$107.69} \\
&= \text{\$64.61 per week for life}
\end{aligned}
$$

(3) Green sustained injury to his back on April 14, 1973, resulting in a PD rating of 82%. Earnings were maximum for PD.

$$
\begin{aligned}
LP &= (82\text{-}60) \times 1.5\% \times \$107.69 \\
&= 22 \times 1.5\% \times \$107.69 \\
&= 33\% \times \$107.69 \\
&= \$35.54 \text{ per week for life}
\end{aligned}
$$

[NOTE: For injuries occurring before September 18, 1959, the life pension for PD ratings of 70% to 100%, inclusive, is 1% of "statutory average earnings" for PD for each 1% the rating exceeds 60%.]

§ 6.6   Payment of Permanent Disability Benefits

LC 4650
4661

Permanent disability benefits are payable in addition to any temporary compensation paid. For injuries occurring during the period April 1, 1974, through December 31, 1989, this benefit is payable beginning on the fourth day after the condition becomes permanent or on the fourth day after the last payment of temporary compensation, whichever is earlier. (For injuries occurring before April 1, 1974, payment commenced on the eighth day after the earliest of the stated factors.) Payment continues twice each calendar month unless otherwise ordered by the W.C.A.B.

For injuries occurring on or after January 1, 1990, payment for perma-   *LC 4650*
nent disability must be commenced within 14 days after the last payment of temporary compensation. Thereafter, payments are made every two weeks on a day designated by the employer with the first payment unless the employer continues the employee's wages under a salary continuation plan. Payment of the PD benefit continues until the employer's reasonable estimate of perma-nent disability or a determined rating has been paid. If any payment is late, the late payment must be increased 10%, without application, unless the em-ployee has not filed a written claim with the employer. Nor does the penalty   *LC 5401*
apply to any payment due prior to or within 14 days after the date a claim form is submitted to the employer. LC 4650 puts the onus on the employer or carrier to monitor, estimate, and pay permanent disability benefits without official action by any state agency. This provision follows previous W.C.A.B. and appellate court decisions which have placed this responsibility upon employers and carriers per the penalty provisions of LC 5814 which permits the W.C.A.B. to assess a 10% penalty if compensation benefits are unreasonably withheld or delayed. See Chapter 9, PENALTIES, § 9.5, *Delay or Failure to Provide Benefits*, for details.

Weekly payments are based upon the formula of $2/3$ times actual weekly earnings, subject to minimum and maximum limits in effect at time of injury. These values are usually lower than the limits for temporary compensation except for permanent total disability for which the same rate as temporary compensation is paid for life. Benefit increases legislated in the Reform Act of 1989 include a proviso increasing the maximum for permanent partial disability if the PD rating is 25% or more. By way of illustration, limits for PD weekly compensation payments in effect in 1984 and subsequent years are set forth below. These values may also be found in Table A, Appendix.

For injuries occurring during the period January 1, 1984, through December 31, 1989:

Permanent Total Disability: Maximum of $224 per week based upon maximum earnings of $336 per week. Minimum of $112 per week based upon minimum earnings of $168 per week.

Permanent Partial Disability: Maximum of $140 per week based upon maximum earnings for PPD of $210 per week. Minimum of $70 per week based upon minimum earnings for PPD of $105 per week.

For injuries occurring during the period January 1, 1990, through December 31, 1990:

Permanent Total Disability: Maximum of $266 per week based on maximum earnings of $399 per week. Minimum of $112 per week based on minimum earnings of $168 per week.

Permanent Partial Disability: Maximum of $140 per week based on maximum earnings for PPD of $210 per week. Minimum of $70 per week based on minimum earnings for PPD of $105 per week.

For injuries occurring on or after January 1, 1991.

Permanent Total Disability: Maximum of $336 per week based on maximum earnings of $504 per week. Minimum of $112 per week based on minimum earnings of $168 per week.

Permanent Partial Disability: Maximum of $140 per week based on maximum earnings for PPD of $210 per week; provided that for final adjusted permanent disability ratings of 25% or more the maximum is $148 per week based upon maximum earnings for PPD of $222 per week. Minimum of $70 per week based on minimum earnings for PPD of $105 per week.

[NOTE: Permanent disability payments are not payable while an employee is receiving rehabilitation temporary compensation or rehabilitation maintenance allowance. Payment of PD is deferred in such cases until the conclusion of the vocational rehabilitation plan. The Court of Appeal has ruled that if an injured worker sustains a second injury while performing on-the-job training under a vocational rehabilitation plan resulting in permanent disability, the compensation rate for payment of PD compensation is the rate in effect at the time of the second injury.]

§ 6.7 Commutation; Lump Sum Payment

LC 5100-5106

The W.C.A.B. has authority to order commutation of weekly permanent disability payments, that is, to order such payments to be paid in a lump sum by an employer or carrier. However, because the employer's basic obligation is to make weekly payments when they are due, the law provides that the employer is entitled to a 3% per annum discount as to each future weekly payment which the employer is required to pay in advance. This percentage of discount is not favorable to employers or carriers when the interest rates of financial institutions are generally higher. Thus, a request for commutation is often opposed, or an employer or carrier endeavors to obtain a compromise and release in exchange for paying a lump sum. The code requires an employee to file a request with the W.C.A.B. and give the employer or carrier notice of his or her request. The employee must show that commutation is to his or her best interest.

In making its determination, the Board must consider the employee's general financial condition, including his or her ability to live without periodic compensation payments and to pay debts incurred before the date of injury. The Board must also find that commutation will avoid inequity and not cause undue hardship on the employee. In essence, the Board looks to protect the employee from improvident decisions. The Board may grant a partial commutation to cover mortgage payments or accumulated debts or to provide funds for payment of the employee's attorney for services rendered in the industrial accident case. The Board and the appellate courts have ruled that it is not a good reason for commutation that the employee may invest the money at interest rates higher than 3%.

The Board may also commute compensation if the employer has sold or disposed of most of his or her assets or is not a resident of California.

§ 6.8 Rating Permanent Disability

The injured employee's permanent disability is assigned a rating by a rating specialist of the Disability Evaluation Bureau. These experts have received extensive training in measuring the effect of physical and mental disability upon ability to compete in the labor market, and in computing the amount of benefits involved. Their "bible" is the "Schedule of Permanent Disability Ratings" originally adopted by the commission and readopted following the reorganization by the Administrative Director. It is the result of many years' study of bodily functions, occupational requirements, age factors, and rehabilitation problems. It reflects the cooperative effort of commission personnel and the medical profession. The schedule may be obtained from the California Publications and Documents Division. Copies are available for perusal at all Appeals Board offices and county law libraries.

The schedule and the ratings computed by the rating specialists are *LC 4660* "prima facie" evidence in any proceeding. Other evidence may be introduced to rebut the scheduled rating, but the Board rarely digresses from it. Most *R 9750* rebuttal evidence does not challenge the schedule but points to the various *10602* factors involved in the computations. Where evidence is offered which shows *10900* the effect of the employee's disability upon his work-performance, such evidence is admissible in rebuttal to a rating report.

The basic premise is that disability is rated, not the pathological condition. Thus, an industrial disease is not rated, rather its permanent effect on the employee's working ability. The factors of permanent disability may be either "objective" or "subjective." Objective factors are usually set forth in medical reports as measurements of findings showing losses of bodily functions or as descriptions of losses of portions of the anatomy. Such factors form the basis for mathematical computations utilizing the values assigned in the schedule. For example,

loss of major arm above elbow rates	75%
loss of sight in one eye rates	25%
loss of major index finger rates	8%
immobility of index finger rates	6%
amputation of ankle joint rates	50%
immobility of ankle joint rates	20%

Under LC 4662 the following are conclusively presumed total disability, *LC 4662* that is, to rate 100%:

(a) loss of both eyes or the sight thereof

(b) loss of both hands or the use thereof
(c) practically total paralysis
(d) incurable imbecility or insanity

(While disability from one injury cannot be rated more than 100%, it is possible for an employee to receive ratings for disabilities caused by separate injuries which may total more than 100%. However, if rating factors involved in separate injuries overlap, there may be an apportionment under the principles of the *Hutchinson* case. See subsequent discussion.)

The effect of subjective factors of disability is also included in the rating if of sufficient severity to interfere with work efficiency. A subjective factor is one which depends upon the expression by the injured person. The term includes pain, numbness, tenderness, and various other manifestations such as a feeling of pins-and-needles, headaches. Again the symptom (subjective factor) is not rated. Its effect may be considered if it is a significant cause of lessening the employee's ability to work.

§ 6.9   Adjustment of Rating for Age and Occupation

Thus far we have spoken of the "standard rating." The first portion of the schedule lists disabilities with a number assigned similar to a Dewey decimal system number. The PD rating shown for each disability is the "standard rating." The standard rating is then adjusted either upward or downward according to factors assigned for occupation and age at the time of injury. (The use of the rating schedule is the subject of a 15-hour course of instruction. The reader can thus appreciate that we can explain here little more than the rudiments of theory.) Hundreds of occupations have been categorized, according to the relative importance of various functions of the body in such occupations, into 12 basic occupational variants. These variants are given letter designations A through L. Variant F is the central point and indicates no adjustment for occupation. A through E lower the rating, and G through L raise the rating. To adjust a rating for occupation, find the disability and the disability number. In the next section, find the occupation and occupation number. Then turn to the next section and locate the disability number, and across the page under the occupation number will be found the applicable letter designation of the occupational variant. Using these designations, the rating, as adjusted for occupation, will be found in the next section.

Another variant is based upon age. The standard rating represents that of the average-aged worker, namely 39 years of age. Ratings increase as age increases over 39, and vice versa, for it is assumed the task of rehabilitation will be much more difficult as age exceeds 39. The chart in the next section of the schedule will further adjust the rating (as adjusted for occupation) for age at time of injury.

EXAMPLES:

(1) Assume a laborer, aged 55, who loses his major index finger and has residual tenderness at the amputation site. His rating would appear Schedule

No. 8.211: 8 (std. rat.) 1 (occ. no.) F (occup. var.) 8 (adj. for occ.)

9:3 (Adj. for Age)
1:0 (pain)
10:3*

For this man the occupational variant did not change the standard rating, but the age variant raised it by 1³/4%. An additional 1% was added for the subjective factor of tenderness, making the total rating 10³/4%.

(2) If the problem involved a machinist aged 60, the rating would be

8.211: 8(25)I 12 15:2
1 (The occupation no. for machinist is 25.)
16:2*

Here the occupational variant upped the rating by 4%, and age added another 3¹/2%. (The subjective rating is usually not adjusted for age or occupation.) This rating adjusted to 16¹/2%.

(3) A 20-year-old typist has continuous slight pain in her back; the rating for this is a standard 10%. [NOTE: Slight pain in the back is not the same as a slight back disability.] The rating is expressed

Schedule No. 18.1: 10(40)C 7 5:1*

Age and occupation variants reduced the 10% standard rating to 5¹/4%.

(4) For a 45-year-old laborer the same standard rating would adjust

18.1: 10 (1) H 13 14

Age and occupation variants increased the 10% standard rating to 14%.

*(The figure after the colon in Rating Bureau computations indicates fourths of 1%.)

§ 6.10 Age and Occupation as Issues

Since age and occupation at time of injury are integral parts of the rating process, they are important issues in any Appeals Board proceeding or in the handling of a claim. Age usually is taken as that given by the employee, although there have been cases where birth certificates, affidavits, or family records have been required.

Particular attention should be given the matter of occupation, because the job-title may not be sufficiently descriptive of the employee's duties. Occupational groupings in the rating schedule are indicative of the hazards of the position, the effort or dexterity involved and the relative importance of the portion of body injured. The employer's job-title may overstate or understate these factors. Thus, it is pertinent to know whether the job involves heavy lifting, repeated bending or motions, working at heights, below ground, at different levels, on scaffolds or ladders, types of machines operated, or tools used.

A decision of the California Supreme Court illustrates the possibilities (and their effect on the rating) which can arise from a list of duties as compared to job title:

Group No.	Occupation	Rating
47	Heavy Equipment Operator	50%
50	Gantry Crane Operator	46½%
22	Operating Engineer	46½%

If an injured employee is performing more than one occupation as shown in the permanent disability rating schedule, that occupation will be used which produces the highest rating after adjustment for occupation. If the employee has two occupations for two different employers, the occupation in which the employee was working at the time of the injury will be determinative.

§ 6.11   Pain

Pain is not rated as such, only its effect. It is necessary to presume that certain degrees of pain will result in certain definite handicaps. The division has established the following definitions for degrees of pain:

minimal (mild)	— a mere annoyance and not ratable
slight	— some handicap in activity causing pain
moderate	— marked handicap in activity causing pain
severe	— precludes activity precipitating the pain

By analogy, these definitions can be applied to other subjective symptoms.

§ 6.12   Judgment Ratings

The schedule itself refers only to broad divisions of disabilities in many instances. Standard ratings for conditions of the spine, for instance, are

slight   30%   moderate   50%   severe   100%

It is necessary for the rater to place the particular case within these limits.

§ 6.13   Judgment Rating "Plateaus"

The judgment rating has been the subject of much misunderstanding and thus the Disability Evaluation Bureau has established so-called rating "plateaus" by assigning specific values to certain of the more common descriptions of disability. These are also referred to as judgment rating "guidelines" and were originally utilized in back cases. By analogy, they may also be used where overall disability is caused by other conditions. Many of these "plateaus" or "guidelines" have been incorporated into the rating schedule. Thus, there follows two lists. The first is the one developed informally and the second as set forth in the schedule. It is the author's opinion that the official list does not rule out use of the informal list to the extent that they may differ.

Disability Description	Standard Rating
1. Minimal to slight pain in back	3%-5%
2. Post-laminectomy back without other symptoms	5%
3. Intermittent slight pain in back	5%
4. Inability to do sustained heavy lifting	10%
5. Constant slight pain in back	10%
6. Inability to do very heavy work	15%
7. Inability to do heavy lifting	20%
8. Inability to do repeated bending and stooping	25%
9. Inability to do heavy work	30%
10. Inability to do heavy work but with ability to do more than light work	40%
11. Limitation to light manual labor	40%
12. Limitation to light work	50%
13. Limitation to light to sedentary work	60%
14. Limitation to sedentary work	70%
15. Limitation to very light work	50%-100%
16. Incapacity to do any work	100%

[NOTE: Variations of these instructions may raise or lower the standard rating applied. Item 15 requires further instructions to place the rating between the extremes of the range shown.]

Graduations between these "plateaus" may result, depending upon variations in descriptions of disability. For instance, continuous slight pain in the back with moderate pain after work involving heavy lifting or exertion would rate about 15% standard. Constant minimal to slight pain in the back would rate about 5% standard. Usually, there are additional factors set forth which aid the rater in placing the rating in the correct category. The description "limitation to light to sedentary work" will result in a rating of 60%, standard.

In considering these "plateaus," the 1965 report of the Workmen's Compensation Study Commission states:

> In an effort to standardize the descriptions of back disabilities presented to the rating specialists, the Rating Bureau has issued guidelines to the referees. The Study Commission is advised that *these guidelines are well known to persons who have a regular amount of contact with the Industrial Accident Commission but they have not been formally published.* (Italics added.)

Most of these guidelines are now outlined in the rating schedule, as follows:

Disability precluding very heavy lifting (also: constant slight pain, spine or abdominal weakness)	10%
Disability precluding very heavy work	15%
Disability precluding heavy lifting	20%
Disability precluding heavy lifting, repeated bending and stooping	25%
Disability precluding heavy work (also: constant slight to moderate pain, spine or abdominal weakness)	30%
Disability precluding more than light work (also: constant moderate pain, spine or abdominal weakness)	50%
Disability precluding more than semi-sedentary work	60%
Disability precluding more than sedentary work	70%

Guidelines were also established for certain disabilities of the hip, such as, ununited fracture of the neck of the femur with residual symptoms. The guidelines established for these hip problems are as follows:

Disability precluding more than semi-sedentary work	60%
Disability precluding more than sedentary work	70%

Definitions of these various terms may be obtained from the Division of Industrial Accidents. Except as otherwise specified, the schedule guidelines apply to chronic affections of the pulmonary tissues, heart disease, impaired function of the neck, spine or pelvis, weakness of abdominal muscles.

If the medical evidence indicates that there are work restrictions which must be placed on the employee's working conditions, such restrictions must be taken into consideration in rating the injured employee's disability. This principle applies even though the physician may have placed such restrictions upon the employee's activities in an effort to avoid further injury. Similarly, where a W.C.A.B. judge must use a "plateau" or guideline to rate the employee's permanent disability, selection of the guideline will not be upheld if the record indicates a different degree of disability. Where the W.C.A.B. rated an employee on "limitation to sedentary work" and use of back brace resulting in a 63% rating, the record showed without contradiction that, in addition, the employee could not work for more than one hour at the time or at all after 3 p.m., and that medication was required for relief of pain. The appellate court held that such restrictions must be included in the instructions to the Rating Bureau. This case points out the advisability of describing the disability shown by the record, especially the medical reports, and also selecting the guideline which is felt to be applicable. In this way the rating specialist has the entire picture and can assign the correct disability rating. However, where a description of the physical disability clearly shows the employee's permanent condition, it is not mandatory that one of the guidelines be used.

Total disability does not signify an absolute state of helplessness. A person may be considered totally disabled if he cannot perform the substantial and material acts necessary for the customary completion of the tasks incident to his business or occupation, according to a recent decision of the Court of Appeal.

According to Board and appellate court decisions, a judgment rating will be upheld if it is "within the range of ratings" indicated by the evidence.

§6.14 Specific Disabilities and Standard Ratings

1. *Head*: Injuries to the head comprise a large number of the cases. Scalp injuries may involve a cut, bruise, laceration or, in some cases, loss of the scalp itself. If the injury is such that the exposure to the air causes irritation, the employee may be awarded medication or toupees on a lifetime basis. When the skull is injured severely enough to cause apertures to remain which cannot be adequately protected or closed through surgery, a permanent disability rating will be awarded. The schedule contains standard ratings based on the area of the aperture, ranging from 10% for 1 square inch to 50% for 8 square inches.

Head trauma may be followed by a post-traumatic syndrome. This condition is a combination of symptoms which cannot always be substantiated objectively by physical findings of tests. Their presence is usually established subjectively, that is, through the patient's complaints. They include such symptoms as headaches, disturbed vision, vertigo, drowsiness, or mental disturbances. A judgment rating is indicated and may range from 0 to 100%, depending on severity.

[NOTE: Administrative Director Rule 9726 has been amended by deleting the previous detailed criteria for measurement of psychiatric disability and providing that measurement of "elements of disability" is to follow the Report of the Subcommittee on Permanent Psychiatric Disability. This report which contains "Psychiatric Protocols" is available through the office of the Medical Director of the Division of Industrial Accidents. Rating of psychiatric permanent disability for injuries occurring on or after July 1, 1988 is to follow the chart and formulae set forth on page 1-B of the Schedule for Rating Permanent Disabilities (disability number 1.4). The procedure is geared to Rule 9726 and the psychiatric protocols and provides for rating of a single work function impairment and of multiple work function impairments.]

2. *Eyes*: Partial loss of visual acuity is rated according to the extent of the loss. Total loss of vision in one eye rates 25% standard, in both eyes, 100%. There are also ratings for associated conditions including cosmetic

defects, blurring, loss or diminishing of the field of vision, double vision, and chronic irritation.

There is an additional rating of 5% if the eye must be removed (enucleated). An award may include lifetime false eye (prosthetic eye) or glasses. If glasses improve vision, the permanent disability rating is based upon the corrected vision, and lifetime glasses will be awarded. Visual acuity of $20/200$ is considered industrial blindness.

3. *Ears*: Loss of an ear rates 10%, standard; loss of hearing in one ear, 10%; loss of hearing in both ears, 50%. Hearing-loss cases seem to be causing quite a problem in industry of late, and it has moved many firms to do everything possible to reduce the noise level in their plants. The impact of noise on the ear's mechanism is called acoustic trauma. These cases involve the question of apportionment for hearing loss due to the aging process.

4. *Nose*: Treatment of nose injuries may involve plastic surgery. Permanent disability factors may include scarring, pain, numbness, or impairing of breathing. Loss of smell or taste may be the result of head or nerve injuries. Loss of either of these senses rates 5%, standard; loss of both rates 10%.

5. *Mouth, Teeth*: Injury to the mouth may involve plastic surgery and dental work. The rating for permanent disability might consist of any residual pain, numbness, or other subjective symptom plus any factors of cosmetic disfigurement. If the jaw is damaged with resultant difficulty in speech or eating, these would be ratable depending upon their degree. Severe malocclusion rates 30%. In the usual case, there is no permanent disability rating for damage to or loss of teeth, but the employee is entitled to their repair or replacement.

6. *Throat*: With throat injuries or disease one may encounter interference with the power of speech. Complete loss of speech rates 50%; difficulty in speaking, 10%.

7. *Neck*: (See 11, *Back*.)

8. *Arms*: The shoulders, arms, and hands are referred to as "upper extremities." If one is right-handed, the entire right upper extremity will be termed the "major" extremity; for a left-handed person, his left is his major upper extremity. The significance of the distinction between major and minor extremities is that permanent disability in a major extremity rates higher than the same disability in a minor extremity. If the injured is ambidextrous, the level of any rating will be somewhat between those for major and minor. Loss of, or loss of function in, a major extremity may change the status of the minor extremity to that of a major extremity.

In the case of amputations, the surgeon tries to obtain a good pad of tissue over the end of the bone to eliminate irritation and to permit the use of any prosthetic appliance indicated. Loss of both hands or arms rates 100%.

Loss of the major arm at the elbow or between the elbow and shoulder, 75%; at the wrist or between the wrist and elbow, 70%. Deduct 5% if loss is of the minor extremity. Deduct 5% if the use of a prosthetic appliance is possible. Any necessary appliance will be furnished on a lifetime basis.

The arm joints represent a variety of motions, and loss of function in the joints is rated upon the measurable losses plus any subjective symptoms. Such ratings may be small if the loss of function is not too extensive but may equal the rating for amputation in very severe cases.

9. *Hands and Fingers*: Injury to a hand or to arm muscles may affect the overall function of the hand. One method of measuring loss of hand function is through the use of a grip-tester, such as the Jamar. Three readings are taken for both hands, then averaged and compared. It is assumed that the major hand is 10% stronger than the minor hand. Complete loss of grasping power in the major hand rates 40%, in the minor, 36%. Partial losses are rated according to a scale set forth in the schedule.

Finger disabilities are extensively covered in the schedule as to both amputation and loss of motion. Ratings are computed for these conditions and for loss of grasping power, and the employee is awarded the greater of the two. Formulae have been developed for rating partial amputations and partial loss of motion, as well as for multiple finger disabilities.

Amputations of fingers		Major	Minor
Thumb:	at carpal joint	16%	14%
	at proximal joint	12%	11%
	at distal joint	6%	5%
Index:	at proximal joint	8%	7%
	at middle joint	6%	5%
	at distal joint	4%	3%
Middle:	at proximal joint	8%	7%
	at middle joint	6%	5%
	at distal joint	3%	2%
Ring:	at proximal joint	6%	5%
	at middle joint	4%	3%
	at distal joint	2%	1%
Little:	at proximal joint	6%	5%
	at middle joint	4%	3%
	at distal joint	1%	1%

Generally, disability involving two or more digits rates more than the sum of the ratings for each. For instance, loss of the major thumb rates 16% and the major index finger, 8%; the rating for loss of both in one injury is 30%.

The major middle, ring, and little fingers, single rate 8%, 6%, 6%; loss of all three rates 35%.

Loss of all fingers rates 55% for major, 50% for minor, 95% for both hands.

10. *Legs and Feet*: Lower extremities are rated in much the same manner as upper extremities, except that no distinction is made between major and minor. The rating for loss of both legs is 100%, but 95% if a prosthetic appliance can be used. If the amputations are below the knees, it is 100% without and 85% with a prosthesis.

Loss of one leg rates 80% without and 65% with a prosthesis; if the amputation is below the knee, 75% and 50%, respectively.

Other ratings are loss of all toes, 20%; loss of a great toe, 10%; any other toe, 2%.

Limitation of motion, shortening of the leg, instability, and subjective symptoms are additional factors which are ratable and in severe cases may rate as much as loss of the involved extremity.

11. *Back*: We have already discussed one feature of rating back disability, the judgment rating. Many conditions which affect the general condition of the body are set out in the schedule with ratings indicated for the degree of disablement. For backs these are: slight—30%, moderate—50%, and severe—100%. The judgment rating places the description of disability within these ranges. As stated, this may be accomplished through the use of the rating "plateaus."

Ordinarily, a description of disability will include the objective or measurable factors of disability, such as bending, twisting, leg-raising, and any atrophy of the muscles, along with a statement of the subjective symptoms considered valid. These factors are rated according to the loss of function. If the effect of the disability of the employee's working capabilities is also described, the applicable rating "plateau" may also be used. The greater of the two ratings will be awarded.

The schedule refers to disabilities of the spine, and, thus, back cases include injuries from the neck to the coccyx.

12. *Other Disabilities*:	*Slight*	*Moderate*	*Severe*	*Pronounced*
Paralysis	20%	60%	100%	
Epilepsy	25	75	100	
Neurosis	25	75	100	
Post Traumatic				
Head Syndrome	20	50	100	
Vertigo	10	50	100	
Headaches	5	15	60	100%
Mental Deterioration	20	50	75	100
Abdominal Weakness	10	30	50	
Lungs	10	40	75	100

	Slight	Moderate	Severe	Pronounced
Heart	40%	70%	100%	
Ribs (Chest Mobility)	40	70	100	
Head, Face, Cosmetic	5	20	50	80%
Limited Motion, Jaw				
or Malocclusion	0	10	30	
Inoperable Hernia				
Truss possible	-one: 10%		two: 25%	
Truss not possible	-one: 25%		two: 50%	
Loss of Kidney - 20%				

13. *Special Tables*: The schedule contains tables for computing ratings for partial loss of vision, partial loss of hearing, limitation of motion in the shoulders, fingers, and ankles; for rating leg-shortening, partial loss of grasping power, and multiple disabilities resulting from one injury.

§ 6.15 Permanent and Stationary Condition

When an injured employee's condition becomes permanent and stationary (P & S), it is ready for rating. This is a useful "rule of thumb" in determining whether disability is permanent or temporary; in some cases whether temporary compensation should be continued, rather than a rating issued. Usually, the treating physician will report to the employer or carrier whether the condition has reached this point. Other indications are whether the employee himself has noted any change in his condition after a reasonable period for convalescence. *R 9735*

The code itself does not require that the condition be "stationary," the basic inquiry being the permanency of disability. Thus, where necessary, factors may be rated even though it may not be clear whether there will be some improvement or worsening. The California Supreme Court has decreed that in cases involving an "insidious, progressive disease" resulting in a continual worsening condition the W.C.A.B. may reserve jurisdiction to issue successive awards for permanent disability benefits. Some cases are such that an award for permanent disability benefits also includes additional medical treatment. Ratings may also be issued where the employee dies before there has been full recovery or where the condition is irreversible and consistently worsening. It should be stressed in all these situations that there must be adequate medical evidence that ratable factors of permanent disability do exist.

[NOTE: Effective January 1, 1991, the term "permanent and stationary" is given statutory recognition, particularly in LC 4061(a)(2), (3), and LC 4062(b). These sections deal with administrative-medical findings per procedures which are operational as of that date for initial determination of permanent disability and medical issues. However, these provisions do not appear to impinge upon the principles discussed above.] *LC 4061- 4067*

§ 6.16   Apportionment of Permanent Disability

LC 4663
4750,
4750.5

LC 4663 provides that an aggravation of a pre-existing disease or condition may constitute an injury. This section and LC 4750 further provide that the employer is liable only for that portion of disability reasonably attributable to the aggravation. Therefore, in assigning a permanent disability benefit, apportionment is proper. An example would be a back case where the employee had 50% loss of motion in the back due to arthritis. If an injury aggravated this condition so that he had 75% loss of motion, only the 25% of such loss due to the injury would be ratable and assessed to the employer. On the other hand, if the employee had no such previous disability even though he had an arthritic condition, an apportionment would not necessarily follow.

Assume, further, that before the injury, the employee never experienced pain in the back. It would be proper to apportion the loss of motion since some of it pre-existed, but it would not be proper to apportion the disability caused by pain since pain would not be present except for the aggravating injury. In apportionment problems, therefore, it is necessary to establish if any disability pre-existed rather than whether any disease existed previously. Similarly, apportionment would be proper if it established that a certain degree of disability would have resulted from the pre-existing condition in the absence of any injury.

Whether there should be an apportionment in cases decided by the W.C.A.B. depends upon the evidence presented on this point. The issue is a factual one, and the courts will not reverse the Board unless the evidence shows the decision to be clearly erroneous. Whether disability results in whole or in part from a pre-existing disease or is fully compensable as a "lighting up" of a dormant or non-disabling prior condition comes within the Board's authority as the final arbiter of the facts.

Often, the question of apportionment must be resolved by medical evidence. It is not unusual for a medical report to indicate that a percentage of a disability is due to a pre-existing condition. However, the appellate courts have said that where the factors of permanent disability are fully set forth in the record, an apportionment made on a percentage basis may not be upheld. Further, an apportionment is not valid if based on a doctor's report which does not take into consideration all of the pertinent facts. When ratable factors of pre-existing disability are set out in the record, the rating for such factors should be subtracted from the rating for the combined disability.

A 1959 amendment provides that law enforcement and fire fighting personnel who qualify for the presumptions of injury are not subject to apportionment of permanent disability ratings based on a "presumption-disability."

140

§ 6.17   Apportionment—Successive Injuries; The *Hutchinson* Case

In the *Hutchinson* case, the California Supreme Court established a rule to be applied in apportioning permanent disability resulting from successive injuries. This case involved two injuries to the back, one to the upper back and one to the lower back. The injuries occurred close together in point of time so that payments for the two PD ratings would overlap. The rating in each case was 26%. The court held that in these cases the disabilities overlapped and that when this situation arises the combined disability must be rated in the second case, and the rating for the first injury subtracted from the rating for the combined disability to get the rating for the disability attributable to the second injury. The significance of rating combined disability is that the multiple disability table is used in many such cases, and the effect of this table is to merge or "telescope" two or more ratings to an amount less than the sum of the ratings. This table is found in the back of the rating schedule. Hutchinson, instead of getting two 26% ratings totalling 52%, would, under this table, get 26% for the first rating. Under the multiple disabilities table, his second rating would be the combined rating less 26%, or 48% − 26% = 22%. This principle could work the other way if the multiple disability table is not used, but overall disability is rated according to a plateau or guideline giving a value exceeding the sum of two separate ratings. Needless to say, the *Hutchinson* decision has created some confusion in subsequent appellate decisions. The Supreme Court recognized that its decision could result in a previously handicapped person's getting less for a subsequent industrial injury than a previously non-disabled person and discussed the need to evaluate disability properly so that the intent of the law be carried out. However, some appellate courts have followed this decision literally and have required combining ankle and heart disability and other non-connected disabilities. On the other hand, the Supreme Court found in another case that disabilities involving a back and knee were separate from serum hepatitis condition and that the disabilities did not overlap. The court indicated that the use of the multiple disability table would take care of any element of overlap in any event. The court recognizes that as a result of the injury and the contracting of the hepatitis the employee had two separate and individual physical abnormalities which should be given recognition in rating permanent disability. In a case decided by the Court of Appeal, the employee suffered a previous aphakic eye condition with a correction to 20/25 which would rate 20% standard, adjusting to 29½% for age and occupation. He later had an injury to that eye resulting in its being removed. The loss of this eye without apportionment would rate 41½% after adjustment for age and occupation. The insurance carrier sought apportionment. The court upheld the W.C.A.B. decision refusing any apportionment. The court holds that the factors of disability involved here did not overlap because of the different periods of rehabilitation required for the two conditions. If the corrected vision had been impaired by the later industrial injury, perhaps there would be some ground for an apportionment. The court seems to recognize that loss of a damaged but useful part of the body can be just as disabling as loss of a healthy portion of the body.

In a 1963 decision, the Court of Appeal decided a case in which the overall condition was rated. The award attributed half to each injury. After the first injury, the employee received a rating of 65% for his back condition. After the second injury his back condition rated 78%. If the insurance carrier covering the second injury had received full recognition of the first rating, its liability would have been a rating of 13%, or 52 weeks of compensation. The 50% apportionment made its liability a rating of 39%, or 156 weeks of compensation. In affirming the award of the larger amount, the appellate court pointed out that the record revealed that after the issuance of the first rating, the employee's condition had improved. Therefore, it is very important in apportionment cases to be able to prove the degree of actual disability or improvement just prior to the second injury. Illustrating this point is the *Newman* case. Newman was disabled from childhood because of amputation of a leg above the knee due to osteomyelitis. But, he worked for 40 years as a jeweler, then suffering a cerebral vascular accident resulting in permanent total disability. The Court of Appeal held that there was no overlapping of disabilities requiring apportionment under the *Hutchinson* rationale. These were separate and distinct injuries. The employee was fully rehabilitated to work with the first disability. Thus, there was no overlapping of factors affecting the same abilities to compete and earn.

§ 6.18 Disabilities in Same Part of Body; The *Wilkinson* Case

The California Supreme Court in the *Wilkinson* case has held that when a worker suffers successive injuries to the same part of the body, and the conditions resulting from these injuries become permanent and stationary at the same time, the employee is entitled to have the overall condition rated in one combined rating. The effect is to increase the value of the rating because of the expanding value of larger ratings, and the question of weekly compensation rates is determined as of the time of the most recent injury. One exception to this rule is that any prior injury resulting in a W.C.A.B. award for permanent disability over which the Board has lost jurisdiction through passage of time (5 years from date of injury) is not to be included.

§ 6.19 Formal and Informal Ratings

R 9739
10602

A "formal" permanent disability rating is one which is prepared by the Disability Evaluation Bureau (now a part of the Office of Benefit Determination (O.B.D.) of the Division of Workers' Compensation) at the request of the Appeals Board or a W.C.A.B. judge. In the report-form sent to the Bureau, the Board or judge sets forth the factors of permanent disability to be rated. The Bureau assigns a recommended rating including the formula used and transmits the form to the Board or judge for filing in the proceeding and service upon the parties. The form contains a notice that the matter will be submitted for decision within seven days after service unless written objection to the report is received within that time. The recommended rating is evidence only of the percentage of permanent disability based upon the description of disability factors and is not proof of the existence of such factors. (See Chapter 14, PROCEDURE, § 14.28, *Rating Reports*, § 14.29, *Cross-Examination of Rating Specialist*.)

An "informal" rating is one which is prepared where no proceeding has been filed with the W.C.A.B. Those who may request an informal rating are an Information and Assistance Officer or an employer and employee (or his or her representative) jointly. All medical reports must be filed with the Bureau, and the Bureau may request the employee to submit to a medical examination. The form used by the Bureau states that it is not a finding or award of the W.C.A.B. and is not evidence of the existence of the described factors of permanent disability. An informal rating is not binding on any party. It provides the basis for concluding a case where there is no real dispute. If an employee later feels that he or she has greater disability than that described in the informal rating, he or she may file a formal proceeding with the W.C.A.B. *R 9742* *R 9750*

If an employee is represented in connection with the informal procedure and a fee is requested for the attorney or other representative, the matter will be transmitted to the W.C.A.B. for the endorsement on the report of a reasonable fee. *R 9753*

Where the informal rating indicates the likelihood of a life pension or a right to future medical treatment, a copy will be sent to an Information and Assistance Officer for the purpose of obtaining a stipulated award (per the W.C.A.B.) or taking any other appropriate action. *R 9750*

The Bureau also provides consultative service in situations where an official report is not issued but information regarding a PD rating or range of possible ratings would be helpful in resolving a case. A request for this service may be made by an employee or by his or her representative; also by an employer or carrier or representative, by W.C.A.B. judges, mediators, arbitrators, pro tem judges, and Information and Assistance officers. If a case is pending before the W.C.A.B. and a declaration of readiness to proceed has been filed, one requesting consultative service must obtain authorization by a W.C.A.B. judge or other official assigned to hear or mediate the matter. *R 9758*

Other services rendered by the Bureau include preparation of ratings for the W.C.A.B. pre-trial rating calendar. Medical reports must be submitted to the Bureau ten days before the date of the pre-trial conference. A rating specialist will be on hand to assist in resolving matters at the conference. The Bureau also reviews compromise and release agreements for their adequacy in regard to permanent disability and commuted values of possible ratings or ranges of ratings. *R 9756* *R 9759*

§ 6.20   Administrative Determination of Permanent Disability Issues

LC 4061-4067

Effective January 1, 1991, industrially injured workers are entitled to an administrative determination of permanent disability benefits and need for continuing medical treatment by the Office of Benefit Determination. This procedure involves notice to the employee of his or her right to seek such a determination. The notice is to be given by the employer or insurer with the last payment of temporary compensation or within five working days after receipt of information indicating that the employee's condition is permanent and stationary. If the employee so requests, a medical evaluation will be made by an agreed medical evaluator or a qualified medical evaluator. A permanent disability rating will be issued based upon the medical evaluators report. Either party may request the Administrative Director to reconsider any rating issued or challenge the findings of the medical evaluator. When a final determination is made, the employer or insurer must either commence payment on the rating or file an application with the W.C.A.B. The mandated procedure is a prerequisite to the filing of an application for adjudication regarding the issues of permanent disability and continuing medical care. For details of this procedure, see Chapter 14, PROCEDURE.

[NOTE: The administrative procedure instituted by LC 4061-4067 raises some questions relevant to "formal" versus "informal" ratings. Under the procedure in place, formal ratings have been issued on the basis of factors of disability found by a workers' compensation judge. In informal ratings, the description of disability factors is prepared by a disability evaluator. Since LC 4061 and 4062 are not specific as to who selects these factors, it appears that a member of the staff of the Office of Benefit Determination, probably a disability evaluator, will prepare the disability description. Also, these sections will require the Administrative Director to review R 9732-9759, specifically R 9739 and 9742 dealing with formal and informal ratings.]

§ 6.21   Subsequent Injuries Fund

LC 4750, 4750.5

As previously discussed, LC 4750 provides that the employer is liable only for that portion of permanent disability which is attributable to the industrial injury. The problem of apportionment has often caused hardships because, while the employee may have been able to work with his previous disability, the amount added by an industrial injury effectively kept him from working at all.

To assist such an employee in his job of rehabilitation, the legislature passed a law creating a Subsequent Injuries Fund. This fund is available in certain cases to make payment to previously handicapped people who have been industrially injured. Another reason for the fund is to encourage employers to hire handicapped people, the fund's existence showing the employer that he would not be held liable for an employee's entire condition in the event of a work injury.

The legislature first created the Subsequent Injuries Fund in 1929 to provide compensation in the more severe cases for the factors of disability which pre-existed the industrial (subsequent) injury. The California Supreme Court struck down this law because of the wording of the provisions of the California Constitution relating to workmen's compensation. The law was no different from those of many other states or jurisdictions. It provided that the fund would be supported by a small payment to the fund by employers or their carriers in any case in which an employee without dependents died from the effects of an industrial injury. But the court held that when the California Constitution provided for a complete program of workers' compensation and created a "liability on the part of any or all persons to compensate any or all of their workmen for injury or disability," the provision was limiting and did not permit legislation requiring employers to provide indirect benefits to employees of other employers. *Cal. Const. Art. XIV, Sec. 4*

The fund was re-created in 1945 as a tax-supported program. It withstood a constitutional attack as a gift of public funds. It was limited to opposite members, i.e., anyone losing sight of an eye with previous loss of sight of an eye. It included loss of use of hand, foot, arm, or leg. In 1949, it was amended to provide for payments if combined industrial and pre-existing permanent disability factors rated 70% or more. In 1955 and 1959, amendments were enacted which placed additional conditions on obtaining the benefit. The combined disability must be 70%, or more, and also meet *one* of the following provisions: *LC 4751*

(1) The first disability must have affected hand, arm, foot, leg or eye, and second injury the opposite member and must rate 5% or more without adjustment for age or occupation; or

(2) Permanent disability from industrial injury must be 35% or more without adjustment of rating for age or occupation.

From any recovery against the State for the prior disability shall be deducted any payments from any other source for such prior disability. *LC 4753*

Not to be deducted, however, are any armed forces pensions for prior disability and any attorneys' fees paid to recover any type of payment for prior disability. Also, there shall not be deducted any assistance to which employee may be entitled under the California Welfare and Institutions Code.

A claim is initiated by filing an application with the W.C.A.B. setting forth facts demonstrating entitlement to the benefit. The state may be represented before the Appeals Board by the State Attorney General's Office or the Division of Industrial Accidents' attorneys. If settlement of a claim appears proper, the office representing the S.I.F. has authority to enter into compromise and release agreements. Such settlements must be approved by the Board. Per W.C.A.B. rules, applications for the S.I.F. benefits must be *LC 4753.5 4754.5* filed with the Board and served upon the "Division of Industrial Accidents, Subsequent Injuries Fund." Any document to be served on the fund, including any medical report, is to be sent to the Division.

Payment of this benefit begins on the 8th day after the last payment of permanent disability compensation due from the employer or insurance carrier. The state then begins paying until all of the award has been paid.

EXAMPLE:

Suppose that a worker's overall condition, including the preexisting disability, rates 80%. The amount attributable to the industrial injury was 40%. The employee will thus obtain an award against the employer based on a 40% permanent disability rating. Against the Subsequent Injury Fund, he will be awarded a 40% rating; and since the total rating of 80% would qualify the employee for a life pension, the Subsequent Injuries Fund is also liable for the life pension.

[At one time the Subsequent Injuries Fund was required to make payment in silicosis cases involving underground metal mining. Effective September 18, 1959, this statute was repealed and the state no longer makes payments in such cases.]

§ 6.22   SIF Apportionment

The courts hold that the employee's partial disability need not have been known by him, if the evidence shows that it did exist and was "labor disabling" (or ratable) at the time of the subsequent industrial injury. This benefit is not applicable, however, to progressive diseases which were not symptomatic or disabling. Where full recovery of workers' compensation benefits is obtained, or is obtainable, by an employee under LC 5500.5, for an occupational disease, and no other condition is responsible for the employee's disability, the Subsequent Injuries Fund is not liable for any portion of the disability. In such a case, there is no "prior disability" which would qualify the employee for these benefits. Therefore, the employee may not compromise his case against the employers involved and then obtain a recovery from the Subsequent Injuries Fund. To permit such a procedure would be to sanction a double recovery which the law will not permit, according to an appellate court decision.

If the condition which pre-existed was "labor disabling," it is immaterial that it was not stationary. The proof necessary is whether the prior permanent impairment was present, not whether it was, or was not, changing in severity. In rating the pre-existing condition, the Appeals Board must determine the extent of any rehabilitation or adjustment to the condition which permitted the injured person to become employable. Where the record shows rehabilitation, the rating fixing the fund's liability must be adjusted accordingly, the effect being to lessen the rating.

§ 6.23   SIF—Statute of Limitations

The California Supreme Court has established the rule that the statute of limitations begins to run when the employee knows or reasonably should know of his or her entitlement to Subsequent Injuries Fund benefits. Even so, there is no statute of limitations, as such, which is applicable but a reasonable time after such knowledge is obtained. (For further discussion see Chapter 14, PROCEDURE, § 14.7, *Time Limitations for Appeals Board Proceedings*.)

§ 6.24   SIF Benefit—Survival

This benefit is payable only to the employee, and the fund's liability for any accrued but unpaid compensation does not survive and thus is not payable to his dependents, in the event of his death. This is an exception to the general rule which is discussed in the next chapter.

§ 6.25   Attorney's Fees—SIF Recovery

An attorney is entitled to a fee for his work in processing a claim against the Subsequent Injuries Fund before the W.C.A.B. The payment of a fee out of the normal benefits does not necessarily recompense the attorney fully where the hearing regarding the fund's liability took place after the issues regarding the employer's liability have previously been resolved or settled. The employee pays the fee by way of a lien allowed by the W.C.A.B. against the SIF benefit.

§ 6.26   Financing the SIF

The subsequent injuries fund is basically financed by taxes. However, in 1972, Article XIV, Section 4 of the State Constitution was amended to provide for additional financing by requiring payment to the state in any case of industrial death without a dependent.

This provision was implemented by the enactment of LC 4706.5 which, as amended by an urgency measure effective April 12, 1973, and operative as of March 7, 1973, requires the following payments to the state by employers and carriers in industrial death cases in which there are no dependents:

1. Total dependency death benefit, without dependent minor children;

2. Accrued and unpaid disability compensation.

If it is later determined by the W.C.A.B. that the deceased employee left a dependent entitled to a death benefit, the amount paid by an employer or carrier shall be returned by the state.

Rules (including forms) for reporting such death cases have been promulgated by the Administrative Director.

§ 6.27   Scholarship Benefits for Dependents of Law Enforcement Officers

By virtue of Section 4709 of the Labor Code, dependents of any chief of police, police officer, sheriff, deputy sheriff, marshal of the Municipal Courts, or member of the California Highway Patrol who dies or is totally disabled as a result of an industrial injury caused by external violence or physical force incurred in the performance of his duty may be entitled to scholarships for institutions of collegiate grade located in California. The scholarship would include payment of tuition and fees, a monthly allowance, books and supplies, to a maximum of $6,000 for a period not to exceed six years, with a maximum of $1,500 per year. The scholarships are awarded on the basis of financial need. This benefit is also available to each child of officers or employees of the Department of Corrections and Department of Youth Authority and those of firefighters employed by counties, cities and counties, districts, and other political subdivisions of the state. LC 4709 defines dependent as the children of the law enforcement officer.

According to an opinion of the California Attorney General, the W.C.A.B. has jurisdiction to determine whether total disability is present in a particular case.

§ 6.28   Social Security Disability Benefit

The Social Security Act provides that an individual who is insured under Social Security who has not attained age 65 and is disabled is entitled to a disability insurance benefit for each month, beginning with the first month after the waiting period. The disability benefit shall be equal to the primary insurance amount as though the applicant had attained age 62. This benefit applies to those who are fully insured or who are insured for disability. There is a waiting period of five months after the filing of the application, and benefits are payable only so long as the disability exists.

The term "disability" means inability to engage in any substantial gainful activity by reason of any medically determinable physical or mental impairment which can be expected to result in death or which has lasted or can be expected to last for a continuous period of not less than 12 months, or, in the case of an individual who has attained age 55 and is blind, unable, by reason of such blindness, to engage in substantial gainful activity requiring skills or abilities comparable to those of any gainful activity in which he has previously engaged with some regularity for over a substantial period of time.

An individual will be determined to be under a disability only if his or her physical or mental impairment is of such severity that he or she is not only unable to do his or her previous work, but cannot, considering age, education, and work experience, engage in any other kind of substantial gainful work which exists in the national economy regardless of whether such work exists in the immediate area in which the person lives, whether a job vacancy exists, or whether the person would be hired if he or she applied for work. An applicant may be required to furnish medical evidence of disability.

Under the act, the total of benefits based on wages and self-employment income will be reduced (but not below zero) by the amount by which the sum of the total of Social Security disability benefits and periodic disability benefits payable under a workers' compensation law or plan exceeds the higher of 80% of his "average current earnings" or Social Security benefits. This reduction will not be effective if the workers' compensation law or plan provides for a reduction of compensation benefits by reason of the receipt of any disability Social Security benefits.

Average current earnings are defined as the higher of:

a. The average monthly earnings used for computing the primary insurance amount; or

b. The average monthly earnings from employment and self-employment during his highest five consecutive years after 1950.

This offset is effective for benefits for months after 1965 based on periods of disability which began after 6-1-65. The amount of the reduction will be adjusted periodically to take account of increases in national earnings levels, but in no event will the total amount of benefits payable on the worker's earnings record be decreased.

The statute applies the offset to benefits under a workers' compensation law or plan of the U.S. or a state. The offset thus clearly applies to the Longshoremen's Act but, by administrative decision, not to recoveries under the Jones Act. It has also been held to apply to the "Black Lung Act." The regulations of the Department of Health, Education and Welfare provide that amounts in compensation awards which represent medical and legal expenses are excluded from any offset. The offset applies to commutation of periodic payments. In the case of compromise and release, there must be a determination of how much is for periodic payments and how much for past and future medical expenses. (See 42 U.S. Code, Sections 414, 423, 424.)

Chapter 7
DEATH BENEFITS

§ 7.1   Introduction

If an injured employee having a right to compensation payments for either temporary or permanent disability dies, his or her death terminates the disability, and the liability of the employer for further disability payments ceases. Any payments due and unpaid at the time of death, however, are paid to the employee's dependents. Further, in the event the death is a result of the industrial injury, the dependents are entitled to a death benefit. A payment for burial expense is also provided. *LC 3501-3503 4700-4706*

Dependents are referred to as either "total dependents" or "partial dependents." A total dependent is one who was wholly dependent upon the deceased employee at the time of the industrial injury. A partial dependent is a person who received only a portion of his support from the deceased employee at the time of the injury. The distinction between these two classes of dependents may affect both the size of the benefit and the determination of entitlement or preference.

§ 7.2   Date of Injury Controls

LC 3502   The date of injury (rather than the date of death where they are not the same date) controls the amount of the death benefits. This is another result of the principle that the law in effect on the date of injury is applicable. Similarly, the question of dependency is referrable to the date of injury. A 1944 decision of the California Supreme Court illustrates this principle. After his injury, an employee married. Later, he died, and his widow filed for death benefits. The court held that she did not qualify for benefits, since she was not a dependent at time of injury.

LC 3501, 3502   However, as to deaths resulting from injuries occurring on or after January 1, 1990, a presumption of total dependency is granted a surviving spouse, subject to an earnings test, to whom the deceased is married at the time of death. See subsequent topic in § 7.9, *Dependents: Total and Partial Dependency*, for further discussion.

Pursuant to a 1990 Court of Appeal decision, in a case involving continuous exposure to asbestos where two separate conditions are caused by the exposure, there can be two dates of injury, one for determining disability benefits relating to one condition and one for determining death benefits by virtue of industrial death resulting from the other condition.

§ 7.3   Caused or Hastened

LC 4663 4700   The death benefit is not apportioned if the injury is an aggravation of a pre-existing condition. Therefore, where any industrial cause speeds the employee's demise for any appreciable amount, and even though he would have died from the prior condition within a short time anyway, the applicable death benefit is payable to the dependents. The court's reasoning here is that LC 4663 defines an injury as including an aggravation of an existing condition, but limits the employer's right to an apportionment to *benefits payable to the employee* because of his disability.

Proof of aggravation or hastening is required through medical reports or testimony. If there are conflicting medical opinions in the record, a determination by the W.C.A.B. based upon "substantial evidence" will be upheld by the appellate courts.

§ 7.4   Accrued Disability Compensation

LC 4700   Any accrued and unpaid compensation due an employee at the time of his death from the employer or insurance carrier is payable to the employee's dependents, personal representative, heirs, or other person entitled to it, in that order of preference. No probate or other administration of the benefits is necessary. An order of the Workers' Compensation Appeals Board is sufficient.

Death terminates the employee's disability so that only the disability payments due as of the date of death are payable whether for temporary or permanent disability.

EXAMPLE:

Suppose an employee has an award for a permanent disability benefit of 160 weeks of payments and that he dies after 100 weeks' payments have been paid. The employer or insurance carrier is not liable for the remaining 60 weeks of payments. Assume that the same employee dies after 100 payments had accrued but only 90 payments had been received, leaving 10 payments unpaid. The employee's dependents would be entitled to the ten weekly payments, but, as stated, not the 60 payments which had not yet accrued.

Likewise, if an employee dies while receiving temporary compensation, only those payments which are due and payable at the time of death are paid to the dependents. This is true regardless of the fact that further temporary compensation and possibly a permanent disability rating were anticipated. If, however, permanent disability payments would have been due if the condition had been rated, it can be rated after death to determine the number of such accrued payments.

The dependents are entitled to receive accrued compensation regardless of the cause of death, that is, whether the death was caused by the industrial injury or was due to causes unrelated to the industrial accident.

EXAMPLES:

(1) A suffers an industrial hip injury and during convalescence is killed in an accident while a passenger in a friend's car. Since the death was unrelated to A's hip injury, no workers' compensation death benefit would be paid, but A's dependents would be entitled to A's accrued but unpaid disability compensation.

(2) Assume B suffers from an industrial disease contracted in the course of his employment. After long period of treatment, the disease causes his death. Here the dependents would be entitled to any accrued but unpaid disability payments in addition to any death benefits to be paid.

As stated in the previous chapter, the liability of the Subsequent Injuries Fund does not survive to the dependents, nor do any accrued but unpaid benefits due from the fund. The reason is that LC 4700 applies only to benefits from employers, and the fund is not the employer.

§ 7.5 The Death Benefit

When an industrial injury causes or hastens death, the employee's dependents receive a sum, payable in weekly installments, as a death benefit. *LC 4701,* Only one death benefit is payable. The size of the benefit depends upon who *4702* the dependents are and whether total or partial dependents. Since benefits have been increased periodically, one should keep in mind that the benefits in effect on the date of injury are controlling, not the benefits in effect on the date of death.

§ 7.6   Death Benefits On or After January 1, 1991

The following are applicable to deaths resulting from injuries occurring on or after January 1, 1991:

LC 4703
- Two or more total dependents regardless of the number of partial dependents: $115,000. (If there are two or more total dependents, the benefit will be divided equally among them, and any partial dependents will receive no part.)

- One total dependent and one or more partial dependents: $95,000, plus four times annual support for partial dependents, not to exceed a total of $115,000. (In this situation, the total dependent will receive $95,000, and partial dependents four times annual support not to exceed an aggregate of $25,000 per LC 4703.)

- One total dependent and no partial dependents: $95,000.

- No total dependents and one or more partial dependents: Four times annual support, not to exceed a total of $95,000. (If insufficient to cover all partial claims, the $95,000 will be divided proportionately.)

- Maximum burial allowance: $5,000.

LC 4703.5
- Continuation allowance for dependent minor children: The Reform Act of 1989 provides for a continuing benefit for dependent minor children where an employee's death results from an injury occurring on or after January 1, 1990. This benefit is payable after the payment of the death benefit provided in LC 4702 and regardless of the maximum limitations set for death benefits by LC 4702 and 4703. Payment will continue until the youngest child reaches the age of 18. It is payable in the same manner as temporary compensation at a rate of not less than $224 per week.

§ 7.7   Death Benefits for Period January 1, 1984 Through December 31, 1990

The following are applicable to deaths resulting from injuries occurring during the period January 1, 1984, through December 31, 1990:

- Two or more total dependents regardless of the number of partial dependents: $95,000. (If there are two or more total dependents, the entire death benefit will be divided equally among them, and any partial dependents will receive no part.)

- One total dependent and one or more partial dependents: $70,000 plus four times annual support for partial dependents not to exceed a total death benefit of $95,000. (Where there is one total dependent and one or more partial dependents, the total dependent will receive $70,000, and the partial dependents will receive four times annual support not to exceed a total of $25,000. If insufficient to cover all the partial-dependent claims, the $25,000 will be divided proportionately.)

- One total dependent and no partial dependents: $70,000.

- No total dependents and one or more partial dependents: four times annual support not to exceed a total of $70,000. (If insufficient to cover all partial claims, the $70,000 will be divided proportionately.)

- Maximum burial allowance: $1,500. For deaths resulting from industrial *LC 4701* injuries occurring on or after January 1, 1986, the maximum allowance is $2,000. For employees of local public agencies through December 31, 1988, the maximum is $1,500 unless the parties have agreed to a larger amount not to exceed $2,000. Beginning January 1, 1989, the statutory maximum for such public employees is $2,000.

- Continuation allowance for dependent minor children: The Reform Act of *LC 4703.5* 1989 provides for a continuing benefit for dependent minor children where an employee's death results from an injury occurring on or after January 1, 1990. This benefit is payable after the payment of the death benefit provided in LC 4702 and regardless of the maximum limitations set for death benefits by LC 4702 and 4703. Payment will continue until the youngest child reaches the age of 18. It is payable in the same manner as temporary compensation at a rate of not less than $224 per week.

§ 7.8 Death Benefits for Period January 1 Through December 31, 1983

The following death benefits are applicable to deaths resulting from in- *LC 4702,* juries occurring during the period January 1, 1983 through December 31, *4703* 1983:

- Two or more total dependents regardless of the number of partial dependents: $85,000. (If there are two or more total dependents, the entire death benefit will be divided equally among them, and any partial dependents will receive no part.)

- One total dependent and one or more partial dependents: $60,000 plus four times annual support for partial dependents not to exceed a total death benefit of $85,000. (Where there is one total dependent and one or more partial dependents, the total dependent will receive $60,000, and the partial dependents will receive four times annual support not to exceed $25,000. If insufficient to cover all partial-dependent claims, the $25,000 will be divided proportionately.)

- One total dependent and no partial dependents: $60,000.

- No total dependents and one or more partial dependents: four times annual support not to exceed a total of $60,000. (If insufficient to cover all partial claims, the $60,000 will be divided proportionately.)

LC 4701
- Maximum burial allowance: $1,500.

[NOTE: For death benefits in effect before January 1, 1983, see Appendix, Table F.]

§ 7.9   Dependents: Total and Partial Dependency

LC 3501-
3503
A claimant for a death benefit must be a person who was dependent upon the deceased employee at the time of the injury resulting in the employee's death. The code makes a distinction between total dependents and partial dependents. A total dependent is one who was wholly dependent upon the deceased employee at the time of the injury, that is, who looked to and was dependent upon the employee for necessities such as food, shelter, and clothing, for sustenance of life and comfort. A partial dependent is one who received assistance from the deceased employee, but such assistance formed only a part of the dependent's income or provision of necessaries.

To be a qualified dependent, a person must also come within one of the several categories of relationships listed in LC 3503:

1. A member "in good faith" of the employee's family or household
2. Husband or wife
3. Child or posthumous (born after the employee's death) child
4. Adopted child or stepchild
5. Grandchild
6. Father or mother
7. Father-in-law or mother-in-law
8. Grandparent
9. Brother or sister
10. Uncle or aunt
11. Brother-in-law or sister-in-law
12. Nephew or niece

LC 4703
Regarding the allocation of benefits as set forth in LC 4702, the law provides that if there is one total dependent, and one or more partial dependents, the total dependent will receive the benefit for one total dependent, and partial dependents are limited to an aggregate amount of $25,000. If there are two or more total dependents, the applicable death benefit is to be divided equally among them, and partial dependents receive no part thereof. If there is no total dependent, any partial dependents will receive four times annual support, and if the total of such claims exceeds the maximum allowable death benefit, the maximum amount will be divided among them "in proportion to the relative extent of their dependency." These provisions of LC 4703 are subject to LC 4704 regarding assignment or reassignment of death benefits. (See subsequent topic in § 7.13, *Distribution of Death Benefits*.)

LC 3501 provides that a minor child (under 18 years of age) of a deceased employee is entitled to a conclusive presumption of total dependency. A child over 18 years of age also qualifies for this presumption if physically or mentally incapacitated from earning where the child is living with the employee-parent or the employee is legally liable for his or her support, there being no surviving totally dependent parent. *LC 3501*

Before 1977, LC 3501 also granted a widow a conclusive presumption of dependency, but in that year the California Supreme Court in the *Arp* case ruled the provision unconstitutionally discriminatory against men (husbands) who had no such presumption. The court voided the presumption for widows leaving it to the legislature to determine whether a presumption should be granted to both husbands and wives. The legislature amended LC 3501 by removing the widows' presumption and retaining the presumption of total dependency only as to the deceased's minor children or incapacitated adult children subject to the conditions noted above. Also at one time, the size of the death benefit for "a widow and one or more minor children" was greater than that for other total dependents. Effective in 1981, the legislature changed its approach in setting the amount of the death benefit to that apparent in the present version of LC 4702-4703.5. Benefits are awarded on the basis of total versus partial dependency. Further, the repeal of the provision regarding a presumption of total dependency for widows requires that husbands and wives prove the extent of their dependency as do other claimed dependents who have no presumption. The California Supreme Court established the principle that in determining the extent of dependency of one spouse upon the other the earnings of both are considered as they relate to the contribution made to the "community" of the family or household. (See discussion of the *Arvizu* case in the next topic, *Proving Dependency*.) Effective as to deaths resulting from injuries occurring on or after January 1, 1990, a conclusive *LC 3501(b)* presumption of total dependency applies to the case of a surviving spouse who is married to an industrially deceased worker at the time of the worker's death where the surviving spouse earned $30,000 or less during the 12 months immediately preceding the death.

[NOTE: As a general rule, a claimant must have been dependent upon deceased employee at the time of the injury causing death rather than the date *LC 3501* of death. However, as to the spousal presumption in LC 3501(b) (effective *(a), (b),* January 1, 1990), the presumption accrues to one who "is married at the time *3502* of death." Also, proof of a claimant's earnings ($30,000 or less) relates to the "twelve months immediately preceding the death."

The effect of a conclusive presumption of total dependency is that the person having the benefit of the presumption is deemed to be a total dependent even if the facts show otherwise. For example, a minor child may be self-supporting or supported by someone other than the employee-parent. These facts are immaterial, for a conclusive presumption may not be controverted. (In law, a presumption is either conclusive or disputable. A disputable presumption may be challenged and controverted by evidence.)

Also, as a matter of history, the presumptions of total dependency in LC 3501 did not apply to non-resident aliens. This exclusion was repealed in 1978. The effect of this repeal, along with the other legislative changes, is that the presumption is available to a non-resident alien child of a deceased worker. Other non-resident alien dependents may qualify if within one of the categories listed above, but they must prove the extent of their dependency.

§ 7.10   Proving Dependency

All claimants for a workers' compensation death benefit must prove their entitlement, both as to to the qualifying relationship and the extent of the support afforded by the deceased worker. Those having the benefit of a conclusive presumption of total dependency need not prove extent of dependency; however, they must prove that they qualify for the presumption. Therefore, a claimant should produce any pertinent documentary evidence, such as, a marriage license, birth certificate, financial records, or letters from the deceased employee. A surviving husband or wife claiming total dependency has the burden to show that he or she received all his or her support from the deceased. Where both husband and wife were working or otherwise had income, the determination rests upon the extent of each one's contribution to their total expenses. This is not always a mere matter of arithmetic, for the appellate courts have ruled that the amount necessary to maintain the standard of living achieved by the couple must be considered.

The California Supreme Court ruled in the *Arvizu* case that in marital situations where both husband and wife have income, an analysis is necessary to determine the extent of the contribution made by the deceased to the survivor at the time of injury. Various factors to be taken into account are household expenses such as maintaining the home and transportation. Cost of purely personal expenses of the deceased worker are not included. Also not included would be such personal expense of the deceased as pre-marital debts, alimony or child support referable to a previous marriage. If the surviving spouse's income was very small and not crucial to the family's financial situation, it is still possible for the spouse to claim total dependency.

LC 3501(b)   With regard to the conclusive presumption of total dependency applicable to spouses of workers deceased by virtue of injuries sustained on or after January 1, 1990, proof is needed of marriage at the time of an employee's death and the extent of the claimant's income ($30,000 or less) during the 12 months preceding the death.

Similar problems arise where claimants other than husbands or wives contend that they are total dependents. Inquiry must be made into all sources of income or support. One appellate decision holds that one may prove total dependency even though the claimant may have a small income, where such income is insignificant as compared to the extent of the support provided by the deceased worker. Where two or more people are sharing expenses, the "family pot" concept is looked to, and it becomes necessary to analyze the extent to which the amount which the deceased contributed to the "pot" inured to the benefit of each claimant. If the claimant is determined to be a partial dependent, the death benefit is four times the annual amount so contributed.

EXAMPLES:

(1) John and Mary Jones have two children under 18 years of age. John is killed in an accident at work. At the time of John's injury, Mary was principally a homemaker, and she also was developing a side business of selling yarn dolls which she made as she had time. Sales of her dolls usually coincided with Christmas and other holidays. The proceeds from this endeavor were used to purchase supplies, and the net was put into a savings account to be used for emergencies or ultimately the children's post-high school education. This net income amounted to an average of about $50 per month. The two children are presumed total dependents. Mary is also a total dependent because her earnings were insignificant in relation to her dependency upon her husband for necessaries, and her earnings played no part in the family day-to-day financial picture.

(2) Assume the same facts as above, but assume also that Mary ran a business at a store location and contributed as much to household expenses as John. Here Mary would be a partial dependent, the children total dependents. If John's injury and death occurred in 1984, the maximum death benefit of $95,000 would be applicable and awarded to the children because there are two or more total dependents and a partial dependent. LC 4703 directs payment to total dependents and nothing for partial dependents. In this fact-situation, Mary would be made guardian and trustee of the funds under direction to use them for the care and benefit of the minor children.

(3) Fred and Phyllis Smith both have salaried positions, each earning about $18,000 per year. There are no dependent children. Each spouse takes care of his or her own car and other incidentals such as clothing, cosmetics, and recreation. They share the expenses of the household, vacation trips, and major purchases for the home such as appliances, carpeting, and drapes. However, Fred pays the house payment of $600 per month, and Phyllis pays taxes and insurance, as well as insurance on both cars. Phyllis does the grocery-shopping, and Fred gives her $200 per month as his share of the food budget. Each has a checking account and savings account, all accounts being held jointly. Under these facts, if either spouse suffers death from an industrial injury, the survivor is a partial dependent. Neither is totally dependent upon the other for support, and each one earns enough to be self-supporting. But, they have developed a life-style and standard of living which takes both salaries to maintain. In determining the amount each is dependent upon the other on an annual basis, one may ascertain and eliminate those expenses which are purely personal to each, especially the personal items taken care of

individually. The crucial question of extent of dependency rests upon the amount which the deceased employee contributed to their joint effort and which was required to sustain a standard of living which neither spouse could support individually. Therefore, dependency would probably exceed 50% of such contribution and would be a weighted proportion in view of the standard of living and the extent of the family liabilities to be assumed by the survivor. This amount is to be determined by the W.C.A.B. judge after all these factors are placed into evidence. As the Supreme Court stated in its *Arvizu* decision, questions related to partial dependency situations must be determined on a case-by-case basis.

(4) A lives at home with his parents. His father has an income of over $10,000 per year, but A pays room and board by agreement with his parents. When he was not working, he did not pay anything. The parents were not dependent upon A for their own support. A was killed in a work-accident, and the parents filed for the death benefit. The burial expenses would be paid either to the parents, or to the mortuary if the bill was not yet paid. But no death benefit could accrue to the parents who were not dependents. Some effort might be made to find partial dependency because of the payment of room and board. However, these payments were in the nature of purchase of services rather than a contribution to support.

(5) X, Y, and Z are brothers sharing an apartment to economize their small incomes. X sustains a head injury at work which causes his death. No one or pair of them could afford the standard of living that the pooling of their three incomes provided. Assuming there were no other dependents, each could qualify as a partial dependent of the others. The benefit would be four times the annual contribution of the deceased brother to each of the others. This determination involves the amount put into the household "kitty" by each and how much the contribution of the deceased inured to the support of the others. The total of the benefits could not exceed the limit set for partial dependents by the law in effect on the date of injury.

§ 7.11   Member of Household or Family in Good Faith; Non-Marital Situations

A member of an employee's household or family in good faith may be any person whom the employee considers a part of his family or household. It is not necessary that the person be related to the employee by blood or marriage. The code stipulates that there must be good faith, so that any lack of good faith, such as deception, could rule out a particular situation. Several cases have reached the appellate courts in quasi-marital or contract situations. The leading case is *Marvin v. Marvin* which was not a workers' compensation case but has been pointed to by the courts and the W.C.A.B. as precedent. In *Marvin*, the California Supreme court held that a live-in companion who knew that the relationship did not constitute a marriage, but was a matter of convenience for both parties, could bring an action against the other for breach of contract if he or she could prove the existence of a contract. Based upon the apparent change in court philosophy over older decisions, the courts and the Board began liberalizing their views of what constitutes good faith in workers' compensation death cases involving various live-in arrangements. It appears at this juncture that any arrangement entered into willingly and knowledgeably is deemed valid, regardless of marriage, absence of marriage, gender, or lifestyle. This overrules or supersedes previous decisions to the effect that live-in arrangements without marriage or facts indicating a putative-spouse situation were considered "meretricious" and not in good faith. (See next topic for definition of "putative spouse.")

§ 7.12 Marriage Problems

If a person proves a marriage relationship, it is presumed to be valid, and it is incumbent upon the person challenging the marriage to prove its invalidity.

There is no such thing as a common-law marriage in California. A common-law marriage is recognized if the marriage were valid in the state in which it is contracted. Our law does recognize a putative marriage which is based upon the good faith of the person claiming a marriage relationship and his or her ignorance of the impediment to the validity of the marriage. A putative spouse qualifies as a husband or wife under LC 3503. Persons living together in a non-married situation, would not qualify as putative spouses although they may be considered members of the family or household in good faith. [NOTE: According to a 1989 decision of the Court of Appeal, a putative spouse has all the rights the law grants to a spouse including those conferred by Probate Code Sec. 6560 upon a spouse who has been omitted from the other spouse's will.]

What claim does a former spouse have to the death benefit? If the divorce or dissolution is final, and the parties are living apart, a former spouse has no claim. This is true even if support payments are a part of the decree, for a former spouse is not a husband or wife and is not a member of the family or household. In the case of an interlocutory decree which has not become final, there is still a marriage, and dependency would turn on the extent of support payments.

This discussion of divorce situations assumes the parties are living apart. Should they reconcile before the decree and resume cohabitation, the wife is a total dependent. If the resumption follows a final decree without a marriage ceremony, the former wife must prove she was a putative spouse or a member of the household in good faith.

Because of disputes which often arise between claimed dependents, most employers and insurance carriers require an Appeals Board Findings and Award before payments of accrued compensation or death benefits are made to any dependent. At the Board hearing, proof of marriage as to a husband or wife or birth certificates of children are the usual matter of evidence presented. Employers' representatives will also inquire regarding any other possible dependents of the deceased. While documentary proof is best, relationships may be established by credible testimony.

§ 7.13   Distribution of Death Benefits

LC 4703
The Appeals Board has very broad authority in ordering payment of the death benefit. Preference is given to total dependents over any partial dependents, and if there is more than one total dependent, the benefit should be divided equally.

LC 4703
The law further provides that when only partial dependents are claimants, the division of the benefit is on a pro rata basis, according to "the relative extent of their dependency." If the aggregate amount of four times the annual contribution of the deceased for their support does not exceed the allowable maximum, each receives his or her entire death benefit. The necessity for pro rata distribution to partial dependents is present only where the aggregate of such benefits exceeds the maximum allowance for this class of dependents.

LC 4704
Regardless of these preferences, the Appeals Board may "set apart" or "reassign" the death benefit to any one or more dependents equitably in accordance with their needs. This provision injects a social philosophy into the awarding of death benefits and permits the Appeals Board to consider the relative economic situations of the dependents. If the monetary needs of the dependents are about equal, the Appeals Board does not ordinarily deviate from the preference of total over partial dependents, or equal distribution among total dependents, proportional distribution as to partial dependents. The Court of Appeal has ruled that the Appeals Board must make specific findings based upon substantial evidence regarding the needs of the dependents before reassigning a death benefit under LC 4703 and 4704.

§ 7.14   Statute of Limitations—Death Claims

LC 5406
Death claims are "outlawed" if not filed with the Workers' Compensation Appeals Board within one year after date of death and also within 240 weeks (i.e., 4^{32}/$_{52}$ years) after the date of injury. For discussion of principles involved in the application of LC 5406, see Chapter 14, PROCEDURE, § 14.7, *Time Limits for Appeals Board Proceedings*, item 4, *Death Cases*.

§ 7.15   Payment of Benefit

LC 4702(b)
Like other workers' compensation payments, the death benefit is paid on the basis of a weekly compensation rate. The code directs that payment be made in the same manner and amounts as temporary compensation unless the W.C.A.B. otherwise directs. The death benefit has been expressed in LC 4702 as a flat amount since 1955; however, the benefit is paid at the weekly rate of temporary compensation in effect on the date of injury. The W.C.A.B. routinely orders payment at the maximum rate for temporary compensation regardless of the actual earnings of the deceased worker. The California

Supreme Court approved this approach to payment of death benefits because of the discretion granted the Board by LC 4702(b). As to deaths resulting from injuries occurring on or after January 1, 1990, no payment of a death benefit is to be less than $224 per week.

Before 1990, payments were to be made at least twice per month. Under LC 4650(c), effective January 1, 1990, payment is to be made every two weeks on the day designated with the first payment. *LC 4650*

Where the benefit is to be divided, so must the weekly installment. This is to provide each beneficiary with a regular specific amount to carry out the purpose of the law.

§ 7.16   Death of a Dependent Beneficiary

If, after an award is made, a dependent beneficiary dies, the Appeals Board may reassign his or her share to any other surviving dependent or dependents. In the event there are no surviving dependents, the payments terminate, and the remaining payments do not survive to the deceased dependent's estate. There is one instance wherein a portion of such beneficiary's share may survive. This is the situation where payments have accrued up to the time of death but have not yet been paid. The accrued but unpaid portion may be ordered by the Appeals Board to be paid to the heirs of the dependent, or, if none, to the heirs of the deceased employee. *LC 4706* *LC 4704*

§ 7.17   Commutation of Death Benefit

If a dependent desires a death benefit to be paid in a lump sum, any payments which have not yet accrued must be commuted—that is, discounted at the rate of 3% per annum. The dependent must show a good and provident reason for an order of commutation. Such an order may issue only after notice of the parties and an opportunity to be heard on the matter. The W.C.A.B. has ruled that the fact that the commuted amount could earn interest in excess of 3% is not sufficient reason to commute a death benefit. *LC 5100- 5106*

§ 7.18   No Dependents—Payment to State

Before March 7, 1973, if a deceased worker had no dependents, no death benefit was payable except the burial allowance. Effective on that date, a new program came into existence. In such cases, a death benefit is paid to the state to assist in financing the Subsequent Injuries Fund. A lump sum is to be paid equivalent to the commuted value of the allowance paid to a total dependent. In addition, any accrued but unpaid disability payments are paid to the state. Employers and insurance carriers must notify the Administrative Director of all such death cases with no dependents. If a claimant later shows up and is awarded a death benefit as a bona fide dependent, the state will repay the employer or carrier. The burial allowance is payable to the person incurring the expense. The appellate courts have ruled that if there is any *LC 4706.5* dependent, even if only a partial dependent, the state is not entitled to a death benefit of any amount not awarded to such dependent. The reason for this ruling is that the constitutional directive speaks only of a payment to the state in any death case in which there is no surviving dependent.

R 9900   An employer (or carrier) must report the death of any employee to the Administrative Director, regardless of the cause of death, except where the employer (or carrier) has knowledge or notice that the deceased employee left a surviving minor child. The report is to be made on DIA Form 510 within 60 days of the employer's notice or knowledge of an employee's death.

The W.C.A.B. has ruled that the state must be joined as a party in any death case whenever it appears that there is no applicant entitled to a presumption of total dependency.

§ 7.19   Employee's Settlement Before Death

LC 5000(b)   LC 5000(b) provides that an employee may release any and all claims which might be made by his or her dependents regarding an injury to the employee. If an employee's settlement is approved prior to his death, the dependents have no right to a death benefit. The California Supreme Court has ruled that this provision is constitutional and does not deprive such dependents of due process of law or equal protection of the law. However, the Supreme Court has also ruled that unless it can be shown that the employee made a knowledgeable waiver of his or her dependents' possible claim for death benefits, the mere fact of signing a compromise and release will not preclude a later application for death benefits. As a result of this holding of the court, the W.C.A.B. has provided form-language to be incorporated into every compromise and release agreement entered into by an employee. This language is to the effect that the employee has been informed and understands that the settlement will release all claims of dependents for death benefits relating to the injury or injuries covered by the settlement. (For additional discussion and form-language, see Chapter 11, SETTLEMENTS, § 11.2, *C&R Requirements*.)

§ 7.20   Public Employees' Retirement Systems— Special Death Benefit

Widows or children of certain members of the California Public *LC 4707*   Employees' Retirement System are covered by a special death benefit, should such member suffer an industrially caused death. The amount is determined by the System. The Workers' Compensation Appeals Board has the function of determining whether death was due to an industrial injury. The award to the widow or children follows the language of LC 4707 to the effect that if the special benefit is less than would be awarded under the workers' compensation law, the employer or insurer shall pay the difference. LC 4707 also provides for burial expense reimbursement, not to exceed $1,000. These special benefits apply to "safety members" and their widows and children. A recent decision of the appellate court holds that the W.C.A.B. has jurisdiction to award a minor child of a deceased safety member a workers' compensation death benefit even though the widow has received the special retirement system allowance in lieu of workers' compensation. (In this case, the child was of a previous marriage.)

Under the County Employees' Retirement Law, widows and children of any member are eligible for a "continuation" allowance which is somewhat larger than their normal allowance if the member's injury was service-connected. Entitlement under the county plan is determined by the retirement board of the particular county.

§ 7.21   Scholarship as Death Benefit

Dependents of any police officer, sheriff, deputy sheriff, marshal, deputy marshal, or highway patrol officer who dies or is totally disabled by *LC 4709* external violence or physical force in the line of duty may be entitled to scholarships to colleges in California. The maximum amount is $6,000 for a period not to exceed six years. Scholarships are awarded on the basis of financial need. This benefit is also available to each child of officers or employees of the Department of Corrections and Department of Youth Authority, and those of firefighters of counties, cities and counties, districts, and other political subdivisions of the state. LC 4709 defines dependent as the children of the law enforcement officer. The W.C.A.B. has jurisdiction to determine the disability issue.

§ 7.22   Special Death Benefit to Dependents of Assassinated Elective Officeholder

A special death benefit is payable by the state of California to certain surviving dependents of a person holding elective office who suffers death by *LC 4720-* reason of assassination. This benefit applies to dependents of public officials *4727* holding any federal, state, local, or special district elective office by virtue of winning an election in California or by being appointed to fill a vacancy in such an office. Dependents who qualify for the benefit are a spouse, dependent minor children, or if no spouse and no such children, a dependent parent. A timely claim must be filed with the state Board of Control. Any person or persons eligible must, within one year of the date of the decedent's death by assassination, choose either of two options: (1) one-half decedent's salary, payable until death or remarriage of the spouse or until the youngest minor child reaches 18 years of age, any payments to decedent's parents to continue during dependency; or, (2) a lump-sum benefit of $150,000. There will be deducted from any benefit paid under this program any death benefit provided from public funds with the exception of workers' compensation.

Chapter 8
THE INJURY

§ 8.1   Introduction

Industrial injuries are referred to in various terms: industrial accident, compensable injury, work injury, injury arising out of and occurring in the *LC 3600* course of employment. These terms refer to the Labor Code requirement that the payment of compensation depends upon the existence of an injury which not only occurs during the course of the employee's duties but which also arises out of the employment. The code further provides the injury must be

167

"proximately caused by the employment." These statutory provisions appear to limit compensable injuries to those which were caused by the particular activity for which the employee was hired. For some time after the passage of the Boynton Act, the courts held to a rather literal interpretation of the proximate cause requirement. Recent court decisions have "liberalized" the interpretation of Section 3600 to mean that an injury is compensable if it is considered "on the job" or in the course of some activity which is "work-connected."

A reading of some of the older court decisions indicates the difficulty encountered in trying to apply the traditional legal concept of proximate cause in this field. The meaning of this term has long been that liability for an act follows only if the act was an effective cause of injury or damage. In applying this requirement, then, injuries which were sustained during the work period would be compensable only if an effective cause of the injury was some function or occurrence normally a part of the employee's duties or incidental activities of the employment. This view ruled out many cases which arose during the course of the job but in which the actual cause of injury did not arise from the job.

The courts began to enunciate a rule similar to the zone of danger doctrine which is sometimes applied in the negligence field. They recognize that in the industrial areas and other types of employment, jobs involve bringing the employees to places of danger or hazard. The trend seems to be to compensate for injury which has any connection with work activity.

It is interesting to note that while the Labor Code language seems more restrictive than the rules recently enunciated by the courts, the California Constitution does not require a stringent test for compensability. The Constitution provides that the legislature may—

> ". . . create and enforce a complete system of workmen's compensation . . . and . . . a liability on the part of any or all of their workmen for injury or disability, and their dependents for death incurred or sustained by said workmen *in the course of their employment, irrespective of the fault of any party.* . . ."

Thus, the Constitution contains no requirement that the injury must arise out of the employment or be proximately caused by the employment. The California Supreme Court has defined "regardless of fault" as meaning "regardless of negligence."

Perhaps one of the most controversial cases to be decided by the California Supreme Court was the *Reinert* case in 1955. Miss Reinert was a girl scout counselor at a summer camp. The owner of a nearby riding stable permitted the counselors to ride his horses at a special low price. The girl scout officials encouraged the counselors to take advantage of the special price so that they could become more proficient in their handling of horses and thus more useful in helping the girl scouts in their charge to learn to ride.

At the end of the season, the camp was closed, and Reinert and her supervisor were the last to leave. Just before departing, Reinert expressed a desire to take one last horseback ride at the special rate. This she did. During the ride she was thrown from the horse and severely injured. The insurance carrier denied benefits claiming that the girl was injured while enjoying a personal activity not within the scope of her employment as a counselor. This was not a case of injury during enjoyment of a benefit provided by the employer, for the camp did not furnish the horses or contribute anything to the charge for the horse. The counselors had to pay the charge, and any lowering of the rate was done by the owner of the horses, an act which he was not required to do. The season was over, and the camp closed, so that the ride was strictly a personal act on Reinert's part.

The commission and the Court of Appeals both denied benefits, but the Supreme Court reversed their decisions and granted benefits. The court's rationale was that Reinert was injured while engaged in an activity which was an integral part of the camp program. Further, she had been permitted and encouraged to take advantage of the low-cost riding for training purposes which provided an indirect benefit to the employer.

Over the years, the former commission, the Appeals Board, and the appellate courts have placed common recurring fact situations in categories with descriptive terminology. While the word "rule" is used in connection with some of the terms, they are merely devices used for determining whether an injury is one arising out of and occurring in the course of employment. Additionally, in defining industrial injury, Labor Code Section 3600 sets forth six special defenses. In the following discussion, we take up these special defenses first, then proceed to the other categories.

§ 8.2   Intoxication

An injury is not compensable if it is caused by "the intoxication, by alcohol or the unlawful use of a controlled substance" as defined by H & S 11007. This rule is calculated to discourage drunkenness and illegal use of drugs on the job. It reflects a moral standard of the community that one should not benefit from insobriety. The difficulty with the rule is in its application. The courts have said that whether intoxication caused the injury is a question of fact for the commission to determine. It is not enough to show that the employee was intoxicated when injured; it must be shown that the injury would not have occurred except for the intoxication. *LC 3600(a) (4)*

In one case, a plant worker was injured by falling from a motor scooter. The evidence of intoxication was clear, but the commission found that this fact was not the cause of the accident. The Supreme Court upheld this decision, saying that the commission's (now W.C.A.B.) conclusion on the facts was final.

Another hurdle in most cases is that proof of partaking of alcohol does not necessarily establish legal intoxication, assuming the same test is used as in drunk-driving cases. There are many factors to consider such as the person's size, capacity, and actions.

The employer or carrier who seeks to establish this affirmative defense has the burden of establishing a complete record showing

1. That the employee imbibed an intoxicant;
2. That he was in fact intoxicated;
3. That the intoxication caused the injury.

If the record is conflicting, the employer must convince the W.C.A.B. judge or Appeals Board of the soundness of this position. Should the finding of the Appeals Board be for the employer, this decision would probably be upheld as a factual determination.

§ 8.3   Self-Inflicted Injury

LC 3600(a)
(5)

Injuries which are "intentionally self-inflicted" are not compensable. This provision of the code rules out the individual who may try to obtain compensation benefits by self-help. If a worker causes his own injury, he still may recover compensation benefits, for they accrue regardless of who was at fault or in the absence of any fault. He is denied benefits only if the self-infliction was intentional.

§ 8.4   Suicide

LC 3600(a)
(6)

No benefits are payable if the employee's death was a suicide. This provision was added to the code in 1961. Previously suicides could be found compensable if the injury was the cause of the state of mind which culminated in the taking of one's own life. This addition to the code was undoubtedly enacted to prevent the granting of benefits in such cases. Difficulty in the application of this rule is foreseen, for the code language rules out the case in which the employee has "willfully and deliberately caused his or her own death." The term "willfully" in legal parlance means that the person intended to do the act; it does not connote any particular or specific purpose for the act. The word "deliberately" means that the person thought about the matter, weighed the pros and cons, reached a decision, reflected upon the decision, then proceeded to commit the act. If the injury resulted in a mental condition preventing the forming of a rational intent, the employer would have a difficult task establishing a defense.

A 1960 decision of the Court of Appeal considered the case of a technician who worked long hours under great strain and who took his own life. The court ruled out application of the so-called M'Naghten's Rule of criminal law to compensation cases. (Did he know right from wrong when he committed the act?) The commission must, the court said, determine whether the employee, despite knowing the effect of his act, have the mental capacity to resist the suicidal impulse in view of the mental condition (manic depressive) caused by work pressures. According to a 1968 decision of the appellate court, reviewing a decision of the Appeals Board, the 1960 decision states the correct principle to be applied in suicide cases. These decisions in effect stress the failure of the 1961 amendment to define the type of defense which may be established in such cases. Recent decisions of the California Supreme Court and appellate courts have followed the 1960 decision (*Burnight* case). The courts ruled that if "but for" the industrial injury the employee's mental capacity would not have resulted in the suicide, this death will be held compensable. The W.C.A.B. must make specific findings on the elements defined by the courts. Therefore, if the facts show that the injury affected the employee mentally to the extent that he or she did not have the capacity to resist the suicidal impulse, a compensable case may be found.

§ 8.5 Altercations

Personal disputes between employees or between an employee and the employer are not considered within the scope of employment. Any injuries occurring because of a fight arising from such a dispute are non-compensable. While this is the general rule, the courts have modified it by providing that if the dispute has some connection with the work or the duties of the participants, a resulting injury is compensable, for it is deemed to arise out of the employment, and compensation is payable regardless of the fault of any party.

The 1961 legislature enacted an amendment which provides that the "initial physical aggressor" may not receive benefits if injured in an altercation. This provision raises questions of how one determines which of the participants was the initial physical aggressor; whether there are degrees of initial physical aggression; whether the employer condoned the activity; whether one should foresee the occurrence of altercations under the particular circumstances, considering human propensities; whether there was provocation to the extent of excusing aggression; whether there is a point at which the initial physical aggression ceases to be relevant to the particular injury sustained. Recent decisions indicate that the "positional risk" doctrine is applied in California under which these questions will be resolved in favor of the injured employee. Under this theory, the fact that the altercation resulted from a personal dispute takes on diminishing importance. *LC 3600(a) (7)*

In a case decided by the appellate court, there was a coffee-period free-for-all in which it was difficult to determine the identity of the initial aggressor. The facts indicate that there may have been some "horseplay" preceding the accident. Under these facts, the appellate court determined that the victim of a coffee-scalding incident was not the aggressor and awarded benefits.

But where there is no question as to the identity of the injured worker as the initial aggressor, LC 3600(a)(7) operates as a bar to recovery of benefits, and, according to the Supreme Court, this code section is not in conflict with Article XIV, Section 4, of the California Constitution. This constitutional provision establishing a system of workers' compensation "regardless of the fault" of any person means liability "regardless of negligence" so that the legislature may enact a provision penalizing an employee for an intentional act (as opposed to a merely negligent act) resulting in his own injury.

§ 8.6   Felonious Act

LC 3600(a) (8)   An injury is not compensable if it results from the commission of a felonious act by the injured worker for which he or she has been convicted.

§ 8.7   Recreational Activities

Ordinarily recreational activities of employees are personal matters and would not be the basis for compensation if injuries occur.

LC 3600(a) (9)   This general rule is now embodied in LC 3600(a)(9) which provides that an injury is not compensable if it arises out of "voluntary participation in any off-duty recreational, social, or athletic activity not constituting part of the employee's work-related duties. . . ." An exception to this principle is expressed in the code provision "where [such] activities are a reasonable expectancy of, or are expressly or impliedly required by, the employment."

R 9883   Every employer must post notice that such off-duty activities may not be compensable. Failure to post notice is not deemed to be a waiver of the code provision. The required notice, as promulgated by the Administrative Director is this: "Your employer or its insurance carrier may not be liable for the payment of workers' compensation benefits for any injury which arises out of an employee's voluntary participation in any off-duty recreational, social, or athletic activity which is not a part of the employee's work-related duties."

When a claim is filed asserting an injury while engaged in the described type of off-duty activity, it is incumbent upon the employee to show that the activity was expressly or impliedly required by the employer or supervisor, or that the activity was "a reasonable expectancy of the employment." The issue of whether the employer or a supervisor ordered or "pressured" an employee to participate is fairly understandable. But the issue of whether the activity was a "reasonable expectancy" creates an area calling for interpretation of statutory meaning. Thus far, the appellate courts have defined this term as raising the issue of whether the employer expected the employee to participate in outside activity. The courts say that if an employee subjectively thought he or she was expected to participate, this subjective belief is sufficient to support a finding of compensability if the subjective belief is objectively reasonable under the attendant circumstances. In other words, did the employee think his or her participation was required or expected, and was he or she justified in this belief? It has been held that an employee was justified where one in a supervisory role kept suggesting that she play on the office's mixed softball team because league rules required a certain number of women on a team. On the other hand, it has also been held that an informal invitation to join fellow-employees at a hunting lodge for a weekend did not create a "reasonable expectancy" or a requirement to attend.

In a leading case which rose before the adoption of subdiv. (a)(9), a company picnic was held not to be in the course of employment, because attendance was voluntary and no direct benefit to the employer was apparent. Other cases indicate that a more liberal approach would probably be taken if the same factual situation were before the appellate court today.

If an employer sponsors a program of recreation for his employees, such as a bowling or baseball team composed of employees, injuries from participation would be compensable. The issue may arise whether a particular activity was sponsored by the employer. If he encourages the activity and furnishes equipment for advertising reasons, it will be deemed to be in the course of the participants' employment. Should the contrary appear; that is, the employer furnishes nothing and has no interest in the activity, he would have no liability, even though he may have indicated he had no objection to it or the use of his business name by the employees for team identification.

Under 1965 legislation, one who sponsors bowling teams or other types of sports or athletic activity does not thereby become an employer of the participants, even though he may furnish subsistence and equipment, where the participants are not otherwise employed by the sponsor.

LC 3301
3352

An employer may have a rule prohibiting forms of recreation during work hours or on the employer's premises. If rules are enforced, activity constituting a violation would be deemed outside the course of employment. But should the employer condone violations of such a rule, either expressly or impliedly, the conduct may be considered to be in the course of employment and any resulting injury to arise out of employment. Recently, the California Supreme Court deemed that an injury sustained while the employee was engaged in unauthorized swimming was compensable inasmuch as there was evidence that the employer had condoned such activities in the past. The court likened this situation to the coffee or comfort break. It is therefore apparent that injuries sustained while employees are using recreational facilities furnished by their employers are compensable. In this category are cafeterias, eating areas, patios, swimming pools, recreation rooms.

The appellate courts have also ruled that activities in connection with conventions, dinners (such as a company awards dinner), picnics, and other similar affairs are in the course of employment if attendance is required or encouraged by the employer. An appellate court upheld an award where an employee on a business trip was injured while returning from a visit to a relative's house. This visit had been discussed with the insured's supervisor who suggested that the employee should visit the relative on this trip.

§ 8.8   Employer Assault

In the 1966 case of *Azevedo v. I.A.C.*, the employer struck his saleslady manager in the sacro-coccyx area with his knee, inflicting serious injury. The commission denied benefits on the basis of a 1951 decision of the Court of

Appeal which held that a personal assault by an employer was outside the scope of employment (thus permitting the employee to bring a court action for damages). In *Azevedo*, the court disapproved its previous opinion, reversed the commission, and held such injuries to be compensable under the compensation law. The employer was also declared liable for the serious and wilful misconduct penalty. In a later decision, the Court of Appeal ruled that Mrs. Azevedo could not bring a personal injury action against her employer since he had "secured" payment of workers' compensation benefits. Presumably, the court felt that the right to recover a penalty for serious and wilful misconduct was a sufficient remedy. Subsequent court decisions held otherwise and permitted legal actions against employers guilty of assaults on *LC 3602(b)* employees. Effective January 1, 1983, LC 3602(b)(1) was enacted which pro-*(1)* vides for such suits subject to credit for any workers' compensation benefits received.

§ 8.9   Place of Danger; Hazards; Assaults by Third Persons; Difficulty of Rescue

Injuries sustained in the course of employment from external causes are compensable on the theory that it is foreseeable that employments often bring employees in proximity with circumstances, conditions, risks, or hazards they would not otherwise encounter. Such risks include collapse of buildings, explosions, customers, a customer and a co-employee or employer. Should an employee deviate materially from his duties for personal reasons, however, the attendant risks would not be considered as arising from the employment.

Injuries from assaults upon a worker during the course of employment are compensable under the zone or place of danger principle. However, if the assault (in several cases, murder) arises from purely personal matters not connected with the employment, the injury or death has been ruled non-compensable as not arising from the employment. The assailant is said to have made use of the victim's place of employment as the locale for an act which he or she is bound to do wherever he or she could. But if the employer has become involved in the set of circumstances leading up to the assault, compensability may be found.

Another principle established by the California Supreme Court is that if the circumstances and peculiarities of one's job-duties are such that rescue from the attack-efforts of an assailant is made extremely difficult, a resulting injury may be deemed to arise from employment even though the attack was personally motivated.

Recent cases have evidenced difficulty on the part of the courts and the W.C.A.B. in applying these principles. In several cases, it has been held that if the motive of the attacker was "personal" toward the employee-victim (general victim) rather than as against the employee because of his or her capacity as a representative of the employer (employment-connected victim), resulting injury is not compensable as not arising from the employment. It is the view here that these decisions are incorrect and are contrary to the principles established by the Supreme Court. A stranger who attacks a worker in the course of the worker's employment is a hazard similar to other hazards such as stray bullets, flying glass, or lightning. The "personal" aspect of the exclusionary rule is not the private motive of the attacker but the personal activity or relationship of the employee. In other words, injuries at work resulting from a stranger's attack should be considered compensable unless it can be said that the employee's activity was such as to constitute a material deviation from duty. This approach is illustrated by a 1990 decision of the W.C.A.B. (*Myers* case, writ denied). The Board holds that an assault by a third person having no connection with the employee is compensable, such an assault being deemed a "neutral risk" of the employment. If the attacker is not a stranger but bears a relationship to the victim not connected with the victim's employment, then there is ground for a finding of non-compensability. Even in this latter type of case, the Supreme Court has said that the requirements or peculiarities of job-duties may make possibility of escape or rescue so difficult as to support a finding of employment-proximate cause.

§8.10 Acts of Convenience or Necessity; Coffee Breaks; Lunch Periods

Personal matters to which an employee attends may result in a noncompensable deviation, but the courts early gave recognition to various activities which must be deemed as work-connected. These include rest room visits, rest periods, coffee breaks, getting a drink of water.

An employee is considered on the job if he eats lunch or takes his rest period at the employer's premises. If he leaves the premises he does so at his own risk. Compensation coverage is suspended during his absence from the premises unless the facts show a special errand for the employer or activity for the employer during such a period.

EXAMPLES:

(1) A case was held compensable where the employee was injured while crossing the street to get his lunch from his car. He was also getting a pair of dividers which he used in his job as draftsman.

(2) In another case, a secretary injured herself while stepping onto the curb in front of her employer's place of business. She was returning from a coffee break, and was carrying a soft drink which she was going to give to her employer. There was some dispute as to whether the employer had asked her to obtain the refreshment for him. This case could be explained on the theory that the employer had sent the secretary on a special errand. The employee was granted benefits.

(3) A 1964 Court of Appeal decision makes injuries during off-premises coffee breaks compensable where the employer acquiesces in the conduct.

Here, bus drivers with the employer's knowledge took coffee breaks outside the employment area. The employer had not objected to this practice.

(4) The rearrangement of rest periods or lunch periods may cause otherwise noncompensable activity to be within the course of employment. Thus, it has been held by the Court of Appeal that if an employer permits an employee to work through her lunch hour to make up time previously granted off work, she is acting in the course of her employment while getting sandwiches to bring back to work so that she could continue working. Also, a salaried employee whose lunch hour was extended because she worked through breaks and the regular lunch-period was held to be in the course of employment while off-premises during her extended lunch-break. But in another case in which a lunch-period was extended merely for the employee's own convenience and not because of the needs of the business, the basic rule was applied and an off-premises injury was held to be noncompensable.

(5) An employee who sustains injury while engaged in recreational activities during his coffee break may be considered in the course of his employment if this type of activity is to be reasonably anticipated, as where crews work out-of-doors, and their breaks are taken in open areas. Also, implied permission for such conduct may be present if the employees' supervisors know of such practices and do not object to it.

§ 8.11   The Going and Coming Rule; Parking Lots; Entrance and Exit

While enroute to or away from work, an employee is not considered as being on the job, i.e., is not in the course of employment. This principle is called "the going and coming rule." Under this rule, injuries which occur during travel to and from work are not compensable. This rule also applies to any personal, uncompensated, time away from work, such as unpaid lunch periods. There are exceptions to the going and coming rule which have also been designated as "rules." As to all these "rules," the chief inquiry should always be whether the injury occurred in and arose out of the employment.

Many employers provide parking for employees. An injury on the parking lot is compensable. The theory here involves the consideration of enjoyment of a benefit granted by the employer and the court's conclusion that the place of employment extends to the perimeter of the property owned or controlled by the employer which is devoted to the plant, office, or other business facility.

The "entrance and exit cases" provide another exception. If the employee reaches the entrance of the place of employment and is injured, such injury is within the course of employment. The question of whether the employee has reached the entrance or exit is often a difficult factual issue.

EXAMPLES:

(1) In 1946, the Supreme Court held that an employee had reached the

entrance, because his car was near the gate to the company parking lot when the accident occurred.

(2) In 1965, the Supreme Court went a step further and decided that a case can be compensable under certain circumstances where an employee is injured after reaching a point adjacent to the place of employment even though he has not actually reached the entrance. The circumstances must indicate that the place of employment was an element in the chain of causation. In the case before the court, the employee was injured while driving his car on a public street and in the act of turning to enter the employer's driveway. In granting benefits, the court stressed the fact that in turning the employee's car was lined up with the barn in which he was going to work.

(3) Mary, a cafeteria worker, was accosted late at night as she sat in a co-employee's car which was parked in a lot near their place of work. They had just completed their shift, and Mary's friend was going to drive her home. In trying to elude the robber, Mary ran toward the street, but unfortunately tripped on a defect in the lot pavement, fell and was seriously injured. The employer was a concessionaire who operated the cafeterias for a large corporation but did not control any other part of the premises. The employer defended on the basis of the "going and coming" rule, pointing out that the corporation's parking lot was not that of the employer; that to get to the lot one had to leave the property through a gate, traverse several feet on the public sidewalk, then enter the parking lot; that Mary did not park there, her friend did. All that Mary knew about her friend's right to park on the lot was, "She said that's where she had to park." The decision was rendered for Mary on the basis of the place of danger theory, consideration being given to the area, the time of night, and the right of Mary to be on the lot by virtue of her employment. The commission affirmed the decision after additional evidence was taken from the employer to the effect that the corporation made the lot available to the cafeteria employees.

If an employer changes an employee's work routine so as to affect the time of his return home, a delayed trip may be compensable which would otherwise be excluded under the going and coming rule. Factors to be considered are time element, increase in danger, extension of course of employment and activities condoned or commenced by the employer. The case establishing this principle involved requiring the employee to return late at night to attend a meeting with his supervisor at which alcoholic beverages were consumed.

§ 8.12 Furnishing Transportation

If the employer furnishes transportation to and from work, the employee is covered when he leaves home and until he returns. Sometimes an employer furnishes a car. In other cases of this type, one employee may pick up several in a company car or truck. Compensable cases have also involved use of the employee's car or a co-employee's car where the employer makes some type of reimbursement for its use. An injury suffered on the way to work is not made compensable by the fact that the employer in a union contract has agreed to pay stated sums for public transportation, according to the location of the job-site. Such payments are deemed additional wages rather than the furnishing of transportation. However, if an employee is paid regular wages while traveling, he is deemed to be in the course of employment. Also, where an employer usually furnishes transportation, but makes other arrangements for an employee, the arranged transportation is in the course of employment.

If an employer requires that the employee furnish transportation for the job, an injury while using a car on the job is compensable. But, if the employer has transportation available, and the employee is injured while using his own car because of personal preference, the injury is not compensable.

§ 8.13   Special Errand or Assignment

When an employee is sent on an errand for the employer, an injury occurring during its performance is compensable. The same rule applies to special assignments requiring work after hours or work at home.

Often such tasks are done without specific direction of the employer, but compensation coverage applies if the work is within the scope of the employee's duties and the employer gives his assent to the assignment. In certain categories of employment, such extra effort is anticipated. Again, the customs or usages of the business or trade may be a determining factor.

One common example is the errand consistently accomplished by an employee on his way home, such as mailing business correspondence. Another involves executive, professional, or technical personnel who take a briefcase full of work home as a matter of course. A recent appellate decision has applied this rule to continuing education efforts of employees if a part of a company program and reasonably related to their job requirements or specifications.

If a regulation requires that a police officer be considered on duty at all times while wearing his uniform, and he is injured going to or coming from work while dressed in the uniform, the injury is to be considered in the course of employment. Two recent Supreme Court decisions illustrate this rule. In one case, a Pomona police officer was traveling to a special assignment at the Los Angeles County Fair when he was injured. In another case, the officer was killed while travelling to his own home when struck by a hit and run motorist. The test is whether the conduct is reasonably directed to the fulfillment of the employer's requirements, to the benefit and advantage of the employer. The court reiterates the general rule that one is ordinarily not in the course of employment while travelling to and coming home from work and states that other situations may not qualify under this exception, as where the officer is not in uniform or is engaged in purely personal activities.

Whether or not an assignment is in the course of employment is a question of fact. If an assignment is one of mixed business and pleasure, the courts ordinarily will determine the question liberally to permit recovery of benefits.

§ 8.14   Commercial Traveler

Traveling salesmen or other employees attending conferences, meetings, or training sessions at the employer's direction are covered by the compensation law at all times during such travel. Coverage also extends to travel in the nature of mixed business and pleasure if the arrangement is permitted by the employer. Ordinarily, however, coverage is limited to those acts which are reasonably necessary to the sustenance, comfort, and safety of the employee. Should the employee engage in personal activity not contemplated by the employment which results in injury, it will be deemed not within the course of his employment. Cases will vary according to the requirements of the job, acts permitted or condoned by the employer, or customs and usages in the trade or business.

§ 8.15   Bunkhouse Rule

An employer may provide housing for his or her employees either because of the nature of the job or because of difficulty in obtaining a work force otherwise. Any injury occurring while an employee is in such housing is deemed to arise out of the employment. Since living on-premises or in employer-furnished housing is a condition of employment in such cases, the rationale is that any activity involved in reasonable use of the premises is in the course of employment. However, if an employee engages in personal activity which would constitute a material deviation from duties or which would be contrary to the interests of the employment, he or she may forfeit the protection of the bunkhouse rule.

A recent line of appellate decisions has injected a factor into bunkhouse cases which involve attacks on employees by robbers and other third-party assailants. It was held that resulting injuries did not arise from employment because such attacks were "personal," i.e., the motive of the assailant was directed at the employee, not the employer or the business. However, if an employee is making proper use of the premises and is not guilty of a material deviation from duty, he or she should have the protection of the bunkhouse rule. One of the reasons for this rule is that a requirement that an employee live on-premises makes him or her a "sitting duck" in relation to many types of hazards. (See previous discussion under Section 8.9, *Place of Danger; Hazards; Assaults by Third Persons; Difficulty of Rescue.*) One appellate court has said that, notwithstanding its ruling, if an employee could show that the location of the bunkhouse so isolated him as to make rescue unlikely, he still might be able to make a case for compensability.

EXAMPLES:

(1) In one case, the Court of Appeal held even wholly unforeseen outside causes of injury will not prevent recovery of compensation under this rule. In that case a man and wife were caretakers of property and lived on the

premises. While they were asleep, a boy started a bulldozer which had been parked on adjacent property by a contractor. There was no connection between the work being done there and the property upon which the man and his wife lived and worked. The bulldozer crashed into the couple's apartment injuring them both. The decision of the court granting benefits seemed to combine the bunkhouse rule and the zone or place of danger rule.

(2) Another unusual case dealt with the function of the commission in deciding the question of industrial injury for the State Employees' Retirement System. The employee in the case was a state fish and game warden who was on night duty in a state park. He was assigned a state-owned station wagon to use in his work. On this night he took his girl friend with him. The next day, they were both found in the car dead from carbon monoxide, their bodies being in a state of undress. The Retirement System asserted that the case was non-industrial, because it was clear that the employee was engaged in immoral conduct and thus the injury did not arise from the employment. The court decided for the claimant widow, stating that the employee had been in the course of employment and was killed by an instrumentality used in the job. The causative factor was not the immoral conduct.

(3) In a later decision, the California Supreme Court reached a similar conclusion. The deceased employee was a bank official who was sent to New York on a special assignment. A fire started in his hotel room, and as a result he and a paramour were suffocated. The evidence of immoral conduct was clear. The court granted the applicant-widow the death benefit, holding that there was no evidence the immoral conduct started the fire. This being true, the court stated, this was the same as any other commercial traveler or bunkhouse case. The employee was rightfully occupying the room furnished by the employer. If the death had occurred while the employee was alone, it would be compensable without question. Absent any proof that the presence of the paramour was a factor in the starting of the fire, the immoral aspect of the case was immaterial.

In the last two examples, the courts seemed to resolve every intendment in favor of compensability. Note that these were not cases in which an employee would benefit. Rather, they involved claimants who were the innocent or wronged widows.

(4) A different facet of the problem is pointed up by a 1966 decision. A landlord hired a tenant on a part-time basis to perform certain services on the premises. He was injured while on a personal errand and contended that the bunkhouse rule applied. The Court of appeal said "No" to this assertion, holding that the work was only incidental to the basic relationship of landlord-tenant.

§ 8.16   "Skylarking" or "Horseplay"

The terms "skylarking" and "horseplay" refer to man's innate sense of humor or playfulness which are not always expressed in a harmless or productive way. Injuries resulting from such conduct during working hours are considered not to arise from the employment. Exceptions are made only in the case of any innocent victim or bystander who may be injured when such activity occurs. Cases have involved all sorts of games, races, and practical jokes.

EXAMPLES:

(1) One of the most severe injuries the author has considered in a compensation case involved misapplication of a high pressure air hose to an unsuspecting aircraft worker.

(2) An unusual injury occurred to a part-time bartender from "indian-wrestling." It seemed that he was adept at this sport, and the employer's clientele included many who likewise enjoyed it. It was therefore made a condition of employment that the bartender wrestle any customer desiring a contest of this skill. Unfortunately, the employee met his match and suffered a severe muscle strain. The case was compensable since he was injured while engaged in a task required by the employer.

(3) In a 1967 case, the Court of Appeal upheld a decision of the Appeals Board in an opinion which discusses the bunkhouse rule as affected by the horseplay rule. The two employees involved were apparently both at fault in causing the injury suffered by one of them. Prior case-law is analyzed, and an award upheld on the basis of apparent condonation of such activity by the employer. There is also an indication that such activity was not unusual and could be foreseen by the employer due to the fact that these employees, who were about 16 years of age, were horse handlers, living in a bunkhouse on a horse ranch.

§ 8.17 Work Outside Regular Working Hours

When an employer requires an employee to work overtime, or return to the plant, or perform work at home, injuries occurring in the course of such work are compensable. Questions arise when an employee engages in this type of activity without any direct order or request from the employer. A rule has evolved that if an employee engages in work activity in a particular way, and the employer knows about it and doesn't object, the activity will be deemed to be in the course of employment. In a case that arose some years ago, the court ruled that an injury was compensable where the injured worker had returned to the plant during his off hours to check the operation of some equipment.

Appellate court decisions in New York, New Jersey, and California have applied these principles to work at home and in continuing education situations. In one case, the employee was taking recording tapes home to edit them with the knowledge of his employer. In another, a claims adjuster was taking files home to work on them. In a 1972 California decision, the employee was taking a class after work with the knowledge and approval of his employer. The employer also had a tuition reimbursement program.

These were sufficient facts to bring the activities within the course of employment, including the travel to and from class.

Several recent cases have involved injuries resulting in the course of taking work home. In one case, a teacher customarily took work home but without the approval or requirement by her supervisor. An adequate work area was available at the school, and it was not required that teachers take work home. In this situation the court held that the employee while transporting materials for continuing her work at home was not in the course of her employment and that her injury was not compensable. This holding of the Supreme Court appears to present the general rule for such cases. But, it must be recognized that each case turns on its own facts. There may be variations, as where there is employer-knowledge and condonation of an employee's practice which is beneficial to the employer. Thus, subsequent cases have been found compensable where an employer or supervisor knew of an employee's taking work home and either approved or raised no objection.

§ 8.18   Deviation From Duties

Where an employee is injured during a material deviation from his or her assigned duties, he or she is not entitled to compensation benefits. The employer has the right to expect performance of a job and the following of instructions. This rule is not easily applied in every case of apparent departure from an assignment. One commercial traveler may have a route specifically mapped out by the employer. A side trip taken for personal reasons would take that portion of the travel outside the course of employment. But if the traveler has been given wide latitude on selection of routes, the defense of deviation becomes more difficult to establish. And if the employer encourages or condones a policy of mixing pleasure with business, the activity may then be considered as within the scope of employment. The Court of Appeals also makes a distinction in some cases between unauthorized departure from the course of employment and the performance of duty in an unauthorized manner. In the latter type of case the injury is compensable, but the employer is entitled to a reduction in his liability for compensation to the extent of 50% on the basis that the employee's conduct constitutes serious and wilful misconduct under LC 4551.

EXAMPLES:

(1) The Court of Appeal applied the deviation principle to a case which appeared to involve the bunkhouse rule. Two employees of an American oil company in Saudi Arabia, after finishing their day's work, decided to drive to a beach some distance from the "company town." They were using a company vehicle with apparent permission of the employer. Getting to the beach required going over a sand dune trail off the main road. One dune did not have a slope on the far side, the vehicle dropped several feet injuring the applicant severely. The court's decision ruled out compensability, stating that the employees were not in the course of employment when injured. The per-

sonal purpose of the trip was not a benefit granted by the employer and was considered a deviation from the normal routine on the employer's premises. One may question application of this case to similar situations today in view of the more liberal cases we have discussed. One implication from this decision would be that if the employer's negligence were involved, the employees could bring suits for damages in the courts of general jurisdiction and the employer would not have the protection of the compensation law.

However, a reading of this opinion indicates the displeasure of the appellate court with the conduct of the parties in placing themselves in danger unnecessarily, the court pointing out all of the recreational facilities back at the company town. (Compare this case with the *Reinert* case, discussed earlier in this chapter.)

(2) A case which arose in Riverside County illustrates this point. Workers living on the premises of a company mining operation, drove toward town on their off hours to visit a tavern. Before getting off the property, they were struck by a company train as they drove across the tracks. Their widows brought suit in the Superior Court to recover damages which they claimed to have suffered from the negligent operation of the train. The court determined that because of the bunkhouse rule, the men's injuries were industrial and that the court had no jurisdiction. These findings limited the dependents to their compensation benefits and placed jurisdiction over the case in the Industrial Accident Commission (now W.C.A.B.).

(3) An employee in the course of employment was injured in an accident which was caused by speeding to elude an officer. The Court of Appeal held this not to be a material deviation from duties but rather the performance of duty in an unauthorized manner. Benefits were awarded subject to the right of the employer to seek a 50% reduction on the basis of the employee's serious and wilful misconduct.

(4) Where a messenger took a route back to the plant other than that mapped out by the employer, an injury was held compensable since it was in the same general area of the city, thus not a "material" deviation. It was contended that the deviation was material, because the employee was looking for a place to eat lunch, a personal activity. The court overruled this contention, saying that in "borderline" cases of mixing personal activities with business while traveling for the employer, "no nice inquiry will be made" as to which business he was engaged in at the time of injury, "unless it clearly appears that neither directly or indirectly could he have been serving his employer." This principle was relied upon by the California Supreme Court in another decision involving the case of an employee of a real estate firm. She had previously deviated from her route while viewing property for possible listing, but at the time of injury she was returning to the regular route and was looking for a restaurant at which to eat dinner. The court held that there was no material deviation at the time of the injury.

(5) The U.S. Supreme Court has held that injuries occurring during off-duty recreation outside the working area are compensable under the Defense Bases Act where the employee is subject to 24-hour call, 365 days per year, while overseas. The court applies the "zone of danger doctrine," although it seems to be more of an overseas-bunkhouse rule.

(6) A worker was held to be in the course of employment where he visited relatives while on a business trip, where such visit was contemplated in the arrangements for the trip with the approval of the employee's supervisor.

(7) Injury from an attack and rape of an airline stewardess during a lay-over in Hawaii was held not to be in the course of employment where she accepted the attacker's invitation to go to his apartment in order to change clothes for their later date. This case was decided on the attacker-personal-motive theory, but the correct rationale is that she was guilty of a material deviation from duties.

§ 8.19　　Types of Injuries

LC 3208
3208.3
4663

The code provides that "injury" includes these occurrences:

1. Injury to the body
2. Injury to artificial members
3. Injury to dentures
4. Injury to eyeglasses but only if as incident to an injury causing disability
5. Injury to hearing aids but only if incident to an injury causing disability
6. Contracting or developing a condition classified as a disease
7. Aggravation of a pre-existing disease or condition
8. Psychiatric injury, also referred to as injury to the psyche

§ 8.20　　Traumatic Injuries

The most common type of injury is the traumatic injury. The terms "trauma" and "traumatic" refer to injuries caused by application of force. These forces include blows, falls, cuts, twists, or strains which result in physical damage to the body. The terms are also applied to mental conditions, denoting a traumatic neurosis, hysteria, or other medical condition resulting from a physical injury, from shock, or from an emotional experience.

Repetitive trauma refers to gradual onset of damage to some part of the body caused by repeated activities occurring in the employment. Ordinarily, the incidents would not be sufficiently severe to cause injury, but their cumulative effect over a long period causes a condition and symptoms requiring medical attention.

Trauma which might be insufficient to cause injury or which might cause an injury from which recovery would be expected in a healthy person may aggravate or "light up" a pre-existing condition or disease.

EXAMPLES:

(1) During the course of his work, an employee had an idiopathic seizure, fell to the floor and sustained bodily injuries. The seizure itself was not work-connected. Compensation was awarded for the bodily injuries, and the award was upheld on appeal. The Supreme Court stated that when one falls against or strikes an object at the place of employment (here the floor), there is sufficient causal connection to render the case compensable.

(2) Where strain and tension caused, or aggravated, a present condition resulting in a stroke, it was held to be an industrial injury.

(3) The Court of Appeal upheld the commission (now W.C.A.B.) in a physical labor-heart case which was found compensable. Five of the six doctors reporting on the matter were of the opinon that the heavy labor performed by the employee aggravated his arterio-sclerotic condition. The rating was 70% based on limitation to sedentary labor; however, the commission attributed only one-fourth of the disability to the injury. Since there was conflicting evidence on the issue of apportionment, the commission's finding was affirmed.

Regarding aggravation by mental or emotional strain or stress, the most recent appellate court decisions establish the principle that a compensable condition need not be the result of stress due to some "unusual" or "extraordinary" event or type of work. Some of the older cases seemed to stand for the opposite proposition. However, it is now well-settled that the pertinent question in a case of this type is whether there were stresses which did affect an employee physically, mentally, or psychologically, thereby resulting in disability. If the medical evidence requires an affirmative answer, the case is compensable, even if the work-activity was usual or ordinary. This principle is applicable in various kinds of cases, especially those involving heart, vascular, or psychological injuries.

(5) Stomach trouble resulting from an emotional stress or strain brought about by working conditions is compensable and may result in a permanent disability rating if the employee must avoid further emotional stress or strain. Even though the evidence may not make out a case of bodily injury caused by mental stress, it may sustain an award based on aggravation of a neurosis. For instance, although in a case before the Court of Appeal the court held that while the record did not support a finding of an industrial heart condition, it did support a finding of "cardiac neurosis."

(6) Repetitive trauma consisting of cumulative back strains or work activity which gradually worsens the employee's back condition is an injury of the occupational disease type and is compensable.

§ 8.21   Mental Disorders

LC 3208
3208.3
4663

Mental disorders are recognized as industrial injuries if caused or aggravated by an industrial physical injury, a so-called "traumatic experience," or factors inherent in the work environment. Permanent disability benefits may be awarded in such cases as justified by the medical evidence. (See Chapter 6, PERMANENT DISABILITY, § 6.14, *Specific Disabilities and Standard Ratings*, item 1.) Effective as to injuries occurring on or after January 1, 1990, a "psychiatric injury" is compensable if it is a mental condition which causes disability or need for medical treatment and is diagnosed pursuant to procedures promulgated under LC 139.2(i)(4). Further, in order to establish compensability of a psychiatric injury, an employee must demonstrate by a preponderance of the evidence that "actual events of employment" were responsible for at least 10 percent of the total causation from all sources contributing to the injury. Legislative intent is expressed that this criterion is to establish a "new and higher threshold of compensability" for psychiatric injuries. The Industrial Medical Council establishes procedures for determining the compensability of psychiatric injury in a manner compatible with the provisions of LC 3208.3. A diagnosis of a mental disorder must be expressed using the terminology and criteria of the American Psychiatric Association's Diagnostic and Statistical Manual of Mental Disorders, Third Edition, Revised, or other psychiatric diagnostic manual generally approved and accepted nationally by practitioners in the field of psychiatric medicine.

Effective July 17, 1991, LC 3208.3 has been amended by adding subdivision (d) which establishes another limitation on psychiatric injury claims. It provides that notwithstanding any other provision of law no compensation is payable for a psychiatric injury unless the employee has been employed by the employer for at least six months, either continuously or intermittently. However, this requirement is not applicable if the psychiatric injury is caused by "a sudden and extraordinary employment condition as distinguished from a regular and routine event." A "regular and routine event" includes, but is not limited to, lawful, non-discriminatory, good faith personnel actions, such as, discipline, work evaluation, transfer, demotion, layoff or termination. Further, the requirement of six months' employment does not apply in the case of a psychiatric injury which occurs in connection with any physical injury. LC 3208.3(d) by its terms may not be construed to authorize an employee or dependent to maintain a lawsuit (action in law or equity) against the employer for damages for psychiatric injury.

[NOTE: The proviso in LC 3208.3 that legislative intent in the enactment of the section is to establish a new and higher threshold of compensability raises the question of the object of the comparatives. It is popularly believed that this section was enacted to overrule the holding of the appellate court in the *Albertson's–Bradley* case which established the so-called "honest perception rule" regarding the industrial nature of mental disorders. Under the rationale of LC 3208.3, there must be one or more actual events at work comprising at least 10 percent of the total causation of a mental disorder for there to be a compensable industrial injury. In the *Albertson's-Bradley* case, the court held that mental or psychological disability resulting from asserted job stress is compensable even where the employee's reaction to events at work is purely subjective and the result of a mistaken belief of job harrassment. The court recognized the difficulty such a rule could generate. The court also noted the concerns of the W.C.A.B. that such a holding not be taken as precedent for making every "after-the-fact rationalization" compensable. The court does hold that the record must demonstrate a work-related causal connection where such rationalization is apparent, and there were no untoward events at work. The latter type of case is demonstrated by the *Power* case, wherein the Court of Appeal sustained a denial of benefits by the W.C.A.B. In *Power*, the court held that the record, especially the opinion of the Agreed Medical Examiner, supported the Board's conclusion that the asserted depression and overweight problem of the employee were non-work-related but were, rather, due to a "nonpathological consequence of unhappiness with one's life situation."]

§ 8.22 Industrial or Occupational Disease— Special Exposure

"Disease" is a very general term and may include any condition which adversely affects good health. More particularly it is considered as including conditions other than traumatic, but this differentiation is often inconclusive. If a nurse contracts polio or tuberculosis from a patient, she has sustained an occupational disease-injury. However, inflammation of a carpet-layer's knees from constant kneeling, a repetitive trauma, is also considered an occupational disease. Toxic poisoning from industrial chemicals is a disease. So also is silicosis which is a lung condition resulting from the abrasive effect of silica dust on lung tissue.

A single day's exposure to polio has been held not to be an occupational disease but a single injury involving a contagious disease. The effect of this holding was adverse to the employee, because it meant her claim was barred by the statute of limitations, since the running of the statute began with the date of exposure rather than the date she discovered she had disability from polio. An occupational disease, said the court, is the effect of repetitive exposure or activities as natural to or inhering in the work by a special exposure or risk. The employee lost because of the court's opinion that exposure to polio was not natural to or inherent in the job of recreational director in charge of a group of children. This case seems to be an exception to the trend which is illustrated by the cases discussed next.

In 1946 the California Supreme Court held in an occupational disease case that when the employee's exposure was in successive employments, any *LC 5500.5* of the employers could be held liable for the entire condition. The employer would then be entitled to obtain contribution on a pro rata basis from the other employers according to periods of exposure. This principle was then codified as LC 5500.5. A 1952 decision of the Supreme Court applied this principle to a case of continuous strain and tension in several employments which resulted in a stroke. In 1959, the Court of Appeal rendered the decision mentioned above which brings back injuries within the definition of occupational disease where the condition is the result of cumulative back strains or activities. More recent decisions have solidified the principle that this type of injury is an occupational disease in all aspects including apportionment of liability among employers under LC 5500.5 and determination of date of injury.

By commission (now W.C.A.B.) decision, acoustic trauma; i.e., hearing loss from industrial noise, is also considered in this category.

More recent decisions of the W.C.A.B. and the appellate courts have expanded on the types of conditions which may be considered as being "work-connected," particularly in the area of mental and emotional stress resulting in either physical or mental disabilities.

"Special exposure" refers to the rule that if the disease in question is one to which everyone is exposed in daily activities, whether at work or elsewhere, the employee may not recover workers' compensation benefits unless he has undergone an exposure particularly related to his work. We all are subject to colds, virus, polio, measles, and other contagious diseases. That symptoms come on or appear during working hours does not establish a compensable case. It must be shown that the job put the employee in a situation of increased exposure to contagion. Nurses can show special exposure to a variety of diseases in their contacts with patients. Agricultural workers in several Southern California areas can show special exposure to San Joaquin Valley Fever (Coccidiomycosis), caused by organisms which lie dormant in the soil and enter the body through the breathing of dust when the ground is disturbed.

Special exposure may consist of increased contact with the elements because of the employment. We refer to such activities as working in the windy, rainy, or cold weather which tends to increase one's susceptibility, or lower one's resistance, to the effects of disease. It has been held that a teacher's increased susceptibility to germs carried by students justified granting her a disability retirement.

§ 8.23   Occupational Disease; Cumulative Trauma; Apportionment Among Employers

LC 5412

This area of the law presents questions such as: Which of successive employers are liable? What is the date of injury? What compensation rates apply? When does the statute of limitations start to run? These questions are answered by a determination whether successive injuries, repetitive trauma or exposure constitutes an "occupational disease" or separate and distinct injuries.

LC 5412 and 5500.5 now specifically include cumulative trauma (CT) and occupational disease in the same category. Thus, in determining date of injury in order to ascertain which law and benefits apply and to fix liability, the provisions of LC 5412 are applicable to occupational disease and cumulative trauma cases. This section defines date of injury in such cases as that date when the employee was disabled and at the same time knew or should have known that his or her condition was due to exposure, stress, or repetitive trauma in his or her present or prior employment. However, it has been held by the courts that the determination of earnings for computing compensation payable is to be based upon those earnings during the time of actual exposure rather than any later earnings when not subject to such exposure. This principle accords with the further holding of the W.C.A.B. and appellate courts that actionable exposure must be shown to have been "injurious exposure." That is, it is not enough to fix liability that a potential exposure was existent at the workplace. The facts must show that there was actual exposure and that this exposure caused or aggravated the employee's condition. Thus, the burden of proof involves showing that there was a deleterious substance or stress at work; that the employee did in fact undergo exposure to the substance or was in an emotional or physical stress situation; that such exposure did in fact relate causally to the worker's asserted injury or disability.

To abrogate appellate decisions permitting the inclusion of specific injuries within the finding of exposure or stress in repetitive trauma cases, the *LC 3208.1,* legislature enacted LC 3208.1, 3208.2, and 5303 which prohibit such action *3208.2* by the W.C.A.B. This legislation also was designed to remove employee *5303* knowledge as a condition regarding date of injury in repetitive trauma cases. Subsequent decisions of the Supreme Court have limited the effect of these code sections in holding that since repetitive or cumulative trauma is an occupational disease, the LC 5412 definition of date of injury is controlling; that the sections merely require separate decisions as to specific injuries.

Procedurally, in filing for a W.C.A.B. hearing, an applicant suffering an *LC 5500.5* occupational disease or cumulative trauma may elect to proceed against any employer in whose employment there was stress or exposure resulting in the particular disability. The W.C.A.B. is required to issue a decision placing all the liability on the employers (or their insurance carriers) so joined in the action. Any employer or carrier so held liable may then request subsequent proceedings to join other employers so that this liability can be apportioned among the employers on the basis of periods of stress or exposure. This procedure permits an award without undue delay in providing benefits and merely defers sometimes lengthy procedures in discovering, joining, and hearing the contentions of employers regarding appropriate apportionment.

Apportionment of liability among employers or insurance carriers is now limited to those employments during the one-year period before the date of injury or the date of last exposure to the hazards of occupational disease or cumulative trauma. As previously indicated, "last exposure" has been construed to mean "last injurious exposure." This one-year limitation has been in effect beginning January 1, 1981, and applies to claims filed or asserted on or after that date. This provision is the culmination of a legislative effort begun in 1974 to simplify the procedure in this type of case and reduce the delays which occurred in endeavoring to ascertain and possibly join as defendants other employers and carriers. An applicant has had the right of election as mentioned earlier since 1959. However, the legislature deemed procedures still too complex and, effective January 1, 1974, reduced liability under LC 5500.5 to exposures during a five-year period. In 1977, effective January 1, 1978, an amendment was enacted setting up a schedule of decreasing periods for assessing liability. Therefore, as to claims filed or asserted according to the dates listed below, apportionment is limited to the period of time indicated for each date. The periods are counted either before the date of injury or the date of last injurious exposure, which ever occurs first:

> January 1, 1978—4 years
> January 1, 1979—3 years
> January 1, 1980—2 years
> January 1, 1981—1 year

In this respect, subrogation rights accrue to those held liable as against an uninsured employer, and protection is provided where a self-insured employer sells a place of work, and the buyer retains substantially all of the employees. This provision will be in effect until 1986.

The principles governing the apportionment of liability in occupational disease and cumulative trauma cases also apply to the situation where an employer has several workers' compensation insurance carriers. The employee has the right to elect to proceed against any one or more of such carriers.

LC 5275 (a)(2) 5273(b)(2)   Effective January 1, 1990, the issue of contribution under LC 5500.5 is subject to arbitration proceedings if the employee is represented by an attorney. Costs of arbitration in such cases are borne by the parties litigating this issue. (See Chapter 14, PROCEDURE.)

LC 5005   Under legislation effective January 1, 1975, an employer and employee may settle an occupational disease claim without affecting the employee's right to proceed against other employers. The extent of the liability of the employer released under the settlement must be taken into consideration by the W.C.A.B. in determining liability of other employers.

LC 5500.6   As to injuries under the homeowners' coverage, which became effective on January 1, 1977, if a claim involves an occupational disease, apportionment is limited to employers for whom the employee worked on the last day of exposure or cumulative trauma. If no such employer had compensation insurance, the last employer for whom the employee actually worked shall be liable. This provision does not, however, rule out apportionment of disability to non-work-related causes or disability previously compensated for under the workers' compensation law.

§ 8.24   Treatment as Aggravation; Secondary Injuries

If the medical treatment provided aggravates the injury, whether or not negligence is involved, the employee is entitled to benefits for the resulting condition. If the practitioner is guilty of malpractice, the employee may recover damages in a third-party suit. Of immediate interest to the employee is that he or she is entitled to workers' compensation benefits where treatment or other causative factor connected with treatment results in a worsening of the industrially caused condition or results in another condition complicating treatment or adding to disability. Any suit for malpractice against a doctor or other medical provider is subject to limitations discussed in Chapter 12, DAMAGE SUITS-SUBROGATION, Section 12.14, *Medical Treatment—Malpractice*, both as to extent of recovery and limitations on any lienclaim of an employer or workers' compensation insurance carrier. If the medical provider involved is the employer, the employee faces the limitations discussed in Chapter 12, under the topic in § 12.11, *Actions Against Employers*.

In a similar vein, it has been established that injuries secondary to the industrial injury are compensable where there is a sufficient causal relationship. In one case, the carrier's doctor told his patient to get out and be more active so as to improve vision in an injured eye. The employee amputated a finger while cutting wood with a power saw. The court held that the fact that he couldn't see well and that he was following the doctor's advice was sufficient causal connection with the original injury. Other compensable cases have involved injuries resulting from weakness of an injured limb and accidents occurring en route to medical treatment for industrial injuries. Drug addiction resulting from treatment has been deemed to be an extension of the injury in many cases. Even though an employee's personality or emotional problems may also contribute to a drug addiction problem, if the addiction would not have materialized but for the injury and the medical treatment furnished in the form of prescription of certain drugs, the employee is entitled to recover based on the addiction and attendant problems.

The California Supreme Court has held that where the employer requires an employee to present a work-return release from the treating physician, the act of the employee in bringing that slip or report to the supervisor arises out of and occurs in the course of employment, and, therefore, an injury in that effort is compensable. Where the treatment involved was rendered in connection with an industrial injury, such an injury is considered secondary to the original injury.

§ 8.25 Medical Evidence of Injury

It bears repeating at every opportunity that the heart of a claim or a defense to a claim is the medical file. It requires medical proof to connect a condition or disability with some activity in the course of employment. Even where certain presumptions apply, medical proof that the condition exists is required. A good medical report is one which relates to the factual situation at hand and is not based upon mere surmise and conjecture. The California Supreme Court has said that a medical opinion without a complete history of injury is a mere hearsay. As such, it is not entitled to weight if other medical evidence includes a correct history. It is especially significant if injury is an issue, and applicant's testimony regarding the occurrence of an injury and subsequent disability is corroborated by other evidence. For example, the Supreme Court characterized a medical report as being unsupported by the facts where the independent medical examiner indicated that the fall did not precipitate the employee's symptoms because he did not seek medical assistance for two months after his fall. The report did not indicate why this was necessarily true or offer any cogent reason for the employee's back condition which required surgery.

§ 8.26   Presumption of Injury

The circumstances of the occurrence of an injury may give rise to an inference or presumption that it was work-connected. If an employee is working under a highly dangerous condition, and if there is a death under circumstances which raise the inference of a causal connection, in the absence of evidence to the contrary, it will be presumed that the dangerous condition was the cause of death. For instance, in a case involving work around a charged electric capacitor, the employee was found dead near the capacitor. The capacitor had been discharged. There was no evidence to rebut the inference that the death was caused by electrocution. The appellate court held that these facts raised a presumption that discharge of the capacitor caused the death.

§ 8.27   Presumption of Injury for Law Enforcement Officers

LC 3212-3212.7 3213

The code provides that as to various law enforcement officers, certain disabling conditions are presumed to result from an industrial injury. These presumptions are not conclusive, however, and may be countered with other evidence. However, a public employer is limited in the type of evidence which may be offered in presumption cases in view of recent decisions of the appellate courts. The cited code sections contain a provision that a presumption-disability "manifesting itself in such cases shall in no case be attributed to any disease existing prior to such development or manifestation." A 1965 decision held that this language prevents apportionment of permanent disability to prior disease. Decisions rendered in 1968 go further and construe the limitation as preventing evidence of any pre-existing disease to rebut the presumption. In other words, a medical report which states that all of an officer's disability is due to underlying pathology and was not affected by his work is not now considered proper rebuttal to the presumption. The courts recognize that this rule makes such presumptions practically conclusive, but hold that the employer is still free to prove that non-occupational effort or tension caused or aggravated the employee's condition. Assuming an employer is able to present permissible rebuttal evidence, the Appeals Board may consider it and the presumption in determining the question of causation. In the absence of any such evidence, the presumption is controlling. For the presumption to be operative, however, the medical report must show that the employee does suffer a heart condition. Where the medical evidence is to the effect that the employee does not have heart difficulties but does have a psychoneurotic syndrome described as "cardiac neurosis," the presumption of heart injury is not applicable. There is also an indication in one appellate decision that if the condition had manifested itself before employment as a police officer or fireman, the presumption might not apply, or the employer might be entitled to an apportionment based upon medical evidence.

Since it is sufficient if the condition either manifests itself or develops during employment, LC 5412 permits an officer or former officer to file an application when he knows or should know of such manifestation or development (*Soby* decision). In response to the *Soby* decision, the Legislature amended LC 3212-3212.7, 3213 to provide that where a worker has terminated or retired from his employment in one of the positions covered by these code sections the applicable presumptions continue to be effective for three additional months for each year of employment in such a position not to exceed a total of 60 months. Also, because this is a limitation on the principle announced in the *Soby* case, the Legislature also adopted LC 4458.5 which *LC 4458.5* guarantees to such employee earnings at the maximum level for computing compensation benefits.

The Court of Appeal in two cases has ruled that hypertension without any evidence of heart pathology or difficulty does not give rise to a presumption of "heart trouble." Therefore, for the heart trouble presumption to be applicable, it is necessary that there be medical evidence showing that the heart has been affected.

The officers and the conditions which are presumed industrial are:

Deputy Sheriff	—	hernia, pneumonia, tuberculosis, heart trouble
Police Off.	—	" " " "
State CI&I and Narcotics Off.	—	" " " "
Dist. Atty. Investigators	—	" " " "
Firefighters	—	" " "
Fish and Game Warden	—	" " "
Foresters	—	" " "
Univ. Cal. Firefighters	—	" " "
Highway Patrol	—	" "
Univ. Cal. Police Off.	—	" "

State Police Off.	—	”	”
Dept. of Corr. (Custodial)	—		”
Youth Auth. (Grp. Spvr.)	—		”
Atascadero Hospital (Sec. Off.)	—		”

The heart trouble and pneumonia presumptions do not apply to certain of these officers until they have served in their jobs for five years. Officers subject to this proviso are city policemen, sheriffs and deputy sheriffs, highway patrol officers, district attorney investigators, University of California policemen. Also, the duties of all the officers shown in the above chart must be in the active law enforcement or active firefighting category. The presumptions do not apply to "those whose principle duties are clerical or otherwise do not clearly fall within the scope of active law enforcement service such as stenographer, telephone operators, and other office workers. . . ." The Court of Appeal has held that identification technicians are not engaged in active law enforcement work; but a bulldozer operator engaged in actual fire suppression work qualifies as a firefighter.

LC 3600.3
GC 18300
50921
55634

Various sections of the Labor Code and Government Code extend coverage of the workers' compensation law to situations wherein law enforcement or firefighting personnel are called into active duty during their regular off-duty hours, or pursuant to cooperative agreements for assistance or because of emergencies in areas outside their regular jurisdictions. Thus, coverage is provided while performing as such officers anywhere in the state. [NOTE: Per LC 3352, 3366, 3367, a law enforcement officer of an adjoining state, temporarily deputized to work under the supervision of a California peace officer, is excluded from coverage under the California workers' compensation law.]

§ 8.28   Cancer Presumption—Firefighters, Peace Officers

LC 3212.1

In addition to the presumptions shown above for firefighters, active firefighting members of fire departments have been granted a disputable presumption that any cancer developing or manifesting itself is work-connected, but the presumption only arises where a firefighter can prove that he or she was exposed to a known "carcinogen" in the line of duty and that it "is reasonably linked to the disabling cancer." The Court of Appeal has ruled that if an employee cannot prove that his or her cancer condition is "reasonably linked" to such exposure, the presumption does not apply. "Carcinogen" means a substance so defined by the International Agency for Research on Cancer or as defined by the director. Those having the benefit of this presumption, subject to the conditions noted, are firefighting members of fire departments of cities, counties, public districts, municipal corporations, or political subdivisions; also, the University of California, the California State University, and the California Department of Forestry. The presumption applies to these firefighters whether volunteers, partly paid or fully paid. [A statutory provision which would have cancelled this presumption in 1989 was repealed by 1987 legislation. Thus, the presumption continues in force unless further action is taken by the legislature.]

Effective January 1, 1990, the above-described presumption regarding cancer applies to peace officers, as defined by PC 830.1 and 830.2(a), who are primarily engaged in active law enforcement activities.

This presumption is extended to a firefighter or peace officer following termination of service for a period of three months for each full year of active firefighting or active law enforcement duties, not to exceed a total extension of 60 months.

Chapter 9
PENALTIES

§ 9.1 Introduction

Many of the provisions already discussed include penalties for non-compliance. An employer's failure to provide adequate medical treatment may subject him to loss of medical control and payment of medical costs much higher than those available to the employer or carrier under the medical fee schedule. We have seen that the employee is penalized if he unreasonably refuses treatment or examination or if the injury is wilfully self-inflicted. In another chapter we will discuss the detrimental effects of not filing an application within the time limits provided by law. The penalties discussed in this chapter are those specifically set forth in the code or the rules as penalties which may affect compensation benefits awarded or result in criminal prosecution.

§ 9.2 Penalties for Non-Insurance

As indicated in Chapter 3, INSURANCE, every employer must "secure" payment of workers' compensation benefits, and there is a host of penalties which may result for a failure to do so in one of the ways provided by the law. An employer who has not "secured" workers' compensation obligations through insurance or permissible self-insurance is deemed illegally uninsured and presumed to be wilfully uninsured unless such an employer can show bona fide efforts to obtain insurance coverage or otherwise comply. These penalties would not apply to homeowners and occupants in connection with home-related or personal service because in most cases their obligation ordinarily arises only if they have a comprehensive personal liability insurance policy. But since the legislature has provided for liability where terms of *LC 3715(b)* employment exceed the conditions of exclusion of casual labor, domestic service, and part-time gardeners, there is the possibility of some penalties in these situations.

LC 3706-3732   Possible penalties for illegal uninsurance include:

-Prosecution for misdemeanor

-Damage suit and presumption of employer-negligence

-Administrative order or court injunction stopping business operation

LC 4554   -A 10% penalty on award for compensation

LC 4555   -Payment of applicant's attorney's fee

-Attachment of property

-Penalties and collection action by Administrative Director on behalf of employee and the Uninsured Employers' Fund

-A possible additional 10% penalty or penalties on compensation awarded for failure to provide or delay in providing benefits

(For additional discussion, see Chapter 3, INSURANCE, § 3.19, *Failure to Insure; Uninsured Employers' Fund.*)

§ 9.3   Failure to Inform Employees

The workers' compensation law contains numerous provisions requiring employers to provide their employees with information about their rights under this law. These notices are discussed in other chapters and we list here but a brief summary of penalizing consequences where such notices are not given.

LC 3550-3552   • Failure to post notice of compensation insurance carrier, or notice of self-insurance, name of claims person and list of benefits:

-Loss of medical control at the outset

-Possible misdemeanor prosecution

-Presumption of non-insurance

(These penalties are not applicable to home-owners or occupants' coverage.)

- Failure to notify injured worker or claimant of rights under workers' compensation, status of claim or payments: *LC 3551, 5402*

    -Extension of statute of limitations *R 9810-9882*

    -Re rehabilitation rights, payment of rehabilitation temporary compensation retroactively *R 10004(c), 10016(b)*

    -Possible 10% penalty if failure to give notice results in delay of benefits *LC 5814*

    -Enforcement by Administrative Director *R 9816*

§ 9.4 Employee's Failure to Notify Employer

When an employee (or dependent) fails to notify his or her employer of an injury, claim of injury, reason for being off work, or other pertinent information, he or she may suffer loss or delay in receiving benefits. Here are some of the ramifications:

- Failure to report injury or claim;

    -Employer's possible defense of prejudice for lack of notice *LC 5403*

    -The bar of the statute of limitations *LC 5400-5412*

    -Loss of reimbursement for self-procured treatment

    -No compensation being paid

    -No authorized medical treatment

    -Lack of credibility in making a late claim

- Failure to keep in touch with employer or claims personnel, especially as to change of address:

    -Delay in receiving compensation

    -Delay in receiving reports and notices, especially regarding medical examinations or notices re rehabilitation

    -Misunderstandings re reason for missing work and possible discipline under company rules or union agreement

§ 9.5 Delay or Failure to Provide Benefits

The code in LC 5814 empowers the W.C.A.B. to assess a 10% penalty *LC 5814*
on an award if the Board finds that benefits have been unreasonably refused or delayed by an employer or insurer. Also, effective January 1, 1990, LC 4650 provides for an automatic 10% penalty on any late payment of tempo- *LC 4650*
rary or permanent disability compensation, as discussed later in this topic. The penalty authorized by LC 5814 is applicable only on a finding by the

Board that any delay or failure is unreasonable. Resolution of the question of reasonableness depends upon the circumstances on a case-by-case basis. If the position of the employer or insurer is found reasonable because of a bona fide dispute, as where there is conflicting medical evidence, or there is a bona fide legal issue, the penalty is not assessed. Most contested cases involve bona fide disputes. Thus, usually the 5814 penalty is not sought nor assessed unless the unreasonableness is clear. The issue is present in many uninsured employer cases. If the employer is insured and fails to notify his insurance carrier of a reported injury, any penalty assessed under this provision is payable by the carrier. A carrier is also subject to this penalty if it is responsible for a violation of Section 5814. In the case of an uninsured employer, this penalty is in addition to any penalties assessed for noninsurance. The penalty is computed by taking 10% of all benefits delayed or refused, including medical treatment. Computing earning capacity incorrectly may constitute unreasonable delay. But if there is a bona fide dispute on an issue, this penalty will not be assessed. If an employer or carrier continually delays or fails to provide benefits which are clearly due, the Appeals Board may assess successive penalties until compliance is obtained. However, a previous penalty is not to be included in computing a later penalty.

This penalty is assessed against future benefits awarded in a W.C.A.B. decision. It is not applied to those benefits which the employer has previously paid on a voluntary basis. Where the penalty is assessed, future benefits to which it applies include any future medical treatment awarded. However, if the W.C.A.B. in one decision determines that an employer was guilty of an unreasonble delay or refusal of making temporary compensation payments, and the Board issues a subsequent award for a permanent disability rating, the penalty imposed in the first decision is not to apply to a subsequent decision awarding permanent disability benefits, for the employer cannot be presumed to be guilty of delaying these payments. The record in the second proceeding would have to show that the employer knew permanent disability payments were due and delayed or refused payment.

In the *Gallamore* case, the California Supreme Court has outlined its interpretation of LC 5814. The penalty is to be assessed under the following criteria:

1. Both pre-award and post-award delinquencies are equally subject to the 10% penalty.
2. The penalty is mandatory even where the amount is very small (minimal).
3. Multiple penalties must be assessed for successive delays or failures so long as they are separate and distinct acts of misconduct.
4. The penalty is to be computed by assessing 10% of the entire amount ultimately awarded for the particular class of benefit which has been unreasonably delayed or withheld.

The Supreme Court thus interprets LC 5814 as referring to penalties for various classes of compensation benefits so that the delay or failure to provide a particular benefit such as temporary compensation will not be effective as to other benefits which have not been unreasonably delayed. Further, under previous decisions, the courts have indicated that the penalty is not to be assessed against benefits which have been provided voluntarily. In *Gallamore*, the Supreme Court also indicates that as to the cases involving seemingly minimal amounts of money, the Board may achieve equity through its authority to decide the question of the unreasonableness of any delay or failure in providing a particular benefit.

The 10% penalty is applicable if the employer's medical file shows that the employee has some degree of ratable permanent disability. Payments must be tendered at least to that extent to escape the penalty.

If an employer having knowledge of any industrial injury claim pays unemployment disability benefits pending determination of certain aspects of the claim, no satisfactory excuse is presented for not paying compensation payments. Also, if an award for compensation benefits has issued, but there is a delay or failure to pay the interest on the award as required by law, the 10% penalty is applicable. In order to excuse a delay in making payments, and thus not assess the 10% penalty, there must be a genuine doubt as to the employer's liability for benefits. This doubt must arise from either a medical or legal standpoint (for instance a *bona fide* dispute over the jurisdiction of the W.C.A.B.). But if the record does not reveal any such reason for delay, the penalty must be assessed under the mandatory terms of Section 5814.

An appellate court held the penalty was not applicable where a complex order of the W.C.A.B. required the issuance of several checks, the court being of the opinion that the employer followed standard business procedures. But, if the delay is caused by paying with a draft which is not immediately negotiable as required by law, the penalty is to be assessed.

The Appeals Board has the authority to assess a 10 percent penalty *LC 5814.1* against an uninsured employer to be applied to any discretionary payments made by the Director from the Uninsured Employers' Fund. This penalty is payable to the Director and is in addition to any penalty assessed against the employer under LC 5814.

If a self-insured local public agency delays payment under an award, an *LC 5814.5* additional penalty is to be assessed in the form of payment of a fee to the applicant's attorney for his or her efforts in enforcement of the award.

Effective January 1, 1990, LC 4650(d) provides for a 10 percent penalty *LC 4650(d)* to be paid if any payment of temporary compensation or permanent disability benefit is not made in a timely manner. In the words of the statute, "the amount of the late payment shall be increased 10 percent and shall be paid, without application, to the employee. . ." The penalty does not apply to any payment due before or within 14 days after the employee submits a claim form per Labor Code Sec. 5401. Also, no increase is payable within the 14-day period specified under Sec. 4650(a) if the employer is unable to determine whether the employee is entitled to temporary compensation and gives the employee notice of this fact and also advises the employee what additional information is needed and when the employer expects to have the information. Further, this penalty does not apply if the employee receives wages or salary pursuant to a salary continuation plan paid for by the employer as required by a collective bargaining agreement, memorandum of understanding or established employer policy, not less than the applicable compensation. The accrual of the penalty for such late payments is subject to the employee's having filed a claim with the employer on a form supplied by the employer. (Labor Code Sec. 5401(a), (c).) The "late payment supplement" (as it is denominated in Sec. 5401) is payable "without application." Presumably, this proviso puts the onus on an employer or carrier to pay the penalty voluntarily and differentiates it from the 10 percent penalty under LC 5814 which requires application to the W.C.A.B. for an order or award assessing that penalty. Failure to pay the 4650 penalty when appropriate might subject an employer or carrier to further penalty under LC 5814.

IC 11661.6
(a)
LC 4650
(e), (f)

Beginning January 1, 1991, if an employer is insured, the employer must reimburse the insurance carrier for any penalty paid under LC 4650 if the late payment of compensation is due less than seven days after the carrier receives the completed claim form from the employer. The carrier is to notify the employer of the obligation to reimburse within 30 days of payment and bill and collect the amount no later than at final audit. There is no obligation to pay or collect such amounts unless their aggregate exceeds $100 during the policy year. The notice to the employer must include a notice of the employer's right to appeal the carrier's decision to the Department of Insurance within 60 days. An employer's obligation to reimburse a carrier for this penalty is not insurable.

§ 9.6   Serious and Wilful Misconduct

LC 4551

Employee: If an injury results from the serious and wilful misconduct (S & W) of the employee, his compensation must be reduced one-half. Four exceptions to this rule are set forth in the code.

An employee's serious and wilful misconduct will not result in any reduction of compensation if

(1) The injury results in death or
(2) A permanent disability rating of 70% or more;
(3) The injury is caused by the employer's failure to comply with safety laws or regulations;
(4) The employee is under 16 years of age.

LC 4552

No reduction may be made until the Appeals Board determines that it should be made.

A charge of serious and wilful misconduct on the part of an employee may be brought by an employer if the employee was engaged in some illegal activity at the time of the injury, as where an accident is caused by speeding to elude a traffic officer. But, if the employer condones the activity, he may not rely on this defense.

Employer: Where an injury is caused by the serious and wilful miscon-   LC 4553
duct of the employer, the compensation payable to the employee is increased one-half. Since January 1, 1983, there has been no ceiling on the amount of the 50% penalty. Before that date, there was a limit of $10,000. Costs of suit before the W.C.A.B. may be awarded not to exceed $250.

The W.C.A.B. has ruled in the *Cabarales* case (1989) that in computing the amount of the 50% penalty, the cost of medical treatment is not included. However, in the 1977 case of *Krekelberg*, the Board held that the statutory definition of "compensation" is controlling and that vocational rehabilitation benefits are subject to the S & W penalty by virtue of the LC 3207 definition. In that case, the inclusion of rehabilitation benefits in the computation increased the penalty from $7,911.25 to the then maximum of $10,000.

An employer's liability for the S & W penalty is not insurable. How-   IC 11661
ever, the expense of defending an action for this penalty is insurable. Thus, an insurance carrier may provide a defense for an insured but may not provide insurance for the penalty.

While in the past the appellate courts have given a stringent definition to the term "serious and wilful misconduct," recent decisions have shown a more liberal trend. Under prior decisions, only extreme cases of misconduct would be recognized whether charged against the employee or the employer. When an employer seeks reduction of an injured employee's benefits he must show a course of conduct very nearly equivalent to intentional self-infliction of the injury. By the same token, an employee seeking the 50% increase in benefits must prove that the employer's conduct involved almost an intent to injure or evidenced a reckless disregard for the safety of his employees. An employer has a good deal more exposure to such a claim because of the safety requirements of the Labor Code and the regulations of the Division of Safety, Department of Industrial Relations. Negligence, even gross negligence, does not constitute wilful misconduct.

To define terms, "misconduct" is "bad behavior." "Wilful" means that the conduct was intended. Thus, to be actionable, the conduct must be a serious and intentionally bad behavior. Further, the conduct must be a material cause of the injury. A showing of misconduct is of no avail if it was not a causative factor in the occurrence of the injury.

If an employer knowingly violates a safety order, and the violation is the cause of the injury, it will constitute serious and wilful misconduct. Also, if   LC 6400
the employer fails to provide a safe place to work, as required by law, the   6406

LC 6414   requisite intent may be inferred. (Such a violation is also a misdemeanor.) Since it is usually necessary to prove intent by inferences from circumstantial evidence, the degree of proof of this issue is very high. However, it is not necessary to prove a violation of a safety order if the facts show that the employer permitted a hazardous situation to exist regarding the place of work or equipment used in the work. Where a violation of a safety order has been proven, it is no defense that the state did not enforce the regulation consistently. Nor is it a defense that the employer's safety committee knew of an unsafe practice and did not make any recommendation for a change. If one in a supervisory capacity is responsible for an unsafe condition, such as use of a machine with the guard removed during cleaning operations, the employer is guilty of serious and wilful misconduct even though the practice was a standard procedure in the plant or an industry-wide practice. In a situation of this kind, supervisory personnel take a calculated risk with the safety of the employees for the sake of convenience and may be held for the S & W penalty if injury results.

When a public agency employer is guilty of serious and wilful misconduct, it must pay the 50% penalty in the same manner as any other employer. The assessment is not in contravention of Government Code Section 818 prohibiting the assessment of penalties against a public agency. While called a penalty, this particular workers' compensation benefit merely recognizes that basic benefits do not fully recompense an injured employee, and the S & W penalty merely provides for more adequate compensation to the employee. The court points out that when the Public Agency Tort Liabilities Act was before the legislature, the Law Revision Commission commented that the act was not to affect rights under the workers' compensation law. In reaching its decision the California Supreme Court stated, "Our conclusion that such an award is merely more adequate compensation rather than punishment avoids that result."

Another principle recently announced is that the standards for required safety measures increase in relation to the intensity of the peril involved.

EXAMPLES:

(1) An example of such misconduct would be the caving-in of a ditch because of a failure to install shoring of the sides as required by safety orders.

(2) Another example would be an employer who was shown to have disregarded the safety of his employees by the manner in which he kept the work premises. While negligence does not constitute serious and wilful misconduct, carelessness in maintaining a safe place to work could be so aggravated as to be equivalent to actionable misconduct.

(3) Putting an employee in a situation of grave danger and forgetting his plight constitutes serious and wilful misconduct.

§ 9.7 Employer Misconduct—Findings

The code provides that misconduct is actionable if it is that of: *LC 4553*

(1) The employer or his managing representative;

(2) A partnership, one of the partners, a managing representative, or general superintendent;

(3) A corporation, an executive, managing officer, or general superintendent.

These positions may be called by various names so that one must examine the duties to determine if the violator has sufficient authority to bind the employer. A foreman is not a general superintendent, generally speaking, but if he has the same duties he will be deemed such.

If the misconduct is the violation of a safety order, the award must contain these specific findings: *LC 4553.1*

(1) The specific manner in which the safety order was violated.

(2) That the violation was the proximate cause of injury or death and the specific manner in which the violation constituted the proximate cause.

(3) That the safety order and conditions making it applicable were known to and violated by particular named person, either the employer or person in one of the above categories, or that the condition was obvious, created a probability of serious injury and that the failure of the employer or person in one of the above categories to correct the condition constituted a reckless disregard for the probable consequences.

§ 9.8 S & W Application—Time Limit

A separate application for this penalty is required by Appeals Board *R 10440* rules which must clearly state facts putting the employer on notice that he is *10445* charged with serious and wilful misconduct. Where technically incorrect, an application may be amended to conform to the rule if it contains such notice of the charge. If insufficient as notice, the application may not be amended if the statute of limitations has run. An allegation of gross negligence is not sufficient notice.

The statute of limitations for S & W is 12 months and is not extended by *LC 5407* furnishing of benefits or the filing of an application for normal benefits.

§ 9.9 Settlement of Normal Benefits—Effect on S & W Claim

When the employer's insurance carrier settles the liability for normal benefits, the settlement does not affect the employee's right to pursue an S &

W claim against the employer. The basis for this principle is the fact that the S & W penalty is not non-insurable.

§ 9.10   Cal OSHA

LC 6401.7
6427
6310

Every employer must establish, implement, and maintain an effective injury prevention program. Such a program is to include education of employees in safe work practices. It may include employer and employee safety committees (Labor Code Secs. 6401.7, 6427, 6310).

LC 140-
156
2626.5
6300
6708

The California Occupational Health and Safety Act of 1973 provides for state enforcement of industrial safety regulations which must be at least as stringent as the standards under the federal act of 1970 (OSHA). The state law applies to state and local entity employers (which are exempt from the federal OSHA), except that the civil penalty provisions do not apply to governmental employers. Cal OSHA is enforced by the California Division of Industrial Safety. The Division must include in its safety regulations and enforce the provisions of 1986 Proposition 65 requiring notice to persons in any place of work of any chemical "known to the state" to be a cause of cancer or reproductive toxicity.

§ 9.11   Illegal Hiring of a Minor

LC 4557

If the injured employee is under 16 years of age and was illegally employed at the time of his injury, compensation shall be increased 50%. (This penalty does not apply if the employer is the State or any of its political subdivisions or districts.)

The employer can escape the penalty if he can show that he employed the minor on the basis of a birth certificate, driver's license, or other reasonable evidence that the minor was over 15 years (sic) of age at the time. This defense is good even though the minor employee falsely obtained such evidence.

Because of this penalty and possible criminal sanctions, it behooves every employer to double-check the age of any minor employee. If the minor is a student, he should present a work permit from his school principle. Whenever a doubtful situation appears, the employer can contact the Division of Industrial Welfare, Department of Industrial Relations. This penalty is not insurable.

§ 9.12   Discrimination Because of Claim

LC 132a

It is the declared policy of the state of California that there should be no discrimination against workers who are injured in the course and scope of their employment. Implementing this policy is LC 132a which contains several enforcement provisions including both criminal and civil penalties.

Any employer is guilty of a misdemeanor if the employer discharges, threatens to discharge, or in any way discriminates against an employee because he or she has filed or made known his or her intention to file an application for adjudication, or because the employee has received a rating, award, or settlement. As an additional penalty, the employee's compensation is to be increased by one-half, not to exceed $10,000, and costs not in excess of $250. Any such employee shall also be entitled to reinstatement and reimbursement for lost wages and work benefits resulting from any such discrimination. The W.C.A.B. has jurisdiction to assess the compensation penalty and to order reinstatement and restoration of wages and benefits. Any insurance carrier who advises, directs, or threatens an insured employer to discharge an employee for any of the above reasons is also guilty of a misdemeanor and subject to the 50% penalty and costs.

If an employer discharges, threatens to discharge, or otherwise discriminates against an employee because the employee has testified or made known his or her intention to testify in another employee's case before the W.C.A.B., the employer is guilty of a misdemeanor, and the employee is entitled to reinstatement and restoration of any lost wages or benefits. Should an insurance carrier advise or pressure an insured employer to discriminate in the above manner, the carrier is also guilty of a misdemeanor.

As to injuries occurring on or after January 1, 1990, LC 132a has been modified to include as actionable discrimination related to an employee's filing a claim with his or her employer or an employee's testifying before a workers' compensation judge.

Proceedings for the 50% penalty, or for reinstatement of employment, lost wages and benefits are commenced by filing a petition with the W.C.A.B. However, there is a one-year statute of limitations which runs from the date of the discriminatory act or date of termination of the employee. The Board or the employee may report an alleged violation to the Division of Labor Standards Enforcement or the office of the public prosecutor. W.C.A.B. rules require that any petition seeking relief under LC 132a must *R 10447* separately state violations and set forth the facts upon which any alleged violation is based.

Appellate court decisions construing LC 132a indicate that an employer does not violate this section if an employee is not reinstated where the disability resulting from injury prevents the injured worker from performing the duties of the job—or where, in the normal operation of the business, there is no available job which the employee can do. However, the courts have held that if an injured worker is treated differently from other employees regarding retention, reinstatement, classification, promotion, or demotion, the employer runs the risk of being found to have discriminated. Important in such cases are company rules and union contracts, along with custom and practice and consistency or inconsistency of application. For example, the California Supreme Court held in one case that even though the employer acted in accordance with its right under a union contract, the facts showed a consistent policy and practice of waiving this provision in industrial accident cases. Thus, its action of termination in contravention of this practice was held to be discriminatory. It has also been held (*Barns* case, 1990) that termination is not justified where the employee is still temporarily disabled and undergoing vocational rehabilitation.

§ 9.13   Unsuccessful Petition to Reduce or Terminate Award

LC 4555.5   Whenever a petition to reduce a final award of permanent disability is denied, the W.C.A.B. may require the petitioner to pay any cost incurred by the employee for medical evidence in the proceeding based on the petition. Here the term "petitioner" would mean the employer, insurance carrier, or the Subsequent Injuries Fund, depending upon who filed such a petition. This provision was enacted in 1959 to discourage petitions of this nature except upon clear evidence of good cause to reduce a rating for permanent disability.

LC 4651.3   In the event an employer or carrier unsuccessfully petitions to reduce or
4607   terminate an award for continuing compensation benefits or an award for continuing medical treatment, the applicant is entitled to be reimbursed for
LC 5710   attorneys' fees incurred in successfully resisting the petition. (An employee is also entitled to payment of attorneys' fees involved in the taking of the employee's deposition by the employer or carrier.)

§ 9.14   Unsuccessful Appeals

LC 5801   A similar penalty is contained in the law to discourage employers from filing baseless petitions for writs of review with the courts of appeal. If the reviewing court finds for the employee, or his dependents, and also determines that the petition of the employer had no reasonable basis, the court may return the case to the Appeals Board for the purpose of awarding the employee or his attorney a reasonable fee for the attorney's services rendered in connection with the petition. However, if an employer's petition raises a bona fide legal issue, there is a reasonable basis for the appeal, and attorney's fees will not be assessed against the employer.

§ 9.15   Refusal of Autopsy

LC 5706,   In any alleged industrial death matter, the Appeals Board has the
5707   authority to order an autopsy and, if necessary, an exhumation of the employee's body. If the body is in the possession of the coroner, compliance is mandatory. When the coroner does not have possession, the order cannot be made if a majority of the dependents refuse to allow an autopsy. In the event the dependents refuse, a disputable presumption arises that the injury or death was not compensable.

§ 9.16   Suppression of Medical Reports

R 10622   A party to an Appeals Board proceedings has a continuing duty to file all medical reports in his possession which are pertinent to the case. If wilfully suppressed, any medical report not produced will be deemed adverse to the party possessing it. Also, in litigated cases, the W.C.A.B. has jurisdiction to hold any party or attorney in contempt for failure to file medical reports as required by W.C.A.B. rules.

§ 9.17 Contest of Administrative Medical Findings— Attorney's Fee

Legislation operative January 1, 1991, as to injuries occurring on or after January 1, 1990, establishing administrative procedures for initial resolution of the issues of extent of permanent disability and need for continuing medical care, requires employers or insurers to pay employees' attorney's fees in certain situations. While not denominated as penalties, these provisions create a liability as a consequence of exercising the right to contest administrative medical findings made under the procedure of LC 4061-4067. If an employer or insurer wishes to contest such findings, LC 4061(k) requires the employer or insurer to file an application for adjudication with the W.C.A.B. Under LC 4064(a), if an unrepresented employee desires to contest such findings administratively, he or she may obtain a report from a qualified medical evaluator to rebut the medical report of the first Q.M.E. at the expense of the employer or insurer. Where the employer or insurer files an application for adjudication with the W.C.A.B., and the unrepresented employee has not obtained a rebuttal medical report per that section, LC 4064(d) requires the employer or insurer to pay any attorney's fee incurred by the employee in connection with the application. *LC 4061- 4067*

Where an agreed medical evaluator selected pursuant to LC 4061-4062 renders a report, and the evaluator's formal medical findings are contested by the employer or insurer by the filing of an application for adjudication with the W.C.A.B., "regardless of outcome," the fee for the employee's attorney will be assessed against the employer or insurer. *LC 4066*

§ 9.18 Fraudulent Claims

Effective January 1, 1992, the Legislature has enacted Chapter 116, Statutes 1991, in an effort to eliminate fraudulent workers' compensation claims. Sections of several codes have been amended or added by this legislation. Central to this effort are IC 1871 outlining the need for the legislation, IC 1871.4 defining the crime of making a fraudulent claim or fraudulent denial of a claim for workers' compensation, IC 1872 establishing the Bureau of Fraudulent claims within the Department of Insurance, IC 1872.3 delineating the investigative and prosecutorial functions of the Bureau and IC 1872.83 establishing the Fraud Assessment Commission for determining the employer assessments to be made under LC 62.6 to fund enforcement efforts. Other provisions deal with criminal and disciplinary penalties to be enforced against persons licensed by the state, including medical providers and attorneys, and also against public employees who may be involved in prohibited activity. The use of "runners" or "cappers" in the referral of cases to medical *IC 1871- 1877.5* providers or attorneys is prohibited as is false or misleading advertising related to compensation matters. This legislation also covers the reporting of suspected compensation fraud and warnings concerning possible criminal liability on certain official forms. It is well to keep in mind that this legislation addresses itself to both fraudulent claims and fraudulent activity calculated to discourage claims or deny benefits.

IC 1871.4   The statute makes it unlawful to make or cause to be made any knowingly false or fraudulent material representation for the purpose of obtaining or denying any workers' compensation as "compensation" is defined in LC 3207; to present or cause to be presented any knowingly false or fraudulent written or oral material statement in support of, or in opposition to, any claim for compensation for the purpose of obtaining or denying any compensation; to knowingly assist, abet, solicit or conspire with any person who engages in any unlawful act under IC 1871.4; to make or cause to be made any knowingly false or fraudulent statements with regard to benefits with the intent to discourage an injured worker from claimimg benefits or pursuing a claim. "Statement" includes any notice, proof of injury, bill for services, payment for services, hospital or doctor records, X-ray, test results, medical-legal expense per LC 4620, or other evidence of loss, injury, expense or payment. Violation of IC 1871.4 may be a misdemeanor or a felo-
IC 11760   ny depending on the circumstances and a sentence may include a fine not
11880   exceeding $50,000. [NOTE: Any person who willfully misrepresents any fact in order to obtain workers' compensation insurance at less than the proper rate is guilty or a misdemeanor or felony depending on the circumstances.]

LC 5803.5   Any conviction under IC 1871.4 which materially affects the basis of any order, decision or award of the Appeals Board is sufficient grounds for a reconsideration of that order, decision or award.

LC 5401.7   The forms required by LC 5401, 5401.5, 5401.6 and the reports required
6410.5   by LC 6409(a), 6409.1(a) and 6413 must contain a prominently stated warning. [NOTE: The forms mentioned in these sections include the claim form of an employee or his or her dependents, notice of possible benefits, an application for adjudication, a lienclaim, a request for information served on an employer or carrier, a response to such a request served by an employer or carrier, physician's first report of injury, employer's report of injury, report of a prisoner's injury incurred while performing labor.] The required warning statement is as follows:

> Any person who makes or causes to be made any knowingly false or fraudulent material statement or material representation for the purpose of obtaining or denying workers' compensation benefits or payments is guilty of a felony.

IC 1872,   The Bureau of Fraudulent Claims is to aid in the enforcement of IC
1872.3   1871.4 and may conduct both private and public investigations of alleged violations. The Bureau may utilize administrative subpoenas and testimony under oath. It may cooperate with other agencies including those of other

states. The Bureau's files and records are privileged but may be made public on order of the superior court upon a finding of paramount public interest and non-interference with an ongoing investigation. Such information may be shared with law-enforcement agencies upon request. Funding for investigation and prosecution of workers' compensation fraud is established through employer assessments per LC 62.6 in amounts to be determined by the Fraud Assessment Commission composed of representatives of insurers, self-insurers and insured employers appointed by the Governor. Half the funds are to be allocated to the Bureau and half to district attorneys upon application. A report of the Bureau's activities will be included in the Insurance Commissioner's annual report. *IC 1872.9*

The anti-fraud legislation includes the Workers' Compensation Insurance Fraud Reporting Act. This act requires insurers and their agents to release information relating to specific workers' compensation fraud investigations to authorized governmental agencies upon request. These agencies include a district attorney, the Attorney General, the Department of Insurance, the Department of Industrial Relations and any licensing agency governed by the Business and Professions Code. An insurer having knowledge or reasonable belief that a person has committed fraud relating to a workers' compensation claim and that the matter has not been previously reported to an appropriate enforcement agency must report it to the local district attorney, the Bureau of Fraudulent Claims or other authorized agency within 30 days. The communication (notice) is to contain the basis of the report. This report is privileged and not to be disclosed as a public record. A violation of the non-disclosure provision is a misdemeanor. An insurer or agent complying with this reporting requirement is not subject to any civil action where the report is made in good faith, without malice and with a reasonable belief that the report is required. *IC 1877-1877.5*

The fraudulent claims legislation prohibits false or misleading advertising concerning services or benefits to be provided to an injured worker. By 1993, the Department of Consumer Affairs will adopt regulations governing advertising published or broadcast by both individuals and entities. Specifically, LC 139.43 prohibits advertising, printing, displaying, publishing, distributing, or broadcasting in any manner, any statement concerning services or benefits afforded an injured worker which is false, misleading, deceptive, or omits material information "necessary to make the statement not false, misleading or deceptive." A violation of this provision is a misdemeanor but includes a possible fine of up to $10,000. LC 139.43 does not apply to physicians or attorneys since their conduct is governed by other provisions of law. LC 139.4 permits the Industrial Medical Council to review advertising copy of qualified medical evaluators. If the Council disapproves of any such copy and so notifies the physician in writing, it may not be used. Violation of LC 139.4 is a ground for termination, suspension or probation of a qualified medical evaluator. Regulations regarding advertising are to be adopted by the *LC 139.4, 139.43, 139.45*

LC 139.45
B&P 651

Council, as well as by physician licensing boards and with respect to attorneys the State Bar. These regulations are to address themselves to elimination of advertisements which do any of the following:

1. Contain an untrue statement.

2. Contain any matter in a manner or format which is false, deceptive or tending to confuse, deceive or mislead.

3. Omit any fact necessary to make the statement made, in the light of the circumstances under which the statement is made, not misleading.

4. Are transmitted in any manner that involves coercion, duress, compulsion, intimidation, threats or vexatious or harassing conduct.

5. Entice a person to respond by the offering of any consideration, including a good or service but excluding free medical evaluations or treatment, that would be provided either at no charge or less than market value. No free medical treatment can be offered for the purpose of defrauding any entity.

B&P 810,
2273,
2314,
2315,
6106.5,
6151,
6153, 6154
IC 750-
750.5
LC 3215-
3218

The anti-fraud legislation also adds restrictions on professional conduct of health care professionals and attorneys, as well as claims personnel and public employees. Any involvement in the presentation of a false insurance claim or violation of LC 1871.4 (as discussed above) may result in disciplinary action regarding the licenses of physicians, osteopaths or chiropractors. The employment of "runners," "cappers," "steerers" or other persons to procure patients is unprofessional conduct and a misdemeanor or felony. Similar provisions in the Labor Code make it a misdemeanor or felony when accomplished with respect to a workers' compensation claim. [NOTE: LC 3215-3218 do not apply to physicians or attorneys whose conduct is governed by other provisions of law.]

B&P
6106.5
6151-
6154
IC 750,
750.4

Attorneys may be disbarred if guilty of violating LC 1871.4. Also, any attorney is prohibited from obtaining clients through "runners" or "cappers." In this connection, the latter are defined as persons or entities who solicit or procure business for an attorney or law firm. Any public officer or employee engaging in such activity may forfeit the right to his or her office or employment. It is also a crime for any person involved in the processing, presentation or negotiation of claims, including insurance claims, to refer or procure clients, cases, patients or customers for a consideration; however this provision does not apply to persons or entities acting on behalf of insurers or self-insurers operating within the scope of their licenses or consent certificates; nor does it (or PC 549) prevent an attorney from dividing fees with another attorney or making an unrequested non-monetary gift for a referral or an

PC 549

unpromised employee bonus in line with Rule 2-200 of the Rules of Professional Conduct of the State Bar. PC 549 makes it a misdemeanor or felony to refer any business to an individual or entity with knowledge, or reckless disregard, that the individual or entity intends to violate IC 1871.4.

When the Appeals Board rescinds or reduces a decision or award on the *LC 5908(b)* ground that it was procured by fraud, the Board must refer the case to the Bureau of Fraudulent Claims if the employer is insured. If the employer is self-insured, the matter is to be referred to the district attorney in the county in which the fraud occurred.

The W.C.A.B. may not award a fee for legal services to any representa- *LC 4903* tive in a workers' compensation proceeding who is not an attorney. [Query *5710* whether LC 4906(b), dealing with the approval or setting of fees, should not also have been amended since it recognizes both attorneys and agents as possible representatives of employees or dependents.] Fees for representing an employee or dependent whose deposition is being taken at the request of an employer or carrier are payable by the employer or carrier if the representative is an attorney licensed by the State Bar. [NOTE: It is not made clear in the anti-fraud legislation why these provisions regarding fees are deemed necessary.]

Chapter 10
LIENS

§ 10.1   Introduction

Payment of compensation must be made directly to the injured worker, or in an industrial death case to the dependent or dependents. In the words of the statute, compensation is payable only "to the claimant entitled thereto unless otherwise ordered by the appeals board." An employer or carrier runs the risk of receiving no credit for payments made to the wrong person, even though that person is an agent, attorney at law, or attorney in fact of the claimant. There is also the likelihood of a 10% penalty under LC 5814 if an incorrect method of payment results in an undue delay in paying the proper person. *LC 4902 4651*

Further, a claimant may not assign his or her claim or accrued payments to any other person or creditor before payment. After payment is received by a claimant, he or she may use it as he or she sees fit. To protect claimants still further, the law prohibits the taking of compensation for debts, either by way of attachment or by execution. *LC 4900* *LC 4901*

In this way the code removes compensation from the operation of the usual remedies used by creditors to reach the assets of their debtors. In place of these remedies, the legislature has provided certain creditors with the right to file a lien claim with the Appeals Board. The lien claim must be served upon the employee and the employer or carrier. The Appeals Board provides *LC 4903* forms which may be used for this purpose. The allowance of such a lien by an order of the Appeals Board is the only exception to the requirement that the compensation be paid directly to injured workers or to their dependents. A lien may be allowed only for obligations set forth in LC 4903 which arise after the industrial injury in question. For example, a lien for an alleged overpayment under the uninsured motorist coverage of a vehicle insurance policy may not be allowed since such a lienclaim is not set forth in the section. Likewise, liens for legal services or medical treatment having no connection with an industrial injury may not be allowed. Also, a lien must be based upon an obligation which the employee is legally required to pay by agreement or by a statute other than LC 4903.

The Supreme Court has ruled that in order for a lienclaim to be valid, the lienclaimant must prove that the claim involves a debt or obligation which the employee must pay. The obligation may arise by contract or by a mandatory provision of law. But, if a lienclaim involves assistance, such as certain types of welfare, the lienclaim's allowance depends upon a legal requirement to repay or a specific authorization for a lien.

LC 4903.1
(b),(c)

The parties to a W.C.A.B. proceeding, including the submission of a compromise and release agreement or stipulated award, have the duty to submit all known lienclaims to the Board in a timely manner.

Any lienclaim filed with the Board must be accompanied by a full statement or itemized voucher supporting the lien and justifying the right to reimbursement with proof of service upon the injured worker, or if deceased the worker's dependents, the employer, the insurer and the respective attorneys or other agents of record.

LC 5401
(c),(d)

After an employee or dependent files a completed claim form as required by LC 5401, a lienclaimant may file an application for adjudication with the W.C.A.B. under the following conditions: A lienclaim form must have been filed and served as outlined above. With the exception of lienclaims for medical-legal services per LC 4620-4628, a period of 90 days must have elapsed since the filing of the lienclaim without the filing of an application for adjudication by the employee, the employee's dependents or the employer. Also, the lienclaimant must attach a copy of the claim form filed with the employer by the employee or a dependent of a deceased employee—or specify in a declaration efforts made to secure a copy or to encourage the filing of a claim form.

The W.C.A.B. has ruled (*Lien Collections, Inc. v. W.C.A.B.; Murdock* (1989)) that where the validity of a lienclaim is at issue, and the lienclaimant fails to appear at a regularly noticed hearing, the Board may deny the lien.

§ 10.2   Attorney's Lien

In the event of a dispute over the right of an employee or other person to compensation, the services of an attorney may be necessary. Experience shows that attorneys are retained in about 90% of the cases coming before the *LC 4903(a)* Appeals Board. An attorney for an employee or dependent is entitled to a *4906* reasonable fee for his or her services as determined by the Board. The code provides that a fee set by the Board is a lien on compensation awarded, with the exception of certain ancillary fees which are assessed against an employer or insurer. Principles governing attorney's fees are established by statute, rule, and appellate decisions. Superimposed upon this body of law are the requirements set forth in LC 4906 as amended, effective January 1, 1990, as discussed in the latter part of this topic.

Routinely, attorneys for employees or dependents in workers' compensation cases inform their clients that the W.C.A.B. will set a reasonable fee so that advance payment or retainer is not necessary. If the client makes a prepayment, or if there is some agreement on the extent of a fee, the attorney has the duty of informing the Appeals Board so that it can be considered when the fee is set by the trial judge or panel of the Appeals Board.

When an award is made, a reasonable attorney's fee is determined and is allowed as a lien against the compensation award. "Reasonable" has been defined by the Court of Appeal as meaning on a par with fees charged in other legal matters. Fees should not be excessive, nor should they be so low as to discourage practitioners from representing applicants for benefits. In fixing a fee, the Appeals Board has before it the record made by the attorney, the number of hearings, his or her effectiveness and results. A reasonable fee can be determined on a time or per diem basis using the local bar association's minimum fee schedule. Many attorneys file a statement of time spent on a case, amount of correspondence and legal documents prepared, with any incidental expenses such as travel or investigation. Since the Appeals Board has sole authority in the matter of fees and since any agreement is void if not approved, any additional fee or bonus paid by a client over that allowed by the Board or workers' compensation judge should not be accepted unless it is reported and approved by supplemental order. Any violation of these provi- *LC 4907* sions is ground for disciplinary action by the W.C.A.B. Recently, the W.C.A.B. has exercised its disciplinary powers against applicants' attorneys for "exacting" additional fees from a client and for attempting to obtain additional fees through a small claims action. (The appellate court has ruled that the small claims court has no jurisdiction over matters involved in an industrial injury case.) Discipline of attorneys may be by way of a contempt proceeding.

Fees may be allowed by the Appeals Board for all legal services and incidental expenses or disbursements, including services rendered before the *LC 4903a* appellate courts. Occasionally the attorney will be called upon to appeal a

LC 5801

decision or to defend against an appeal. If the employee prevails in any appeal taken by an employer and the reviewing court finds there is no reasonable basis for the employer's appeal, it must remand the case to the Appeals Board for a supplemental award for legal services for the applicant's attorney.

In the usual case, an award for compensation will include some payments which have already accrued as of the date of decision. The attorney's lien will be assessed against this portion of the recovery rather than against any future payments. If no compensation has accrued, but future payments are awarded, a portion of each installment may be applied to the fee. Another approach would be to "commute" enough payments off the "far end" of the award to equal the fee. Special problems arise where the applicant recovers nothing or is awarded further treatment but no compensation payments. In such cases, the Appeals Board may enter a finding of the reasonable value of the attorney's services which he may use as a basis for billing his client. If it appears that the Board's decision is an interim one, the Board may defer decision on the fee question until the time of subsequent proceedings. The most common case of this type is one which has been brought to hearing before the applicant's condition has reached a stationary point so that the extent of permanent disability cannot be determined.

As a general rule, if an employer is properly insured (or permissibly self-insured), it is error to assess the employer or carrier with the applicant's attorney's fee. However, there are certain situations calling for assessment of fees for an applicant's attorney against employers or carriers as an added benefit or penalty. They are:

LC 5801

1. Where an appeal to the appellate courts is taken by an employer or carrier, the appeal is not successful and the court finds that there was no reasonable basis for such appeal; [NOTE: If an employer's petition for writ of review sets forth a bona fide legal issue, there is a reasonable basis for the appeal, and attorney's fees will not be assessed against the employer.]

LC 4607
4651.3

2. Where an employer or carrier unsuccessfully petitions the W.C.A.B. to terminate a continuing award;

LC 4555

3. Where the employer is illegally uninsured;

LC 5710

4. Where an injured worker's attorney is required to attend the taking of a deposition of the injured worker by the employer or carrier;

LC 5814.5

5. Where a self-insured local public agency unreasonably delays or refuses payment under an award, fees for award-enforcement services.

Such fees are determined by the W.C.A.B. either on its own motion or upon request of the applicant or his or her attorney. The same test of reasonableness applies, and the employer or carrier has a right to notice and a right to be heard before the W.C.A.B. in cases in which such additional fees are requested or ordered.

The jurisdiction of the Appeals Board to award fees for additional legal services continues so long as there is any compensation remaining due or payable to the employee. In a decision of the Court of Appeal, it was held that additional fees are proper for work done by an applicant's attorney in defending an award against efforts of an employer to decrease the applicant's recovery, even though the Appeals Board had lost jurisdiction to grant further benefits or decrease the award.

Fees may also be allowed for services rendered on behalf of an injured *R 9742* worker in proceedings before the Rehabilitation Bureau, in obtaining an in- *9929* formal permanent disability rating, or for participation in proceedings before an Information and Assistance Officer. These fees are set by the W.C.A.B.

The Board applies the "common fund" principle where an applicant's attorney's efforts are responsible for the establishment of a fund against *LC 4903.2* which a lienclaimant's lien applies. Under these circumstances, the Board may require that a lienclaimant pay a portion of the fee for the applicant's attorney. The common-fund principle is embodied in LC 4903.2 which provides for a fee to applicant's attorney from a lienclaimant's recovery where the lienclaimant has received all notices of hearing and a notice of intent to allow such a fee, the lienclaimant has not participated in the W.C.A.B. proceedings, the attorney's services were reasonably required to effect a recovery for the lienclaimant, and the case is not disposed of by way of compromise and release. Any fee allowed is to be based upon the attorney's effort on behalf of the lienclaimant, and the fee-benefit ratio is to be no greater than that applied to the applicant's award. The provisions of LC 4903.2 apply to lienclaims for unemployment benefits under LC 4903(f) & (g), and to medical-provider and wage-loss policy lienclaims under LC 4903.1.

Attorneys' fees for service rendered in matters other than the compensation case are not allowable as liens.

As a general rule, the Appeals Board has no authority as to fee arrangements between employers or carriers and their attorneys. The one exception arises in third-party actions. (See Chapter 12.)

As to cases involving injuries occurring on or after January 1, 1990, *LC 4906* many of the principles discussed above are codified in LC 4906 as amended. In addition, the amendment requires an attorney to furnish a client a written disclosure form. No attorney may demand or accept any fee until the amount has been approved or set by the W.C.A.B. Any fee agreement must be submitted to the Board for approval within 10 days after the agreement is made. In establishing a fee, the Board shall consider the responsibility assumed by the attorney, the care exercised by the attorney, the time involved, and the results obtained. A disclosure form promulgated by the Administrative Director [Disclosure Statement] must be furnished to the client. The

Disclosure Statement must prominently describe the procedures available to an injured worker or his or her dependents. The form is to describe LC 4906, the range of attorney's fees customarily approved by the Board and the attorney's fee provisions of LC 4064, also the extent to which the client may receive compensation without incurring attorney's fees. The form must include the telephone number of the Office of Benefit Assistance and Enforcement along with a statement that the client may receive answers to questions concerning entitlement to compensation or the procedures to follow to receive compensation. A copy of the disclosure form signed by the client and the attorney is to be sent to the employer by the attorney.

R 10987   W.C.A.B. rules require that when a case involving an injury occurring on or after January 1, 1990, is resolved without the filing of an application with the W.C.A.B., and an attorney or agent representing an employee or dependent requests a fee, a request must be filed with the Board on an approved form. The attorney or agent must indicate the activity or activities for which the fee is sought, the nature of the dispute, responsibility assumed, care shown in representation, an estimate of the time involved, and the results obtained. The form is to include an order of approval to be signed by the Presiding Judge or designated judge. A copy of the signed disclosure form must accompany the request.

LC 4061-
4062   As noted above, LC 4906 requires that the Disclosure Statement include reference to the attorney's fee provisions of LC 4064. This section is a part of the legislation setting up administrative-medical initial determination of permanent disability and medical issues. This legislation is effective January 1, 1991, as to injuries occurring on or after January 1, 1990. An attorney representing an injured worker will be involved in the process, and the matter of his or her fee for services will be referred to the W.C.A.B. and be a part of any determination of the adequacy of any settlement or stipulated award per LC 4061(k). In two instances, an employer or carrier will be liable for the fee of an employee's attorney for services required by the filing of an application for adjudication with the W.C.A.B. by the employer or carrier in lieu of furnishing benefits indicated by a formal medical evaluation or rating: (1) per LC 4064(d), where the employee is unrepresented when the application is filed, has not obtained a rebuttal medical report at the expense of the employer or carrier, and incurs attorney's fees in opposing the application; (2) per LC 4066, where an employer or carrier files an application contesting the formal medical evaluation prepared by an agreed medical evaluator (A.M.E.), regardless of outcome. Regarding possible sanctions for involvement in a fraudulent workers' compensation claim, see Chapter 9, PENALTIES, § 9.18, *Fraudulent Claims.*

LC 4903,
5710   The W.C.A.B. may not award a fee for legal services to any representative in a workers' compensation proceeding who is not an attorney. [Query whether LC 4906(b), dealing with the approval or setting of fees, should not also have been amended since it recognizes both attorneys and agents as possible representatives of employees or dependents.] Fees for representing

an employee or dependent whose deposition is being taken at the request of an employer or carrier are payable by the employer or carrier if the representative is an attorney licensed by the State Bar.

§ 10.3   Medical and Hospital Liens

The Appeals Board may grant a lien against compensation for reasonable expenses incurred by or on behalf of the injured employee for medical or *LC 4903b* hospital care. This provision safeguards the rights of those furnishing self-procured treatment to the employee. If the Appeals Board orders reimbursement to an applicant for the cost of treatment, the order may provide for payment directly to the physician or the hospital in question. If a lien has been filed, some workers' compensation judges order such payment in satisfaction of the lienclaim; others dismiss the lien since payment has been ordered directly.

Disputes regarding lienclaims for medical, medical-legal, or hospital *LC 4903.4* expenses are to be resolved in a separate proceeding which may include binding arbitration upon agreement of the parties including the employee if he or she remains a party to the dispute. This procedure applies to injuries occurring on or after January 1, 1990.

If the employee is denied recovery for self-procured treatment, the lien for treatment may be assessed against any compensation which may be awarded. The lien right may be exercised by any practitioner coming within the definition of "physician" as contained in LC 3209.3 (Chapter 4, MEDICAL TREATMENT). [NOTE: If a provider of medical services has knowledge that an employee has filed a claim of injury with the employer *LC 3751(b)* under LC 5401, the medical provider may not collect money directly from the employee unless the provider obtains a written notice of rejection of the claim by the employer and has furnished the employee a copy of the notice. Any medical provider who violates this provision of LC 3751(b) is liable for three times the amount collected.

Most private medical plans or insurance policies exclude benefits for industrial injuries and have subrogation rights in the event they have provided treatment for such an injury. They may file lienclaims for the cost or value of any treatment. Since the Appeals Board has permitted such liens where self-procured treatment awards are made, the plans have been very liberal in providing treatment first and waiting for a determination of the industrial nature of the injury.

LC 4903.1 was enacted to provide procedures for allowance of liens of health care providers, including allocation of funds where the amount *LC 4903.1* awarded under a compromise and release agreement is not sufficient to provide for full payment to one or more of such lienclaimants. Specifically, this section is applicable to a "health care provider, a health care service plan, a group disability policy, including a loss of income policy, a self-insured employee welfare benefit plan, or a hospital service contract." The category "health care provider" was added to the section effective January 1, 1991. Liens are to be allowed under this section on the following basis:

1. If reimbursement for self-procured medical or hospital treatment is denied because of lack of notice of injury to the employer, the named health plans will nevertheless be awarded a lien against other compensation awarded the employee.

2. If reimbursement for self-procured treatment is awarded, such liens shall be awarded.

3. If a case is disposed of by way of a compromise and release agreement, a workers' compensation judge may adjust such a lien by the same ratio as the applicant's recovery under the settlement bears to the potential recovery. [NOTE: This provision for settlement allocation does not apply to "health care providers" who are not one of the listed plans or policies.] The amount allowed will be full satisfaction of the lienclaim. Before the adoption of LC 4903.1, the W.C.A.B. had no jurisdiction to reduce a lien for the reasonable value of medical or hospital services rendered for an industrial injury, even where the issue of industrial causation was bitterly contested. In establishing this rule, the Supreme Court stated that the lien claimant did have the burden of a prima facie showing that the treatment was rendered for an alleged industrial injury, especially where the case is concluded by a compromise and release agreement. The new legislation creates an exception to the court-made rule and permits the W.C.A.B. to reduce medical plan liens when a workers' compensation case is settled for less than the potential recovery; i.e., as shown by the employee's evidence without reference to opposing evidence.

The legislation in LC 4903.1 regarding medical-provider liens has been held to apply to such liens even where the medical services were provided before the effective date of the section, i.e., before January 1, 1976.

The courts have also determined that under subdivision (c) of Section 4903.1, the Appeals Board may approve a settlement between an employee and his or her employer even though the settlement excludes from consideration the lienclaim of a medical provider, so long as the Board's order is without prejudice to the right of such lienclaimant to proceed independently with an action before the W.C.A.B. against the employer. In this situation, the lienclaimant must be able to prove that its medical services were provided for a work-related injury or condition.

LC 4903.2   As noted in the previous topic, the W.C.A.B. may allow an applicant's attorney a fee out of the recovery of a medical provider who files a lien under LC 4903.1.

The courts also hold that the so-called *Gregory* formula complies with the section in settlement situations. This formula is:

$$\frac{\text{Settlement}}{\text{Potential Recovery}} \times \text{Lien} = \text{Lien Recovery}$$

The "potential recovery" as used in the formula must be a legitimate appraisal of the applicant's potential rights under the workers' compensation act. It must be a "reasonable evaluation" based upon "reasonably probable" recovery by the employee.

In submitting these proposals under the *Gregory* formula, the parties must make proper service upon the lienclaimant of the settlement agreement, the proposal, and supporting documents. Further, the lienclaimant must be given the opportunity for a hearing if the lienclaimant objects to the amount which would be allocated to it under its claim.

With regard to the duty of an insurer of a health plan with an exclusionary provision as to workers' compensation cases, the Supreme Court has also said that since such a plan has a right to a lien in such cases, it may not withhold benefits where an alleged employer of the insured employee denies employment. The health plan insurer may not wait until the W.C.A.B. decides the case and may have to respond in damages if it denies payment or services.

Both private and public hospitals file lienclaims when they find they have treated an industrial case.

The lienright applies only to treatment for the industrial injury; therefore, liens for unrelated illnesses will be denied.

A medical provider may file a lienclaim to recoup fees and costs in providing medical-legal services (examinations, reports, tests, X-ray, etc., as provided in LC 4620-4627) to the extent that the employee is entitled to reimbursement under LC 4621. (Also see Chapter 4, MEDICAL TREATMENT, § 4.21, *Payment or Reimbursement for Cost of Medical Reports*.) *LC 4903(b)*

§ 10.4 Living Expenses

The code provides lien protection for those who extend credit to the employee or his family for living expenses following the injury. The basis for the lien may be a personal loan, overdue rent, groceries on credit, or necessary clothing. The usual case involves rent and groceries. The applicant in one case asked for a supply of lienclaim forms pending approval of his settlement because of his family's need for the necessities of life. He must have thought the forms could be used as cash, since they are printed on green paper, for he then proceeded on a lienclaim spending spree. When all the claims were filed, there was very little left of the settlement, and he then asked that the liens be denied. It was later learned that he had tried to "oversell" the settlement by offering lienclaim forms, with his signed consent affixed, in exchange for an automobile, a watch and other jewelry. Fortunately, the merchants declined these offers. Liens for the necessaries furnished were allowed. *LC 4903(c)*

Any expense incurred before the injury cannot be allowed as a lien.

LC 4903(e)

If the employee has deserted or is neglecting his wife or minor children, the Appeals Board may allow a lien against compensation for their reasonable living expenses. This lien is levied only upon application of the wife or guardian for the minor children. Again, it is only effective for expenses incurred after the date of injury. This provision brings the Appeals Board into the domestic relations field, the family members mentioned becoming parties to the litigation. Upon proper proof, the Appeals Board may divide the compensation between the parties in a manner it deems equitable.

W&I 11477
11478.4

LC 138.5(a)

Effective in 1984, LC 4903(e) has been amended to provide that an "assignee" (i.e., the state or county) under W & I 11477 may also claim a lien against workers' compensation for sums paid to support an employee's spouse and children. In this connection, the state Department of Social Services and the Division of Industrial Accidents are to cooperate in exchanging information concerning workers receiving permanent disability payments or who have filed an application for adjudication. These provisions appear to be a legislative response to court decisions denying liens based upon advancements of welfare funds under the AFDC program. A county may also recoup general assistance by way of a lienclaim since the law permits a county to require repayment. But the courts have ruled that the state may not obtain a lien for living expenses where the expenses were for institutional aid given in a mental hospital in connection with treatment. Such care is treatment, here for an illness unconnected with the industrial injury, and not living expenses within the meaning of LC 4903(c).

LC 4903.1

Payments made under a group disability policy providing loss of time benefits are the proper subject of a lienclaim, but any lien allowed is limited to temporary compensation awarded for the same day or days of payment of the disability policy benefit. A lien for such benefits will not be allowed unless the group disability provides for reduction, exclusion, or coordination of workers' compensation. Recovery of wage-loss payments may be subject to payment of a fee to applicant's attorney if the attorney's efforts effected recovery, and the lienclaimant did not participate in the proceedings. (See prior topic, § 10.2, *Attorney's Lien*.)

Except as provided in LC 4903.1, wage-loss payments under disability policies have been held not be lienable as advancement of living expenses. The same principle has also been applied to employer-provided, non-industrial disability benefits. The rationale is that such benefits are provided under a contract for which premiums have been paid or are a fringe benefit granted without expectation of repayment. This is true even if the program or policy contains an exclusion of industrially caused disability. In considering these decisions one should keep in mind that they involved particular policies or programs and their wording. It may well be that the terms of such coverage could be worded to make it clear, as do many sick-leave provisions, that the payments are deemed not in addition to workers' compensation and that the employee agrees that if the disability is determined to be industrial, such payments shall be considered as advances under LC 4903(c) and that he or she will reimburse the disability carrier or employer fund.

§ 10.5 Burial Expenses

The reasonable burial expense of a deceased employee may be the basis of a lien against compensation. The amount of the lien may not exceed the limit for burial expense as set forth in LC 4701. The lien procedure is permitted those who incur the burial expense and may be used whether or not the death is compensable, if any compensation has accrued. In a compensable case, the lien is assessed against the award of burial expense. (See Chapter 7, DEATH BENEFITS.)

LC 4903(d)
4701

§ 10.6 Unemployment Insurance

There are two kinds of unemployment insurance in California. One insures benefits in the case of unemployment because of the non-industrial disability of an employee; the other provides benefits where the unemployment is the result of reasons other than disability. The disability variety is referred to as UCD (unemployment compensation disability benefits) or DI (disability insurance) and is financed by the 1% deductions from the paychecks of wage-earners. The non-disability kind is supported by a payroll tax on employers and is called UI (unemployment insurance benefits). State employees, including state officers, are entitled to a special non-industrial disability benefit after use of sick-leave under UI 2781 and GC 18135.

Each day of unemployment due to disability is compensated at $1/7$ of the weekly rate. The maximum period of payment is 26 weeks. In times of economic stress, this period may be extended by the state as part of either a state or federal program. Legislation was passed in 1975 amending UI 4003 to permit an extension of more liberal federal criteria until December 31, 1976, under the Federal-State Extended Unemployment Compensation Act of 1970 as amended by the Emergency Unemployment Compensation Act of 1974 (P.L. 93-572).

UI 2653
2655
UI 4003

Under certain circumstances, the Labor Code provides the California Department of Employment with the right to a lien if an employee has been paid either type of unemployment benefit, and he later is awarded workers' compensation benefits for the same period of unemployment. The California Supreme Court in interpreting these code sections has stated they evidence an intent on the part of the legislature to provide an integrated social program of benefits for persons unemployed for reasons beyond their control. It is intended that a worker shall not receive double benefits for the same period of unemployment. Thus, where the record in a particular case before the Appeals Board shows that the Department of Employment has met the conditions for allowance of a lien, the Board is under a mandatory duty to allow it.

LC 4903(f),
4903(g),
4904
4901.4

LC 4903.2   Recovery under a lienclaim for UI or UCD may be subject to payment of a fee to applicant's attorney if the attorney's efforts effected recovery, and the lienclaimant did not participate in the proceedings. (See prior topic, § 10.2, *Attorney's Lien*.)

[NOTE: Under UI 1255.7 and 1342, spousal and child support obligations are partially lienable against unemployment insurance benefits.]

LC 4904   Where a compromise and release agreement (C & R) or stipulation proposes a certain amount to be allocated to a lien for unemployment benefits, and the lienclaimant objects, the W.C.A.B. will determine the appropriate lien to be allowed and enter findings of fact regarding the issue. The Board may approve a C & R or stipulation which proposes disallowance of the lien, in whole or in part, only where the lienclaimant has been served the C & R or stipulation along with all medical and rehabilitation documents 15 days before the Board's action. However, the Board may approve a C & R on all other issues and defer determination of the lienclaim for subsequent proceedings if the defendant agrees to pay the amount ultimately determined to be due the lienclaimant.

When the Employment Development Department has served an employer or insurance carrier with a lienclaim, the department must be notified of the commencement of disability indemnity payments not later than 15 working days after payments are begun and also notified of the filing of any application for adjudication, stipulated award or compromise and release agreement within 10 working days of the date of filing.

§ 10.7   UI Lien

LC 4903(g)   In screening applications for unemployment benefits, the department is careful to ascertain whether an industrial disability is involved. Should the employee later be awarded workers' compensation where UI has been paid, the code provides that the department may recover such payments by filing a lienclaim with the Workers' Compensation Appeals Board. A 1967 amendment removed the requirement that the department must prove that the UI payment was made erroneously. This lien may be allowed only from temporary compensation. In case of partial disability, no lien is allowed, but the compensation carrier is given credit for any UI benefits received for the same period.

UI 1280,   Weekly benefits range from $40 to $190 during 1990, $210 during
1281   1991, and $230 on and after January 1, 1992. The amount of the weekly benefit depends upon the earnings of the employee during the highest quarter of his or her base period.

R 10770   If a lien for UI has been filed, it is the duty of the trial judge or the W.C.A.B. to permit the Department of Employment to update its lien before a decision is issued.

§ 10.8   UCD Lien

Most lienclaims filed by the Department of Employment are for UCD *UI 2629* payments. Under the provisions of the Unemployment Insurance Code, the employee is entitled to the difference between UCD and temporary compensation payments if the UCD benefit rate is the larger of the two. The department's lien applies only for each day the employee received UCD and for which he or she is also awarded temporary compensation for an industrial injury. Under both plans, the daily benefit rate is 1/7 of the weekly rate. If the daily rate of UCD is smaller than the temporary compensation rate, the department will be allowed its lien for that day, and the employee will retain the difference. As a result, it may be said generally that the disabled employee recovers the greater of the two benefits.

Like workers' compensation, the weekly rate for UCD (and for UI) is based upon earnings. The plans differ in that UCD is determined by the *UI 2655* highest amount earned in one quarter of the employee's base year. Thus, earning capacity at the time of injury under workers' compensation may be maximum, but UCD less than maximum if the employee has had a spotty record of employment covered by the UCD law. It is also possible for one with a maximum UCD rate to have minimum earnings under the workers' compensation law.

Benefits range from $50 per week to $266 per week during 1990, $343 *UI 2653* per week on and after January 1, 1991—or the maximum limit set for *2655* workers' compensation temporary disability indemnity, whichever is less. The extent of the benefit depends on the earnings of the employee during the highest quarter of his or her base period. The limit on payments during the period of disability is 52 weeks.

Other differences affect the amount of recovery under a UCD lien. One is that the workers' compensation law provides for two distinct types of disability payments based upon two distinct purposes: (1) temporary compensation, payable to support the employee during his recovery from an industrial injury; (2) permanent disability compensation, a payment to assist the employee to adjust to competing on the labor market with his permanent handicap. UCD is not based upon specific purposes. It represents a payment made to relieve the hardship of unemployment caused by any type of disability regardless of the cause of that disability.

It is quite apparent, then, that the Supreme Court's statement about the two programs forming an integrated social plan has very limited application. In one decision, the court ruled that a UCD lien must be paid if its payment coincided with a period of payment of permanent disability benefits. In another decision, it was held mandatory to allow all of the UCD lien out of any sums received under a compromise and release agreement. Since an industrial accident case may be settled because of one or more disputed issues, this decision appeared unrealistic and prevented settlement in many cases.

LC 4904   In 1957, LC 4904 was amended to relieve the situation resulting from these court decisions. Now, UCD may be a lien only against any recovery for temporary compensation; it cannot be a lien against any permanent disability benefits. As to settlements, the parties may designate how much of the money to be paid the employee is for temporary disability, how much for permanent disability, medical expenses, or attorneys' fees. The Department of Employment is then served with a copy of the settlement agreement, and, if no objection is raised, it may be approved by the Appeals Board. If the department objects that the proposal is not in keeping with the evidence on record with the Appeals Board, it may request a hearing for the purpose of establishing a period of temporary disability more favorable to its lien claim. The final decision is up to the Appeals Board subject, of course, to the right of a party, including the Department of Employment, to seek review by the appellate courts.

The Unemployment Insurance Appeals Board rendered a decision early in the UCD program to the effect that if a workers' compensation settlement is based only upon the employee's medical expenses and a reasonable sum for his attorney's fee, the employee could properly be paid UCD benefits. The board's reasoning was that UCD does not include any such benefits, and thus there is no necessary inference that loss of time through an industrial injury has been established or compensated for. This principle is also contained in the 1957 amendment to LC 4904. Such agreements are referred to as "medical only" settlements.

In case the settlement appears to contain some recovery for temporary disability and permanent disability in addition to medical expenses, the total medical expense is deducted from the settlement figure. The balance must then be allocated between the two types of disability. Any UCD lien is applied to the portion allocated to temporary disability. Any attorney's fee is then allowed out of the balance.

What happens if an employee is awarded only a short period of temporary compensation, and the record shows he has been paid UCD for that period? The Appeals Board must order all the compensation paid to the Department of Employment, unless there is a difference in the weekly rates. But what if the employee's attorney is responsible for the recovery and requests a fee? There is not enough compensation for both liens. The Court of Appeal ruled that the UCD lien takes precedence, and the attorney cannot recover his fee by way of a lien under LC 4903a. In that case, the UCD insurer, a private insurance company, was represented by its own attorney so that the argument of the attorney for the employee that he was responsible for any recovery for the UCD insurer was not persuasive to the court. Since it is extremely rare for a lienclaimant to be represented at an Appeals Board hearing, the Board has limited the application of the decision to those cases in which a lienclaimant is represented. In most cases it can be said that the work of the employee's attorney does not benefit lienclaimants' interests and that, in the event there is not enough recovery to satisfy all liens, the attorney should be given consideration. The appellate court decision has been criticized even though the lienclaimant has its own attorney. At any rate, both views are represented in LC 4903.2 permitting the Board to allow a fee out of recovery under a UI or UCD lien if the lienclaimant is not represented in the proceeding.

If a UCD lien has been filed, the trial judge or the W.C.A.B. must con- *R 10770* tact the lienclaimant, whether the Department of Employment, a private U.C.D. carrier, or an employer self-insured for UCD, and permit the lienclaim to be updated.

EXAMPLES:

(1) A claims an industrial hernia. The workers' compensation carrier denies the claim on the ground that no effort was required in A's job which would cause such a condition. A applies for UCD and is paid for the six weeks necessary for the operation and convalescence. He files for a hearing before the Appeals Board. At the hearing, the evidence shows that although his regular duties did not require heavy exertion, he was asked to lift some panels; that he felt a sharp pain in his groin while doing so. The W.C.A.B. judge awards six weeks' temporary compensation and the cost of medical treatment. Many hernia cases do not reach the Appeals Board, because often an employee's benefit under UCD and a group medical policy are the same as compensation benefits. If in the example the UCD was $100 per week for a total of $600, but the temporary compensation awarded was at the rate of $119 per week, the industrial accident award would net the employee $19 per week, or $114 plus the medical expense.

(2) Pending determination by the Appeals Board of his disputed back injury, B receives 13 weeks of UCD. These payments were at the rate of $70 per week ($10 per day) because of his quarterly earnings record. At the time of his injury, his earning capacity under the workers' compensation law gave him a compensation rate of $100 per week for temporary disability and $70 per week for permanent disability. B was ultimately awarded 25 weeks of compensation. Six weeks of the UCD has been paid after the last date for which temporary compensation was awarded. In this case, the UCD lien would be honored only for the last seven weeks of the temporary compensation. This situation can be represented graphically:

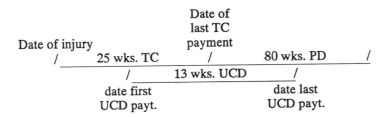

The amount of the lien would be 7 × $70 or $490. Under the W.C.A.B. award, the temporary compensation would be 25 × $100 or $2500, of which $490 would be ordered paid to the UCD lienclaimant. From the amount for temporary compensation, the employee nets $2010. He is also paid all of the 80 weeks of permanent disability payments which total $5600.

(3) C is awarded 16 weeks of temporary compensation for an industrial aggravation of an allergy. The evidence of record does not support any finding of permanent disability. C's earnings were minimum under the workers' compensation law for a compensation rate of $35 per week for the particular date of injury. Pending determination of the compensation benefits, the Department of Employment paid 13 weeks of UCD at the rate of $50 per week based on his earnings record with the department. In this case, the department, in satisfaction of its lien, would recover 13 × $35 or $455. The employee would receive the compensation for the three weeks during which he was not paid any UCD, or $105. His total recovery under both plans is $755, whereas under the compensation award he would have received only $560.

§ 10.9   Allocation to UCD or UI Lien; *Baird* Formula

Since a lien for unemployment benefits may be allowed only from temporary compensation, where a case involves a claim of permanent disability, it is necessary to decide the allocation to be made from an employee's recovery. If a formal decision issues, findings will be made regarding any period of temporary disability and any portion of such period subject to a UCD or UI lien. In the case of settlements, however, the task is more difficult because LC 4904 permits the parties to suggest a reasonable sum to be allocated to such lienclaims but does not set forth specific criteria. In 1958 the commission developed an approach known as the *Davis* formula (*Davis v. Blaser*) which recognized the priority of the cost of medical treatment and allowed unemployment liens on the basis of a ratio computed from an estimated period of temporary disability. In 1963, the commission modified this formula in the *Baird* case which was upheld by the Supreme Court. *Baird* follows the same basic premise as *Davis* but eliminates some of the arithmetic.

EXAMPLE:*

A disputed case is settled by a compromise and release (C & R) for $2,500. The W.C.A.B. judge approves the settlement including a proposal to allow $86 in full satisfaction of a UCD lienclaim of $300 on this basis:

Potential value of case:	
Estimated temporary disability indemnity	$2500.00
Estimated permanent disability indemnity	$4000.00
Past and future medical expense	500.00
TOTAL potential value	$7000.00
Amount of UCD lien	300.00

Amount of Compromise and Release . . .	$2500.00
Less: past and future medical expense . .	500.00
Adjusted C&R figure	$2000.00

FORMULA: $\dfrac{\text{Amount of lien}}{\text{Potential Value}} \times \text{Adjusted C\&R figure} = \text{Amt. allowable as lien}$

(Baird)

$$\frac{300}{7000} \times 2000 = \$86.00$$

---

*Example courtesy David I. Lippert, W.C.A.B. Judge

Under proposed changes of the C&R form this method of allocation will apply to both UCD and UI. The form provides spaces for the parties to propose sums to be allocated to temporary and permanent disability, accrued, and future medical expense for the purpose of determining such lienclaims under the Baird formula.

§ 10.10   UI and UCD Pending Appeal

If unemployment insurance payments continue while a workers' compensation case is being reviewed by the W.C.A.B. on petition for reconsideration, the lien will be allowed as of the date the Board is ready to issue its final decision. If temporary compensation is not being received, unemployment payments are to continue while the matter is pending on reconsideration.

§ 10.11   Satisfaction of Unemployment Lienclaim

Taken together, the provisions of the Labor Code and the Unemployment Insurance Code render conclusive the findings of the Workers' Compensation Appeals Board, not only as to the amount to be allocated to a UCD or UI lien, but also as to the entitlement of the employee to the unemployment benefit in the first place. If the Appeals Board allows only a portion of the claimed lien, such partial allowance shall be in full satisfaction of the entire lienclaim of the Department of Employment or private UCD carrier. Further, no overpayment to the employee may be declared because of any sums not recovered through such a lienclaim. *LC 4904 UI 2741 2735.5*

§ 10.12   UCD Hospital Benefits

The unemployment disability hospital benefit has been repealed as of January 1, 1979. In repealing this provision of UI 2800, and following, the Legislature made a trade-off for a waiver of the unemployment compensation disability waiting period so long as the employee claimant is hospitalized for one day or more. (Before 1979, the benefit was $12 per day not to exceed 20 days and included confinement in a nursing home. Liens for this benefit were allowed only if the cost was recovered as self-procured medical treatment.) *UI 2627, 2627.5*

§ 10.13   Private UCD Carriers

UI 4354

UI 3258

UI 3264,
3265
2712

The unemployment insurance law permits private insurance coverage or self-insurance for UCD benefits if the private plan contains better benefits than the state plan administered by the Department of Employment. Under a private plan, the employee's 1% deduction is paid to a private insurance carrier. An employer may also be self-insured for UCD, in which event it retains the 1% for use in this program. These private carriers have the same lien-rights as the Department of Employment. In disputed UCD cases, however, the department may make payments pending determination of the merits of the claim. If the department deems the claim to be proper, the private carrier must reimburse the department. If an industrial injury is involved, the department may file a lien to protect the rights of the private UCD carrier. An employer self-insured for UCD is not subject to a damage suit based upon a denial of benefits, for the UCD law and its appeal procedures provide the exclusive remedy. This principle is particularly applicable where the plaintiff in such an action has appealed the employer's adverse decision and has been awarded benefits.

§ 10.14   Unrequested Liens

LC 4905

Where it appears that a person would be entitled to a lien but has not requested it, the Appeals Board may allow it and order payment to the proper person from the employee's award of workers' compensation benefits. This provision permits the Appeals Board to allow a lien where the right to it is established in the record by evidence presented by the employee or the employer. This authority permits a speedier procedure since it is not necessary to hold up a decision to permit the creditor to file a lienclaim.

This procedure is used where the employee presents unpaid bills to prove the amount of self-procured medical treatment. An employee may ask that a payment be directed to his grocer or landlord. In some cases, a lender will mail the Appeals Board a promissory note or a letter alleging an oral agreement for repayment of a loan from compensation. When questioned about such a matter, the employee may agree to payment out of any compensation award, or the W.C.A.B. judge, in his or her discretion, may require the filing of a lienclaim along with information justifying its allowance.

Of course, no such lien will be allowed, whether requested or not, unless it is in one of the categories previously discussed. Again, liens will be denied if the claims are for obligations which are not listed in LC 4903, and liens will be denied for obligations which arose before the date of the employee's industrial injury.

§ 10.15   Notice of Lienclaim

When a lienclaim is properly filed and served on the parties to an Appeals Board proceeding, the employer or insurance carrier continues to pay compensation at the possible risk of paying twice. Notice of a lienclaim places the burden on the employer or carrier to ascertain which compensation payments would be subject to the lien if found to be valid by the Board, and to make only such further payments as will not jeopardize the lien. If full compensation is paid under these circumstances, the employer or carrier may be required to pay the lienclaimant.

§ 10.16 Employer's Lien

The employer has a lien against any recovery realized by the employee from any third person whose negligence or wilful act caused the industrial injury. This lien is limited to the extent of the benefits conferred upon the employee by the employer. The same lienright accrues to the employer's workers' compensation insurance carrier. (See Chapter 12, DAMAGE SUITS —SUBROGATION.)

LC 3856-3858

§ 10.17 Liens of Public Assistance Funds

In addition to the benefit or assistance programs previously discussed, there are others which have lienrights against a recipient's workers' compensation award. The Uninsured Employers' Fund may obtain a lien for discretionary compensation paid and medical treatment furnished pending an award in a case in which the Fund is a party. The Asbestos Workers' Account may recoup the cost of medical treatment and other "recoverable costs." The Restitution Fund created by the legislature to aid victims of crime and their families may recover expenditures made to a claimant who is entitled to workers' compensation.

LC 4903.3

LC 4903(i)
LC 4414
LC 4903(h)
GC 13959, et seq.

Chapter 11
SETTLEMENTS—COMPROMISE AND RELEASE

§ 11.1   Introduction

About one-third of all decisions rendered by the W.C.A.B. are orders approving settlements. The Board furnishes printed forms called "Compromise and Release" agreements. (W.C.A.B. forms 15, 16, and 17.) In compensation vernacular, a settlement is referred to as a "C & R." When a case is settled, it is "C & R'd." The W.C.A.B. forms, or forms containing the same provisions, must be used in submitting any settlement for approval. *R 10870-10886*

An employee does not waive any rights by accepting voluntary payment of benefits. Likewise, an employee may not waive or be compelled to waive such rights through any contract, rule, or regulation. The parties may settle, subject to statutory conditions, and only with W.C.A.B. approval. The California Supreme Court has stated that, within the parameters of the statutory guidelines, the W.C.A.B. has a great deal of discretion in approving or disapproving C & R's. Under Board rules, no release of liability is valid unless approved by a judge, a commissioner, a panel of the Board, or the entire Board. *LC 4909 5000, 5001* *R 10870*

A case may originate by the filing of a C & R, or a settlement may occur at any stage of an Appeals Board proceeding. It will not be approved unless adequate under all the circumstances. Agreements providing for less than the full amount of compensation which could be awarded for a particular injury or disability are approved only if a reasonable doubt exists as to the rights of the parties, or if the settlement appears to be in the best interests of the parties.

LC 5502(d)   Effective January 1, 1991, regarding injuries occurring on or after January 1, 1990, a mandatory settlement conference must be held in 10 to 30 days after the filing of an application with the Appeals Board where an employee or dependent is represented by an attorney. This conference will be conducted by a referee appointed by the Board. If an employee or dependent is not represented, a workers' compensation judge may conduct a settlement conference. A judge presides at a settlement conference only in cases involving unrepresented employees or dependents. The Board may also, in its discretion, set a case for a conference hearing.

§ 11.2   C & R Requirements

LC 5003   The provisions of a C & R must include the following information: date of accident, statutory average earnings, nature of disability, benefits paid or due, future benefits (amount of settlement), proposed days and amount of temporary compensation allocated to any lienclaim for unemployment benefits.

LC 5004   If a death case is involved, the C & R must also show date of death, name of widow, names and ages of all children, names of other dependents, whether dependents are total or partial, amount to be paid, and to whom.

R 10886   The W.C.A.B. form further requires this information: age and occupation of injured employee, whether returned to work and when, respective claims of parties (reasons for settlement), an agreement of the parties that the C & R may be considered an application on behalf of the employee and that *10878*   the matter may be set for hearing on all issues, including adequacy of the settlement, proof of service of a copy of the C & R upon any lienclaimant whose lien is proposed to be disallowed in whole or in part, plus all medical reports.

LC 5003   The formalities of executing the document are also governed by statute and rule. They must be

R 10874   Signed by the employee or other beneficiary;

Signed also by an attorney for the employee or beneficiary with a statement of any fee paid or arrangement made for one. (Usually the word "reasonable" is inserted in the blank on the form.);

Signed by any guardian ad litem for any minor beneficiary, as well as by any minor over 14 years of age;

Attested (witnessed) by two disinterested witnesses as to the signature of the employee or any beneficiary, or be acknowledged before a notary public.

By W.C.A.B. directive, a C & R entered into by an employee must incorporate in the document or in a separate addendum signed by the employee a statement that the employee has been informed and understands that the C

& R releases any claim of his or her dependents to death benefits relating to the injury or injuries covered by the agreement.

Substantial compliance with these requirements is sufficient if a technical omission can be supplied later, such as the seal of a notary who witnessed the employee's signature.

§ 11.3 Original C & R

The term "original C & R" refers to one which is submitted for approval where there is no proceeding then pending before the Appeals Board. In most instances, these will be accompanied by the entire medical file of the employer or carrier. Sometimes a claims examiner will also include a written statement taken from the employer or other beneficiary. A file is prepared by the Appeals Board, numbered and docketed as a formal case. It is then referred to a W.C.A.B. judge for review. If he or she feels the settlement is adequate, it may be approved without further proceedings. Should the record be deemed inadequate, the judge may require a further medical examination or other information.

Settlements often involve questions of rating permanent disability and computing probable present or commuted value of the benefits. Such cases are then sent to the Disability Evaluation Bureau for a report. A joint reference to this bureau and the medical bureau is often made. It is not unusual for these reviews to result in an additional medical examination to supply missing information such as diagnostic workups or more complete measurements of residual function.

If at any point the judge is not satisfied with the record, the C & R may be considered as an application, and the matter may be set for hearing on all *R 10878* pertinent issues. After such a hearing, the judge may approve the settlement or disapprove it and issue a decision or award consistent with the evidence presented. The Appeals Board will ordinarily exhaust the informal steps described before requiring a hearing. In many cases the employer or carrier, after being notified of the judge's analysis of the various issues, will authorize an increase in the settlement or renegotiate with the employee.

§ 11.4 Adequacy of C & R

A case may be settled at any stage of the proceedings. At whatever point it is submitted, the test is the same: Is it a fair and adequate settlement under *R 10870* the circumstances of the case? The authority to approve does not include the authority to change the terms of a C & R. The W.C.A.B., or a judge, may not alter the terms of the agreement or strike a provision then approve it as changed. If the Board or a judge is not satisfied with the agreement, has suggested changes, or requires a better factual record, the parties must be notified and given the opportunity to provide the information or make a record.

The adequacy of a C & R depends upon the issues to be resolved or settled. If there is a serious question of compensability, jurisdiction, statute of limitations, or other issue which could preclude any benefits, the board will consider such an issue in making its determination. If there is no such legal issue, as where injury is admitted, and the only question is extent of permanent disability, the Board will scrutinize a C & R closely with regard to the range of permanent disability ratings justified by the medical file, other facts in the record and the report of the Disability Evaluation Bureau. Such a settlement will be compared to the commuted value of the potential rating.

§ 11.5   Settlement of Rehabilitation Rights

R 10870

The W.C.A.B. has ruled that an injured worker's right to rehabilitation under LC 139.5 may not be settled by a C&R unless there is a serious question concerning the compensability of the alleged injury. (See Chapter 16, REHABILITATION.)

§ 11.6   Third-Party C & R

A settlement made between the employee, the employer, and a third party is called a third-party compromise and release agreement. If such a settlement is approved, it relieves the employer from further liability under the workers' compensation law, and the third-party from further liability under both general law and the compensation law. The function of the Appeals Board in reviewing or approving these settlements is to determine whether the net recovery by the employee is adequate as compared to his rights under the compensation law. A more detailed discussion of this topic will be found in the next chapter.

§ 11.7   Liens Against C & R

Liens may be allowed out of the settlement amount. The most common are attorneys' fees, physicians' fees, hospital expenses, and unemployment liens, subject to the limitations discussed in the previous chapter.

§ 11.8   Finality of C & R; C & R as Defense
in Other Actions

LC 5000

When a C & R is approved, it settles all matters relating to that particular injury. Thereafter, the employee cannot ask for further treatment or file an application based upon a new and further disability. If he should later die from the injury, his dependents cannot recover any death benefits. In serious cases, the likelihood of further benefits including a death benefit is considered in arriving at the settlement figure. In a recent case which reached the California Supreme Court, this aspect of LC 5000 was challenged as unconstitutional. The court upheld the provision, holding that it does not deny dependents equal protection or due process of law. However, the court expressed dissatisfaction with the W.C.A.B. form which did not inform the employee that the C & R, when approved, would have this effect. In the later *Sumner* case, the Supreme Court held that a C & R without such a notice would not be effective to bar the right of a dependent to file a death claim. As a result of this holding, the W.C.A.B. has developed the following language

238

for incorporation into the C & R or added by an addendum signed by the employee: "I have been advised and fully understand that this compromise and release agreement releases any and all claims of my dependents to death benefits relating to the injury or injuries covered by this compromise agreement." The Board holds that if an approved C & R entered into by an employee conforms to the notice requirements, it settles any possible death benefit or claim, and a later claim filed by a spouse or other dependent is barred.

In a 1956 decision, the appellate court stated that an approved C & R is a good defense to a later suit against the employer where both actions grew out of the employer's alleged assault on the employee. The C & R contained this language: ". . . to settle any and all claims on account of . . ." the employee's injuries. Thus, the employee had made an election of remedies and had released the employer from all further liability. Note here the fact that both the employer and his compensation insurance carrier were parties to the agreement. Where the action is based on negligence (rather than a direct assault), the insurance coverage for workers' compensation prevents recovery against the employer in a damage suit, and an approved C & R merely puts this protection in a different form. However, where the employer and a third person are charged with joint negligence, the third person may not use the employer's C & R as a defense in a negligence action.

Another action which may grow out of an industrial injury is the penalty for serious and wilful misconduct. Often the carrier will settle its liability on the normal issues, the employer having to defend the S & W claim. In this situation, the employer cannot use the carrier's C & R as a defense. Similarly, it has also been held that an approved C & R on "normal" issues does not bar an employee from seeking relief under LC 132a for alleged discrimination by an employer. The general release clause in the W.C.A.B. form does not cover this separate cause of action. Therefore, if a settlement is to cover all possible causes of action connected with an injury, they should be specifically stated in an addendum to the standard form.

Regarding occupational disease or cumulative trauma cases, the appellate court has considered the question of whether an applicant under the provisions of Labor Code Section 5500.5 may settle with one employer, then proceed against others. If he should settle, does he release the other employers? Here, the W.C.A.B. had approved a settlement (C & R) as to one of the defendant employers. The Court of Appeal reversed an award against the other employers, holding that in an occupational disease case any settlement recovery is to be taken into account in determining the pro rata liability of the various defendants. To rule otherwise would be to permit a double recovery of compensation benefits. Amounts received under a C & R are defined as compensation under previous appellate decisions. A 1974 statute makes this *LC 5005* rule a part of the Labor Code and provides further that, in determining the liability of the other employers or carriers, the W.C.A.B. must take into account the liability of the employer or carrier released under the C & R.

The Supreme Court has ruled that if an employer is going to rely upon an approved C & R (if further proceedings are brought or if pertinent to some other action) as a matter of defense, the employer must give appropriate notice in the proceeding and introduce evidence of the C & R and its approval by the W.C.A.B.

§ 11.9   Setting Aside a C & R

A settlement which has been approved may not be set aside except for fraud, duress, undue influence, incompetency, or mutual mistake. Because of the care exercised by the Appeals Board in reviewing these agreements, a case of this type would be rare. Even where incompetency is apparent, the employee's guardian must make a timely application to set aside the settlement.

In one case, the employee sought to set aside a C & R claiming that he did not sign the document. A handwriting expert proved that the signature was that of the employee. In another case, the employee asserted that her attorney did not explain that the settlement would prevent her from pursuing her claim for further medical treatment. She testified, however, that her doctor looked the papers over and recommended that she accept; that her attorney told her that under the circumstances this was the best she could do. The medical evidence showed that all the facts had been known to the parties, and thus there was no mutual mistake or fraudulent conduct involved.

As a general rule, acceptance of a benefit provided by a settlement forecloses an appeal from a judgment enforcing the terms of the settlement, absent facts demonstrating severability of the terms. A person attempting to withdraw from a settlement or set it aside might be required to tender a return of any money or other benefit received thereunder.

§ 11.10   Advantages of Settling

From an applicant's point of view, there may be many reasons for settling a case. Often these are the same reasons an employee may want to commute an award to a lump-sum payment, that is, to start a business, to make up delinquent payments on a home or to pay off debts which have piled up during the employee's disability. If there is little question about the extent of the worker's compensation benefits, the settlement must be equal to the commuted value of those benefits. If there are disputed issues, and the evidence is conflicting, the worker may wish to accept some recovery rather than risk getting nothing or the lower end of any range of possibilities indicated by the record. The W.C.A.B. judge, of course, will pass upon the fairness and adequacy of the C & R.

On the defense side, settlements are desirable because of their finality. It is advantageous for an employer to settle many cases because of the five-year continuing jurisdiction of the Appeals Board. The same reasoning applies to awards with lifetime benefits. It is true, of course, that many employees are cognizant of the value of the continuing jurisdiction and of lifetime awards and may not wish to settle for any amount. This is particularly true of continuing awards for medical treatment, prosthetic appliances, or institutional care. The settlement of cases not only allows the closing of a file and the attendant cost of handling, but also frees the reserves being held to cover anticipated future benefits. It is not unusual for an employer or carrier to pay more than the commuted value of an award for a C & R, the overage being an amount to purchase the employee's rights to file for new and further disability under LC 5410 or to petition to re-open under LC 5803.

Settlements which set up a periodic payment plan in lieu of a lump-sum cash payment are called "structured settlements." Such settlements may involve payment through an annuity or other type of investment. The incentive for an employer or carrier is that the overall cost of a case or administration of an award may be reduced, and the differential between the commuted value of a PD rating and potential earnings in the marketplace can work for the benefit of both parties. Also, a structured settlement permits more flexibility in the setting of a periodic payment adequate to meet the needs of the employee or dependent. With the setting of such payment, the claimant has an assured income and is not subject to the risk of over-spending or rash spending which could occur if a lump-sum were paid. As a cautionary note, an employee should carefully examine the consequences of settling if entitled to continuing or lifetime medical treatment.

If the employee is in bad health from non-industrial causes, this may have some bearing on how much is offered. So, also, will the likelihood of eventual industrial death. A case is recalled in which a dairy worker suffered an industrial aggravation of a diabetic condition. All examining doctors indicated the necessity of amputation of the injured leg. The employee was 75 years of age and the prognosis was not good. A C & R in a large sum was submitted and approved. Five years later this employee filed an application setting forth his most recent injury—a back strain suffered while pitching hay. Thus, there is always the unusual case to cause one to pause and reflect. Nevertheless, there is a great deal of truth in the adage that a good settlement is the best solution to any dispute.

Chapter 12
DAMAGE SUITS—
SUBROGATION

§ 12.1   Tort Actions

"Tort" is a legal term meaning "wrongdoing" or "harm." It is applied to wrongs which cause injury to a person or property or to personal or property rights. It is usually differentiated from breach of contract, although the courts have recognized hybrid situations wherein both contract law and tort law are applicable. The word "tortfeasor" means "wrongdoer." ("Tort" is a French word based upon a Latin word for wrongdoing.) A tort action is a civil lawsuit brought in a court of general jurisdiction, viz. municipal court or superior court. (The W.C.A.B. is a special court of limited jurisdiction which hears and decides only litigated cases involving workers' compensation benefits or allied issues such as serious and willful misconduct, discrimination because of a claim or causation in certain retirement cases. See Chapters 13 and 14.)

There is a potential tort action in just about every industrial accident case. Therefore, both an injured worker and his or her employer should be sensitive to this possibility—the employee in seeking full redress and the employer because of the right to recoup workers' compensation expenditures from a third-party tortfeasor. In this chapter, we consider tort actions which *CC 1714* *LC 3852* may be maintained against third parties and those which may or may not be brought against employers, insurance carriers, or their employees or agents.

In any tort action, one must consider legislation which serves to restrict recovery in certain types of cases. We refer to Proposition 51 of 1986 designed to limit liability in multiple defendant cases (i.e., the "anti-deep pocket" law), the Tort Reform Act of 1987 regarding punitive damages and product-liability, and MICRA, which limits recovery in medical malpractice cases. MICRA is discussed in Section 12.14, *Medical Treatment—Malpractice.*

CC 1431.2   Proposition 51 is a measure adopted by the initiative process, effective June 4, 1986. It provides that in an action based upon comparable fault "the liability of each defendant for non-economic damages shall be several only and shall not be joint. Each defendant shall be liable only for the amount of non-economic damages allocated to that defendant in direct proportion to that defendant's percentage of fault, and a separate judgment shall be rendered against the defendant for that amount." Economic damages are defined as "objectively verifiable monetary losses," and non-economic damages are defined as non-monetary losses such as pain, suffering, inconvenience, mental suffering, emotional distress, loss of society and companionship, loss of consortium, injury to reputation and humiliation.

CC 3294,   The Tort Reform Act of 1987 sets tighter parameters for punitive dam-
3295   age claims, including claims against medical providers. Proof of the extreme
2860   conduct justifying punitive damages must be established by "clear and con-
1714.45   vincing" proof. Controls are established regarding an insurance carrier's
CCP   obligation to furnish an insured separate and independent counsel for legal
425.13   representation, as well as fees paid to such counsel. In product liability cases, a manufacturer or seller is not liable if the product involved is a common consumer product known to be unsafe, such as sugar, tobacco, alcohol, butter, castor oil, or a similar product. In medical malpractice cases, attorney's fees are increased for recoveries over $100,000.

§ 12.2   Third-Party Actions

When an industrial injury is caused by the negligence or intentionally
LC 3852   wrongful act of some person other than the employer, the injured employee has two rights (causes of action): (1) the right to workers' compensation benefits; (2) the right to sue the wrongdoer for damages in a court action. However, these rights are governed so as to give the employee only the greater of the two recoveries. Because no one knows until the completion of both procedures which is greater, and because workers' compensation is recoverable more quickly, as a rule, the code contains a rather complicated series of provisions to accomplish this result. The damage suit is called a "third-party action."

The employer also has a right to sue the wrongdoer for damages which
LC 3852   consist of any compensation payments made to the employee. In addition, the

employer may include in the damage claim any "salary, wage, pension, or other emolument paid to the employee or his dependents." This right is both a subrogation right and an independent cause of action.

A workers' compensation insurance carrier has the same right of action as an employer. In this respect it is said to be "subrogated" to the rights of the *LC 3850* employer whom it insures. The carrier's right is limited to the extent of the *IC 11662* compensation payments made or medical treatment furnished.

The Uninsured Employers' Fund is subrogated to the right of the unin- *LC 3732* sured employer to bring actions against third parties, and, likewise, the Self-Insurers' Security Fund is subrogated to the rights of any employer whose *LC 3850(c)* obligations it has assumed.

Others having possible subrogation rights include the Insurance Commissioner or guarantee fund in handling claims of an insolvent insurer. The Public Employees' Retirement System also has limited subrogation rights with respect to disability pensions. The Asbestos Workers' Account *LC 4417* may seek to recover its expenditures by filing a lien in any third-party action maintained by a claimant.

If an employer or carrier has made payment to the state as required by LC 4706.5 in an industrial death case wherein the deceased employee left no one qualified as a dependent, the employer may seek recoupment in a third-party action.

Firefighters, peace officers, and emergency medical personnel are specifically granted the right to maintain suit against anyone who causes in- *LC 3852* jury wilfully or through negligent use of property after knowing of the pres- *CC 1714.9* ence of such personnel. An employer of an injured employee in one of these categories has subrogation rights as to workers' compensation paid.

If either the employee or employer (or carrier) brings an action against a third person, the person bringing the action must serve the other with a copy *LC 3853* of the complaint, either by personal service or certified mail. Proof of service is to be filed in the action. If both file actions they must serve each other. At any time before trial on the facts in such a suit, an employee-plaintiff may join the employer as a party-plaintiff. If the employer brings suit, the employer may join the employee as a party-plaintiff. If both have filed actions, either may make a motion asking the court to consolidate the actions.

§ 12.3 Employer's Lien; Credit Against Compensation

If the employee alone brings suit, the employer or carrier may enforce a lien for compensation benefits furnished against any judgment in favor of the *LC 3853-* employee. In most cases the employers, carriers, and employees' attorneys *3855* have a working arrangement whereby recoveries from third parties are shared *LC 3856* in a three-way split. The attorneys are compensated for their work in obtaining the recovery; the employer or carrier gets a partial reimbursement; the employee gets part as to his cause of action. These arrangements result from the practicalities in bringing suit against the alleged wrongdoer. First, the employer or carrier cannot bring suit without the co-operation of the employee who usually is the chief witness. Secondly, if the employer or carrier joins in the employee's suit or files a lien, the jury will learn that the employee has already received some benefits and that an insurance company or employer is going to get all or part of any judgment. It is deemed best, therefore, to permit the employee to proceed alone under an agreement on the disposition of any recovery. If the parties decide to proceed in this fashion, it is important that the employer (or other person or entity claiming subrogation rights) notify the third party of its claim.

In case the employee proceeds alone against the third party, the employer or carrier may intervene in the suit and request that a lien be granted. A 1971 amendment to the code permits the employee and the third party to settle their case, leaving the employer or carrier to their remedy of suing the third party directly. However, the Court of Appeal has held that where the statute of limitations has barred the employer's right to pursue an action independently, the new law will be construed so as not to foreclose the employer from litigating the issues.

LC 3857,
3858
    If a judgment is obtained in which such a lien is allowed, but there are more compensation payments due, the employer or carrier has the right to add to the lien before the judgment is paid by the third party.

EXAMPLE:

A sues B for damages because of injuries received in an automobile accident, and he recovers a judgment for $50,000. B has a $30,000 insurance policy, but is otherwise judgment-proof.

LC 3858
    If A were receiving compensation benefits by reason of the accident, the employer's lien would be effective only against the actual amount received under the judgment. The employer's right to recoup is continuing, however, and if A should ever collect more than the $30,000 from B's insurer, the employer must be given notice and a right to perfect his lien.

LC 3858,
3861
    As to compensation due after the satisfaction of a judgment against or settlement with a third party, the employer or workers' compensation insurer has the right to credit, i.e., is relieved of further payment of compensation up to the amount received under the judgment or settlement after payment of costs and fees. The W.C.A.B. has ruled that this credit applies to future liability for vocational rehabilitation services. However, the Board has also held that if the third-party action is a malpractice action against a medical provider, and the medical provider has indicated an intent to introduce evidence in that action of the employee's receipt of workers' compensation benefits, by virtue of CC 3333.1 the employer may not receive credit for a settlement in the malpractice action.

§ 12.4   Attorneys' Fees

In 1949, LC 3856–3860 were amended to permit the employee's attorney's fee to be deducted from the third-party recovery before assessment of the employer's lien for workers' compensation. However, this right applied only to court actions and not to third-party settlements.

The law was changed in 1959 to permit payment of the employee's attorney out of the proceeds if the attorney's work benefitted the employer or carrier in recovering on the lien. The court has authority to set fees for employee's attorney and that of the attorney for the employer or carrier. *LC 3856 3860*

An employee and employer may agree that the employee's attorney will represent both in a third-party action. While these arrangements have been approved by the appellate courts, the courts have also pointed out that the employee and his attorney have the duty of protecting the rights of the employer or carrier. Thus, where the defendant in such a case raises issues which could affect the compensation lienclaim, the employer or carrier must be notified and given the opportunity to litigate those issues. LC 3859 and 3860 govern the matter of fees giving the court authority to set fees for both the employee's attorney and, if represented in the action, the attorney for the employer or carrier. If the case is settled without a court action, the W.C.A.B. sets these fees.

In 1975, the California Supreme Court ruled that both LC 3856 and LC 3860 are to be construed to require the payment of a portion of the employee's attorney's fee out of the lien recovery if the attorney was principally responsible for obtaining recovery for both the employee and employer or compensation carrier, whether or not there is an agreement for dual representation. The trial court in approving and setting the fee is to determine a reasonable fee for obtaining the judgment or settlement, then apportion the fee between the employee's net recovery and the amount realized by the employer or carrier on its lien. The court recognized that circumstances will vary as to the amount of work involved and the degree of assistance to a lienclaimant. For example, the Court of Appeal has held that where a lienclaimant was represented at all stages of the proceeding by its own attorney, the lienclaimant cannot be required to pay a part of the fee for the employee's attorney out of its lien recovery.

Because of the attorney's fee issue, the employer's right to a setoff as to future compensation benefits and the employee's right to settle without the employer's approval (leaving the employer with the right and task of pursuing an independent action against the third party), both the employee and the employer or carrier should analyze third-party case potentials very closely. In most cases, it will probably benefit both to make an agreement for representation by the employee's attorney.

§ 12.5   Settlement of Third-Party Actions

LC 3859,
3860

The same analysis is required on third-party settlements, for the lien of the employer or carrier applies to any sums received from the third party. Also, the third party must be sure to recognize the lien, obtain a waiver or give notice to the employer or carrier. [NOTE: It is also important that one claiming subrogation rights give notice to the third party.]

Where the settlement is made after suit is commenced, the court must approve and set attorneys' fees. Where the settlement is made without court action, the approval and fee-setting is done by the Workers' Compensation Appeals Board. The former I.A.C. always had authority to pass upon the adequacy of third-party settlements but did not have any authority over attorneys' fees until the law was amended in 1959. Before this change, the commission compared the net amount after deducting attorneys' fees and any costs with the present value of the employee's compensation benefits. Approval was given if the net was equal to or greater than these benefits. If less, the settlement was not approved. In this event, the parties would either re-negotiate, or if the difference permitted, the employee's attorney might reconsider the fee. Now that the W.C.A.B. has authority to fix fees, it may determine all issues connected with a third-party settlement submitted for approval.

When a third-party settlement without suit is approved by the Board, the employer or carrier and the third party are relieved of any further liability regarding the injury in question. However, if a settlement is insufficient to cover all of the potential workers' compensation benefits, this situation can be recognized in the C & R document, and the third-party settlement considered as a partial recoupment for the employer or carrier. Also, if the settlement is for an amount greater than accrued benefits, and the document does not specifically cover future benefits, the employer or carrier may obtain additional credit against its liability for such future benefits. As held by the Court of Appeal, where an employer seeks a W.C.A.B. decision granting credit for an employee's recovery in a third-party settlement, the Board must determine the reasonableness of the attorney's fee proposed in the settlement. The issue is raised when the employer's request and pertinent documentation are submitted to the Board. The credit is limited to the net amount after deduction of reasonable attorney's fees and costs. Also, if a settlement

CC 3333.1
involves a medical malpractice case, and the settlement is negotiated so as to result in a reduced amount to reflect the employee's collateral sources, including workers' compensation, the settlement recovery may not be taken as a credit by the employer against liability for workers' compensation. This ruling by the Court of Appeal is grounded upon the fact that CC 3333.1 prohibits liens for workers' compensation benefits in medical malpractice cases.

Many settlements are approved by the W.C.A.B. without much question, such as those involving a relatively small amount of compensation as compared with the amount of the settlement with the alleged wrongdoer. A third-party compromise may be larger in some cases because of the difference in the theory between compensation payments and damages for a wrongful act. The latter may include the entire wage-loss, permanent impairment, as well as pain and suffering. As has been stated, the workers' compensation plan does not compensate for pain and suffering, as such, and this may be the largest item of damages in a negligence case. Pain itself is not considered in computing compensation benefits. Its effect on the ability of the employee to work may be a factor in setting the permanent disability rating.

Many varying elements are involved in negotiating these settlements and in their approval. One is the question of how much liability insurance the wrongdoer has. Before executing any papers, the employee and the employer or compensation carrier should make a comparison with compensation benefits, for it is quite possible that the limits of liability coverage do not equal the present or commuted value of these benefits. This is particularly true if the employee is entitled to continuing or lifetime medical treatment. Review of a third-party C & R involves the same principles discussed in Chapter 11, SETTLEMENTS—COMPROMISE AND RELEASE.

§ 12.6   Settlement Without Employer's Consent

In LC 3859(b), the law provides that an employee may settle and release *LC 3859,* any claim he or she may have against a third party, without the consent of the *3860* employer or the employer's workers' compensation insurance carrier. Such a settlement is subject to the right of the employer or carrier to proceed against the third party in order to recoup the cost of benefits provided to the em- *LC 3852,* ployee or to his or her dependents.   *3854*

The settlement provision of LC 3860 requires notice to the employer and an opportunity to recover the amount of compensation paid for special damages. However, Subsection (b) of this section has been amended to provide that except as provided in Section 3859 (as amended above) the settlement amount is subject to the full claim of the employer. Thus, while the employer ostensibly has a lien, an employee or dependent may now settle and release his or her particular claim with the third party and leave the employer to proceed against the third party by an independent suit. This legislation seemingly overrules the prior statute and appellate court decisions upholding the priority of an employer's lien against settlement recoveries where the employer is not guilty of contributory negligence. Compensation lienclaimants in such cases must negotiate in good faith. The courts have allowed settlements between the employee and the third party without recognition of the lien if there is a factual determination by the court or jury that the employer was guilty of contributory negligence.

If there is a general verdict without indication that the employer was negligent, the compensation lien must be allowed against the verdict so rendered. Under this legislation, the parties may settle without the lienclaimant's participation, so long as the lienclaimant's right to maintain a separate action is preserved. The basic rules pertaining to verdicts and judgments are applicable, and in order to have all issues resolved, adequate notice of the issues and proceedings must be given to a lienclaimant. The plaintiff and the defendant cannot foreclose the employer or carrier where such notice has not been given, and this is particularly true where, because of the time element involved, the statute of limitations has run against the right of the employer or carrier to proceed alone in a separate action.

§ 12.7   Contributory Negligence of Employer or Employee; Comparative Negligence Rule

Under the common-law rule of contributory negligence, a person's cause of action against another for negligently causing injury or damage could be defeated if the latter could establish that the injured party's own negligence was wholly or partly responsible for the injury or damage. Thus, a plaintiff in a personal injury action would recover nothing if it were found that he or she was guilty of contributory negligence, even though it was also *CC 1714* established that the defendant was negligent. Court decisions adopted this rule for California, although CC 1714, which calls for consideration of an injured party's own fault, does not appear to require the strict common-law test. In 1975, the California Supreme Court, in *Li v. Yellow Cab Co.*, overruled these previous decisions and established a rule of comparative negligence. Under this rule, a negligent plaintiff may have his or her recovery against a negligent defendant reduced, but all recovery is not denied as it was under the previous rule. In applying the comparative negligence rule, a court or jury must determine a percentage of responsibility based upon the relative degree of negligence of the parties.

The court in the *Li* case overruled a century of court decisions which had applied the common-law rule of contributory negligence established by an English court decision in 1809. The *Li* case also eliminates the "last clear chance" doctrine as a possible defense to a charge of contributory negligence and supersedes the "assumption of risk" defense as it pertains to contributory negligence. The Supreme Court states that CC 1714, which was enacted in 1872, did incorporate in California law the English negligence rules but that the code language is broad enough to permit a more equitable interpretation by the courts, that the courts have developed the expertise necessary to apportion liability as required by a pure comparative negligence rule. Thus, the court has abated the harshness of the rules previously applied in cases of concurrent negligence. It still remains the case that if the defendant is found not to have been negligent, the plaintiff takes nothing. If the defendant did negligently cause the plaintiff's injury, and the plaintiff was not negligent, the judgment is not reduced.

Since rules regarding negligence and concurrent negligence impinge upon third-party actions growing out of industrial injuries, the courts have established a set of rules governing consideration of the subrogation rights of employers and carriers. Until the Supreme Court's decision in *Witt v. Jackson*, liens of employers were given priority regardless of any concurrent negligence. In 1961, in *Witt v. Jackson*, the court had before it a case in which both an employee and his employer sought recovery from a third party. The facts indicated that negligence attributed to the employer was partly responsible for the employee's injuries. Applying the maxim that one should not benefit from his own wrong, the court held that the lien of a contributorily negligent employer should be denied. In order that this rule not result in a windfall, double recovery by the employee (i.e., full receipt of full compensation benefits), the judgment against the third party would be reduced by the amount of the workers' compensation benefits already received. The employee's net recovery would not be affected since the rule deals only with that portion which would otherwise be paid to the employer under the lien.

The *Witt v. Jackson* rule affected settlement negotiations because an employer's consent was necessary, and if the parties asserted that the employer was negligent and should be denied a lien, such consent was often difficult to obtain. It was for this reason that the law was changed to permit settlement between an employee or dependent and a third-party defendant, leaving the employer or carrier the option of bringing a separate suit against the third party. The rationale is that the plaintiff (employee or dependent) and the defendant can negotiate liability, damages, and any *Witt v. Jackson* credit claimed by the defendant. If the employer was not negligent, the right of the employer or carrier to seek recovery from the third party is not adversely affected. If the employer was negligent, the employer or carrier would have lost in any event. Also involved is the likelihood that if an employer or carrier realizes from the factual situation that its position on the employer-negligence issue is weak, it may forego any further litigation.

With the advent of the comparative negligence rule, it became necessary to determine its effect upon the *Witt v. Jackson* principle. In the *Cole* case, the Supreme Court affirmed the basic philosophy of *Witt v. Jackson*, holding that comparative negligence rules also apply to the question of the employer's negligence. Where an employer and the third party are concurrently negligent, the employer's right to a lien is recognizable only to the extent that workers' compensation benefits furnished exceed that portion of the judgment which is attributable to the employer's negligence. By way of example, suppose that an employee recovers a $100,000 judgment against a negligent third party; that the employer has paid out $20,000.00 in workers' compensation benefits; and, that the employer's negligence has been found to be 50% responsible for the employee's injury. In this example, the employer would not recover anything on his lien, for he was responsible for $50,000.00 of the damages in the third-party suit. He would recover on his lien only to the extent that worker's compensation benefits exceeded $50,000.00.

The Supreme Court also holds that where the issue arises before the W.C.A.B. in a compensation proceeding in which the employer claims credit *LC 3857* for the employee's recovery in a third-party suit, the same principle applies. In this situation, the W.C.A.B. has authority to determine the degree of negligence and to apply the principles of the *Cole* decision.

The next major issue determined by the Supreme Court was whether an employer's lien in a third-party action or claim for credit in a W.C.A.B. proceeding should be further reduced by the amount attributable to the employee's own negligence. In the *Rodgers* case, the court holds that the claim of an employer or carrier is not subject to reduction by virtue of the employee's own negligence. Again, if the employer is not guilty of contributory negligence, there is no reduction of its lienright, and the lien of an employer applies to the recovery of the employee or dependent even if the net received by the employee or dependent is an amount reduced because of the employee's negligence.

If a defendant in a third-party action claims that a *Witt v. Jackson-Cole* issue rules out the subrogation right of an employer or other subrogation claimant, the latter must be given adequate notice. The Court of Appeal has said that such notice in a lawsuit must be by way of an adequate "pleading" filed and served no later than the pretrial procedure or the trial-setting date. Further, in the conduct of a trial, the parties may not prejudice the rights of the employer or carrier seeking a lien so as to preclude presentation of a defense to the charge of contributory negligence. Even though the parties have a right to settle a case without the consent of the employer, leaving the employer or carrier to pursue a claim by separate suit, where the statute of limitations has run as to any such suit, the parties must permit litigation of *Witt v. Jackson-Cole* issues before settling. A trial court in a third-party case will not try to determine future compensation benefits and will leave this phase of the case to the W.C.A.B. If the employer was found guilty of contributory negligence by the trial court, this finding will be binding upon the parties in any later W.C.A.B. proceedings. If the issue was not decided, the W.C.A.B. has jurisdiction to decide it.

§ 12.8   Reimbursement of Third Party by Employer

A decision of the appellate court illustrates this problem. A school district engaged a maintenance company to wash the windows of its high school. The contract provided that the company was to be "held responsible for payment of any and all damages" resulting from its operations. There was also a proviso that Hauser windows were to be washed from the inside using stepladders. A maintenance company employee washed a Hauser window without a ladder and without any safety equipment of any kind. Instead, he stood on the sill and held onto the window as he washed it. A bolt sheared, the window came loose and he fell two stories. He received compensation benefits from the company's compensation carrier. Later the employee and the carrier brought suit against the school district on the theory that the window was not in safe condition for such work. A judgment was entered against the district which it settled for $25,000. The school district then sued the company asserting that the language quoted above constituted an agreement to indemnify the district. The appellate court held that there was evidence to indicate that both the district and the employer were negligent. If a jury found this as fact, there was an implied indemnification clause in the contract so that the district could recover from the company. Thus, in a circuitous manner, an employee and the employer's compensation carrier could recover from the employer on the theory of negligence, in spite of the provisions and policy of the workers' compensation law.

Presumably because of this case, the 1959 legislature amended the code to prohibit such lawsuits against employers unless the employer has agreed in writing, before the injury occurs, to reimburse or hold the third party harmless. It will no longer be possible to hold an employer to an implied indemnification agreement. Under the new law it must be expressly stated in the agreement. *LC 3864*

"Hold-harmless" or indemnity clauses are common and are inserted in contracts to safeguard the parties from the consequences of acts for which they are not directly responsible. The 1959 change in LC 3864 gives the contracting parties the additional burden of foreseeing the possibilities and also to prevent the result in the window case unless the employer was given an opportunity to consider it beforehand and agree or refuse to agree to such a clause.

Two decisions of the appellate court point up the effect of LC 3864. In the first case, the court holds that a third party held liable in a damage suit may obtain indemnity from the employer of the injured plaintiff in concurrent negligence cases if the third party is merely passively negligent as opposed to being actively negligent. The indemnity may be on either a contractual or an equity basis. LC 3864 would limit this type of recovery to cases of express contractual indemnity, but that provision is not retroactive to cases arising before its enactment in 1959. Passive negligence is involved where the third party controls the place of employment, has knowledge of a special danger actively created by the plaintiff's employer. The right to indemnity may apply to a settlement with the third party if possible liability is apparent. The statute of limitations regarding the indemnity right begins to run where the settlement is made. The other case dealt with a newspaper's route manager (Sweat) who employed a person named Deal. Through Sweat's negligence, Deal was injured. Sweat had covered Deal under his workers' compensation insurance policy. The newspaper sued Sweat to recover amounts paid under a judgment obtained on the basis of the doctrine of *respondeat superior* (liability for act in "scope" of agency). The basis for the newspaper's suit against Sweat was the liability of an agent or a contractee who, through a wrongful act, causes loss on the part of the other without the other's fault being involved. While the court recognizes this general rule, it holds that in the absence of a specific contract of indemnity, LC 3864 prohibits the application of the doctrine of implied indemnity where the resulting injury is industrial.

§ 12.9   When a Third-Party Action?

A surprising number of third-party actions go by the board, because they are not recognized by the employee or by the employer or carrier. A first report of an industrial injury may show merely that an employee was hit by a falling object, was struck by a piece of equipment or fell because of defective work performed by others. If a full investigation is not made soon after the injury, the parties may miss the fact that the employer and the injured's fellow workers were not responsible for the cause of the injury and that instead the cause was the negligence of a third person or firm. When the facts come to light at a hearing on compensation benefits, it is often too late for the employee to bring suit against the third party because of the one-year statute of limitations in personal injury cases.

For discussion of possible liability of a city or a county in issuing a building permit to an uninsured contractor or property owner, see: Chapter 3, INSURANCE, § 3.23, *Workers' Compensation Requirement for Building Permit.*

§ 12.10   Actions Against Fellow Employee

LC 3601
Where a worker's industrial injury or death results from an act of a co-worker, no third-party damage suit may be maintained against the co-worker by the injured worker or his or her dependents except in two situations. Such a suit may be brought where:

(1)   The injury or death is proximately caused by the willful and unprovoked physical act of aggression of the other employee

(2)   The injury or death is proximately caused by the intoxication of the other employee

Except in these two instances, the right to recover workers' compensation benefits is the exclusive remedy. In no event, either by legal action or agreement, is the employer to be held liable in any way for damages awarded or liability incurred by the other employee.

LC 3852
No employee may be held liable to his or her employer for causing the injury or death of a co-employee as a general rule. However, if an injured worker or a dependent obtains a judgment against an employee under one of the above exceptions, the employer may seek recovery for compensation payments and other damages per LC 3852.

The restrictions against employer-liability for the acts of employees does not prevent a claim for the serious and wilful misconduct penalty if the co-employee causing the injury comes within the definition of top management personnel set forth in LC 4553. (See Chapter 9, PENALTIES, § 9.6, *Serious and Wilful Misconduct.*)

Further, it should be noted that before the revision of LC 3600-3602 effective January 1, 1983, appellate court decisions held both employees and their employers liable for negligence or malpractice without considering the statutory limitations on such suits in LC 3601. The theory was that both the employees and the employer acted in "dual capacities," which doctrine was abrogated by legislative amendment effective on the above date. Therefore, in considering appellate court decisions regarding suits against co-employees one should note whether the facts arose before or after January 1, 1983.

§ 12.11 Actions Against Employer

As a general rule, an employer who has "secured" payment of workers' compensation is immune from suits brought in the general courts by employees or dependents on the basis of a work-injury or death. Workers' compensation is the exclusive remedy. The present law contains several exceptions to this general rule. Because amendments effective January 1, 1983, were enacted in response to certain decisions of the California Supreme Court and appellate courts, a review of the court holdings is in order to fully appreciate their effect. *LC 3600- 3602*

In the case of *Duprey v. Shane* (1939), the Supreme Court ruled that an employee of a doctor could bring a personal injury action (malpractice) where the doctor treated her for a work-injury. It was said that there was a dual relationship between them: (1) employer-employee and (2) doctor-patient. The employee was permitted to maintain her action on the basis of the doctor-patient relationship, and thus the doctor's right to immunity from suit as an employer was not abridged. He could be held liable for damages because he intentionally chose to assume another role vis à vis the employee. The *Duprey* case did not create much controversy since it appeared to be limited to malpractice cases, and doctors could escape the potential by having other physicians treat their employees. But, in the 1970's the courts began applying the so-called "dual capacity" doctrine to various types of situations. In one case, it was held that if an employee was injured by a product manufactured by the employer for use by the general public, the employer as manufacturer bore a second relationship to the employee who was considered as a member of the consuming public. However, if the injurious item was manufactured only for use in the business and not for the general trade, there was no liability other than that for workers' compensation. Also, suits were allowed if based upon the alleged deceit of an employer in misrepresenting an injured worker's rights or in failing to disclose the known deleterious effect of substances used in the employer's operations. Another line of decisions overruled a previous decision and allowed actions against employers who were guilty of willfully assaulting an employee. In *Unruh v. Truck Ins. Exch.*, a worker's action against a carrier was upheld on the basis of fraudulent and deceitful actions of the carrier's investigators in investigating the workers' compensation claim. Thus, the number of court-declared exceptions to the statutory provision for employer-immunity from actions at law in industrial accident matters was increasing. The "straw" that moved the legislature to step in was the Supreme Court decision in *Bell v. Vangas.* The court held that the dual capacity doctrine applied to the driver of a truck used to haul wholesale quantities of propane gas to retailers. A dissenting opinion pointed out that there was no way Bell could have been a member of the consuming class, for he was not a retailer buying truckloads of propane from Vangas.

LC 3600,
3601,
3602
4558

In 1982, effective January 1, 1983, the legislature adopted a "package" which included increasing workers' compensation benefits, removing the ceiling from the serious and wilful misconduct penalty, giving the W.C.A.B. increased authority in discrimination cases, and, finally, removing the "dual-capacity" doctrine from the law. The Legislature did find some merit in the court decisions outlined above and retained a limited number of exceptions.

LC 3600, 3601, and 3602 were amended to emphasize that workers' compensation is the exclusive remedy for injuries in the course of employment "in lieu of any other liability whatsoever to any person . . ." (3600); "exclusive remedy" (3601); "the sole and exclusive remedy" (3602). LC 3602 provides: "(T)he fact that either the employee or the employer also occupied another or dual capacity prior to, or at the time of, the employee's industrial injury shall not permit the employee or his or her dependents to bring an action at law for damages against the employer."

The exceptions provided in LC 3602 are:

LC 3602(b)
(1)

Assault: Suit may be brought against an employer where the employee's injury is the result of a wilful physical assault by the employer.

LC 3602(b)
(2)

Fraudulent Concealment: Suit may be brought against an employer if an employee's injury is aggravated by the employer's fraudulent concealment of the existence of the injury and its connection with the employment. Damages are limited to those caused by the aggravation, the burden of proof being on the employer regarding apportionment of damages between the initial industrial injury and the aggravation due to the concealment. In order to maintain a suit under this provision, an employee must prove that he or she sustained an initial industrial injury and that this initial injury was aggravated by the employer's fraudulent concealment of the injury and its connection with the employment.

LC 3602(b)
(3)

Defective Product: An action may be maintained against an employer where injury or death results from a defective product manufactured by the employer, but only if the product is furnished to the employee by a third person. This exception applies only to a product manufactured by the employer and sold, leased, or otherwise transferred to "an independent third person" for a valuable consideration, and then that product is furnished the employee by a third person.

Unguarded Power Press: An action may be brought against an employer if the employer knowingly removes or fails to install a "point of operation guard" on a power press. In order to maintain this action it must be shown that the manufacturer of the press installed or required the guard and so informed the employer. Under this exception, "employer" means "a named identifiable person who is, prior to the time of the employee's injury or death, an owner or supervisor having managerial authority to direct and control the acts of employees." It must also be established that the failure to install or the removal was through an affirmative instruction conveyed by the employer. That the employer subsequently acquiesced in or ratified the removal of a guard is not sufficient. There is no right of contribution by another defendant against the employer unless there is a judgment against the employer, and the employer fails to discharge his or her comparative share of the judgment. *LC 3602(a) 4558*

An appellate court decision has determined that a power hand saw is not a power press; thus, an employee injured while using such a saw may not maintain a personal injury action against the employer. It has also been held that an employment agency furnishing temporary help is not liable under this exception since liability is predicated upon a direct act of the employer in the removal or failure to install a point of operation guard.

Uninsured Employer: An employer who is illegally uninsured for workers' compensation is subject to an action at law for damages brought by an injured worker or his or her dependents in the event of death. This exception is discussed in more detail in Chapter 3, INSURANCE, § 3.19, *Failure to Insure; Uninsured Employers' Fund.* *LC 3602(a) LC 3706*

Credit for Compensation: If an employee or dependent obtains a judgment or settlement by virtue of a claim or action under any of the above exceptions, the employer receives credit for any workers' compensation payments made and is relieved from future workers' compensation obligations to the extent of actual payments made in accordance with a judgment or settlement. *LC 3600(b) 3709*

[NOTE: Some appellate court decisions since January 1, 1983, may appear to be applying the "old law." These cases involve injuries occurring before that date. Thus, noting dates of injury will help to put post-1982 decisions in perspective. There is anticipation that a new line of cases interpreting the 1983 amendments will emerge.]

The protection afforded employers against actions at law brought by their employees presupposes the existence of compensable injuries under the workers' compensation law. LC 3602(c) provides: "In all cases where the conditions of compensation set forth in Section 3600 do not occur, the liability of the employer shall be the same as if this division (the workers' compensation law) had not been enacted." *LC 3602(c)*

If a plaintiff in a personal injury action was a gratuitous volunteer, rather than an employee, a suit may be brought even though the defendant had "secured" payment of compensation benefits. However, in the case of a volunteer defined as an employee under the compensation law, a "secured" employer is protected from such suits. This protection also applies to suits brought by persons injured during physical fitness or agility tests which are part of an examination for a job, although they would receive compensation benefits as "non-gratuitous volunteers."

While the Supreme Court has held that a spouse may bring an action against a defendant in a personal injury action for loss of "consortium" (conjugal services) of the injured spouse, thus far, the appellate courts have refused to permit this type of suit against an employer in an industrial accident case. The courts hold that compliance with the compensation law is a complete defense to such actions.

Appellate court decisions following the 1982 legislation indicate the courts' acknowledgment that the dual-capacity doctrine has been nullified and that the exemption from tort actions of an employer who has "secured" workers' compensation coverage has been strengthened. The courts have ruled that an employee may not maintain a suit against his employer and a co-employee for harrassment on the job resulting in physical impairment, and that employee's wife may not bring an action for loss of consortium (Supreme Court *Cole* decision). Also precluded are suits brought by heirs of a deceased worker whether or not the heirs are deemed dependents under the workers' compensation law. Where a suit is based upon the alleged fraud or deception of the employer or carrier, and the "Unruh Theory" is asserted, the courts hold that *Unruh* will not be extended to cases in which the facts show only a refusal of or delay in payment of workers' compensation for which the normal procedures for enforcement and appeal are adequate. [The same prohibition against tort actions versus an employer has been applied to suits predicated upon denial of unemployment disability compensation; the right to an administrative appeal being deemed a sufficient remedy.] Likewise, where a property-owner or a general contractor has "secured" workers' compensation benefits and is determined to be the employer as the "ultimate hirer" of an unlicensed uninsured building contractor, such an employer status carries with it immunity from a tort action brought by the unlicensed contractor or his or her employee. The appellate court now seems to be satisfied that in tort cases predicated upon harrassment or unsafe practices resulting in bodily injury or discrimination because of a claim the workers' compensation law affords adequate remedies in view of the 1982 amendments regarding penalties for serious and willful misconduct and discrimination.

In the case of *Shoemaker v. Myers* (1990), the California Supreme Court has ruled that injuries assertedly caused by an employer's wrongful termination of an employee and attendant post-termination activities are compensable under the workers' compensation law. Thus, a civil suit against the employer based upon such allegations is barred even though the employer's actions were intentional or "egregious." The court overruled a prior appellate decision which had held to the contrary. Also barred are suits against an employer based upon allegations of breach of the covenant of good faith and fair dealing, inducement of breach of contract and infliction of emotional distress whether or not intentional. However, the Supreme Court recognizes other exceptions to the exclusiveness of the workers' compensation remedy. These include lawsuits based upon defamation, fraudulent deprivation of a claim against a third party, acts of employers or carriers wherein they have stepped out of their proper roles (*Unruh* case), where there is a questionable relationship between an employer's actions and employment, or where the activity was not a risk of the employment. A statute which grants a specific right of suit for enforcement purposes may also provide an exception. For example, suits are permitted under the federal and state civil rights acts and the California "whistleblower" law. Similarly, the United States Supreme Court has held that the suit permitted under federal law pertaining to seasonal and migratory agricultural workers for failure to provide safe transportation is not barred by a state's workers' compensation law. Other appellate court decisions have ruled out suits against an employer where the injury aspects of a case indicate compensability under the workers' compensation law, but have permitted them where the damages sought are for non-injury effects. In any permitted suit in which there is recovery for the effects of injury, the employer must be given credit for any workers' compensation benefits provided.

The question of whether a general-special employer situation exists may arise in a damage action by way of defense. For instance, if an employee of a contractor is injured through the negligence of a sub-contractor, he has a right of action against the sub-contractor. But if the "sub" was either a general or special employer; i.e., a joint employer who has "secured" compensation benefits, the employee's sole remedy is under the workers' compensation law. A salary reimbursement agreement between contractors does not make out a case of joint employment where the defendant exercised no control over the injured employee. One who is determined to be the "ultimate hirer" of an unlicensed, uninsured building contractor or the contractor's employees is immune from a personal injury damage suit filed by either on the basis of an industrial injury. See discussion of "ultimate hirer" in Chapter 2, EMPLOYMENT, § 2.8, *Employee or Independent Contractor*.

Where one of the joint wrongdoers is an employer who has settled with the employee in a compensation case, another wrongdoer cannot set up the settlement as defense in the damage action. However, if the employer is a partnership which has complied with the compensation law, and the defendant in a damage suit is one of the partners, there can be no recovery, for the plaintiff is deemed to be an employee of each partner. He is thus limited to his remedy for compensation benefits. Of course, if the plaintiff is also a partner not receiving wages, he may maintain an action against any partner who negligently caused his injury.

LC 2801

In any personal injury action permitted by law which is based upon asserted negligence of an employer, or officer or agent of the employer, the defenses of assumption of risk and fellow-servant rule are not available. As to the defense of contributory negligence, LC 2801 sets up a comparative negligence test. See the prior discussion of contributory and comparative negligence.

An overly broad pre-employment release of future liability required of an employee by an employer which includes release of liability for intentional acts, violation of law or fraud is contrary to public policy and void, according to a ruling of the Court of Appeal.

§ 12.12 Third Party as "Employer" Under Safety Laws

LC 6304, 6304.5 6400

Prior to 1971, the definition of "employer" for the purposes of the state safety laws included persons or organizations not defined as employers under the workers' compensation law. These sections of the Labor Code defined those who have a duty to provide workers with a safe place to work as "every person having direction, management, control, or custody of any employment, place of employment, or any employee." Thus, an owner-builder owed a duty to workmen of a sub-contractor to provide a safe place to work and could be sued for damages for a failure to do so. This provision was applied by the courts to property owners and construction contractors particularly.

In 1971, LC 6304 was amended to provide that one who is not an actual employer of an injured person is no longer a "statutory employer" under California safety laws. Section 6304.5 was added to the Labor Code which provides that the safety laws are not to "have an application to, nor be considered in, nor admissible into, evidence in any personal injury or wrongful death action arising after the operative date of this Section except as between an employee and his own employer."

The removal of the prior definition of "employer" from the safety laws and inadmissibility of safety laws and regulations in any personal injury or wrongful death action constitutes a compromise between labor and management. In the "trade," labor received increased benefits in the form of higher maximums for compensation rates and a new permanent disability conversion table, along with increased death benefits for dependents. Was it a trade? Previous appellate court decisions have grounded liability of property owners, lessees, or general contractors on two bases: (1) the general duty owed to "invitees" and (2) the duty placed by the former statute upon "statutory employers" to provide a safe place to work. It may be doubted that this

CC 1714

amendment will have any effect upon the success or failure of personal injury litigation. The obligation of a property owner or contractor is contained in Civil Code Section 1714, and employees working on a premises under contract have been defined as "invitees." As an example, the Restatement of Torts, Section 416, states: "One who employs an independent contractor to do work which the employer should recognize as likely to create during its progress a peculiar risk of physical harm to others unless special precautions are taken, is subject to liability for physical harm caused to them by the failure of the contractor to exercise reasonable care to take such precautions, even though the employer has provided for such precautions in the contract or otherwise."

§ 12.13 Liability of Compensation Carrier; Self-Insured Employer; Claims Personnel

As a general rule, a workers' compensation insurance carrier is not liable in personal injury actions brought by employees of an insured employer. Some years ago the Court of Appeal ruled that a compensation carrier's liability is limited to that set forth in the terms of its policies as required by the Insurance Code. Thus, a carrier was not liable for the alleged malpractice of a doctor furnished by it to treat an industrial injury, although the doctor would be subject to such a suit. This same principle has been applied to suits seeking to hold a carrier liable for the alleged negligence of a safety inspector employed by it to inspect the premises of its insureds. However, it has been held by the appellate courts that an insurance carrier can incur a liability for activities following an injury, such as investigations or claims handling. One case involved the invasion of privacy of the injured worker through the carrier's method of investigation and motion picture taking. Other cases have involved carriers' failure to handle claims of good faith. The same protection against personal injury actions applies to the California Workers' Compensation Insurance Rating Bureau which has authority to make safety inspections.

IC 11750.3 11758, 11759

In the *Unruh* case, the California Supreme Court held that an employee who was a victim of the fraud, deceit, and invasion of privacy perpetrated by investigators for her employer's workers' compensation insurance carrier could maintain an action against the carrier. The court pointed out that ordinarily in the investigation and administration of a workers' compensation claim, the carrier would be immune from suit. But here, the acts of the investigators were intentional and went beyond normal procedures. In practicing fraud and deceit, they acted in a dual capacity and removed themselves and the carrier from the protection of the law. The court also pointed out that the injurious acts were separate from and subsequent to the employee's initial injury. Considering the 1983 legislation removing "dual capacity" as a ground for suit, there is an obvious defense to be asserted in any future *Unruh* type of case. However, it must be kept in mind that the court stressed that the investigators intentionally changed their roles from investigators to active antagonists willing to practice fraud and deceit. Therefore, it is possible that a court might hold that the *Unruh* principle continues to be viable. It may also be noted that many recent decisions have upheld the immunity of employers and carriers where plaintiffs have sought to bring their cases under the *Unruh* holding. In those cases, the facts alleged showed that the only dereliction, if proved, involved normal claims procedures for which there is adequate remedy under the workers' compensation law. The same result has occurred in cases alleging failure to handle claims in good faith.

An appellate court has held that the *Unruh* case does not apply to a self-insured employer; that in handling workers' compensation claims the employer is not an insurance carrier, even though subject to similar rules.

There has been a good deal of litigation concerning whether claims representatives for workers' compensation insurance carriers and self-insured employers can be held personally liable for so-called "bad faith" handling of claims. Thus far, the courts have declared that claims personnel who are employees of carriers or employers are immune from such suits. The same is true of independent adjusters retained by carriers. According to the California Supreme Court's decision in the *Marsh & McLennan* case (1989), independent ("third-party") administrators for self-insured employers are also immune from damage suits brought by employees based upon alleged faulty claims-handling. The court stated that, absent a showing of outrageous conduct per *Unruh*, a workers' compensation claimant has no tort cause of action against an independent administrator for a self-insured employer on the basis of non-payment of compensation. Remedies are provided under the workers' compensation law for such defaults, and jurisdiction resides in the W.C.A.B. This decision is consistent with previous decisions of the Court of Appeal in the *Denning, Rodriguez,* and *Santiago* cases. A contrary decision in the *Dill* case was disapproved.

A general issue regarding so-called "bad faith" lawsuits against insurance carriers has been resolved by the California Supreme Court in the case of *Moradi-Shalal v. Fireman's Fund,* namely, that IC 790.03 does not create a bad faith cause of action in favor of a third-party claimant (i.e., one who is not the insured) against an insurance carrier in handling the claim. In other cases, appellate courts have continued to hold that neither insurance carriers nor their agents and employees may be sued for damages for matters growing out of handling workers' compensation claims. Nevertheless, in *Jablonski v. Royal Globe,* the Court of Appeal has held that allegations of an injured worker in a civil suit against a workers' compensation insurance carrier and its agents that they wrongfully denied insurance coverage and destroyed evidence of such coverage with the intent to deprive the employee of workers' compensation benefits were sufficient to bring the case to trial, and that these allegations bring the case within the criteria set in the *Unruh* decision.

§ 12.14　Medical Treatment—Malpractice

The right to bring an action for negligence against a physician, as defined by the Labor Code, arises out of the duty of the physician to his patient to use that degree of skill employed by members of his profession in the community. Even though a physician furnished by an employer or carrier is their agent, he is also subject to the physician-patient relationship with the injured employee whom he is treating. Not only are injuries suffered by reason of any malpractice of such physician compensable as a continuation of the original industrial injury, the employee may bring a damage action against the physician. If the employee recovers a judgment, the employer has *LC 3852* a lienright to the extent of any added compensation payments made. However, this lienright is subject to the provisions of CC 3333.1. The employee does not have any right to bring a damage action against the employer or carrier for malpractice, the employee's sole remedy as to these parties being under the compensation law.

While LC 3852 provides for a lien, the California Supreme Court has ruled that CC 3333.1 supersedes LC 3852, and if in a malpractice suit a de- *CC 3333.1* fendant medical provider introduces evidence of the plaintiff's receipt of workers' compensation benefits, the employer has no lien or any subrogation rights. The court also held that CC 3333.1 is not unconstitutional, for the need to lessen potential liability in medical malpractice cases in order to assure malpractice insurance at reasonable premium rates is a valid legislative purpose. As previously noted, if a settlement in a medical malpractice case is negotiated for a reduced amount because a workers' compensation lien is not permitted per CC 3333.1, an employer may not obtain credit against workers' compensation liability on the basis of the employee's recovery under the settlement.

§ 12.15 Other Insurance

If a plaintiff in a personal injury action also recovers benefits under a personal insurance policy for which he has paid premiums, the defendant is not entitled to any credit for the sums received, even though payment under the policy was brought about by the very injury which is the subject matter of the lawsuit. Such policies are extrinsic of any connection with the defendant. In most cases any double recovery aspect is prevented through an exclusion in the insurance policy for industrial injuries and for subrogation rights in case the carrier has paid on the basis of an industrial injury. (Compare: LC 3752.)

The uninsured motorist law provides for a reduction of its benefits by amounts payable to a claimant under the workers' compensation laws. Uninsured motorist insurance is not to benefit any workers' compensation insurer or self-insured employer, the United States, or any state or political *IC 11580.1,* subdivision. The amount paid under a policy may be reduced by the present *11580.2* value of all amounts payable to the insured under any workers' compensation law, exclusive of any non-occupational disability benefits. If arbitration is necessary under the policy, the arbitrator is not to proceed with the matter until the workers' compensation questions, including permanent disability, are determined. The insured must file a statement under penalty of perjury stating whether the insured has a pending claim for workers' compensation arising from the accident and, if so, whether there has been an award or settlement. If there has been no award or settlement, arbitration will not proceed unless the insured can show good cause why it should proceed.

In *Coltherd v. W.C.A.B.* (1990), the Court of Appeal holds that payment under the uninsured motorist coverage of a policy of vehicle insurance is properly received without deduction of workers' compensation benefits where the policy terms do not require it. Further, any overpayment made by virtue of such a policy may not be a lien against workers' compensation benefits since LC 4903 does not include such a lien.

Chapter 13
JURISDICTION

§ 13.1   Introduction

The term "jurisdiction" refers to the authority of a governmental body to exercise control over persons or things. Its precise meaning must be gained from the context in which it is used. Disputes concerning jurisdiction in workers' compensation cases may involve state versus federal authority, state versus state, Workers' Compensation Appeals Board versus general courts' jurisdiction, exclusive jurisdiction, concurrent jurisdiction, or jurisdiction as limited by time or subject matter.

§ 13.2   California's Jurisdiction

The California workers' compensation law applies to all industrial in- *LC 3203* juries occurring within this state. It also applies to any injury occurring out- *5305* side the state if the contract of employment was made in California. Under *3600.5* this authority, cases have come before the commission and the Appeals Board involving injuries occurring in most parts of the world.

If an out-of-state employee is working temporarily in California, and if the employer is covered by workers' compensation in the other state, and further, if the other state gives reciprocal recognition to similar situations for California employers, the employee is limited to the benefits and remedies provided by the laws of the other state.

The State Compensation Insurance Fund has been granted the right to cover employees who are temporarily out of California under the laws of *IC 11779* other states on condition that the Fund also insures the employer's California *11780.5* employees. The Fund may also issue policies covering an employer's liability under the Longshoremen's and Harborworkers' Act and for compensation or damages under other federal or maritime laws.

California law applies to employments in interstate commerce unless *LC 3203* they are deemed to come under federal coverage for similar benefits.

Congress has provided a number of laws based upon various aspects of federal authority, and in those areas of activity state law does not apply. If a state tribunal has determined that it has jurisdiction, the federal courts ordinarily will not interfere where the record indicates that the question is a doubtful one. The courts will give the employer credit for any payments made under the wrong law.

§ 13.3　　Federal Legislation

The federal compensation laws present a picture of legislative patchwork in approaching the problem of work injuries. Some employments are covered by provisions similar to the California compensation law, others by a right to sue the employer on the basis of negligence. Under the federal Constitution, the United States government has jurisdiction over navigable water, interstate and foreign commerce, and bases or lands owned or controlled by it. Federal legislation has provided that if Congress has not acted in a particular field of activity, the state compensation law may be applied. Confusion has resulted from the reluctance of some states to exercise this authority with the result that many injuries have gone uncompensated. As these problems come to the attention of the legislators, new federal laws result in an effort to fill the need.

The Longshore and Harbor Workers Act is a workers' compensation law providing payments similar to those of the California laws and covers persons employed on docks and ships while the ships are being loaded and unloaded or repaired. It has also been made applicable to any employee working at a defense base in territory acquired from a foreign government, persons employed by firms doing work for the United States outside this country's boundaries, workers engaged in exploring and developing the natural resources of the United States' outer continental shelf, all civilian employees of "non-appropriated funds" on U.S. defense bases (post exchanges, servicemen's clubs, and similar activities). A similar type of law applies to all federal civilian workers. Except as to federal employees, these laws all refer to private employment, and as to these benefits may be afforded through private insurance. Disputes are determined by a commissioner or deputy commissioner of the U.S. Department of Labor.

In 1972, Congress amended the Longshore and Harbor Workers Act to bring it in line with the report of the recommendations of the National Commission on State Workmen's Compensation Laws. These changes include:

> Broadening jurisdiction to include shoreline, maritime-connected operations, such as a terminal, marine railway, or other adjoining area customarily used in loading, unloading, repairing, or building a vessel.

> Weekly compensation to be paid is 66²/3% of earnings with a maximum of 200% of the national average weekly wage.

Minimum compensation to be 50% of the national average weekly wage or actual wage of injured worker, whichever is less.

Compensation payable for temporary disability, permanent partial, and permanent total disability.

All necessary medical treatment with employee choice of physicians from an approved list.

Attorneys' fees to be paid by employer as an added benefit if and to the extent compensation awarded exceeds amount paid or offered by the employer.

Increased use of "Special Fund" for subsequent injury cases, medical, and vocational rehabilitation.

Death benefits to widow or widower are 50% of average earnings, for each minor child, 12⅔%; total of benefits not to exceed 66⅔% of average earnings. Funeral allowance up to $1,000.

Benefits to survive to workers' dependents.

Suits against vessels for "unseaworthiness" are prohibited to longshoremen and others under this act. Hold-harmless and indemnification agreements between vessel owners and stevedoring firms prohibited.

Railroad workers are protected by the Federal Employers' Liability Act, the remedy being a suit at law based on a showing of negligence. The doctrine of comparative negligence applies, which means that if the employee is also negligent, he does not necessarily lose out altogether. His recovery will be reduced only to the extent that his own conduct played a part in causing the injury. A similar law, the Jones Act, governs injuries to seamen. Employees of shipowners are also protected by Convention 55, an international agreement, which provides benefits for injuries occurring while on board ship in maritime navigation. The benefits include wages, board and lodging, and medical treatment ("maintenance" and "cure"). The courts also permit suits against shipowners for "unseaworthiness" if seamen are injured on shipboard.

Where state and federal jurisdiction seem to overlap, or where it is not clear which law applies, the United States Supreme Court has applied the concept of a "twilight zone" in which either may take jurisdiction. Many cases of this type come from local activities in navigable waters.

The federal courts have applied the California compensation law as a defense in a damage suit under the federal High Seas Death Act. In the reported case, the facts show that the dependents of an airline's San Francisco flight supervisor sued the airline under the federal act because of the employee's death which occurred when one of the airline's planes on which he was a passenger went down in the Pacific. Referring to the fact that the employee was traveling on company business, the court decided: California had jurisdiction and its compensation law applied. The employer had complied with the law and, therefore, could not be made subject to damage suits. The employee's duties were non-maritime in nature, and there was no conflict with any federal workers' compensation law.

§ 13.4 Jurisdiction of the Workers' Compensation Appeals Board

LC 5300, 5304

      The California Workers' Compensation Appeals Board has exclusive jurisdiction over all disputes arising under the California workers' compensation law. The exercise of this authority is dependent upon the existence of an injury out of and occurring in the course of an employment relationship. If any element of this requirement is missing, the Appeals Board does not have jurisdiction. Thus, if employment is not proven, or if the employment is exempt, the Board's jurisdiction ends upon the making of such a finding. Likewise, if employment is proven, but an injury in the course of it cannot be substantiated, the Appeals Board can proceed no further. When such negative findings are made, the power to adjudicate rests in the general courts.

      When jurisdiction attaches in the W.C.A.B. because of an industrial injury, the Board has exclusive jurisdiction over all issues arising under the compensation law. For example, appellate court decisions have established that a physician may not seek additional fees in the small claims court where a fee for his services had been set by the W.C.A.B., and the same rule has been applied to attorneys' fees. However, if a compensation-like benefit is furnished by an employer to supplement compensation, the W.C.A.B. has no jurisdiction over that benefit. Also, service-connected disability benefits under retirement laws are also outside the W.C.A.B.'s jurisdiction unless a statute grants such jurisdiction, as in the case of the Public Employees Retirement System where the jurisdiction is limited to determining whether the employee suffered a work injury.

LC 134
R 10606
10608
10615
LC 4628

      A party or an attorney representing a party may be punished for contempt in failing to follow the W.C.A.B. rules governing the filing of medical reports. Contempt may also be an appropriate remedy or punishment for an attempt to circumvent the exclusive jurisdiction of the Board. For example, an attorney may be held in contempt for exacting a fee from his client in excess of that allowed by the Board or for suing his client in small claims court for such a fee. A physician who violates W.C.A.B. Rule 10606 and LC 4628 in failing to identify a person or persons other than the physician responsible for substantive portions of medical reports may be cited for contempt of the

CCP 1209

Board. An appellate court will not interrupt W.C.A.B. contempt proceedings so long as the Board complies with the provisions of CCP 1209.

      LC 134 requires that the W.C.A.B. proceed in contempt proceedings in the same manner as courts of record. Accordingly, the W.C.A.B. must follow the applicable provisions of CCP 1209. Where the Board itself is conducting contempt proceedings, it is error for the Board to have one Commissioner hear the evidence and all seven members adjudicate the issue.

A petition for reconsideration is not a prerequisite for seeking review by the appellate court of a decision of the Board re contempt. A person found guilty of contempt may, however, petition the Board to reconsider its decision.

The W.C.A.B. has authority per LC 5309(c) to direct and order workers' *LC 5309* compensation judges to issue writs, summons, warrants of attachment, warrants of commitment, and all necessary process and proceedings for direct and hybrid contempt in like manner and to the same extent as courts of record. "Hybrid contempt" is defined as "a charge of contempt which arises from events occurring in the immediate presence of the workers' compensation judge for reasons which occur outside the presence of the workers' compensation judge."

§ 13.5   Determining Jurisdiction

The Appeals Board is a court, but because of the need for a finding of the above jurisdictional facts, it is termed a court of limited jurisdiction. Every court has the authority to determine its own jurisdiction, and its final decision on this point is binding on the parties in any later litigation involving the same right or transaction.

The question of the binding effect of an Appeals Board decision requires inquiry into the finality of the decision and identity of issues decided with those raised in a subsequent court action. For example, it has been held that a Board finding of no disabling injury does not preclude proof of injury in a damage action arising from the same incident. The appellate court's reasoning was that under the compensation law a disabling injury must be "work disabling," there being no recovery under the law for pain and suffering as such; whereas, in a negligence case, there can be recovery for pain and suffering even though not necessarily work disabling.

A case reached the California Supreme Court in which actions had been filed in the superior court and before the Appeals Board based upon the same injury. The Supreme Court ruled that the tribunal in which an action was filed first had jurisdiction to determine jurisdiction. In answer to criticism that this rule would make the power to adjudicate depend upon a race to the court house, the court stated that this was better than a race between tribunals to see which would decide the jurisdictional question first. Subsequent decisions indicate that if a W.C.A.B. matter comes on regularly for hearing, the Board should proceed to decide any jurisdictional issues and not delay its proceedings merely because of another proceeding filed or contemplated in another judicial forum. The W.C.A.B. is considered as having "precedential" jurisdiction to determine jurisdiction where no action has been taken in another forum. For example, a final finding by a workers' compensation judge that an alleged uninsured employer was covered by a workers' compensation insurance policy precludes jurisdiction of the superior court in a personal injury action brought by the employee against the employer.

In another case, a superior court ruled that an action by a widow for wrongful death of her husband could not be maintained where the facts showed it to be an industrial death under the bunkhouse rule. This decision was upheld by the appellate court. The result was that the court determined the compensability of the injury. The decision became final and thus binding on the parties in a later action before the Appeals Board. All that was necessary thereafter was placing into evidence a certified copy of the judgment and proof of dependency to obtain an award for the death benefit.

If an applicant's status in performing the service in the course of which he is injured is exempt, such as one rendering voluntary service to a charitable organization without pay, the Appeals Board lacks jurisdiction, and the injured may bring suit in the general courts.

Where an employer in Utah, also doing business in Wyoming, used an employment agency in Denver to locate technical personnel, a phone call from the agency to the employee in California which was accepted by phone in California was sufficient to constitute the creation of a contractual relationship in California. Thereafter, the employee was injured in Utah in the course of his employment. He received workers' compensation under the Utah law, then returned to California and filed with the California Appeals Board. In his application he sought to obtain the difference between the extent of Utah benefits and California benefits. The award of the additional benefits was affirmed, the court holding that California had jurisdiction. But where a worker residing in another state receives a phone call from his union in California offering him work in his own state, California does not have jurisdiction even though the worker must make a round-trip to California to get the work-slip.

§ 13.6   Jurisdictional Time Limits

Generally, it may be said that the Appeals Board has continuing jurisdiction over an industrial injury case for five years after the date of injury. It may determine questions of new and further disability or amend its decisions within that period of time. There are exceptions, as where no benefits have been paid or application filed with the Board within one of the applicable statutes of limitation. Also, in some cases, the Appeals Board may reserve jurisdiction on undecided issues beyond the 5-year period. This problem is discussed in more detail in Chapter 14, PROCEDURE, § 14.7, *Time Limits for Appeals Board Proceedings,* and § 14.9, *Jurisdictional Time Limits, et al.*

§ 13.7   Jurisdiction of the Person

A party who is not subject to California's jurisdiction may make a special appearance before the Appeals Board to test its jurisdiction. Such a party may go into the issue of employment in questioning witnesses without its constituting a general appearance, for employment is a jurisdictional issue. A party may waive this defense by appearing in the proceeding without objection, and if it does so the Board may make a binding decision on the merits.

If an out-of-state person or firm derives a significant amount of income from sales to businesses in California, service of process may be made upon the California Secretary of State, and thus jurisdiction may be gained over such person or firm. (See also Chapter 14, PROCEDURE, § 14.12, *Service of Process.*)

Chapter 14
PROCEDURE

§ 14.1   Introduction

The procedural aspects of the California workers' compensation law include required notices, claims handling by employers, insurance carriers or administrators for self-insured employers and resolution of disputes by an agency or tribunal. Traditionally, employer claims handling was not subject to a great deal of governmental oversight, but gradually over the years more regulation has been established through the office of the Administrative Director by virtue of requirements for additional notices, procedures for change of physician, litigation reduction efforts including those of Information and Assistance Officers, rules and procedures governing vocational rehabilitation plans, rights, and liabilities. The jurisdiction of the Workers' Compensation Appeals Board as a judicial body was recognized by providing for appeal to the Board of any quasi-judicial determinations of the Director. Otherwise, disputes over entitlement to benefits were brought directly to the W.C.A.B. through the filing of an application to obtain a judicial decision on the merits.

The Workers' Compensation Reform Act of 1989, effective January 1, 1990, superimposes upon the procedural picture an increase in administrative oversight and as of January 1, 1991, additional administrative-medical procedures with respect to the issues of permanent disability and medical treatment, subject to resort to the Board by any party dissatisfied with the administrative result. The procedures inaugurated by the Act are specifically made applicable to injuries occurring on or after January 1, 1990. Generally, it may be said that the procedures in place for pre-1990 injuries will be followed for injuries occurring during 1990 until such time as the administrative-medical procedure for initial determination of permanent disability and medical issues becomes operative in 1991. As will be seen, the W.C.A.B. retains its ultimate jurisdiction with some restrictions on the admissibility of medical evidence. Also, some issues will be determined by referees or arbitrators appointed by the W.C.A.B. or by a workers' compensation judge.

§ 14.2   Notice to Employer; Claim Form; First Reports

LC 5400-
5401
LC 5402

As a prerequisite to recovery of benefits, a worker must give his employer notice of any injury within 30 days of its occurrence. While the code requires a written notice, it also states that knowledge of the injury by the employer is equivalent to the giving of written notice. Failure to give notice may be a bar to later recovery, but only if the employer can prove that he or she was misled or affected detrimentally in defending against a claim. In

W.C.A.B. proceedings this is called the defense of "prejudice for lack of notice." It is often raised by the defense, but rarely is it of any avail because of the difficulty in proving any real detriment. The reluctance of the Appeals Board to invoke this bar to an action, except in very extreme cases, stems from the fact that upon finding prejudice it must deny the employee any benefits. Lack of notice may be considered, however, in evaluating the applicant's claim of industrial injury.

The cases in which written notice of injury is given are rare. Usually the employee reports to his foreman or to the plant dispensary. He or she may then be referred to a company insurance office to complete forms required by *LC 3760* the employer. Under 1967 legislation, an employer must report an injury to his workers' compensation insurance carrier within five days. The Appeals Board may enforce this duty by orders for contempt.

Effective January 1, 1990, within one working day after receiving notice *LC 5401,* of an injury or knowledge of injury or claim of injury from any source, the *5402* employer must notify the injured worker, or dependents if death ensues, of possible workers' compensation benefits and include a claim form requesting the employee's name and address, the time and place of the injury, and nature of the injury. This notice is to include information on procedure for collection of compensation and the phone number of the Office of Benefit Assistance and Enforcement (O.B.A.E.) of the Division of Workers' Compensation and the right to consult an attorney or the O.B.A.E. The employee or dependent or agent is to complete the form and file it with the employer who must send a dated copy to the claimant or agent who filed it and to the insurer, if any. Filing of the completed claim form is a prerequisite to the receipt of the *LC 4650* penalty for late payment of compensation or the right to request a formal *4061,* medical evaluation under LC 4061 or 4062. [NOTE: LC 4061 and 4062 are *4062* operative as of January 1, 1991.] Claim forms may also be obtained from other sources including the O.B.A.E. and offices of the Department of Employment Development.

The claim form and notice must contain a warning that making a *LC 5401.7* fraudulent claim or fraudulent denial of a claim is a felony. See Chapter 9, PENALTIES, § 9.18, *Fraudulent Claims*, for details.

Under amendments enacted by the 1990 legislature effective January 1, *LC 5401,* 1991, provision of a claim form and notice of possible eligibility for workers' *5402* compensation is mandatory only where the injury results in lost time from work beyond the date of injury or where medical treatment is more extensive than first aid. "First aid" is defined as any one-time treatment of minor scratches, cuts, burns, splinters or other minor injury by other than a physician or other licensed health care provider providing services in consultation with a physician. Serious exposure to a hazardous substance is not a minor industrial injury.

LC 5401,
5402
Further, the filing of the claim form constitutes commencement of proceedings, establishes the jurisdiction of the Workers' Compensation Appeals Board, and permits the parties to commence discovery procedures including subpoena of records, deposition of witnesses and receipt of records of treating physicians. Lienclaimants may file applications with the W.C.A.B. If the employer does not reject liability within 90 days after the date of the

LC 5500(b) written claim, the injury is presumed to be compensable. This presumption is rebuttable only by evidence discovered subsequent to the 90-day period. An application may be filed with the W.C.A.B. if there is a bona fide dispute after the service of the completed claim form.

LC 5401,
5402
A claim form is deemed to be furnished to an employee or dependent when the employer personally delivers it or mails it by first class mail. With regard to the 90-day period for rejecting a claim (after which if not rejected there is a rebuttable presumption of compensability), the period commences after the completed claim form is filed with the employer by an employee or dependent. The claim form is deemed filed for this purpose when personally delivered or when it is received by the employer by first class or certified mail. As to commencement of proceedings and establishment of W.C.A.B. jurisdiction, the completed form is deemed filed when personally delivered or placed in the mail by first class or certified mail addressed to the employer.

LC 5401.5,
5401.6
If an employee is represented by an attorney, the attorney must send an information request form to the employer, insurance carrier or third-party administrator and a copy of the attorney disclosure form required by LC 4906(e). The employer must respond within 30 days. See subsequent topic, *Discovery; Depositions; Deposition of Employee or Dependent.*

LC 6409.1
If an occupational injury or illness results in the employee's loss of work-time beyond the date of injury or illness, or requires medical treatment beyond first aid, from information supplied by an injured worker or by others, the employer must prepare a report of injury on a form prescribed by the Division of Labor Statistics and Research. This report is filed with that division unless the employer is insured, in which case, the report is filed with the insurance carrier, and the carrier sends a copy to the division. The employer is to file this report within five days, and a carrier receiving an employer's report must file the original with the division immediately. In

LC 6409
case of "serious injury or illness, or death," the employer must also report immediately to the Division of Occupational Safety and Health by telephone or telegraph. "Serious injury or illness" means one which necessitates hospitalization in excess of 24 hours for other than medical observation or which involves loss of any member of the body or any serious degree of permanent disfigurement. Every physician as defined in LC 3209.3 who attends an injured worker must file a physician's first report of injury on a form prescribed by the Division of Labor Statistics and Research with the employer, or if the employer is insured with the insurance carrier. A portion of this form is to be completed by the employee, if able, describing how the injury or illness occurred. It is to be filed within five days of the initial examination.

Inability or failure of the employee to complete his or her portion does not affect compensation rights or excuse a delay in filing the report. If pesticide poisoning is suspected, a copy of the report is sent to the division, and the physician must also file a "complete report" with the division.

The reports required by LC 6409 and 6409.1 must contain a warning that making a fraudulent claim or fraudulent denial of a claim is a felony. See Chapter 9, PENALTIES, § 9.18, *Fraudulent Claims*, for details. *LC 6410.5*

The employer's first report is not open to public inspection, is not to be made public, and is not admissible in evidence in any adversary proceeding before the W.C.A.B. However, a physician's first report of injury is admissible as evidence and is often the most important piece of evidence in a case. However, no physician's report required by LC 6409.1 is admissible "as evidence to bar proceedings for the collection of compensation," and the portion completed by the employee is not admissible. *LC 6412*

Civil penalties may be assessed against employers or physicians who fail to file the reports required by LC 6409 and 6409.1, subject to the right to appeal to the director under LC 3725. *LC 6413.5*

If an insured employer has not furnished the insurer a report of injury per LC 5402 and 6409.1 for a claim received by the insurer, the insurer must so notify the employer who must then provide the report in a timely manner. *LC 3761*

Of practical significance to the employee is the fact that benefits will not be furnished unless the employer knows about the injury. It is not necessary that he or she file a formal claim. Notice to or knowledge of the employer regarding the injury is sufficient to impose the duty to furnish benefits. Of course, if the employee is asked to fill out a claim form, he or she should do so to assist the employer or carrier in adjusting the matter and completing the forms required by the state. Also, if the employee's difficulty turns out to be non-industrial, many employers have insurance departments which can be of assistance in providing unemployment or group insurance benefits.

§ 14.3   Notice to Employee; Claim Form

An employer must notify all employees of their right to workers' compensation benefits along with a description of all benefits, including medical treatment, compensation payments, rehabilitation, and death benefits for dependents. Instructions on how to obtain these benefits must also be included. This information is also to be posted at every work location. The posted notice must be in the form prescribed by the Administrative Director. It must inform employees of the current compensation insurance carrier, or the fact that the employer is self-insured if that is the case, and who is responsible for claims adjustment, identify to whom injuries should be reported and give the location and telephone number of the nearest Information and Assistance Officer. Insurers are to provide this notice to all policyholders and inform them of the LC 3550 requirements and possible penalties for failure to post. *LC 3550-3552*

LC 5402
138.4
R 9810-
9883

Also, when an employer or carrier is notified of injury to an employee, knows of an injury from any source, or is in possession of facts indicating an injury or exposure to harmful substances or stress, notice of workers' compensation rights and benefits must again be given the employee, or, in the case of death, to his or her dependents. Further, a knowledge of an injury or facts suggesting a possible injury is the same as if the employee or dependent has made a formal claim, and the employer or carrier is obligated to commence appropriate benefits. As outlined in the previous topic, for

LC 5401,
5402
4650

injuries occurring on or after January 1, 1990, the employer must also provide an injured worker, or dependent in a death case, a claim form to be completed and returned to the employer. Also, as noted, beginning January 1, 1991, the claim form is required only for lost-time injuries or injuries not requiring medical treatment beyond first aid.

R 9812

An employer is also required to send an injured worker or dependent additional written notices, as follows:

1. Notice of the commencement of temporary compensation within 14 days of the first day of disability, or of the death benefit within 14 days of death.
2. Notice of any delay in the determination of the employee's entitlement (or dependent's entitlement) within 14 days of the employer's receipt of notice of a claim (or knowledge as previously outlined), delay not to exceed 90 days.
3. Notice of information in 1. above, to accompany first payment of compensation or death benefit.
4. Notice of termination of benefits within 14 days of termination giving reason for the action and an accounting of all payments.
5. Notice of denial of claim, if claim denied, within 14 days of disability or death unless notice of delay given and then no more than 90 days.

Copies of the listed notices (1 through 5, above) must be filed with the Administrative Director's office. These notices are not required if an application has been filed with the W.C.A.B.; or a compromise and release has been approved; or if payment has been resumed following a notice of termination. The forms used for the notices need not be in any particular format, but they must be approved by the Administrative Director.

LC 138.4
139.6

A pamphlet published or approved by the Administrative Director outlining in some detail workers' compensation rights, benefits, and procedures must be included with the first notice of payment or notice of delay in payment sent to an injured worker. The pamphlet is to be available in both English and Spanish and written in easily understood terms. The pamphlet must also inform employees of procedures for resolving disputes and the right to seek information and advice from an Information and Assistance Officer or an attorney.

[NOTE: Other notices are required with respect to vocational rehabilitation. See Chapter 16, VOCATIONAL REHABILITATION.]

§ 14.4   Administrative-Medical Evaluation; Permanent Disability; Medical Treatment Issues

Operative January 1, 1991, and applicable to injuries occurring on or after January 1, 1990, is a formalized administrative-medical evaluation procedure which is mandatory for initial determination of permanent disability and continuing medical treatment issues. The procedure is set out principally in LC 4061 and 4062. LC 4061 applies to both unrepresented employees and employees represented by attorneys with some differences between the two categories. Neither of the above issues may be the subject of an application for adjudication before the W.C.A.B. unless there has been a finding by an agreed medical evaluator (A.M.E.) or a qualified medical evaluator (Q.M.E.). LC 4062 applies only to employees represented by attorneys and sets up a procedure for initial resolution of the additional issues of an employee's permanent and stationary status, preclusion or likely preclusion to engage in his or her usual occupation, extent and scope of medical treatment, and existence of new and further disability. None of the 4062 issues may be the subject of an application for adjudication before the W.C.A.B. unless there has first been an evaluation by an A.M.E. or a Q.M.E. [NOTE: The filing of a claim form by the employee is a prerequisite to any request for a formal medical evaluation.] *LC 4061-4067* *LC 4061(1)* *LC 4062* *LC 5401(c)*

The procedure begins with an employer or carrier giving notice to an injured worker with the last payment of temporary compensation of the employer's position regarding payment of permanent disability benefits and procedures available to the worker. This notice must be on a form approved by the Administrative Director and convey one of the following notices: *LC 4061 (a), (b)*

1. Notice that no permanent disability indemnity will be paid because of the absence of any permanent impairment or limitation. This notice must inform the employee on how to obtain a formal medical evaluation.

2. Notice that PD compensation may be payable but the amount cannot be determined because the condition is not permanent and stationary (P & S); that the condition will be monitored and the employee notified re evaluation for PD or medical treatment. If the employer later believes that there is no ratable PD, the notice in item 1, above, must be given in 14 days.

3. Notice that the employee's condition is P & S and that PD payments may be or are payable.

Additionally, the employer must notify an injured worker within five working days of any information coming to the employer's attention indicating that the employee's condition is P & S and notify him or her of the procedure for obtaining a formal medical evaluation regarding PD or continuing medical care.

An unrepresented employee may, utilizing a prescribed form furnished by the employer or carrier, request a formal medical evaluation by a Q.M.E. selected from a panel of three Q.M.E.'s. If an employee is represented, the parties must make an effort to select an A.M.E. If no agreement is reached within 10 days or any agreed extension not to exceed 20 days, they may not select an A.M.E., but each party may select one Q.M.E. to conduct a formal medical evaluation, i.e., one Q.M.E. each for each appropriate medical specialty or subspecialty. This limitation does not apply to reports of treating physicians or where the W.C.A.B. later permits a party to obtain an evaluation from another physician. The employee is responsible for making an appointment with an A.M.E. or Q.M.E. The physician must discuss his or her professional qualifications with the employee and permit him or her to ask questions. An examination may be terminated if it appears that the evaluator is biased and the employee permitted to select another Q.M.E. from another panel of three. But, if the W.C.A.B. finds the termination was unjustified, the *LC 4061(a)* cost will be deducted from any award. [NOTE: Per LC 139.2(g), the Medical *139.2(g)* Director is to assign panels of three Q.M.E.'s of appropriate specialties within five days of receiving a request. If not assigned in 15 days, the employee may select any Q.M.E. of choice. A form will accompany notice of panel members and their qualifications. The notice will inform the employee of the right to transportation expense, compensation for the day of examination and of the fact that the evaluation will be considered if the matter goes before the W.C.A.B.]

[NOTE: An agreed medical evaluator need not be a qualified medical evaluator.]

LC 4061 The O.B.D. issues a permanent disability rating based on the evaluator's *(h), (i), (j)* report. The parties may request the O.B.D to reconsider the rating. Questions concerning apportionment of PD are submitted to the W.C.A.B. When the report of a designated A.M.E. or Q.M.E., or a PD rating issued by the O.B.D. requires the employer to provide benefits, such benefits must be furnished, or the employer or carrier must file an application for adjudication with the *LC 4063* W.C.A.B. Except for evaluations made by a treating physician, no medical *LC 4061* evaluation obtained prior to service of the report of an A.M.E. or Q.M.E. is *(k), (l)* admissible as evidence. Records and reports of A.M.E.'s and Q.M.E.'s and *LC 4062.2* treating physicians are admissible. The parties may submit previous medical information to the A.M.E or Q.M.E.

LC 4062.2 There is to be no communication with an evaluator except in writing with service upon other parties.

LC 4064 The employer or carrier pays the cost of a formal medical evaluation including the cost of any rebuttal report obtained by an unrepresented employee from a Q.M.E. If an employer or carrier files an application with the W.C.A.B., and the employee is unrepresented and has not obtained a rebuttal Q.M.E. evaluation, the employer or carrier is liable for any attorney's fee thereafter incurred by the employee in connection with the application. If an employee is represented by an attorney, and the employer or carrier files an application contesting the findings of an A.M.E., the employer or carrier is liable for the employee's attorney's fee regardless of outcome.

LC 4064(d)
4066

If a petition is filed pursuant to LC 5803 on the basis of a change in the employee's condition, a formal medical evaluation must be obtained. If the judge does not refer the matter to the original A.M.E. or Q.M.E., the 4061 and 4062 procedures are applicable.

LC 4067

§ 14.5 Workers' Compensation Appeals Board Procedure

Proceedings before the Workers' Compensation Appeals Board have been described as "informal," a description which can be deceptive. When the compensation act was adopted, it was hoped that hearings could be handled informally by the commissioners, but it eventually become apparent that the commissioners could not hear all the cases. Attorneys were appointed to act as referees, to conduct hearings and submit reports, and recommended decisions. In 1951, there were 60 referees issuing about 45,000 recommended decisions per year. To comply with the code, the commission issued blanket minute orders adopting these decisions. To bring the code in line with the procedure which had evolved over the years, the Legislature that year enacted amendments permitting referees to make final decisions. The Appeals Board implemented these provisions in its rules, reserving to itself certain special orders along with its function as a reviewing court. By virtue of LC 123, the designation "referee" was changed to "workers' compensation judge."

LC 115
5001
5309-5313

R 10345
10340-
10352

LC 123

Hearings before the workers' compensation judges are similar to trials in the general courts before a judge sitting without a jury. Certain procedural rules are less formal than court rules, but there is the same requirement for a record based upon both sworn testimony and documentary evidence. As part of the reorganization of the commission to the Appeals Board, the commission's rules were revised and adopted by the Board. Many of the commission's rules dealing with the medical bureau and the Disability Evaluation Bureau are found in the rules of the Administrative Director. The workers' compensation judge has authority to appoint guardians and trustees where necessary and to issue subpoenas and other process. (Per 1987 SCR 40, workers' compensation judges may wear judicial robes while presiding over hearings. The robes are to be purchased at the judges' own expense.) The Appeals Board has authority to punish for contempt.

LC 5700-
5710
LC 132

LC 134
LC 5307.5
R 10530

LC 5309(c) empowers the W.C.A.B. to direct and order workers' compensation judges to issue writs, summons, warrants of attachment, warrants of commitment, and all necessary process and proceedings for direct and hybrid contempt in like manner and to the same extent as courts of record. "Hybrid contempt" is defined as "a charge of contempt which arises from events occurring in the immediate presence of the workers' compensation judge for reasons which occur outside the presence of the workers' compensation judge."

LC 5309

LC 5500.3   The W.C.A.B. is directed by statute to establish uniform court procedures, uniform forms, and uniform time of court settings for all offices of the Board. No office or judge is to require any forms or procedures other than as established by the Board.

LC 115   There are specific rules about filing papers and documents, but the
LC 5703   Appeals Board has never required that they be presented in any prescribed format. W.C.A.B. rules do require that documents filed with the Board be on
R 10392 $8^1/2 \times 11$ inch paper with two holes punched at the top and centered so as to fit the Board's file. Medical reports should be submitted with a transmittal letter, and all documents must include a heading showing the name of the in-
R 10395   jured worker and the W.C.A.B. case number. Certain documents are not to be filed with the Board. These include letters between the parties or their attorneys; subpoenas; notice of taking deposition; medical appointment letters; any document not required by the rules or which does not request action by the Board. This rule is intended to keep extraneous matters out of the Board's files and is not to be considered as inhibiting the submission of relevant or otherwise appropriate evidence or documentation. If there is doubt about a particular document, it is better to file it if a party's rights could be involved.

R 10400-   For applications and most petitions, the Appeals Board provides printed
10520   forms without charge. Hearings or other action may be requested or motions
LC 5708   may be made by letter so long as copies are served upon the other parties to the litigation. Medical reports, wage reports, and permanent disability rating
R 10600-   reports may be used instead of direct testimony. Any party may require the
10635   presence of the person preparing such a report so that he may be cross-examined. Common law or statutory rules of evidence do not apply; thus hearsay testimony is admissible. There are no filing fees charged, although parties must pay the cost of any certified copies of official documents desired and any transcripts of testimony requested. If the Board has a transcript prepared for its own use, the parties may have access to it but must pay for any copies ordered by them.

Although there is flexibility of procedure, a litigant should employ the same degree of preparation as he would for a case in the general courts. The Appeals Board has issued a directive to its trial judges to make sure that there is some evidence in the record on every issue raised at a hearing. Ordinarily, the parties supply the necessary evidence, but occasionally the judge must remind them to cover a certain issue, or he may quiz a witness himself. This does not differ from court procedure, for judges of the general courts often exercise the same prerogative. The courts are enjoined by law to assure the most expeditious ascertainment of the truth. The judge's role in covering any issue not covered by the parties does not relieve a litigant from preparing his case thoroughly, for the interrogation by the judge must be of a general nature in order that he or she maintain objectivity and render a just decision.

While common law or statutory rules of evidence do not apply, experience has shown that evidence which would be inadmissible in the general courts usually lacks weight or probative value. Hearsay evidence, for instance, is admissible before the Appeals Board, but it is most often not convincing evidence unless it comes within one of the common law or statutory exceptions to the hearsay rule which is applied in the general courts. The best approach to an industrial accident case is to determine the issues and prepare to meet those issues with competent evidence.

Flexibility of procedure refers to the ability of the Appeals Board to hold hearings on short notice and in almost every part of the state. Riding circuit has been alluded to as "have gavel; will travel." This description certainly applies to the trial judges. The establishment of Appeals Board branches throughout the state has reduced the number of circuits, but a certain amount is necessary. Hearings may be held in various locations, in city council chambers, county supervisors' chambers, or in courtrooms. A hearing may also be held in prison if the applicant is incarcerated there at the time of his hearing. If the applicant is in very serious condition, and it appears necessary to expedite matters, a bedside hearing may be requested.

When it appears impractical to bring witnesses a great distance to the hearing, the matter may be transferred to the branch nearest to their location for the taking of additional testimony, after which it is returned to the original judge with a transcript of the testimony, or, if the parties agree, with the second judge's resume of the proceedings. For out-of-state witnesses, it is often possible to obtain testimony in the same manner through the offices of state industrial commissions or boards. Specific information on this point is available at Appeals Board headquarters or branches. Some states will provide the Board with transcripts without charge. Others require the parties to defray the expense. If a particular state does not provide this service, the parties must arrange for depositions, or the witnesses must be brought to California. Our code contains a reciprocity arrangement regarding the conduct of hearings for other jurisdictions. As a result, the California compensation judges hold many hearings in out-of-state cases. Other testimony often *R 10727* presented by deposition is that of a physician or a rehabilitation consultant. *10957*

A workers' compensation judge is subject to the rules of judicial conduct. A judge is prohibited from ex parte contact with parties or witnesses *LC 123.6* where notice and opportunity to be present has not been given. It has been held to be reversible error for a judge to visit an accident scene, talk to witnesses or call a doctor for clarification of a report where these contacts take place outside the presence of the parties.

§ 14.6 Burden of Proof; Liberal Construction Rule

LC 5705 provides: "The burden of proof rests upon the party holding the *LC 5705* affirmative of the issue." An employee, a dependent, a lienclaimant, or other party seeking to establish rights against an employer or carrier has the burden of proof of an injury arising out of and occurring in the course of employment and of entitlement to benefits in connection with such an injury. If the evidence tends to support a claim, the burden of going forward with evidence to the contrary shifts to the defendant (employer or carrier). If the evidence is conflicting the judge will make a decision resolving the conflict. An employer or carrier defendant has the burden to proof on any affirmative defenses raised in a proceeding. (See subsequent discussion in § 14.18, *Answers; Affirmative Defenses; Pre-trial Statement.*)

LC 3202

LC 3202.5

An applicant has the benefit of the liberal construction rule. This rule provides that the laws are to be "liberally construed by the courts with the purpose of extending their benefits for the protection of persons injured in the course of their employment." This rule does not relieve a claimant of the necessity to present evidence and to establish his or her case by a preponderance of evidence. However, the appellate courts and the W.C.A.B. apply the liberal construction rule both to the interpretation of the law and to the weighing of the evidence.

§ 14.7　Time Limits for Appeals Board Proceedings

The law does not favor the litigation of stale claims, and this policy is put into effect by statutes which limit the time within which a person may bring suit. The various code sections containing these limits are referred to singly and collectively as the "Statute of Limitations." If the period of time for the filing of a particular suit goes by, and the claimant has not filed his action, his claim is barred. In popular parlance, people usually say that the claim or debt is "outlawed." Lawyers say that "the statute of limitations has run." The claim is barred because if the time has expired, the courts will not exercise their authority to assist the claimant. On the other hand, if the party

LC 5409

in whose favor the statute has operated does not raise the point, that party is deemed to have waived the defense, and the courts will act. Thus, the defense of the statute of limitations is called an affirmative defense, one which a party must assert and prove, or it will not be considered.

The same general principles apply to proceedings before the Appeals Board. The Labor Code sets forth various time limits for the filing of applications or other requests for relief. The first time period involved has already been discussed; namely, the 30 days for giving notice of injury. Other provisions regarding time present a set of rules which has required considerable interpretation by the appellate courts, the former commission, and the Appeals Board. (REMINDER: Under the *Reynolds* decision, these time limits do not start to run against an employee unless the employer has given the employee notice of rights and benefits under the compensation law.)

1. *Normal Benefits:*

LC 5405(a)

(a) If no benefits, compensation, or medical treatment have been furnished by the employer or carrier, the application must be filed with the Appeals Board within one year from the date of injury. It has been held that if an industrially injured worker fails to notify his employer of the injury or reveal facts concerning it, but instead files a personal injury suit against a third person, his application for workers' compensation benefits filed with the W.C.A.B. more than six years after the injury is barred by the statute of limitations. Under these circumstances, the period is not extended by the pendency or outcome of the personal injury action.

(b) If benefits, compensation, or medical treatment have been furnished by the employer or carrier, the application must be filed within one year after the date of the last payment or other benefit.

Furnishing a benefit which brings (b) into effect is any benefit provided by the employer or carrier because of the injury. If the employer renders first aid, furnishes pain pills or pays wages during a period of disability, he has furnished a benefit. If a considerable amount of time goes by, and some form of treatment is given at the plant dispensary for the injury, the one year within which to file with the Board is counted from that date. Thus it is possible for the employer to give new life to a claim which would otherwise be barred.

An insurance carrier would undoubtedly refuse further treatment if the original period of limitation has expired. In many cases, however, the carrier *LC 3755* is not notified that the employee is seeking treatment from the employer. Nevertheless, treatment or other benefit given by the employer on account of an industrial injury can revive a dead claim as to both the employer and his insurance carrier. The code provides a procedure whereby the carrier can take control of the case and give the employee and the employer notice that it has assumed liability in the case. The employer may be dismissed as a party in any proceeding, and the matter may continue only as to the insurer. In practice, however, most carriers do not file such notices or seek to have the employer dismissed as a party to the proceeding.

Another problem involving the statute of limitations occurs when the claims examiner or adjuster has failed to notify the treating physician that a case has been closed. In giving the physician authority to treat, the employer or carrier makes him its agent. If this agency is not terminated by specific notice, the physician may continue to be in a position to bind the parties and extend the period within which the employee may file an application with the Appeals Board. In some cases the doctor has told the employee to return in a year for a checkup or to make an appointment whenever he feels the symptoms returning, and the claims department has not been informed of these instructions. The better procedure is to give written notice to both the employee and the doctor when benefits have been terminated with a specific statement that no further benefit or treatment is to be given without prior authorization.

If in treating an injury the doctor furnished by the employer must also treat a condition caused by a prior injury, the medical treatment will be deemed rendered for both conditions, and, therefore, the statute of limitations will not run on the first injury until one year from the date of the last treatment. Other acts by an employer which constitute the furnishing of a benefit, and thus tolling the statute of limitations, include a recommendation by a plant nurse that an employee take aspirin, where given after a timely report of an industrial injury, and the act of a foreman in taking the employee to a doctor for treatment of an industrial injury, even though the doctor was not paid for his services.

2. *New and Further Disability:*

LC 5410

An employee has five years from the date of injury within which to begin Appeals Board proceedings to collect compensation for any "new and further disability" caused by the injury. This provision is meant to cover instances in which unforeseen disability results after an apparent cure or after all benefits were paid which were thought to be due. Also, by court decision it includes permanent disability. LC 5410 states that the jurisdiction of the Appeals Board is continuing during the 5-year period. The California Supreme Court has ruled that it is basically a statute of limitations, and, in defining "new and further disability," the court stated that the term refers to those cases in which an application for benefits had already been filed or in which the employer has recognized the injury and has furnished some benefit. The result is that the employee may file an application with the Appeals Board on the basis of new and further disability at any time within one of these periods:

LC 5404, 5405

(a) If no benefits have been furnished, within one year from the date of injury. In this type of case, any kind of claim is barred if an application is not filed within the year.

(b) If any compensation benefit was furnished by either the employer or his insurance carrier, or if an application is filed within one year from date of injury, the application for new and further disability may be filed within one year from the date of the last benefit *or* within five years from the date of injury, whichever is later.

As previously mentioned, the statute of limitations does not begin to run until the employer, on receiving notice of or knowledge of an injury, gives the injured worker notice of his or her rights under the compensation law.

EXAMPLES:

(1) Mary Jane complained to her immediate supervisor that her right shoulder and neck were giving her trouble and that she was having difficulty in operating her drill press. The supervisor told her that she probably should see a doctor. The condition persisted, and Mary Jane quit her job. Thereafter, she consulted a doctor who diagnosed her condition as resulting from repetitive motions in operating the drill press. She did not file her application for compensation benefits until two years later when the doctor told her the condition was permanent. In her application, she sought both temporary and permanent disability benefits and reimbursement for self-procured treatment.

The insurance carrier for the employer raised the statute of limitations. Under the *Reynolds* principle, the statute of limitations had not run since the employer had knowledge of facts indicating physical difficulty in performing her work. These facts required investigation by the employer and notice to Mary Jane of her possible rights under the compensation law.

(2) When Smith was hired, his employer gave him a booklet which explained company policies, sick leave, vacation, holidays, group health and life insurance, the company retirement plan, and the workers' compensation *LC 5402* program, benefits, and procedures. Information about workers' compensation was posted on the wall above the coffee pot at Smith's work location. Smith twisted his knee at work, but thinking it to be minor he did not report it or mention it to any of his co-workers. Two years later, he filed an application with the W.C.A.B. At the hearing, the carrier's attorney raised the defense of the statute of limitation as an issue. This claim was barred because the application was filed more than one year after the injury.

(3) Jones was injured on February 2, 1975, and was afforded treatment for the next seven years. His application for additional benefits filed in 1982 *LC 5405* was not barred since within one year after the last furnishing of treatment.

(4) Hansen strained his back at work on November 16, 1979. He received 12 weeks of temporary compensation and medical treatment for a pe- *LC 5410* riod of five months. His application for a permanent disability award was filed on October 31, 1984. If the defense urged the statute of limitations, the ruling would be that the request was timely, for *permanent disability is deemed to be a new and further disability.*

(5) Palmer caught his hand in a milling machine sustaining a severe injury. The date was June 16, 1976. Adequate treatment was furnished through December 10, 1976, and he returned to work the next day. Some stiffness of his fingers resulted. During the period of recuperation, he had consulted an attorney about his rights, and on July 25, 1976, he filed an application. One of the benefits requested was a permanent disability rating. A hearing was scheduled, but the matter was placed "off calendar" when the referee was informed that Palmer was currently receiving temporary compensation and medical treatment. Palmer dismissed his attorney shortly after his return to work. In 1977 he took a job in another state and did not return to California until the spring of 1982. He retained another attorney and filed another application requesting the permanent disability benefit. At the hearing the defense asserted the statute of limitations on the basis that the second application was filed more than one year after the date of the last benefit and more than five years after the date of injury. The ruling would be here that the original application was in time, raised the issue of this benefit which was *LC 5404* never decided; the second application was not necessary and served only as a request for a hearing on the original application. This example illustrates the continuing jurisdiction of the Board to decide any issue which is raised in

timely fashion but never litigated. It would have made no difference in this case if the hearing had been requested 20 years after placing the matter "off calendar."

In example (3), permanent disability was used to illustrate a "new and further disability." The appellate courts have ruled that any change in the nature of the employee's disability is "new and further," whether temporary or permanent. If an applicant receives an award based on a rating, he may file for an additional award if his condition worsens to a greater degree and if the 5-year period after the injury has not expired.

"New and further" may also include additional temporary disability which is not merely a continuation of the original period of such disability. The commission, the Appeals Board, and the courts have given this term a very broad definition which can be deemed to include any change in condition as giving rise to a right to file within the LC 5410 5-year period. However, if one year from date of injury (or date of last benefit) has expired before the filing of an application, and the temporary disability involved is continuous and not new and further disability, the claim for temporary compensation is barred. This principle is without prejudice to seeking further temporary benefits, should a change in condition occur, or permanent disability benefits within five years after date of injury. Fortunately, "new and further" cases usually involve future temporary benefits or a permanent disability rating, and this particular problem does not arise too often. In view of the court's ruling on this point, most applicants' attorneys file their clients' applications as soon as possible, even though they may be receiving full *R 10414* benefits at the time. The matter will not be calendared for hearing until one of the parties files a Declaration of Readiness to Proceed.

LC 5410   That an injury has caused the need for vocational rehabilitation benefits is a ground for instituting proceedings under LC 5410.

3. *Subsequent Injuries Fund:*

The California Supreme Court has ruled that in cases involving the Subsequent Injuries Fund, the statute of limitations begins to run as to the fund's liability when the employee knows or reasonably should know of his or her entitlement to those benefits. Even so, there is no statute of limitations, as such, which is applicable to subsequent injuries fund cases. The employee has a reasonable time after having such knowledge to file against the fund or to join it in a proceeding. What is a reasonable time is to be governed under the same principles applicable to the doctrine of *laches*. Under this doctrine, a reasonable time is usually measured by a statute of limitations period, but such a comparison is not mandatory in all cases.

This decision of the Supreme Court seemingly lays to rest problems which were apparent in prior cases. The W.C.A.B. and the appellate courts had been applying the 5-year period under LC 5410 to claims against the subsequent injuries fund. This approach led to some conflicting decisions because the Labor Code does not expressly set out a statute of limitations for such claims.

4. *Death Cases:* A dependent must file any application for death benefits   *LC 5406*

(a) Within one year from the date of the employee's death, *and* it must also be filed

(b) Within 240 weeks from the date of the injury.

Both of these periods must be complied with. The controlling language in LC 5406 is that no proceedings for death benefits "may be commenced more than one year after date of death, nor more than 240 weeks from the date of injury." This section of the code also contains statements about types of factual situations which are all covered by the periods in (a) and (b) because of the all-encompassing effect of the quoted limitation. In cases involving prolonged illness, the 240-week period may be significant. The Supreme Court has ruled that should death occur after 240 weeks from date of injury, a claim for death benefits is barred unless the dependents have filed their application with the W.C.A.B. within the 240-week period. The court recognized that the application would be filed before the death of the employee, but the court stated that its decision was in accord with the clear language of the last paragraph of LC 5406.

Under LC 5402 as amended, effective January 1, 1976, upon receiving   *LC 5401,* notice or knowledge of a claim of injury (or, as under the *Reynolds* decision,   *5402* facts which would put an employer on notice of a possible claim of injury) resulting in death, an employer must give the employee's dependents notice that they may be entitled to death benefits. Under the *Reynolds* rule, the statute of limitations does not start to run until such notice is given. Recognizing that the running of either of the above periods could foreclose a death claim, the Court of Appeal has ameliorated the harshness of LC 5406 by ruling that neither period starts to run until the dependent knows or should know that the deceased employee's death was industrially related. [NOTE: The requirement for giving notice of possible death benefits to dependents is now set forth in LC 5401.]

In case of death of an asbestos worker from asbestosis, the period for   *LC 5406.5* commencing death-benefit proceedings is one year from the date of death. The Court of Appeal has ruled that where exposure to asbestos results in two distinct pathologies through separate processes, there can be two dates of injury: one for determining benefits for disability caused by one condition, and one for determining benefits due dependents by virtue of death caused by the other condition.

5. *Serious and Wilful Misconduct:*

(a) An application charging the employer with serious and wilful mis-   *LC 5407* conduct and seeking the 50% penalty must be filed within "twelve months from the date of injury." [NOTE: The code specifically states that this period is not extended by the payment of compensation, any agreement to pay or the filing of an application for normal benefits. This prohibition does not rule out an extension of the period by fraud or an estoppel, as will be discussed later.]

As indicated in the chapter on penalties, cases have arisen wherein the employee has not properly alleged the charge of serious and wilful misconduct, and the question before the appellate court is whether the allegations serve as notice of such a claim or whether they merely make out a claim of negligence. If the allegations indicate the wilfulness of the asserted wrongdoing, the application may be amended even though the amendment is made more than one year from date of injury. An allegation of negligence, however, may not be amended to a claim of wilful conduct if more than one year has elapsed from the injury date. (See subsequent discussion of rule on S & W applications.)

LC 5407.5   (b) If the employer charges the employee with serious and wilful misconduct, his action must also be brought within "twelve months from the date of injury." This period of limitation is not applied if the employee has commenced proceedings for an increase in benefits as mentioned in (a) above.

6. Discrimination Because of Claim:

LC 132(a)   Proceedings to recover the penalty for discrimination because of a workers' compensation claim or to obtain reinstatement and reimbursement for lost wages and work benefits must be instituted within one year from the discriminatory act or the date of termination of the employee.

7. Rehabilitation:

LC 5405.5   The period of limitations for requesting vocational rehabilitation is one year from the date of the last finding of permanent disability by the W.C.A.B. or one year from the date of approval of a compromise and release of other *LC 5410* issues. Also, a request may be filed with the Board within 5 years from date *5803* of injury.

8. Date of Injury; Occupational Disease; Cumulative Trauma:

LC 5411   Where it is necessary to determine the date of injury in computing time limits or which schedule of benefits applies, the code provides that it is the date on which the alleged incident or exposure took place. In most cases there is a single incident and the date is easily ascertained. The appellate court has also ruled that a single exposure to a contagious disease is not to be governed by the occupational disease provisions, but is to be considered as a single injury the date of which is the date of the exposure.

LC 5412   The date of injury in cases of occupational disease or cumulative injuries (cumulative or repetitive trauma) is the "date upon which the employee first suffered disability therefrom and either knew, or in the exercise of reasonable diligence should have known that said disability was caused by his present or prior employment."

The inquiry often becomes a question of when the employee knew or should have know he suffered disability. In many cases doctors have reported that a person suffering a disease may not realize it and the extent of his condition until he has difficulty performing his work. He may then visit a doctor who, after a diagnosis, may advise him to terminate or change his employment. Many cases of silicosis have been brought to light by the routine chest x-rays conducted by state and local health departments.

Per a 1990 Court of Appeal decision, in a case involving continuous exposure to asbestos where two separate conditions are caused by the exposure, there can be two dates of injury, one for determining disability benefits relating to one condition and one for determining benefits due dependents by virtue of death resulting from the other condition.

9. *Minors; Incompetents:*

None of the periods of limitation applies to any person under 18 years of age or any incompetent person until a guardian or trustee is appointed. The appointment may be made by a court or the Appeals Board. In a death case the statute of limitations might run as to the rights of a widow and still be ineffective against any minor dependents until the appointment of the guardian, guardian ad litem, or trustee. There have been cases of this type in which the death benefit is awarded the children and paid to the widow as trustee for the use and benefit of the children. The Appeals Board retains continuing jurisdiction over trusteeships it creates and may require an accounting by the trustee.

LC 5408

10. *Estoppel:*

This term as applied to time limits means that the person who asserts that a claim is barred, because the application or other document filed to commence proceedings was filed late, has done something to prevent or delay the filing, and it would be unjust to permit him to raise this defense. In legal parlance, we say that where the defendant has misled a claimant or made a promise upon which the claimant relied to his detriment, the defendant is estopped from raising the defense of the statute of limitations. The conduct may be a promise, such as, "Fill out these papers, and we'll take care of everything;" or "As soon as we check this out, you'll be hearing from us." It may take the form of misdirection—"Your claim is for unemployment insurance, not compensation;" or "Since this was a federal project, you have to file under the federal compensation law." Estoppel may result from the conduct of either the employer or the insurance carrier. The time starts running when the employee discovers the fraud or other conduct giving rise to the estoppel. The time also starts running when the employee in the exercise of reasonable diligence should have discovered these facts. A flat denial of liability is not the basis for an estoppel.

The program started in 1965 requiring employers to give employees notice of acceptance, denial, or termination of compensation raised the question whether a failure to comply could create an estoppel to plead the statute of limitations. The Supreme Court answered this question in 1974 in the *Reynolds* case in holding that the statute will not start to run until such notice is given. However, an appellate court has held that where an employee is aware of his or her rights and makes an informed decision to forego workers' compensation in favor of pursuing only a third-party action, an employer is not estopped to raise the statute of limitations as a defense, even though the employer did not notify the employee of workers' compensation rights.

§ 14.8   Filing Early; Stating the Issues; Declaration of Readiness to Proceed

LC 5404

From the foregoing, the advantage of filing an application with the Appeals Board as soon as any dispute arises is apparent. Under LC 5404 upon the timely filing, the various time limitations discussed are no longer in the picture as a bar to recovery regarding any benefit requested in the document. They continue to be applicable, however, as to any right or benefit not mentioned as an issue in the application or Appeals Board record. Therefore, if Jones should file because the employer's carrier is not paying temporary compensation, and in his application he only asks for this particular benefit, the 5-year period under LC 5410 is still running as to any permanent disability benefit or other type of new and further disability. If he does not file an amended application or an amendment to the original application within the 5-year period raising these additional issues, they will be barred. This rule emphasizes the need for careful analysis of the applicant's case and a comprehensive stating of the issues in the original application. This is not difficult to do because the official application form lists the basic benefits, and all the employee or his representative has to do is place a check mark after benefits desired of those listed on the form. There is also a space for writing in any benefit or issue not listed.

Alluding to an earlier statement, if all possible issues are set forth, and if the employer or insurance carrier is providing current benefits, the employee may request that the matter be placed off calendar at the time of the filing. This action will save the carrier the task of preparing a defense unnecessarily and the Appeals Board the setting of a case for hearing in which there is no immediate dispute. At the same time, the employee has protected his or her rights against the running of the various periods of limitation. In a case of this nature it is possible that five years may elapse without any formal proceedings. If so, the application should be reviewed before the expiration of the period to check the adequacy of the issues raised in the light of existing circumstances. Any issue properly raised within the 5-year period may be decided at any time after the expiration of that period.

LC 5502
R 10414

The off-calendar approach is evident in W.C.A.B. rules regarding setting a hearing only after the filing of a Declaration of Readiness to Proceed.

For pre-1990 injuries, an application is not set for hearing unless a declaration of readiness is filed. As to injuries occurring on or after January 1, 1990, a hearing is to be held not less than 10 days nor more than 60 days after the filing of the application. However, Board rules require a declaration of *R 10966* readiness for subsequent proceedings.

Where a case is not calendared through a required declaration of readiness, it is placed on inactive status. It may be placed on calendar by the filing *R 10582* of a declaration of readiness. If a case is in inactive status in excess of one year, it may be dismissed, but only if notice and an opportunity to be heard is given the applicant. CAUTION: Such dismissals are probably "without prejudice;" that is, without foreclosing a party's right to set aside the order of dismissal and reinstate the case. It is doubted that an appellate court would uphold a purported dismissal for lack of prosecution "with prejudice," for vested rights are involved.

§ 14.9 Jurisdictional Time Limits; Altering or Amending Decision; Petition to Reopen

The statutes of limitation discussed thus far are affirmative defenses; that is, they are deemed waived if not asserted by the defendants before the *LC 5409* workers' compensation judge or the Appeals Board submits a matter for decision. Jurisdictional time limits are not deemed waived and may be urged at any point in the proceedings, even on appeal. The reason for this distinction is that the latter are limits on the power of the Appeals Board to act rather than merely limits on the right of a party to commence a proceeding.

The code provides in LC 5404 that the timely filing of an application makes inapplicable any statute of limitation and that thereafter the right to *LC 5404* present further claims is governed by LC 5803-5805. These sections in turn give the Appeals Board continuing jurisdiction over all its decisions for a period of five years from the date of injury. Under these sections, a party may *LC 5803-* petition to reopen his case after a decision has been made to present further *5805* evidence. Defendants may seek to reopen to reduce an award. If the evidence shows that the decision should be changed, the Appeals Board may, "rescind, alter or amend" its original decision. We have seen that under LC 5410, the issue of "new and further disability" may be raised before the end of five years from date of injury and decided at any time thereafter. Similarly, if a petition to reopen a W.C.A.B. decision is filed within five years from date of injury, the Board's authority to determine the issues raised by the petition continues beyond the five years. Also, if a petition is filed within five years, another party may file a counter-petition within 30 days after the filing of the original petition. It has been held that a petition filed after five years based upon a medical report received within the five years is timely. When a decision is rendered after five years on a timely petition, the continuing jurisdiction of the Board is limited to ancillary orders which do not change basic rights and obligations.

LC 5803-
5805

R 10454
10458

A petition to reopen under LC 5803-5805 must show good cause to re-open. The allegations are to include a detailed statement of the facts demon-strating good cause. Assertions based upon evidence which is merely cumulative of that already in the record do not suffice. But, even though a petitioner is entitled to notice and an opportunity to be heard before a decision issues, a petition should also include as an exhibit or exhibits any documentation upon which the petitioner relies, such as, medical reports or affidavits or declarations under penalty of perjury of parties or witnesses.

LC 5803

"Good cause" to reopen includes the prevention of inequitable results, correction of previous procedural errors, consideration of a charge of perjury, increased or decreased disability, discovery of suppressed evidence. The need for vocational rehabilitation services may be the subject-matter of a petition to reopen, and in this connection reopening applies to decisions of the Rehabilitation Bureau. Where the ground for reopening is newly discovered evidence, due diligence in obtaining it must be shown, as well as the materi-ality of it to the petitioner's case. Merely cumulative evidence is insufficient. In one case, the Court of Appeal held that new evidence in the form of testi-mony of a disinterested witness who would corroborate the applicant's testi-mony was good cause to reopen.

LC 4067

On and after January 1, 1991, with respect to injuries occurring on or after January 1, 1990, if the jurisdiction of the W.C.A.B. is invoked per LC 5803 on the ground of a change in an injured worker's condition, a formal medical evaluation must be obtained in accordance with the administrative-medical procedure required under LC 4061-4067.

A petition to reopen may not be used as a belated appeal where the time for appeal (petition for reconsideration) has expired or where the W.C.A.B. has denied reconsideration.

As previously mentioned, there are orders which are not restricted by the five-years-from-date-of-injury rule, for they do not amount to an altering or amending of the award. These include:

(1) An order enforcing the furnishing of a continuing benefit.
(2) An order setting an attorney's fee for work done after the 5-year period.
(3) An order commuting an award to a lump sum payment.
(4) An order approving a compromise and release agreement.
(5) An order converting an award for further medical treatment to an award for lifetime medical treatment.

It is not unusual for the W.C.A.B. to reserve jurisdiction to determine certain issues in the future as where temporary benefits are awarded and ju-risdiction is reserved to rate permanent disability. The Supreme Court has ruled in the *Jackson* case that the Board may reserve jurisdiction to issue successive awards for permanent disability where an employee suffers an in-sidious, progressive, disease and his or her condition is continually deteriorating; that in such a case the Board's authority is not limited to the five-year period set forth in LC 5410 or 5804 but is continuing. The court denominates the five-year period as a statute of limitations.

The Supreme Court in *Nickelsberg v. W.C.A.B.* (1991) has ruled that the removal of the time constraints in LC 4656 regarding payment of temporary total compensation for injuries on or after January 1, 1979, does not permit an employee to petition to reopen an award after five years from date of injury in order to obtain a further award of such compensation. The court applied the five-year limitation in LC 5410 and 5804 on petitions to reopen an award and so ruled even though the temporary disability resulted from surgery performed pursuant to an award of further medical treatment. The court held that these provisions are jurisdictional. It was also ruled that an award for further medical treatment does not amount to an implied award for further compensation for disability resulting from such treatment. The removal of the time limit in LC 4656 was intended only to permit timely awards of temporary total compensation where the disability is continuous.

§ 14.10 Statutes of Limitation; Third-Party Actions

In bringing any action in court against a third party who is claimed to be responsible for the injury, the employee is confronted with a one-year period *CCP 340* in which to file the action. The employer or carrier may also bring action against the third party to recover compensation benefits paid the employee because of the injury, and by virtue of the appellate court decision they, too, are limited to one year in which to bring their action. A 1967 Court of Appeal decision holds that the employee's timely filing of action against a third party removes any bar of the statute of limitations regarding the subrogation lien of the employer or carrier for compensation benefits furnished because of the injury in question. Also, this one-year period may be extended if the parties were delayed in filing by the fraud or other conduct of the third party which would constitute actionable estoppel.

§ 14.11 Filing and Service of Application

The jurisdiction of the Appeals Board attaches to a case when a person having an interest in the matter files an application. The printed form is the result of years of study and experience. Every effort has been made to permit the stating of most workers' compensation cases through the use of one side *LC 5500* of one legal-size form. Some of the more complicated matters require addi- *R 10400-* tional material, but for the most part the one document is sufficient. *10447*

For injuries occurring on or after January 1, 1990, an application may be *LC 5401* filed with the W.C.A.B. after a claim form has been completed, filed with the *5500(b)* employer, and served upon the parties. Note that the filing of the claim form constitutes the "commencement of proceedings" and establishes the jurisdic- *LC 5401(c)* tion of the Board. Thereafter, the parties may commence discovery, including the subpoena and deposition of witnesses. Lienclaimants may file an application. The parties have the right to receive copies of the records of the treating physician or physicians. Additionally, effective January 1, 1991, the obtaining of a formal medical evaluation and PD rating, if applicable, under the administrative-medical procedures set out in LC 4061 is necessary before the issues of permanent disability or further medical treatment may be the subject of an application filed with the W.C.A.B. This is also true for the issues listed in LC 4602 where an employee is represented by an attorney. These issues are: permanent and stationary status of the employee's condition, preclusion or likely preclusion from his or her usual occupation, scope and extent of medical treatment, and existence of new and further disability.

LC 4061(l)
LC 4062(e)

LC 5401(d)

Beginning January 1, 1991, a lienclaimant may file an application for adjudication only if the lienclaimant has filed and served a lienclaim, 90 days have elapsed since the filing of the lien, and no application for adjudication has been filed by the employee, a dependent or the employer. These restrictions do not apply to lienclaims for medical-legal expenses under LC 4620-4628. If an application is filed by a lienclaimant, it must be accompanied by a copy of the claim form filed with the employer by the employee or a dependent if the employee is deceased. If the lienclaimant has not been able to secure a copy, or no claim form has been filed, the lienclaimant must attach a declaration to the application specifying efforts made to secure a copy or encourage the filing of a claim form.

LC 5401.5,
5401.6

Where an employee is represented by an attorney, the attorney must send an information request form to the employer, insurance carrier or third-party administrator and the attorney disclosure form as required by LC 4906(e). The information request form must include information required by LC 5401.5. Within 30 days after receiving the form, the recipient must furnish the information delineated in LC 5401.6. For details see subsequent topic in § 14.20, *Discovery; Depositions; Deposition of Employee or Dependent.*

LC 5501
R 10360

Any party affected by the occurrence of an industrial injury may file an application for determination of liability. Thus, an application may be filed by an employer, an insurance carrier, or a lienclaimant. In these situations the applicant must prove the jurisdictional facts, i.e., the employee's industrial injury.

R 10500
LC 5501
R 10505
10514
10520

Upon filing of an application, if the applicant is represented by an attorney or agent, the W.C.A.B. will serve a conformed copy showing the filing date and the case number upon the attorney or agent who is then required to serve all other parties. If the applicant is not represented, the Board will make the service. Service of the application may be made by mail or by personal service. Proof of service must be filed with the Board.

LC 5502
R 10414

Under LC 5502 as it read before 1990, an application is not set for hearing unless a Declaration of Readiness to Proceed is filed. This section was amended effective as to cases involving injuries occurring on or after January 1, 1990. The amended version requires that a hearing be held not less than 10 days nor more than 60 days after the filing of an application. The *R 10415* previous reference to a Declaration of Readiness to Proceed was deleted; however, W.C.A.B. rules require the filing of a declaration of readiness for *R 10966* proceedings subsequent to the original hearing. The form for the declaration procedure is available at W.C.A.B. offices.

An application subject to the 1990 changes may also indicate issues which require a mandatory settlement conference by a referee or reference to an arbitrator. (Also see § 14.32, *Hearings by Referees; Arbitrators.*)

§ 14.12 Service of Process

The rules provide that the parties are to serve all documents except those *R 10500* reserved for service by the Board. The Board serves notice of hearing and all *10520* findings, orders, decisions, and awards upon the parties and their attorneys or agents of record. Service of documents on Board proceedings is usually made by mail, copies being sent to the parties and their attorneys or agents at their addresses of record. Personal service may also be made. Proof of service is to be filed with the Board, and documents served by the Board must show proof of service. The parties may prove service by an affidavit or declaration of service, a written statement on the original filed with the Board and signed by the party making the statement, or by a letter of transmittal. Proof of service must show the names and addresses of persons served, whether service was personal or by mail, the date of service, the place of personal service or the address to which mailing was made. The Board indicates service by endorsement on the document showing service on the persons listed on the official address record on the Board's case file. This endorsement is to state whether service was personal or by mail and include the date of service and the signature of the person making the service. The Board's procedure has been approved by the Court of Appeal.

Service of process by the Appeals Board is limited by the code to the confines of the state. Out-of-state service may be made by serving the party's *LC 5501* designated agent within the state or the California Secretary of State if the *LC 134* party has sufficient contact with this state to indicate that no unfairness would result through such service. If valid service has not been effected, the Appeals Board has authority to quash service on a showing of good cause. A party may waive any defect in service by making a general appearance in the case, but a special appearance to test the validity of service does not amount to such a waiver. Thus a party appearing on a motion to quash service of an application on the ground that the Board lacks jurisdiction may ask questions regarding the alleged employment relationship without its constituting a general appearance, for employment is a jurisdictional issue.

§ 14.13 Contents of the Application

The printed form of application supplied by the Appeals Board should be used where practicable. Any application should contain: *R 10412*

(1) The names and addresses of all parties.
(2) The material facts in controversy regarding any right or benefit.
(3) The estimated time required for trial and the number of lay and professional witnesses.
(4) In occupational disease cases involving more than one employment, a chronological listing of names and addresses of all employees and their compensation insurance carriers; also the places and periods of exposure to the "hazards of said disease."
(5) The benefits sought by the applicant; other issues.

LC 5500(b)   Where a case involves an injury occurring on or after January 1, 1990, the application must also specify the nature of the dispute, the action being requested of the W.C.A.B., and the efforts previously made to resolve the issue in dispute. The application must be accompanied by medical reports or other documents indicating the basis for the dispute and supporting the action being requested.

§ 14.14   Separate Applications

R 1040   A separate application must be filed for each separate injury. If an employee files one application alleging a series of injuries of the same type, it is often difficult to determine whether they are separate injuries or constitute an occupational disease or condition. Where he is uncertain of his theory, the employee may file an application asserting an occupational disease theory and separate applications for each of the separate incidents on the separate injuries theory. In one back case, for instance, an employee filed an application on the basis and 13 other applications on that number of back strains. The judge's decision was that they were separate and distinct injuries rather than an occupational disease. This finding had an effect on the applicant's recovery, for earning capacity was different in each employment.

§ 14.15   Filing Application and Venue

R 10390   An application for adjudication of a claim may be filed at any office of the W.C.A.B. It will be deemed filed as of the date that it is received by the Board, not as of the date of mailing if mailed to the Board. An application

R 10403, 10404   filed in the "wrong" office under venue rules will be sent to the "correct" office. "Venue" refers to the appropriate location for holding a hearing considering the residence of the parties and the convenience of witnesses. Preference is given to the office in the county of residence of the employee or dependent of a deceased employee or, if there is no office in that county, to the nearest office. Also appropriate is the office in the county of, or nearest office to, the place of the alleged injury or exposure. Any party may petition for a change of venue for good cause. If the request is based upon the convenience of witnesses, the petition must set forth the names and addresses of the witnesses and the substance of their testimony.

LC 5501.5, 5501.6   Beginning January 1, 1991, an application for adjudication may be filed in any of the following locations:

1. In the county of residence of an employee or dependent.

2. In the county where the injury occurred or where the last injurious exposure occurred in cumulative trauma or occupational disease cases.

3. In the county of the principal place of business of the attorney for an employee or dependent.

If the county selected has more than one W.C.A.B. office, the written consent of the employee or dependent must be filed with the application. Where the county is that of the attorney's office, this information must be included in the request for information form. If the employer or carrier objects within 30 days of the receipt of this information, the venue site must be as set forth in either item 1 or item 2, above. In the event that there is no W.C.A.B. office in any of the counties mentioned, the application is to be filed in the office nearest one of the places described in items 1, 2 and 3, above, but an employer or carrier may object to the selection of the place nearest the applicant's attorney's office.

A change of venue may be granted for good cause on a petition setting forth specific reasons therefor filed by an applicant or a defendant. If the request is for the convenience of witnesses, the petition must include the names and addresses of the witnesses as well as the substance of their testimony.

§ 14.16 Alleging Serious and Wilful Misconduct or Discrimination

An application or other document filed in a case alleging serious and wilful misconduct must set out the facts upon which the change is based in sufficient detail so that the parties may be fully advised regarding the basis for the claim. Each theory of liability must be separately stated. For instance, if one theory is the violation of a safety order, and second theory is a failure to provide a safe place to work generally, there must be separate detailed allegations which tend to support the charges. *R 10440 10445*

The correct citation or reference to any safety order or regulation allegedly violated must be set forth, along with all the particulars required for the findings discussed in the chapter on penalties. Failure to comply with this procedure may be grounds for a continuance.

Similar rules require factual allegations in a petition for an S & W penalty under LC 132(a) based upon alleged discriminatory acts of an employer or insurance carrier. Such discrimination is actionable if taken because the employee filed an application for workers' compensation benefits or was involved in a compensation proceeding as a witness. (See Chapter 9, PENALTIES.) *LC 132(a)* *R 10447*

§ 14.17 Petition for Subsequent Injuries Fund Benefits

LC 4751
R 10940-
10946

An applicant claiming the special benefit from the subsequent injuries fund must file a separate application or petition setting forth the facts upon which he bases his claim. A copy must be served on the Division of Industrial Accidents, Subsequent Injuries Fund, and no hearing may be set sooner than 30 days thereafter. Medical reports or other documentary evidence must also be served upon the Fund. The Fund may be represented by the state Attorney General or the DIA's attorneys (LC 4753.5).

§ 14.18 Answers; Affirmative Defenses; Pre-Trial Statement

LC 5500-
5505
R 10480-
10488

The employer or insurance carrier must file an answer challenging the accuracy or completeness of the application. Issues may be raised by way of denial. The answer may contain statements or allegations of factual matter and any special or affirmative defenses. Evidence on matters not set forth in any answer may be allowed only upon such terms as the workers' compensation judge or Appeals Board may impose.

R 10480
10414
10488

An answer to an application is to be filed no later than 10 days after service by the applicant of a declaration of readiness to proceed. A form provided by the W.C.A.B. may be used.

No default may be taken for failure to file an answer. Oral answers or amendments may be permitted at the time of the hearing—again, on such terms as the workers' compensation judge may impose. According to the Court of Appeal, where a default consists of a failure to appear at a hearing, an award may be issued.

R 10492

Both the application and the answer are superseded by the trial judge's statement of the facts and issues which is dictated into the record at the commencement of the hearing. Attorneys will recognize this procedure, for it is the same as, and actually a forerunner of, the "pre-trial and pre-trial order" now used in the general courts. Since the principle of "due process of the law" governs any legal proceeding, any issue raised at a hearing without previous notice to the opposing party may not be tried if objection is raised. In that event the matter must be continued to permit the objecting party to prepare to meet the issue. Fortunately, both applicants and defense attorneys cooperate to agree on facts which are not disputed so that the trial may proceed only on those matters actually in dispute. The advantage of the answer is that it assures a timely notice to the applicant of defense issues, including affirmative defenses, and avoids continuances. (For a discussion of the trial judge's statement of facts and issues, see the later topic in § 14.34, *The Hearing.* The statement will include any affirmative defenses raised by the defendants.)

LC 5705

The affirmative defenses listed in the code are:

(1) That the applicant is an independent contractor.

(2) That the applicant's injury was caused by his intoxication.

(3) That the applicant's unreasonable conduct aggravated the injury.

(4) That the employer was prejudiced by lack of notice of the injury.

(5) That the claim is barred by the statute of limitations.   *LC 5409*

Other affirmative defenses are:

(6) That the Appeals Board lacks jurisdiction.

(7) That the injury was caused by the serious and wilful misconduct of the employee.

(8) That the injury was wilfully self-inflicted.

(9) That the death of the employee was a wilful suicide.

(10) That the injury resulted from an altercation in which the employee was the initial aggressor.

(11) That the employee was a non-salaried partner of the defendant.

(12) That the employment was one of those specifically excluded from the compensation law.

(13) Credit for compensation paid or for employee's third-party recovery.

(14) Aggravation by subsequent injury.

(15) Refusal to submit to examination.

(16) Horseplay or non-industrial recreation.

(17) Apportionment, disability or liability.

(18) By carrier, lack of insurance coverage of the employer.

(19) By carrier, absence of liability under the general-special employer rule.

(20) By carrier, lack of coverage under an exclusionary endorsement or policy provision.

If these defenses are not alleged in an answer or raised in some other manner before submission of the case for decision, they are deemed waived. *LC 5409* One exception to the waiver rule is the question of jurisdiction which may be *5705* raised at any time before the decision becomes final. At the hearing, the em- *R 10484* ployer or carrier has the burden of proving these affirmative defenses. If the applicant's evidence reveals facts upon which such a defense may be based, it is not necessary for the defense to add to this evidence, although it is best to have as strong a record as possible.

§ 14.19 Petitions

R 10450

All requests for Appeals Board action other than applications or answers are termed petitions. The rules require that a petition contain the title and number of the case and that it indicate the type of relief or action sought.

Petition to Reopen. See prior discussion under *Jurisdictional Time Limits.*

LC 5311

R 10452

Petition for Disqualification of Judge. A petition to disqualify a judge for cause must be filed not more than 10 days after service of notice of hearing and be accompanied by affidavit or declaration under penalty of perjury giving detailed facts showing grounds for disqualification of the judge to whom a case or proceeding has been assigned.

R 10453

Petition for Automatic Reassignment of Judge. An injured worker, a dependent of a deceased worker, or a defendant may file a petition for automatic reassignment not more than 5 days after service of notice of hearing, or, if the case is set for hearing before a named judge at a conference hearing, the petition may be made orally at that time. An affidavit or declaration under penalty of perjury in the form set out in R 10453 must be filed with a written petition but not with an appropriate oral petition.

R 10458
LC 5410

Petition for New and Further Disability. This petition must set forth specifically and in detail the facts relied upon to establish new and further disability.

R 10462
10464

LC 4651.1
5410.1

Petition to Terminate Liability. A petition for an order terminating the liability of an employer or carrier under an award for continuing benefits must be filed within 10 days of the termination. All medical reports not previously filed must accompany the petition. The petition must contain a statement in underlined capital letters that an order terminating liability for temporary total disability indemnity will issue unless objection is made in writing within 14 days of service. If an objection is filed, the matter will be set for hearing. If it appears that the liability for temporary compensation should be terminated, the Board will proceed to adjudicate any residual permanent disability. It will also be presumed that temporary disability continues for at least one week after the filing of the petition. Any party who unsuccessfully petitions to terminate an award or to reduce an award for permanent disability benefits must pay attorney's fees incurred by the employee in resisting such a petition.

R 10608
10615

In connection with the filing of any petition and answer, all medical reports not previously filed must be filed and copies served on adverse parties.

[NOTE: Other petitions are discussed elsewhere in connection with specific topics.]

§ 14.20 Discovery; Depositions; Deposition of Employee or Dependent

In the past, pre-trial discovery procedures have been limited to service of medical reports as well as information and documents admissible as evidence under LC 5703-5706. These include official records and publications, transcripts of testimony, autopsies, permanent disability rating reports issued under LC 4660, wage and other employer reports, special investigations, medical and hospital records and depositions. Deposition of witnesses is permitted under LC 5710 which specifically provides for the deposition of an employee or a dependent, subject to the conditions noted below. The W.C.A.B. consistently ruled that the discovery procedures applicable to actions in the general courts as set for in the CCP are not applicable to workers' compensation proceedings. In the Reform Act of 1989 and 1990 amendatory legislation, effective January 1, 1991, discovery, including depositions, receipt of reports of treating physicians and subpoena of records, is permitted after the filing of a claim form with the employer by an employee or dependent. Per LC 5502, discovery closes on the date of the mandatory settlement conference. Evidence not disclosed or obtained thereafter is not admissible unless the proponent of the evidence can demonstrate that it was not available or could not have been discovered with due diligence before the conference. *LC 5401 (c) LC 5502 (d)(3)*

Effective January 1, 1991, if an employee is represented by an attorney, the attorney is required to send an information request form, along with a copy of the attorney disclosure form required by LC 4906(e) to the employer, insurer or third-party administrator. The employer, insurer or third-party administrator must then serve a response upon the attorney within 30 days. Information contained in these forms is not admissible in any W.C.A.B. proceeding. The information request served by the employee's attorney must provide information and indicate issues as follows: *LC 5401.5, 5401.6*

1. Name and address of the attorney.
2. Social Security number of the employee [and name and address of the employee].
3. Date of injury.
4. Part or parts of the body affected.
5. Insurance carrier or third-party administrator of the employer, if known.
6. Date of birth of the employee.
7. Earnings at time of injury.
8. Occupation at time of injury.
9. Dates of disability.
10. Names and addresses of doctors or hospitals providing self-procured medical treatment.
11. Other cases filed for industrial injuries by the employee.

12. Whether the employee is claiming temporary disability indemnity, permanent disability indemnity, medical treatment, reimbursement for medical expenses, compensation at the proper rate, vocational rehabilitation.
13. Other issues raised.
14. A demand for medical records or reports in the possession of the employer, insurer or third-party administrator.
15. A listing of medical reports or records or other information being provided.
16. Whether the employee will agree to arbitration.
17. The venue selected by the employee if an application for adjudication is filed with the W.C.A.B.
18. Notice of the employer's right to object only within 30 days of receipt of the request for information form.
19. Notice that a response to the request must be served on the attorney within 30 days of the receipt of the request form.
20. Copies of all medical reports and records in the possession of the employee must accompany the request.

Within the 30-day period, the employer, insurer or third-party administrator must serve upon the employee's attorney a response to the request for information. The response must include:

1. Name and address of the attorney, if any.
2. Name and address of the injured worker.
3. Date of the claimed injury.
4. Name and address of the employer.
5. Name and address of the insurer or third-party administrator.
6. Earnings of the employee.
7. Whether compensation was paid including total, weekly rate, and the date of last payment.
8. Whether medical treatment was provided, including date of last treatment.
9. Whether the employer denies liability for injury arising out of and in the course of employment.
10. Whether the employer disputes the issues of temporary diability, weekly rate, permanent disability, further medical treatment, self-procured medical treatment, vocational rehabilitation services.
11. Whether the employer disputes any other issue.
12. Whether the employer agrees to arbitration.
13. Whether the employer objects to the employee's choice of venue.
14. A listing of medical reports, records or other evidence being served. [NOTE: Presumably, copies of all defense medical reports and records must be served with the response.]

A not uncommon procedure in compensation cases is the taking of depositions of witnesses. This involves taking the statement of a witness under *LC 5710* oath and the recording of the statement by a court reporter. A deposition taken on notice to the other side may be used at a hearing to impeach the testimony of a witness if it differs from the deposition. Under certain circumstances, a deposition may be introduced into evidence in lieu of the testimony of the witness. Depositions most frequently taken are those of injured workers, dependents in death cases, physicians in lieu of cross-examination at a hearing, and, as authorized, rehabilitation consultants.

If an employer or insurance carrier takes the deposition of an injured employee or dependent for use in the employee's workers' compensation *LC 5710* proceeding, the employee is entitled to:

(1) All reasonable expenses of transportation, meals, and lodging incident to such deposition.

(2) Reimbursement for any loss of wages incurred during attendance at such deposition.

(3) A copy of the transcript of the deposition without cost to the employee or dependent.

(4) A reasonable allowance for attorney's fees if the employee or dependent is represented by an attorney at the deposition. This fee is discretionary upon order of the W.C.A.B. and if ordered is payable by the employer or the employer's insurance carrier.

[NOTE: As to injuries occurring on or after January 1, 1990, the parties may *LC 5401* take depositions of witnesses after a claim form is filed with the employer by an employee or dependent.]

§ 14.21 Filing Medical Reports: Hospital Records

When an application is filed and served, the parties are governed by rules regarding the filing of medical reports or other written evidence, such as *R 10600-* payroll records. Medical reports must be filed and copies served on the other *10635* parties within 10 days after the service of the declaration of readiness to proceed. This requirement serves as a discovery procedure before trial. A good medical report will have a complete history of the injury, thus parties will be fairly well alerted to the position and the evidence of their opposition.

When an application is filed in connection with an injury occurring on *LC 5500(c)* or after January 1, 1990, the application must be accompanied by all medical reports which are pertinent to the issues in dispute. Note should be taken of the restrictions on the admissibility of medical reports other than those of an A.M.E., Q.M.E., or a treating physician set forth in LC 4061-4067. These sections seem to rule out reports of physicians obtained unilaterally by the parties, both before and after the report or reports of the officially designated physician, with the exception of the reports of treating physicians, or where the Board determines that there is good cause to permit a party to obtain an evaluation by another physician.

With regard to the restrictions mentioned, LC 4061(c), (d), provides in part: "Evaluations obtained prior to the period to reach agreement [on an A.M.E.] shall not be admissible before a workers' compensation judge or appeals board. . . ." This limitation does not apply to reports of treating physicians or where the Board determines that there is good cause to permit a party to obtain an evaluation from another physician.

LC 4061(*l*) provides in part: "With the exception of an evaluation or evaluations prepared by the treating physician or physicians, no evaluation of permanent impairment and limitations or need for continuing medical care resulting from the injury shall be obtained prior to service of the formal medical evaluation on the employee and employer if the employee is unrepresented, or prior to the attempt to select an agreed medical evaluator if the employee is represented. Evaluations obtained in violation of this prohibition shall not be admissible before a workers' compensation judge or the appeals board. However, the testimony, records, and reports offered by the treating physician or physicians . . . and formal medical evaluations prepared by a qualified medical evaluator selected by an unrepresented employee from a three-member panel shall be admissible."

LC 4062(f) provides in part: "With the exception of a report or reports prepared by the treating physician or physicians, no report determining disputed medical issues set forth in subdivision (b) [permanent and stationary status of employee's condition, preclusion or likely preclusion to engage in usual occupation, extent and scope of medical treatment, existence of new and further disability] shall be obtained prior to service of the formal medical evaluation of the agreed or qualified medical evaluator on the employee and employer. Reports obtained in violation of this prohibition shall not be admissible in any proceeding before a workers' compensation judge or the appeals board. However, the testimony, records, and reports offered by the treating physician or physicians . . . shall be admissible.

[NOTE: LC 4061(c)(2) and (d)(2), as well as LC 4062 (b)(2) provide for admissibility of reports by treating physicians and where the W.C.A.B. determines there is good cause to permit a party to obtain an evaluation "from another physician." Presumably, the reports of an agreed medical evaluator are also admissible. Note should be taken that LC 4050, giving an employer and the W.C.A.B. the authority to require medical examinations of an injured worker, and LC 4620, giving claimants the right to obtain necessary medical examinations and reports at the expense of the employer, were not amended.]

Any party desiring to cross-examine a physician on his or her report must arrange for the physician's presence at the hearing by subpoena or otherwise. Some question has arisen whether the request for this opportunity may be made at the hearing or whether the party has waived his right by a failure to subpoena the witness before the hearing. The Appeals Board and the appellate courts hold that the request need not be made until the medical report has actually been taken into evidence by order of the judge, for until that point in the proceedings the report is not officially in the record as direct testimony. R 10610 provides that the right to cross-examination of a physician is deemed waived where the report is filed and served 20 days before the hearing unless the physician is produced at the hearing, or unless good cause is shown for not producing him. The party producing the physician must pay any witness fee involved. The validity of this rule is subject to question. However, an appellate court reviewing this rule merely mentioned it and held that it did not apply to the situation before the court. Because of the rapidity with which matters are set for hearing, it requires close attention to invoke this rule. Per the rules of the W.C.A.B., an applicant must file his or her medical reports at the time the applicant's declaration of readiness to proceed is filed. All other parties are to file their medical reports within 10 days after service of the declaration of readiness. Copies of all medical reports must be served on the other parties. Because of the time element involved, a party has to act quickly if a doctor is to be subpoenaed for cross-examination on his or her report. *R 10610* *10615* *R 10606* *10610* *R 10608*

After a proceeding is commenced, each party has a continuing duty to file and serve any medical report within five days after its receipt. In case of wilful suppression of any medical report, it is presumed that the report is adverse to the party possessing it. *R 10615* *10622*

The mandatory filing of medical reports does not apply to X-rays or hospital records. Nevertheless, the Board receives a large number of such unsolicited items which it must return. X-rays should be transmitted only under specific order directing their production. Only two situations should cause production of X-rays and hospital records. One is if the physician-witness will use them in giving testimony. The second would be a request from the Appeals Board, a judge, or an independent medical examiner. A party may, of course, subpoena any evidence which has a bearing on the case. The rules also govern withdrawal or return of exhibits. *R 10608* *10618* *10620*

When hospital records are offered into evidence, the party offering them must designate the portions he believes are pertinent and state where in the records they are to be found. The purpose of this rule will be apparent to anyone who had dealt with these records. Many of the pages and entries are on an hourly or daily basis and set forth the patient's temperature, the giving of medicine, whether he rested or slept. X-ray reports, laboratory findings and the reports of any examining or operating physician will also be included. The determination of what is pertinent or helpful to a party may often be made by one of the parties' medical witnesses. The rule is designed to permit the judge to focus quickly upon those matters which have probative value without the necessity of examining every page of the records. *R 10626*

Perusal of hospital records may be made by attorneys or investigators prior to the hearing if the employee has given written permission.

There are occasions when a doctor's office records are subpoenaed by one of the parties, and confusion results because it was not made clear that only the records were required at the hearing and not the doctor, his nurse, or other assistant. Ordinarily, it is sufficient if the doctor sends the records to the Appeals Board, or has someone deliver them, at any time prior to the date of the hearing. In the event a party requires the doctor's presence, the subpoena and the person serving it should clearly state this requirement. *LC 4055.2* Under a 1974 amendment, a copy of any subpoena for medical records must be served on all parties of record.

§ 14.22   Medical Examiners Appointed by the W.C.A.B.

LC 139
5703.5
R 10700-
10716

LC 28
4061-4067

Before 1990, the law permitted the W.C.A.B. and its judges to appoint independent medical examiners (I.M.E.'s) either at state expense or the expense of one of the parties, also medical examiners agreed upon by the parties (A.M.E.'s) at the expense of one of the parties. With amendments effective as to injuries occurring on or after January 1, 1990, the nomenclature has been changed; "independent medical examiner" becomes "qualified medical evaluator" (Q.M.E.) and "agreed medical examiner" is "agreed medical evaluator" (A.M.E.). Q.M.E.'s are selected through the Medical Director from an official list approved by the Industrial Medical Council. LC 5703.5, as amended, seemingly repeals the previous broad authority of the Board and judges to appoint official medical examiners, limiting it to appointment of a Q.M.E. or A.M.E. at the expense of one of the parties only in the case of an unrepresented employee, and then only with regard to clinical issues other than the issues specified in LC 4061-4062, i.e., other

LC 4067

than permanent disability and medical treatment issues. Also, LC 4067 provides that in Board proceedings subsequent to the initial evaluation under LC 4061 or 4062, further references to a Q.M.E. or A.M.E. will be made to the same physician unless the Board or a judge makes a finding that the physician's opinion was not relied upon or that the physician is no longer available, in which case the procedures of initial medical evaluation under those sections are applicable. To be considered in this connection, however, are the

LC 4050-
4056
5703

possible inherent authority of the Board as a court and Labor Code sections which were not not changed in the Reform Act. Medical examinations at the direction of the Board are authorized in LC 4050, and, under LC 5703(b), the Board has authority to appoint "special investigators" to report upon "any scientific or medical question." Note may also be taken, as discussed in the previous topic, that LC 4061 and 4062 provide for the authority of the Board to "permit a party to obtain an evaluation from another physician" upon a showing of good cause. In any event, the practice has been to appoint official medical examiners only where there is a conflict in the medical evidence sufficient to require expert medical assistance in resolving an issue.

As a general rule, a party may offer medical evidence in rebuttal to the report of a Board-appointed medical expert, assuming that the party conforms to the time limitations set by the judge for further proceedings. However, as of January 1, 1991, with respect to injuries occurring on or after January 1, 1990, this principle is subject to the limitations placed upon the Board's authority and the necessity for a judge to find good cause per LC 4061 and 4062 in order to permit a party to obtain a report from another physician.

[NOTE: By virtue of 1990 legislation, the W.C.A.B.'s authority to appoint independent medical examiners continues until January 1, 1991, at which time the above changes and limitations take effect as to injuries occurring on or after that date.]

LC 28
5703.5
139.1

Any party may request a further hearing to cross-examine an independent or special medical examiner. R 10727 states: "The Workers' Compensation Appeals Board favors cross-examination of medical witnesses by way of deposition. Reasonable costs in connection with such deposition shall be allowed under Labor Code Section 4600." [Re medical-legal costs, see Chapter 4, § 4.21, *Payment or Reimbursement for Cost of Medical Reports*.]

R 10726
19727

R 10978-
10980

Communication with a medical examiner appointed by the Board or a judge is prohibited, except for the necessary interview of the employee by the examiner as an incident to the examination. All contact is made by or through the official making the appointment. The appellate court has held that a violation of this rule requires that the resulting report be stricken from the record.

R 10718

A party has the right to rebut the report on an I.M.E. with a report by his own physician covering a later examination.

§ 14.23 Contents of Medical Reports

As we have stated, the Appeals Board and compensation judges must decide medical questions upon medical evidence. In most cases, the evidence will be presented in the form of medical reports. Claims examiners base their handling of cases on the treating physician's progress reports and the more complete reports of special examinations. Medical reports vary in their value as evidence. They may be excellent and complete; or they may be terse, uncertain or ambiguous. Each report must be analyzed carefully, and if any uncertainty results from a particular report, it should be clarified either by the physician submitting the report or by some other consultant. Such analysis and clarification is the job of the person who expects to rely upon the report, whether he be an employee, an employer, a claims examiner or an attorney representing a party before the Appeals Board or compensation judge.

R 10606
R 10978-
10980

A good medical report will contain detailed descriptions of the injury, the parts of the body affected, the employee's symptoms and complaints, and the result of the physician's examination. The report will also contain a description of any disability, the cause, and whether temporary or permanent. In rendering his opinion, it is well for the physician to give the reasons for his conclusions. To be of value, opinions should be based upon medical probabilities. A conclusion based on possibilities is usually characterized as mere conjecture. A medical possibility may, however, support a finding if corroborated by compelling non-medical evidence.

R 10606 provides the following:

The Workers' Compensation Appeals Board favors the production of medical evidence in the form of written reports. Direct examination of a medical witness will not be received at a hearing except upon a showing of good cause and written notice to the parties filed and served at least 20 days before the hearing.

These reports should include where applicable:

(a) the date of the examination;

(b) the history of the injury;

(c) the patient's complaints;

(d) source of all facts set forth in the history of complaints;

(e) findings on examination;

(f) opinion as to the extent of disability and work limitations, if any;

(g) cause of the disability;

(h) medical treatment indicated;

(i) opinion as to whether or not permanent disability has resulted from the injury and whether or not it is stationary. If stationary, a description of the disability with a complete evaluation;

(j) the reasons for the opinions; and,

(k) the signature of the physician.

If any person other than the physician who has signed the report has participated in the examination of the injured employee or in the preparation of the report, the name or names of such persons and their role shall be set forth, including the name of person or persons who have taken the history, have performed the physical examination, have drafted, composed, or edited the report in whole or in part.

In death cases, the reports of non-examining physicians may be admitted into evidence in lieu of oral testimony.

Failure to comply with the requirements of this section will not make the report inadmissible but will be considered in weighing such evidence.

R 9725,
9726   The rules of the Administrative Director set forth certain criteria for describing disability in medical reports. R 9725 provides that the method of measuring physical disability should follow the report of the Joint Committee of the California Medical Association and Industrial Accident Commission as contained in *Evaluation of Industrial Disability*, edited by Packard Thurber,

Second Edition, Oxford Press, New York, 1960. R 9726 details the format for describing pychiatric disability in medical reports. Psychological testing and a work function impairment analysis are recommended. This rule's criteria include a complete history of injury or illness and the patient's occupational, mental, medical, social, and developmental background; also, review of medical, employment, and personnel records. Diagnoses are to be expressed in DSM-III terminology. An evaluation report should contain a summary and conclusion with regard to possible total or partial permanent disability.

§ 14.24 Late Filing of Medical Reports

The rules provide that the judge may allow the late filing of medical reports in a compensation proceeding on such terms and conditions as his *R 10622* discretion dictates. A late report shall not be refused admission into evidence if the party offering it has been diligent in scheduling the examination and he receives it within the preceding seven days. This problem arises many times because of last minute activity of the parties to obtain up-to-date medical reports for a forthcoming hearing. Receipt of an application or notice of hearing usually triggers further medical examinations. The compensation judge's exercise of discretion will undoubtedly depend on the state of the medical file and the issues raised. Formerly, the practice was to take testimony and such medical evidence as was presented at the hearing, then give the parties time to file and serve other reports along with seven days after service within which to request further proceedings. Too often the late reports not only change the picture presented by the medical evidence, but also indicate that additional interrogation of witnesses is necessary to obtain a complete record. And in many instances upon receiving these reports, the parties will settle. In cases of this type, the first hearing may have been unnecessary, or the procedure becomes one of trying a case on a piecemeal basis. For these reasons, the practice has been instituted of giving the parties a short continuance to a date certain to permit the presentation of all evidence at one hearing and to encourage the parties to be more efficient or diligent in their preparation.

[NOTE: Under the W.C.A.B. rules, a medical report received by a party too late for filing before a hearing, or a report received after a hearing but before *R 10615* a decision has issued, must be filed and served even though the report might not be taken into evidence.]

§ 14.25 Medical Reports of Lien Claimants

When a lienclaim of the department of employment or of a private UCD carrier is contested, the lienclaimant must file any medical reports in its pos- *R 10608* session which are pertinent to the case. Even though the lien is not objected to by any party, the Appeals Board or judge may order the production of *R 10978* these reports. Since a lienclaimant is a party to the litigation, he must prove the validity of his lien, and if it becomes material, he must file any medical evidence in his possession. In this category would be included physicians, hospitals, or medical plans seeking recovery for medical charges.

§ 14.26   Cross-Examining Physicians

R 10727   As previously noted, R 10727 states that the W.C.A.B. favors cross-examination by way of deposition; that reasonable costs will be allowed per LC 4600. (See also LC 4620-4627.) This procedure makes it possible to schedule cross-examination in a physician's office or other convenient location with due consideration for the time constraints of all concerned.

In cross-examining a physician on his report, the examiner should keep in mind that doctors are more interested in diagnosis and treatment of the condition than they are in, what may be to them a purely academic question, whether an incident or exposure in employment caused or aggravated the condition. Doctors are usually on a tight schedule, and the loss of income represented by time spent in court or during a deposition must be considered. One independent medical examiner testified, in a case heard by the author as a referee, that medicine is the art of applying medical knowledge and science to varying situations and is not an exact science; that a more satisfactory situation results in the courtroom when both the doctor and the attorney realize this fact. The medical profession presents the same cross-section of human traits, foibles, or prejudices as any other group. The attorney, therefore, need not feel apprehensive about cross-examining a physician if he or she has adequately prepared his line of questioning. Likewise, the physician need not feel that cross-examination is an inquisition if he testifies in a straight-forward manner. Preparation by the attorney includes analyzing the medical reports, checking the meaning of medical terms in a medical dictionary, reading publications dealing with the condition in question, and conferring with one's own medical witness or witnesses.

The cross-examination concerning a report should begin with a discussion of the doctor's qualifications and experience, unless the attorney is satisfied with the witness' stature as an expert in the particular field of medicine. Next it is necessary to discuss terminology used in the report. This is of utmost importance, for, while the written report is deemed direct testimony, it was prepared some time before the hearing and may contain typographical errors or may not clearly and fully set forth the doctor's thoughts or opinions. The exact meaning of the report must be established so that the attorney and witness are semantically together. Otherwise, if the report is not clarified, the effect of the cross-examination is lessened to a great degree.

There is usually more than one school of thought on any medical problem, so that it is possible for the physician to give a series of "yes" answers when asked whether various theories are possible. This assumes that the witness is candid. If he is not, he may get into difficulty if he does not concede the possibilities.

In building a foundation for later questions, it is best to keep questions short. Attorneys usually get into trouble when they ask an expert witness long, complex, or hypothetical questions before they are really ready to ask them. It helps to bring in one at a time those items or factual facets of the problem which may not be revealed by the medical report and to record the doctor's opinion as to the importance or effect of each fact upon his opinion. When all the facts are in the record which are pertinent, then the hypothetical question may be put to the witness. One heart case is recalled in which the specialist for the defense had rendered the opinion that ditch digging did not cause or aggravate the employee's heart condition, even though his heart attack occurred while he was in the ditch. On cross-examination, facts not previously called to the doctor's attention were brought out. Thus, he testified that it was a hot day which could have been a significant factor; also the fact that it was humid; that the employee had just finished a good-sized lunch. Then in answer to a hypothetical question based on all these facts, the witness reversed his opinion and stated that coupled with them the strenuous exertion probably aggravated the condition, resulting in the attack.

In one back case, the independent medical examiner was shown motion pictures of the employee performing bending motions he had told the doctor he could not do. Other motions of the employee in the pictures appeared to be somewhat guarded. The witness did not reverse his opinion about the employee's having disability as a result of the back strain, but he did change his conclusion about the extent of his disability, stating that it was probably minor in view of the apparent ability to perform deep flexion.

It also makes the examination of the medical witness more understandable and effective if he is asked to explain the mechanics of the theory expressed in his report. The doctor may be asked to detail it in relation to the anatomy so that a medical layman can understand it.

Cross-examination questions should be studied and written out before the hearing, so that a talkative or argumentative witness does not distract the attorney from his line of inquiry. Hypothetical questions containing many facts or assumptions should be typed and a copy given to the witness, opposing counsel, and the judge. Before the answer is given, it helps to determine whether the doctor understands it and can give his answer. Many times an expert will argue about the facts or assumptions, especially if the question contains errors of terminology or medical theory, so that these matters should be squared away before the question itself is put to the witness for the record.

One requirement is to know when to quit, when the witness has said all that he has to say on the subject that will be beneficial to the cross-examiner's position, or the least detrimental. If the witness keeps referring to his report as containing his opinion, the most that may be gained are some affirmative answers to possibilities. If he will not admit that there are other possibilities or theories, the stopping point would be where it was apparent that the witness is less than candid or is assuming the role of an advocate.

Care should also be taken not to overdo references to the physician's status if he is not a specialist or a diplomate of the board of the particular specialty involved. If a medical witness is candid and credible and has experience in the field, an attorney may be surprised if he pushes the point too strongly. Two examples come to mind from cases heard by the author as a referee. In both cases, the doctor's hands were used eloquently:

1. Q: Now, doctor, you are not an orthopedist—isn't that correct?
   A: That is true, but in my forty years' experience as team physician for various schools and colleges, I should judge that with these hands I have treated as many injured bones, muscles, and tendons as any orthopedic specialist.

2. Q: Doctor, you are a pathologist, not a heart specialist, according to your previous testimony?
   A: I have not treated a heart patient. But I have held as many hearts in my hand as a heart specialist listens to. I have studied hearts, the pathology involved on the onset of disease, and the cause of failure.

Since testimony on cross-examination is an extension of the physician's report, an applicant may obtain reimbursement for the cost involved.

§ 14.27   Filing of Other Reports

R 10600, 10601

Payroll or other reports submitted in lieu of direct testimony must be filed with the Appeals Board and served on the other parties five days before the hearing. Due process of law requires that the right to cross-examine the person preparing the report be afforded the parties.

§ 14.28   Rating Reports

R 10602

Reports of recommended permanent disability rating prepared by the Disability Evaluation Bureau are filed in the case by the workers' compensation judge, and copies are served upon all the parties. Unless any objection to a report *and* any request for cross-examination of the rating specialist, or for further proceedings, are filed within seven days after service of the report, the matter will be submitted for decision.

§ 14.29   Cross-Examination of Rating Specialist

R 10602

Appeals Board procedure requires that the compensation judge decide which factors of disability are caused by the injury and thus to be included in the instructions to the rating bureau. When the parties are served with the rating report, they will have notice of the judge's determination of ratable factors, as well as the formula for the computations of the rating specialist in addition to the amount of the final rating. If the factors selected are the type which require only mathematics to get the rating, it would serve little purpose to cross-examine the rating specialist. In a case of this kind, the cross-examiner's quarrel may be with the factors selected by the judge, in which event he or she should file objections to the rating and set forth his or her reasons.

If the judge's instructions in any respect require the exercise of judgment by the rating specialist regarding extent of disability, age, or occupation of the employee, a proper subject for cross-examination is presented.

A decision of the California Supreme Court shows that cross-examination can bring out and underscores the need to analyze the employee's classification and duties before entering into a stipulation on the issue of "occupation." At the hearing the parties stipulated to an occupation of "operating engineer." The matter was referred to the permanent disability rating bureau, and, as is the usual practice, the judge sent the entire file along with his instructions. The rater in reviewing the judge's summary of testimony concluded that the occupation was more akin to "heavy equipment operator," which would result in a higher permanent disability rating and thus a larger award. The following are the occupations he considered and their effect on the rating:

Occupational Group No.	Occupation	Rating (as adj. for occ.)
47	heavy equipment operator	50%
50	gantry crane operator	46$\frac{1}{2}$%
22	operating engineer	46$\frac{1}{2}$%

The court held that it is true that the judge was not bound by the stipulation, but that he could not ignore it and select another occupation unless the parties had been put on notice that occupation was in issue, and the parties afforded the opportunity to present evidence on the issue.

Of course, the same attention should be given to all elements of a rating both at the time of the hearing and in analyzing the rating report when it is received: to whether the disability is scheduled (in the rating schedule) or nonscheduled; whether it is based on objective factors, or subjective factors, or both; and, in general, whether the result is consistent with all instructions given.

Suppose, for instance, that the judge's instruction is, "Disability prevents employee from performing heavy labor." These are words of art and require the rater to assign a rating of 30%, standard. (This is one of the "plateaus" of subjective disability evaluations discussed in Chapter 6.) Cross-examination would merely bring out the information that the Appeals Board uses such a definition.

Another issue can be "apportionment," if a pre-existing condition or prior injury is involved in the case. Care should be taken to ascertain whether the rating report reveals the apportionment. If not, the judge will decide the issue in his findings.

Appellate court decisions stress the parties' right to cross-examine the rating specialist and the right to notice and a hearing if the judge or the Board intends to ignore a stipulation of facts as matters of constitutional due process of law. Where proper procedural steps have been taken, the rating schedule and the rating report are prima facie evidence. Further, the judge or the Board can fix permanent disability and determine the issue of apportionment without expert testimony because of their "great experience," making them "better qualified than the average laymen" in determining these questions.

§ 14.30　Screening the Application; Rating Calendar; Conference Calendar; Priority Calendar

R 10301

Most often, the application is filed by the injured employee or a dependent. Some are filed by employers, some by physicians, hospitals, or other lienclaimants. Regardless of who files, the case is carried under the name of the employee. The clerk's office prepares the case file, a docket sheet, and index cards. A number is assigned the case with lettered prefix indicating the location of the headquarters or branch in which it is filed. The index of employees will indicate any previous cases filed by or on behalf of the employee. The file is then referred to a screening unit which checks the adequacy of the information alleged in the application and the benefits sought. If deficiencies are noted, the applicant or his or her attorney will be notified and directed to supply the correct information or straighten out any ambiguities. One of the most common omissions is the failure to name or join the insurance carrier of the employer as a party. Should there be any difficulty in obtaining the name of a carrier, Appeals Board personnel will follow the routine which has developed to get this information. First, the employer will be contacted for the name of his insurer. If unsuccessful, the clerk's office may then check the list of self-insureds. The Board or the parties may contact the California Worker's Compensation Insurance Rating Bureau which has records of all employers who are insured. Finally, if these efforts are of no avail, it will be considered that the employer is wilfully uninsured.

Cases are also screened to select those which appear to have easily determinable issues for a special short-cause calendar which the Appeals Board calls its "rating calendar." These cases are reviewed by a rating specialist who makes recommendations to the parties on the ranges of the possible benefits as revealed by the medical evidence then on file. If the parties find a common ground, they may stipulate to an award of a certain amount or file a compromise and release agreement. If they cannot agree, the rating calendar judge will transfer the case to another judge for trial the same day. If the matter has been scheduled prematurely, or if good cause is shown for a continuance, it can be continued to a date certain or continued on notice.

LC 5502(d)

A "conference calendar" includes cases set for discussion between the parties and a compensation judge in an effort to resolve issues by agreement. Sometimes issues are resolved or clarified, and cases are settled as a result of these conferences. Cases not settled are referred to the regular calendar the same day, although a continuance is permitted if the parties request it on a showing of good cause. If a case involves an injury occurring on or after January 1, 1990, a mandatory settlement conference will be scheduled before a referee appointed by the Board if the applicant is represented by an attorney. If the applicant is not represented, the judge to whom the case is as signed may hold a settlement conference. A settlement conference in such a case will be conducted not less than 10 days nor more than 30 days after the filing of the application. If the dispute is not resolved, the regular hearing will be held within 75 days after the filing of the application. (See subsequent topic in Section 14.32, *Hearings by Referees; Arbitrators.*)

The Administrative Director may establish priority calendars for expedited W.C.A.B. hearings in cases involving injuries occurring on or after January 1, 1990, regarding the issues of entitlement to medical treatment, entitlement to temporary compensation, appeal from the Rehabilitation Unit, disputes re liability among employers or insurance carriers, or other issues as determined by the Director. An expedited hearing is to be held within 30 days. Per R 10136, a request for an expedited hearing is made by completing, filing, and serving the official form set forth in R 10137 with the application or within five days days thereafter. The O.B.A.E. will review the request and refer it to the Presiding Judge within two days. An expedited hearing will be set within 15 days from the filing of the application. Any subsequent request is to be directed to the Presiding Judge by petition setting forth good cause.

LC 5502(b)
R 10136,
10137

§ 14.31 Regular Calendar

The bulk of the cases is set on the regular trial calendar. Every effort is made to schedule a hearing within six weeks after the filing of the application and declaration of readiness to proceed or other request for relief. Many are set within four weeks. The rules require at least 10 days' notice of hearing. If it takes a week to prepare the file, screen, and serve notice, three weeks is the minimum time within which a hearing could be held after the filing of an application. Any continuance would probably mean an additional four to six weeks. Calendars are prepared so as to leave a few hearing dates open for continuance to a date certain.

Preparation of a defense by the defendants becomes a problem if the application, declaration of readiness, and the notice of hearing are served together. The short notice and the volume of cases handled stresses the need for as much notice as possible. Most attorneys familiar with Appeals Board practice serve a copy of the application on the defendants on the same day the original is filed. The fact of service and the parties served must be shown on the lower part of the application. Service by mail is sufficient. Since most carriers receive service of many Appeals Board documents daily, the clerk's office has facilitated notice of a pending action by placing a copy of any application ready for processing in the envelope prepared for the applicable carrier. This service will be shown on the original application. These efforts by the attorneys and the clerk's office have materially reduced the number of continuances. So also has the keeping of cases off-calendar until a declaration of readiness to proceed has been filed.

LC 5500
R 10966

The foregoing discussion is subject to the rule of automatic setting for hearing of cases involving injuries occurring on or after January 1, 1990. Requests for subsequent proceedings must be accompanied by a Declaration of Readiness to Proceed.

§ 14.32   Hearings by Referees; Arbitrators

The Reform Act of 1989 provides for the appointment of referees and arbitrators to hold hearings on certain issues in order to expedite the resolution of cases pending before the W.C.A.B. These procedures are applicable to cases involving injuries occurring on or after January 1, 1990.

LC 5502(d)

Referees. Effective January 1, 1991, through December 31, 1993, regardless of the date of injury, where an applicant is represented by an attorney, a referee is to conduct a settlement conference in 10 to 30 days after the filing of an application. If the dispute is not resolved, a regular hearing is to be held within 75 days. A referee must be one who is eligible to be a workers' compensation judge or an arbitrator per LC 5270. A referee has authority to approve a settlement (C & R) or issue a stipulated findings and award or frame issues for trial. Within 10 days prior to a conference, the parties must submit statements re issues, exhibits, and witnesses. Evidence not disclosed will be inadmissible unless it could not be discovered with due diligence. Discovery closes on the date of the conference. If an applicant is not represented by an attorney, a settlement conference may be held by the workers' compensation judge to whom the case is assigned for regular hearing.

LC 5270-
5278

Arbitrators. LC 5270-5277 provide for the appointment of arbitrators and both mandatory and agreed arbitration of certain issues for injuries occurring on or after January 1, 1990. An arbitrator is an attorney who is either a certified workers' compensation specialist, a retired workers' compensation judge, a retired Appeals Board member, or certified pro tem workers' compensation judge, appointed to a list of arbitrators by a Presiding Workers' Compensation Judge. An arbitrator has the same authority as a workers' compensation judge except as to reference to a Q.M.E. or the power of contempt. Parties select an arbitrator by agreement or by striking two names each from a panel of five submitted by a Presiding Workers' Compensation Judge. Additional names will be included if there are multiple applicants, defendants or lienclaimants. If the litigated issue is insurance coverage, any attorney may be selected by agreement of the parties.

LC 5275

Mandatory arbitration applies to the issues of insurance coverage and contribution by employers or carriers in occupational or cumulative trauma cases under LC 5500.5. It also applies to the issue of permanent disability where an informal rating indicates 15% standard or less, and the case cannot be set for hearing in 110 days from the date of the application—or 20% standard and no hearing in 150 days—where applicant has not requested a continuance. [NOTE: Inclusion of the PD issues is operative only for the period January 1, 1991 through December 31, 1993, and regardless of the date of injury.]

Other issues may be submitted to arbitration by agreement or by a Presiding Judge. Proceedings may be held at any agreed time or place or as ordered by the arbitrator. An arbitrator's decision will be based upon evidence submitted by the parties and issued within 30 days of submission. If a decision is not issued within that time, or a time agreed to by the parties, the arbitrator forfeits his or her fee, and the submission order and all stipulations are vacated. Costs of arbitration are borne by the employer or carrier in disputes involving an employee. In other cases, costs are borne as follows: equally by an employer or carrier and a lienclaimant; equally in proceedings under LC 5500.5; by dependents per proportionate shares of death benefits if there is no dispute as to injury causing death. Disputes over arbitrators' fees or costs are resolved by the Presiding Workers' Compensation Judge. An *R 10999* arbitrator's fee will be judged according to responsiblity assumed, experience, number and complexity of the issues, time involved, and expeditiousness and completeness of issue resolution.

W.C.A.B. rules implement the arbitration process. If an application in- *R 10995-* cludes issues to be resolved by mandatory arbitration, a request for arbi- *10999* tration on the approved form must be submitted with the application. If the parties have agreed on an arbitrator, the Presiding Judge will, within six days, order the issue or issues submitted to arbitration. Where a party requests a panel of arbitrators, the Presiding Judge will provide each party an identical list of five arbitrators. Each party is to strike two names from the list and return it to the Presiding Judge within six days. Failure of a party to return his or her list within that time will constitute a waiver of the right to participate in the selection process. If one arbitrator remains, the judge will, within six days, order submission of the issue or issues to arbitration before that arbitrator. If more than one arbitrator remains after the parties exercise their right to strike two names, the judge will make a random selection of an arbitrator from the remaining names. If all names have been stricken (as where more than two parties are involved), a new panel of five will be submitted. This procedure will continue until an arbitrator can be selected.

If a case is set for hearing before a workers' compensation judge, arbitration must be requested within six days after receiving notice of hearing. Arbitration will not be permitted after the taking of testimony in a proceeding before a judge. Disqualification of an arbitrator will be on grounds stated in CCP 170.1. No disclosure of any offer of settlement is to be made to an *LC 5278* arbitrator before the filing of an award. Also, there is to be no ex parte communication (i.e., by one party only) with an arbitrator except for scheduling a hearing or requesting a continuance.

§ 14.33   Interpreters

It is the responsibility of any party producing a witness requiring an in- terpreter to arrange for the presence of a qualified interpreter at a hearing. *R 10564* The Board or a judge may appoint an interpreter and fix his or her compensa- *LC 5811*

LC 4620 tion or fee for the appearance. The amount charged by an interpreter will be deemed reasonable unless proved to be, or is manifestly, unreasonable. The fee will be assessed as costs under LC 5811 or LC 4620.

[NOTE: The above provision under R 10564 is in addition to the provision for an interpreter in connection with medical treatment or examination under LC 4600 and 4620.]

§ 14.34   The Hearing

An Appeals Board hearing room is a courtroom furnished in a utilitarian manner. It contains the judge's bench, a witness stand, a counsel table, a reporter's table, and additional seats for witnesses and any spectators. A court reporter is present at every hearing to record a verbatim account of all the testimony given and the orders or rulings of the judge. The reporter doubles as court clerk and court reporter. The Board does not employ bailiffs.

A hearing begins with a pre-trial conference conducted by the judge. The judge has before him or her the file containing the application, any answer filed by the defendants, the medical or other reports filed by the parties. The judge is already familiar with the contentions of the parties and in a general way the factual situation. The judge proceeds to examine the parties, or their counsel if they are represented, about the facts which they will agree on and the issues which they intend to raise. In doing so, the judge uses a printed trial sheet which contains a listing of the most common issues:

1. Employment
2. Age
3. Occupation
4. Injury
5. Insurance or wilful non-insurance
6. Medical
7. Earnings
8. Compensation paid
9. Extent of disability
10. Attorney's fee or arrangement
11. Lien claims
12. Affirmative defenses
13. Misconduct of employer
14. Death
15. Dependency
16. Burial expense
17. Other issues
18. Submission or disposition
  (a) Need for medical treatment
  (b) Liability for self-procured medical treatment
  (c) Medical-legal costs

Starting down this list, the judge asks if these items are admitted as alleged in the application. The parties admit those matters they agree to be true, and any pertinent matter not agreed upon is deemed in issue. When the admitted facts and the issues are determined, the judge dictates for the record an order which the reporter includes in the minutes of the hearing. It might appear thus:

"John Doe, born April 9, 1949, while employed as a carpenter by Richard Roe Construction Co., Inc., a corporation, on July 10, 1984, at Glendale, California, sustained an injury arising out of and occurring in the course of said employment, consisting of a comminuted fracture of the right femur. At that time, the employer's workers' compensation insurance carrier was the Target Insurance Co., a corporation. Some medical treatment was furnished. Temporary compensation has been paid in full through January 4, 1985. Earnings are maximum.

"The issues are:

1. Nature, extent and duration of disability
2. Reimbursement for self-procured medical treatment
3. Reimbursement for medico-legal costs (medical costs, X-rays, etc.)
4. Unreasonable refusal of medical treatment offered by the defendants
5. Apportionment of disability
6. Aggravation of disability by employee's unreasonable conduct
7. Statute of Limitations"

Suppose that the applicant is claiming that he injured his back when he broke his femur; our hypothetical minutes do not show this claim or issue. Whether back disability resulted from the admitted injury is in issue under general issue of "nature, extent and duration of disability," and specialists in workers' compensation matters would undoubtedly so understand the issues. Those unfamiliar with workers' compensation practice have evidenced difficulty when the issues concerning the precise disability or disabilities are not stated. Sometimes, when the defense counsel states, "We admit injury," the applicant or his counsel believes that there is nothing more for him to prove concerning causation of disability. Such is not the case. This admission on the part of the defense means only that an incident at work occurred; it does not constitute an admission or stipulation that all of applicant's claimed disability is to be attributed to that incident without a contest. The record in John Doe's case would be clearer if the pretrial order began:

"Applicant, John Doe, claims a compensable injury to his back and leg on July 10, 1984. It is admitted that applicant was born April 9, 1949, etc." The statement of the issues would further clarify matters if another were added:

"The issues are:

1. Whether applicant suffered a back injury on July 10, 1984, at the time of the injury to his right leg.
2. Nature, extent, etc."

An issue on which the applicant should be particularly well prepared is that of "earnings." An employer or insurance carrier is not bound by any rate of payment that has been made before the hearing. If compensation payments have been paid at the maximum rate because of inaccurate information about applicant's earning capacity at the time of injury, this issue can be raised at the hearing. There have been many cases of an applicant's being caught off-guard because he assumed that the defense would stipulate that earnings were in accordance with the rate at which compensation had been paid in the past. An applicant should always be ready to *prove* his earning capacity at the time of injury.

After completing the pre-trial statement, the judge usually turns the matter over to the attorney for the applicant if he has one. (About 90% of the applicants are represented by counsel.) If not, the judge asks questions of the applicant who testifies under oath concerning his injury, compensation, disability, and other issues. If the case is difficult or complex, the judge will discuss with the applicant the advisability of a continuance to permit him or her to retain counsel. In most of these cases, the applicants desire to be represented, but have not previously been advised of procedural rights. Those who do not know an attorney are referred to the lawyers reference service of the local bar association.

The applicant testifies on direct examination and then is cross-examined by the defense. This procedure is repeated as to any other witnesses the applicant may have. The defense puts on its case after the applicant has rested his case. The documentary evidence may be admitted into evidence as it is offered by the parties. Some judges prefer to have all medical reports introduced at the beginning of the hearing. Each party should be careful to ascertain which reports are going into evidence and whether as applicant's exhibits or defendants' exhibits, for the filing of a report by a party does not necessarily indicate that he will offer it into evidence. All reports must be filed under the Board's rules of discovery, but it is not uncommon for a party to disown a report. When this happens, the other party may offer it, or the judge may make it a part of the record as an Appeals Board exhibit.

When both sides have rested their cases, the judge makes an order of disposition. If the evidence is deemed complete on all issues, the order is merely, "Submitted." This order means that the judge will decide the matter later and issue a "Findings and Award" if the applicant is awarded anything, or "Findings and Order" if the applicant is to receive nothing. Except for cases on the Pre-trial Calendar, judges rarely enter a decision at the hearing. There are several procedural reasons for orders of submission. All decisions are prepared by the judge. The judge must also prepare a resume of all the testimony at the completion of the hearing. At the time the decision is issued, the judge is also required to prepare a memorandum opinion giving the reasons for the decision. Most cases involve detailed computations either by the judge, a senior legal stenographer or a rating specialist. The decision, the resume of testimony, and the memorandum opinion are served on the parties by the Appeals Board.

R 10700

At the conclusion of the hearing, one of the parties may request reference of the case to an independent medical examiner or an agreed medical examiner. In the latter reference, one or both of the parties must defray the expense. If the judge is not satisfied with the medical record, the judge may initiate a reference to an independent medical examiner or a medical bureau staff physician. In the alternative, the judge might suggest that the parties consider the appointment of an agreed medical examiner. In a case of this nature, the judge's order of disposition would provide:

"Matter to be submitted to an independent medical examiner (or to an agreed medical examiner at the expense of the defendants with authority for necessary tests and x-rays). His report will be filed, served and made a part of the record without further order. The parties shall have 7 days following service to request cross-examination or further proceedings; thereafter the matter to stand submitted."

A similar reference to the Disability Evaluation Bureau may be made if there is an issue of a rating. On occasion, an order of disposition will contain references to both. Such an order might read:

"Matter to be referred to an independent medical examiner . . . etc., and thereafter, if indicated, to the Disability Evaluation Bureau. Each report will be filed, served and made a part of the record without further order. The parties shall have 7 days following service of each report to request cross-examination or further proceedings; otherwise submitted."

§ 14.35 Hearing in Occupational Disease or Cumulative Trauma Cases

Hearings in occupational disease and cumulative trauma cases involve the principles and procedure set forth in LC 5500.5 as discussed in Chapter 8, THE INJURY, Section 8.23, *Occupational Disease; Cumulative Trauma; Apportionment Among Employers.* Some procedural points are stressed here. The applicability of the exposure-periods set out in LC 5500.5 depends upon the date of filing or assertion of a claim. Also, "exposure" means "injurious exposure" as determined by proof of actual exposure and by medical opinion. "Employer" includes insurance carriers on the risk during periods of exposure. An applicant may elect which employer or employers (and carrier or carriers) to proceed against. The defendant or defendants named in the application have the right to no more than one continuance for the purpose of joining others. The employee may then elect to proceed against the parties so joined, and the Appeals Board may enter an award against one or more of them if the evidence is sufficient. If any employer or carrier held liable wishes to obtain a contribution from other employers, it must do so in supplemental proceedings which will not affect the requirement to make payments under the original award. The same result can be effected by stipulation, if the defendants will agree that one is to assume the burden of initiating payments or furnishing medical treatment. *LC 5500.5*

Date of injury for occupational disease (including cumulative trauma) is that date a worker is disabled and knows or with reasonable diligence should know that his or her condition was caused by his or her employment. However, an appellate court has ruled that date of injury for the purpose of determining earnings or earning capacity at time of injury is the date of last exposure or exertion having a causal connection with the condition. *LC 5412*

LC 5005

If an applicant and a defendant in an occupational disease or cumulative trauma case settle that defendant's potential liability through an approved compromise and release agreement, the period of exposure involved must be considered in fixing the liability of the other defendants in the case.

§ 14.36   Hearings on Serious and Wilful Misconduct

LC 4551
4553.1
R 10440
10445

The issue of serious and wilful misconduct is tried as a separate case apart from the other or "normal" issues. More cases arise charging the employer with misconduct than those charging the employee. If the trial judge finds that the injury was caused by such conduct, he orders the payment or deduction of the penalty, as the case may be. As against an employer, it sometimes happens that this issue is the only one litigated, for the employer or carrier may have accepted the case as compensable and is currently furnishing normal benefits. If so, the award of the penalty will be in general language assessing a penalty of "50% of compensation." When the full extent of normal benefits can be determined, another order may issue setting the exact amount of the penalty.

An employer in an S & W case may be represented by an attorney supplied by his insurance carrier since defense of an S & W claim is insurable. However, the penalty itself is not insurable.

From the applicant's point of view, S & W is a very difficult issue to prove. Not only are there many factors to prove, but there are problems in producing evidence to prove them. The most difficult factor is the knowledge of the employer or managing representative of a violation of a safety order, although it is possible to prove it by circumstantial evidence. Most applicants' attorneys start their proof by calling as the first witnesses the employer or managing representatives under a provision of law which permits one party to call the opposing parties, their officers, or agents and interrogate them as if on cross-examination, without being bound by their answers. Good preparation includes the subpoenaing of these witnesses, for there is no guarantee that they will be present at the hearing otherwise. (See previous discussion, Chapter 9, PENALTIES, § 9.6, *Serious and Wilful Misconduct.*)

§ 14.37   Hearings in Discrimination Cases

R 10447
LC 132(a)
4453

Discrimination by an employer against an employee for filing a workers' compensation claim, testifying in a compensation proceeding, or receiving an award or settlement may be the basis for an action before the W.C.A.B. to obtain additional compensation in the form of a 50% penalty. If a violation of LC 132(a) is proven, the penalty is 50% of the compensation awarded, not to exceed $10,000 plus costs not to exceed $250. Insurance carriers may also be liable for this penalty if they bring pressure upon an employer to obtain the discharge of an employee who files a claim, testifies, or receives an award or settlement. An employee may also petition the Board for an order of reimbursement for wages lost by reason of such discrimination or reinstatement to his or her position if termination was due to discrimination.

Petitions for enforcement of LC 132a must allege each violation separately and factually. At the hearing on such petition the employee has the burden of proof of any alleged violation and his or her right to the relief sought. (See previous discussion, Chapter 9, PENALTIES, § 9.12, *Discrimination Because of Claim.*)

§ 14.38 Hearings in Death Cases

In a death case, the usual issues are whether death resulted from an industrial injury, dependency, amount of the death benefit, and burial expense. *LC 3501-* The defendants may raise additional issues including any affirmative de- *3503* fenses. When filing an application, the dependents or their attorney may also *4700-* file a petition for guardian ad litem or trustee for any minor dependents. *4706* Normally this appointment is the first order of business at the hearing.

Proving dependency involves introducing into evidence the marriage *R 10372* license of the widow and the deceased employee and the birth certificates of *10412* any children. If these documents do not exist, it is incumbent upon the applicants to prove dependency through testimony, letters, or other evidence. Employers and carriers investigate to discover all possible dependents and may ask that additional persons be joined as parties to the litigation. The same burden of proof and problems of evidence rest with any person claiming to be a dependent within the statutory definition of that term as previously discussed.

When the fact of industrial death is in issue, the main problem of the parties may be a medical question of causation. R 10606 provides in part: "In *LC 5703(a)* death cases, the reports of non-examining physicians may be admitted into *R 10606* evidence in lieu of oral testimony." A physician is subject to cross-examina- *10610* tion on his or her report. *10727*

In a death case, as in any other type, the Appeals Board or a compensa- tion judge may direct that a special investigation be made on any scientific or *LC 5703(b)* medical question and take into evidence a report of the results. Such an in- vestigation need not include an examination of the employee or his remains, although the Appeals Board may order an autopsy or exhumation for this purpose. As has been stated previously, if the dependents do not give their *LC 5706-* consent, there arises a disputable presumption that the death was not indus- *5707* trially caused.

In undisputed cases, the parties may file a stipulation that the death award be issued to the claimants. This procedure is useful where the defen- dants' investigation shows there are no other dependents, but they do not *R 10496* wish to make payment without the protection of a formal award or order.

(See also, Chapter 7, DEATH BENEFITS.)

§ 14.39 Investigation and Motion Picture Evidence

Insurance carriers and self-insured employers do a considerable amount of investigating in cases requiring large reserves and those which are suspected of being false claims. The first contact will be with the employee or other claimants, and the investigator will take the statements of these individuals. In this task, the investigator has the initial burden of covering the possible issues which may later arise or be pertinent to litigation. This requires attention to such details as age, occupation, injury, disability, failure to give notice of injury, statute of limitations, and other matters. If the information gained from this source and others justifies further investigation, the defendants may authorize a "sub-rosa" investigation and the taking of motion pictures of the employee where practicable. These techniques often prove valuable in ferreting out the dishonest applicant or the exaggerating applicant. Problems are also encountered which make pictures of little value. When this occurs it is better not to show them at a hearing; however, problem "movies" have been shown often enough to suggest the need for discussion.

Under recent decisions of the appellate courts, care must be taken in conducting investigations so as not to violate a person's constitutional right of privacy. The courts have permitted damage suits to be brought against persons or firms responsible for invading the right of privacy in such a way that it becomes oppressive. Also, evidence obtained through invasion of the right of privacy has been ruled inadmissible in a W.C.A.B. proceeding.

There are also technical problems which can affect the utility of motion picture evidence. Bad lighting or focus can obscure what the subject is doing. In one case, the pictures showed the applicant moving about in his yard, but distinct motions could not be made out because all shots were taken by telephoto lens through a picket fence. In another case, the subject appeared only as a silhouette, and identification would have been difficult if the applicant had not been so taken by starring in a movie that he exclaimed, "Hey, that's me."

The pictures must relate to the disability under consideration by the Appeals Board. To be effective, bodily motions which are pertinent to the case must be revealed. In a wrist case, the defense presented excellent color pictures showing the applicant wielding a sledge hammer for several hours. The commission medical examiner testified, however, that this activity was consistent with a stiff wrist. None of the pictures showed any flexing of the wrist. These would have been excellent shots if the applicant had had a back or shoulder case.

Before pictures are shown at a hearing, the applicant must be cross-examined to establish testimony which will make the pictures effective. If he testifies that he did or can do the things recorded on film, the showing is not necessary. If he testifies that he cannot do the activity in question, the testimony must cover a sufficient period of time to prevent his destroying the effectiveness of the investigation when he testifies on redirect examination.

Many an expensive investigation has been devalued when the applicant testifies on redirect, "Yes, I tried the things shown in the pictures, but I paid for it. I was laid up for weeks afterwards and had to take pain-killers."

The all-seeing eye of the camera will also record disability if it in fact exists. In such cases, showing the pictures at a hearing simply helps the applicant prove his case. Sometimes the subject knows that he is being followed. In one case, the applicant testified that the defense showed all of the pictures but the ones of him calling the auto club for service in fixing a flat tire. In the pictures which are shown, it was quite obvious that the subject was wearing his rigid, chair-type back brace. The defense can be assisted materially in selecting cases for the motion-picture technique by close liaison with one of its examining physicians. The doctor will be able to advise whether the pictures show an ability inconsistent with the applicant's claim or whether they merely corroborate the claim.

§ 14.40 Evidence Code

The Evidence Code by its terms does not apply to special courts, such as the Appeals Board or to administrative agencies (EvC 300; Comments of *EvC 300* Law Rev. Com). But — there are provisions in this code which are specifically made applicable to all courts, tribunals, and agencies. Others may be applied by implication. Any tribunal or agency may adopt all or part of the code by rule. Those provisions applicable to Appeals Board proceedings are:

Procedure for appointment of interpreters and oath of interpreters and *EvC 570.4* translators.

Rights regarding privileged communications and the privilege not to testify in certain cases. These include the privilege against self-incrimination, lawyer-client, testimony of spouses, marital communications, physician- *EvC 900-* patient, psychotherapist-patient, clergyman-patient, official information, *1070* political vote, trade secret, newsmen's source, sexual assault victim, and counselor-victim.

An exception to the physician-patient privilege occurs when the patient, or one claiming through him, causes a litigated issue to be raised in a suit or proceeding, such as an Appeals Board hearing.

An exception to the marital communications privilege arises when spouses are involved in litigation against each other or when there is an action between a spouse and one claiming through a deceased spouse.

Also applicable to Appeals Board proceedings is the detailed procedure for response to subpoenas duces tecum; i.e., by sending business records to the courts or other tribunals. This is similar to a procedure followed informally by the Appeals Board (and former I.A.C.) for many years. One may doubt that the Appeals Board, or parties appearing before it, will insist on the more formal procedure of the Evidence Code. The subpoena duces tecum *EvC 1560* usually has the notation placed thereon: "Appearance Not Necessary—Records May Be Brought or Sent to W.C.A.B."—or a notation of similar import. This procedure is used for hospital and other types of records.

EvC 600

In defining presumptions, the comments of the Assembly Committee on Judiciary and the Law Revision Commission discuss certain aspects of the workers' compensation presumptions. This, plus an indication that classification of presumptions not listed in the Evidence Code is the job of the appellate courts, implies that this portion of the code may be applied to the Appeals Board proceedings. There are many presumptions in the compensation law: that regarding employment when performance of a service is shown; presumptions of dependency in death cases; of injury in certain cases involving law officers; of wilful non-insurance and negligence if employer uninsured. How the courts will classify these presumptions; i.e., as presumptions affecting the burden of proof or as presumptions affecting the burden of producing evidence, remains to be seen.

§ 14.41 Enforcement of Awards

There is no particular problem of award enforcement if the defendant is an insurance carrier or a permissibly self-insured employer. Whenever an overdue payment is reported to the Appeals Board or Administrative Director, a phone call to the claims department is sufficient. For many years the commission followed a rule of thumb that if payment is not made within 48 hours after commission notification, the 10% penalty for unreasonable delay in payment will be assessed.

Before the creation of the uninsured employers' fund, difficulties were often encountered in enforcing an award against an uninsured employer. If the employer did not furnish the benefits awarded, the applicant had to pursue the remedies of attachment or execution on a judgment obtained by filing a certified copy of the W.C.A.B. award with the County Clerk. Regarding present procedures involving the uninsured employers' fund, see Chapter 3, INSURANCE, § 3.19, *Failure to Insure; Uninsured Employers' Fund.*

LC 96(i)

The Labor Code also provides for assignment of a W.C.A.B. award to the Labor Commissioner for enforcement against an uninsured employer. If an applicant is not represented, he or she may make the assignment, or the applicant may authorize his or her attorney or other representative in writing to make the assignment.

LC 5800

Appellate courts have established the principle that a class action may be brought in the Superior Court to enforce the payment of interest due on W.C.A.B. awards, if an insurance carrier or self-insured employer makes a practice of not adding such interest. Interest is to be paid at the rate provided for civil judgments and only upon that portion of an award which is currently due and payable but of which payment is delayed. Interest begins to accrue only after an award is issued and continues to accrue until paid. Interest is not payable on future benefits if paid in a timely manner when the date for payment arrives. In the usual case, then, any interest on an award would be a small, even minimal, amount. However, the courts indicate that it must be paid, and they permit class actions to enforce LC 5800. The court in such an action may require members of the class (applicants) to file certified copies of their awards with the court.

§ 14.42 Costs

The Labor Code provides in LC 5811 that the Appeals Board may allow *LC 5811* "costs as between the parties." The Board, however, limits its application of this provision, viz. R 10564 allowing interpreter's fees as a cost item. Generally, the W.C.A.B. confines allowance of costs to those costs specifi- *LC 4600* cally provided for in other sections of the code. Thus, costs are allowed to *4620-* applicants under LC 4600 for medical reports, medical testimony, tests and *4627* X-rays, or photocopying of medical records. However, a Supreme Court decision ordering that an employee be reimbursed for the cost of printing an answer to a petition for writ of review which was summarily denied will require a re-examination of the LC 5811 question. The court holds that contrary dictum in a previous Court of Appeal opinion is not controlling.

In a serious and wilful misconduct case or a discrimination case, an *LC 4553* award against an employer for the 50% penalty may include an award of *132(a)* costs of suit, not to exceed the sum of $250.

Where an employer is required to pay a fee for an applicant's attorney, *LC 5801* such fees may be considered costs. This would not apply to the fee the ap- *4607* plicant pays out of his or her award, but would include those fees assessable *4651.3* against an employer or carrier in the taking of an employee's deposition and *4555* other fees previously discussed which are assessed as penalties. (See Chapter *5710* 10, LIENS, § 10.2, *Attorney's Lien*.)

Chapter 15
APPEALS

§ 15.1 Introduction

The Labor Code and the rules provide for appeals to the W.C.A.B. from decisions of workers' compensation judges, commissioners, panels of commissioners, and deputy commissioners. A party may also petition for reconsideration of a decision of the full Board, that is, a decision in which all seven members participate. This method of appeal is called "reconsideration." Decisions of arbitrators and referees appointed by the Board are appealable by way of petition for reconsideration. The rules also provide for appeals to the Board from decisions of the Administrative Director regarding medical control and from decisions of the Rehabilitation Unit (formerly Rehabilitation Bureau), these appeals being referred to as "Review of Administrative Orders" in the W.C.A.B. rules. If a party feels aggrieved by a decision of the Board, further appeal may be taken to the California Court of Appeal or Supreme Court by filing a petition for a writ of review. Most appeals do not go beyond the Appeals Board level. *LC 5900-5956* *R 10840-10864* *LC 5270-5277* *R 10988 10990* *R 10950-10958*

§ 15.2 Administrative Appeals

Administrative Director. Within 30 days after service of an order of the Administrative Director denying or granting an employer's petition for an Order Requiring Employee to Select Employer-Designated Physician, an aggrieved party may appeal to the W.C.A.B. Under W.C.A.B. Rule 10950, this appeal is taken to the Board "in the same manner specified for petitions for reconsideration." When appeal is filed with the Board, it will be referred to a workers' compensation judge for further proceedings including the taking of additional evidence. The judge will determine the merits of the appeal both factually and legally. Further appeal to the Board may be taken by way of petition for reconsideration. *R 9787* *R 10950* *LC 5900*

Rehabilitation Unit. A party to a proceeding before the Rehabilitation Unit (formerly, Rehabilitation Bureau) may appeal to the W.C.A.B. within 20 days after the service of a Bureau determination, decision, or order. A copy *R 10014(e)* *10955-10958*

LC 4645(d)   of this appeal is to be served on the other party or parties and the Bureau. Within 20 days thereafter, the Bureau may submit a report and recommendations to the Board, serving the parties as well. The appeal is made by filing a petition with the Board and serving copies on the other parties and the Bureau. If an application for adjudication of other workers' compensation benefits is already on file with the Board, only the petition is required. If no such application is on file, one must be filed with the petition. The record before the Board is to be made by the parties. The party filing an appeal must file and serve copies of the Bureau's decision and any other document deemed relevant. Additional documents may be filed by the opposing parties within 5 days thereafter. If a party wishes to present the testimony of a Bureau consultant by deposition, an order for such deposition must be obtained from a workers' compensation judge. The burden of proof is upon the person disputing the Bureau's decision. The merits of an appeal will be determined by a judge on both a legal and a factual basis. Further appeal may be taken by petitioning for reconsideration from the judge's decision.

Declaration of Readiness. Since the two types of administrative appeal discussed above come on for hearing before a judge, these appeals will not be calendared for hearing unless and until one of the parties files a Declaration of Readiness to Proceed with the Board.

§ 15.3   Reconsideration

The petition for reconsideration is usually an appeal from a decision of a workers' compensation judge, but it may also be utilized in appealing from a decision rendered by an arbitrator or referee appointed by the Board, a commissioner, a panel, or the Appeals Board itself. Under the present procedure of rotating panels of three commissioners, a decision of a panel is deemed to

LC 115   be a decision of the Board. If a matter of great importance to uniformity of decision, the Appeals Board may consider it *en banc,* that is, with all commissioners taking part in the deliberations and subsequent decision.

LC 5906   The petition for reconsideration has been likened to a combination ap-
5908   peal and motion for a new trial. This is an apt description, for the Appeals Board has authority to grant reconsideration, re-open the evidence, conduct further hearings, take additional testimony, accept additional medical evidence, or refer the case to a medical examiner or the Disability Evaluation
R 10860   Bureau for reports. When a petition for reconsideration is filed, the judge
10989   whose decision is being appealed reviews it and prepares a Report on
10991   Reconsideration for the Board. Any arbitrator or referee having a decision appealed to the Board must also review and report on the petition. When reconsideration is granted, any further proceedings are conducted by compensation judges. If the trial judge has recommended the order granting reconsideration, he or she may officiate; if the trial judge has recommended
LC 5908.5   denial, another judge will probably hear the matter. The judge conducting
R 10862   further proceedings has authority to re-open the record and to permit the introduction of additional evidence even though reconsideration has been

granted for a more limited purpose. The subsequent decision will be made by a panel or the board as a whole. If the decision after reconsideration is a continuing award, future issues may be determined by a trial judge, subject to the same right of the parties to seek reconsideration by the Appeals Board.

In reaching its decision, the Board has before it the record made at the original hearing and any additional evidence taken at further hearings ordered by the Board. The judge holding subsequent hearings provides a report of additional testimony or other evidence, along with any recommendation he feels is warranted. The Board may order transcripts of any hearing, but this is not a legal requirement if neither party challenges the sufficiency of the judge's report or reports of the evidence. The Board may re-weigh the evidence and make a determination of the facts different from that of the trial judge. Its decision on the facts, including the question of the credibility of the witnesses, is conclusive in any further appeal. The Appeals Board may also decide questions of law, subject to the authority of the appellate courts as final determiners of the law and interpretation of statutes.

Appellate court decisions have added some provisos to the Board's exercise of authority on reconsideration. In a 1971 decision, the Supreme Court stated:

> Although the Board is entitled to reject the referee's findings on credibility matters if substantial evidence supports contrary findings the degree of substantiality required to sustain the Board in such cases should be greater than that afforded by the evidence relied upon herein. . . . We conclude that the Board failed to accord to the referee's findings the great weight to which they are entitled, and instead rested its decision upon circumstantial evidence which, at best, is speculative and conjectural and which petitioner's uncontradicted testimony rebutted. . . .

Petitioner had testified that he had sustained an injury and did not report it for 11 days, because he feared loss of his job for not disclosing a prior back injury which was aggravated. Also, the Court of Appeal holds that if substantial evidence supports the compensation judge's findings, and the W.C.A.B. on reconsideration does not overturn such findings in its decision, a question of law is presented, and the appellate court may order the original decision of the judge reinstated.

On the other hand, if the only medical evidence supporting the trial judge's decision consisted of reports and testimony of a physician which were conflicting and in certain aspects inaccurate, the W.C.A.B. acts properly in re-weighing the evidence, giving weight to the other medical evidence in the record which was not subject to these weaknesses.

The W.C.A.B. must state the reasons for its decision including the evidence relied upon and the applicable law. If a trial judge's report on recon- *LC 5908.5* sideration adequately sets forth the required elements of a decision, the Board may adopt the report as its statement of reasons for decisions. However, if the judge's report is insufficient, adoption of the report does not constitute compliance with LC 5908.5.

LC 5908(b) In any case wherein the Appeals Board rescinds or reduces an award on the basis that the order, decision, or award was procured by fraud, the Board must refer the case to the Bureau of Fraudulent claims per IC 12990 and following, if the employer is insured, or to the district attorney of the county in which the fraud occurred if the employer is self-insured.

§ 15.4   Petition for Reconsideration

LC 5903 The Labor Code sets forth these grounds for reconsideration:

1.   Acting in excess of powers granted to the Appeals Board.
2.   Fraud in procuring decision.
3.   Insufficient evidence to support findings of fact.
4.   Insufficient findings of fact to support the decision.
5.   Newly discovered evidence which with reasonable diligence could not have been discovered and produced at the hearing.

LC 5803.5 6.   Conviction pursuant to IC 1871.4 (fraudulent claim or fraudulent denial of claim).

LC 5902 The petition for reconsideration must be verified; that is, the petitioner must certify before a notary public or upon penalty of perjury that the petition *R 10850* contains facts known to the petitioner to be true, except such matters as he *LC 5905* alleges upon mere information and belief. Copies of the petition must be served upon the opposing party or parties. Service may be made by mail; proof of service must be shown on the petition or by letter of transmittal. (See Chapter 14, PROCEDURE, § 14.12, *Service of Process*.)

LC 5903 Any point not raised in the petition is deemed waived and may not be as- *R 10507* serted at a later date. The petition must be filed within 20 days after the issu- *CCP 1013* ance of the decision which is the subject of the appeal. This period is extended five additional days if service is made by mail in California, 10 additional days if outside California but within the United States, and 20 additional days if outside the U.S. [NOTE: Mailing a petition for reconsideration to the Board is not equivalent to filing. The petition must be received by the Board within 20 days, plus the additional days allowed. Thus, a petition mailed to the Board from within California must be received by the Board on or before the 25th day after the date of the service of the decision being appealed.]

LC 5906 The Appeals Board has 60 days after any decision to grant reconsideration on its own motion. The Board has limited the exercise of this authority to those cases in which a miscarriage of justice may be involved or which appears to present novel and important questions of law. The fact that the Board has this authority is of no avail to one filing a late petition for reconsideration. If the Board elects to grant reconsideration, it may do so only on one of the grounds listed in LC 5903. (See above.)

A petition to reopen under LC 5804 (5-year continuing jurisdiction to alter or amend a decision) may not be used as a substitute for a petition for reconsideration. This type of petition must be predicated upon allegations of an increase or decrease in disability—or other good cause, such as newly discovered evidence or fraud. If a petition for reconsideration appears to be in reality a petition to reopen, it can be treated as such and be set down for hearing on the issues raised in the petition. In one case, a petition to reopen was used as a belated appeal, being filed 45 days after the judge's decision. The appellate court held that it was not a proper petition to reopen, that it was too late as a petition for reconsideration. However, complicating the picture somewhat is a recent decision of the Court of Appeal holding that where the Appeals Board inadvertently let its 60-day time limit on deciding whether to grant or deny a petition for reconsideration go by without action (thereby resulting in automatic denial), the Board could grant reconsideration because of its continuing jurisdiction to reopen for good cause. In this case the Board had intended to grant reconsideration but had failed to do so in time through "inadvertence."

If a party has filed for reconsideration within the 20-day period, the 5-year time limit under LC 5804 does not apply, and the Appeals Board has full authority after granting reconsideration to render its decision following further proceeding in review of the record.

"Skeleton petitions" or "bare allegations" of the statutory grounds for *R 10846* reconsideration are insufficient, and such petitions are customarily denied. On the other hand, if the Appeals Board feels that a miscarriage of justice may occur, it may grant reconsideration even though the petition does not comply with the rules as to form and content. If the petitioner asserts that the *R 10852* evidence is insufficient to support the decision, that the decision was *10856* procured by fraud, or that petitioner has newly discovered evidence, the petitioner will ordinarily be held to the rule-requirement of detailed factual recitals or suffer a summary denial of his petition.

§ 15.5   Primary Authority of W.C.A.B.

The authority of a workers' compensation judge is a delegated authority *LC 5310* via statute and rule. Thus, on reconsideration, the Board has authority to reweigh the evidence, as well as, pass upon legal points. The authority of the *LC 5900(b)* Board to grant reconsideration on its own motion has been previously noted. Also, the Board may "remove to itself" the proceedings on any claim. *LC 5310* "Removal" is rare, but the authority exists to correct any grave error which might transpire at the trial level which could affect vested rights or cause undue expense or hardship.

§ 15.6   Appellate Courts—Writ of Review

A party in a W.C.A.B. proceeding who deems himself or herself ag- *LC 5950* grieved by a decision of the Board may petition the Court of Appeal for a writ of review. This petition must be filed within 45 days after the issuance of the Board's decision. The time is extended, according to an appellate court ruling, if service of the Board's decision was by mail per the time periods provided in CCP 1013, i.e., 5 additional days if service was made in California, 10 days if outside California, and 20 days if outside the United States. The Board customarily serves its decisions by mail. If a petition is not filed within 45 days plus any extension, the Board's decision becomes final. A writ cannot be granted unless the aggrieved party has previously filed a petition for reconsideration with the Appeals Board. If reconsideration is denied, the petitioner has 45 days from the order denying reconsideration within which to seek a writ of review. In the event the Appeals Board grants reconsideration, the period is 45 days after the issuance of the Board's decision after reconsideration. [NOTE: The ruling that the time extensions in CCP 1013 apply to the time to file a petition for writ of review under LC 5950 is being questioned in a case pending in the Court of Appeal. Until this question is finally resolved, a petitioner should file a petition within the 45-day period.]

CCP 1013

The writ of review is called an "extraordinary" remedy. In law, this means that the appellate courts need not grant a writ or review the matter presented. A writ is usually granted only where it appears that an important question of law is involved or that the Appeals Board has exceeded its authority. Thus, there is no right to a direct appeal to the higher courts as there is from a decision of a superior or municipal court. When a person appeals from a judgment of one of these courts, he or she files a notice of appeal with the court clerk and requests the clerk and the court reporter to prepare the record which will be certified to the reviewing court. Briefs are filed, and the case is argued before the appellate court which will later issue its decision in the form of a written opinion.

LC 5950-5956

The procedure for a writ of review is just opposite. The aggrieved party files his brief in the form of a petition and a memorandum of points and authorities. The opponent files an answer. The petitioner has the burden of showing the appellate court that there is some reason for reviewing the decision and the record of the Appeals Board. It is not enough to assert that the Appeals Board decided the facts incorrectly, for the Labor Code makes the Board's determination of fact conclusive even when a compensation case is being reviewed by a higher court. The appellate court has no authority regarding the facts unless there is no evidence to support the Board's determination, the evidence is not conflicting, or there is no dispute as to the facts. Where the evidence introduced by an applicant regarding his new and further disability is uncontroverted in a proceeding on a petition to reopen, the Appeals Board may not rely on medical reports received at an earlier hearing before applicant's change in condition. But if there is any evidence of a cogent and material nature in the record tending to support the findings of fact of the Appeals Board, the court will deny the writ. On the denial of a writ, the court issues an order but ordinarily does not issue a written opinion, although

LC 5951

LC 5953
Rule 57,
Cal. Rules
of Court

it may. When a writ of review is granted, the clerk of the appellate court issues the writ directing the Appeals Board to certify its record to the court. *LC 5951* The Board then prepares a transcript of the testimony, the decision, minutes, and exhibits. When this record reaches the appellate court, the parties may peruse it in order to prepare further briefs or oral argument. Like the Appeals Board's action in granting reconsideration, the granting of a writ of review does not mean that the court will reverse the decision under review. It merely means that the court will carefully consider the record and the arguments of the parties to determine whether there are any errors of law. The court will then announce its decision in a written opinion.

Any person affected or aggrieved by a decision of the W.C.A.B. may petition for a writ of review regarding any material issue in the case. However, a petition for reconsideration to the W.C.A.B. is a prerequisite to a petition for a petition for a writ of review. In other words, the only decisions of the W.C.A.B. which may be appealed to the appellate courts are decisions made after the filing of a petition for reconsideration. Further, any issue not raised before the W.C.A.B. in a petition for reconsideration is deemed waived and may not be raised in a petition for writ of review.

If a party petitions for a writ of review, and the petition is filed in time, it is immaterial that the petition did not follow the rules on the form of the petition. The petition will be considered as timely filed, and the petitioner under other rules of court will be required to file an amended petition in correct form.

In this type of proceeding, the Appeals Board is deemed a party; thus, the title of a compensation case in the appellate court would appear in this manner: *"John Doe v. Workers' Compensation Appeals Board."* The Labor Code provides that the Legal Bureau of the division of industrial accidents will represent the Appeals Board in appellate review proceedings. The bureau's attorneys answer petitions, file briefs, and make oral arguments before the appellate courts in support of the Board's decision. The petitioner's opponent before the Appeals Board is also a party and has both the right and the duty to appear and seek to uphold the Board's decision.

The Court of Appeal in the district in which the applicant lives or in which an employer or insurance carrier has an office has jurisdiction and venue to consider a petition for a writ of review.

The grounds for review are similar to the grounds for reconsideration. The jurisdiction of the appellate court is limited, however, to questions of law regarding these points:

1. Workers' Compensation Appeals Board exceeding its authority.
2. Fraud in the procurement of the decision.
3. Reasonableness of the decision. *LC 5952-*
4. Whether substantial evidence supports the decision. *5953*
5. Whether findings of fact support the decision.

Substantial evidence means any evidence which would tend to support the Board's determination, even though the evidence is weak and even though the reviewing court might have decided the facts differently. The complete absence from the record of any evidence of probative value presents a question of law for the court's determination. A question of law also arises where there is no dispute regarding the facts or the evidence. The question for the court to determine may be whether there is a conflict in the evidence. If the court rules that the evidence of one party is not material or is too remote to create a conflict, the court will base its resolution on the case on the facts and inferences established by the evidence presented by the other party. In any event, the reviewing court will presume that the Appeals Board considered all the evidence in the record.

LC 5953

In its decision, the reviewing court may affirm, modify, or annul the decision of the Appeals Board. If the court deems the record incomplete, it may send the case back for further proceedings.

Rules 27.5, 29 29.2-29.9, 44, Cal. Rules of Court

If a party is dissatisfied with a decision of a Court of Appeal, he or she may petition the California Supreme Court to review the matter within 10 days after the decision becomes final as to the Court of Appeal. Formerly, a party petitioned for a "hearing" in the Supreme Court; however, the Rules of Court were amended to denominate this procedure as "Petition for Review" by the Supreme Court. The rules limit the petition to 30 pages, although additional briefs are permitted if Supreme Court review is granted.

Regarding the time when a Court of Appeal decision becomes final, if the decision is rendered after the granting of a petition for writ of review filed in that court, the decision is final as to that court 30 days after issuance of the decision. In this situation an aggrieved party has 40 days within which to petition the Supreme Court for further review. In the case of a Court of Appeal order denying a writ of review, the order is final immediately. In this latter situation, an aggrieved party has only 10 days within which to petition the Supreme Court.

If the Supreme Court grants review, the decision of the Court of Appeal becomes a nullity, although the Supreme Court is authorized to approve all or part of the decision or reverse it and enter a new and different decision. Where the granting of Supreme Court review follows the denial of a writ of review by the Court of Appeal, the Supreme Court may itself grant the writ or remand the matter to the Court of Appeal with instructions to grant the writ and render a decision on the merits.

The right of appeal applies to every award, order, or other decision of the Appeals Board and to each party who may be affected by a decision. Parties who should have appealed but did not when another similarly affected did appeal may find themselves foreclosed from taking advantage of any success the appealing party may have in the appellate court.

Because of the continuing jurisdiction of the Appeals Board and the possibility of a number of decisions in one case as disputes arise, there is also the possibility of a number of appeals in one case. Not many decisions are reversed by the Appeals Board, and not many decisions of the Appeals Board are reversed by the appellate courts, statistically speaking. While the number of appeals has increased, the percentage of cases appealed is relatively small in comparison to the number of decisions issued each year. Even though the appellate courts have indicated more interest in this field recently, most petitions for a writ of review are denied. From this, one can easily see the necessity for thorough preparation of his case at the trial level; i.e., for the hearing before the workers' compensation judge, and the extent of the Appeals Board's authority as an appellate tribunal.

Costs on Appeal; Attorney's Fees. The Supreme Court has ruled that an *LC 5811* employee may recoup the reasonable cost of printing an answer to a petition for writ of review where the petition is summarily denied. The order allowing such costs is to be issued by the W.C.A.B. under LC 5811. The Board must also determine the reasonableness of the cost based upon evidence taken on the issue. The court holds that contrary dictum in a previous Court of Appeal opinion is not controlling.

If an attorney is called upon to appeal a decision of the W.C.A.B. by *LC 4903(a)* way of petition for writ of review or to defend against such an appeal taken by another party, he or she is entitled to additional compensation for his or her efforts. On remand from the appellate court or on denial of a writ, the attorney's procedure is to file a request with the Board that the fee be included in the Board's final order or be set forth in a supplemental order. If an employee prevails in an appeal taken by an employer or carrier, and the reviewing court finds that there is no reasonable basis for the appeal of the employer *LC 5801* or carrier, the court must remand the matter to the Board for a supplemental award of an attorney's fee to be paid by the appealing party as additional compensation.

Chapter 16
VOCATIONAL REHABILITATION

§ 16.1   Introduction

A rehabilitation concept has always been integral to the philosophic base for workers' compensation. This purpose is most readily apparent in the provision for all medical treatment necessary to cure or relieve the effects of industrial injury. Also, when permanent disability is rated, consideration must be given to any diminished ability to compete in an open labor market. Effective January 1, 1975, the workers' compensation program was enhanced by the inclusion of the right of qualified injured workers to vocational rehabilitation in addition to the other benefits. This legislation established vocational rehabilitation benefits by the following language of LC 139.5(c):

LC 4600

LC 4660

LC 139.5

341

When a qualified injured workman chooses to enroll in a rehabilitation program, he shall continue to receive temporary disability indemnity payments, plus additional living expenses necessitated by the rehabilitation program, together with all reasonable and necessary vocational training, at the expense of the employer or the insurance carrier, as the case may be.

LC 139.5(a) and (b) provided for the establishment of a rehabilitation unit within the Division of Industrial Accidents and authorized the Administrative Director to promulgate rules and regulations and to coordinate and enforce the implementation of vocational rehabilitation plans. Rules were adopted defining "qualified injured worker" (Q.I.W.) and established criteria for entitlement, payment of vocational rehabilitation temporary disability indemnity (VRTD), preparation and approval of vocational rehabilitation plans, procedures, and appeals. The rehabilitation unit was designated the "Rehabilitation Bureau."

As a part of the Reform Act of 1989, LC 139.5 was amended and LC 4635-4647 enacted to delineate benefits, definitions, and procedures, including many items covered in the rules. This legislation is effective for injuries occurring on or after January 1, 1990. The Rehabilitation Bureau is redesignated the Rehabilitation Unit and is a part of the Office of Benefit Determination (O.B.D.) of the Division of Workers' Compensation (formerly, Division of Industrial Accidents). The amended LC 139.5 as further amended by the 1990 Legislature reads as follows:

139.5. (a) The administrative director shall establish within the Office of Benefit Determination a vocational rehabilitation unit, which shall include appropriate professional staff, and which shall have the following duties:

(1) To foster, review, and approve vocational rehabilitation plans developed by a qualified rehabilitation representative of the employer, insurer, state agency, or employee.

(2) To develop rules and regulations, to be promulgated by the administrative director, which would expedite and facilitate the identification, notification and referral of industrially injured employees to vocational rehabilitation services.

(3) To coordinate and enforce the implementation of vocational rehabilitation plans.

(4) To develop a fee schedule, to be promulgated by the administrative director, governing reasonable fees for vocational rehabilitation services provided on and after January 1, 1991. The initial fee schedule promulgated under this paragraph shall be designed to reduce the cost of vocational rehabilitation services by 10 percent from the level of fees paid during 1989.

(5) To develop standards, to be promulgated by the administrative director, for governing the timeliness and the quality of vocational rehabilitation services.

(b) The salaries of the personnel of the vocational rehabilitation unit shall be fixed by the Department of Personnel Administration.

(c) When an employee is determined to be medically eligible and chooses to enroll in a vocational rehabilitation program, he or she shall continue to receive temporary disabilty indemnity payments, and, after his or her medical condition becomes permanent and stationary, a maintenance allowance. The employee also shall receive additional living expenses necessitated by the vocational rehabilitation services, together with all reasonable and necessary vocational training, at the expense of the employer.

(d) The amount of the maintenance allowance due under subdivision (c) shall be two-thirds of the employee's average weekly earnings at the date of injury payable as follows:

(1) The amount the employee would have received as continuing temporary disability indemnity, but not more than two hundred forty-six dollars ($246) a week for injuries occurring on or after January 1, 1990.

(2) At the employee's option, an additional amount from permanent disability indemnity due or payable sufficient to provide the employee with a maintenance allowance equal to two-thirds of the employee's average weekly earnings at the date of injury subject to the limits specified in subdivision (a) of Section 4453 and the requirements of Section 4661.5. In no event shall temporary disability indemnity and a maintenance allowance be payable concurrently.

If the employer disputes the treating physician's determination of medical eligibility, the employee shall continue to receive that portion of the maintenance allowance payable under paragraph (1) pending final determination of the dispute. If the employee disputes the treating physician's determination of medical eligibility and prevails, the employee shall be entitled to that portion of the maintenance allowance payable under paragraph (1) retroactive to the date of the employee's request for vocational rehabilitation services.

(e) . . . [1975 Provisions not applicable to injuries occurring before 1975.]

(f) The time within which an employee may request vocational rehabilitation services is set forth in Sections 5405.5, 5410, and 5803.

The discussion in this chapter includes consideration of the applicable statutes and rules and decisions of the W.C.A.B. and appellate courts. At the conclusion of this chapter are found the rules of the Administrative Director relating to vocational rehabilitation and the rules of the W.C.A.B. regarding pertinent Board procedures and rehabilitation appeals. Also included are the official color-coded forms, as well as approved form letters for use by employers or carriers and their claims administrators, examiners, or adjusters. These forms are applicable to pre-1990 injuries and will be pertinent to later injuries until such time as new forms are available. Rules adopted pursuant to the 1989 legislation are also included.

Since the Reform Act legislation is superimposed upon a body of law developed from 1975 through 1989, our discussion in this chapter will identify the previous law followed by a discussion of the provisions effective as of January 1, 1990, and applicable to injuries occurring on or after that date.

Substantively, the statute and the rules revolve about these rights and benefits for a qualified injured worker (Q.I.W.):

1. Notice of potential vocational rehabilitation rights,
2. Diagnostic services and determination of status as a qualified injured worker (Q.I.W.),
3. Services of a qualified rehabilitation representative (Q.R.R.),
4. Vocational training or education reasonably necessary for a return to work pursuant to an approved rehabilitation plan, and
5. Vocational rehabilitation temporary disability indemnity (compensation; VRTD) while undergoing diagnostic procedures and vocational rehabilitation; also, additional living expenses necessitated by a plan and for injuries on or after January 1, 1990, the maintenance allowance.

Procedurally, the law provides for:

1. Employer's giving notice of rights and benefits,
2. The employer's obtaining medical advice regarding the employee's medical eligibility for vocational rehabilitation,
3. Appointment of a Q.R.R.,
4. Preparation of a plan,
5. Approval of a plan by the Rehabilitation Bureau or unit,
6. Resolution of disagreements or disputes by the Bureau or unit; orders concluding plans, and
7. The right to appeal to the W.C.A.B. and appellate courts.

§ 16.2   Historical Background

The idea that the disabled or handicapped person should be assisted to be self-supporting, either wholly or partially, is longstanding in the United States. In 1920, Congress established a policy of assisting states in their rehabilitation programs. In California, the State Department of Rehabilitation has carried on this function, including both medical and vocational services in its program. Before 1975, the department included industrially disabled persons among its clientele, but it was hampered in having a comprehensive industrial plan because of budget limitations. Within the framework of workers' compensation at the present time, the Department of Rehabilitation is considered an important resource agency, along with professional providers (sometimes referred to as vendors) in the private sector.

In 1965, LC 139.5 was enacted as a limited, voluntary, program under which a worker would be afforded a vocational rehabilitation plan only if initiated by the employer. Any standard permanent disability rating was to be adjusted according to the new occupation, but only if the employee had been advised of this eventuality before his or her agreement to accept a plan.

In 1971, legislation was enacted requiring public agencies to develop rehabilitation programs for public employees in cooperation with the State Department of Rehabilitation. Any plan developed is to include an adequate subsistence allowance if the employee is required to be away from home. This program, however, is voluntary on the part of both the employee and the employer. While these provisions are still on the books, they have, in effect, been superseded by the 1975 amendment to LC 139.5. The Court of Appeal has ruled that the 139.5 mandatory provisions are applicable to employees of the state and local public entities (counties, cities, districts). *LC 6200-6208*

The Report of the National Commission on State Workmen's Compensation Laws filed with Congress in 1972 included a strong recommendation for mandatory vocational rehabilitation as a worker's compensation benefit. Many states had already included this element within their programs. Two years later, effective in 1975, California amended LC 139.5 to make vocational rehabilitation a matter of right for qualified employees and a mandatory obligation of employers or their carriers. Stress should be laid upon the fact that not every industrially injured worker has this entitlement. He or she must be found to be a "qualified injured worker" (Q.I.W.) under the administrative guidelines.

Definitive rules were adopted to implement LC 139.5, and forms prescribed for Bureau procedures and plan submission. These rules were completely revised effective July 1, 1988, and the previous forms replaced by new forms and form numbers. Changes made by the 1988 rules eliminated the necessity of filing a disability status report (former form RB-1) with the Bureau; added a requirement that treating physicians render reports about an injured worker's medical eligibility for vocational rehabilitation services; established specific time frames for development of rehabilitation plans and other procedures; indicated priority for plan types; stressed a contractual concept as between the employer and employee in plan development; with certain exceptions restricted multiple plans.

As previously discussed, the Reform Act of 1989, effective for 1990 and later injuries, codified, with certain modifications, many items covered by existing rules, provides for the maintenance allowance, and for mandatory monitoring of an employee's condition and status with respect to medical eligibility through the efforts of an assigned qualified rehabilitation representative along with appropriate notices to the employee at various intervals.

§ 16.3   Notice of Vocational Rehabilitation Rights

Pre-1990 Provisions

LC 3550
3551
138.3
138.4
139.6
R 9800
LC 5402

R 10005
10006

An employer must provide employees with information regarding all workers' compensation benefits, rights, and procedures as outlined in Chapter 14, PROCEDURE, § 14.3, *Notice to Employee; Claim Form*. This information is to be given each employee either when hired or by the end of the first pay period. When injury occurs, the injured worker must be advised again of his or her workers' compensation rights including the right to receive vocational rehabilitation services if a "qualified injured worker" (Q.I.W.). [See approved form letters at the end of this chapter.] Under the rules of the Administrative Director, a special notice regarding vocational rehabilitation services and the procedure for requesting such services must be given the injured worker on a form prescribed by the Director. This notice is to be given immediately upon knowledge that the employee's medical condition may permanently preclude a return to his or her usual and customary occupation or the position in which the employee was engaged at the time of injury. If this medical criterion is not readily ascertainable, the notice must be given immediately following 180 days of aggregate total disability. If, after giving this notice, the employer or insurance carrier deems the employee not to be a qualified injured worker, a further notice to the employee must be given setting forth the reasons for denial of vocational rehabilitation services. The notice of denial must inform the employee of available remedies and his or her right to seek information and advice from an Information and Assistance Officer or an attorney. (This notice is not required if the Bureau determines that the employee is not eligible.)

R 10007
(a)(6)

R 10006

Where vocational services are to be provided, the employer or carrier in the form and manner prescribed by the Director (through the Bureau) must give notice to the employee of the commencement of the services within 10 days of the date when the commencement or determination is operative or should be operative. Where there is a delay in making the required determination of eligibility, notice of such delay must be given the employee within 10 days of the date when the determination should have been made.

If services are provided, and then services are interrupted, the employer or carrier must give notice of any interruption of 15 or more days, the notice to be given within 10 days of the date of first knowledge. This notice must include reasons for interruption and projected resumption date.

R 10006
10007

If an injured worker has a legal representative (attorney or other representative), copies of all notices required by R 10006 must be provided the representative. Likewise, copies of all other notices and all reports, plans, and requests for action filed with the Rehabilitation Bureau as prescribed by the rules are to be furnished the legal representative.

An employer or carrier must retain in its file exact copies of all notices (and, inferentially, all reports and other pertinent documents) for submission to the Bureau on request. Thus, these initial procedures do not involve filing with the Bureau but are confined to giving notice. This eliminates the previous requirement of filing a report with the Bureau after 180 days of disability (former RB-1). Now, in that same time-frame, the employer or carrier gives notice to the employee, retaining exact copies for submission if the Bureau is called upon to make an official determination.

The giving of required notices is important to the employer or carrier because if such notice is not given, the statute of limitations will not begin to run until it is given. Also, as held by the Supreme Court in the *Webb* and *Renfro* cases, the employee's obligation to choose or not to choose to receive vocational rehabilitation services, i.e., to make a demand for such services, does not arise until proper notice is given. As a result, an employer or carrier may be required to pay compensation retroactively to the time when such notice should have been given. Another facet of timely notice is that early identification of likely candidates for vocational rehabilitation is important in order to assure maximum motivation on the part of the employee. As for the employee, his or her rights may be adversely affected by not giving the employer notice of injury or notice of a claim for vocational rehabilitation services after receiving appropriate notices from the employer, carrier, or the Bureau.

[NOTE: "Employer" includes a workers' compensation insurer and the adjusting agency of a self-insured employer.] *R 10003(b)*

1990 Provisions

Effective as to injuries occurring on or after January 1, 1990, in addition to the required notices and claim form, as discussed in Chapter 14, PROCEDURE, a written notice on an officially approved form regarding possible eligibility for vocational rehabilitation services (VRS) must be given an industrially injured worker whenever the employer or carrier receives a physician's report indicating that an employee is medically eligible for vocational rehabilitation. This notice must be given within 10 days of knowledge of the employee's medical eligibility and must contain: *LC 4637* *R 10123*

1. An explanation of VRS available including the maintenance allowance and the effect of any delay in the acceptance of VRS.
2. Instructions as to how the employee may apply for VRS.
3. Notice that failure to apply within 90 days of receipt of notice of medical eligibility may terminate the employee's entitlement unless the treating physician determines medical inability to participate, except as provided in LC 5410.
4. Notice of the employee's right to an agreed qualified rehabilitation representative (Q.R.R.) and the right to request a preliminary evaluation of vocational feasibility before any acceptance or rejection of VRS, and the right to request a change of Q.R.R. per LC 4640.
5. Notice that VRS may not be settled or otherwise converted to cash payments.

If the employer or carrier believes that the employee is not eligible for VRS after giving the above notice, a further notice of this conclusion is to be given the employee along with instructions on how to contest the determination.

LC 4636

Immediately upon receipt of a treating physician's final report regarding medical eligibility for VRS, the employer must provide the employee with a copy and a notice on an officially approved form containing information on how to contest the physician's findings and advice that the employee may be eligible for VRS if unable to return to his or her usual occupation or the occupation in which injured. [NOTE: It appears that where the physician's report mentioned in LC 4637 is that of the treating physician monitoring the employee's condition under LC 4636, the employer or carrier must give both notice of how to contest the physician's conclusion and the more extensive notice required under LC 4637.]

LC 4641,
4643

Other written notices of rights and procedures must be given if the employee wishes to decline (refuse) to accept VRS and where an employer or carrier seeks to withhold payment of the maintenance allowance because of alleged non-cooperation by the employee.

R 10123

R 10123 lists the following notices and time frames:

1. The 90-day Q.R.R. assignment notice—within 10 days subsequent to 90 days of aggregate total disability.
2. Notice of Potential Eligibility—within 10 days of knowledge of medical eligibility.
3. Reminder Notice—45 to 70 days after employee's receipt of Notice of Potential Eligibility.
4. Notice of Non-Eligibility—within 10 days of knowledge of non-eligibility for VRS.
5. Notice of Interruption — within 10 days of agreement to interrupt.
6. Notice of Intent to Withhold Maintenance Allowance—15 days before withholding benefits.
7. Insurer's notice to employer of potential refund per LC 4638— within 60 days of Unit approval of plan.

An employer is to retain copies of all notices to an employee and provide the Rehabilitation Unit with copies upon request.

§ 16.4   Qualified Injured Worker; Medical Eligibility; Vocational Eligibility or Feasibility

Pre-1990 Provisions

LC 139.5
R 10003(c)
R 10011

In order to be eligible for workers' compensation vocational rehabilitation services, an industrially injured worker must meet the criteria for "qualified injured worker" (Q.I.W.). Under the rules, there are two aspects to determining whether an employee is a Q.I.W. He or she must have both "medical eligibility" and "vocational eligibility."

One is deemed to have "medical eligibility" if the effects of injury (whether or not combined with residuals of any prior injury or disability) permanently preclude, or are likely to preclude, the employee from engaging in his or her usual or customary occupation or the position in which the employee was engaged at the time of injury.

As noted above, upon receiving notice or knowledge of an industrial injury, the employer or carrier must make a timely determination regarding the likelihood that the injured worker will qualify for vocational rehabilitation services. In the interest of expediting this determination, the rules require the employer or carrier to request the employee's treating physician to provide a report (on a form prescribed by the Administrative Director) whether the employee is medically eligible for these services. [Forms RB-90 and RB-91 (buff color)] "Medical eligibility" means that the effects of the injury, whether or not combined with a prior injury or disability, permanently preclude or are likely to preclude the employee from engaging in his or her usual and customary occupation or the position in which engaged at the time of injury. This request is to be made where aggregate temporary total disability continues for 90 days. If the treating physician is unable to make the determination, the employer or carrier must repeat this request no less frequently than every 90 days until the physician provides the report or the employee is released to return to work at his or her usual and customary occupation. *R 10008, 10003 (c)(1)*

Upon receiving information indicating that the employee is medically eligible, the employer or carrier must give the employee the notice previously discussed and begin the procedure for providing vocational rehabilitation services. [NOTE: The notice regarding the employee's rights must be given after 180 days of total disability even though there may be no report of medical eligibility.] *R 10009*

"Vocational eligibility" is based upon a determination that the employee can reasonably be expected to return to suitable gainful employment or self-employment through the provision of vocational rehabilitation services. Thus, it is not enough that an employee cannot return to his or her previous type of work. It must also appear that training or retraining will be effective in returning the worker to the labor market to a meaningful extent. The principle of feasibility is evident in the rules. "Suitable gainful employment," or self-employment, must be "reasonably attainable" and offer an "opportunity to restore the employee as soon as practicable and as near as possible to maximum self support, due consideration being given to the employee's qualifications, vocational interests and aptitudes, pre-injury earnings and future earning capacity, and future labor market." All the stated factors are to be weighed, and no one factor is to be "considered solely in determining suitable gainful employment." The overall policy is to provide the services if *R 10003(h)* it is at all possible to restore the worker to some form of full-time or part-time employment or self-employment.

Decisions of the W.C.A.B. and the appellate courts demonstrate that each case must be determined on its own merits because the combinations of factors described above differ from case to case. For example, in one case it was held that sporadic self-employment using an alternate skill did not preclude a Q.I.W. finding; whereas, where a worker had developed a going business and was already self-supporting, he was not a Q.I.W. and not entitled to vocational services. It has been held that a totally disabled worker may be a Q.I.W. if medical and other facts show that the worker can become partially self-supporting. But a retired worker who had other medical problems was held not to be a Q.I.W. because he would not be able to work even if retrained. Also, if an industrial injury merely causes a temporary aggravation of a preexisting condition, and any disability is attributable only to the prior pathology, the worker is not a Q.I.W.

R 10011

R 10004

Rulings in several decisions have established the employee's right to receive and the employer's obligation to provide such diagnostic services and compensation as may be necessary to determine whether an employee is a qualified injured worker. This principle is evident in the 1988 rules in both the substantive and procedural provisions. There may be a medical issue or a vocational issue as previously illustrated. There may be a question concerning the employee's incentives and commitment. [The rules state that an employee is not required to accept vocational rehabilitation services if the employee does not choose to do so. See form RB-107, STATEMENT OF DECLINE OF VOCATIONAL REHABILITATION BENEFITS (buff color).] Another issue might be whether the employee is permanently disabled or whether the disability actually renders him or her unable to perform his or her regular occupation or the job in which injured. An employer may provide work within the capabilities of the worker, or the worker may possess a secondary capability making training unnecessary. But if training or education is required to qualify the worker for modified work or to update a secondary field of expertise, the employee is a Q.I.W. and entitled to such training or education. In any event, the employer must furnish any professional services required to resolve such Q.I.W. issues.

Undocumented aliens may qualify for vocational rehabilitation benefits since their immigration status may change, or they may seek work in their home countries.

1990 Provisions

LC 4635

The concept of the previous definition of Q.I.W. in R 10003 has been retained in LC 4635(a); however, "vocational eligibility" has become "vocational feasibility." Thus, a Q.I.W. is one who has both "medical eligibility" and "vocational feasibility."

A worker is medically eligible if the expected permanent disability resulting from his or her injury, whether or not combined with the effects of a prior injury or disability, permanently precludes or is likely to preclude the employee from engaging in his or her usual occupation or the position in which he or she was injured. Note that "expected permanent disability" replaces the term "effects of whose injury" of the previous rule, thus making it clear that one must have permanent disability to qualify as a Q.I.W. for VRS.

When total disability continues for 90 days, an employer or carrier must *LC 4636* assign a qualified rehabilitation representative (Q.R.R.) to explain to the employee his or her rights and obligations re vocational rehabilitation. The Q.R.R. will contact the treating physician, provide him or her a description of the employee's job at time of injury, including the physical requirements of the job, and request the physician to determine the employee's medical eligibility for vocational rehabilitation services (VRS). The job description is to be developed jointly by the Q.R.R., the employer, and the employee. The physician's determination must take into account medical condition, potential limitations, ability to accept and participate in VRS, ability to engage in modified or alternative work, recommendations regarding evaluation and services. If the physician is unable to assess medical eligibility, the Q.R.R. will continue to monitor the situation and request the opinion of the physician. The treating physician must report every 60 days until he or she can report either that the employee is released for his or her usual occupation or the one engaged in at time of injury or has disability precluding such work activity. [NOTE: When total disability exceeds 365 days, there is a rebuttable presumption that the employee is medically eligible.]

Upon receipt of the final report from the physician, the employer or car- *LC 4637* rier sends a copy to the employee along with notice of the procedure to fol- *4640* low in contesting the physician's determination and that the employee may *4643* be eligible for VRS. If the physician finds medical eligibility, the employer *4646* must notify the employee within 10 days about VRS, maintenance allowance, how to apply, that failure to apply in 90 days may terminate entitlement unless the physician reports medical inability to participate, the right to reopen under LC 5410, the right to an agreed Q.R.R. and to request preliminary evaluation before any acceptance or rejection of VRS, the right to request a change of Q.R.R. per LC 4640, that vocational rehabilitation benefits may not be settled or converted into cash payments. (See LC 4646.)

If the employee is able and does not decline services, the employer and *LC 4637* employee are to agree to a Q.R.R. to ascertain vocational feasibility. If the employee is determined to be a qualified injured worker (Q.I.W.), the employer shall so notify the employee and include a statement describing the procedure to contest a determination. If the employee is a Q.I.W., an agreed vocational rehabilitation plan must be submitted to the O.B.D. Rehabilitation Unit for review and approval within 90 days, or the parties must request the

Rehabilitation Unit to resolve any dispute. If the employee is determined not to be a Q.I.W., the employer or carrier must give the employee written notice on an approved form of that conclusion and the procedure for contesting it before the Rehabilitation Unit. (Regarding required notices, see previous topic in § 16.3, *Notice of Vocational Rehabilitation Rights.*)

LC 4641
R 10131,
10131.1

An employee cannot be required to accept or undergo vocational rehabilitation, and he or she may decline VRS by completing a Form RU-107. The statute and rules require that both the employee and his or her representative, if any, sign the declination form. In order for the declination to be effective, the employee must have received the notice of rights required by LC 4637 and a full explanation by a Q.R.R. The employer must submit to the Unit a request for termination on Form RU-105 along with the signed declination (Form RU-107), a Form RU-500W (Notice of Potential Eligibility) and documentation showing that a Q.R.R. had been assigned. The Unit is to act upon the request within 30 days.

§ 16.5   Rehabilitation Benefits; Temporary Compensation; Maintenance Allowance

Pre-1990 Provisions

LC 4600

LC 139.5

Rehabilitation benefits are in addition to all other workers' compensation benefits. Thus, a plan may recognize the employee's need for any further medical treatment or, perhaps, any assistance required because of any psychological barriers to a vocational effort (as, for example, a problem of motivation due to the employee's age or handicapped condition). In the language of the statute, a Q.I.W. is entitled to "reasonable and necessary vocational training." As previously noted, these substantive rights include notice, diagnostic services for determination of Q.I.W. status, vocational training under an approved plan, the payment of vocational rehabilitation temporary compensation (VRTD), along with any additional living expenses necessitated by a plan. According to LC 139.5, the right to these benefits accrues when a Q.I.W. "chooses to enroll in a rehabilitation program." However, appellate court decisions have established the principle that one cannot "choose to enroll" until he or she is aware of his or her right to such benefits. This awareness depends upon the employer's giving the required notices. It may be expected that the courts will apply this same rule to the employer's obligation to move forward regarding the resolution of the initial question of the employee's medical eligibility and other required procedural steps under the 1988 rules.

R 10003(i),
10009(e),
10018

The rules provide that an employee's right to receive VRTD is continuous "during the period of his or her entitlement to vocational rehabilitation services, including the period of participation in eligibility evaluation, participation in plan development and during pendency of plan approval and implementation." R 10018 also states: "However, entitlement to such payment shall be contingent upon the employee's voluntary participation in and availability to receive vocational rehabilitation services. Vocational rehabilitation temporary disability indemnity shall be payable in the same manner and at the same rate as temporary disability indemnity." Decisions have indicated that where proper notice has been given the employee must make out a *prima facie* case of entitlement before he or she is eligible to receive VRTD and other rehabilitation benefits. This holding will undoubtedly be affected in future cases by the employer's obligation to determine, through the treating physician, whether there is medical eligibility, for the rules require definite steps to be taken, depending upon the physician's opinion.

Again, if an employer has failed to give the employee proper notice of his or her rights regarding vocational rehabilitation, payment of VRTD is to begin from the date of such breach of duty. This principle was established by the California Supreme Court in the *Webb* and *Renfro* cases based upon the rationale that while ordinarily the obligation to pay rehabilitation temporary compensation arises when the employee makes known to his or her employer that he or she "chooses to enroll in a rehabilitation program," the employee cannot make known a choice or request if he or she has not been advised that this benefit is available.

Principles distilled from appellate court and W.C.A.B. decisions govern various aspects of the compensation benefit. Permanent disability payments are not to be made concurrently with rehabilitation temporary compensation and are deferred until completion of a plan. Rehabilitation compensation is payable while the worker is undergoing rehabilitation, including evaluation *LC 139.5* and diagnosis, and is not subject to any restrictions in duration which might apply to regular temporary disability indemnity. Any payment of rehabilita- *LC 4656* tion compensation after two years from date of injury is to be made at the rate *LC 4661.5* in effect when such payment is made. A petition to terminate temporary compensation will not be entertained by the W.C.A.B. during rehabilitation. *LC 4651.2* Rehabilitation temporary compensation is to be considered in the assessment of a penalty for serious and willful misconduct and any penalty for unrea- *LC 5814* sonable delay or failure to provide rehabilitation benefits.

If an employee receives a retirement allowance while undergoing rehabilitation, no deduction is to be made from his or her compensation unless authorized by a specific law, regulation or provision of the retirement plan. *LC 4853* Such a law is LC 4853 which provides for the termination of temporary compensation to local public safety members of the Public Employees' Retirement System after their retirement. However, it has also been held that LC 4853 applies only to disability pensions under P.E.R.S., not to regular service retirements or to retirements under county or other retirement programs.

1990 Provisions

The principles discussed above concerning entitlement questions are viable, except as modified by statute, with regard to 1990 and later injuries. The most significant changes relate to the maintenance allowance (in place of

VRTD), the maximum set for the allowance, and the right to use a portion of permanent disability accrued payments to bring the allowance up to the applicable temporary compensation rate.

LC 139.5
(c), (d)

For injuries occurring on or after January 1, 1990, when an employee is determined to be medically eligible and chooses to enroll in a vocational rehabilitation program, in addition to his or her right to other VR benefits, he or she continues to receive temporary compensation, and, after his or her condition becomes permanent and stationary, a maintenance allowance, plus any living expenses necessitated by the program. This would include the right to payment during the period necessary to determine vocational feasibility in view of the decisions previously discussed establishing the right to VRTD in connection with diagnostic procedures and also because investigation of vocational feasibility is mandatory if an employee is determined to be medically eligible.

The maintenance allowance is two-thirds of average weekly earnings at time of injury subject to a maximum compensation rate of $246 per week. The maintenance allowance may be supplemented, at the employee's option, by advances of permanent disability benefits sufficient to equal the applicable temporary compensation rate. Payment is subject to LC 4661.5 regarding payments made after two years from date of injury. In no event are temporary compensation and the maintenance allowance to be paid concurrently. Other than the partial use of permanent disability entitlement permitted by the amended LC 139.5, the pre-1990 ruling that permanent disability payments and VRTD are not to be paid concurrently would also apply to the maintenance allowance for injuries occurring in 1990 and after. This basic principle is recognized by permitting an employee to supplement the maintenance allowance with only that amount of his or her permanent disability entitlement to equal the temporary compensation rate. [NOTE: An employee is entitled to receive unemployment disability benefits to the extent that the total of the maintenance allowance plus the permissible amount of permanent disability advance is less than the applicable disability benefits.]

UI 2629

LC 4850

City, county, and district law enforcement officers and firefighters, investigators of a district attorney's office, and lifeguards of a county of the first class who are members of the Public Employees' Retirement System or subject to the county retirement law of 1937 are entitled to receive salary, not to exceed one year, in lieu of temporary compensation or maintenance allowance under LC 139.5.

If the employer disputes the treating physician's determination of medical eligibility, the employee is to be paid the basic maintenance allowance pending final determination of the dispute. If the employee challenges the treating physician's conclusion and prevails, he or she is entitled to the basic allowance retroactive to the date of the employee's request for VRS. If the employer causes a delay in the provision of services, the full maintenance allowance is payable for the period of the delay, including the amount of any

LC 4642

opted permanent disability advance.

The maintenance allowance may not be settled or commuted to a lump *LC 4646* sum unless a workers' compensation judge finds that there are good faith issues which if decided against the employee would preclude all workers' compensation benefits.

If an employee unreasonably refuses to cooperate in the provision of *LC 4643* VRS, the employee is not entitled to the basic maintenance allowance for the period of unreasonable failure to cooperate. In order to effectively withhold payment under these circumstances, the employer or carrier must first give the employee notice of intent to withhold payment and the reasons therefor. *R 10123* This notice is to be given to the employee at least 15 days before the with- *(f)(4)* holding of payment. The employee has 10 days after receipt of the notice to object by seeking a resolution of the dispute by the Rehabilitation Unit of O.B.D. Following an expedited conference, a decision is to be served on the parties by certified mail within 10 days after the employee's objection. The basic maintenance allowance is payable until receipt of the determination.

§16.6 Qualified Rehabilitation Representative

Pre-1990 Provisions

The rules place the impetus upon the employer or carrier to move forward in the development of a rehabilitation plan for an employee having "medical eligibility." The first step is the appointment of a "qualified rehabil- *R 10003(d)* itation representative" (Q.R.R.) to assist in the preparation of a plan. A qualified rehabilitation representative is defined as a "person capable of developing and implementing the vocational rehabilitation plan, whose experience and regular duties involve the evaluation, counseling or placement of indus- *R 10009* trially injured workers." The procedure calls for a cooperative effort on the part of the employer or carrier and the employee in the selection of a Q.R.R. In practice, an employer or carrier usually selects the Q.R.R. and refers the employee to him or her. R 10009(a) requires the employer to make the selection in consultation with the employee immediately after giving the notice required by R 10006(a). The initial task of the Q.R.R. is to evaluate the employee's "vocational eligibility" in order to determine his or her status as a Q.I.W.

If the parties cannot agree upon a Q.R.R., either party may request the Rehabilitation Bureau to assign one. Upon receiving such a request, the Bureau will appoint an independent vocational evaluator (I.V.E.) from a list *R 10010* prepared by the Chief of the Bureau. [The educational and experience qualifications of I.V.E.'s are set forth in R 10003(e).] Under instructions from the Bureau, the I.V.E. is to report to the Bureau, with copies to the parties, regarding the issues submitted. If the employer fails to provide services, the Bureau may determine that the I.V.E. is to develop a plan, assuming the employee is found to be a Q.I.W. Another alternative, where an employer or *R 10009(f)* carrier has failed to provide services, is for the employee to request the Bureau to approve the appointment of a Q.R.R. selected by the employee. In this event, the employee must substantiate his or her entitlement to vocational

R 10009(h)   rehabilitation services. Also, the parties may agree to a change of or consultation with a Q.R.R. This could include a situation where the parties are

R 10009(b)   seeking a second opinion. Within 15 days of a referral, the parties are to supply the Q.R.R. with copies of all extant medical and vocational reports.

R 10009(c)   If it is determined that the employee is a Q.I.W., the Q.R.R. will proceed to develop a plan and the employer or carrier must submit the plan to the employee within 90 days of the initial evaluation. But, if the evaluation results in the employer's taking issue with the employee's entitlement, the employee must be given notice within the 90-day period that he or she is not a Q.I.W. and the reasons for this conclusion. The employer or carrier may also request resolution of the question by the Bureau.

R 10009(f)   Where the employee requests the appointment of a Q.R.R. of his or her choice, a copy of the request must be served on the other party or parties, and within 20 days of the Bureau's notification, the employer or carrier must either agree to provide vocational services or establish through medical and vocational reports that the employee is not a Q.I.W. If the employer or carrier does not respond within the prescribed period, the Bureau has authority to order an examination by an independent medical examiner, or, if it appears that the employee is medically eligible, order the provision of vocational rehabilitation services by a Q.R.R. selected by the employee or by the Bureau at the employee's request, all at the expense of the employer or carrier. [NOTE: All employee requests for Bureau action are to be submitted using Form RB-104 (yellow).]

1990 Provisions

LC 4635(b)   "Qualified rehabilitation representative" is now defined by statute. A person who may qualify as a Q.R.R. is one who is capable of developing and implementing a vocational rehabilitation plan, whose experience and regular duties involve the evaluation, counseling, or placement of disabled persons, and who is familiar with the provisions of LC 4635-4647. This definition differs somewhat from that in R 10003(d) in that under LC 4635(b) a Q.R.R.'s experience may be related to "disabled persons" rather than to "industrially injured workers," thus broadening the sector from which they may be drawn.

LC 4635(c)   The definition of "independent vocational evaluator" (I.V.E.) under LC 4635(c) is the same as that set forth in R 10003(e) as outlined above with the exception, however, that psychological evaluation or assessment is no longer qualifying experience.

LC 139.5   The Rehabilitation Unit is to recommend for adoption by the
(a)(4)   Administrative Director governing reasonable fees charged for vocational rehabilitation services (VRS) on and after January 1, 1991. The initial fee

schedule is to be designed to reduce the cost of VRS by 10 percent from the level of fees paid during 1989. Regarding the Reasonable Fee Schedule, see R 10131.1 for rules applicable to injuries on or after January 1, 1990.

R 10132.1

The 1990 provisions bring a Q.R.R. into the picture earlier than the prior rules, i.e., after 90 days of aggregate total disability. The Q.R.R. will assist in obtaining a determination from the treating physician regarding the question of an employee's medical eligibility for VRS. If the employee is determined to be medically eligible either by the treating physician under LC 4636 or by "a physician's report" under LC 4637 received by the employer or carrier, the employee has the right to an agreed upon Q.R.R. to determine vocational feasibility. If this appointment does not transpire, the employee may request the Rehabilitation Unit of O.B.D. to appoint an I.V.E. to provide VRS.

LC 4636, 4637

LC 4640

When a Q.R.R. is assigned per LC 4636(a), there must be an initial consultation within 25 days. The Q.R.R. is to explain VRS and assist in the development of a job description per Form RU-91 or a narrative job description, whichever is deemed appropriate. The Q.R.R. will then submit a Form RU-90 and the job description to the treating physician for a determination of the employee's medical eligibility for VRS.

R 10124

If an employer or carrier fails to assign a Q.R.R. or otherwise fails to meet requirements, an employee may request the Rehabilitation Unit to order the provision of VRS at the expense of the employer or carrier through a Q.R.R. selected by the employee or by an I.V.E. appointed by the Unit. The parties may agree to a change of Q.R.R. Where agreement on a change cannot be reached, either the employee or employer (or carrier) may request the Unit to appoint an I.V.E.

LC 4639

The rules provide that if the parties cannot agree upon a Q.R.R., either party may request the appointment of an I.V.E. by the Rehabilitation Unit within 15 days. The requesting party files a request for dispute resolution (Form RU-103) with the Unit. Within 15 days of the filing, the Unit will appoint an I.V.E. with notice to the parties. An assignment is made in rotation from a panel in the geographic area included within the venue of the correct Unit office. The evaluator chosen will meet the language and specialty requirements of the employee. All medical and vocational reports are to be forwarded to the I.V.E. by the employer within 10 days. If the I.V.E. cannot meet with the employee within 10 days of receipt of these documents, another I.V.E. will be appointed. No party may communicate with an I.V.E. except for communications initiated by the evaluator or as otherwise directed by the Unit. All communications will be confirmed in writing by the I.V.E. The Unit may order that VRS be provided by an I.V.E. at the employer's expense if (1) the employer fails to provide them in a timely manner after the employee's request; (2) necessary to determine vocational feasibility or to determine if a plan meets requirements; or, (3) the employee and his or her Q.R.R. cannot agree on a vocational goal.

R 10125

§ 16.7　Vocational Rehabilitation Plan; Types of VR Plans; Agreement to VR Plan

Pre-1990 Provisions

R 10011

　　　A vocational rehabilitation plan is set forth in a document prepared by a Q.R.R. [Form RB-102 (blue), 4 pages.] This document is to contain a description in some detail of occupational goals, vocational services contemplated, and the type of plan, placement, and possible earnings, including any modified or alternative work for the same or new employer. Medical information necessary includes a description of the employee's limitations and ability to participate in the plan and function in the proposed occupation, along with the name of the treating physician. The plan document is to contain a statement of certain financial matters, such as the rate for payment of VRTD, any additional living expenses, and costs for books, supplies, tools, equipment, or tuition. It will also include expected dates for commencement and completion of the program, as well as the responsibilities of the Q.R.R. and the parties. Various other required details are names, addresses, phone numbers, and signatures of the Q.R.R., the parties, and any legal representatives. (See R 10011(b) for full details re plan preparation.)

R 10012
(d), (e)

　　　As a matter of D.I.A. and Bureau policy, plans which utilize an employee's transferable skills and experience for modified or alternative work with the same employer, or for direct job placement with another employer, and provide wages, hours, and working conditions similar to those enjoyed by the employee when injured are preferable to plans which propose training for an occupation in which the employee has no skills or experience. In such situations, due consideration is given to an employee's skills and opportunities to earn similar wages should the modified or alternative work later become unavailable. Also, where a question arises concerning the comparative length of alternative plans of equal merit, preference will be given to the plan which expedites the worker's return to suitable gainful employment. According to official rulings, a plan may include education, language courses to remove language barriers, and technical training or courses, or employment coupled with on-the-job training or technical courses. Any tools or equipment customarily furnished by a worker in the new occupation are to be included in the plan. However, an employer is not required to furnish equipment which would be classified as a "capital investment."

R 10011(a)

　　　When the plan document [RB-102] is completed, a copy must be submitted to the employee who has 15 days to review it and either agree or object. If either the employee, employer, or carrier objects to the plan, and agreement cannot be reached within 15 days of the objection, the plan, a statement of the disagreement, and a request for resolution are to be submitted to the

R 10011
(c), (d)

Bureau by the employer or carrier. If the parties agree, it is deemed that they intend to comply with all its provisions. A material breach of the agreement by the employer could result in the Bureau's ordering an extension or modification. The employee will continue to be entitled to VRTD during the period of time involved in these procedures. A material breach by the employee may result in an order terminating entitlement if the employer has given the employee a written warning explaining the breach and possible consequences, *R 10011(e)* and the employee fails to correct it within 10 days. Types of breaches of agreement include failure of an employer to provide necessary funds or services; also, failure of an employee to notify the Q.R.R. within 5 days of any inability to participate in his or her plan or attend a class per the plan. If unforeseen *R 10011(g)* circumstances bring about a need for plan modification either party may apply to the Bureau for approval of a change.

1990 Provisions

A vocational rehabilitation plan is, "the written description of and *LC 4635(e)* rationale for the manner and means by which it is proposed that a qualified injured worker may be returned to suitable gainful employment. The plan may contemplate modification of the employee's occupation at the time of injury, provision for alternative work with the same employer, direct job placement assistance, on-the-job training, formal training, academic instruction, job placement assistance, or self-employment." A plan must specify the anticipated completion date and the amount and source of payments to be made during pendency of the plan. Also, a plan must define the responsibilities of the employee, the employer, the Q.R.R., an insurance carrier, or other parties in implementing the plan. [NOTE: Per R 10126, where a question arises concerning the duration of alternate plans of equal merit, preference is given to the plan which expedites a return to suitable gainful employment.]

"Suitable gainful employment" is, "employment or self-employment *LC 4635(f)* which is reasonably attainable and which offers an opportunity to restore the employee as soon as practicable and as near as possible to maximum self-support, due consideration being given to the employee's qualifications, likely permanent disability, vocational interests and aptitudes, pre-injury earnings and future earning capacity, and the present and projected labor market."

[NOTE: The foregoing definitions are similar to those of R 10003(g), (h), and certain requirements of R 10011. In the LC 4635(f) definition of suitable gainful employment, the term "projected labor market" replaces "future labor market" of R 10003(h).]

When an employee is determined to be a Q.I.W., the Q.R.R. and the *LC 4638* employee jointly will develop an "agreed upon vocational rehabilitation plan." The employer or carrier must also be involved, for the employer or carrier must submit the plan to the Rehabilitation Unit of O.B.D. within 90 days after the determination of the employee's vocational feasibility. If no plan is submitted within that time, any dispute regarding the furnishing of VRS must be submitted to the Unit for determination.

Plans which utilize an employee's transferable skills and experience in modified or alternative work with the same or similar employer, and with wages, hours, and working conditions similar to those at time of injury, are preferable to those plans which propose training for an occupation in which the employee has no skills or experience. If an insured employer, in whose employment the injury occurred, provides such modified or alternative work for 12 months, the employer is entitled to a refund of premium from the insurer. The refund is calculated as equal to the standard premium per $100 of payroll applied to wages paid during the 12-month period as adjusted for the experience modification factors applicable to the employer.

R 10126,
10131,
10012

LC 4644

A VR plan (or modification of a previous plan) is to be submitted to the Rehabilitation Unit on Form RU 102 with appropriate attachments. [NOTE: If the matter requires dispute resolution, Form RU 103 is to be utilized with an attached summary of any informal conference and the results thereof including identification of issues resolved, issues pending, positions of the parties, and the rationale and supporting information for each such position.] A plan is to be submitted within 15 days of agreement. A plan which is based upon modified or alternative work for the same employer is not subject to approval prior to implementation. However, an employer or carrier may be required to file a modified or alternative work plan upon its completion under R 10012(b) or in order to obtain Unit approval of termination of VRS under LC 4644 and R 10131.

R 10126(c)

Within 30 days after receipt of a VR plan which is properly submitted, documented, and signed, the Rehabilitation Unit will either approve or disapprove the plan. If approval or disapproval is not made in 30 days, it will be deemed approved. However, plan commencement is not deemed approval. This latter provision undoubtedly refers to early commencement of a plan either before submission to the Unit or before the 30-day period has expired.

§ 16.8   VR Plan Approval and Implementation

Pre-1990 Provisions

R 10011
(f), (g)
R 10012

R 10005

Except for plans involving modified or alternative work within present capabilities, all vocational plans must be submitted to the Bureau for approval within 15 days of agreement. The Bureau is to approve or disapprove a plan within 30 days of receipt and advise the Q.R.R. and the parties of its action. In making its determination, the Bureau may request additional information including medical or vocational reports. If no notice of Bureau action is received by the parties within 30 days, a plan is considered approved, assuming all plan requirements have been met and that no one has filed a written objection with the Bureau. A plan is to be implemented when the employee's medical condition permits and the Bureau has given its approval, or on the date specified in the plan, whichever date first occurs. Therefore, if the parties have agreed upon a plan, it may be put into operation before official action is taken, but preapproval commencement must be explained in the plan and Bureau approval sought as indicated.

While plan commencement is not deemed approved, if the plan is not disapproved within the 30-day period, the parties may consider it approved. As to *R 10011(b)* agreed plans involving modified or alternative work with the same employer, such plans do not require Bureau approval before implementation. This type of plan is to be submitted to the Bureau upon completion along with a request for an order approving conclusion of services. [Form RB-105 (pink).]

Employee Self-Procured Plans. Official decisions have established the principle that an employee must follow the procedures set forth in the rules if he or she desires to undergo a rehabilitation program of his or her own choosing. [Employee requests are submitted on Form RB-104 (yellow).] As a general rule, an employer or carrier is not liable for the costs of a self-procured plan and the payment of VRTD where the employee has not sought agreement and Bureau action. All plans, whether employer-initiated or employee-initiated must be submitted to the Bureau for approval. If a plan is submitted subsequent to an approved plan, it will not be approved unless the employee can substantiate that the original plan is no longer feasible because of a change of permanent disability, or because conditions in the original plan cannot be met, or the original plan has not prepared the employee for suitable gainful employment. Because of the required procedures, it would be difficult for an employee to obtain reimbursement for the cost of an unapproved plan. A case might be made if the employer or carrier has failed completely in carrying out notice requirements. This points up the importance of an employer's or carrier's giving the required notices and obtaining the treating physician's opinion regarding the employee's medical eligibility. Reported cases dealing with claims for reimbursement have involved fact situations in which employees had turned down approved plans to seek other forms of training or education. In these cases, reimbursement was denied.

1990 Provisions

As noted in the previous topic, a VR plan is to be submitted to the *R 10126* Rehabilitation Unit for review within 15 days after agreement on the plan. The Unit will approve or disapprove the plan within 30 days; however, the parties may assume approval if no order is received within the 30-day period. Early commencement of a plan is not deemed approval. Again, plans calling for modified or alternative work with the same employer are not subject to prior approval before implementation, but see the NOTE under the prior topic regarding filing the plan after completion. Upon approval, the parties may move forward with the plan, and if circumstances require an early commencement because of motivational factors or availability of resources, this information should be included in the plan document or otherwise conveyed to the Rehabilitation Unit at the earliest opportunity.

The principles concerning employee self-procured plans remain the *R 10127,* same as for pre-1990 cases. An employee seeking a plan of his or her own *10128* choosing would file a request on a Form RU 104 with the Rehabilitation

Unit. If the matter involves a dispute regarding a plan, a form RU 103 would be used to obtain a Unit determination. If the case is not already pending with the Unit, an RU-101, Case Initiation Document, must also be filed. Because of the required procedures and remedies provided by LC 4635-4647, there is little chance that an unapproved self-procured plan will be reimbursable.

§ 16.9   Interruption of VRS

Pre-1990 Provisions

R 10015   Should a circumstance arise resulting in or requiring an interruption in the provision of vocational rehabilitation services, the parties must agree to an interruption, or approval must be sought from the Bureau. There must be good cause for any hiatus in carrying out a plan, and it may not exceed six months without the Bureau's assent. If the interruption is requested by the employee, he or she has the responsibility to make a written request for resumption of services before the expiration of the period of interruption, and may seek Bureau assistance if the employer refuses. [Form RB-104.] Where the employee fails to make a timely request, the employer or carrier may seek an order concluding the obligation.

1990 Provisions

LC 4644(b)   A deferral or interruption of VRS is authorized if the parties agree or if
R 10129   the Rehabilitation Unit so orders for good cause. If there is agreement, the employer or carrier must provide the employee with a letter of agreement notice within 10 days. An employee may make a written request for further interruption or may request the reinstatement of services. If the employer or carrier does not respond to an employee request, the employee may request that the Rehabilitation Unit make an appropriate order utilizing a Form RU 104. If the matter involves a dispute, resolution of the dispute by the Unit is requested on a Form RU 103. Where an employee fails to make a timely request for reinstatement of VRS, the employer may request a Unit order approving termination of liability.

§ 16.10   Conclusion and Termination of VRS

Pre-1990 Provisions

R 10016   Upon completion of a plan, the employer or carrier may file a request
           with the Bureau for a determination and order approving the conclusion of
R 10007   vocational rehabilitation services. [All requests for termination of vocational
(a)(5)   rehabilitation services and other entitlements must be filed with the Bureau and include an accounting of all benefits provided. Form RB-105 (pink).] A copy of the request is to be sent to the employee. It will be deemed granted unless the employee files a written objection, with a copy to the employer or carrier, within 20 days. In the latter event, the Bureau will, within 30 days, obtain through a conference or other means the employee's reasons for objection and substantiating evidence, then issue its decision. If no timely objection is filed, the request of the employer or carrier will be deemed granted,

and a decision will issue within 30 days. Other grounds for seeking an order approving conclusion of services are: that the employee is not a Q.I.W. or has failed to cooperate in efforts to determine that question; that the employee failed to complete an approved plan; that the employee declined to accept vocational rehabilitation services; that the employee failed to request timely reinstatement of services; that all necessary and reasonable services have been provided; or, as previously noted, that a plan for modified or alternative work with the same employer has been completed.

1990 Provisions

Liability of the employer or carrier terminates if an employee, having received notice of potential eligibility, declines VRS by completing a Form RU-107, Employee Statement of Declination of Vocational Rehabilitation. This form must be signed by the employee and his or her representative, if any. In order to obtain Rehabilitation Unit approval of termination of liability on this ground, the employer or carrier must file the completed form with the Unit along with a request for an order of termination (Form RU-105), a copy of a notice of potential eligibility (Form RU-500W) and documentation of assignment of a Q.R.R. The record must show that the employee received adequate notice and explanation of his or her right to VRS. *LC 4644 R 10131, 10131.1*

Liability for VRS also ceases when a Q.I.W. completes an approved plan or whenever a Q.I.W. unreasonably fails to complete an approved plan.

In addition, if an employee does not request VRS within 90 days after notification of medical eligibility per LC 4638, liability will terminate. However, in order for this ground of termination to be effective, the employer or carrier must give the employee a reminder notice not earlier than 45 days nor later than 70 days after receipt by the employee of the medical eligibility notice. This ground for termination is not applicable if the employee is unable to comprehend the consequences of failing to make a timely request or if conditions beyond his or her control prevent compliance.

The rules require that a Request for Termination (Form RU-105) be filed with the Unit within 10 days after the occurrence of the circumstances giving rise to the right of termination. A copy is to be served upon the employee who then has 20 days to file an objection utilizing Form RU-103, Request for Dispute Resolution. If there is no timely objection, the Unit will approve the request within 30 days unless it appears inappropriate under the circumstances of the case. Where an objection is filed, the Unit must hold a conference within 30 days to consider the evidence and render a decision. *R 10131*

§ 16.11   Reinstatement of VRS

Pre-1990 Provisions

Where by order, the Bureau has approved conclusion of services per R 10016, an employee may petition the Bureau for a determination of his or *R 10017* her need for and entitlement to reinstatement of vocational rehabilitation benefits (Form RB-104). Such a request must be timely in accordance with the provisions of LC 5405.5, 5410 and 5803. (See subsequent discussion in § 16.14, *Statutes of Limitation; Reopening.*) The grounds for such requests set out in R 10017 are: that the W.C.A.B. has determined that additional rehabilitation services may be required because of a change in the employee's disability; that the W.C.A.B. has ordered an entitlement question to be determined by the Bureau; that the W.C.A.B. has vacated an order concluding services; that the employee can substantiate that a plan was not provided; that circumstances causing a refusal or non-availability for participation have changed; that the plan did not prepare the employee for suitable gainful employment; or that an order concluding services was based upon incorrect information or error of the Bureau. If an employer or carrier and the employee wish to agree to reinstatement of services, they may do so, subject to plan-approval requirements.

1990 Provisions

LC 4644
R10130

In addition to the provision for reinstatement of VRS after deferral or interruption of a VR plan, as previously noted, the code provides for reinstatement on these grounds: Where there has been a finding that original plan was inappropriate because of a change in the employee's medical condition; where there are facts which were not reasonably discoverable or available; where there has been a failure on the part of the employer or carrier to provide timely services per an approved plan; or, where circumstances beyond the control of either the employee, the employer, or carrier render a plan inappropriate. Further, if a plan is based upon modified or alternative work with the same or similar employer, and that employment terminates within 12 months, and such work is unavailable on the labor market, the employee may be entitled to additional VRS. In this situation, the employee has the burden to establish an inability to compete for suitable gainful employment with his or her existing skills. In order to request a reinstatement of VRS, the employee must initially make a demand upon the employer or carrier and, if not reinstated, seek an order from the Unit utilizing a Form RU-104, Employee Request for Order of Vocational Rehabilitation Services.

[NOTE: The 1990 LC provisions and the 1990 supplemental rules do not specifically address the question of O.B.D. or Rehabilitation Unit procedure for seeking reinstatement of VRS following a final order approving termination of liability. Presumably, this procedure is to be addressed before the W.C.A.B. under LC 5405.5, 5410, or 5803. However, R 10017, discussed previously, is still extant, and it may be argued that this procedure is available for injuries during and after 1990—or that Unit jurisdiction is inherent in the statement of grounds for reinstatement in LC 4644.]

§ 16.12   Rehabilitation Unit Jurisdiction; Procedure in Contested Cases

Pre-1990 Provisions

In addition to the plan-approval function outlined above, the Rehabilitation Bureau has original jurisdiction over disputed or contested cases and issues. We have seen that either an employee or an employer or insurance carrier may invoke this jurisdiction by filing a written request for determination. Requests for action, plan approval, approval of conclusion of benefits and other determinations are to be submitted on forms prescribed by the Bureau. Forms and information may be obtained from the Bureau. In any matter pending before it, the Bureau may require any party to file and serve pertinent documents, medical reports or vocational reports. It has authority to prepare a list of qualified independent vocational evaluators (I.V.E.'s) and make appointments to resolve impasses or to provide services.   *R 10014, 10007*   *R 10005*   *R 10010*

The Administrative Director and the Bureau have developed and approved the following forms for submission of requests for Bureau consideration and action:

RB-101—CASE INITIATION DOCUMENT
      (goldenrod (dark yellow) form)
RB-102—VOCATIONAL REHABILITATION PLAN
      (blue form, 4 pp.)
RB-103—REQUEST FOR DISPUTE RESOLUTION
      (green form)
RB-104—REQUEST FOR ORDER OF REHABILITATION
      (yellow form)
RB-105—REQUEST FOR CONCLUSION OF REHABILITATION
      BENEFITS
      (pink form)
RB-107—STATEMENT OF DECLINE OF VOCATIONAL
      REHABILITATION
      (buff color form)

[NOTE: A completed RB-101, CASE INITIATION DOCUMENT, is to accompany any of the other forms filed with the Bureau if a Bureau case number has not previously been assigned. (Forms RB-90 and RB-91 (buff color) are used by the employer or carrier and the treating physician to ascertain medical eligibility. They would be submitted to the Bureau as evidence upon the filing of an appropriate request for Bureau action.)]

When Bureau action is desired to resolve a dispute or disagreement, the request for action is submitted utilizing the appropriate form. All medical and vocational reports not previously filed with the Bureau must also be submitted and served. Any position an opposing party wishes to advance must be in written form and filed with the Bureau and served within 15 days of service   *R 10014* of the request for action. The Bureau may make its determination based upon the record, conduct a conference, or require the parties to meet and confer for resolution by agreement or to frame issues. The Bureau will either issue a decision in 45 days or schedule a conference. If a conference is held, the Bureau will submit the matter at the conference or upon receipt of additional information requested at the conference. Its decision will issue in 30 days after submission. A Bureau order becomes final unless an appeal is filed with the W.C.A.B. within 20 days after service of the order.

R 10006(d),
10013   Where it appears that the employer or carrier denies liability for any workers' compensation benefits, as where there is a question of industrial injury or other issue which would preclude all benefits if decided adversely to the employee, the matter must be referred to the W.C.A.B. for resolution of such an issue before the Bureau may proceed with rehabilitation issues.

R 10014(c),
10020,
10014(e)   If either party fails to comply with the findings, the Bureau may petition the W.C.A.B. for enforcement and assessment of any appropriate penalty. Any finding, decision or order of the Bureau is appealable to the W.C.A.B.

R 10007(c)   Filing of documents, including medical and other reports, with the W.C.A.B. does not constitute a filing with the Bureau.

R 10014(e)
CCP 1013   Time extensions for action following service of matters by mail are governed by section 1013 of the Code of Civil Procedure, i.e., 5 additional days from the date of mailing, or 10 additional days from date of mailing if service is made to an out-of-state party.

1990 Provisions

LC 4645   The Legislature has codified the approach of R 10014 in that all disputed matters regarding the provision of VRS must be submitted to the Office of Benefit Determination, and under both statute and rule, this means
LC 139.5
R 10127   the Rehabilitation Unit.

LC 4643   When a dispute arises from an employee's objection to the intention of an employer or carrier to withhold the maintenance allowance, the employee is to file a request for dispute resolution (Form RU-103) with the Unit with service upon other parties. The request is to include a full explanation of the employee's position. A conference will be held and a determination made by the Unit within 10 days.

R 10127   All other requests for dispute resolution are submitted on a Form RU-103, Request for Dispute Resolution, with attached vocational reports not previously submitted and a format summary of any informal conference. The summary must identify both resolved and unresolved issues, supporting information and the positions of the parties. Where an informal conference has not been held, the requesting party must attach all pertinent medical and vocational reports and other information not previously submitted, identify why an informal conference is inappropriate and state the issues and the positions of the parties relative to the issues. The other parties have 15 days to file and serve position papers along with supporting data. Upon receipt of the request, the Unit may make a determination, request additional information or set the matter for a formal conference.

The Unit is to issue a determination within 45 days of the receipt of the original request or within 30 days after the receipt of any required or permitted additional information. Any determination or recommendation is binding unless an appeal (petition) is filed with the W.C.A.B. within 20 days after service of the Unit decision. *R 10123 10124 LC 4645(d)*

Generally, all papers and documents filed with the Rehabilitation Unit must contain the Unit file number. If no number has been assigned, a Case Initiation Document (Form RU-101) must be attached as a cover for the document being filed. Incomplete forms may be returned to the sender. All forms must be on the color stock approved by the Administrative Director.

If an employer or carrier has raised a good faith issue of injury arising out of and occurring in the course of employment, no documents are to be filed with the Rehabilitation Unit until the employer or carrier accepts liability or there has been a finding of compensable injury by the W.C.A.B. Any documents tendered to the Unit without such acceptance or finding will be returned to the sender. *R 10123 (e)(1)*

The following forms established by Administrative Director rule apply to injuries occurring on or after January 1, 1990: *R 10133*

RU-90—Treating Physician's Report of Disability Status

RU-91—Description of Employee's Job Duties

RU-101—Case Initiation Document (Goldenrod color form)

RU-102—Vocational Rehabilitation Plan (Blue Form)

RU-103—Request for Dispute Resolution (Green form)

RU-104—Employee Request for Order of Vocational Rehabilitation Services (Canary color form)

RU-105—Request for Termination of Rehabilitation (Pink form)

RU-107—Employee Statement of Declination of Vocational Rehabilitation Services

RU-500W—Notice of Potential Eligibility

RU-500W.1—Reply Card

RU-500X—Reminder Notice

RU-500Y—Denial of Vocational Rehabilitation Services

RU-500Z—Intent to Withhold Maintenance Allowance

R 10123.2   Except for Form RU-107, any person or entity may reproduce all required forms and notices but may only modify the heading to permit imprinting the name, address, telephone number, logo-type or other identifier of an employer, insurer or third-party administrator. The reproduction must be otherwise identical in typestyle and format using the designated color. If the form is computer generated, a minimum of a one-half inch border in the designated color is required.

The following forms have been adopted as indicating a recommended format:

RU-AA—Notice of Assignment of Qualified Rehabilitation Representative

RU-AB—Notice of Interruption

RU-AC—QRR Verification of Vocational Rehabilitation Explanation

R 10127.1   Upon receipt of a request for dispute resolution (Form RU-103), the Rehabilitation Unit will determine if a formal conference is necessary. Notice of the time and place of any conference will be served upon the parties. If the
LC 4643   matter consists of an objection to withholding the maintenance allowance, the Unit will hold an expedited conference to determine entitlement, and a determination will issue within 10 days of the receipt of the objection. If any party is unable to attend a conference, his or her position on any issue may be submitted in writing. Following the conference, the Unit will issue a determination based upon its file, information provided during the conference and any written positions submitted prior to or at the time of the conference. A determination of issues other than the withholding of the maintenance allowance will be issued within 30 days of the date of the conference or within 30 days of receipt of any required additional information. Where a dispute is resolved before a conference, upon notification the Unit will cancel the conference on notice to the parties.

§ 16.13   Jurisdiction of the W.C.A.B.; Appeals

Pre-1990 Provisions

R 10014(e)   The rules give effect to the judicial jurisdiction of the W.C.A.B. in pro-
10013   viding for appeal to the Board from a Bureau decision. Also, the rules recognize that a rehabilitation issue may arise in an original proceeding before the Board, and provision is made for reference to the Bureau in such a case.

R 10955-   When a Bureau decision is appealed, the parties must follow the proce-
10958   dure set out in the W.C.A.B. rules. These rules require a petition in the nature
R 10842   of a petition for reconsideration. If no application has been filed, an applica-
10392   tion for hearing must be filed as well. The matter comes on for hearing before a workers' compensation judge who has authority to review the matter anew and make a determination on all rehabilitation issues. The appealing party has the burden of proof. Any party aggrieved by the judge's decision may appeal further to the Board and to the appellate courts. (See Chapter 15, APPEALS.)

It is important to keep in mind that filing an objection with the Rehabilitation Bureau concerning one of its orders does not constitute an appeal. Also, an appeal properly taken to the W.C.A.B. will not be calendared for hearing unless a party files a Declaration of Readiness to Proceed with the Board.

When a rehabilitation issue arises in a W.C.A.B. proceeding regarding *R 10013* other workers' compensation issues or benefits, and if it appears that the resolution of one or more issues could defeat the entire claim, the judge is to determine these issues, and then, if appropriate, refer the matter to the Bureau on the question of entitlement to vocational services. On the other hand, if there is no issue which would bar the employee's right to workers' compensation, the judge is to refer the rehabilitation question to the Bureau which will advise the judge of its recommendations. After receiving these recommendations, the judge may then enter a decision regarding rehabilitation.

If an employee seeks to reopen his or her permanent disability award on the ground that he or she has been found by the Bureau not to be a Q.I.W., the employee must file a timely appeal from the Bureau decision with the W.C.A.B. Such a finding by the Bureau, if upheld, is good ground to reopen the award for permanent disability (*LeBeouf* case).

1990 Provisions

Reference to the jurisdiction of the W.C.A.B. is set forth in LC 4645. An *LC 4645* appeal may be taken from a determination or recommendation of the *R 10992* Rehabilitation Unit by filing a petition with the W.C.A.B. within 20 days after service of the Unit's decision. R 10992 provides that if an application is already on file with the Board the appeal is taken by filing a petition setting forth in detail the reasons for the appeal. In order to obtain a setting for hearing in such case, a declaration of readiness to proceed must also be filed. If no application is on file, an application for adjudication must accompany the petition. A copy of each pleading (i.e., application, petition, answer, etc.), and each notice or order must be served upon the O.B.D. Rehabilitation Unit.

The subject-matter of R 10013 is covered in LC 4645(a)-(c). Under the LC provisions, all disputed issues regarding VRS are to be submitted initially to the O.B.D. Rehabilitation Unit for its recommendation, except in the following instances: Where a question regarding VRS is first raised before a workers' compensation judge, and there are good faith issues which if resolved against the employee would defeat his or her right to all workers' compensation benefits, the judge will determine those issues and, if appropriate, refer the question of entitlement to VRS to the O.B.D. Rehabilitation Unit for its recommendation. Where there is no issue concerning compensability of the injury, the VRS entitlement issue will be referred to the Unit for its recommendation before entering a finding, decision, or award on VRS. [NOTE: LC 4635(b) and (c) seem to limit the function of the Unit to making a recommendation to the workers' compensation judge who then makes the final determination regarding VRS entitlement where the issue is first raised before the judge. Formerly, under R 10013, the Bureau made a "determination" rather than a "recommendation."]

§ 16.14   Statutes of Limitation; Reopening

Pre-1990 Provisions

LC 5405.5
5410
5803
5804

An employee must request vocational rehabilitation within one year after the date of the last finding of permanent disability by the Appeals Board or within one year after the issuance of a Board order approving a compromise and release of other issues or benefits. Also, the employee may file an application seeking rehabilitation benefits within 5 years from the date of injury. Further, a petition to reopen a W.C.A.B. award or a decision of the Rehabilitation Bureau on this ground may be filed within 5 years from date of injury. If there is a pending proceeding before the Bureau in which the Bureau reserved jurisdiction, the Bureau may entertain a request for further benefits even though the request is received more than five years from date of injury. It is to be noted that the time-limit sections contemplate some type of procedure before the W.C.A.B. It appears that if the Board has made no decision in a case, the only time restriction is 5 years from date of injury under LC 5410. If the Board has made a determination regarding permanent disability, or approved a C & R, then the time is either one year after the Board decision or 5 years from date of injury, whichever is later.

R 10017

An employee may petition the Rehabilitation Bureau to reinstate vocational rehabilitation services after an order approving conclusion of such services has issued (Form RB-104). A request for reinstatement is subject to the time limits set forth in LC 5405.5, 5410, and 5803. Grounds for seeking reinstatement are: that the W.C.A.B. has determined that the employee's disability has changed to an extent requiring additional services; that the W.C.A.B. has ordered determination of entitlement or has vacated a previous decision concluding services; that the employee can substantiate that a plan was not provided; that the employee can demonstrate a change in circumstances which caused his or her nonavailability or refusal of services; that the previous plan did not prepare the employee for suitable gainful employment; that the order concluding services was based on incorrect information or error of the Bureau. The employer or carrier may agree to reinstatement after reviewing the employee's request.

Under the principles established by the Supreme Court in the *Reynolds, Webb,* and *Renfro* cases, these time periods do not begin to run unless the employee has been made aware of the potential right to vocational rehabilitation benefits. If an application or petition for rehabilitation benefits is filed with the W.C.A.B., either by way of original application or petition to reopen, the provisions of R 10013 will govern reference to the Bureau for its determination or recommendations.

1990 Provisions

Subdivision (d) of LC 4645 relating to appeals from decisions of the *LC 4645* O.B.D Rehabilitation Unit reserves to the parties the rights and limitations set forth in LC 5405.5, 5410, and 5803.

The one-year statute of limitations in LC 5405.5 remains unchanged; *LC 5405.5* however, the section was amended to make clear that it applies to vocational rehabilitation services as provided in LC 4635-4647.

The term "vocational rehabilitation services" is included in LC 5410, *LC 5410* and two grounds for invoking the right to seek such services within five years from date of injury have been added: that such services are feasible "because the employee's medical condition has improved," and, secondly, that they are feasible "because of other factors not capable of determination at the time the employer's liability for vocational rehabilitation services otherwise terminated." Note that this section deals with the jurisdiction of the W.C.A.B.

The provisions of LC 5803 were not changed since the section includes *LC 5803* decisions and orders of the Rehabilitation Unit within the authority of the Appeals Board for reopening upon the ground that an employee's disability has recurred, increased, diminished, or terminated.

§16.15 Rehabilitation Settlements; Lump-Sum Payments

Pre-1990 Provisions

The Appeals Board may not permit the commutation (lump-sum pay- *LC 5100.6* ment) or settlement of compensation or indemnity payments or other benefits to which the employee is entitled under rehabilitation. This statutory provision evidences the public-policy concern that benefits be utilized for the purpose for which intended, namely, to return the employee to suitable gainful employment or self-employment.

The W.C.A.B. has recognized a class of cases in which there are issues *R 10870* which if decided adversely to the employee would preclude him or her from receiving any workers' compensation benefits. In such cases, it would not serve the interests of justice to permit settlement on other issues, and leave the same issues open regarding rehabilitation. Such an issue would be whether there was, in fact, an industrial injury. Another would be whether the whole claim is barred by the statute of limitations. Based on this rationale and prior decisions, the Board promulgated the following language as a part of R 10870:

> . . . No agreement shall relieve an employer of liability for vocational rehabilitation benefits unless the Workers' Compensation Appeals Board makes a finding that there is a good faith issue which, if resolved against the injured employee, would defeat the employee's right to all workers' compensation benefits.

In applying this rule, the judges and the Board examine the record to ascertain the "good faith" of the parties in terms of facts showing the questionableness of the employee's case. For example, if, in a previous decision, industrial injury has already been established, no settlement of rehabilitation rights or waiver of them included in the C & R document would be deemed to be in "good faith." On the other hand, the Board may not arbitrarily disapprove such a settlement or strike the provision concerning rehabilitation. If the Board deems the record inadequate to determine the "good faith" issue, the parties must be given an opportunity to supply information or make a record to serve as the basis for the Board's review and determination.

1990 Provisions

LC 4646

The Legislature has adopted the rationale of the above-mentioned W.C.A.B. rule in LC 4646 which provides that settlement or commutation of VRS is not permitted (per LC 5100.6) except where there is a finding by a workers' compensation judge that there are good faith issues which if decided against the employee would defeat the employee's right to all workers' compensation benefits. Information regarding these provisions must be included in the notice given the employee as required by LC 4637(a)(5).

§ 16.16   Legal Representation; Attorneys

Pre-1990 Provisions

R 10014(d)

The vocational rehabilitation rules recognize that an employer, carrier, or employee may be represented by a "third party," i.e., an attorney or other representative. In this event, the name, address, and phone number of the representative must be filed with the Bureau. Notice of such representation filed

R 10007
(a)(6)

with the W.C.A.B. is not considered notice to the Bureau. Any notice of denial of liability for the provision of vocational rehabilitation benefits sent by an employer or carrier must inform the employee of his or her right to seek advice from an information and assistance officer of the D.I.A. or an attorney. A copy of every notice given an employee must be sent to his or her legal representative. A legal representative for an employee is to sign the

R 10006(d)
R 10011
(b)(12)
R 10007
(c), (e)

acceptance of an agreed plan. On submission of any disputed issue to the Bureau, the employer or carrier must serve copies of the request and all pertinent reports and notices upon the employee's legal representative. [NOTE: Due process principles require that a copy of any request or other document filed with the Bureau by an employee be served upon the employer or carrier and any legal representative of that party of record with the Bureau.]

If an employee's attorney or representative requests a fee, the matter will be referred to the W.C.A.B. for fee-setting in accordance with the Board's decision in the *Ponce DeLeon* case. The fee will be a lien against the employee's compensation and is not an obligation of the employer or carrier.

1990 Provisions

LC 4906
R 10122
10134
10987

The definition of VR "parties" in the rules includes the designated representatives of an employer or employee. An attorney representing an employee must give the employee a written disclosure statement on the form set out in R 10134. Fees for representation in a vocational rehabilitation matter are set by the W.C.A.B. The procedure in obtaining a fee determination involves submitting the question to the W.C.A.B. on an official form where there has been no prior proceeding before the Board. One requesting the setting of a fee must include information indicating the activity, nature of dispute, responsibility assumed, care shown in representation, estimate of the time involved, and the results obtained. A copy of the signed attorney disclosure statement must accompany the request form.

§ 16.17 Rehabilitation of Inmates of State Penal or Correctional Institutions

Inmates of state penal or correctional institutions who are injured while engaged in assigned work or employment during incarceration are entitled to vocational rehabilitation services in order to prepare them for suitable gainful employment upon their release. "Assigned work or employment" includes work performed in any pay or non-pay position in a work program under the direction and approval of an authorized inmate leadman, or supervisory leadman, or Department of Corrections employee. It includes physical fitness training and forestry training involved in fire-suppression assignments, but does not include activities in skill centers, vocational training, or academic education programs or other activities which are not encompassed within the assigned duties. "Inmate" means a person committed to the custody of the Department of Corrections and who is in a facility, camp, hospital, or institution of the department for the purpose of confinement, treatment, employment, training, or discipline. The term includes one who has been temporarily removed from a facility for the performance of assigned work, but does not include a prisoner who has escaped or who has been released on parole. Eligibility for services depends upon a finding that an injured inmate is a qualified injured worker. In addition to the notice requirements of R 10005, 10006, and 10007, the Director of Corrections is required to give formal notice of the availability of vocational rehabilitation services to industrially injured inmates disabled 28 calendar days or more. A copy of this notice is sent to the state Department of Rehabilitation. A vocational rehabilitation plan for a Q.I.W. inmate will be prepared by a qualified rehabilitation representative, chosen by the Department of Corrections, who may be an employee of the department or the Department of Rehabilitation. A plan may be based upon modified work or a work-position available at a place of incarceration or detention. Services are to be provided as soon as feasible and, if possible, before the inmate's release from custody. Notwithstanding R 10018, an inmate is not entitled to vocational rehabilitation temporary disability indemnity (VRTD) while serving in a state penal or correctional institution.

PC 5069
R 10021

§ 16.18 Fair Employment Practices

LC 1420 (Fair Employment Practices Act) was amended, effective July 1, 1974, to prohibit discrimination on the basis of "physical handicap." Exceptions are made where the handicap renders one unable to do the job or where the health or safety of others would be endangered. The law permits inquiry regarding physical fitness of applicants for peace officer positions.

§ 16.19 Administrative Director Rules and Forms

The following rules relating to vocational rehabilitation include Article 12 (Sections 10001 through 10021) of Subchapter 1, Title 8, California Code of Regulations. Approved forms are also set forth. These rules and forms apply to injuries occurring before 1990. The Article 12 regulations are followed by rules which include forms applicable to injuries occurring on or after January 1, 1990, comprising Article 7, (Sections 10122 through 10133) of Subchapter 1.5, Chapter 4.5, Title 8, California Code of Regulations. Also included are W.C.A.B. Rules 10955-10958 and 10992 applicable to appeals from Rehabilitation Unit determinations.

§ 16.20 Article 12: Vocational Rehabilitation

10001. Authority

The Rules and Regulations contained in Article 12 are adopted pursuant to the authority contained in Sections 133, 138.4, 139.5, and 5307.3 of the California Labor Code. (Reference: Chapter 1435, 1974 Stats.)

10002. Operative Date

The provisions of this article apply to industrial injuries or diseases occurring on or after January 1, 1975. The 1988 amendments to this article shall be effective on July 1, 1988 and shall apply to all pending and reopened cases on and after the date of adoption; provided, however, nothing in these amendments shall require the reopening on reconsideration of a final order of the bureau or appeals board.

10003. Definitions

As used in this Article:

(a) "Bureau" means the rehabilitation unit established within the Division of Industrial Accidents pursuant to Labor Code Section 139.5.

(b) "Employer" includes the insurer providing the security for the compensation required by Divisions 4 and 4.5 of the Labor Code, and the adjusting agency of a self-insured employer.

(c) "Qualified injured worker" means an employee:

(1) The effects of whose injury, whether or not combined with the effects of a prior injury or disability, if any, permanently preclude, or are likely to preclude the employee from engaging in his or her usual and customary occupation or the position in which he or she was engaged at the time of injury (hereinafter referred to as "medical eligibility"); and

(2) Who can reasonably be expected to return to suitable gainful employment through the provision of vocational rehabilitation services (hereinafter referred to as "vocational eligibility").

(d) "Qualified rehabilitation representative" means a person capable of developing and implementing the vocational rehabilitation plan, whose experience and regular duties involve the evaluation, counseling or placement of industrially injured workers.

(e) "Independent vocational evaluator" means a qualified rehabilitation representative who, in addition to the requirements of subsection (d), meets one of the following qualifications:

(1) A doctorate or master's degree in vocational counseling or its equivalent and one or more years full-time experience in vocational counseling of industrially injured employees.

(2) A doctor of medicine degree and one or more years full-time experience in psychiatric or psychological evaluation of disabled adults in relation to rehabilitation counseling.

(3) A doctorate or master's degree in counseling or psychology or their equivalent and two or more years full-time employment using rehabilitation counseling techniques and conducting vocational evaluations or psychological assessments of disabled adults under the direct supervision of an independent vocational evaluator.

(4) A baccalaureate degree in any field and three or more years full-time employment using rehabilitation counseling techniques and conducting vocational evaluations or psychological assessments of disabled adults under the direct supervision of an independent vocational evaluator.

(f) "Vocational rehabilitation services" means those services required to determine an employee's vocational eligibility and those services reasonably necessary to provide a qualified injured worker with the opportunity to return to suitable gainful employment. Such services may include, but are not limited to: vocational and medical evaluation; counseling; job analysis; assistance with job modification, alternative employment or job placement assistance; and retraining, including on-the-job training.

(g) "Vocational rehabilitation plan" means the written description of and rationale for the manner and means by which it is proposed a qualified injured worker may be provided the opportunity to return to suitable gainful employment. The plan may contemplate modification of the employee's occupation at the time of injury, provision for alternative work with the same employer, direct job placement assistance, on-the-job training, retraining, job placement assistance or self-employment.

(h) "Suitable gainful employment" means employment or self-employment which is reasonably attainable and which offers an opportunity to restore the employee as soon as practicable and as near as possible to maximum self support, due consideration being given to the employee's qualifications, vocational interests and aptitudes, pre-injury earnings and future earning capacity, and the present and future labor market. No one factor shall be considered solely in determining suitable gainful employment.

(i) "Vocational rehabilitation temporary disability indemnity" means the continuing temporary disability indemnity payments made during the time period in which the employee is entitled to receive vocational rehabilitation services and is no longer entitled to receive temporary total disability indemnity.

10004. Participation Not Required

Nothing in these rules shall require an employee to accept vocational rehabilitation services if the employee does not choose to do so.

10005. Reporting Requirements

All reports and notices required by this article shall be in the form and manner prescribed by the administrative director. The employer shall retain in its file an exact copy of all notices sent to the employee, and shall provide the bureau with a copy upon request. Forms and information concerning reporting procedures may be obtained from the bureau. Incomplete or improperly completed reports and notices submitted to the bureau may be returned to the sender for proper resubmission.

10006. Notice to Employee

(a) The employer shall advise the employee of his or her potential entitlement to vocational rehabilitation services and the procedure for requesting such services:

(1) Immediately upon knowledge that the employee's medical condition may permanently preclude a return to his or her usual and customary occupation or the position in which he or she was engaged at the time of injury; or

(2) When notice was not given as provided for in subsection (1), immediately following 180 aggregate days of total disability.

(b) When the employee has been notified as required by subsection (a) and it is subsequently asserted by the employer that the employee is not a qualified injured worker, the employer shall notify the employee that he or she is not entitled to vocational rehabilitation services, the reasons therefor, and the procedure for contesting the assertion; provided, however, notice shall not be required when the determination is made by the bureau.

(c) The employer shall also provide the employee, in the form and manner prescribed by the administrative director, with written notice and a copy submitted to the bureau of:

(1) The commencement of the provision of vocational rehabilitation services within 10 days of the date on which such services commenced.

(2) A delay in the determination of the employee's entitlement to vocational rehabilitation services or of the commencement of such services within 10 days of the date on which the determination or commencement should have occurred as provided for in this article.

(3) An interruption of 15 days or more of vocational rehabilitation services within 10 days of the date of first knowledge of such interruption. The notice shall contain the reasons for the interruption and the projected resumption date.

(d) The employer shall provide the employee's representative, if any, with copies of all notices.

10007. Reports to Bureau

(a) The employer shall submit to the bureau:

(1) All unresolved disputes concerning entitlement to and provision of vocational rehabilitation services and other entitlements provided for in this article.

(2) All vocational rehabilitation plans developed in accordance with Section 10011.

(3) All requests for interruption of vocational rehabilitation services which exceed 180 days in accordance with Section 10015.

(4) All requests for substantive changes in the amount or type of vocational rehabilitation services or other entitlements provided for in this article.

(5) All requests for termination of vocational rehabilitation services and other entitlements provided for in this article. Such requests shall include an accounting of all vocational rehabilitation benefits provided.

(6) All denials of liability for the provision of vocational rehabilitation services. Such reports shall inform the employee of the available remedies and the employees' right to seek information and advice from an information and assistance officer or attorney.

(b) The bureau may require submission of necessary medical and vocational reports to make determinations provided for in this article.

(c) Upon submission of an issue to the bureau, the employer shall concurrently provide to the bureau, to the employee, and to his or her representative, if any, copies of all pertinent reports and notices. Filing of such reports with the appeals board shall not constitute filing with the bureau.

(d) When liability for an injury is in dispute, neither the employer nor the employee shall report to or request the services of the bureau until the employer accepts liability or the appeals board finds the injury is compensable.

(e) The employer shall provide the employee's representative if any, with copies of all reports to the Bureau.

10008. Identification or Need for Vocational Rehabilitation Services

Where aggregate temporary total disability continues for 90 days, the employer shall request the employee's treating physician to report, based on a description of job duties furnished by the employer, whether the employee meets the requirements of medical eligibility specified in Paragraph (1) of subsection (c) of Section 10003 and report the opinion to the employer on a form prescribed by the administrative director. If the treating physician is unable to make the determination at that time, the employer shall request the treating physician to report, as soon as possible but no less frequently than every 90 days thereafter, until either the physician provides the opinion or the employee is released to return to work at his or her usual and customary occupation.

10009. Initiation of Vocational Rehabilitation Services

(a) The employer is responsible for the selection of the qualified rehabilitation representative in consultation with the employee. Within 10 days of knowledge that an employee may be medically eligible for vocational rehabilitation services, the employer shall provide the employee with the notice required by subsection (a) of Section 10006. Immediately thereafter, unless the employee's medical condition precludes participation or the employee refuses the provision of vocational rehabilitation services, the employer shall, in consultation with the employee, assign a qualified rehabilitation representative to evaluate the employee's vocational eligibility.

(b) If agreement cannot be reached, either the employer or employee shall request the bureau to assign a qualified rehabilitation representative. Within 15 days of the date of request, the bureau shall appoint an independent vocational evaluator in accordance with subsection (b) of Section 10010.

(c) A referral to a qualified rehabilitation representative shall be accompanied by all medical and vocational reports. Within 15 days of receipt of a request, the qualified rehabilitation representative shall conduct an initial evaluation. When the vocational eligibility evaluation establishes that the employee is a qualified injured worker, the qualified rehabilitation representative shall immediately proceed with the provision of vocational rehabilitation services to develop a proposed vocational rehabilitation plan. Within 90 days of the qualified rehabilitation representative's initial evaluation, the employer shall either:

(1) Submit a vocational rehabilitation plan to the employee as provided for in this Article; except as provided for in subsections (d) and (e);

(2) Notify the employee that he or she is not a qualified injured worker and the reason for such determination in accordance with subsection (b) of Section 10006; or

(3) Request the bureau to resolve a dispute concerning qualified injured worker status or the provision of vocational rehabilitation services.

(d) When the qualified rehabilitation representative cannot develop a vocational rehabilitation plan for the employer to submit to the bureau within 90 days of the initial evaluation, the qualified rehabilitation representative shall notify the employer and employee of the reason why a plan could not be developed and of the estimated time to complete plan development. The notification must contain satisfactory explanation of good cause for the extension of time. A copy of the notification shall be attached to the plan provided for in Section 10011 when the plan is submitted to the bureau for approval.

(e) The employer or employee, when able to substantiate that plan development is not proceeding expeditiously, may request the bureau to determine if the process should be expedited and to resolve any disputes concerning the provision of vocational rehabilitation services. Pending a determination by the bureau, the employee shall continue to receive vocational rehabilitation services and vocational rehabilitation temporary disability indemnity. Within 30 days of the submission of necessary information by the employer, employee and qualified rehabilitation representative, the bureau shall issue its decision, including the reasons therefor and set the date by which the plan shall be submitted to the bureau.

(f) If the employer fails to voluntarily provide vocational rehabilitation services and the employee can substantiate the need for such services, the employee may request the bureau, on a form prescribed by the administrative director, to order the provision of vocational rehabilitation services at the expense of the employer. The employee may request that vocational rehabilitation services be provided by a qualified rehabilitation representative of his or her choice. Copies of such requests shall be served on the other parties by the employee. Within 20 days of the date of the bureau's notification, the employer shall either:

(1) Agree to provide vocational rehabilitation services; or

(2) Establish through medical and vocational reports that the employee is not a qualified injured worker.

(g) If the employer fails to respond within 20 days of the date of the bureau's notification, the bureau shall:

(1) Order an examination by an independent medical examiner at the expense of the employer if the opinions expressed in the medical record do not enable the bureau to determine medical eligibility; or

(2) If the employee is medically eligible, order the provision of vocational rehabilitation services at the expense of the employer by a qualified rehabilitation representative selected by the employee or, at the employee's request, by the bureau.

(h) Nothing in this section shall preclude the employer and employee from agreeing to a change of or a consultation with a qualified rehabilitation representative. If agreement cannot be reached within 15 days of the request, the employer or employee may request the bureau to order a change or a consultation. The bureau, within 15 days of receipt of the employer or employee's request, shall order a change or consultation if it finds the need to be in the best interests of the parties.

10010. Independent Vocational Evaluators

(a) The bureau chief shall develop a procedure for compiling a list of qualified independent vocational evaluators. Such evaluators shall meet the requirements of subsection (e) of Section 10003 and present evidence of their ability and experience in the evaluation, plan development and placement of industrially injured workers. The listing may include the evaluator's second language, if any, and other information pertinent to the provision of vocational rehabilitation services. The list shall be reviewed annually and revised as needed.

(b) The bureau chief shall establish a procedure that requires the appointment of an independent vocational evaluator on a rotational basis from a list of all independent vocational evaluators in a designated geographic area determined by the bureau chief. The bureau shall make the appointment within 15 days of either its determination of the need for the evaluation or receipt of a request for an independent vocational evaluation. When necessary and appropriate vocational rehabilitation services cannot be provided within 15 days of appointment, the bureau shall appoint the next evaluator on the list.

(c) The bureau may order that vocational rehabilitation services be provided by an independent vocational evaluator at the expense of the employer upon a finding of any of the following:

(1) The employer failed to provide vocational rehabilitation services in a timely manner.

(2) An independent evaluation is necessary for the bureau to determine if an employee is vocationally eligible.

(3) An independent evaluation is necessary to determine if a vocational rehabilitation plan meets the requirements of this article.

(4) The employee and qualified rehabilitation representative cannot agree on a vocational goal.

(d) The independent vocational evaluator shall report directly to the bureau and serve copies of the report on all parties to the case. Except for communications between the evaluator and the employee or employer which are necessary for the evaluator to complete the evaluation, no party shall communicate with the independent vocational evaluator regarding the case unless otherwise directed by the bureau.

10011. Vocational Rehabilitation Plans

(a) Unless the qualified injured worker refuses vocational rehabilitation services, the employer shall, within the time specified in subsections (c) and (d) of Section 10009, submit a vocational rehabilitation plan, developed by a qualified rehabilitation representative, to the employee. The employee shall review the plan and either agree or object within 15 days of its submission by the employer.

(b) The plan shall define the responsibilities of the employer, employee, qualified rehabilitation representative and other parties or facilities in implementing the plan. The plan shall contain the following information:

(1) The names, addresses and telephone numbers of the insurer, self-insured employer or adjusting agency; the qualified rehabilitation representative; the employee; and the employee's representative, if any.

(2) The DIA identification number of the insurer, self-insured employer or adjusting agency; the bureau case number; and the appeals board case number, if any.

(3) The employee's birthdate, social security number, occupation, average weekly earnings at the time of injury, date of injury and a description of the nature of the injury.

(4) The date disability commenced; a description of the employee's medical limitations, ability to participate in the plan and function in the proposed occupation; and the name of the reporting physician.

(5) The suitable gainful employment objective of the plan, the rationale for choosing the plan objective, a projection of employment opportunities and an estimate of earnings expected upon successful completion of the plan.

(6) The type of plan: either modified job or alternative employment with the same employer; direct placement with a new employer; on-the-job training; vocational training; or self employment.

(7) The expected dates of commencement and completion of the plan.

(8) The nature, extent and duration of vocational rehabilitation services, including training, placement assistance and counseling to be provided during the plan.

(9) The weekly rate at which temporary disability indemnity will be paid; transportation expenses; additional living expenses; funds for purchase of books, supplies, tools, equipment and tuition; other items or services required by the plan, if any; and the time and manner of payments to be made to the employee or provider of services.

(10) The responsibilities of the employer, employee, qualified rehabilitation representative and any other persons and entities involved in implementing and completing the plan.

(11) The signature of the qualified rehabilitation representative who developed the plan.

(12) Acceptance of the plan and signatures of the employer, employee, and employee's representative, if any.

(c) When the employer or employee object to a proposed plan and agreement cannot be reached on modification within 15 days of the objection, the employer shall immediately submit the plan and a statement of the disagreement to the bureau with a request that the bureau aid in the resolution of the dispute.

(d) Subject to the approval of the bureau as provided in Section 10012, agreement of the employer and employee to a proposed plan shall be deemed to be an agreement that the employer and employee intend to comply with all of the plan's provisions. Material breach of the agreement by the employer may result in the bureau ordering either an extension of the plan or development of a new plan, during which time the employee shall continue to be paid vocational rehabilitation temporary disability indemnity. Material breach of the agreement by the employee may result, after the employer has provided the employee with a written warning explaining the breach and the possible consequences and the employee does not terminate the breach within 10 days of the warning, in the bureau ordering the termination of entitlement to vocational rehabilitation benefits.

(e) The following shall be presumed to be evidence of a material breach of the agreement:

(1) Failure of the employer to provide the employee with necessary funds or services in sufficient time to enable the employee to participate in the vocational rehabilitation services specified in the plan.

(2) Failure of the employee to notify the qualified rehabilitation representative within 5 days of his or her inability to comply with the provisions of the approved plan; and the reason why he or she was not available to

receive the vocational rehabilitation services specified in the plan, including attendance at classes.

(f) As soon as the qualified injured worker's medical condition permits, implementation of the vocational rehabilitation plan shall begin upon bureau approval, when required, or the date specified in the plan, whichever date first occurs; however, plan commencement shall not be deemed approval.

(g) Nothing in this section shall preclude the employer or employee from requesting the bureau to approve a modification of the plan because of unforeseen circumstances arising subsequent to the prior plan agreement.

10012. Plan Approval

(a) All vocational rehabilitation plans shall be submitted to the bureau for approval within 15 days of agreement to the plan by the employer and employee except as provided for in subsection (b).

(b) A vocational rehabilitation plan that provides for modified or alternative work with the same employer and has been agreed to by the qualified injured worker shall not be subject to bureau approval prior to implementation. The employer shall submit such plans to the bureau upon completion, together with a request to conclude vocational rehabilitation services as provided for in Section 10016.

(c) Within 30 days of receipt of a plan, the bureau shall approve or disapprove the plan and advise the employer, employee and qualified rehabilitation representative of its action. In reaching a decision, the bureau may request additional information, confer with the employer, employee and qualified rehabilitation representative, and otherwise seek agreement on the terms and conditions of the plan. If approval or disapproval is not made by the bureau within 30 days of receipt of the plan and all requirements of this article have been met, the plan shall be deemed approved unless the employer or employee files a written objection within 30 days of the bureau's receipt of the plan.

(d) Rehabilitation plans which utilize an employee's transferable skills and experience for placement in modified or alternative work with the same employer or propose direct job placement with a similar employer, providing the employee will have wages, hours, and working conditions similar to those at the time of injury, due consideration being given to suitable gainful employment, shall be preferable to those plans which propose training for an occupation in which the employee has no skills or experience, provided the employee has the skills necessary to compete for other available employment at wages similar to those at the time of injury if the modified or alternative work later becomes unavailable.

(e) Where a question arises concerning the comparative length of alternative training plans of equal merit, preference shall be given to the plan which expedites the worker's return to suitable gainful employment.

(f) A vocational rehabilitation plan submitted subsequent to an approved plan shall not be approved by the bureau unless the qualified injured worker can substantiate one of the following:

(1) The original plan is no longer feasible because of a change of permanent disability;

(2) The original plan was not completed because conditions provided for in the plan could not be reasonably met; or

(3) The original plan has not prepared the qualified injured worker for suitable gainful employment.

10013. Entitlement Issues

(a) All matters regarding the question of entitlement to and provision of vocational rehabilitation benefits shall be submitted initially to the bureau, except as otherwise provided for in this section.

(b) Where the question of entitlement to vocational rehabilitation benefits is first raised before a workers' compensation judge and there are good faith issues which, if resolved against the employee, would defeat his or her right to all compensation, the judge shall first determine the compensability of the injury and, if the injury is compensable, then refer the question of entitlement to vocational rehabilitation benefits to the bureau for determination.

(c) Where the question of entitlement to vocational rehabilitation benefits is first raised before a workers' compensation judge and there are no issues which would bar the employee's right to compensation, the workers' compensation judge shall refer the question of entitlement to vocational rehabilitation benefits to the bureau for its determination before making a finding, decision or award on the issue of the employee's entitlement to vocational rehabilitation benefits.

10014. Bureau Resolution of Disputes

(a) Where there is a question concerning an employee's entitlement to vocational rehabilitation benefits, or the employer's alleged failure to provide vocational rehabilitation services as required by this article, or where a proposed vocational rehabilitation plan is unacceptable to the employer or qualified injured worker, either the employer or the employee may request the bureau to make a determination. All such requests shall be submitted to the bureau on a form prescribed by the administrative director together with all medical and vocational reports not previously submitted to the bureau. A copy of the request shall be served concurrently on the other parties. The opposing party shall, within 15 days of service of the request, submit its written position on the request together with copies of all medical and vocational reports not previously submitted to the bureau.

(b) To make its determination, the bureau may make a decision based on the records submitted, conduct a conference or require the employer and employee to meet and confer to either resolve the issues or frame issues for consideration by the bureau. The bureau shall either issue its decision or schedule a conference to be held within 45 days of the request provided for in Subsection (a). When a conference is held, the case shall be submitted for bureau decision at the conference, or upon receipt of additional information requested by the bureau at the conference; and the bureau shall issue its decision within 30 days of submission.

(c) If either the employer or employee fails to comply with the findings, the bureau may petition the appeals board for enforcement and, where appropriate, assessment of any penalty permitted by the Labor Code.

(d) When an employer or employee chooses to be represented by a third party in matters before the bureau, the bureau shall be notified immediately, in writing, of the name, address and telephone number of said representative. Notice to the appeals board of representation shall not be considered notice to the bureau.

(e) Any finding, decision or order of the bureau shall be binding unless a petition to appeal the finding, decision or order is filed with the appeals board within 20 days after service of the bureau's findings, decision or order. A copy of the petition shall be served concurrently on the bureau. The time requirements of Section 1013 of the Civil Procedure Code shall govern all service by mail.

10015. Interruption of Services

(a) The provision of vocational rehabilitation services may be interrupted for good cause upon request of the employee and agreement by the employer or, in the absence of agreement, upon a determination by the bureau as provided for in Section 10014. In no event shall the duration of interruption of services exceed six months, except when approved by the bureau.

(b) Where vocational rehabilitation services have been interrupted, either by agreement or a determination of the bureau, the employee shall have the responsibility to request in writing that the employer reinstate services before expiration of the period of interruption. If the employer fails to resume services, the employee may request the bureau to resolve the dispute as provided for in subsection (b) of Section 10014. If the employee fails to request reinstatement timely, the employer may request bureau determination of conclusion of vocational rehabilitation services as provided for in Section 10016.

10016. Conclusion of Vocational Rehabilitation Services

(a) The provision of vocational rehabilitation services to an employee may be concluded when the bureau determines that:

(1) The qualified injured worker completed an approved vocational rehabilitation plan;

(2) The employee is not a qualified injured worker or the employee failed to cooperate in the provision of vocational rehabilitation services to determine the employee's eligibility as a qualified injured worker;

(3) The qualified injured worker unreasonably failed to complete an approved vocational rehabilitation plan;

(4) The employee declined, in the form and manner prescribed by the administrative director, to accept the provision of vocational rehabilitation services;

(5) The employee failed to request timely reinstatement of vocational rehabilitation services; or

(6) All necessary and reasonable vocational rehabilitation services have been provided.

(b) Requests for bureau approval of conclusion of vocational rehabilitation services shall be submitted by the employer to the bureau and a copy served concurrently on the employee.

(c) The employer's request for bureau determination of conclusion of vocational rehabilitation services shall be deemed granted unless: the employee, within 20 days of the employer's request, submits a written objection to the bureau and serves a copy on the employer; or the Bureau determines that the request for conclusion of vocational rehabilitation services was inappropriate. The bureau shall, within 30 days of receipt of the request, issue its decision on all requests for approval of conclusion of vocational rehabilitation services, except as provided in subsection (d).

(d) When the employee objects to the employer's request for bureau determination of conclusion of vocational rehabilitation services, the bureau shall, within 30 days of the employee's objection, hold a conference or otherwise obtain the employee's reasons for objection together with substantiating evidence and issue its decision on the employer's request.

10017. Reinstatement of Vocational Rehabilitation Benefits

(a) The employee may, following bureau determination of conclusion of vocational rehabilitation services as provided for in Section 10016 and subject to the limitations of Sections 5405.5, 5410, and 5803 of the Labor Code, request the bureau to make a determination on his or her need for and entitlement to reinstatement of vocational rehabilitation benefits when:

(1) The appeals board has determined that the employee's disability has changed to the extent that additional vocational rehabilitation services may be required;

(2) The appeals board has ordered that the entitlement to vocational rehabilitation services is to be determined by the bureau or that a prior determination by the bureau to conclude vocational rehabilitation services is vacated;

(3) The employee can substantiate that either a vocational rehabilitation plan was not provided; the circumstances which caused the qualified injured worker to be unavailable for or decline the provision of vocational rehabilitation services have changed; or the plan did not prepare the employee for obtaining suitable gainful employment, as required by this article; or

(4) The conclusion of vocational rehabilitation services was based on incorrect information or error of the bureau.

(b) The employer and employee shall not be precluded by this section from agreeing to the reinstatement of vocational rehabilitation services, contingent upon their compliance with other applicable provisions of this Article.

10018. Vocational Rehabilitation Temporary Disability Indemnity

An employee shall be entitled to continuous payment of vocational rehabilitation temporary disability indemnity during the period of his or her entitlement to vocational rehabilitation services, including the period of participation in eligibility evaluation, participation in plan development and during pendency of plan approval and implementation. However, entitlement to such payment in addition to any other requirement shall be contingent upon the employee's voluntary participation in and availability to receive vocational rehabilitation services. Vocational rehabilitation temporary disability indemnity shall be payable in the same manner and at the same rate as temporary disability indemnity.

10019. Bureau File Retention

(a) The bureau shall retain its files until five years from date of injury, one year from the last request for vocational rehabilitation services, or one year from date of conclusion of vocational rehabilitation services, whichever occurs last, except that the retention time shall be extended to 90 days beyond a final decision of the appeals board on a petition which appeals a bureau finding, decision or order.

(b) When the parties, subsequent to the time limits in subsection (a), request a determination by the bureau, the bureau may require the parties to provide copies of pertinent notices, reports and documents which are necessary for the bureau to make its determination.

10020. Enforcement of Notice and Reporting Requirements

(a) Where an insurer, self-insured employer or adjusting agent has habitually and as a matter of custom and practice failed to meet the notification and reporting requirements of this article, the administrative director may request the insurance commissioner or the Director of Industrial Relations, as the case may be, to audit and enforce such requirements pursuant to the authority provided for in Section 129 of the Labor Code.

(b) The administrative director may, at any time, require submission of specific reports that he or she deems necessary to effectuate the purpose and provisions of this article.

10021. Rehabilitation of Industrially Injured Inmates

(a) Under the provisions of Chapter 1347 of the Statutes of 1976, inmates of a state penal or correctional institution may be eligible for workers' compensation benefits, including the provision of vocational rehabilitation services, for injuries which occur during their incarceration and while engaged in assigned work or employment. As used in this section:

(1) "Assigned work or employment" means work performed in any pay or nonpay position in a work program under the direction and with the approval of a duly authorized inmate leadman or supervisory leadman or Department of Corrections employee. The term does not include skill centers, vocational training or academic education programs (except for physical fitness training and forestry training which are authorized by Labor Code Section 3365 as prerequisites to fire suppression duties) or activities which are clearly not encompassed within the duties and responsibilities of the position to which assigned.

(2) "Inmate of a state penal or correctional institution" means a person committed to the custody of the Department of Corrections; and who is in a facility, camp, hospital, or institution of the Department of Corrections for the purpose of confinement, treatment, employment, training, or discipline; or who has been temporarily removed by the Department of Corrections from a facility under its jurisdiction with or without custody, for the performance of assigned work. The term does not include a prisoner who has escaped or who has been released on parole.

(3) "Qualified rehabilitation representative," notwithstanding subsection (d) of Section 10003, means a person capable of developing and implementing the plan submitted pursuant to Section 10011, and employed by the Department of Rehabilitation or the Department of Corrections.

(4) "Director," as cited in subdivision (b) of Section 5096 of the Penal Code, means the Director of Corrections. In addition to the requirements of Sections 10005, 10006 and 10007, the Director of Corrections shall provide notice of the availability of vocational rehabilitation services to inmates dis-

abled for 28 calendar days or more, on a form prescribed by the director. A copy of such form shall be sent to the Department of Rehabilitation.

(b) Notwithstanding Section 10018, an injured inmate who otherwise qualifies for vocational rehabilitation services shall not be entitled to vocational rehabilitation temporary disability indemnity while serving in a state penal or correctional institution.

(c) Vocational rehabilitation services to determine an inmate's eligibility as a qualified injured worker, and to develop any required vocational rehabilitation plan, shall be provided by a qualified rehabilitation representative chosen by the Department of Corrections. Such services shall be provided the inmate as soon as it is feasible and prior to the inmate's release from custody, if possible, with the intent of preparing the inmate for suitable gainful employment upon release. Nothing shall bar the development and implementation of a plan, however, prior to the inmate's release, using modified work or an otherwise suitable work position meeting the definition of assigned work or employment under subsection (a) of this section.

FORM COLOR: BUFF

STATE OF CALIFORNIA
DEPARTMENT OF INDUSTRIAL RELATIONS
DIVISION OF INDUSTRIAL ACCIDENTS
REHABILITATION BUREAU

**TREATING PHYSICIAN'S REPORT OF
DISABILITY STATUS**

TO: _____

_____

_____

_____

INSTRUCTIONS FOR PHYSICIAN: The employer or its insurer is required by the California Administrative Code to solicit the treating physician's opinion concerning the injured worker's ability to return to work for all industrial injuries which caused disability exceeding 90 days. The physician shall complete this form and return it to the sender listed below within 15 days of receipt of this request.

SENDER NAME (Employer/Insurer/Adjusting Agent):		
ADDRESS:		
CITY:	STATE:	ZIP:
EMPLOYER NAME:		CLAIM #:
EMPLOYEE NAME: (First) (Middle) (Last)		DATE OF INJURY:

Attached is a description of the job duties (on DIA Form RB-91) furnished by the employer. Based on your examination, including the history provided by the patient and the enclosed job description, choose one of the following:

1. ☐ The employee should be able to return to his or her previous employment on or about ___ / ___ / ___.

2. ☐ The employee will be precluded or is likely to be precluded from engaging in his or her previous employment.

3. ☐ It is premature to give my opinion concerning the employee's ability to return to his or her previous employment. I should be able to provide such an opinion on or about ___ / ___ / ___.

Physician's comments:

PHYSICIAN'S NAME:	DATE:
PHYSICIAN'S SIGNATURE:	

DIA FORM RB-90

FORM COLOR: BUFF

STATE OF CALIFORNIA
DEPARTMENT OF INDUSTRIAL RELATIONS
DIVISION OF INDUSTRIAL ACCIDENTS
REHABILITATION BUREAU

**DESCRIPTION OF EMPLOYEE'S
JOB DUTIES**

INSTRUCTIONS FOR EMPLOYER: This form shall be completed by the employer or by the insurer in consultation with the employer for inclusion with the request for the Treating Physician's Report of Disability Status (DIA Form RB-90) for all industrial injuries which caused disability exceeding 90 days. This description shall delineate the specific duties performed by this employee.

EMPLOYEE NAME: (First) (Middle) (Last)	CLAIM #:
EMPLOYER NAME:	LOCATION/DEPARTMENT:
JOB TITLE:	NO. OF HOURS PER WORK DAY:

DESCRIPTION OF JOB DUTIES:

MAKE THE APPROPRIATE ENTRY FOR EACH OF THE FOLLOWING ITEMS TO DESCRIBE THE EXTENT OF THE SPECIFIC ACTIVITY PERFORMED BY THIS EMPLOYEE.

NUMBER OF HOURS
0   1-2   3-4   5-6   7+

1. SITTING
2. STANDING
3. WALKING
4. BENDING OVER
5. CRAWLING
6. CLIMBING
7. REACHING OVERHEAD
8. CROUCHING
9. KNEELING
10. BALANCING
11. PUSHING OR PULLING
12. LIFTING OR CARRYING
   A. 10 LBS. OR LESS
   B. 11 TO 25 LBS.
   C. 26 TO 50 LBS.
   D. 51 TO 75 LBS.
   E. 76 TO 100 LBS.
   F. OVER 100 LBS.

NUMBER OF HOURS
0   1-2   3-4   5-6   7+

13. REPETITIVE USE OF FOOT CONTROL
   A. RIGHT ONLY
   B. LEFT ONLY
   C. BOTH
14. REPETITIVE USE OF HANDS
   A. RIGHT ONLY
   B. LEFT ONLY
   C. BOTH
15. GRASPING
   A. SIMPLE/LIGHT
      (1) RIGHT ONLY
      (2) LEFT ONLY
      (3) BOTH
   B. FIRM/STRONG
      (1) RIGHT ONLY
      (2) LEFT ONLY
      (3) BOTH
16. FINE DEXTERITY
   A. RIGHT ONLY
   B. LEFT ONLY
   C. BOTH

YES   NO   DESCRIPTION

17. DRIVING CARS, TRUCKS, FORKLIFTS AND OTHER EQUIPMENT
18. OTHERWISE BEING AROUND EQUIPMENT AND MACHINERY
19. WALKING ON UNEVEN GROUND
20. EXPOSURE TO DUST, GAS OR FUMES
21. EXPOSURE TO MARKED CHANGES IN TEMPERATURE OR HUMIDITY.

COMMENTS: (Attach separate sheet or use reverse side if needed.)

PREPARER'S NAME:	TITLE:
PREPARER'S SIGNATURE:	DATE:

DIA FORM RB-91

FORM COLOR: GOLDENROD (dark yellow)

STATE OF CALIFORNIA
DEPARTMENT OF INDUSTRIAL RELATIONS
DIVISION OF INDUSTRIAL ACCIDENTS
REHABILITATION BUREAU

CASE INITIATION DOCUMENT

REHAB BUREAU USE ONLY

INSTRUCTIONS: This form shall be completed and attached to all requests for Bureau action on matters for which no Rehabilitation Bureau case number has been assigned. Form must be typed and submitted to the appropriate Rehab Bureau office.

	First	*Middle*	*Last*

EMPLOYEE NAME: _____ SEX: _____

ADDRESS (include city, state & zip): _____

DATE OF BIRTH: __/__/__   SOC SEC # ___-__-____   PHONE # _____

NATURE OF INJURY: _____ **DATE OF INJURY:** __/__/__

EMPLOYER NAME: _____

MAILING ADDRESS (incl city, state, zip): _____

DIA ID #   _-____-__-___ (___)

INSURANCE CARRIER / SELF-INSURED CERTIFICATE NAME: _____

ADJUSTING AGENCY NAME (if agency adjusted): _____

CLAIMS MAILING ADDRESS (incl city, state, zip): _____

PHONE # _____   INSURER CLAIM # _____

EMPLOYEE'S REP: _____ PHONE # _____

FIRM NAME: _____   DIA FIRM # (if known): __ __ __ __ __

MAILING ADDRESS (incl city, state, zip): _____

EMPLOYER'S REP: _____   DIA FIRM # (if known): __ __ __ __ __

MAILING ADDRESS (incl city, state, zip): _____

QUALIFIED REHAB REP: _____ PHONE # _____

FIRM NAME: _____   DIA FIRM # (if known): __ __ __ __ __

MAILING ADDRESS (incl city, state & zip): _____

SUBMITTED BY: _____   TITLE: _____

SIGNATURE: _____   DATE: __/__/__

DIA FORM RB-101 (new 7/88)

392

FORM COLOR: BLUE

STATE OF CALIFORNIA
DEPARTMENT OF INDUSTRIAL RELATIONS
DIVISION OF INDUSTRIAL ACCIDENTS
REHABILITATION BUREAU

VOCATIONAL REHABILITATION PLAN

REHAB BUREAU USE ONLY

INSTRUCTIONS: This form shall be used for submitting vocational rehabilitation plans to the Rehabilitation Bureau. The form shall be prepared by the qualified rehabilitation representative and presented to the employee. When the plan is signed by the parties, the employer/insurer shall submit this form and all medical and vocational reports, not previously submitted, to the appropriate Rehabilitation Bureau office. If a Rehabilitation Bureau case number has not been assigned, attach a completed Case Initiation Document (DIA Form RB-101).

SECTION A

EMPLOYEE NAME: (First) (Middle) (Last) | RB CASE #:

EMPLOYER/INSURER NAME:

QUALIFIED REHABILITATION REPRESENTATIVE NAME:

This Vocational Rehabilitation Plan (DIA Form RB-102) shall be the written agreement of the employer and employee to a proposed plan developed by the qualified rehabilitation representative and is subject to the approval of the Rehabilitation Bureau. This plan shall contain a written description of and rationale for the manner and means by which it is proposed a qualified injured worker may be provided the opportunity to return to suitable gainful employment.

SECTION B

OCCUPATION AT INJURY: | DOT CODE: | EARNINGS AT INJURY: $_____ per _____ | DATE DISABILITY COMMENCED: ___ / ___ / ___

DESCRIPTION OF MEDICAL LIMITATIONS (Identify the medical report relied upon):

SUMMARY OF EMPLOYEE'S EDUCATIONAL AND VOCATIONAL BACKGROUND:

SECTION C

VOCATIONAL OBJECTIVE: | DOT CODE:

ESTIMATED WEEKLY EARNINGS UPON COMPLETION: $ _____

LIST ALTERNATIVES FOR VOCATIONAL OBJECTIVE AND THE REASON NOT SELECTED:

RATIONALE FOR SELECTION OF VOCATIONAL OBJECTIVE:

INITIALS

DIA FORM RB-102 (4 PAGES) - PG. 1

FORM COLOR: BLUE

SECTION D
TYPE OF PLAN

WITH THE SAME EMPLOYER
1. ☐ MODIFIED JOB
2. ☐ ALTERNATIVE WORK

WITH A NEW EMPLOYER
3. ☐ DIRECT PLACEMENT
4. ☐ ON-THE-JOB TRAINING
5. ☐ EDUCATIONAL RETRAINING
6. ☐ SELF-EMPLOYMENT

DO NOT COMPLETE SECTION "G' OF FORM.

COMPLETE ALL SECTIONS OF FORM

SECTION E

DESCRIBE NATURE AND EXTENT OF REHABILITATION PLAN:

EXPLAIN WHY THE EMPLOYEE SHOULD BE ABLE TO PERFORM THE DUTIES OF THE NEW OCCUPATION. IDENTIFY THE MEDICAL REPORT RELIED UPON:

PLAN COMMENCEMENT DATE:
___ / ___ / ___

DURATION OF PLAN:
Date QRR Selected: ___ / ___ / ___
Date of Initial Evaluation: ___ / ___ / ___
Date Plan Submitted to Employee: ___ / ___ / ___

EXPECTED COMPLETION DATE (including placement assistance):
___ / ___ / ___

Number of weeks training: _____
Number of weeks placement assistance: _____

Explain reason when plan development exceeds 90 days:

INITIALS

DIA FORM RB-102 (4 PAGES) - PG. 2

FORM COLOR: BLUE

SECTION F

RESPONSIBILITIES OF THE EMPLOYER:

The employer or it's insurer shall timely provide all vocational rehabilitation services and benefits necessitated by the approved vocational rehabilitation plan. The rate of payment of temporary disability indemnity shall be modified for wages earned on a wage loss basis and for allowable liens; and adjusted, where applicable, in accordance with Labor Code Section 4661.5.

The employer/insurer shall continue to provide, within ten days of receipt, the employee or his or her representative with copies of all vocational reports during the provision of vocational rehabilitation services.

Other:

RESPONSIBILITIES OF THE EMPLOYEE:

The employee shall be available to receive and participate in the provision of vocational rehabilitation services. The employee shall attend and arrive on time for all scheduled activities; and, if for any reason he or she does not, must immediately notify the qualified rehabilitation representative of the reason therefor.

The employee shall follow the requirements of all facilities and persons providing vocational rehabilitation services. The employee shall notify the Qualified Rehabilitation Representative about anything that may interfere with scheduled completion of this plan.

Other:

SECTION G

List vocational tests conducted and state how the results of such tests led to the selection of the plan objective:

Explain how the employee's transferable skills have been used in the selection of the plan objective:

Explain why the Qualified Rehabilitation Representative predicts that the employee will be employable in the vocational objective of the plan:

INITIALS

DIA FORM RB-102 (4 PAGES) - PG. 3

FORM COLOR: BLUE

SECTION H
PLAN FISCAL PROVISIONS

Temporary disability indemnity will be paid to the employee at the weekly rate of $_____ from ___ / ___ / ___ until completion of the plan. Such payments shall not be made less frequently than twice per month. If any amount is withheld from temporary disability indemnity because of attorney's fees and liens, describe withholding method.

Adequate transportation expenses will be paid to the employee in advance as follows (Describe method of calculation and disbursement.):

Retraining costs will be paid as follows:

Other costs specified in this plan will be paid as follows:

SECTION I
VERIFICATION OF THE Q.R.R.

This plan was developed by me as the Qualified Rehabilitation Representative or as an Independent Vocational Evaluator and I recommend its approval because it is my opinion that the services contained in this plan will provide the employee with the opportunity to return to suitable gainful employment.

QRR SIGNATURE:	DATE: ___ / ___ / ___

SECTION J
PLAN AGREEMENT

Subject to the approval of the Rehabilitation Bureau, agreement of the employer and employee to a proposed plan shall be deemed to be an agreement that the employer and employee intend to comply with all of the plan's provisions. Material breach of the agreement by the employer may result in the Bureau ordering either an extension of the plan or development of a new plan, during which time the employee shall continue to be paid vocational rehabilitation temporary disability indemnity. Material breach of the agreement by the employee may result, after the employer has provided the employee with a written warning explaining the breach and the possible consequences and the employee does not terminate the breach within 10 days of the warning, in the Bureau ordering the termination of entitlement to vocational rehabilitation benefits.

I have read and understand this plan and agree to comply with all of the plan's provisions.

NAME OF EMPLOYER/INSURER:	SIGNATURE:	DATE: ___ / ___ / ___
NAME OF EMPLOYER/INSURER REPRESENTATIVE:	SIGNATURE:	DATE: ___ / ___ / ___
NAME OF EMPLOYEE:	SIGNATURE:	DATE: ___ / ___ / ___
NAME OF EMPLOYEE REPRESENTATIVE:	SIGNATURE:	DATE: ___ / ___ / ___

PERSONS SIGNING THIS SECTION SHALL ALSO INITIAL OTHER THREE PAGES IN INITIALS BOX

DIA FORM RB-102 (4 PAGES) - PG. 4

FORM COLOR: GREEN

STATE OF CALIFORNIA
DEPARTMENT OF INDUSTRIAL RELATIONS
DIVISION OF INDUSTRIAL ACCIDENTS
REHABILITATION BUREAU

REQUEST FOR DISPUTE RESOLUTION

	REHAB BUREAU USE ONLY

INSTRUCTIONS: This form is to be used when either the employer, the employee or their representative is unable to resolve disputed rehabilitation issues and a determination by the Bureau is requested. The completed form must be accompanied by all medical and vocational reports and any other pertinent information not previously submitted to the Bureau. The request must be sent to the appropriate Bureau office. If a Rehabilitation Bureau case number has not been assigned, attach a completed Case Initiation Document (DIA Form RB-101). Do not use this form when liability for the injury is disputed or as an initial request for or reinstatement of rehabilitation benefits.

EMPLOYEE NAME: (First)	(Middle)	(Last)	RB CASE #:

The Rehabilitation Bureau is requested to resolve the following dispute(s) because the parties disagree on:

- [ ] the employee's medical eligibility for vocational rehabilitation services.
- [ ] the employee's ability to benefit from the provision of vocational rehabilitation services.
- [ ] the description of the employee's job duties.
- [ ] the selection of the Qualified Rehabilitation Representative.
- [ ] the payment of vocational rehabilitation temporary disability benefits.
- [ ] the development of a vocational rehabilitation plan.
- [ ] the provisions of the vocational rehabilitation plan.

- [ ] The requesting party objects to the Request for Conclusion of Vocational Rehabilitation Benefits (DIA Form RB-105). The reason is:

- [ ] Other (explain):

SUMMARY OF PARTIES EFFORTS TO RESOLVE DISPUTE(S):

An unsuccessful attempt to resolve the dispute(s) was made by Mr. / Mrs. / Ms. _____ on ___ / ___ / ___.
The results of this attempt were (attach additional page if needed):

Copies of this request with copies of medical and vocational reports have been served on:

Has the employer/insurer accepted this claim?
Yes [ ] No [ ]

Has liability for the injury been found by the WCAB?
Yes [ ] No [ ]

NAME OF REQUESTOR:	TITLE:
FIRM NAME:	
ADDRESS:	
CITY:	STATE:	ZIP:
SIGNATURE:	DATE:

DIA FORM RB-103

FORM COLOR: YELLOW

STATE OF CALIFORNIA
DEPARTMENT OF INDUSTRIAL RELATIONS
DIVISION OF INDUSTRIAL ACCIDENTS
REHABILITATION BUREAU

**REQUEST FOR ORDER OF
REHABILITATION BENEFITS**

REHAB BUREAU USE ONLY

INSTRUCTIONS: This form is to be used only when the employer fails to voluntarily initiate the provision of vocational rehabilitation services and the employee can substantiate the need for such services. This form is also to be used to request a Bureau determination for reinstatement of vocational rehabilitation benefits. The form must be accompanied by all medical and vocational reports and any other pertinent information not previously submitted to the Bureau. The request must be sent to the appropriate Bureau office and served on the parties. If a Rehabilitation Bureau case number has not been assigned, attach a completed Case Initiation Document (DIA Form RB-101). Do not use this form when liability for the injury is in dispute.

EMPLOYEE NAME: (First)   (Middle)   (Last) | RB CASE #:

WHEN EMPLOYER INITIALLY FAILS TO PROVIDE VOCATIONAL REHABILITATION BENEFITS
The employee claims that the employer failed in it's obligation to voluntarily provide vocational rehabilitation services because:

The employee can substantiate his or her medical eligibility as a qualified injured worker in the report of
dated ___ / ___ / ___.
Describe the employee's job duties at the time of injury.

Explain why the employee is unable to perform his or her job at the time of injury.

Did the employee request the employer to provide vocational rehabilitation services?   YES ☐   ___/___/___   NO ☐
Has the employer/insurer accepted this claim?   YES ☐   ___/___/___   NO ☐
Has liability for the injury been found by the WCAB?   YES ☐   ___/___/___   NO ☐
Did the employer provide vocational rehabilitation services?   YES ☐   NO ☐
On what date should the employer have provided vocational rehabilitation services?   ___/___/___
Does the employee wish to choose his or her qualified rehabilitation representative?   YES ☐   NO ☐
    If answer is yes, enter name:

Date last worked: ___/___/___   Date of last payment of temporary disability: ___/___/___

WHEN EMPLOYEE IS REQUESTING REINSTATEMENT OF VOCATIONAL REHABILITATION BENEFITS
The employee requests that the Bureau determine his or her entitlement to reinstatement of vocational rehabilitation benefits because:

How does the employee substantiate this request?

DATE OF INJURY: DATE OF APPROVAL OF COMPROMISE & RELEASE OR
___/___/___   FINDING OF PERMANENT DISABILITY BY THE APPEALS BOARD   ___/___/___

STATEMENT OF EMPLOYEE
In making this request, the employee states that he or she is in need of vocational rehabilitation services, will accept such services and is now able to participate in the provision of such services.

Copies of this notice have been sent to: | EMPLOYEE SIGNATURE:
    | EMPLOYEE REPRESENTATIVE'S SIGNATURE (if represented):
    | DATE: ___/___/___

DIA FORM RB-104

FORM COLOR: PINK

STATE OF CALIFORNIA
DEPARTMENT OF INDUSTRIAL RELATIONS
DIVISION OF INDUSTRIAL ACCIDENTS
REHABILITATION BUREAU

**REQUEST FOR CONCLUSION OF
REHABILITATION BENEFITS**

REHAB BUREAU USE ONLY

INSTRUCTIONS: This form must be used by the employer/insurer to request the Bureau to determine when vocational rehabilitation benefits are concluded. This form is required on all cases in which vocational rehabilitation benefits commenced. This request must be sent to the appropriate Bureau office. If a Rehabilitation Bureau case number has not been assigned, attach a completed Case Initiation Document (DIA Form RB-101). This form should not be used for interruptions of benefits.

EMPLOYEE NAME: (First) (Middle) (Last)	RB CASE #:
EMPLOYEE ADDRESS:	REHABILITATION BUREAU ADDRESS:
CITY, STATE, ZIP:	CITY, STATE, ZIP:

The Employer/Insurer requests Rehabilitation Bureau approval of conclusion of vocational rehabilitation services because:

☐ the qualified injured worker completed a vocational rehabilitation plan.
☐ the employee is not a qualified injured worker or the employee failed to cooperate in the provision of vocational rehabilitation services to determine the employee's eligibility as a qualified injured worker.
☐ the qualified injured worker unreasonably failed to complete an approved vocational rehabilitation plan.
☐ the employee declined, on the prescribed form, to accept the provision of vocational rehabilitation services.
☐ the employee failed to request timely reinstatement of vocational rehabilitation services.
☐ none of the above reasons apply and all necessary and reasonable vocational rehabilitation services have been provided.

The basis for this request is substantiated in the attached reports and is summarized as follows:

NOTICE TO EMPLOYEE

If you object to this request, you (or your attorney, if you are represented) must submit your written objections and the reasons for them to the Rehabilitation Bureau within 20 days of the date of this request. The objection should be made on the "Request for Dispute Resolution" (DIA Form RB-103) and a copy must be sent to the employer/insurer.

Within specified time limits and subject to certain criteria, you may request reinstatement of vocational rehabilitation benefits. Requests must be in writing, accompanied by supporting facts and submitted to the Rehabilitation Bureau within one year of either a finding of permanent disability or approval of a compromise and release by the Workers' Compensation Appeals Board; or within 5 years from the date of your injury. The Rehabilitation Bureau will determine if the vocational rehabilitation services previously provided were sufficient or if you are entitled to additional services.

SUMMARY OF VOCATIONAL REHABILITATION BENEFITS PROVIDED:

Date Rehab Services Commenced: __ / __ / __   Rehab Plan Type: _____   Rehab Plan Goal: _____
Date Rehab Services Completed: __ / __ / __   Return to Work: YES ☐   __ / __ / __   NO ☐
Employee's New Job Title: _____   Wages: $ _____ per _____

1. The employee has been paid $_____ in temporary disability indemnity benefits at the rate of $_____ per week, beginning __ / __ / __ and ending __ / __ / __ for the injury occurring on __ / __ / __.
2. Vocational rehabilitation services provided to the employee include: (check where applicable)

☐ Job Analysis	☐ Vocational Evaluation
☐ Vocational Testing	☐ Situational Assessments
☐ Counseling	☐ Labor Market Survey
☐ Training: Number of Weeks: _____	☐ Financial Analysis
☐ Placement Services: Number of Weeks: _____	☐ Other (Specify): _____

COPIES OF THIS NOTICE HAVE BEEN SENT TO:	SUBMITTED BY (Name):
	SIGNATURE:
	ADDRESS:
	CITY, STATE, ZIP:
	PHONE NUMBER: DATE: ( )

DIA FORM RB-105

FORM COLOR: BUFF

STATE OF CALIFORNIA
DEPARTMENT OF INDUSTRIAL RELATIONS
DIVISION OF INDUSTRIAL ACCIDENTS
REHABILITATION BUREAU

STATEMENT OF DECLINE OF
VOCATIONAL REHABILITATION BENEFITS

REHAB BUREAU USE ONLY

INSTRUCTIONS: This form shall be signed and dated by the employee and the employee's representative (if any) when the employee declines the provision of vocational rehabilitation services/and sent to the employer/insurer. When the choice to decline services occurs subsequent to the commencement of vocational rehabilitation services, this form shall be submitted by the employer/insurer to the Rehabilitation Bureau with the Request for Conclusion of Rehabilitation Benefits (DIA Form RB-105).

EMPLOYEE NAME: (First)   (Middle)   (Last)   RB CASE # (if any):

NOTICE TO EMPLOYEE

Employees who have had industrial injuries may be entitled to receive vocational rehabilitation benefits if they are likely to be precluded from returning to their employment and would benefit from the provision of vocational rehabilitation services.

This benefit, known as vocational rehabilitation, varies with the employee's needs and abilities. This may include an evaluation to identify the type of vocational rehabilitation services which can help the employee to return to suitable employment. These services may involve changing the demands of the employee's usual job; assisting the employee to obtain new employment compatible with his or her abilities, or training the employee for a new occupation.

When the employee is a qualified injured worker, all vocational rehabilitation costs are paid by the employer or its insurer. The employee continues to receive temporary disability indemnity payments during the period of entitlement to vocational rehabilitation services.

The employee has the right to choose whether he or she will accept the provision of vocational rehabilitation services. Regardless of the employee's choice, other workers' compensation benefits will not be affected.

If the employee declines rehabilitation benefits now, he or she may be able to request future consideration of these benefits within statutory time limits. The request must be in writing and submitted to the Rehabilitation Bureau within one year of either a finding of permanent disability or approval of a compromise and release by the Workers' Compensation Appeals Board; or within 5 years from the date of injury. The Rehabilitation Bureau will determine entitlement to services.

STATEMENT OF EMPLOYEE

I have read and understand this notice and I choose to decline the provision of vocational rehabilitation benefits.

EMPLOYEE'S SIGNATURE:

EMPLOYEE REPRESENTATIVE'S SIGNATURE (if represented):

DATE:
__ / __ / __

DIA FORM RB-107

Ace Insurance Company
123 Fourth Street
Center City, CA 94123
(415) 555-1234

Injured Worker
Address
City, State   Zip

Dear Injured Worker:

Dr. _____ indicates you may not be able to return to your usual employment because of your (date) job injury. This qualifies you for a vocational evaluation to determine if the provision of vocational rehabilitation services may help you return to work.

Enclosed is a description of vocational rehabilitation services which are part of the workers' compensation benefits. Your right to receive vocational rehabilitation benefits is voluntary and their commencement is subject to statutory time limits. A choice to accept the provision of vocational rehabilitation services does not affect your other workers' compensation benefits. You have a right to participate in the selection of a rehabilitation counselor. Entitlement to rehabilitation may not normally be "settled" or otherwise converted to lump sum payments.

You should call me at (phone number) to advise me if you are interested in receiving these benefits; to select the rehabilitation counselor; and discuss any questions you may have. For additional information, you may contact the Information and Assistance Officer, provided at no extra charge to you by the State Division of Industrial Accidents, by calling (phone number) or by writing to the Information and Assistance Officer at (address).

If I do not hear from you within 15 days, I will assume that you are not interested in receiving vocational rehabilitation services.

Sincerely,

Susie Swift
Claims Adjuster

cc: Rehabilitation Bureau
        (WEBB - COMMENCEMENT)

401

Ace Insurance Company
123 Fourth Street
Center City, CA 94123
(415) 555-1234

Injured Worker
Address
City, State Zip

Dear Injured Worker:

-    California law requires that we advise injured workers who
are disabled more than 180 days about their potential right to
vocational rehabilitation benefits.

Enclosed is a description of vocational rehabilitation
services which are available to qualified injured workers who
may not be able to return to their usual employment as a part
of the workers' compensation benefits.

The information submitted by your physician indicates that
you should be able to return to your former work. However, if
this should change, you may be entitled to these benefits in
the future.

Your right to receive vocational rehabilitation benefits
is voluntary and their commencement is subject to statutory
time limits.

If you have any questions, please contact me at (phone
number). For additional information, you may contact the
Information and Assistance Officer, provided at no extra charge
to you by the State Division of Industrial Accidents, by
calling (phone number) or by writing to the Information and
Assistance Officer at (address). You may also consult with an
attorney of your choice or seek a resolution of the dispute by
the Rehabilitation Bureau of the Division of Industrial
Accidents.

Sincerely,

Susie Swift
Claims Adjuster

cc: Rehabilitation Bureau
            (WEBB - NOT QUALIFIED)

Ace Insurance Company
123 Fourth Street
Center City, CA 94123
(415) 555-1234

Injured Worker
Address
City, State Zip

Dear Injured Worker:

Reports received from your physician are unable to predict whether you will be able to return to your usual employment. If it is later determined that you may not be able to return to your employment, you may be eligible to receive vocational rehabilitation services.

Enclosed is a description of vocational rehabilitation benefits and your rights concerning this benefit.

I will advise you further within 90 days concerning the status of your entitlement to vocational rehabilitation services.

If you have any questions, please contact me at (phone number). For additional information, you may contact the Information and Assistance Officer, provided at no extra charge to you by the State Division of Industrial Accidents, by calling (phone number) or by writing to the Information and Assistance Officer at (address).

Sincerely,

Susie Swift
Claims Adjuster

cc: Rehabilitation Bureau

(WEBB - DELAY)

Ace Insurance Company
123 Fourth Street
Center City, CA 94123
(415) 555-1234

Injured Worker
Address
City, State Zip

Dear Injured Worker:

Provision of vocational rehabilitation services for you has been delayed because _____ _____ _____ _____.

We expect to be able to provide you with either a resumption of services, or a more satisfactory explanation by _____.

If you have any questions, please contact me at (phone number). For additional information, you may contact the Information and Assistance Officer, provided at no extra charge to you by the State Division of Industrial Accidents, by calling (phone number) or by writing to the Information and Assistance Officer at (address).

Sincerely,

Susie Swift
Claims Adjuster

cc: Rehabilitation Bureau

(DELAY)

Ace Insurance Company
123 Fourth Street
Center City, CA 94123
(415) 555-1234

Injured Worker
Address
City, State Zip

Dear Injured Worker:

As of (date), vocational rehabilitation services are being interrupted until (date) because _____

_____

_____.
During this period you will not be receiving vocational rehabilitation services.

To resume services or to extend the period of interruption, you must notify me, in writing, of your request for reinstatement prior to (date). Your failure to do so could jeopardize your right to receive future vocational rehabilitation services.

If you have any questions, please contact me at (phone number). For additional information, you may contact the Information and Assistance Officer, provided at no extra charge to you by the State Division of Industrial Accidents, by calling (phone number) or by writing to the Information and Assistance Officer at (address).

Sincerely,

Susie Swift
Claims Adjuster

cc: Rehabilitation Bureau

(INTERRUPTION)

405

Ace Insurance Company
123 Fourth Street
Center City, CA 94123
(415) 555-1234

Injured Worker
Address
City, State Zip

Dear Injured Worker:

-     Your request for the provision of vocational
rehabilitation services has been carefully considered. Based
on a review of all available information, we have concluded that
we are not responsible for providing you with vocational
rehabilitation benefits because _____
_____
_____
_____.

The decision on your entitlement to rehabilitation
benefits does not affect your entitlement to other workers'
compensation benefits.   The commencement of vocational
rehabilitation services is subject to statutory time limits.

If you have any questions, please contact me at (phone
number).

If you are not satisfied with my explanation, you may
contact the Information and Assistance Officer, provided at no
extra charge to you by the State Division of Industrial
Accidents, by calling (phone number) or by writing to the
Information and Assistance Officer at (address). You may also
consult with an attorney of your choice or seek a resolution of
the dispute by the Rehabilitation Bureau of the Division of
Industrial Accidents.

Sincerely,

Susie Swift
Claims Adjuster

cc: Rehabilitation Bureau

(DENIAL)

§ 16.21 Article 7: Vocational Rehabilitation

[Applicable to injuries occurring on or after January 1, 1990]

10122. Definitions

The following definitions apply to this Article and are in addition to those as set forth in Labor Code section 4635:

(a) Rehabilitation Unit.

The unit established within the Division of Workers' Compensation, Office of Benefit Determination.

(b) Employer.

Employer includes the insurer and self-insured employer providing the security for compensation required by division 4 and 4.5 of the Labor Code. Employer also includes the third party administrator acting as an agent for the insurer or self-insurer.

(c) Parties.

The employee, employer and their designated representatives, if any.

(d) Case Initiation Document.

The cover sheet that provides the name and address of the party(ies) and their representatives, if any, requesting action from the rehabilitation unit.

(e) Correct Rehabilitation Unit District Office.

The district office venue assigned by the Rehabilitation Unit.

(f) Notices.

Required notices letters generated by the employer and/or insurer and directed to the injured worker.

10123. Reporting Requirements

(a) Except for notices required by this article to be sent to an employee, all forms or correspondence submitted to the Rehabilitation Unit shall include:

(1) Rehabilitation Unit file number, or

(2) Case Initiation Document as the cover sheet for the information being submitted.

Documents which have neither a Rehabilitation Unit file number or a Case Initiation Document will be returned to the sender with instructions for proper filing.

(b) All forms, notices, reports and other communications subject to Labor Code section 139.5 and Article 2.6 commencing with Labor Code section 4635 are to be served simultaneously on all parties.

(c) All forms and reports as required by this article shall be submitted to the correct Rehabilitation Unit District Office in the manner prescribed by the Administrative Director.

(1) Incomplete forms or forms with incomplete information attached may be returned to the sender. Each form has instructions as to the reports/information which must be attached.

(2) A form filed without the attachments and a specific listing of all enclosures as required by the instruction section of the form is deemed incomplete and shall be denied or returned to sender for proper submission. All incomplete requests will be date stamped.

(3) The Rehabilitation Unit shall serve a copy of the transmittal information upon the other parties when a form is returned.

(d) Filing instructions and venue lists shall be provided upon request by the Rehabilitation Unit. Requests shall be submitted to:

Rehabilitation Unit Headquarters
Office of Benefit Determination
P.O. Box 3032
Sacramento, CA 95814-3032

(e) All forms submitted to the Rehabilitation Unit shall bear original signatures and shall be on forms as issued by the Administrative Director or forms approved by the Administrative Director and on the color stock designated by the Administrative Director. Improperly colored copies and/or altered/changed forms will not be accepted by the Rehabilitation Unit.

(1) No forms, notices or reports shall be forwarded to the Rehabilitation Unit when the employer has raised a good faith issue of injury arising out of and occurring in the course of employment, until the employer has accepted liability for the injury or there has been a finding of injury by the Workers' Compensation Appeals Board.

(2) Any requests for provision of rehabilitation services and for intervention/dispute resolution require confirmation by the employee or his/her representative that liability for the injury has been accepted.

Forms sent to the Rehabilitation Unit when a good faith issue of injury exists or where there has been no confirmation of acceptance of injury, shall be returned to the sender.

(f) All required notices shall be sent to the employee on a timely basis by the employer/insurer in the form and manner prescribed by the Administrative Director. The data box portion of the notice shall be forwarded to the Rehabilitation Unit at the same time the notice shall be forwarded to the worker. Failure to provide notices timely shall subject the insurer, third party administrator or self-insured employer to administrative penalties upon audit by the Office of Benefit Assistance and Enforcement. The following notices are timely when sent within the following periods:

(1) The notice of Potential Eligibility is to be sent within 10 days of the employer's knowledge of the employees medical eligibility for vocational rehabilitation services.

(2) The Reminder Notice is to be sent not earlier than 45 days nor later than 70 days after the employees receipt of the Notice of Potential Eligibility.

(3) The Denial of Vocational Rehabilitation Services shall be sent within 10 days of knowledge of non-eligibility for vocational rehabilitation services.

(4) The Notice of Intent to Withhold Maintenance Allowance is to be sent no less than 15 days prior to withholding rehabilitation benefits.

(g) The following shall be sent on a timely basis and maintained in the claims filed:

(1) A 90-day Qualified Rehabilitation Representative assignment letter shall be sent no later than 10 days subsequent to ninety days of aggregate total disability.

(2) A Notice of Interruption shall be sent no later than 10 days of the agreement to interrupt services with copies to all parties.

(h) The insurer shall advise the employer of a potential refund as described in Labor Code section 4638 within 60 days of the approval of the plan by the Rehabilitation Unit.

(i) The employer shall retain a true copy of all notices sent to the employee and shall provide the unit with a copy upon request.

(j) When an employer or an employee chooses to be represented in matters pending before the Rehabilitation Unit, the represented party or representative shall notify the Rehabilitation Unit by completing and filing DWC Form RU-101, "Case Initiation Document." Notice of representation to the Appeals Board shall not be considered notice to the Rehabilitation Unit.

10123.1 Unrepresented Employees

The Rehabilitation Unit shall assist an unrepresented worker in complying with section 10123 of these regulations. Such assistance may include directing the worker to the correct Rehabilitation Unit district office, obtaining all reports and/or obtaining information necessary to make a determination on disputed issues.

10123.2. Reproduction of Forms, Notices

Except for the Employee Statement of Declination of Vocational Rehabilitation Services, DWC Form RU-107, any person or entity may reproduce all the forms and notices required by this article and article 2.6 of chapter 2, part 2 of division 4 of the Labor Code (commencing with section 4635) and may only modify the heading to permit imprinting the name, address, telephone number and logo-type or other identifier of an employer, insurer or third party administrator. The reproduction must be otherwise identical in typestyle and format using the designated color to that promulgated by the Administrative Director in this section. If the form is computer generated, a minimum of a one half inch border in the designated color is required.

10124. Initial Consultation

Within 25 days of receipt of the assignment required by subdivision (a) of Labor Code section 4636, the qualified rehabilitation representative shall:

(a) Meet with the employee to explain the services available to assist the employee in returning to work. If the employee's medical eligibility for vocational rehabilitation services has not yet been determined, the qualified rehabilitation representative shall assist the employee and confer with the employer in the joint development of a job description, using either DWC Form RU-91, "Description of Employee's Job Duties" or a narrative description, whichever is most appropriate given the injury in question.

(b) Submit DWC Form RU-90, "Treating Physician's Report of Disability Status," and the job description to the employee's treating physician and request the physician to determine the employee's medical eligibility for vocational rehabilitation services.

10125. Independent Vocational Evaluator

(a) The Rehabilitation Unit Headquarters shall maintain a list of Qualified Rehabilitation Representatives (QRR) who meet the requirements of an Independent Vocational Evaluator (IVE) pursuant to Labor Code Section 4635(c). A QRR who meets the qualifications specified in Labor Code Section 4635(c) may apply to be included on the IVE list throughout the year. The IVE list shall be reviewed and revised on a yearly basis, and shall be made available upon request.

(b) The parties are encouraged to select a QRR whenever a dispute is raised regarding the assignment of a QRR. If the parties cannot agree on the selection of a QRR within fifteen (15) days, either party may request the Rehabilitation Unit to appoint an IVE. To request an IVE either party must file a Request for Dispute Resolution, DWC Form RU-103, with the correct Rehabilitation Unit district office.

(c) Within fifteen (15) days of receipt of the request, the Rehabilitation Unit shall appoint an IVE with notice served simultaneously on the IVE and all parties. The assignment shall be made in rotation from a panel of all independent vocational evaluators in the geographic area included within the venue of the correct rehabilitation unit district office and who meet the language and specialty requirements, if any, of the employee.

(d) Upon receipt of notification of the IVE appointment, the employer shall forward all medical and vocational reports to the IVE within ten (10) days. If the IVE is unable to meet with the employee within ten (10) days of receipt of the medical and vocational reports, upon notification from either party, the Rehabilitation Unit shall appoint another IVE.

(e) The IVE shall communicate with the injured worker throughout the provision of rehabilitation services. Except as specified in Administrative Rule 10125(d) above, no party shall communicate with the IVE regarding the evaluation unless otherwise directed by the Rehabilitation Unit except for communications initiated by the IVE. All such communications shall be confirmed in writing by the IVE.

(f) The Rehabilitation Unit may order that vocational rehabilitation services be provided by an Independent Vocational Evaluator at the expense of the employer upon a finding of any of the following:

(1) The employer failed to provide vocational rehabilitation services in a timely manner subsequent to the employee requesting vocational rehabilitation services;

(2) An independent vocational evaluation is necessary for the Rehabilitation Unit to determine if an employee is vocationally feasible;

(3) An independent vocational evaluation is necessary for the Rehabilitation Unit to determine if a vocational rehabilitation plan meets the requirements of this article; or

(4) The employee and qualified rehabilitation representative cannot agree on a vocational goal.

10126. Vocational Rehabilitation Plan

(a) Pursuant to Labor Code section 4638, within ninety (90) days after determination of the employee's vocational feasibility, the employer shall either:

(1) Submit Vocational Rehabilitation Plan, DWC Form RU-102, agreed to by the parties with appropriate attachments or;

(2) Submit a Request for Dispute Resolution, DWC Form RU-103, to the Rehabilitation Unit, attaching a summary of the informal conference and the results thereof, including identification of the issues, issues resolved,

issues pending, position of the parties and the rationale/supporting information for the position(s).

(b) Nothing shall preclude the employer or employee from requesting the Rehabilitation Unit to approve a modification of the plan because of an unforeseen circumstance arising subsequent to the initial plan agreement. Such request for approval shall be submitted to the correct Rehabilitation Unit district office on the Vocational Rehabilitation Plan, DWC Form RU-102.

(c) Within 15 days after the employee and employer have agreed to the terms and conditions of a vocational rehabilitation plan, the plan shall be submitted to the Rehabilitation Unit for review and approval. Within thirty (30) days of receipt of a properly submitted, documented and signed plan, the Rehabilitation Unit shall approve or disapprove the plan. If approval or disapproval is not made within thirty (30) days of receipt of a properly submitted plan, the plan shall be deemed approved. Plan commencement shall not be deemed approval.

(d) A vocational rehabilitation plan that provides for modified or alternate work with the same employer and has been agreed to by the employer and employee shall not be subject to Rehabilitation Unit approval prior to implementation.

(e) Where a question arises concerning the duration of alternate plans of equal merit, the unit shall approve the plan that expedites the employee's return to suitable gainful employment.

10127. Dispute Resolution

When there is a dispute regarding the provision of vocational rehabilitation services, either the employee or employer may request the Rehabilitation Unit to resolve the dispute. All requests for dispute resolution shall be submitted as follows:

(a) If the request for dispute resolution results from an employee's objection to the employer's intention to withhold maintenance payment pursuant to section 4643:

(1) The employee shall forward to the Rehabilitation Unit Request for Dispute Resolution DWC Form RU-103 to the correct Rehabilitation Unit district office with copy to all parties;

(2) The employee shall state his/her position with full explanation of his/her objection, and attach the same to the request for Rehabilitation Unit dispute resolution; copies shall be served on all parties;

(3) The Rehabilitation Unit shall schedule and hold a conference and issue a determination within ten (10) days of the date of receipt of the employee's objection.

(b) Excluding (a) above, all other requests for Rehabilitation Unit dispute resolution shall be submitted by completing a Request for Dispute Resolution, DWC Form RU-103, and attaching all medical and vocational reports not previously submitted to the Rehabilitation Unit, along with a format summary of the Informal Conference. The format summary identifies the issues involved, the unresolved issues remaining, and the positions of the parties, including supporting information which shall be attached. The request for dispute resolution and all attached documentation shall be served on the parties.

(c) Excluding (a) above, and in instances in (b) where an informal conference is either impossible or impractical:

(1) The requesting party shall:

(a) Complete the request form;

(bb) Attach all pertinent medical and vocational reports not previously submitted to the Rehabilitation Unit;

(cc) Clearly identify why an informal conference is inappropriate.

(dd) Clearly state the issue(s) and identify supporting information for each issue and position;

(ee) Serve copies on all parties.

(2) Upon receipt of the request above, the opposing party shall have fifteen (15) days to forward their position with supporting information to the Rehabilitation Unit with copies to all parties.

(3) Upon receipt of all information, the Rehabilitation Unit shall either issue its determination based on the record, will ask for additional information, or set the matter for formal conference.

(d) Pursuant to (b) and (c) above, the Rehabilitation Unit shall issue a determination within forty-five (45) days of the receipt of the original request.

10127.1. Conferences

(a) Upon receipt of "Request for Dispute Resolution" DWC Form RU-103, the Rehabilitation Unit shall determine if a formal conference is necessary. Notices shall be served by the Rehabilitation Unit on all parties, identifying the time, date, and location of any conference. Where the request is initiated by an unrepresented employee, the Rehabilitation Unit or an Information & Assistance Officer may assist the employee in completing and serving the form.

(b) Rehabilitation Unit Conferences shall be held on the date and time scheduled. Any party unable to attend the conference, may submit his/her position, on the issue(s) in writing, to the Rehabilitation Unit district office holding the conference. Following the conference, the Rehabilitation Unit shall issue a determination based on its file, information provided during the conference, and any written positions submitted prior to or at the time of the conference.

(c) If the dispute is resolved by the parties before the conference has been held, the party who requested the conference shall contact the Rehabilitation Unit for permission to cancel the conference. If permission to cancel is given, the requesting party shall notify all parties of the cancellation, and forward, in writing to the Rehabilitation Unit, with copies to all parties, notification that the conference has been cancelled. The requesting party shall include in the notification the issue(s) in dispute and the resolution reached by the parties.

(d) Except where the conference is held pursuant to Labor Code section 4643, a determination shall be issued within thirty (30) days of the date of conference unless additional information is requested by the Rehabilitation Unit, in which case, determination shall be issued thirty (30) days from the date of receipt of all further requested information.

10128. Request for Order of Rehabilitation Services

If the employer fails to voluntarily provide services, subsequent to the employee's written demand with substantiation of eligibility for services upon the employer, the employee may, on DWC Form RU-104, "Employee Request for Order of Vocational Rehabilitation Services," request the Rehabilitation Unit to order the provisions of vocational rehabilitation services at the expense of the employer. A copy of the demand and copies of all medical and vocational reports including a listing of documents shall be attached with a completed Case Initiation Document, DWC form RU-101. Medical reports filed by the parties will be returned upon request.

10129. Request for Interruption/Deferral of Services

(a) The provision of vocational rehabilitation services may be interrupted or deferred upon the request of the employee and agreement by the employer, or if the agreement cannot be reached, upon a finding of good cause by the Rehabilitation Unit.

The employer shall within 10 days of the date of the agreement, confirm the deferral or interruption in writing to the employee including advice concerning procedures to be followed by the employee to commence or continue vocational rehabilitation services.

(b) The period of deferral or interruption may be extended upon agreement of the employee and employer. If the employee and employer are unable to agree to an extension of the deferral or interruption period, the Rehabilitation Unit may order an extension of the deferral or interruption period upon a finding that the extension is in the best interests of the employee.

(c) If the employer fails to commence or continue vocational rehabilitation services after receipt of a timely request from the employee, the employee may request the Rehabilitation Unit to order the provision of vocational rehabilitation services pursuant to section 10128.

10130. Request for Reinstatement of Vocational Rehabilitation Services

Request for reinstatement of vocational rehabilitation services following an interruption or deferral shall be made in accordance with Labor Code section 4644(b), and Rule 10131(b).

All other requests for reinstatement of services shall initially be submitted to the employer carrier, or self-insured employer. If the employer carrier, or self-insured employer fails to reinstate services and the employee wishes a determination of entitlement to further rehabilitation services, all such requests shall be directed to the correct Rehabilitation Unit district office on DWC Form RU-104, "Employee Request for Order of Vocational Rehabilitation Services."

10131. Request for Termination of Rehabilitation Services

(a) When employer elects to unilaterally terminate rehabilitation services, prior to such termination, the employer shall, on a DWC Form RU-105, "Request for Termination of Rehabilitation Services," prescribed by the Administrative Director, request the Rehabilitation Unit to approve a termination of services. The request must be filed within 10 days of the circumstances set forth in Labor Code section 4644(a).

(b) Absent objection from the employee within twenty (20) days of receipt of Request for Termination of Rehabilitation Services, the Rehabilitation Unit shall approve the request in thirty (30) days unless the Rehabilitation Unit determines the request for termination of rehabilitation service is inappropriate. The objection must be filed on DWC Form RU-103, "Request for Dispute Resolution."

(c) When the employee objects to the employer's request for Rehabilitation Unit determination of termination of rehabilitation services, the Rehabilitation Unit shall, within thirty (30) days of the employee's objection, hold a conference or otherwise obtain the employee's reasons for objection together with substantiating evidence and issue its decision on the employer's request.

10131.1. Declination of Rehabilitation

(a) A Request for Termination of Rehabilitation Services on the basis that the employee has declined rehabilitation services must be made in the form and manner set forth by the Administrative Director in section 11028.1 of these rules by using DWC Form RU-105.

(b) A Request for Termination of Rehabilitation Services shall be approved when:

(1) the employee has received Notice of Potential Eligibility pursuant to Labor Code section 4637(a); and,

(2) the employee has received a full explanation by a Qualified Rehabilitation Representative of his/her rights and obligations pertaining to vocational services pursuant to Labor Code section 4636(a).

(c) The employee and his/her representative, if any, must sign a declination of rehabilitation on the form prescribed by the Administrative Director.

(d) The employer shall submit a Request for Termination of Rehabilitation Services, Form RU-105, to the correct Rehabilitation Unit district office with copies to all parties. The request shall be accompanied with the signed DWC Form RU-107, "Employee Statement of Declination of Vocational Rehabilitation Services," and a copy of "Notice of Potential Eligibility," DWC Form RU-500W, and documentation of the assignment of the Qualified Rehabilitation Representative required by subdivision (a) of Labor Code section 4636.

(e) Upon receipt of a Request for Termination of Rehabilitation Services pursuant to (a) above, the Rehabilitation Unit will either approve or disapprove the request within thirty (30) days.

10131.2. Notice to Retire Rehabilitation Case File

When there has been no activity on a file reported to the Rehabilitation Unit for 18 months or more, the Rehabilitation Unit shall retire its file subsequent to issuing a Notice of Intention to Retire the file.

Notice will advise the parties that the file will be retired without prejudice and the parties retain the right to request a future determination of eligibility from the Rehabilitation Unit if such request is received within the statutory period.

10132. Fee Schedule

The Fee Schedule promulgated by the Administrative Director shall be deemed reasonable for providers of vocational rehabilitation services pursuant to Labor Code section 139.5. This fee schedule applies to all vocational rehabilitation services performed on or after 1/1/91.

(a) Rehabilitation providers and employers/insurers may enter into agreements to provide services at rates other than those provided by the Fee Schedule. Any agreements, however, shall be made in writing prior to the provision of such rehabilitation services. Fees, however, that are charged back to a file by an in-house QRR shall not exceed this fee schedule.

(b) Disputes pertaining to the application of the Fee Schedule shall be initially determined by the Rehabilitation Unit.

(c) Service provided by persons other than the firm in which the Qualified Rehabilitation Representative is employed must be clearly identified and billed separately.

(d) Qualified Rehabilitation Representatives appointed by the Rehabilitation Unit to act in the capacity of an independent Vocational Evaluator shall strictly adhere to the fee schedule. Use of Service Code 90 should have prior approval from the Rehabilitation Unit.

(e) All billings from vocational rehabilitation service providers are due and payable within sixty (60) days of receipt unless within the sixty (60) day period an objections [*sic*] filed contesting the billing or any portion thereof. Any portion of the billing not contested shall be paid within the sixty day paeriod. Absent objection as described, billings not paid within sixty days from the date of receipt are subject to penalty under Labor Code sections 129 and 129.5.

10132.1. Reasonable Fee Schedule

VOCATIONAL REHABILITATION FEE SCHEDULE

The following fee schedule applies to all services rendered under the Rules and Regulations of the Department of Industrial Relations, Division of Workers' Compensation.

All billings for casework provided are to be itemized in tenths of an hour and submitted using the service code # as listed below.

Non-billable costs include: postage, clerical services, photocopies, in-house waiting time, attempts telephone contacts, and in-house staffing. If detailed documentation of these activities is required, the activity is billable at the normal hourly rate of actual time spent.

Adjustments to the Fee Schedule will be reviewed by the Administrative Director of the Division of Workers' Compensation on an annual basis. Recommendations regarding adjustments to the Fee Schedule shall be reviewed by the Rehabilitation Advisory Committee prior to public hearings.

All billings from vocational rehabilitation service providers are due and payable within sixty days of receipt pursuant to section 10132(e).

Fee Schedule

Professional Hourly Rate	$65.00

Service
Code # Item Description   *Schedule*

21   Travel Rate Not to Exceed $44.00/Hr. + $0.24/Mile

30   90 Day QRR Benefit Call   Actual time, not to exceed 5 Hours
Includes all contacts to schedule appointments, preparation of RU90/91, visit verification, employer contact, first physician contact. Subsequent contacts to be billed at hourly rate.

31   Job Analysis   Actual time, not to exceed 5 Hours
Includes contacts to schedule appointment, site visit, document completion, document review with worker/attorney, securing signatures and completed report. All services not included above will be billed separately.

32   Initial Interview   Actual time, not to exceed 5 Hours
Includes initial file review, scheduling contact with worker, contact with worker and representative, if any, interview, and completed report.

33   Transferable Skills Assessment & Review   Actual time, not to exceed 4 Hours
Detailed work-up of vocational history to include special training, certifications, materials with which worker is familiar, products, subject matter, and services (MPSMS) Worker codes and Guide to Occupational Exploration (GOE) codes developed in this process can lead to vocational exploration alternatives. Includes review with injured worker and report.

34   Vocational Testing & Report   Actual time, not to exceed 4 Hours
Includes administration and scoring of a standard battery of vocational tests.

35   Counseling & Research Service   Actual Time, By Report
Includes professional time meeting with worker, guidance through vocational exploration, plan review, plan monitoring test interpretation with worker, and labor market and resource research.

40   Labor Market Survey   Actual time, not to exceed 3 Hours
Includes up to ten contacts.

41   Job Seeking Skills   Actual Time, By Report
All activity directed to providing the worker with skills, resume preparation, personal presentation, etc.

42   Placement Services   Actual Time, By Report
Job placement services, placement follow-up and placement counseling.

43 DWC Form RU-102, all required documents and cover latter [sic] completion.
Modified or alternate work   Actual time, not to exceed 1 Hour

44 DWC Form RU-102, all required documents and cover letter completion.
Direct placement, OJT,
Training, Self-Employment   Actual time, not to exceed 2 Hours

51 Telephone Calls   Actual Time, By Report
After an initial review, file review is billable activity only for re-opening or re-activation of a file, or for conference preparation purposes. Review of new medical/legal reports, or work evaluation reports, upon receipt, is billable activity.

53 Reporting   Actual time, not to exceed 1.5 Hours
Unless otherwise specified, three-tenths of an hour per page, up to one and one half hour maximum.

54 Rehabilitation Unit Conference, Informal
Conference & Professional Appearance   Actual Time, By Report
Actual time at professional rate. Preparation time up to one hour.

60 Vocational Evaluation:
One Day Module $200.00
Identification of Academic Achievement Levels and Initial Vocational Interests.

61 Three Day Module: $450.00
Screen Learning Ability and Aptitudes for Selected Occupational Goal; Identify Academic Achievement Levels; Assess Vocational Interests; Determine Feasibility of a Proposed Job Modification.

62 Five Day Module: $700.00
Evaluation of Learning ability, Aptitudes, and Physical Capacity for Related Occupational Groups; Situational Assessment for a specific occupational goal; Identification of Academic Achievement Levels and Assess Vocational Interests; Determine Feasibility of Alternate Work with same employer.

63 Ten Day Module: $1200.00
Evaluation of Vocational Feasibility; Comprehensive Assessment of One or a Combination of following: Physical Tolerances and Stamina; Skills and Aptitudes for Several Occupational Groups; Vocational Interests; Worker Characteristics; Evaluate and Propose Functional Job Modification.

64 Work Hardening/Work Adjustment   up to 3 hour/day $75.00
                                         more than 3 hour/day $120.00
Structured goal oriented individualized program using real or simulated work activities in

conjunction with tasks that are graded to progressively improve the functioning of the individual.

65   Situational Assessment   Charged at most appropriate module
Assessment of performance and work related behavior in a controlled work situation.

66   Job or Training Site Modification   Actual time at Professional Hourly Rate

67   Functional Capacity Assessment   Actual time at Professional Hourly Rate
Includes isolated short term structured activities designed to determine parameters of tolerance.

68   Upper Extremity, Hand Evaluation
and Comprehensive Lifting   Actual time at Professional Hourly Rate
Fees for ancillary service providers may be charged separately.

69   Dominance Transfer   Per day charge at $120
Fees for ancillary services providers may be charged separately.
No charge shall be made for cancellations if received within two working days.
Full charge is allowed for absences during a schedule evaluation.
No shows are to be billed at 50% of the scheduled module.
Exit Staffings are to be charged at the professional hourly rate under Service Code 35.
Reports are to be charged under Service Code 53.

Education & Training
The QRR shall insure that the private vocational school selected to provide vocational training to the qualified injured worker has received approval from the State Department of Education, Private Post Secondary Education Division. As between schools of equal merit, preference will be given to those schools who have reduced their tuition rates by 10% from published 1989 tuition rates, in accordance with the reduction required by Labor Code section 139.5(a)(4). Documentation reflecting the tuition reduction shall be available upon request. Private Vocational Schools may not charge a tuition rate for rehabilitation students which is greater than the lowest rate than that given to the general public.

70   Education Tuition/On the Job Training Fees

71   Books & Supplies

90   Extraordinary Services/Expenses: It is recognized that there can occasionally be exceptional circumstances which may require services and fees beyond those listed. Billings above the recommended fee schedule shall require additional documentation. Prior authorization for excess billings should be obtained before service delivery.

10133. Forms & Notices.

TREATING PHYSICIAN'S REPORT OF DISABILITY STATUS

INSTRUCTIONS: Pursuant to requirements of the California Labor Code, please complete this form and return it to the claim administrator listed below within 15 days of receipt with a copy to the Qualified Rehabilitation Representative.

EMPLOYEE NAME:	(LAST)	(FIRST)	(M.I.)	SS#	DATE OF INJURY

EMPLOYER NAME:

Attached is a description of the employee's job duties. Based on your examination, including the history provided by the patient and the enclosed job description, choose one of the following:

_____ I expect to release the employee to return to the pre-injury occupation on or about _____.

_____ The employee's permanent disability as a result of the injury whether or not combined with the effects of a prior injury or disability, if any, is likely to preclude the employee from returning to work at the pre-injury occupation.

Is the employee currently physically able to participate in vocational rehabilitation services? ____ Yes ____ No

If yes, please describe any physical limitations: _____

_____

If employee is not physically able to participate in vocational services, please estimate when participation may be possible:

_____

_____ At this time, I am unable to give an opinion concerning the employee's ability to return to the pre-injury occupation. I expect to be able to

provide an opinion on or about: _____ .

Please advise also if the employee is currently physically able to perform light duties if modified or alternative work is available:

_____ Yes, with the following limitations: _____

_____

_____ No

Physician's Name _____ Date: _____

Physician's Signature _____

Please return to: Employer/Insurer/Adjusting Agent   Claim #:

Address:	(Street)	(City)	(State)	(Zip)

Send a copy to Qualified Rehabilitation Representative:

Address	(Street)	(City)	(State)	(Zip)

STATE OF CALIFORNIA
DWC FORM RU-90 (12/90)

DESCRIPTION OF EMPLOYEE'S JOB DUTIES

INSTRUCTION FOR INSURER/EMPLOYER: This form shall be developed by the QRR jointly with the employer and employee for inclusion with the request for the Treating Physician's Report of Disability Status (DWC Form RU-90) for all industrial injuries which cause disability exceeding 90 days. This description shall delineate the specific duties performed by this employee.

| EMPLOYEE NAME: | (LAST) | (FIRST) | (M.I.) | CLAIM #: |

EMPLOYER NAME: JOB ADDRESS:

| JOB TITLE: | NO. OF HOURS PER DAY: | DAYS PER WEEK: |

GENERAL JOB DESCRIPTION:

SPECIFIC JOB DUTIES:

1. Check the frequency and number of hours a day the worker is required to do the following specific types of activities.

ACTIVITY	FREQUENCY		NUMBER OF HOURS A DAY									
	CONTINUOUS	INTERMITTENT	0	1	2	3	4	5	6	7	8	MORE THAN 8
a. Sitting												
b. Walking												
c. Standing												
d. Bending												
e. Squatting												
f. Climbing												
g. Kneeling												
h. Twisting												

2a. Hand manipulation required?   ___ No   ___ Yes (Check b, c, d.)

   2b. Simple grasping?   ___ Right Yes ___ No ___   ___ Left Yes ___ No ___

   2c. Power grasping?   ___ Right Yes ___ No ___   ___ Left Yes ___ No ___

   2d. Pushing and pulling?   ___ Right Yes ___ No ___   ___ Left Yes ___ No ___

   2e. Fine manipulation?   ___ Right Yes ___ No ___   ___ Left Yes ___ No ___

3. (a) Does the job require worker to reach or work above the shoulder?   ___ Yes   ___ No   Frequency _____

   (b) Reaching at or below shoulder level?   ___ Yes   ___ No   Frequency _____

4. Does the job require use of his/her feet to operate foot controls or for repetitive movement?   ___ Yes   ___ No

5. Are there special visual or auditory requirements?   ___ No   ___ Yes (Describe)

DWC FORM RU-91(PAGE 1 OF 2) (12/90)

DESCRIPTION OF EMPLOYEE'S JOB DUTIES
(continued)

6. LIFTING	FREQUENCY		CARRYING	FREQUENCY
____	____	a. 10 lbs or less	____	____
____	____	b. 11 to 25 lbs	____	____
____	____	c. 26 to 50 lbs	____	____
____	____	d. 51 to 75 lbs	____	____
____	____	e. 76 to 100 lbs	____	____
____	____	f. Over 100 lbs	____	____

Longest distance carried: _____

Heaviest item carried and how far: _____

	YES	NO	DESCRIPTION
7. DRIVING CARS, TRUCKS, FORKLIFTS OR OTHER MOVING EQUIPMENT	__	__	_____
8. WORKING NEAR HAZARDOUS EQUIPMENT AND MACHINERY	__	__	_____
9. WALKING ON UNEVEN GROUND	__	__	_____
10. EXPOSURE TO DUST, GAS OR FUMES	__	__	_____
11. EXPOSURE TO NOISE	__	__	_____
12. EXPOSURE TO EXTREMES IN TEMPERATURE OR HUMIDITY	__	__	_____
13. WORK AT HEIGHTS	__	__	_____

COMMENTS: (Attach separate sheet or use reverse side if needed.)

EMPLOYER CONFIRMATION: NAME OF CONTACT	DATE:
EMPLOYEE'S SIGNATURE:	DATE:
QRR'S NAME:	QRR FIRM NAME:
QRR'S SIGNATURE:	DATE:

MANDATORY FORMAT
STATE OF CALIFORNIA
DWC FORM RU-91 (PAGE 2 OF 2) (12/90)

CASE INITIATION DOCUMENT

TYPE OF ACTION (CHECK ONE)

___ **Initial Filing**
___ **Address Change**
___ **Employee/Employer Atty Firm Change**
___ **Adjusting Agency Change**

INSTRUCTIONS: This form shall be completed and attached to all requests for Rehabilitation Unit action on matters for which no Rehabilitation Unit Case number has been assigned. This form is also to be used to update address changes for any of the parties or to record changes in representation for either the employer or employee and any change of adjusting agency. This form must be typed or printed clearly and submitted to the appropriate Rehabilitation Unit office. See reverse side for Rehabilitation Unit addresses.

EMPLOYEE NAME:	(LAST)	(FIRST)	(M.I.)	SEX:
ADDRESS:	(STREET)	(CITY)	(STATE)	(ZIP)
DATE OF BIRTH:	PHONE #:	SOCIAL SECURITY #:	DATE OF INJURY:	

EMPLOYER NAME: _____   DWC ID #: (If known) _____

MAILING ADDRESS: (inc. city, state & zip) _____

SELF-INSURED CERTIFICATE NAME: _____

INSURANCE CARRIER (if any): _____

ADJUSTING AGENCY NAME (if agency adjusted) _____

CLAIMS MAILING ADDRESS (inc. city, state & zip): _____

PHONE # _____   CLAIM #: _____

QUALIFIED REHAB REPRESENTATIVE, IF ANY

FIRM NAME: _____   REPRESENTATIVE NAME: _____

MAILING ADDRESS (inc. city, state & zip): _____

PHONE #: _____   DWC FIRM # (If known): _____

EMPLOYEE'S REPRESENTATIVE, IF ANY

FIRM NAME: _____   REPRESENTATIVE NAME: _____

MAILING ADDRESS (inc. city, state & zip): _____

PHONE #: _____   DWC FIRM # (If known): _____

EMPLOYER'S REPRESENTATIVE, IF ANY

FIRM NAME: _____   REPRESENTATIVE NAME: _____

MAILING ADDRESS (inc. city, state & zip): _____

PHONE #: _____   DWC FIRM # (If known): _____

SUBMITTED BY: _____

TITLE: _____

DATE: _____

REHABILITATION UNIT USE ONLY

Must be printed on Goldenrod paper or preapproved computer generated with Goldenrod borders.

MANDATORY FORMAT
STATE OF CALIFORNIA
DWC FORM RU-101 (12/90)

VOCATIONAL REHABILITATION PLAN

INSTRUCTIONS: This form shall be used for submitting a vocational rehabilitation plan to the Rehabilitation Unit. The form shall be prepared by the Qualified Rehabilitation Representative (QRR) and presented to the employee. When the plan is signed by the parties, the employer/insurer shall submit this form and all medical and vocational reports, not previously submitted, to the appropriate Rehabilitation Unit office. If a Rehabilitation Unit case number has not been assigned, attach a completed Case Initiation Document (DWC RU-101).

SECTION A

EMPLOYEE NAME:	(LAST)	(FIRST)	(M.I.)	RU CASE #:
ADDRESS:	(STREET)	(CITY)	(STATE) (ZIP)	DATE OF BIRTH
CLAIMS ADMINISTRATOR: (FIRM)				CLAIM #
ADDRESS:	(STREET)	(CITY)	(STATE)	(ZIP)

This Vocational Rehabilitation Plan (DWC Form RU-102) shall be the written agreement of the employer and employee to the proposed plan developed by the QRR and is subject to the approval of the Rehabilitation Unit. This plan contains a written description of and rationale for the manner and means by which the employee shall be provided the opportunity to return to suitable gainful employment.

SECTION B

OCCUPATION AT INJURY:	EARNINGS AT INJURY:	DATE OF INJURY:

DESCRIBE TYPE OF INJURY AND MEDICAL LIMITATIONS: (Also identify the medical report relied upon)

SUMMARY OF EMPLOYEE'S EDUCATIONAL AND VOCATIONAL BACKGROUND:

INITIALS

REHABILITATION UNIT USE ONLY

DWC FORM RU-102 (PAGE 1 OF 4) (12/90)

SECTION C	
VOCATIONAL OBJECTIVE:	ESTIMATED WEEKLY EARNING UPON COMPLETION:

TYPE OF PLAN

WITH THE SAME EMPLOYER	WITH NEW EMPLOYER
1. ____ Modified Job	3. ____ Direct Placement
2. ____ Alternate Work	4. ____ On-the-job Training
	5. ____ Educational Retraining
	6. ____ Self-employment

DESCRIBE NATURE AND EXTENT OF REHABILITATION PLAN:

DATE VOCATIONAL FEASIBILITY DETERMINED: _____

PLAN COMMENCEMENT DATE: _____

EXPECTED COMPLETION DATE (Including placement assistance but excluding monitoring): _____

WEEKS OF TRAINING: _____   # WEEKS OF PLACEMENT ASSISTANCE: _____

INITIALS

DWC FORM RU- 102 (PAGE 2 OF 4) (12/90)

PLAN FISCAL PROVISIONS

Temporary disability indemnity/maintenance allowance will be paid to the employee at the weekly rate of $ _____ through completion of plan. Such payments shall be made every two weeks. If any amount is withheld from maintenance allowance because of attorney's fees and liens, describe withholding method. Specify how much, if any, of the maintenance allowance is a permanent disability supplement.

Adequate transportation expenses will be paid to the employee in advance as follows. Describe method of calculation and disbursement:

Retraining costs will be paid as follows:

Other costs specified in this plan will be paid as follows:

SECTION D

1. Explain how employee's transferable skills have been used in the selection of the plan objective.

2. List results of vocational testing, if any, and how they support the vocational objective.

3. Describe why this employee will be employable in the vocational objective of this plan. Include assessment of labor market.

INITIALS

DWC FORM RU-102 (PAGE 3 OF 4)(12/90)

SECTION E

RESPONSIBILITIES OF THE EMPLOYER:

The employer/insurer shall timely provide all vocational rehabilitation services and benefits necessitated by the approved vocational rehabilitation plan and as required by the Labor Code.

Other:

RESPONSIBILITIES OF THE EMPLOYEE:

The employee shall be available and reasonably cooperate in the provision of vocational rehabilitation services. The employee shall arrive on time and participate in all scheduled activities; if for any reason the employee does not, he or she must immediately provide an explanation to the Qualified Rehabilitation Representative.

The employee shall follow the requirements of all facilities and persons providing vocational rehabilitation services. The employee shall notify the Qualified Rehabilitation Representative about anything that may interfere with scheduled completion of this plan.

Other:

SECTION F

VERIFICATION OF THE Q.R.R.

This plan was developed by me as the Qualified Rehabilitation Representative or as an Independent Vocational Evaluator. I recommend its approval because it is my opinion that the services contained in this plan will provide the employee with the opportunity to return to suitable gainful employment.

QRR Signature	Date:
Address:	

SECTION G

PLAN AGREEMENT

Subject to the approval of the Rehabilitation Unit, agreement of the employer and employee to a proposed plan shall be deemed to be an agreement that the employer and employee intend to comply with all of the plan's provisions.

Failure of the employer to timely provide all services required by the plan may result in the employee being entitled to additional services.

Failure of the employee to comply with the provisions of this plan may result in termination of the employer's liability for rehabilitation services or conclusion of rehabilitation services, whichever is applicable.

I have read and understand all four pages of this plan and agree with all of the plan's provisions.

NAME OF EMPLOYEE:	SIGNATURE:	DATE:
NAME OF EMPLOYEE REPRESENTATIVE:	SIGNATURE:	DATE:
ADDRESS OF EMPLOYEE REPRESENTATIVE:		

PERSON AUTHORIZING THE PROVISION OF THIS PLAN ON BEHALF OF THE EMPLOYER:

NAME:	SIGNATURE:

FIRM NAME AND ADDRESS:

PERSONS SIGNING THIS SECTION SHALL ALSO INITIAL THE OTHER THREE PAGES IN INITIAL BOX.

Must be printed on Blue paper or preapproved computer generated with Blue border.

MANDATORY FORMAT
STATE OF CALIFORNIA
DWC FORM RU-102 ((PAGE 4 OF 4)(12/90)

REQUEST FOR DISPUTE RESOLUTION

DO NOT USE THIS FORM WHEN LIABILITY FOR THE INJURY IS DISPUTED OR AS AN INITIAL REQUEST FOR OR REINSTATEMENT OF REHABILITATION SERVICES.

INSTRUCTIONS: This is to be used when the parties are unable to resolve disputed rehabilitation issues and a determination by the Rehabilitation Unit is required. The completed form must be accompanied by all medical and vocational reports, including an indexed listing, and any other pertinent information not previously submitted to the Rehabilitation Unit. The parties are expected to meet prior to filing this request in an effort to informally resolve disputed issues. This request must be sent to the appropriate Rehabilitation Unit office. If a case number has not been assigned, attach a completed Case Initiation Document (DWC Form RU-101).

EMPLOYEE NAME:	(LAST)	(FIRST)	(M.I.)	RU CASE #:
ADDRESS:	(STREET)	(CITY)	(STATE & ZIP)	DATE OF INJURY:

The Rehabilitation Unit is requested to resolve the following dispute(s) because the parties disagree on:

____ the employee's medical eligibility for vocational rehabilitation services

____ the employee's ability to benefit from the provision of vocational rehabilitation services

____ the description of the employee's job duties

____ the selection of the Qualified Rehabilitation Representative

____ the payment of Vocational Rehabilitation temporary disability or maintenance allowance

____ the development of a vocational rehabilitation plan

____ the provisions of the vocational rehabilitation plan

____ the deferral or interruption of Vocational Rehabilitation Services

____ Other (explain):

____ The employee objects to the Notice of Intent to Withhold Maintenance Allowance and requests an expedited conference. (Attach a copy of the notice.)

____ The employee objects to the Request for Termination (or Request for Conclusion pre 1/1/90 injuries) of Rehabilitation Services. The reason is:

SUMMARY OF PARTIES' INFORMAL EFFORTS TO RESOLVE THIS DISPUTE:

An informal conference was held on _____. A summary of the conference including a list of attendees, issues addressed, agreements reached, and unresolved issues is attached.

Copies of this request with copies of medical and vocational reports have been served on:	Has the employer/insurer accepted this claim? ____ Yes ____ No Has liability for the injury been found by WCAB? ____ Yes ____ No
NAME OF REQUESTOR: TITLE: FIRM NAME: ADDRESS: SIGNATURE: DATE:	**REHABILITATION UNIT USE ONLY**

Must be printed on Green paper or preapproved computer generated with Green border.

MANDATORY FORMAT
STATE OF CALIFORNIA
DWC FORM RU-103 (12/90)

EMPLOYEE REQUEST FOR ORDER OF
VOCATIONAL REHABILITATION SERVICES

(Do not use this form when liability for injury is in dispute or when rehabilitation services are already being provided.)

INSTRUCTIONS TO EMPLOYEE: This form is to be used only when the employer fails to initiate or reinstate vocational rehabilitation services. Please attach a completed Case Initiation Document (DWC Form RU-101) and any medical records that you may have. Only use this form for injuries occurring on or after 1/1/90.

EMPLOYEE NAME:	(LAST)	(FIRST)	(M.I.)	SS #
ADDRESS:	(STREET)	(CITY)	(STATE) (ZIP)	CLAIM #: (if available)

NAME OF EMPLOYER:	ADDRESS OF EMPLOYER	DATE OF INJURY

JOB TITLE:

EMPLOYEE'S SECTION

____ I was not contacted by a Qualified Rehabilitation Representative (QRR).
____ I was not notified of my entitlement to vocational rehabilitation benefits.
____ I was not provided timely vocational rehabilitation services.
____ I would like reinstatement of vocational rehabilitation services.
____ I have been disabled 365 days or more.
____ My QRR preference is (if any) _____.

____ Other: _____

Has the employer/insurer accepted liability for this injury?   YES ____   NO ____   UNKNOWN ___

Date last worked: _____   Date of last payment of temporary disability: _____

I need vocational rehabilitation and will accept such services and will participate in the provision of such services.

EMPLOYEE SIGNATURE: _____   PHONE #: _____

THIS SECTION IS ONLY TO BE COMPLETED IF THE EMPLOYEE HAS RETAINED THE SERVICES OF A REPRESENTATIVE. Attach copies of request to employer/insurer for initiation or reinstatement of services. Complete medical file must be included with listing.

The employee requests initiation or reinstatement of vocational rehabilitation benefits because:

____   L.C. 4639 (a)   Explain:

____   L.C. 4644 (c)   Explain:

____   L.C. 4644 (d)   Explain:

____   L.C. 5410   Explain:

DATE OF APPROVAL OF COMPROMISE & RELEASE OR FINDING OF PERMANENT DISABILITY BY THE WORKER'S COMPENSATION APPEALS BOARD: _____

Send this request to:	Employee Representative Signature (if any)	
___ Rehab Unit		
and a copy to:	Phone #:	Date:
___ Insurer/Employer		
Documents attached:	**REHABILITATION UNIT USE ONLY**	

Must be printed on Canary paper or preapproved computer generated with Canary border.

MANDATORY FORMAT
STATE OF CALIFORNIA
DWC FORM RU-104 (12/90)

REQUEST FOR TERMINATION
OF REHABILITATION SERVICES

To: State of California
Department of Industrial Relations
Division of Workers' Compensation
Rehabilitation Unit

INSTRUCTIONS: This form must be used by the employer/insurer to request the approval of termination of liability for rehabilitation services for those injuries occurring on or after 1-1-90. This request must be sent to the appropriate Rehabilitation Unit office. If a Rehabilitation Unit case number has not been assigned, attach a completed Case Initiation Document (DWC RU-101).

EMPLOYEE NAME:	(LAST)	(FIRST)	(M.I.)		(RU CASE #:)

EMPLOYEE ADDRESS	(STREET)	(CITY)	(STATE)	(ZIP)	(D.O.I.)

The Employer/Insurer requests Rehabilitation Unit Approval to Terminate Liability for Rehabilitation Services because:

_____ The Qualified Injured Worker declined, on the prescribed form, the provision of vocational rehabilitation services. Copies of the following documents are attached: A properly prepared Statement of Declination (RU-107); Notice of Potential Eligibility (RU-500-W); QRR Verification of Explanation of Vocational Rehabilitation.

_____ The Qualified Injured Worker completed an approved plan. Copies of all unsubmitted vocational reports are attached.

_____ The Qualified Injured Worker unreasonably failed to complete an approved plan. Copies of all unsubmitted vocational reports are attached.

_____ The Qualified Injured Worker failed to request vocational rehabilitation services within 90 days of notification of medical eligibility. Copies of the Notice of Potential Eligibility (RU-500-W) and Reminder Notice (RU-500-X) are attached.

NOTICE TO EMPLOYEE

If you object to this request, you (or your attorney, if you are represented) must submit your written objections and the reasons for them to the Rehabilitation Unit within 20 days of receipt of this request. The objection should be made on the "Request for Dispute Resolution" (DWC Form 103) and a copy must be sent to the employer/insurer. The Rehabilitation Unit will determine if vocational rehabilitation services were sufficient or if you are entitled to further services.

Must be printed on Pink paper or preapproved
computer generated with Pink border.

Rehabilitation Unit Use Only

DWC FORM RU-105 (PAGE 1 OF 2) (12/90)

REHABILITATION FIRM/COUNSELOR

a) Firm Name: _____   b) QRR Name: _____

c) Date of Referral: _____   d) Date of Feasibility: _____

e) Date Plan Commenced: _____   f) Date Plan Completed: _____

SUMMARY OF VOCATIONAL REHABILITATION	
Maintenance allowance paid through _____	Return to Work: ___ Yes Date: _____ ___ No
Total maintenance allowance paid not including P.D. Supplement: $ _____	Employee's New Job Title: _____
P.D. Supplement $ _____	Plan Type: _____
Total costs of QRR services $ _____	Employed in plan objective ___ Yes ___ No
Total other costs of rehabilitation services: $ _____	Wages: $ _____ per _____
Amount withheld for Employee's Representative, if any $ _____	
	SUBMITTED BY (Name):
COPIES OF THIS NOTICE HAVE BEEN SENT TO:	FIRM NAME:
	CITY, STATE, ZIP:
	PHONE NUMBER DATE:

PROOF OF SERVICE BY MAIL

I am a citizen of the United States and a resident of the County of _____. I am over the age of eighteen years and not a party to the within matter. My business address is: _____

_____.

On _____, 1990 I served the **Request for Termination of Rehabilitation Services** on the parties listed below by placing a true copy thereof enclosed in a sealed envelope with postage fully prepaid, and thereafter deposited in the U.S. Mail at the place so addressed.

I declare under penalty of perjury under the laws of the State of California that the foregoing is true and correct. Executed at _____ on _____, 19____.

_____
Signature

MANDATORY FORMAT
STATE OF CALIFORNIA
DWC FORM RU-105 (PAGE 2 OF 2) (12/90)

STATE OF CALIFORNIA   DIVISION OF WORKERS' COMPENSATION

EMPLOYEE STATEMENT OF DECLINATION OF VOCATIONAL REHABILITATION SERVICES

INSTRUCTIONS: This form is to be used when the employee declines rehabilitation following notification of medical eligibility. It must be signed by the employee and his/her representative, if any, and submitted by the employer to the Rehabilitation Unit along with a properly completed Request for Termination of Rehabilitation Services (DWC Form RU-105). If a Rehabilitation Unit case does not exist, it must be accompanied by a Case Initiation Document (DWC Form RU-101).

Employee Name	Last	First	M.I.	RU Case #:

NOTICE TO EMPLOYEE

The purpose of this form is to formally record your desire to end your right to rehabilitation benefits. If you decline rehabilitation services, your right for rehabilitation services will end upon the approval of the Rehabilitation Unit. This means your employer will not be required to provide rehabilitation services to you at a later date, unless otherwise determined pursuant to the Rules and Regulations of the Workers' Compensation Appeals Board in accordance with Labor Code Section 5410.

DESCRIPTION OF VOCATIONAL REHABILITATION SERVICES

If you had a work-related injury which prevents you from doing your former job, you are entitled to receive rehabilitation services. The amount of services you receive will depend on your needs and abilities.

Some rehabilitation plans call for your former job to be modified, or for a different job with your same employer or a new employer. Other plans involve training for a new type of work. All of the rehabilitation costs are paid by your employer. During rehabilitation, you will receive a maintenance allowance. You have a right to an evaluation to determine the vocational options available to you prior to making the decision. Your right to rehabilitation is separate from your other Workers' Compensation Benefits and cannot under the Labor Code be terminated by a cash payment to you. If you are not ready to participate now in rehabilitation, but might be later, it is possible to delay your participation in rehabilitation for a period of time.

If you want more information, you may contact the Rehabilitation Unit of the Office of Benefit Determination, at no charge, or contact an attorney.

STATEMENT OF DECLINATION

This form must be signed by the injured employee.

The injured employee states:
I have read this statement of Declination for Vocational Rehabilitation Services.
I have received the pamphlet "Help in Returning to Work".
I decline rehabilitation.
I have met with a QRR.
I understand by signing this form I am giving up a service to which I may be entitled.

EMPLOYEE'S SIGNATURE _____   Date: _____

Representative's signature, if any.
The representative states: I have reviewed this form with my client; and,
I have explained the effects of declining vocational rehabilitation benefits.

EMPLOYEE'S REPRESENTATIVE'S SIGNATURE: _____   Date: _____

REHABILITATION UNIT USE ONLY

DWC FORM RU-107 (12/90)

DO NOT STAPLE   **DATA COLLECTION BOX**   *(Refer to specifications prior to printing)*

Type   DWC No.   Notice Date   Injury Date

Revision   Orig. Date   Claim No.   Employer

Employee Last Name   Employee First Name   So. Sec. No   Identifying Date

Company Name _____

Address _____

_ _ _DETACH HERE _ _ _ THIS PART TO: REHABILITATION UNIT P.O. BOX 429 _ SAN FRANCISCO, CA 94101-0429 _ _ _ _ _
This part to employee

VIA CERTIFIED MAIL

REMINDER NOTICE

On _____ I wrote to let you know about vocational rehabilitation services. I have not received a response from you. **If you are interested, you must let me know by** _____ . **If I do not hear from you by then, you are likely to lose your right to these services.**

Enclosed is another copy of the pamphlet explaining rehabilitation benefits. I am also including another reply card for you to complete. Please return it to me right away.

Please call me if you have any questions. If you want more information, please contact the California Division of Workers' Compensation by calling 1-800-736-7401 or you may consult an attorney.

NAME: _____

cc: Attorney, if represented   SIGNATURE: _____

PHONE #:   _____

MANDATORY FORMAT
STATE OF CALIFORNIA
DWC FORM RU 500-X (12/90)

REPLY CARD

Claim # _____

Employee Name _____

____ Yes, I want vocational rehabilitation. Please contact me about the next step.

____ Yes, I want vocational rehabilitation but not right now.

____ I do not know yet. Please contact me to arrange an evaluation.

____ I do not want vocational rehabilitation services. I realize that if I change my mind, I have only **90 days** from the date I received the enclosed Notice of Potential Eligibility to request rehabilitation. If I do not submit a request within 90 days, my rights to vocational rehabilitation services will likely terminate.

Signature _____

Phone # _____

Date _____

MANDATORY FORMAT
STATE OF CALIFORNIA
DWC FORM RU 500-W.1 (12/90)

435

DO NOT STAPLE   **DATA COLLECTION BOX**   *(Refer to specifications prior to printing)*

Type   DWC No.   Notice Date   Injury Date

Revision   Orig. Date   Claim No.   Employer

Employee Last Name   Employee First Name   So. Sec. No.   Identifying Date

Company Name ———————————————————————————————————

Address ———————————————————————————————————

— — DETACH HERE — — — THIS PART TO: REHABILITATION UNIT P.O. BOX 429 SAN FRANCISCO, CA 94101-0429 — — — —
This part to employee

NOTICE OF POTENTIAL ELIGIBILITY

Dr. _____ reports you will not be able to return to your usual job because of the effects of your work injury. Enclosed is a copy of the Physician's Report of Disability Status (RU-90) (**"OR"** A copy of the Physician's Report of Disability Status will be sent to you when we receive it.) You are now eligible for a vocational rehabilitation evaluation.

Enclosed is a pamphlet that describes these services and maintenance benefits to which you may be entitled and the effect of any delay in accepting these services. Under state law, your right to vocational rehabilitation cannot be settled or traded for cash payments. **Please read the pamphlet carefully.**

Vocational rehabilitation is voluntary on your part - - yours to accept or reject. If you are not interested, you will not lose other workers' compensation benefits. You may request a vocational evaluation to help you decide if you want services. You may also participate in the selection of an agreed upon Qualified Rehabilitation Representative. Please refer to the pamphlet for details.

However, you must make a decision in the next 90 days. That does not mean you have to start rehabilitation within that time. But you do have to make a choice. **If you do not let me know by** _____**, you are likely to lose your right to vocational rehabilitation services.** A reply card is enclosed for your convenience.

Please call me if you have any questions. If you want more information, please contact the California Division of Workers' Compensation by calling 1-800-736-7401, or you may consult an attorney.

cc: Attorney, if represented

NAME: _____

SIGNATURE: _____

PHONE #: _____

MANDATORY FORMAT
STATE OF CALIFORNIA
DWC FORM RU 500-W (12/90)

DO NOT STAPLE **DATA COLLECTION BOX**   *(Refer to specifications prior to printing)*

Type   DWC No.   Notice Date   Injury Date

Revision   Orig. Date   Claim No.   Employer

Employee Last Name   Employee First Name   So. Sec. No.   Identifying Date

Company Name _____

Address _____

_ _ _ DETACH HERE _ _ _ THIS PART TO: REHABILITATION UNIT P.O. BOX 429 SAN FRANCISCO, CA 94101-0429 _ _ _ _ _
This part to employee

DENIAL OF VOCATIONAL REHABILITATION SERVICES

Based on a review of your file, you are not eligible for vocational rehabilitation services at this time. Our decision is based on a determination that you are:

____ Not Medically Eligible - See attached Physicians Report of Disability Status or other supporting documentation

____ Not Vocationally Feasible because:

Our action involves only vocational rehabilitation. It does *not* affect your right to other workers' compensation benefits.

You have the right to disagree with our decision. If you disagree, within fifteen days after receiving this letter, you or your representative must complete the two forms enclosed and return them to the Rehabilitation Unit office closest to you. The addresses and phone numbers of the Rehabilitation Unit of the Division of Workers' Compensation are on the back of the Case Initiation Document (Form No. RU-101).

Under certain conditions you may have the right to reopen your case. Please refer to the enclosed pamphlet for additional information. You have 5 years from the date of injury to make this request.

Please call me if you have questions. If you need more information, you may contact the California Division of Workers' Compensation by calling 1-800-736-7401, or you may consult an attorney.

Attachments: Request for Dispute Resolution   NAME: _____
Case Initiation Document
Pamphlet   SIGNATURE: _____

   PHONE #: _____
cc: Attorney, if represented

MANDATORY FORMAT
NOTICE OF NON-ELIGIBILITY
STATE OF CALIFORNIA
DWC FORM RU 500-Y (12/90)

DO NOT STAPLE　　**DATA COLLECTION BOX**　　*(Refer to specifications prior to printing)*

Type	DWC No.	Notice Date	Injury Date

Revision	Orig. Date	Claim No.	Employer

Employee Last Name	Employee First Name	So. Sec. Nc.	Identifying Date

Company Name _____

Address _____

_ _ _ DETACH HERE _ _ _ THIS PART TO: REHABILITATION UNIT P.O. BOX 429 SAN FRANCISCO, CA 94101-0429 _ _ _ _ _
This part to employee

INTENT TO WITHHOLD MAINTENANCE ALLOWANCE

You've been receiving a maintenance allowance of $ _____ per week during your vocational rehabilitation. We plan to stop these payments because you have unreasonably failed to cooperate by:

_____

_____

_____.

If you object to the withholding of your maintenance allowance, you may request a conference with the California Division of Workers' Compensation to resolve the dispute. YOU HAVE **10 DAYS** FROM THE DATE YOU RECEIVE THIS NOTICE TO MAKE THIS REQUEST. If you do not, the payments will stop until:

_____.

Enclosed is a Request for Dispute Resolution and a Case Initiation Document. These are the forms used to request a conference. There are instructions at the top of each form explaining how to fill them out. Completed forms must be sent to the nearest office of the Rehabilitation Unit. The addresses and phone numbers of the Rehabilitation Unit offices are on the back of the Case Initiation Document.

Please call me if you have questions. If you need help completing the forms, please contact the nearest office of the Division of Workers' Compensation or call 1-800-736-7401, or you may consult an attorney.

Attachments:　Request for Dispute Resolution
　　　　　　　Case Initiation Document

cc:　Attorney, if represented

NAME: _____

SIGNATUFE: _____

PHONE #: _____

DATE: _____

MANDATORY FORMAT
STATE OF CALIFORNIA
DWC FORM RU 500-Z (12/90)

RECOMMENDED FORMAT

NOTICE OF ASSIGNMENT OF
QUALIFIED REHABILITATION REPRESENTATIVE

Under California law, we must assign a Qualified Rehabilitation Representative to meet with any injured worker who is off work more than 90 days to explain vocational rehabilitation services. If you cannot return to your job, I wanted you to know about the services available to find another job because of the effects of your injury. Enclosed is a brochure explaining these services. You should read it in preparation for this meeting.

I have asked _____ , a Qualified Rehabilitation Representative, to contact you to explain these services and answer your questions. _____ also will want to know about your job requirements so he/she can talk to your doctor about your return to work.

Please call me at _____ if you have questions. If you need more information, please contact the California Division of Workers' Compensation by calling 1-800-736-7401.

cc: Attorney, if represented

RECOMMENDED FORMAT
STATE OF CALIFORNIA
D-WC RU-AA (12/90)

RECOMMENDED FORMAT

NOTICE OF INTERRUPTION

I am confirming our agreement to interrupt or defer vocational rehabilitation from (or until) _____.

The reason for this action is: _____.

To start vocational rehabilitation services, you must contact me no later than _____. All that is needed is for you to complete the bottom of this form and return to me. If you do not respond by _____, we will take no further action. You would then have 5 years from the date of injury to request reinstatement.

Please call me at _____ if you have any questions. If you want more information, please contact the California Division of Workers' Compensation by calling 1-800-736-7401.

cc: Attorney, if represented

_____
Signature & Date

- -

TEAR LINE

_____   Claim # _____

_____   Date of Injury _____

_____

YES, I am ready to start rehabilitation services.

Employee Name _____   Signature _____

Address _____

_____

RECOMMENDED FORMAT
STATE OF CALIFORNIA
DWC RU-AB (12/90)

RECOMMENDED FORMAT

Re: Employee Name: _____

Claim No: _____

QRR VERIFICATION OF VOCATIONAL REHABILITATION EXPLANATION

> **INSTRUCTIONS:** This form is to be filled out and signed by the Qualified Rehabilitation Representative who meets with the employee and explains his/her rights pursuant to Labor Code 4636a. This form is to be served on all parties by the QRR.

This is to certify that I have personally met with the employee named above and explained to the employee his/her rights and obligations pertaining to vocational rehabilitation in accordance with Labor Code 4636(a). In addition, I have provided the employee with information required by the Division of Workers' Compensation. This meeting occurred on _____ *at* _____

Street Address

_____	_____	_____
(City)	*(State)*	*(Zip)*

Copies of this form were sent to:	QRR Signature _____
	Name _____ Date: _____
List of documents given to employee:	Firm Name _____
	Street Address _____
	City, State, Zip _____
	Phone Number _____
	QRR Tax ID # _____

RECOMMENDED FORMAT
STATE OF CALIFORNIA
DWC RU-AC ((12/90)

§ 16.22 W.C.A.B. Rules Re Rehabilitation Appeals

10955. Rehabilitation Appeals

Proceedings regarding rehabilitation as provided in Section 10008 [1988 Section 10014(e)] of the Rules of the Administrative Director of the Division of Industrial Accidents shall be commenced as follows:

(a) if an Application for Adjudication is already on file, by filing an appropriate petition.

(b) if no Application for Adjudication is on file, by filing an application and an appropriate petition.

A copy of all pleadings, notices and orders shall be served on the Rehabilitation Bureau.

A hearing on a rehabilitation appeal will not be set unless a Declaration of Readiness to proceed is filed pursuant to Section 10414 (of the W.C.A.B. rules).

10956. Rehabilitation Records

When filing a petition under Section 10955, the party appealing from a decision of the Rehabilitation Bureau shall file and serve copies of the decision and other documents which the appealing party deems relevant. Within five (5) days of receipt of these documents, the opposing party may file and serve copies of whatever additional documents the opposing party deems relevant.

10957. Deposition of Rehabilitation Consultants

Depositions of Rehabilitation Bureau Consultants will not be taken except on terms and conditions as ordered by a workers' compensation judge.

10958. Hearing and Burden of Proof

Proceedings instituted under Section 10955 shall be assigned, heard and determined in the same manner as proceedings instituted for the collection of other compensation except that the burden of proof shall be on the person disputing the finding or determination of the Rehabilitation Bureau.

10992. Rehabilitation Appeals

Proceedings regarding rehabilitation as provided in Labor Code Section 4645 shall be commenced as follows:

(a) If an Application for Adjudication is already on file, by filing a petition setting forth in detail the reasons for appeal from the decision of the Office of Benefit Determination, vocational rehabilitation unit.

(b) If no Application for Adjudication is on file, by filing an Application and a petition setting forth the reasons for appeal.

A copy of all pleadings, notices and orders shall be served on the Office of Benefit Determination, vocational rehabilitation unit.

If an Application for Adjudication is already on file, a Declaration of Readiness to Proceed is required before a rehabilitation appeal will be set for hearing.

This rule applies to injuries occurring on or after January 1, 1990.

APPENDIX

Tables for computing compensation benefits

Table A

Minimum and maximum earnings and compensation rates on or after April 1, 1974

Injury Date	Employee's Actual Earnings	Weekly Compensation Rate	
On or after 1-1-91	$504.00	$336.00	— Maximum for Temporary Disability and Permanent Total Disability[1]
	189.00 or comp. = ²/₃ x 1.5 x av. wkly. earnings, whichever is less	126.00	— Minimum for Temporary Disability
	168.00	112.00	— Minimum for Permanent Total Disability[1]
	210.00	140.00	— Maximum for Permanent Partial Disability[3]
	222.00 *[if PD rates 25% or more]	148.00*	
	105.00	70.00	— Minimum for Permanent Partial Disability[3]
1-1-90 through 12-31-90	399.00	266.00	— Maximum for Temporary Disability and Permanent Total Disability[1]
	168.00 or comp. = ²/₃ x 1.5 x av. wkly. earnings, whichever is less, but not less than	112.00	— Minimum for Temporary Disability
	147.00	98.00	
	168.00	112.00	— Minimum for Permanent Total Disability[1]
	210.00	140.00	— Maximum for Permanent Partial Disability[3]
	105.00	70.00	— Minimum for Permanent Partial Disability[3]

(Table A continued on next page.)

Injury Date	Employee's Actual Earnings	(Table A continued) Weekly Compensation Rate	
1-1-84 through 12-31-89	$336.00	$224.00	— Maximum for Temporary Disability and Permanent Total Disability[1]
	168.00	112.00	— Minimum for Temporary Disability and Permanent Total Disability[1]
	210.00	140.00	— Maximum for Permanent Partial Disability[3]
	105.00	70.00	— Minimum for Permanent Partial Disability[3]
1-1-83 through 12-31-83	294.00	196.00	— Maximum for Temporary Disability and Permanent Total Disability[1]
	126.00	84.00	— Minimum for Temporary Disability and Permanent Total Disability[1]
	195.00	130.00	— Maximum for Permanent Partial Disability[3]
	75.00	50.00	— Minimum for Permanent Partial Disability[3]
1-1-81 through 12-31-82	262.50	175.00	— Maximum for Temporary Disability and Permanent Total Disability[1]
	73.50	49.00	— Minimum for Temporary Disability and Permanent Total Disability[1]
	105.00	70.00	— Maximum for Permanent Partial Disability[3]
	45.00	30.00	— Minimum for Permanent Partial Disability[3]
1-1-78 through 12-31-80	231.00	154.00	— Maximum for Temporary Disability and Permanent Total Disability[1]
	73.50	49.00	— Minimum for Temporary Disability and Permanent Total Disability[1]
	105.00	70.00	— Maximum for Permanent Partial Disability[3]
	45.00	30.00	— Minimum for Permanent Partial Disability[3]

(Table A continued on next page.)

Appendix

(Table A continued)

Injury Date	Employee's Actual Earnings	Weekly Compensation Rate	
1-1-77 through 12-31-77	$231.00	$154.00	— Maximum for Temporary Disability and Permanent Total Disability[1]
	52.50	35.00	— Minimum for Temporary Disability and Permanent Total Disability[1]
	105.00	70.00	— Maximum for Permanent Partial Disability[3]
	45.00	30.00	— Minimum for Permanent Partial Disability[3]
4-1-74 through 12-31-76	178.50	119.00	— Maximum for Temporary Disability and Permanent Total Disability[1]
	52.50	35.00	— Minimum for Temporary Disability and Permanent Total Disability[1, 2]
	105.00	70.00	— Maximum for Permanent Partial Disability[3]
	30.00	20.00	— Minimum for Permanent Partial Disability[3, 4]

TABLE A FOOTNOTES:

1. Total permanent disability (100% rating) payable for life.

2. For period April 1, 1974 through May 6, 1974, minimum temporary and permanent total compensation of $35.89 based on earnings of $53.84.

3. Permanent partial disability entitlement may also be computed at 4 weeks of compensation for each 1% of the rating, with a minimum compensation rate of $52.50 per week based on earnings of $78.75 per week. Employee is entitled to greater value of rating.

4. For period April 1, 1974 through May 6, 1974, minimum permanent partial disability compensation is $20.51 based on earnings of $30.77.

Table B

For computation of compensation rates for injuries occurring on or after April 1, 1974

To obtain weekly earnings for monthly salaried person, multiply monthly salary by 12 and divide the result by 52.

Employee's Actual Earnings	Weekly Compensation Rate	Employee's Actual Earnings	Weekly Compensation Rate	Employee's Actual Earnings	Weekly Compensation Rate
$ 30.00	$ 20.00	$270.00	$ 180.00	$1.00	$0.667
40.00	26.667	280.00	186.667	2.00	1.333
50.00	33.333	290.00	193.333	3.00	2.00
60.00	40.00	300.00	200.00	4.00	2.667
70.00	46.667	310.00	206.667	5.00	3.333
80.00	53.333	320.00	213.333	6.00	4.00
90.00	60.00	330.00	220.00	7.00	4.667
100.00	66.667	340.00	226.667	8.00	5.333
110.00	73.333	350.00	233.333	9.00	6.00
120.00	80.00	360.00	240.00		
130.00	86.667	370.00	246.667	0.10	0.067
140.00	93.333	380.00	253.333	0.20	0.133
150.00	100.00	390.00	260.00	0.30	0.20
160.00	106.667	400.00	266.667	0.40	0.267
170.00	113.333	410.00	273.333	0.50	0.333
180.00	120.00	420.00	280.00	0.60	0.40
190.00	126.667	430.00	286.667	0.70	0.467
200.00	133.333	440.00	293.333	0.80	0.533
210.00	140.00	450.00	300.00	0.90	0.60
220.00	146.667	460.00	306.667		
230.00	153.333	470.00	313.333	0.01	0.07
240.00	160.00	480.00	320.00	0.02	0.013
250.00	166.667	490.00	326.667	0.03	0.02
260.00	173.333	500.00	333.333	0.04	0.027
				0.05	0.033
				0.06	0.04
				0.07	0.047
				0.08	0.053
				0.09	0.06

(Table B continued on next page.)

Appendix

(Table B continued)

To compute compensation rate, separate the components of actual earnings to tens and units of dollars, tens and units of cents. Find the values opposite each in the applicable columns; then add.

EXAMPLE: Find the compensation rate for weekly earnings of $ 157.47.

Earnings	Compensation
$150.00	$100.00
7.00	4.667
.40	.267
.07	.047
Totals $157.47	$104.981
	or $104.98

REMINDER: This table is based upon the formula: compensation = $2/3$ actual weekly earnings. Be sure to check Table A for the minimum and maximum rates in effect on date of injury for the particular benefit being computed.

449

Table C

Minimum and maximum rates since September 22, 1951, to and including March 31, 1974

Injury Date	Employee's Actual Earnings	"Statutory Average Earnings"	Weekly Compensation Rate	
4-1-72	$170.04	$161.54	$105.00	— Maximum for Temporary Disability
through	56.67	53.84	35.00	— Minimum for Temporary Disability
3-31-74	113.36	107.69	70.00 *	— Maximum for Permanent Disability*
	32.39	30.77	20.00	— Minimum for Permanent Disability
1-1-69	141.70	134.62	87.50	— Maximum for Temporary Disability
through	40.48	38.46	25.00	— Minimum for Temporary Disability
3-31-72	85.02	80.77	52.50 *	— Maximum for Permanent Disability*
	32.39	30.77	20.00	— Minimum for Permanent Disability
9-15-61	113.36	107.69	70.00	— Maximum for Temporary Disability
through	40.48	38.46	25.00	— Minimum for Temporary Disability
12-31-68	85.02	80.77	52.50	— Maximum for Permanent Disability
	32.39	30.77	20.00	— Minimum for Permanent Disability
9-18-59	105.26	100.00	65.00	— Maximum for Temporary Disability
through	85.02	80.77	52.50	— Minimum for Temporary Disability
9-14-61	32.39	30.77	20.00	— Minimum for both Temp. and Perm.
9-11-57	80.98	76.93	50.00	— Maximum for Temporary Disability
through	64.78	61.54	40.00	— Maximum for Permanent Disability
9-17-59	24.29	23.08	15.00	— Minimum for both Temp. and Perm.
9-7-55	64.78	61.54	40.00	— Maximum for Temporary Disability
through	56.68	53.85	35.00	— Maximum for Permanent Disability
9-10-57	24.29	23.08	15.00	— Minimum for both Temp. and Perm.
9-22-51	56.68	53.85	35.00	— Maximum for Temporary Disability
through	48.58	46.16	30.00	— Maximum for Permanent Disability
9-6-55	15.75	15.00	9.75	— Minimum for both Temp. and Perm.

*NOTE: For injuries on or after April 1, 1972, employee's permanent disability entitlement may also be computed at 4 weeks of compensation for each 1% of the rating, with a maximum compensation rate of $52.50 per week. Employee is entitled to greater value of rating.

Appendix

Table D

For computing "statutory earnings" and weekly compensation rates from actual earnings, for injuries through March 31, 1974. To obtain weekly actual earnings for monthly salaried person, multiply monthly salary by 12 and divide the result by 52.

Employee's Actual Earnings	Statutory Average Earnings	Weekly Compensation Rate	Employee's Actual Earnings	Statutory Average Earnings	Weekly Compensation Rate
$ 10.00	$ 9.50	$ 6.175	$ 0.10	$ 0.095	$ 0.06
20.00	19.00	12.35	0.20	0.19	0.12
30.00	28.50	18.525	0.30	0.285	0.185
40.00	38.00	24.70	0.40	0.38	0.25
50.00	47.50	30.875	0.50	0.475	0.31
60.00	57.00	37.05	0.60	0.57	0.37
70.00	66.50	43.225	0.70	0.665	0.43
80.00	76.00	49.40	0.80	0.76	0.49
90.00	85.50	55.575	0.90	0.855	0.555
100.00	95.00	61.75			
110.00	104.50	67.925			
120.00	114.00	74.10			
130.00	123.50	80.275			
140.00	133.00	86.45			
150.00	142.50	92.625			
160.00	152.00	98.80			
170.00	161.50	104.975			
1.00	0.95	0.62	0.01	0.01	0.01
2.00	1.90	1.235	0.02	0.02	0.01
3.00	2.85	1.85	0.03	0.03	0.02
4.00	3.80	2.47	0.04	0.04	0.02
5.00	4.75	3.09	0.05	0.05	0.03
6.00	5.70	3.705	0.06	0.06	0.04
7.00	6.65	4.32	0.07	0.07	0.04
8.00	7.60	4.94	0.08	0.08	0.05
9.00	8.55	5.56	0.09	0.09	0.06

(Table D continued on next page.)

To compute "statutory average earnings" or the compensation rate, separate the components of actual earnings to tens and units of dollars, tens and units of cents. Find the values opposite each in the applicable columns; then add.

Example: Find the compensation rate for actual earnings of $88.54 per week.

Earnings	Compensation
$80.00	$49.40
8.00	4.94
.50	.31
.04	.02
Totals 88.54	54.67

REMINDER: Check Table C for minimum and maximum in force on the date of injury. Also, these may differ for temporary disability and permanent disability benefits.

Appendix

Table E

Permanent Disability Compensation Rates for Minors

I. In 1972, the law was amended to provide that a person under 18 years of age is a minor. Prior to 1972, a minor was a person under 21 years of age.

II. As to injuries occurring on or after April 1, 1974, PD compensation rates are computed in the same manner as for adults, depending on actual probable earnings at age 18. (See Tables A & B.) Exception: for the period April 1, 1974 through May 6, 1974, the maximum PD rate is $71.79 based on maximum earnings of $107.69.

III. As to injuries occurring before April 1, 1974, PD compensation rates may be computed per the following table, subject to the maximum and minimum PD compensation rates set forth in Table C.

Actual Weekly Earnings	Minor's PD Compensation Rate	Actual Weekly Earnings	Minor's PD Compensation Rate
$ 10.00	$ 6.50	$ 0.10	$ 0.065
20.00	13.00	0.20	0.13
30.00	19.50	0.30	0.195
40.00	26.00	0.40	0.26
50.00	32.50	0.50	0.325
60.00	39.00	0.60	0.39
70.00	45.50	0.70	0.455
80.00	52.00	0.80	0.52
90.00	58.50	0.90	0.585
100.00	65.00		
1.00	0.65	0.01	0.01
2.00	1.30	0.02	0.01
3.00	1.95	0.03	0.02
4.00	2.60	0.04	0.03
5.00	3.25	0.05	0.03
6.00	3.90	0.06	0.04
7.00	4.55	0.07	0.045
8.00	5.20	0.08	0.05
9.00	5.85	0.09	0.06

To compute compensation rate, separate the components of the minor's actual weekly earnings to tens and units of dollars, tens and units of cents. Find the compensation values opposite each; then add.

(Table E continued on next page.)

EXAMPLE: Find the compensation rate for permanent disability for a minor with actual weekly earnings (or actual probable earnings at age of majority) of $79.23.

Actual Earnings	PD Compensation
$70.00	$45.50
9.00	5.85
.20	.13
.03	.02
Totals $79.23	$51.50

REMINDER: Check table C for minimum and maximum compensation rate for permanent disability in effect on date of injury.

Appendix

Table F

Death Benefits Before 1983

Death Benefits 1-1-81 through 12-31-82

Two or More total dependents: $75,000.

One total dependent and one more partial dependents:
$50,000 plus 4 times annual support for partial dependents not to exceed $25,000.

One total dependent, no partial dependents: $50,000.

No total dependent, one or more partial dependents: 4 times annual support, not to exceed a total of $50,000.

Burial allowance: $1,500

Date of Injury	Widow & Minor Child**	Widow Without Children; Other Total Dependents	Partial Dependents	Maximum Burial Expense*
1-1-77 through 12-31-80	$55,000	$50,000	4 times annual support not to exceed $50,000	$1,000 1,500 on or after 1-1-79
1-1-74 through 12-31-76	45,000	40,000	4 times annual support, not to exceed $40,000	1,000
3-7-73 through 12-31-73	28,000	25,000	4 times annual support, not exceed $25,000	1,000
4-1-72 through 3-6-73	28,000	25,000	4 times annual support, not to exceed $15,000	1,000
1-1-69 through 3-31-72	23,000	20,000	4 times annual support, not to exceed $15,000	1,000

(Table F continued on next page.)

455

(Table F continued)

Date of Injury	Widow & Minor Child**	Widow Without Children; Other Total Dependents	Partial Dependents	Maximum Burial Expense*
9-18-59 through 12-31-68	20,500	17,500	4 times annual support, not to exceed $15,000	600
9-11-57 through 9-17-59	15,000	12,000	4 times annual support, not to exceed $12,000	400
9-7-55 through 9-10-57	12,500	10,000	4 times annual support, not to exceed $10,000	400
9-22-51 through 9-6-55	4 times statutory average annual earnings; maximum benefit $8,750	7,000 max.	4 times annual support, not to exceed $7,000	400

* Burial expense is paid to dependents or other persons incurring funeral expense.
** For year 1980, "spouse" and minor child or two or more minor children, $55,000.

INDEX

Boldface type indicates chapter references.

Index

Index

461

J

K

No index entries

L

M

Index

Index

X, Y, Z

No index entries